Prentice Hall Brief Review for the New York Regents Exam

Geometry

A. Rose Primiani, Ed.D. / William Caroscio

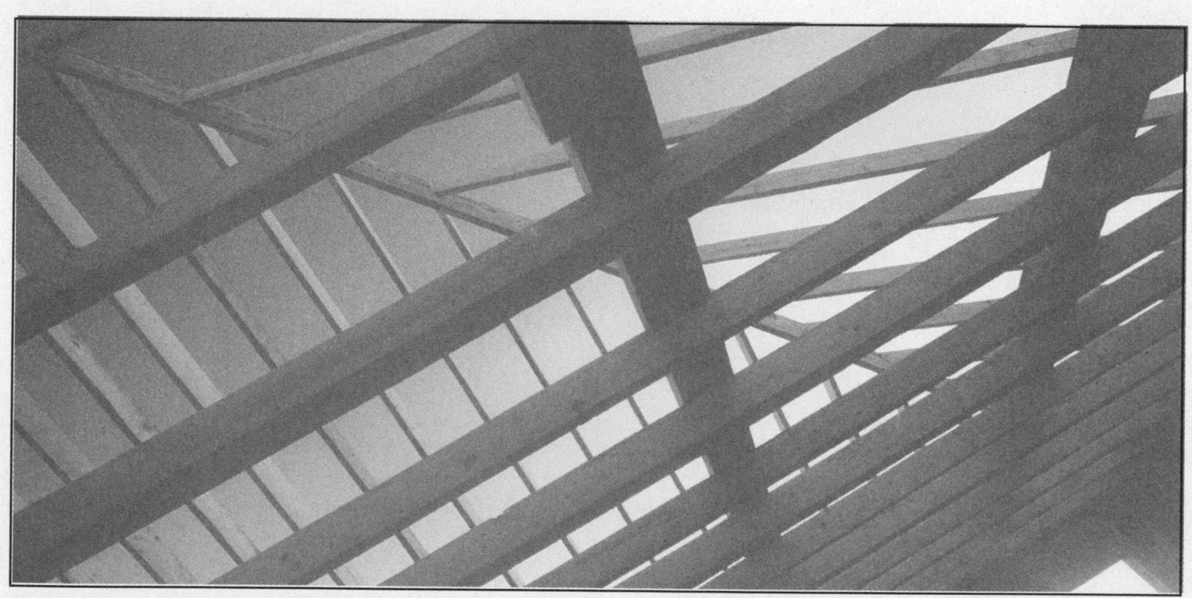

Order Information

Send orders to:
PEARSON CUSTOMER SERVICE
P.O. BOX 2500
LEBANON, IN 46052-3009
or
CALL TOLL FREE 1-800-848-9500
(8:00 A.M.-6:00 P.M. EST)

- Orders can be placed via phone

Order online at k12oasis.pearson.com

Authors

A. Rose Primiani, Ed.D. (1939–2009), was a former Director of Mathematics and Computer Education for District 10, Bronx, NYC, and a Supervisor of Mathematics K–12 for the Yonkers Public Schools, NY. She was an adjunct professor at Manhattan College, Mercy College, CUNY, and Fordham University. Dr. Primiani was a Curriculum and Instructional Materials Consultant for Pearson Publishers, School Division. She consulted extensively on mathematics curriculum development and effective instructional practices and was involved in correlating other states' curriculum to Pearson middle school and high school mathematics texts; including those of New Jersey, Ohio, Maryland, and New York.

William Caroscio has over 35 years of experience in mathematics education. This experience includes middle school, high school, and college teaching experience. Mr. Caroscio is past president of the Association of Mathematics Teachers of New York State and the New York State Mathematics Supervisor Association. He is a member of AMTNYS, NYSAMS, NCTM, MAA, NCSM, NYSMATYC, and AMATYC. Mr. Caroscio is a National Instructor in the T3 (Teachers Teaching With Technology) program. He has conducted sessions and workshops at the local, state and national levels. Mr. Caroscio has served as an item writer for the NYS Education Department assessment committees, as a member of the Commissioner's Committee on the New Mathematics Standards, and the Geometry Committee, writing sample tasks for the new standards.

Reviewers

Irene "Sam" Jovell
Senior Mathematics Specialist
Questar III
Castleton, New York

Dina Kushnir
Mathematics Coordinator 9–12
Fayetteville-Manlius High School
Fayetteville, New York

Kate Nowak
Mathematics Teacher
Fayetteville-Manlius High School
Fayetteville, New York

Acknowledgments appear on p. A-1, which constitutes an extension of this copyright page.

ISBN-13: 978-0-13-320262-5
ISBN-10: 0-13-320262-3

1 2 3 4 5 6 7 8 9 10 V069 15 14 13 12 11

TABLE OF CONTENTS

Chapter 3 Triangles

Chapter 4 Relationships with Triangles

Chapter 5 Quadrilaterals and Other Polygons

Chapter 6 Coordinate Geometry

Chapter 7 Transformational Geometry

Chapter 8 Angles in Circles

Chapter 9 Solid Geometry and Its Applications

INTRODUCTION

In order to receive a New York High School Regents Diploma when you graduate from high school, you must pass the New York State Regents Examination in Geometry. The New York State Education Department has outlined a Core Curriculum for Geometry that focuses on five process strands: Problem Solving, Reasoning and Proof, Communication, Connections, and Representation. The Core Curriculum for Geometry also focuses on six content strands: Geometric Relationships, Constructions, Loci, Informal and Formal Proofs, Transformational Geometry, and Coordinate Geometry. The intent of both the process and content performance indicators is to provide a variety of ways for students to acquire and demonstrate mathematical reasoning ability when solving problems.

This book has been written for you, a high school student in the State of New York. You can use it as a tool for understanding the process strands and applying the content strands of the Geometry Curriculum.

Structure of the Brief Review

Included in the front of the book are brief diagnostic tests for each chapter. These tests will allow you to measure your level of understanding of the content and concentrate on the specific concepts according to your needs.

Each lesson in this book

- addresses specific performance indicators of the Geometry Curriculum.
- includes definitions, formulas, and examples with complete explanations.
- provides practice exercises at the end of every lesson to check for understanding.

At the end of each chapter, review exercises entitled *Preparing for the Geometry Exam* address the entire content of the chapter and include both multiple-choice and open-ended questions in the Geometry format.

Calculator Solutions

Graphing calculators will be made available for use during the Geometry Exam. Graphing calculator solutions are offered throughout the text as an alternative problem-solving method.

Glossary

A complete glossary of terms is included in the back of this book. It offers a complete definition of the term, with examples as appropriate.

Transition to the Common Core

Pearson is committed to supporting the Common Core Standards and the P-12 Common Core Learning Standards for Mathematics in New York. With that in mind, this Brief Review has been updated to include a new Table of Contents, correlated to both the New York standards and the Common Core standards.

Specifications for the Regents Examination in Geometry

The following information was taken from the New York State Education Department Web site.

The Regents Examination in Geometry is a graduation requirement for those students seeking an advanced degree diploma in the State of New York. The first administration of the exam is scheduled for June 2009.

The exam covers both content and process strands of the core curriculum in Geometry and it encompasses one year of study. The examination will assess students' conceptual understanding, procedural fluency, and problem-solving abilities in mathematics.

The following table shows the percentage of total credits that will be aligned with each content strand.

Content Strand	% of Total Credits
Geometric Relationships	8–12%
Constructions	3–7%
Locus	4–8%
Informal and Formal Proofs	41–47%
Transformational Geometry	8–13%
Coordinate Geometry	23–28%

Question Types

The Regents Examination in Geometry consists of 38 questions totaling 86 credits and will include the following types and numbers of questions:

Question Type	Number of Questions	Total Credits
Multiple choice	28	56
2-credit open ended	6	12
4-credit open ended	3	12
6-credit open ended	1	6
Total	**38**	**86**

Calculators

Schools must make a graphing calculator available for the exclusive use of each student while that student takes the Regents Examination in Geometry.

FACTS AND STRATEGIES

Test-Taking Facts and Tips

- You will have up to three hours to complete the exam.
- You should answer all 38 exam questions. If you skip a question, you will receive zero credits for it. Keep in mind that no credit is subtracted for incorrect answers.
- Bring several pens, pencils, and a good eraser to the exam room. All work must be done in pen except for graphs and drawings, which are to be done in pencil.
- You will record your answers to the multiple-choice questions on a detachable answer sheet, which is the last page of the exam booklet.
- In answering the open-ended questions, you must record all of your work in the exam booklet directly below the corresponding item. Your work must include tables, diagrams, and graphs as necessary. You can receive partial credit on these items.
- Scrap paper is not permitted. A sheet of graph paper will be provided for any exam items for which graphing may be helpful but not required.
- A graphing calculator will be made available as will a straightedge and a compass.

Facts and Strategies for the Multiple-Choice Questions

General Facts and Strategies

- Budget your time on the multiple-choice questions to be sure that you leave at least one hour for all other questions. Wear a watch, if possible, because a wall clock may not be in sight during the exam.
- The order in which you answer the items does not matter, so you may go to other parts of the exam before completing the multiple-choice questions. However, give yourself ample time to return to these questions because they are worth 65% of the total credits.
- Each multiple-choice question is worth two credits, but no partial credit is given. Therefore, even if you are unsure of an answer, take a reasonable guess. Do *not* leave any blanks because even by guessing, you have a 25% chance of getting an answer correct.
- Carefully read each question *twice* before answering to be sure that you know what is being asked.
- If you are somewhat unsure of an answer, skip the question and move on to the next one. However, place a mark in your exam booklet next to the question you skipped as a reminder to return to it later. Remember to skip the corresponding location on your answer sheet.
- You can do all your computations in the exam booklet, but be sure to write your answers to the multiple-choice questions in pen in the correct space on the answer sheet provided.

- Before writing an answer, check to see whether it is reasonable.
- After completing all parts of the exam, you must read and sign the statement at the bottom of the answer sheet.

Strategies for Multiple-Choice Questions

- Immediately cross out choices that you know cannot be correct.
- Try to estimate the answer when appropriate. This may help you eliminate some choices.
- Use your calculator for square roots, decimals, percents, and so on.
- Check each choice against the wording of the question itself, just as you would check the solution to a problem.
- Use the problem-solving strategies you have studied. These include the following:
  - drawing a diagram or graph when the question describes a figure,
  - looking for a pattern when you suspect a relationship,
  - making a table when data are given,
  - working backward from the choices given,
  - using guess-and-test or trial-and-error, and
  - writing an equation.

On the following page, you will have an opportunity to examine two multiple-choice questions of the type that might appear on the Geometry Exam. As you solve the questions, the directions will guide you through a few of the strategies listed above. These are only two examples of the many multiple-choice questions that you will find throughout this book.

FACTS AND STRATEGIES

Multiple-Choice Questions (2 credits each)

Complete the statement: If a transversal intersects two parallel lines, then

(1) alternate interior angles are congruent.
(2) corresponding angles are supplementary.
(3) corresponding angles are complementary.
(4) same-side interior angles are complementary.

Problem solving strategies: Draw a diagram; substitute numbers; eliminate choices

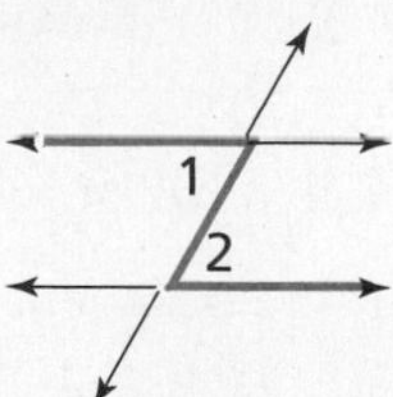

Draw a diagram to illustrate the problem. In the diagram above, $\angle 1$ and $\angle 2$ are alternate interior angles. Two parallel lines cut by a transversal form congruent corresponding angles (forming an "F" shape), congruent alternate interior angles (forming a "Z" shape), and congruent alternate exterior angles. Examine each answer choice to see which one is true.

Answer choice (1) is always true. Choice (2) is true only when $\angle 1$ and $\angle 2$ are 90°; choice (3) is true when $\angle 1$ and $\angle 2$ are 45°. Choice (4) is not true—same-side interior angles are supplementary, not complementary. ***The correct answer is choice (1).***

Which statement can you conclude is true from the given information?

Given: $\overleftrightarrow{AB}$ is the perpendicular bisector of $\overline{IK}$.

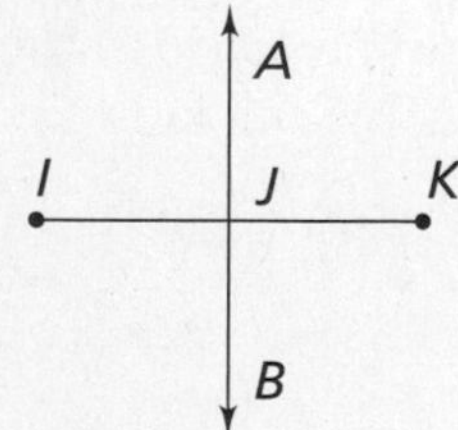

(1) A is the midpoint of $\overline{IK}$.
(2) $\angle AIJ$ is a right angle.
(3) $AJ = JB$
(4) $IJ = JK$

Problem solving strategies: Use a diagram; use a definition of a perpendicular bisector and midpoint

The perpendicular bisector is perpendicular to the base to which it is drawn and it bisects the base. Choices (1) and (2) can be eliminated immediately. Choice (3) is incorrect because you do not know the exact position of A and B from J. Since $\overleftrightarrow{AB}$ bisects $\overline{IK}$, you know that the point of intersection, J, is the midpoint of $\overline{IK}$. Using the definition of a midpoint, $IJ = JK$. ***Therefore, (4) is the correct answer.***

FACTS AND STRATEGIES

Facts and Strategies for Open-Ended Questions

General Facts and Strategies

- Plan your time so that you have at least one hour to answer all of the open-ended questions after completing the multiple-choice questions. Budget your time on each question. Try to spend as much as, but no more than, 5 minutes on each 2-point question, 7–8 minutes on each 4-point question, and 8 minutes on the 6-point question.
- Be sure to write your answer(s) clearly. You must show all of your work in the exam booklet directly under the questions.
- Do all your computations in ink, but use pencil for drawings and graphs.
- If you are using a calculator, estimate your answer to make sure your calculator answer is reasonable. Be sure to explain your work in detail, including those steps you performed on the calculator.
- The "open-ended" questions will be scored by committees of teachers using scoring keys. These keys explain the number of credits that should be awarded for different types of answers.
- If you give a correct numerical answer to a question but show no work, you will receive one credit. However, if you give a correct numerical answer to a question but show an incorrect procedure, you will receive zero credits.
- Some questions have multiple parts. To receive full credit for these questions, you must answer each part completely. If you are unable to answer part (a), you might still be able to answer part (b) or part (c) and receive partial credit.
- Label all answers that are measurements with the proper units of measure, such as inches, feet, square inches, and so on. Items involving measurements might not require you to name the unit of measure in the answer, but it is better to be cautious to be sure you receive full credit.
- After completing all parts, read and sign the statement at the bottom of the multiple-choice answer sheet.

Strategies for Open-Ended Questions

- Use your calculator for square roots, decimals, percents, and so on.
- Use the problem-solving strategies you have studied. These include the following:
  - drawing a diagram when the question describes a figure,
  - looking for a pattern when you suspect a relationship,
  - making a table when data are given,
  - working backward,
  - using guess-and-test or trial-and-error, and
  - writing an equation.

On the following pages are examples of the types of questions that might appear in the open-ended section of the exam. The sample scoring keys provide some insight into how committees score solutions to these questions.

Open-Ended Questions (2 credits each)

This problem is a sample question you might see as a 2-point open-ended question on the exam.

A circular garden has a circumference of 75 feet. A landscaper suggests enclosing the garden in a square fence.

a) To the nearest foot, what is the length of the side of the smallest square that will enclose the garden?

b) How much fencing will be needed?

The sample solutions to this question and the credits awarded are shown below.

0 credits	1 credit	2 credits
No work shown	Correct formula and substitution $C = \pi d$; $75 \approx 3.14d$ $\frac{75}{3.14} \approx d$; $d \approx 24$ ft. d = length of the side of square fence	$C = \pi d$ $d = 24$ ft. = length of side P(fence) $\approx 4(24)$ ≈ 96 ft.

Shown below is another 2-credit sample question. Study the scoring key to see what a complete answer should contain.

This Venn diagram shows the number of students who take various courses.

- Circle A represents all students studying math.
- Circle B represents all students studying science.
- Circle C represents all students studying technology.

What percentage of the students study math or technology?

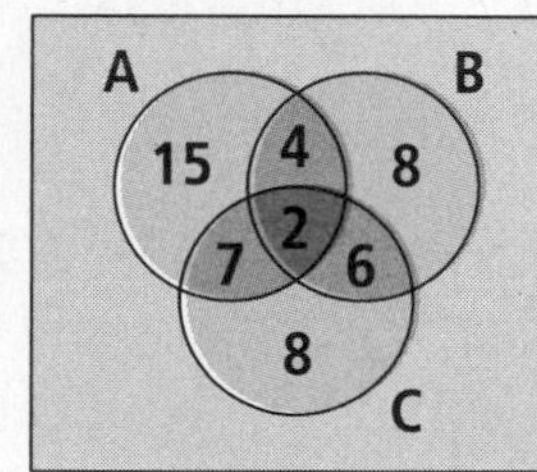

The sample solutions to this question and the credits awarded are shown below.

Scoring Key

2 credits 50 students in all, math or technology.

$$15 + 4 + 2 + 7 + 8 + 6 = 42$$

$$\frac{42}{50} = 84\%$$

1 credit Correct numbers, such as 28 taking math, and 23 taking technology.

0 credits Answer given is incorrect, irrelevant, or incoherent **or** correct response obtained by an obviously incorrect procedure.

FACTS AND STRATEGIES

Open-Ended Questions (4 credits each)

This problem is a sample question you might see as a 4-point open-ended question on the exam.

A forest ranger spots a fire from a 21-foot tower. The angle of depression from the tower to the fire is 30°.

a) Draw a diagram to represent this situation.
b) To the nearest foot, how far is the fire from the base of the tower?

Four sample solutions to this question and the credits awarded are shown below.

0 credits	1 credit	2 credits	3 credits	4 credits
Either: • No work shown • Incorrect diagram • Wrong formula	Diagram of a 30°-60°-90° triangle only Ranger 30° 21 ft Fire x	Show formula only $x = 21\sqrt{3}$	Show formula only and solution without diagram $x = 21\sqrt{3}$ $x \approx 36$ ft. The fire is about 36 feet from the base of the tower.	• Show diagram • Correct formula • Correct solutions

Shown below is another sample. Study the scoring key to see what a complete answer should contain.

Verify that quadrilateral *ABCD* with vertices $A(-5, -1)$, $B(-9, 6)$, $C(-1, 5)$, and $D(3, -2)$ is a rhombus by showing that it is a parallelogram with perpendicular diagonals.

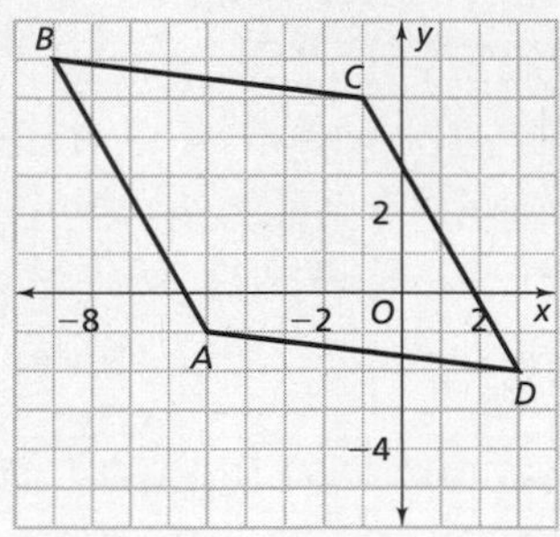

Scoring Key

4 credits Shows *ABCD* is a parallelogram (by any of several methods); then shows diagonals are perpendicular by computing slopes to be $\frac{3}{2}$ and $-\frac{2}{3}$. Includes meaningful commentary on what is occurring.

3 credits Shows *ABCD* is a parallelogram by either opposite sides parallel or one pair of sides are = and parallel and diagonals are perpendicular, but presentation is not clear.

2 credits Work complete and shows correct ideas, but contains errors.

0–1 credit Work incomplete, but shows some understanding of what to do.

Open-Ended Questions (6 credits each)

This problem is a sample question you might see as a 6-point open-ended question on the exam.

Write a proof given the figure below. Study the scoring key to see what a complete answer should contain.

Given: $\overline{BC} \cong \overline{DA}$; $\overline{CF} \cong \overline{AF}$; $\angle 1 \cong \angle 2$

Prove: $\triangle CEF \cong \triangle AEF$

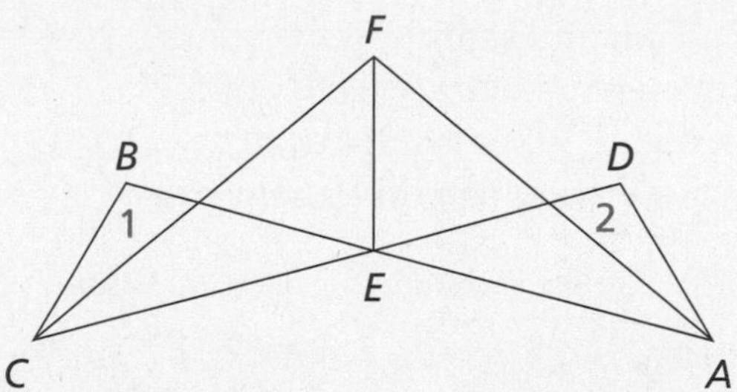

A 6-credit sample solution to this question is shown below.

Statements	Reasons
1. $\overline{BC} \cong \overline{DA}$	1. Given
2. $\angle 1 \cong \angle 2$	2. Given
3. $\angle BEC \cong \angle DEA$	3. Vertical angles are congruent.
4. $\triangle BEC \cong \triangle DEA$	4. AAS
5. $\overline{CE} \cong \overline{AE}$	5. CPCTC
6. $\overline{CF} \cong \overline{AF}$	6. Given
7. $\overline{EF} \cong \overline{EF}$	7. Reflexive Property
8. $\triangle CEF \cong \triangle AEF$	8. SSS

Scoring Key

6 credits All the necessary steps (statements and reasons) as shown above, correct idea, some details inaccurate.

5 credits Correct idea, well organized, some steps missing.

4 credits Correct idea, one or more significant steps omitted.

3 credits Correct statements with incomplete reasons.

2 credits Only triangles *BEC* and *DEA* proven congruent.

1 credit Just steps with no sequence or logic, only given steps listed.

0 credits No attempt made.

Graphing Calculators and Their Potential

The graphing calculator and other interactive software programs are great tools for solving problems and for learning mathematics. This section gives you a concise overview of some of the ways technology can be used to solve problems and investigate mathematical concepts.

Because of the great variety in available technology—graphing calculators, computer programs, Web resources—the discussion and sample activities that follow do not show specific commands. If you need help, consult your user's manual, in which the steps are shown in detail. What is important is that you get to know what interactive geometry software can do to help you explore geometry more easily.

Geometry Enhanced with Technology

Geometry is unlike any other course you have studied in high school. It offers you the opportunity to experience what it is like to work as a mathematician. The use of technology helps make the most of this opportunity. Mathematicians combine their observations with theories and guesses before attempting to carry out a proof. Most often this process requires them to try and try again.

Using effective geometry tools greatly strengthens the experience of studying geometry. Exciting new possibilities exist for exploring geometric concepts. Graphing calculators or computer software are great tools for learning and solving problems. The use of interactive computer software helps you follow a set of procedures while at the same time discover theorems by investigating geometric constructions.

For example, you can construct a triangle using a graphing calculator or interactive geometry software. You can then measure each angle and determine their sum. Then the triangle can be changed by dragging one of the vertices. You can make a conjecture about the sum of the angles. You can then try and prove your conjecture. When you make a discovery like this yourself, you "own" the theorem more than if a teacher simply presented you with it.

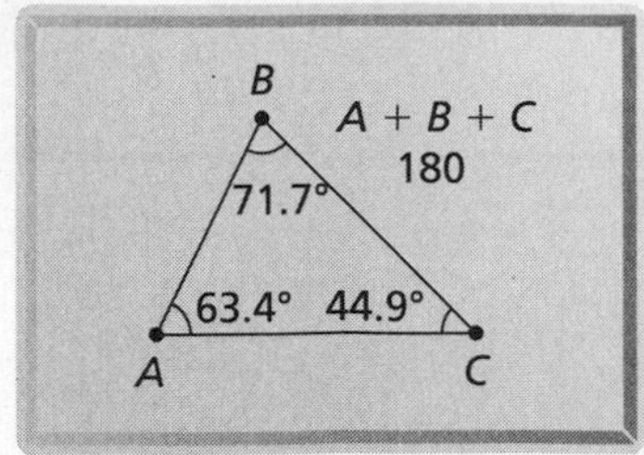

Visual Effect

In geometry, figures are often worth a thousand words. Drawings are essential for descriptions and proofs. An interactive geometry environment allows you to conduct your own investigations and lead you to ask questions about geometric relationships. Your answers to these questions may lead you to important conjectures, properties, and theorems.

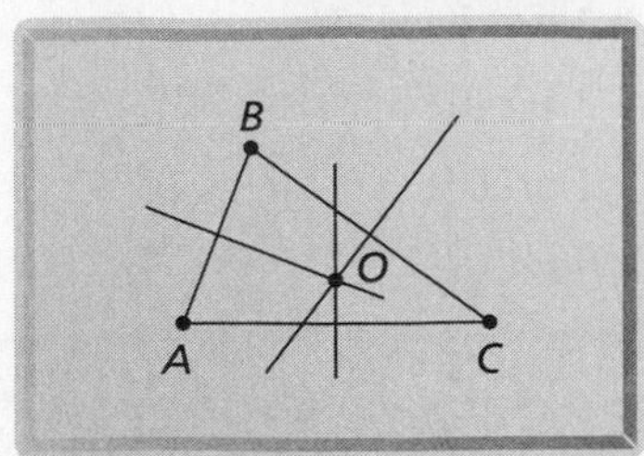

For example, consider the concurrency of the perpendicular bisectors of the sides of a triangle. When constructed within an interactive geometry environment, you can see the common point of intersection. You can manipulate the figure to verify that the concurrency is invariant. As you manipulate the figure, you may ask yourself, "When is the point of concurrency inside, outside, or on the triangle?" You can use interactive geometry software to come up with possible answers to this question.

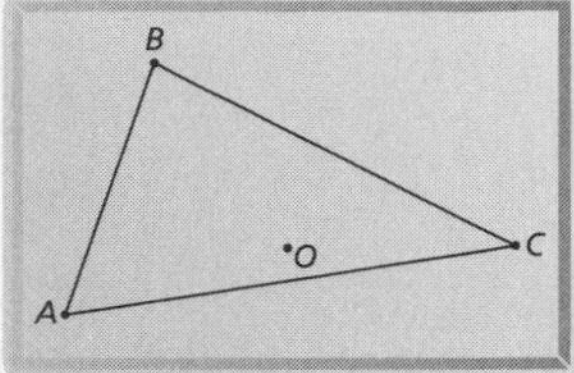

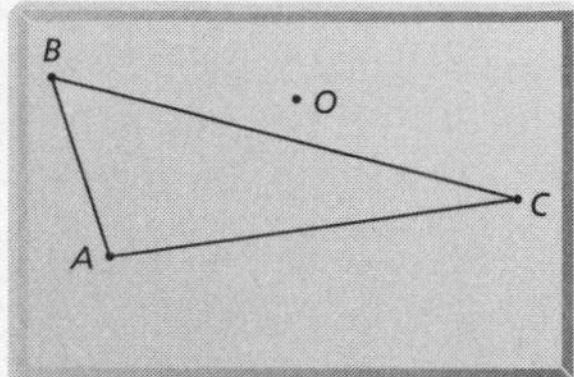

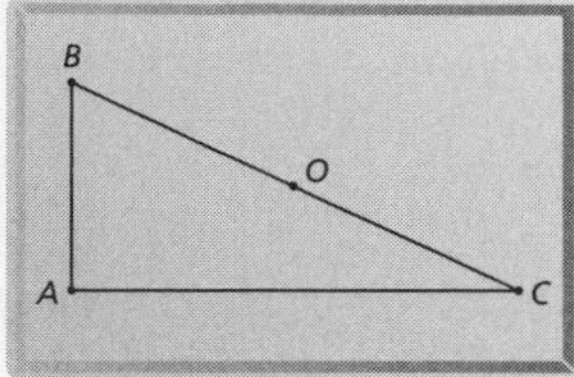

This process of drawing, manipulating, and asking can help you discover important relationships.

By using inductive reasoning—that is, drawing a conclusion from a set logically from a pattern of specific examples—you can decide whether an observed pattern is worth proving. In other words, you can use interactive geometry software to generate a set of examples. If the same properties seem to be true for each of the examples, you can then decide if you want to write a formal proof.

Formal Proof

A formal proof is a cornerstone of the study of geometry. The role of proof in geometry should not merely be to verify the truth of theorems. Rather, proofs are a vehicle to gaining a better understanding of the material. Investigations add excitement and insight into the learning experiences. The geometry course should reflect a flow of observation, conjecture, validation, plausible argument, and then formal proof.

Before you can write a proof, however, you must first guess and verify. When studying geometry, you need to first discover and examine relationships to understand them. Then you can formulate a plan to write the proof. There are no better tools for this kind of conjecturing and guessing than the geometry software available today. You are encouraged to use interactive geometry software prior to attempting the proof of a theorem. Investigating the situation completely can provide the necessary insights required to complete a successful proof. Further, there are several formats you can use to write a formal proof. Using interactive geometry software can help you decide which format you should use to write your proof.

Caution Required

When using figures as part of a proof, you must make sure that the figures are accurate. For example, suppose you were asked to prove that all triangles are isosceles.

Let ABC be a triangle with l the angle bisector of $\angle A$, m the perpendicular bisector of $\overline{BC}$ cutting $\overline{BC}$ at midpoint E, and D the intersection of l and m. Draw perpendicular line segments from D to $\overline{AB}$ and $\overline{AC}$, cutting them at F and G, respectively. Finally, draw $\overline{DB}$ and $\overline{DC}$.

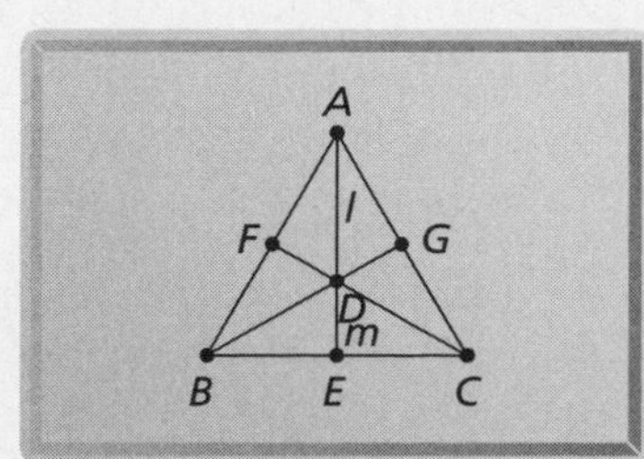

Now, consider the following argument:

Statements	Reasons
1. $\triangle ADF \cong \triangle ADG$	1. AAS
2. $\overline{AF} \cong \overline{AG}, \overline{DF} \cong \overline{DG}$	2. CPCT
3. $\triangle BDE \cong \triangle CDE$	3. SAS
4. $\overline{BD} \cong \overline{CD}$	4. CPCT
5. $\triangle BDF \cong \triangle CDG$	5. HL
6. $\overline{FB} \cong \overline{GC}$	6. CPCT
7. $AB = AF + FB = AG + GC = AC$	7. Definition of midpoint and substitution
8. $\triangle ABC$ *is isosceles.*	8. Definition of isosceles triangle

What could be wrong? Are all triangles really isosceles? There is nothing wrong with the sequence of steps and the reasoning in this proof. The conclusion follows logically from what was given and the figure that was drawn.

This type of erroneous proof illustrates how poorly drawn and inaccurate figures can lead you to a false argument. This example offers a persuasive argument for the need to use accurately constructed diagrams, especially when they are part of a proof. This cxample shows how easily a logical argument can be swayed by what the eye sees in a figure, emphasizing the importance of drawing a figure correctly and accurately. The relation of points is often critical to the proof.

The following sample activities illustrate how to use interactive geometry software to help you make conjectures.

Sample Activity I

1. Construct a triangle with an angle bisector and the perpendicular bisector of the opposite side. Use the space below to outline your steps.

2. What do you notice as you manipulate the drawing? You should notice that the angle bisector and the perpendicular bisector intersect. However, it appears that this point of intersection is not interior to the triangle. The error in the original sketch is readily observed.

Sample Activity 2

1. Construct a triangle containing the circumcenter, *O;* incenter, *I;* centroid, *G;* and orthocenter, *H,* as shown in the accompanying figure. Use the space below to outline your steps.

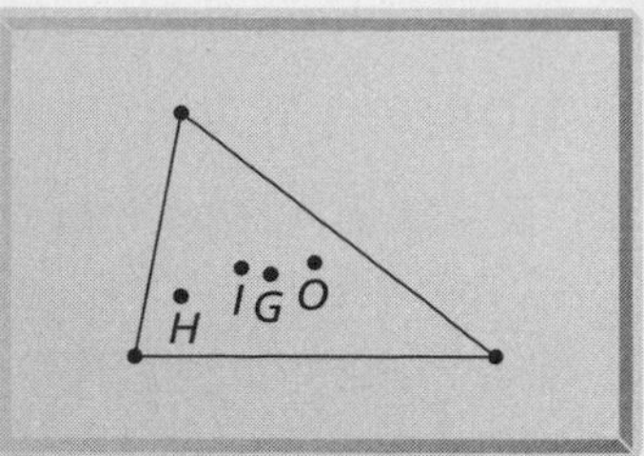

2. Consider the following questions and write your conjectures:
   a. When will all the centers be inside the triangle?
   b. Which ones leave the triangle and when?
   c. Are any of these centers ever on the triangle? When?
   d. Measure the distances between the centers and determine any relationships that exist between the measures.

Sample Activity 3

1. Start with a construction of a parallelogram as shown in the accompanying figure.

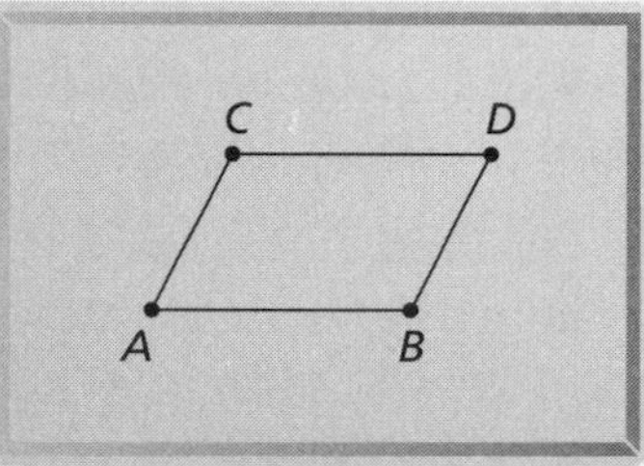

2. List five properties of the parallelogram.
3. Measure quantities in the figure and make conjectures about the relationships you observe. Use the space below to make your conjectures.

4. The accompanying figures show possible stages of exploration.

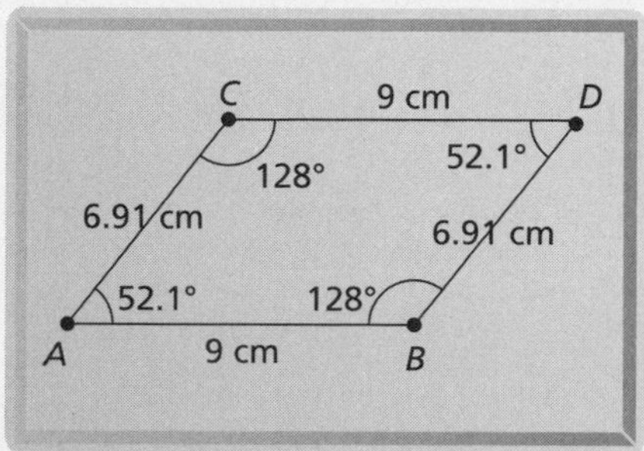

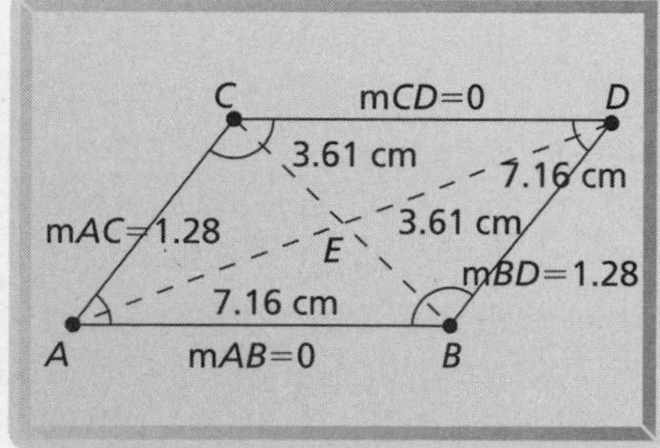

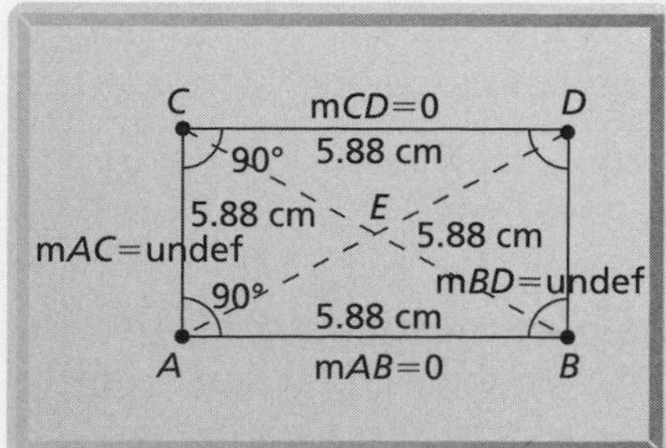

USING A CALCULATOR

Sample Activity 4

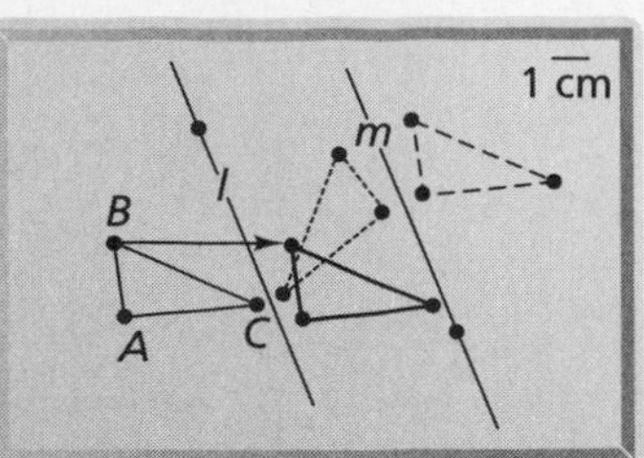

1. Start with the construction as shown in the accompanying diagram.
2. Triangle ABC has been reflected over line l and then over line m.
3. The image of the first reflection is the dotted triangle and the image of the second reflection is the dashed triangle.
4. Then triangle ABC is translated by the vector shown. The image of the translation is the bold triangle.
5. Grab the endpoint of the vector and determine the translation vector such that the image under the translation is the same as the image under the double reflection.
6. Describe your results in complete sentences. Use the space below to describe your observations.

Sample Activity 5

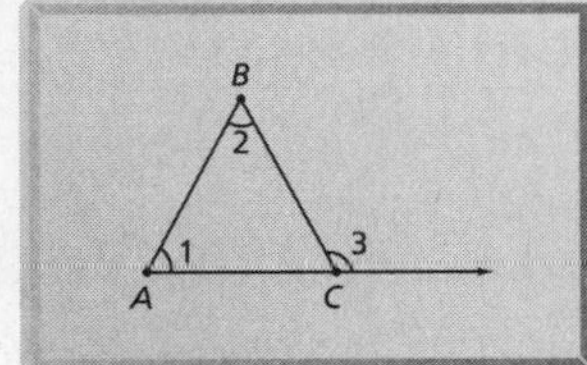

1. Start with the construction of the triangle shown in the diagram to the right.
2. Measure the angles labeled 1, 2, and 3, and compare $m\angle 1 + m\angle 2$ with $m\angle 3$. What do you observe?
3. Grab and drag point C, changing the shape of the triangle. What happens to the measure of each of the angles? How does your answer to the question in step 2 change?
4. Develop a hypothesis that explains your observations and write a proof that proves or disproves your hypothesis.

Use the space below to describe your observations.

Let the Fun Begin

Current technology tools can enable mathematical investigation and trialing. They also enhance the learning of algebraic concepts. This can often provide motivation for improving missing competencies.

People learn in different ways. This technology provides a platform where you can approach problems from multiple perspectives. As you work through this text, challenge yourself to ask how the problem could be approached from a different perspective. Do not hesitate to stop and play with the mathematics. Playing with objects in a construction can be the doorway to new ideas and new theorems. There are many resources for interactive geometry software. Find the tool that best meets your needs and have fun!

Name ______________________ Date __________

Diagnostic Test 1: Chapter 1

Basic Geometry in the Plane

Choose the numeral preceding the word or expression that best completes the statement or answers the question.

1 Which best describes skew lines?

(1) Lines that never meet.

(2) Lines that do not lie in the same plane.

(3) Lines that are coplanar.

(4) Lines that are parallel.

2 If two angles are supplementary and congruent, then they are

(1) acute angles.

(2) obtuse angles.

(3) right angles.

(4) complementary.

3 If two lines cut by a transversal are parallel, what is true of the corresponding angles?

(1) The angles are supplementary.

(2) The angles are complementary.

(3) The angles are right angles.

(4) The angles are congruent.

4 If two or more planes intersect, the intersection is a

(1) point.

(2) line.

(3) plane.

(4) triangle.

5 The locus of points equidistant from 2 parallel lines is

(1) a circle.

(2) the perpendicular bisector.

(3) a line midway to both lines.

(4) 2 intersecting lines.

6 The locus of points a fixed distance from a given point is

(1) a plane.

(2) 2 planes.

(3) 2 parallel planes.

(4) a circle.

7 Circle O has a radius of 3 ft. Line l is 2 ft from the center of O. Line m is 3 ft from l, and m is parallel to l. Lines l and m intersect O in

(1) one point.

(2) two points.

(3) three points.

(4) four points.

8 What is the locus of points equidistant from the ends of a line segment?

(1) the perpendicular bisector

(2) two points

(3) a circle

(4) a triangle

Name ______________________________ Date __________

Diagnostic Test 2: Chapter 2

Mathematical Statements

Choose the numeral preceding the word or expression that best completes the statement or answers the question.

1 Which of the following is the negation of the statement *I don't like spinach*?

(1) I don't like spinach.

(2) I like spinach.

(3) Spinach is good.

(4) Spinach is green.

2 What is the statement called when two simple statements are joined with the word *and*?

(1) disjunction

(2) negation

(3) biconditional

(4) conjunction

3 A disjunction is false when which condition holds?

(1) Both disjuncts are true.

(2) Both disjuncts are false.

(3) The first disjunct is true and the second false.

(4) The first disjunct is false and the second true.

4 Which two statements are logically equivalent?

(1) conditional and disjunction

(2) conjunction and disjunction

(3) conditional and contrapositive

(4) converse and biconditional

5 Which of the following is the inverse of the statement *If you study, then you will pass*?

(1) If you didn't pass, then you didn't study.

(2) You will pass if you study.

(3) If you pass, then you studied.

(4) If you don't study, then you will not pass.

6 Which type of triangle is a counterexample to the statement *The angles of a triangle are never all the same*?

(1) scalene **(3)** obtuse

(2) equilateral **(4)** isosceles

7 What best describes the statement *All triangles are three sided polygons*?

(1) open **(3)** closed

(2) true open **(4)** true closed

8 Which of the following is a biconditional statement?

(1) Today is Tuesday and tomorrow is Wednesday.

(2) Today is Tuesday or tomorrow is Wednesday.

(3) If today is Tuesday, then tomorrow is Wednesday.

(4) Today is Tuesday if and only if tomorrow is Wednesday.

9 What statement is the conjunction of a conditional statement and its converse?

(1) disjunction **(3)** contrapositive

(2) biconditional **(4)** converse

Diagnostic Test: Geometry

Name ______________________________ Date ____________

Diagnostic Test 3: Chapter 3

Triangles

Choose the numeral preceding the word or expression that best completes the statement or answers the question.

1 The measure of two angles of a triangle are 50° and 20°. This triangle must be

(1) right.
(2) isosceles.
(3) acute.
(4) obtuse.

2 What is the measure of $\angle A$ in the accompanying figure?

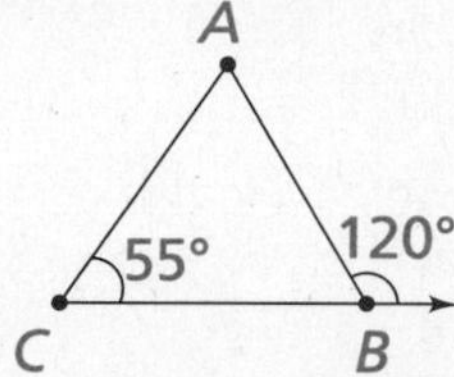

(1) 55° **(3)** 65°
(2) 60° **(4)** 120°

3 A triangle with two complementary angles is classified as which kind of triangle?

(1) obtuse **(3)** complementary
(2) acute **(4)** right

4 Which is a possible length for the third side of a triangle whose other two sides are 10 and 18?

(1) 8 **(3)** 12
(2) 28 **(4)** 35

5 What is the longest side of a triangle with a perimeter of 39 if a similar triangle has sides of length 3, 4, and 6?

(1) 12 **(3)** 18
(2) 13 **(4)** 20

6 Using similar triangles to measure the height of a flag pole is known as

(1) indirect measurement.
(2) direct measurement.
(3) proportional.
(4) similar measurement.

7 Which type of proof begins by assuming the opposite of what you want to prove?

(1) two column
(2) indirect
(3) paragraph
(4) flow

8 What must be true before using CPCTC in a proof?

(1) Two triangles are similar.
(2) Two triangles are congruent.
(3) SAS
(4) AA

9 Which of the following is not a postulate or theorem of congruence for triangles?

(1) ASA **(2)** SAS **(3)** AAS **(4)** SSA

10 What is the value of x in the accompanying figure?

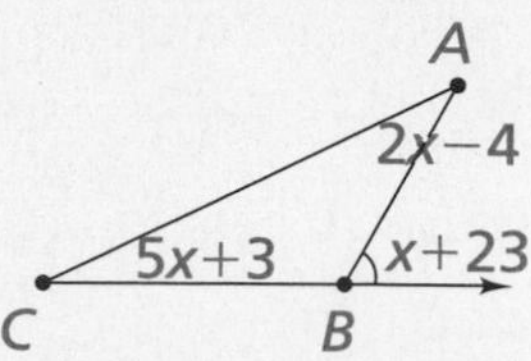

(1) 4 **(2)** 8 **(3)** 10 **(4)** 12

Name ______________________________ Date __________

Diagnostic Test 4: Chapter 4

Relationships with Triangles

Choose the numeral preceding the word or expression that best completes the statement or answers the question.

1 What is the length of TS?

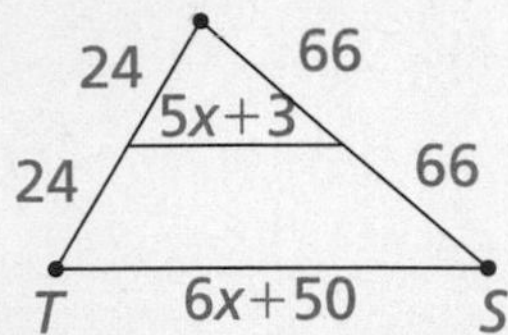

(1) 11

(2) 58

(3) 116

(4) 200

2 The area of a square is 25 units^2. What is the length of the diagonal of the square?

(1) 5 units

(2) $5\sqrt{3}$ units

(3) $5\sqrt{2}$ units

(4) 20 units

3 In a 30°–60°–90° triangle the hypotenuse is 18. Which of the following are the lengths of the legs of this triangle?

(1) 9 and 6

(2) 9 and $9\sqrt{3}$

(3) 9 and $9\sqrt{2}$

(4) $9\sqrt{2}$ and $9\sqrt{3}$

4 Determine the value of x in the accompanying figure.

(1) 6

(2) $6\sqrt{3}$

(3) 9

(4) 18

5 Which proportion is not correct based upon the accompanying figure?

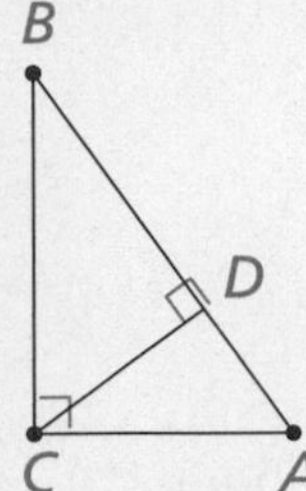

(1) $\frac{AD}{CD} = \frac{CD}{BD}$

(2) $\frac{AB}{AC} = \frac{AC}{AD}$

(3) $\frac{BD}{BC} = \frac{BC}{AB}$

(4) $\frac{BC}{CD} = \frac{CD}{AC}$

6 The orthocenter is on which segment?

(1) altitude **(3)** base

(2) median **(4)** hypotenuse

7 TM is a median of a $\triangle$RST. The length of TM is 24. The distance from T to the center of gravity is ____________?

(1) 12 **(3)** 16

(2) 8 **(4)** 6

Name ______________________________ Date __________

Diagnostic Test 5: Chapter 5

Quadrilaterals and Other Polygons

Choose the numeral preceding the word or expression that best completes the statement or answers the question.

1 The number of degrees in an exterior angle of a regular polygon with n sides is

(1) 180°. **(3)** $(n - 2)180°$.

(2) 360°. **(4)** $\frac{360°}{n}$.

2 The number of triangles found in the interior of any regular polygon is always

(1) n. **(3)** $n - 2$.

(2) $n - 1$. **(4)** $n - 3$.

3 Find the measures of the numbered angles in the parallelogram.

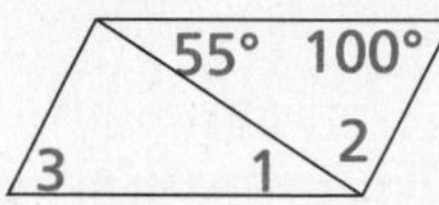

(1) $m\angle 1 = 55, m\angle 2 = 25; m\angle 3 = 100$

(2) $m\angle 1 = 25, m\angle 2 = 55; m\angle 3 = 100$

(3) $m\angle 1 = 45, m\angle 2 = 35; m\angle 3 = 100$

(4) $m\angle 1 = 100, m\angle 2 = 25; m\angle 3 = 55$

4 What is the measure of each exterior angle of a regular hexagon?

(1) 45° **(3)** 120°

(2) 60° **(4)** 90°

5 The sum of the interior angles of a decagon is

(1) 360°.

(2) 1440°.

(3) 1800°.

(4) 720°.

6 Which property is sufficient to show a quadrilateral is always a parallelogram?

(1) It has 4 right angles.

(2) 2 pairs of opposite sides are parallel.

(3) 1 pair of opposite sides is parallel.

(4) 1 pair of opposite sides is congruent.

7 The measure of $\angle ABC$ equals which of the following?

I. $m\angle BCD$ **II.** $180° - m\angle BCD$ **III.** 105°

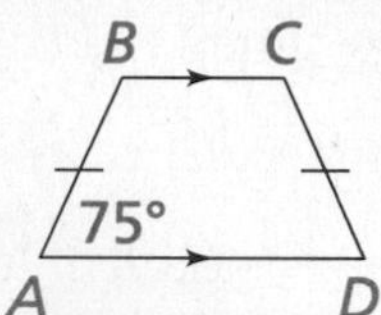

(1) III only **(3)** I and III

(2) I and II **(4)** I, II, and III

8 In the pentagon below $\angle B \cong \angle D$. Find the number of degrees in $\angle C$.

(1) 90°

(2) 100°

(3) 120°

(4) 80°

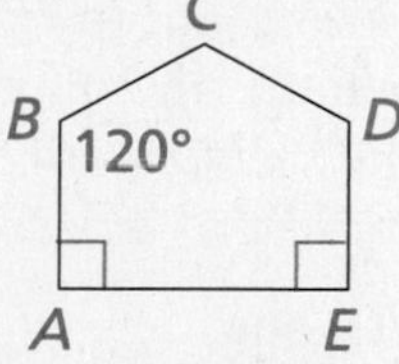

9 The diagonals of an isosceles trapezoid

(1) are congruent.

(2) bisect each other.

(3) are perpendicular.

(4) form 4 congruent triangles.

Diagnostic Test: Geometry

Name ______________________________ Date ____________

Diagnostic Test 6: Chapter 6

Coordinate Geometry

Choose the numeral preceding the word or expression that best completes the statement or answers the question.

1 Which represents the midpoint of the line segment with endpoints (4, −3) and (8, 5)?

(1) (2, 4) **(3)** (−6, −1)

(2) (6, 1) **(4)** (−2, − 4)

2 Find the distance between (1, 5) and (5, −3).

(1) $2\sqrt{13}$ **(3)** $4\sqrt{5}$

(2) 5 **(4)** 10

3 The slope of the line passing through the points (3, −2) and (7, 2) is

(1) 0. **(3)** undefined.

(2) 1. **(4)** −1.

4 If the slope of a line is *zero*, then the line is

(1) rising left to right.

(2) falling left to right.

(3) horizontal.

(4) vertical.

5 What is the maximum number of points in the solution to a system of equations that represent a parabola and a circle?

(1) one **(3)** three

(2) two **(4)** four

6 For which equation will the graph of $y = -x^2 + 2$ and the line intersect in two points?

(1) $y = -2x + 3$ **(3)** $y = 5$

(2) $y = 2$ **(4)** $y = 0$

7 The equation of a line with a slope of 3 and a *y*-intercept of −8 is which of the following?

(1) $y = -8x + 3$ **(3)** $y = 3x + 8$

(2) $y = 3x - 8$ **(4)** $y = 3x - (-8)$

8 Which equation is that of a circle with center (3, −4) and a radius of 5?

(1) $x^2 + y^2 = 5$

(2) $3x^2 - 4y^2 = 25$

(3) $(x - 3)^2 + (y + 4)^2 = 5^2$

(4) $(x + 3)^2 + (y - 4)^2 = 5^2$

9 Which equation represents the line that is parallel to the graph of $3y - 7x = 9$?

(1) $y = \frac{7}{3}x + 1$ **(3)** $y = -\frac{3}{7}x + 1$

(2) $2y = -7x + 6$ **(4)** $y = -\frac{1}{7}x + 3$

10 Which of the following points would make the graph below into a square?

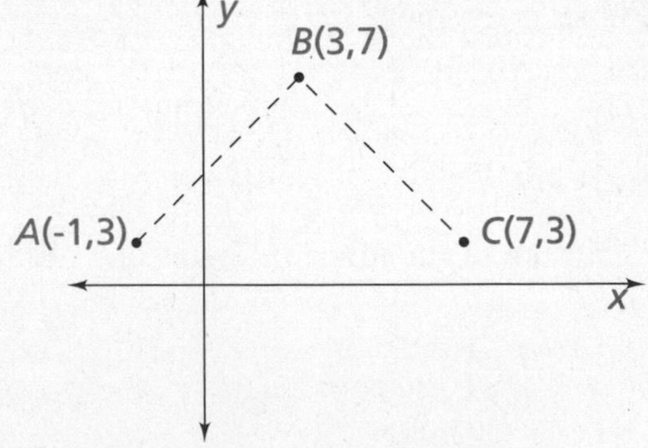

(1) $D(4, -2)$ **(3)** $D(3, 0)$

(2) $D(3, -1)$ **(4)** $D(3, -3)$

Diagnostic Test: Geometry

Name ______________________________ Date ____________

Diagnostic Test 7: Chapter 7

Transformational Geometry

Choose the numeral preceding the word or expression that best completes the statement or answers the question.

1 Which point represents the image of the point (3, −4) when reflected in the x-axis?

(1) (3, 4)
(2) (−3, 4)
(3) (−3, −4)
(4) (−4, 3)

2 A glide reflection is made up of which two transformations?

(1) reflection and rotation
(2) rotation and translation
(3) reflection and translation
(4) dilation and reflection

3 Reflecting a figure over two intersecting lines is the same as what single transformation?

(1) reflection
(2) rotation
(3) dilation
(4) translation

4 Which of the following has rotational symmetry?

(1) isosceles trapezoid
(2) isosceles triangle
(3) right triangle
(4) square

5 What are the coordinates of the image of A (−1, 3) under $T_{2,3}$?

(1) (2, 3)
(2) (−3, 3)
(3) (1, 6)
(4) (1, 0)

6 The accompanying figure is an example of which of the following transformations?

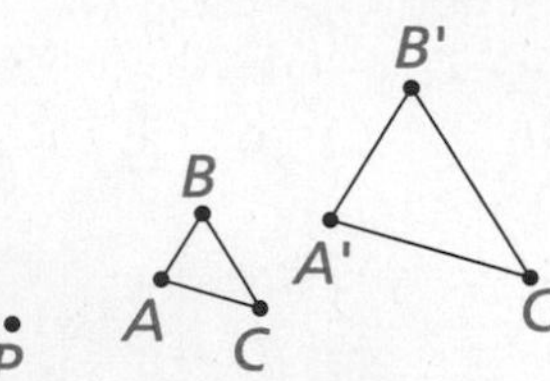

(1) rotation
(2) dilation
(3) reflections
(4) translation

7 $D'(4, 12)$ is the image of $D(6, 18)$ under a dilation. What is the scale factor?

(1) $\frac{2}{3}$ **(3)** $\frac{3}{2}$
(2) $\frac{1}{2}$ **(4)** .66

8 Which of the following is not an isometry?

(1) reflection
(2) translation
(3) rotation
(4) dilation

9 Under what transformation will the image of $Q(-5, 4)$ be $Q'(-4, -5)$?

(1) a reflection about the x-axis
(2) a 90° counterclockwise rotation about the origin
(3) a reflection about the origin
(4) a 90° clockwise rotation about the origin

Name ______________________________ Date ____________

Diagnostic Test 8: Chapter 8

Angles in Circles

Choose the numeral preceding the word or expression that best completes the statement or answers the question. Use the information in the figure to answer questions 1–10.

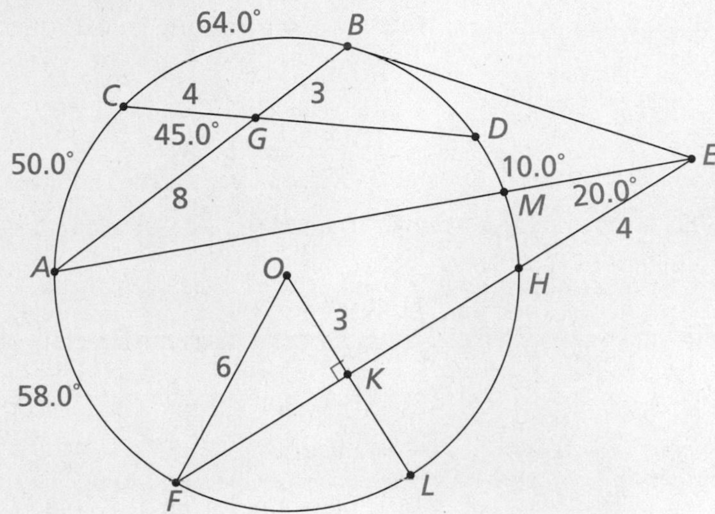

1 Determine the length of $\overline{KL}$.

(1) 6 **(3)** 3
(2) 8 **(4)** 12

2 Determine the $m\widehat{BD}$.

(1) 50° **(3)** 45°
(2) 40° **(4)** 90°

3 $GD = ?$

(1) 6 **(3)** 8
(2) 12 **(4)** 24

4 $m\angle FOL = ?$

(1) 20° **(3)** 45°
(2) 50° **(4)** 60°

5 Determine the length of $\overline{KH}$.

(1) 6 **(3)** $3\sqrt{3}$
(2) $3\sqrt{2}$ **(4)** $3\sqrt{6}$

6 Determine the length of the tangent segment BE (to the nearest integer).

(1) 5 **(3)** 7
(2) 6 **(4)** 8

7 Determine the $m\angle BEA$.

(1) 32° **(3)** 64°
(2) 57° **(4)** 114°

8 Determine the $m\widehat{MH}$.

(1) 18° **(3)** 40°
(2) 20° **(4)** 68°

9 Which of the following is a true statement?

(1) $m\widehat{AF} \cong m\widehat{FL}$ **(3)** $m\widehat{FL} \cong m\widehat{HL}$
(2) $m\widehat{AC} \cong m\widehat{BD}$ **(4)** $m\widehat{DM} \cong m\widehat{MH}$

10 $m\angle BAM$

(1) 15° **(3)** 30°
(2) 25° **(4)** 50°

Name ______________________________ Date __________

Diagnostic Test 9: Chapter 9

Solid Geometry and Its Applications

Choose the numeral preceding the word or expression that best completes the statement or answers the question.

1 Find the surface area of a rectangular prism with $l = 6$ in., $w = 4$ in., and $h = 2$ in..

(1) 48 in.^{2} **(3)** 120 in.^{2}

(2) 88 in.^{2} **(4)** 112 in.^{2}

2 If the volume of a cylinder is 252π ft^3, what is the volume of a cone with the same base and height?

(1) 36π cu ft^3 **(3)** 84π cu ft^3

(2) 126π cu ft^3 **(4)** 252π ft^3

3 Two pyramids are similar and the ratio of their corresponding sides is 5:8. What is the ratio of their surface areas?

(1) 25:64 **(3)** 125:512

(2) 5:8 **(4)** 20:32

Use the following diagram for exercises 4–5. (Answer may be left in terms of π.)

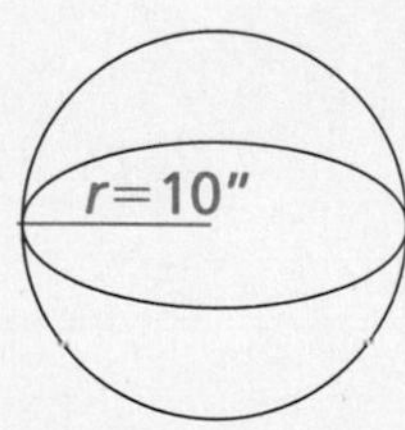

4 Find the surface area of the sphere with radius 10.

(1) $80\,\pi\, in^2$ **(3)** $100\pi\, in^2$

(2) $200\pi\, in^2$ **(4)** $400\pi\, in^2$

5 Find the volume of the sphere above.

(1) $1333.3\pi\, in^3$ **(3)** $133.3\pi\, in^3$

(2) $400\pi\, in^3$ **(4)** $4000\pi\, in^3$

6 Find the volume of the prism below.

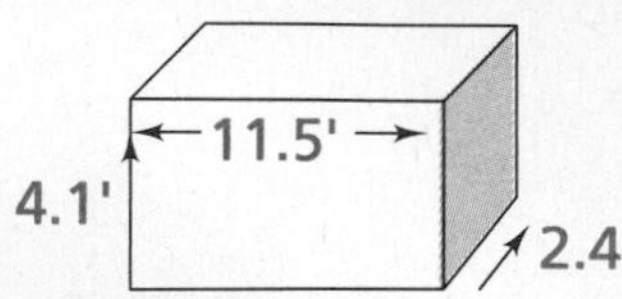

(1) 124.8 ft^3 **(3)** 62.4 ft^3

(2) 113.16 ft^3 **(4)** 162 ft^3

7 If 2 planes intersect, the intersection will be

(1) a point. **(3)** a line.

(2) 2 points. **(4)** 2 intersecting lines.

8 To the nearest integer, find the lateral area of a cylinder whose base has a radius of 7 and whose height is 14.

(1) 154 **(3)** 2156

(2) 308 **(4)** 616

9 To the nearest integer, find the volume of a square pyramid with base area of 36 cm^2 and height of 8 cm.

(1) 144 cm^3 **(3)** 96 cm^3

(2) 44 cm^3 **(4)** 288 cm^3

10 How many lines can be perpendicular to a plane through a given point, not in the plane?

(1) one and only one

(2) up to two lines

(3) up to three lines

(4) an infinite number

1 Basic Geometry in the Plane

Discovering New York

New York City's Subway

In 1904, New York City opened its first underground train line, known as the "subway." Since then, the subway has grown into one of the biggest transit systems in the world, with 26 train lines operating on more than 800 miles of tracks. Laid end to end, the tracks would stretch from New York City to Chicago. More than half of all New Yorkers do not own a car, so public transportation is an essential form of travel. Nearly 5,000,000 passengers ride on New York City's subway system every day. Its trains run 24 hours a day, 7 days a week.

To carry so many people, the system uses more than 27,000 volts of electricity. That is enough power to light the city of Buffalo, New York, for an entire year.

1.1 Points, Lines, Planes, and Segments

New York Standards

Foundational standards coverage

The foundation of geometry begins with three undefined terms: **point, line,** and **plane.** All other terms can be defined by using these terms.

Undefined Terms

A **point** can be described as a location in space. It has no length, width, or height. All geometric figures consist of points. **Space** consists of the infinite set of points. The physical representation of a point is a **dot.** A capital letter next to the dot is used to name the point.

A • point *A*

A **line** is a set of points extending in opposite directions without end. A line indicates direction and has one dimension, length. A line is named by any 2 points on the line, in any order, or by a single lowercase letter.

line *AB* or $\overleftrightarrow{AB}$

A **plane** is a flat surface of points extending in every direction without end. It has two dimensions, length and width. A single letter or at least three points in the plane can name a plane.

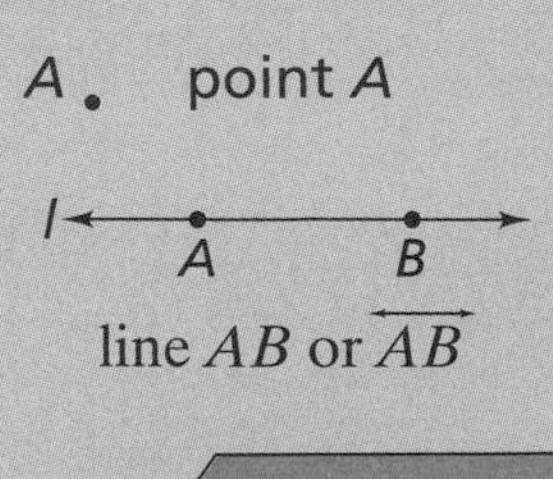

Plane *P* or plane *ABC*

Points and lines that lie in the same plane are **coplanar.** If two lines intersect, then they are coplanar. Lines that do not lie in the same plane are **skew** lines.

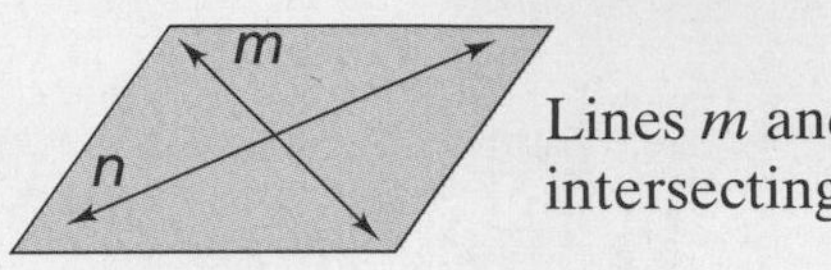

Lines *m* and *n* are intersecting lines.

Collinear points are points that lie on the same line. Points that do not lie on the same line are **noncollinear.**

Assumptions that are accepted as true without proof are called **postulates** or **axioms.**

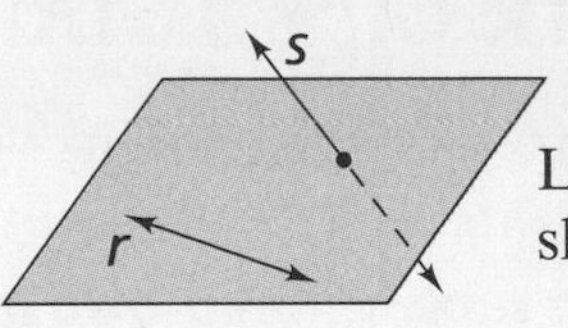

Lines *r* and *s* are skew lines.

Here are four basic **postulates** about points, lines, and planes.

- Through any 2 points, there is exactly one line. (Any two points determine a line.)
- If 2 lines intersect, they intersect in exactly one point.

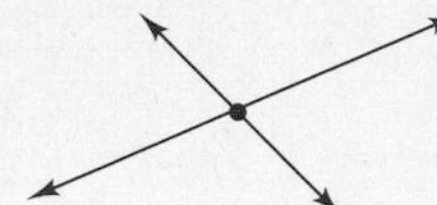

- If 2 planes intersect, they intersect in exactly one line.

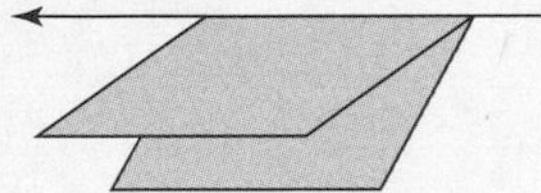

- Through any 3 noncollinear points, there is exactly one plane.

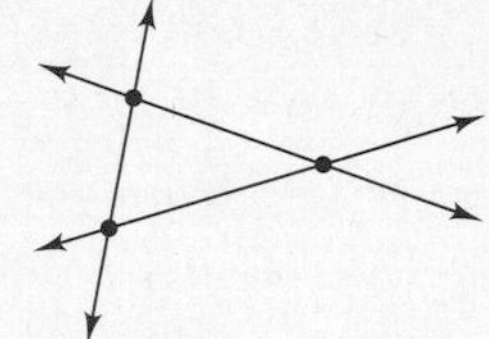

EXAMPLES 1 and 2 **Using the basic postulates for points, lines, and planes**

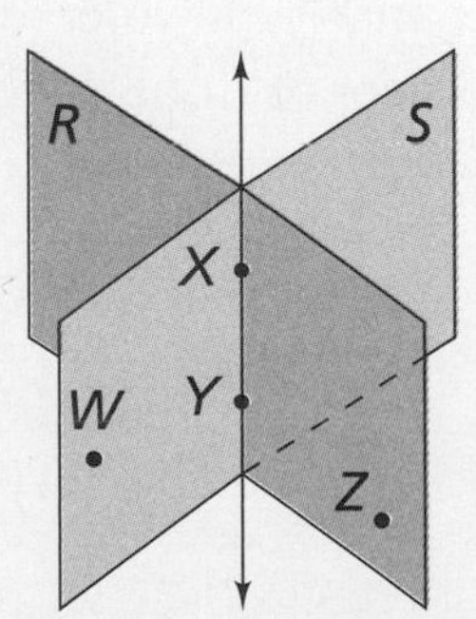

1 Name three labeled points that determine plane *R*.

■ SOLUTION

Because three noncollinear points determine a plane, three points that determine plane *R* are points *X*, *Y*, and *Z*.

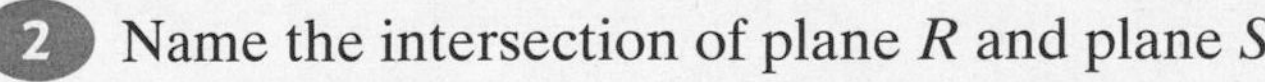

2 Name the intersection of plane *R* and plane *S*.

■ SOLUTION

The intersection of two planes is a line. The intersection of plane *R* and plane *S* is $\overleftrightarrow{XY}$.

Recall that a number line is a line whose points have been placed in one-to-one correspondence with the set of real numbers. This pairing between the points of a line and the real numbers is a fundamental postulate of geometry.

Ruler Postulate

The points of a line can be paired with the real numbers one-to-one so that any two points on the line can be paired with 0 and 1. The real number that corresponds to a point is called the **coordinate** of that point. The **distance** between two points of the line is equal to the absolute value of the difference of their coordinates.

The distance between point *A* and point *B* is denoted *AB* or *BA*.

EXAMPLE 3 Using the Ruler Postulate

3 Find *AB* on the number line at the right.

■ **SOLUTION**

The coordinate of *A* is −4. The coordinate of *B* is 2. Subtract the coordinates in any order, and then find the absolute value of the difference.

$AB = |-4 - 2| = |-6| = 6$ or $BA = |2 - (-4)| = |6| = 6$

The Ruler Postulate provides a basis for the following definitions.

Definitions Related to Segments

A **line segment,** or **segment,** is part of a line that begins at one point and ends at another. The points are called the **endpoints of the segment.** You name a segment by its endpoints.

segment *JK* ($\overline{JK}$)

The **length of a segment** is the distance between its endpoints.

Segments that are equal in length are called **congruent segments.** You indicate congruent segments by marking them with an equal number of tick marks. The symbol for congruence is ≅.

$\overline{CD} \cong \overline{EF}$

The **midpoint** of a segment is the point that divides the segment into two congruent segments.

$\overline{PM} \cong \overline{QM}$

M is the midpoint of $\overline{PQ}$.

Note

The statement *CD* = *EF* is read "The length of segment *CD* is equal to the length of segment *EF*."

The statement $\overline{CD} \cong \overline{EF}$ is read "Segment *CD* is congruent to segment *EF*."

You can use these statements interchangeably.

If the endpoints of a segment on a number line have coordinates A and B, you can find the coordinate of the midpoint by simplifying the expression $\frac{A+B}{2}$.

EXAMPLE 4 **Finding the midpoint of a segment on a number line**

4 Find the coordinate of the midpoint of $\overline{AB}$.

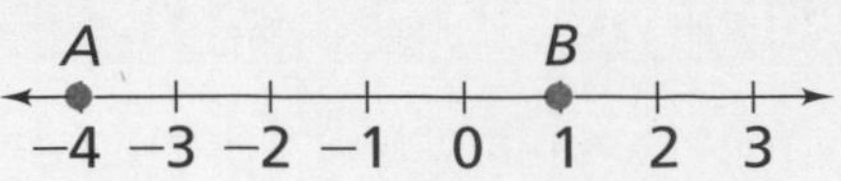

■ **SOLUTION**

The coordinate of A is -4. The coordinate of B is 1.

The coordinate of the midpoint is $\frac{-4+1}{2} = \frac{-3}{2} = -1\frac{1}{2}$.

On a number line, a point C is **between** point A and point B if the coordinate of point C is between the coordinates of points A and B. This leads to an important postulate concerning segments.

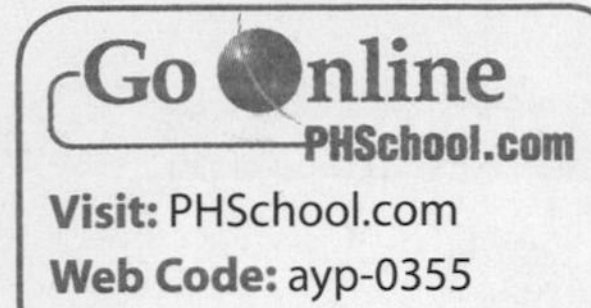

Visit: PHSchool.com
Web Code: ayp-0355

Segment Addition Postulate

If point C is between point A and point B, then A, B, and C are collinear and $AC + CB = AB$.

EXAMPLE 5 **Using the Segment Addition Postulate**

5 In the figure at the right, point U is between point V and point W, and $VW = 31$. Find UW.

■ **SOLUTION**

$VU + UW = VW$ ← **Apply the Segment Addition Postulate.**
$3t - 9 + 2t + 5 = 31$ ← **Substitute.**
$5t - 4 = 31$ ← **Combine like terms.**
$5t = 35$ ← **Solve.**
$t = 7$

Therefore: $UW = 2t + 5 \rightarrow 2(7) + 5 = 19$.

Practice

Choose the numeral preceding the word or expression that best completes the statement or answers the question.

1 Three noncollinear points determine a
(1) plane.
(2) line.
(3) segment.
(4) midpoint.

2 Which of the following statements is true?
(1) Any three points determine a line.
(2) Collinear points are always coplanar.
(3) Skew lines lie in the same plane.
(4) Any two lines determine a plane.

3 On a number line, the coordinate of point A is m and the coordinate of point B is n. Which expression represents the length of $\overline{AB}$?

(1) $n - m$ **(3)** $m + n$

(2) $|m - n|$ **(4)** $\frac{m + n}{2}$

4 Given that point R is the midpoint of $\overline{PQ}$, which statement is false?

(1) $PR = QR$ **(3)** $PR = 2PQ$

(2) $QR = \frac{1}{2}PQ$ **(4)** $PR + RQ = PQ$

In Exercises 5–14, refer to the figure below.

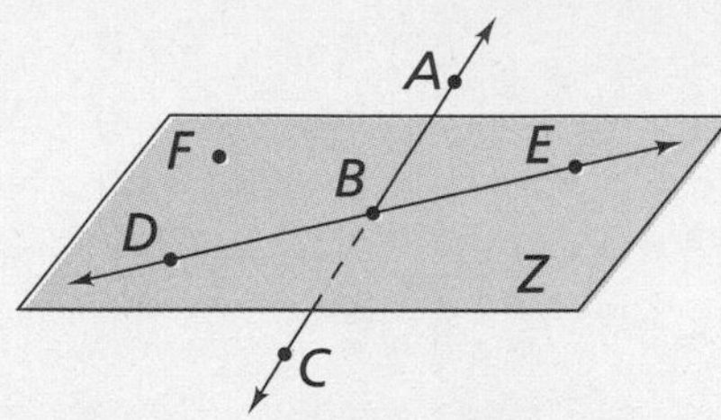

Are the points collinear? Write *Yes* or *No*.

5 B, E, A **6** D, B, E

7 A, B, D **8** A, C, B

Are the points coplanar? Write *Yes* or *No*.

9 C, B, A, E **10** E, F, B, D

11 D, B, F, A **12** D, B, F, C

13 Use the labeled points to name plane Z in three different ways.

14 Name the intersection of $\overleftrightarrow{AC}$ and $\overleftrightarrow{ED}$.

In Exercises 15–20, refer to the figure below. Use the labeled points to answer each question.

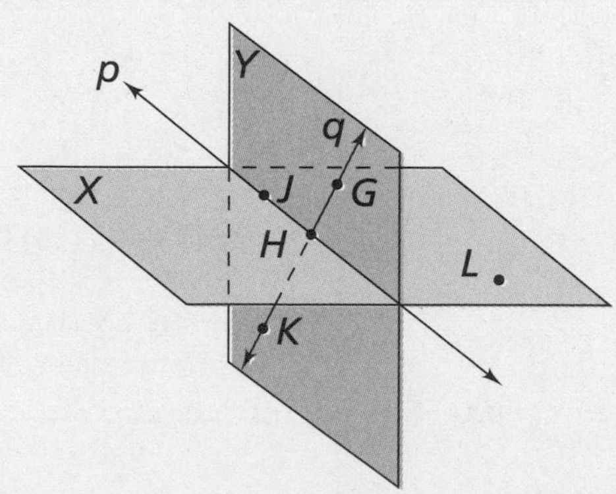

15 Name two points that determine line p.

16 Name three points that determine plane X.

17 Name the intersection of line p and line q.

18 Name line q in three different ways.

19 Name the intersection of planes X and Y.

20 Name the intersection of line q and plane X.

In Exercises 21–24, refer to the number line below. Find each length.

A			B		C		D			E
−7	−6	−5	−4	−3	−2	−1	0	1	2	3

21 AC **22** BD **23** CB **24** AE

In Exercises 25–28, refer to the number line below.

P	Q	R	S	T	U	V	W	X	Y	Z
−5	−4	−3	−2	−1	0	1	2	3	4	5

Give the letter that names the midpoint of each segment.

25 $\overline{QS}$ **26** $\overline{SW}$ **27** $\overline{VZ}$ **28** $\overline{RZ}$

In Exercises 29–30, use the figure below. Point *M* is the midpoint of $\overline{JK}$.

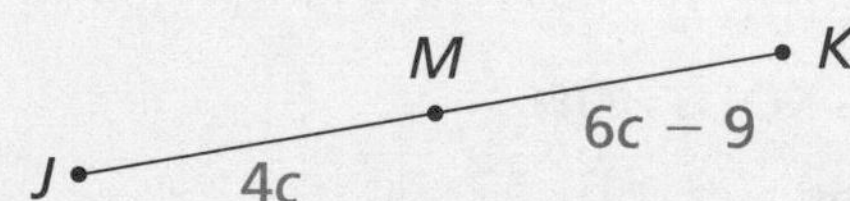

29 Find c.

30 Find JM and JK.

31 The towns of Ames, Bradley, and Carlton lie along the same straight road. Ames is 45 miles due east of Bradley, and Carlton is 10 miles due west of Ames. Which town is between the other two? Draw a diagram to illustrate your answer.

1.2 Rays and Angles

New York Standards
Foundational standards coverage

Another set of definitions and postulates is associated with the concept of a ray.

Definitions Related to Rays

A **ray** is part of a line that begins at one point and extends without end in one direction. The point is called the **endpoint of the ray.** You name a ray by its endpoint and one other point on it.

R S ray RS ($\overrightarrow{RS}$)

On a line, if point B is between point A and point C, then $\overrightarrow{BA}$ and $\overrightarrow{BC}$ are **opposite rays.**

opposite rays $\overrightarrow{BA}$ and $\overrightarrow{BC}$

An **angle** (or **plane angle**) is the figure formed by two rays with a common endpoint. Each ray is a **side** of the angle, and the endpoint is the **vertex** of the angle. The symbol for angle is ∠. There are several ways to name an angle.

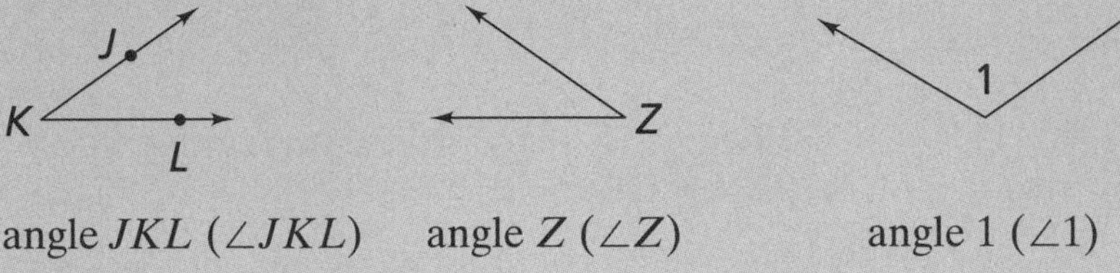

angle JKL ($\angle JKL$) angle Z ($\angle Z$) angle 1 ($\angle 1$)

EXAMPLE 1 **Identifying rays**

1 Identify all the rays in the figure.

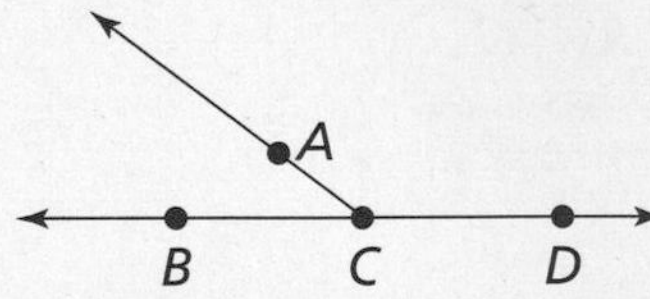

■ **SOLUTION**
$\overrightarrow{CA}$, $\overrightarrow{CD}$, $\overrightarrow{CB}$, $\overrightarrow{BD}$, $\overrightarrow{DB}$

Angles are classified according to their degree measure.

Definitions Related to Angle Measure

An **acute angle** is an angle whose measure is greater than 0° and less than 90°.

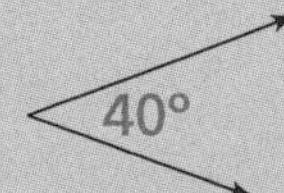

An **obtuse angle** is an angle whose measure is greater than 90° and less than 180°.

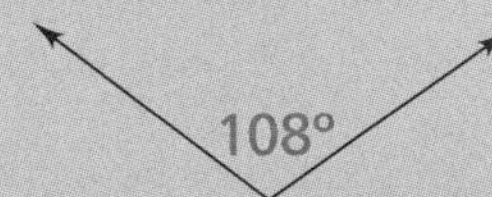

A **right angle** is an angle whose measure is equal to 90°.

This symbol indicates a right angle.

A **straight angle** is an angle whose measure is equal to 180°.

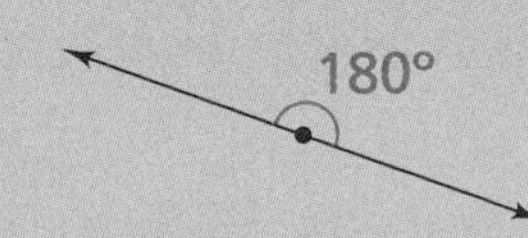

Go Online PHSchool.com
Visit: PHSchool.com
Web Code: ayp-0760

Definitions Relating to Angle Relationships

Congruent angles are two angles that have the same degree measure.

This is written as $m\angle A = m\angle B$; read *the measure of* $\angle A$ *is equal to the measure of* $\angle B$, or $\angle A \cong \angle B$, read $\angle A$ *is congruent to* $\angle B$.

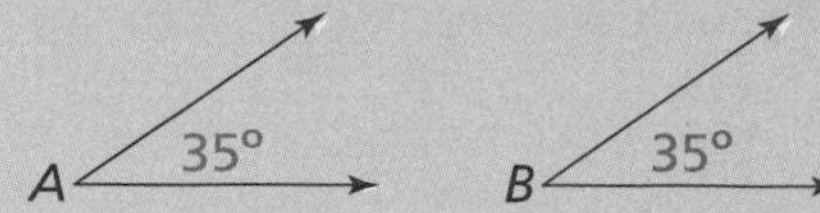

An **angle bisector** is a ray that divides an angle into two congruent angles. $\overrightarrow{CE}$ bisects $\angle DCF$.

Adjacent angles are two angles that share a common side and the same vertex but no common interior points.

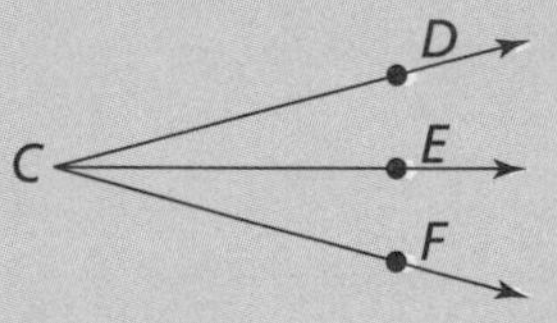

In the diagram on the left, $\angle DCE \cong \angle FCE$ and $\angle DCE$ is also adjacent to $\angle FCE$.

Complementary angles are two angles whose measures add up to 90°. In the diagram at the right, $\angle 1$ and $\angle 2$ are complementary.

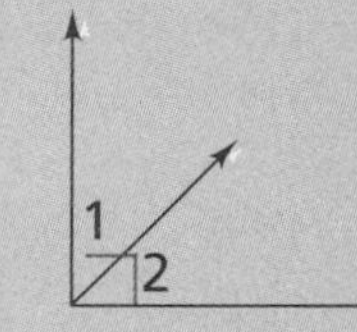

Supplementary angles are two angles whose measures add up to 180°. Supplementary angles that are also adjacent form a **linear pair.** $\angle 3$ and $\angle 4$ are supplementary.

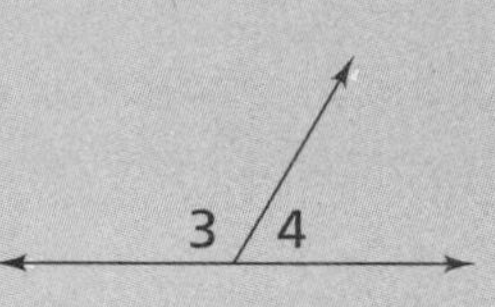

Go Online
PHSchool.com
Visit: PHSchool.com
Web Code: ayp-0762

You can use these definitions to identify the angle relationships in a given figure.

EXAMPLES 2 and 3 **Identifying angle relationships**

2 Use the figure to identify at least one of each of the following:

Angle bisector	Congruent angles
Adjacent angles	Complementary angles
Linear pair	Supplementary angles

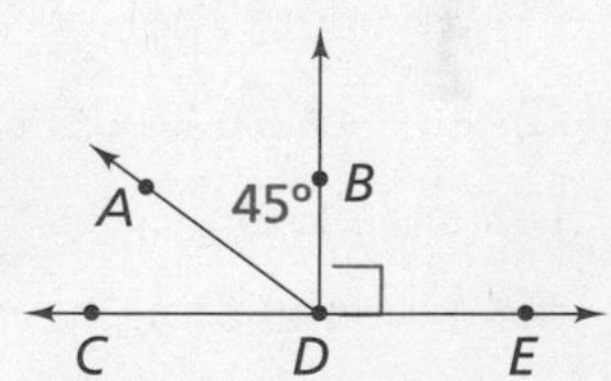

■ **SOLUTION**

Angle bisector:	$\overrightarrow{DA}$ bisects $\angle CDB$ and $\overrightarrow{DB}$ bisects $\angle CDE$
Adjacent angles:	$\angle CDA$ and $\angle ADB$ or $\angle ADB$ and $\angle BDE$
Linear pair:	$\angle CDA$ and $\angle ADE$ or $\angle CDB$ and $\angle BDE$
Congruent angles:	$\angle CDA \cong \angle ADB$ or $\angle CDB \cong \angle BDE$
Complementary angles:	$\angle CDA$ and $\angle ADB$
Supplementary angles:	$\angle CDB$ and $\angle BDE$

3 Find $m\angle ADC$.

■ **SOLUTION**

$\overleftrightarrow{CE}$ forms a straight angle with measure 180°. You are given that $m\angle ADB = 45°$ and $m\angle BDE = 90°$. Therefore, $m\angle ADC = 180 - 45 - 90 = 45°$. The angles $\angle ADC$ and $\angle ADB$ are complementary angles.

An angle separates a plane into three sets of points: the angle itself, the points in the *interior* of the angle, and the points in the *exterior* of the angle.

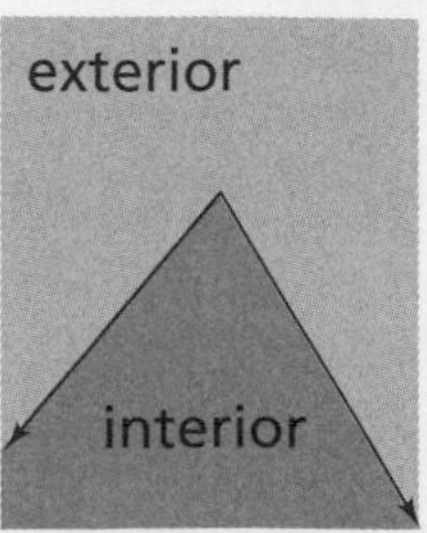

Angle Addition Postulate

If point B is in the interior of $\angle AOC$, then $m\angle AOB + m\angle BOC = m\angle AOC$.

EXAMPLE 4 Using the Angle Addition Postulate

4 In the figure, $m\angle AOB = 74°$ and $m\angle AOC = 106°$. Find $m\angle BOC$.

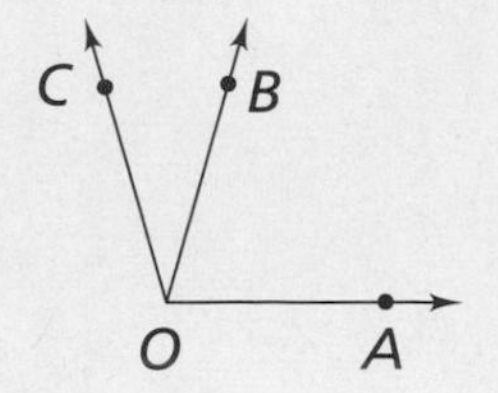

SOLUTION

$m\angle AOB + m\angle BOC = m\angle AOC$ ← **Apply the Angle Addition Postulate.**

$74° + m\angle BOC = 106°$ ← **Substitute.**

$m\angle BOC = 32°$ ← **Solve.**

Practice

Choose the numeral preceding the word or expression that best completes the statement or answers the question.

1 The measure of a straight angle is

(1) less than 90°. **(3)** exactly 90°.
(2) less than 180°. **(4)** exactly 180°.

2 The supplement of an acute angle is

(1) an acute angle.
(2) an obtuse angle.
(3) a right angle.
(4) a straight angle.

3 Which is the most reasonable estimate of the measure of $\angle QRS$?

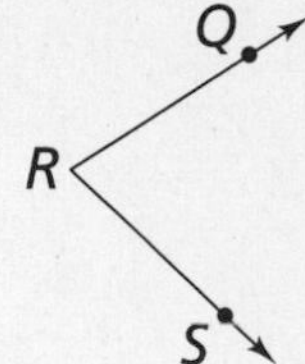

(1) about 115° **(3)** about 75°
(2) about 95° **(4)** about 15°

4 In the figure below, $\overrightarrow{AX}$ and $\overrightarrow{AZ}$ are opposite rays, and $\angle XAY$ is a right angle. Which statement is false?

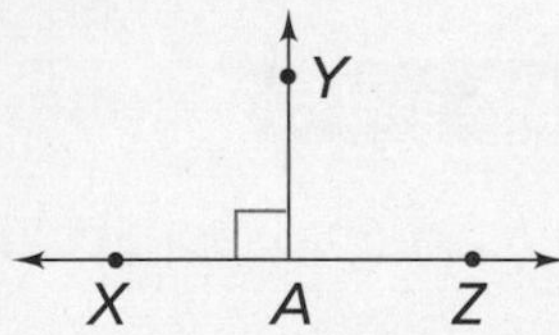

(1) $\angle YAZ$ is the complement of $\angle XAY$.
(2) $\angle YAZ$ is adjacent to $\angle XAY$.
(3) $\angle YAZ$ is congruent to $\angle XAY$.
(4) $\angle XAY$ and $\angle YAZ$ are a linear pair.

5 If $\angle 1$ is supplementary to $\angle 2$ and $\angle 2$ is supplementary to $\angle 3$, which statement is always true?

(1) $\angle 1$ is supplementary to $\angle 3$.
(2) $\angle 1$ is complementary to $\angle 3$.
(3) $\angle 1$ is congruent to $\angle 3$.
(4) $\angle 1$ is adjacent to $\angle 3$.

6 Two acute angles can be which of the following?

I. congruent III. complementary
II. adjacent IV. supplementary

(1) I and II **(3)** I, II, and III
(2) I and III **(4)** I, II, and IV

7 $\overrightarrow{OF}$ bisects $\angle EOG$. Which of the following is not true?

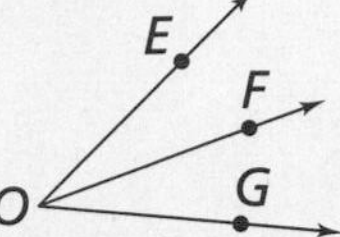

(1) $m\angle EOF = m\angle FOG$
(2) $m\angle FOG = m\angle EOG - m\angle EOF$
(3) $m\angle EOF = m\angle EOG$
(4) $m\angle FOG = \frac{1}{2}m\angle EOG$

8 $\angle YXZ$ and $\angle ZXW$ are adjacent and supplementary angles. If $m\angle YXZ = 37°$, what is $m\angle ZXW$?

(1) 143° **(3)** 53°
(2) 37° **(4)** unknown

9 What is the measure of the angle formed by opposite rays?

(1) 90° **(3)** 180°
(2) 360° **(4)** unknown

10 $\angle AZB$ and $\angle CZB$ are supplementary. The $m\angle AZB = 2x - 4$ and $m\angle CZB = 8x + 4$. What is the measure of each angle?

(1) $m\angle AZB = 32°$ and $m\angle CZB = 148°$
(2) $m\angle AZB = 12°$ and $m\angle CZB = 76°$
(3) $m\angle AZB = 43°$ and $m\angle CZB = 22°$
(4) $m\angle AZB = 68°$ and $m\angle CZB = 292°$

In Exercises 11–13, state the measure of the complement of an angle of the given measure.

11 56° **12** 12.5° **13** $x°$

In Exercises 14–16, state the measure of the supplement of an angle of the given measure.

14 113° **15** 41.5° **16** $y°$

In Exercises 17–18, $\overrightarrow{OA}$ and $\overrightarrow{OB}$ are opposite rays. Find $m\angle AOC$.

17 **18**

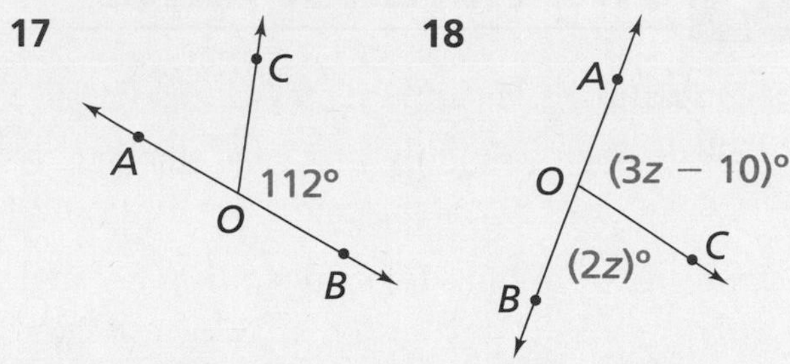

In Exercises 19–20, $m\angle PZR$ is a right angle. Find $m\angle PZQ$.

19 **20**

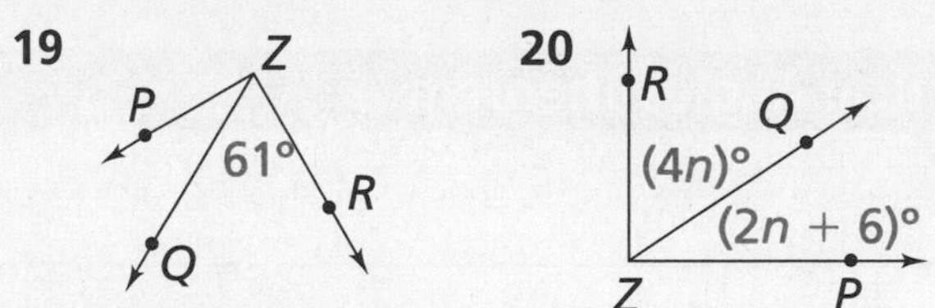

In Exercises 21–24, answer *true* or *false*.

21 Complementary angles are always adjacent.

22 The angles of a linear pair are always adjacent.

23 If $\overrightarrow{PQ}$ and $\overrightarrow{PR}$ are names for the same ray, then Q and R must be names for the same point.

24 If the union of two rays is a line, then the rays are opposite rays.

In Exercises 25–28, solve the problem.

25 The measure of an angle is equal to the measure of its complement. Find the measure of each angle.

26 The measure of an angle is equal to the measure of its supplement. Find the measure of each angle.

27 The measure of an angle is twice the measure of its supplement. Find the measure of the larger angle.

28 The measure of an angle is fourteen degrees less than the measure of its complement. Find the measure of the smaller angle.

1.3 Intersecting, Perpendicular, and Parallel Lines

New York Standards

G.G.35 Transversal of parallel lines

The figure at the right shows intersecting lines ℓ and m. The lines form the following four pairs of adjacent angles, and each is a linear pair.

$\angle 1$ and $\angle 2$ $\quad$ $\angle 2$ and $\angle 3$ $\quad$ $\angle 3$ and $\angle 4$ $\quad$ $\angle 4$ and $\angle 1$

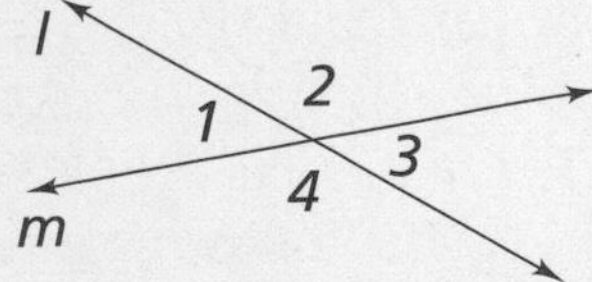

The figure also contains two pairs of *vertical* angles.

$\angle 1$ and $\angle 3$ $\quad$ $\angle 2$ and $\angle 4$

Vertical angles are two angles whose sides form two pairs of opposite rays. There is a special relationship between vertical angles, stated as follows.

Vertical Angles Theorem

If two angles are vertical angles, then they are congruent.

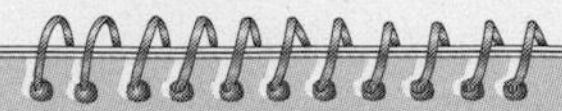

Note

You can prove the Vertical Angles Theorem algebraically.

Notice that the above statement is called a *theorem*. A **theorem** is a statement that can be proved true.

EXAMPLE 1 Using the Vertical Angles Theorem

In the figure at the right, lines s and t intersect at point P, $m\angle 1 = (3n - 14)°$, and $m\angle 3 = (2n + 17)°$. Find $m\angle 2$.

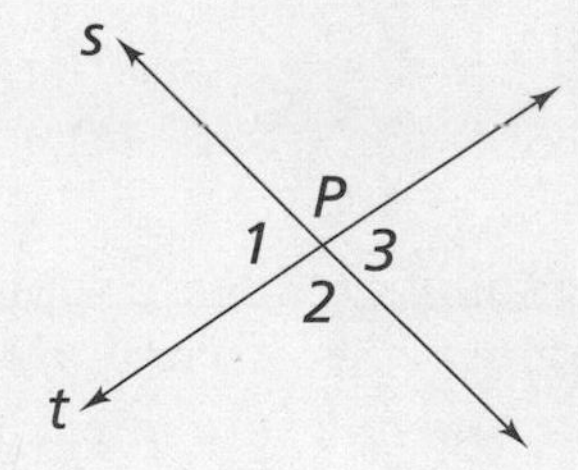

SOLUTION

$m\angle 1 = m\angle 3$ ← **Apply the Vertical Angles Theorem.**

$3n - 14 = 2n + 17$ ← **Substitute.**

$n - 14 = 17$ ← **Solve.**

$n = 31$

Therefore: $m\angle 1 = (3n - 14)° \rightarrow (3[31] - 14)° = 79°$

Because $\angle 1$ and $\angle 2$ are a linear pair, $m\angle 2 = 180° - m\angle 1 = 180° - 79° = 101°$.

Perpendicular lines are two lines that intersect to form right angles. The symbol for perpendicular is $\perp$.

$\overleftrightarrow{EF}$ is perpendicular to $\overleftrightarrow{GH}$, denoted $\overleftrightarrow{EF} \perp \overleftrightarrow{GH}$.

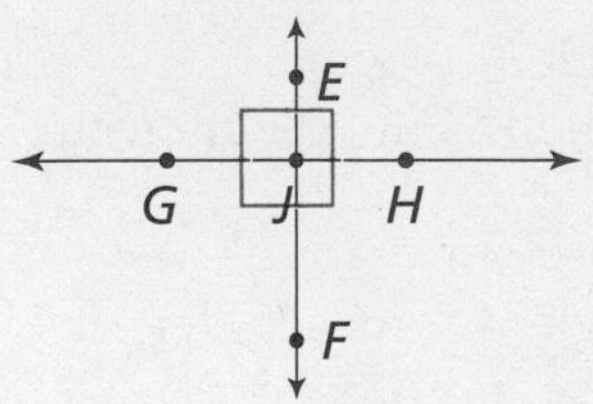

Because $\overleftrightarrow{EF} \perp \overleftrightarrow{GH}$, $\angle$EJG, $\angle$GJF, $\angle$EJH, and $\angle$HJF are right angles and each measures 90°.

Note

A small square at the intersection of two lines denotes a right angle.

EXAMPLE 2 **Working with perpendicular lines**

2 In the figure, $\overleftrightarrow{AB} \perp \overleftrightarrow{CD}$ and $m\angle EZD = 53°$. Find $m\angle AZE$.

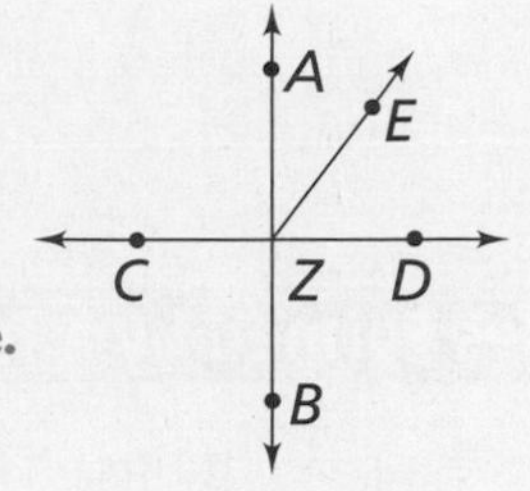

■ **SOLUTION**

Because $\overleftrightarrow{AB} \perp \overleftrightarrow{CD}$, $\angle AZD$ is a right angle and $m\angle AZD = 90°$.

$m\angle AZE + m\angle EZD = m\angle AZD$ ← **Apply the Angle Addition Postulate.**

$m\angle AZE + 53° = 90°$ ← **Substitute.**

$m\angle AZE = 37°$ ← **Solve.**

Coplanar lines that do not intersect are called **parallel lines.** In the diagram at the right, lines p and q are parallel, denoted $p \parallel q$.

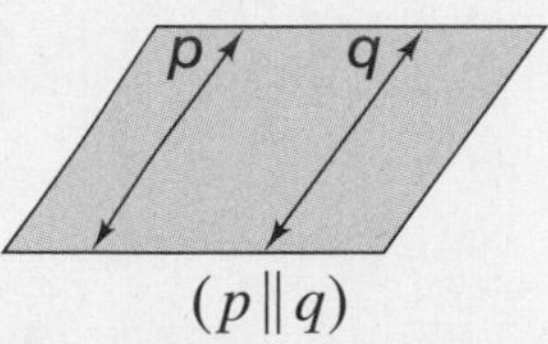

$(p \parallel q)$

Parallel Postulate

Through a point not on a line, there is exactly one line parallel to the given line.

Parallel lines are equidistant; that is, they are the same distance apart at every point. The **distance between two parallel lines** is the perpendicular distance between any point on one of them and the other line.

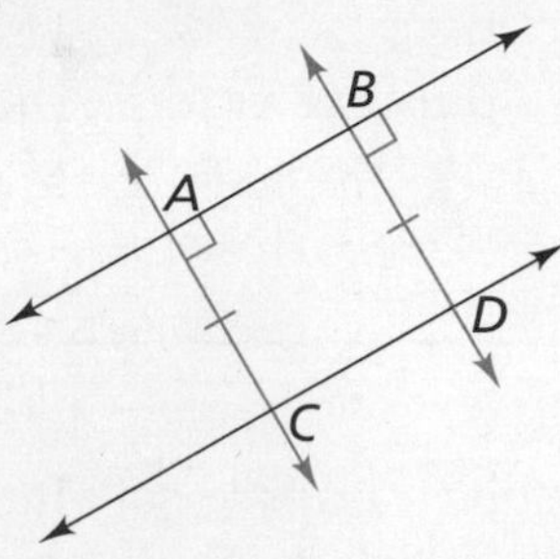

$\overleftrightarrow{AB} \parallel \overleftrightarrow{CD}$ is illustrated by the diagram at the right.

The lines are parallel if they are the same distance apart at every point. The distance between $\overline{AB}$ and $\overline{CD}$ is the equal to the length of $\overline{AC}$ and $\overline{BD}$. If $\overleftrightarrow{AC} \perp \overleftrightarrow{CD}$, $\overleftrightarrow{BD} \perp \overleftrightarrow{CD}$, and $\overline{AC} \cong \overline{BD}$, then $\overleftrightarrow{AB} \parallel \overleftrightarrow{CD}$.

EXAMPLES 3 and 4 **Working with parallel lines**

3 How many lines containing Z are parallel to $\overline{WX}$ and what is the distance between them?

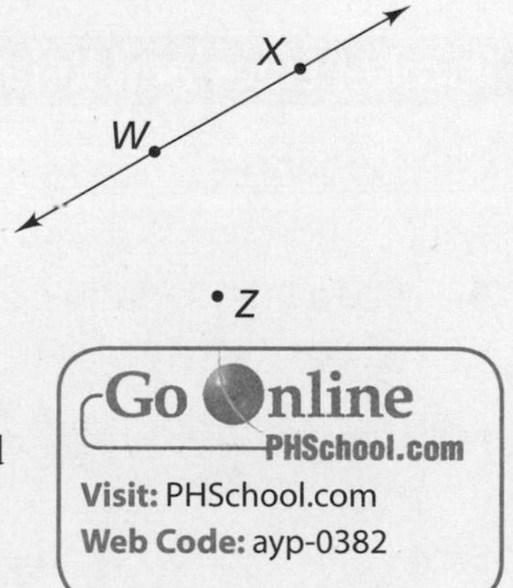

■ **SOLUTION**

Using the Parallel Postulate, there is exactly one line parallel to $\overline{WX}$ that goes through Z. The distance between them is equal to the length of segment WZ.

4 $\overline{WZ}$ is perpendicular to $\overline{WX}$. What is the distance between $\overline{WZ}$ and the line parallel to $\overline{WZ}$ that goes through X?

■ **SOLUTION**

The distance between the line parallel to $\overline{WZ}$ is equal to the length of $\overline{WX}$.

A line that intersects two or more coplanar lines at different points is called a **transversal.**

The following postulate and theorems apply to the angles formed when a transversal intersects two parallel lines.

Angles Formed by a Transversal

In the figure at the right, lines *a* and *b* are intersected by transversal *t*.

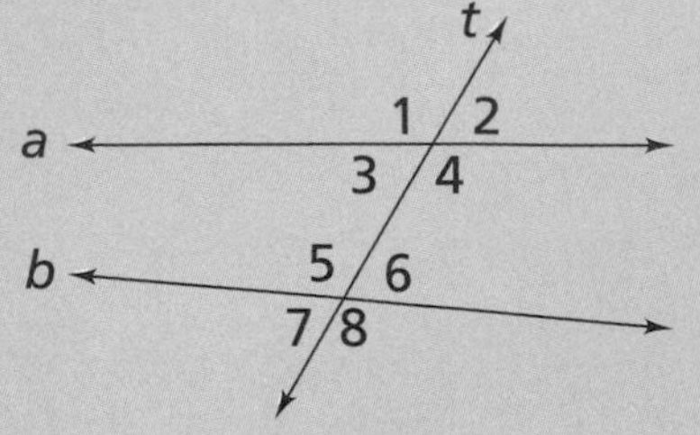

The **interior angles** are:
$\angle 3$, $\angle 4$, $\angle 5$, and $\angle 6$

The **exterior angles** are:
$\angle 1$, $\angle 2$, $\angle 7$, and $\angle 8$

Corresponding angles are a pair of nonadjacent angles, one interior and one exterior, that are both on the same side of the transversal. In the figure above, these are the pairs of corresponding angles.

$\angle 1$ and $\angle 5$ $\angle 2$ and $\angle 6$ $\angle 3$ and $\angle 7$ $\angle 4$ and $\angle 8$

Alternate interior angles are a pair of nonadjacent interior angles on opposite sides of the transversal. The alternate interior angles are:

$\angle 3$ and $\angle 6$ $\angle 4$ and $\angle 5$

Alternate exterior angles are a pair of nonadjacent exterior angles on opposite sides of the transversal. The alternate exterior angles are:

$\angle 1$ and $\angle 8$ $\angle 2$ and $\angle 7$

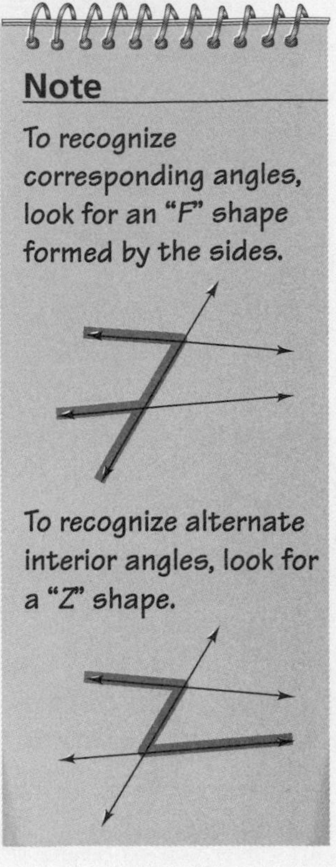

When a transversal intersects parallel lines, the pairs of angles have special relationships. These are summarized by the following postulate and theorems.

Parallel Lines and Related Angles

Corresponding Angles Postulate If two parallel lines are cut by a transversal, then corresponding angles are congruent.

Alternate Interior Angles Theorem If two parallel lines are cut by a transversal, then alternate interior angles are congruent.

Alternate Exterior Angles Theorem If two parallel lines are cut by a transversal, then alternate exterior angles are congruent.

Same-Side Interior Angles Theorem If two parallel lines are cut by a transversal, then interior angles on the same side of the transversal are supplementary.

EXAMPLES 5 and 6 Working with parallel lines and related angles

5 $p \parallel q$ and $m\angle 1 = 118°$. Find $m\angle 7$.

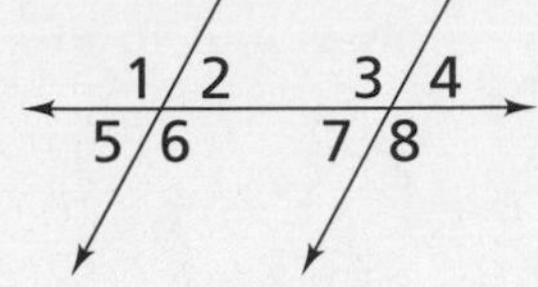

■ **SOLUTION**

Step 1 $m\angle 8 = m\angle 1$ ← **Use Alternate Exterior Angles Theorem.**
$m\angle 8 = 118°$ ← **Substitute.**

Step 2 $m\angle 7 + m\angle 8 = 180°$ ← **Apply definition of linear pair.**
$m\angle 7 + 118° = 180°$ ← **Substitute.**
$m\angle 7 = 62°$ ← **Solve.**

$m\angle 3 = 24(n + 1)$ and $m\angle 5 = 15n$. Find the value of n and the measure of both angles.

■ **SOLUTION**

Step 1 Identify the relationship between $\angle 3$ and $\angle 5$.

$\angle 3 + \angle 2 = 180°$ ← **Use Same-Side Interior Angle Theorem.**
$\angle 2 \cong \angle 5$ ← **Use Vertical Angle Theorem.**
Therefore, $\angle 3 + \angle 5 = 180°$. ← **Substitute.**

Step 2 Solve for n.

$24(n + 1) + 15n = 180°$ ← **Substitute.**
$24n + 24 + 15n = 180°$ ← **Use Distributive Property.**
$39n + 24 = 180°$ ← **Solve.**
$39n = 156°$
$n = 4°$

Step 3 Find the measure of both angles.

$m\angle 3 = 24(n + 1)$ and $m\angle 5 = 15n$ ← **Given.**
$m\angle 3 = 24(4 + 1)$ $m\angle 5 = 15(4)$ ← **Substitute.**
$m\angle 3 = 120°$ $m\angle 5 = 60°$ ← **Solve.**

Therefore, the value of $n = 4$, $m\angle 3 = 120°$, and $m\angle 5 = 60°$.

Go Online PHSchool.com
Visit: PHSchool.com
Web Code: ayp-0379

Perpendicular Transversal Theorem

If a transversal is perpendicular to one of two parallel lines, then it is perpendicular to the other.

EXAMPLE 7 Applying the Perpendicular Transversal Theorem

In the figure at the right, $a \perp c$, $c \parallel d$, $m\angle 1 = (7x - 8)°$, and $m\angle 2 = (4x)°$. Find $m\angle 2$.

■ **SOLUTION**

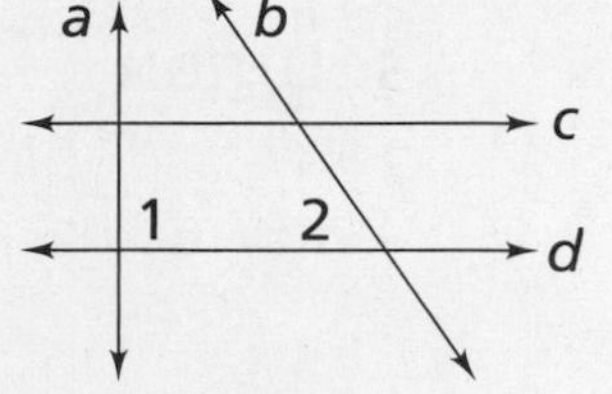

Because $a \perp c$ and $c \parallel d$, it follows that $a \perp d$. So $\angle 1$ is a right angle.

Step 1 $m\angle 1 = (7x - 8)° = 90°$ ← **Apply definition of right angle.**
$7x - 8 = 90$ ← **Solve.**
$x = 14$

Step 2 $m\angle 2 = (4x)°$ ← **Substitute.**
$m\angle 2 = (4[14])°$ ← **Simplify.**
$m\angle 2 = 56°$

You can use the following postulates and theorems to show that two lines are parallel.

Showing That Lines Are Parallel

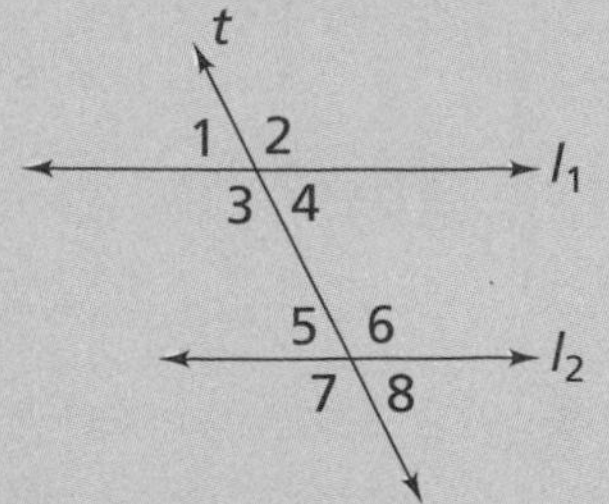

Converse of Corresponding Angles Postulate If two lines are cut by a transversal so that a pair of corresponding angles are congruent, then the lines are parallel.

If $\angle 1 \cong \angle 5$, then $l_1 \parallel l_2$.

Converse of Alternate Interior Angles Theorem If two lines are cut by a transversal so that a pair of alternate interior angles are congruent, then the lines are parallel.

If $\angle 4 \cong \angle 5$, then $l_1 \parallel l_2$.

Converse of Alternate Exterior Angles Theorem If two lines are cut by a transversal so that a pair of alternate exterior angles are congruent, then the lines are parallel.

If $\angle 1 \cong \angle 8$, then $l_1 \parallel l_2$.

Converse of Same-Side Interior Angles Theorem If two lines are cut by a transversal so that a pair of same-side interior angles are supplementary, then the lines are parallel.

If $\angle 3$ and $\angle 5$ are supplementary, then $l_1 \parallel l_2$.

EXAMPLES 8 and 9 Justifying a statement that lines are parallel

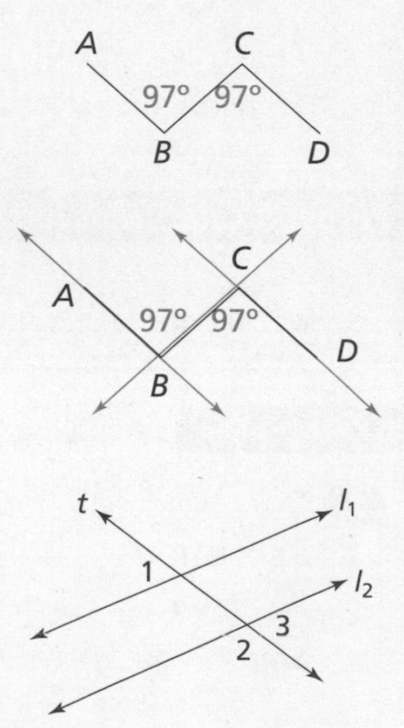

8 Given the figure at the right, state the postulate or theorem that justifies the conclusion $\overline{AB} \parallel \overline{CD}$.

■ SOLUTION

The segments $\overline{AB}$ and $\overline{CD}$ are parts of two lines, $\overleftrightarrow{AB}$ and $\overleftrightarrow{CD}$, that are cut by transversal $\overleftrightarrow{BC}$. You may find it helpful to copy the figure and extend the lines as shown at the right.

The labeled angles, $\angle ABC$ and $\angle DCB$, are a pair of alternate interior angles. Because these angles are congruent, $\overline{AB} \parallel \overline{CD}$.

The justification is that **the Converse of the Alternate Interior Angles Theorem applies.**

9 Given the figure at the right, state the postulate or theorem that justifies the conclusion that $l_1 \parallel l_2$, given that $m\angle 1 = 35°$ and $m\angle 2 = 145°$.

■ SOLUTION

Lines l_1 and l_2 are cut by the transversal t. Therefore, $\angle 2$ and $\angle 3$ are supplementary and $m\angle 3 = 180 - 145 = 35°$. Therefore, $\angle 1 \cong \angle 3$ and $l_1 \parallel l_2$.

The justification is that **the Converse of the Alternate Interior Angles Theorem applies.**

Practice

Choose the numeral preceding the word or expression that best completes the statement or answers the question.

1 If two lines are each parallel to a third line, then

(1) they are parallel to each other.

(2) they are perpendicular to each other.

(3) they are a pair of skew lines.

(4) their relationship cannot be determined.

2 Given the figure below, which statement is true?

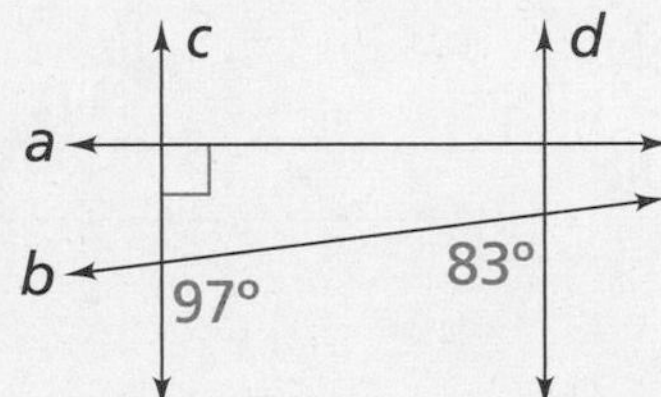

(1) $a \parallel b$ **(3)** $a \perp d$

(2) $a \parallel d$ **(4)** $b \perp d$

3 If two lines are coplanar, then they cannot be

(1) intersecting. **(3)** perpendicular.

(2) parallel. **(4)** skew.

In Exercises 4–6, refer to the figure below. Find each angle measure.

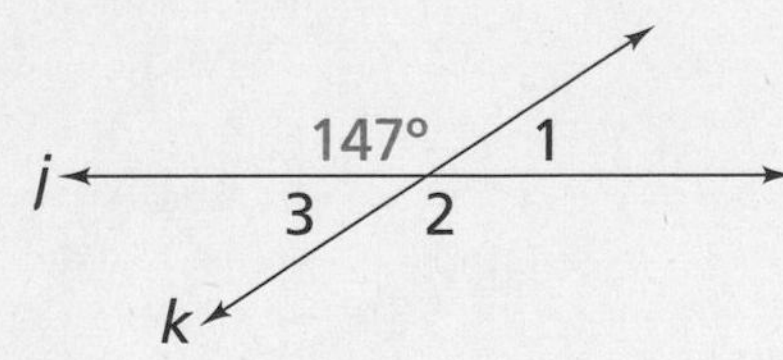

4 $m\angle 1$ 5 $m\angle 2$ 6 $m\angle 3$

In Exercises 7–12, refer to the figure below. Given $r \parallel s$, find each angle measure.

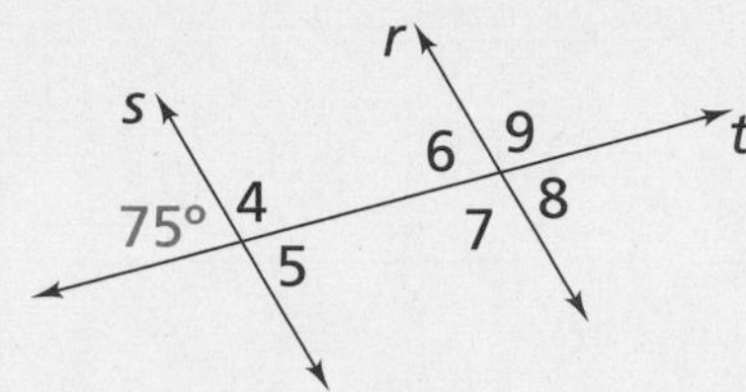

7 $m\angle 4$ 8 $m\angle 5$ 9 $m\angle 6$

10 $m\angle 7$ 11 $m\angle 8$ 12 $m\angle 9$

In Exercises 13–18, refer to the figure below. Given $\overleftrightarrow{BE} \perp \overleftrightarrow{FC}$, find each angle measure.

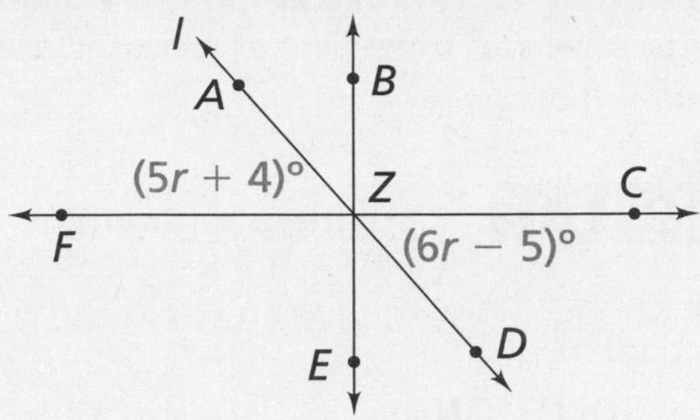

13 $m\angle CZD$ 14 $m\angle AZB$ 15 $m\angle BZC$

16 $m\angle DZE$ 17 $m\angle AZC$ 18 $m\angle AZE$

In Exercises 19–24, refer to the figure below. Given $l \parallel m$, find each angle measure.

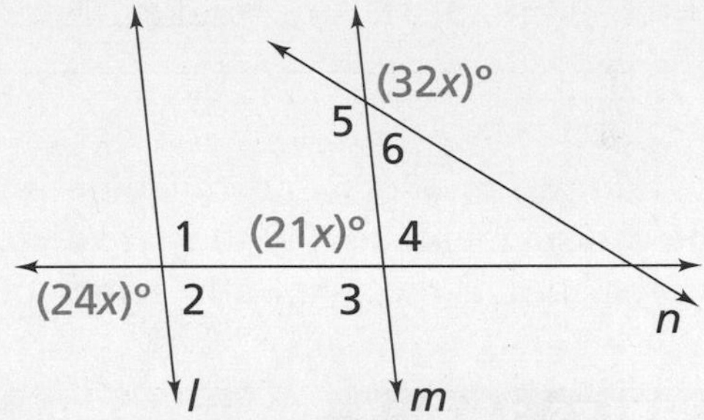

19 $m\angle 1$ 20 $m\angle 2$ 21 $m\angle 3$

22 $m\angle 4$ 23 $m\angle 5$ 24 $m\angle 6$

In Exercises 25–26, state the postulate or theorem that justifies the conclusion $\overline{AB} \parallel \overline{DC}$.

25

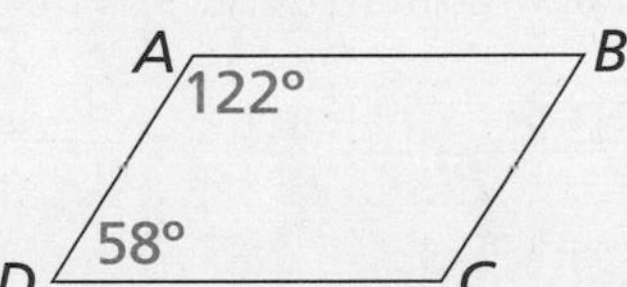

26

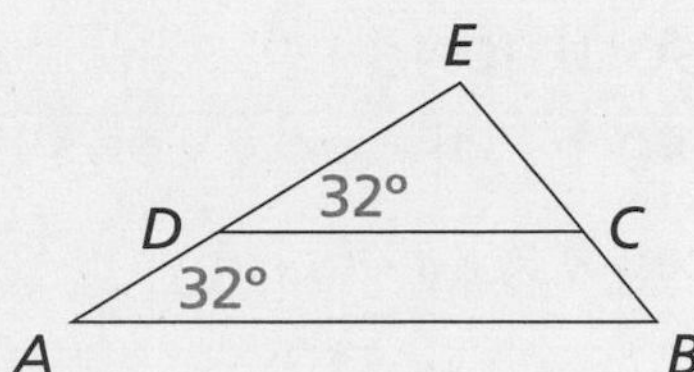

1.4 Constructing Line Segments, Angles, and Triangles

New York Standards

G.G.17 Constructing angle bisectors

G.G.20 Constructing equilateral triangles

A **geometric construction** is a drawing in the plane using only an unmarked **straightedge** (ruler) and a **compass.** The straightedge is used to draw segments, rays, and lines. The compass is used to draw circles and parts of circles called **arcs.**

EXAMPLE 1 **Copying a segment**

1 Make a copy of $\overline{AB}$ shown at the right.

■ **SOLUTION**

Step 1 Draw a line n and place point C on it.

Step 2 Open the compass and place it on $\overline{AB}$ so that the point and the pencil tip coincide with A and B, respectively.

Step 3 Place the compass point at C and mark a point on the line where the pencil tip meets the line. Label this point D. As a result, $\overline{CD} \cong \overline{AB}$.

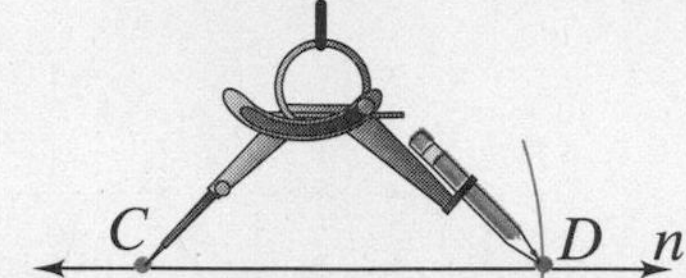

You can add two line segments together using basic constructions. To do this, copy the two segments so that they are placed end-to-end. The length of the final construction is the sum of the length of the two segments.

EXAMPLES 2 and 3 **Constructing a segment from two specified segments**

2 Given $\overline{KL}$ and $\overline{XY}$, construct $\overline{EG}$ so that $EG = KL + XY$.

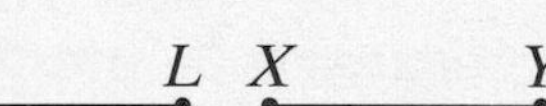

■ **SOLUTION**

Step 1 Draw a line n and place point E on it.

Step 2 Construct $\overline{EF} \cong \overline{KL}$ on n.

Step 3 Construct $\overline{FG} \cong \overline{XY}$ on n with F between E and G. As a result, $EG = KL + XY$.

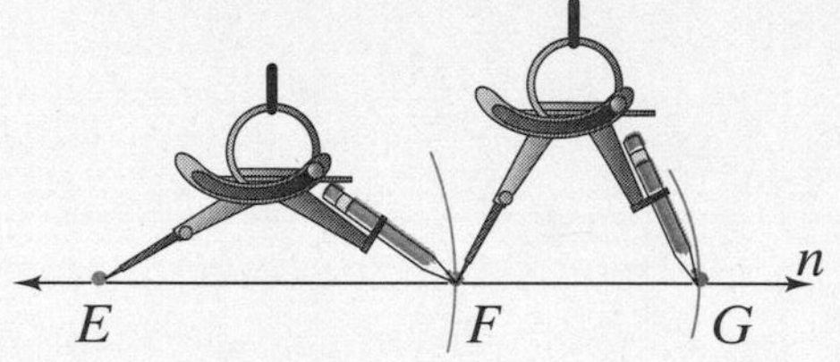

3 Construct $\overline{WZ}$ so that $WZ = 2XY$

■ **SOLUTION**

Step 1 Make a copy of $\overline{XY}$.

Step 2 Add the copy of $\overline{XY}$ to the original segment.

Just like segments, you can also use a straightedge and a compass to make copies of angles and to construct the sum of two angles.

Example 4 shows the construction of an angle congruent to a given angle.

Go Online
PHSchool.com
Visit: PHSchool.com
Web Code: ayp-0090

EXAMPLE 4 **Copying an angle**

4 Make a copy of $\angle PQR$ shown below.

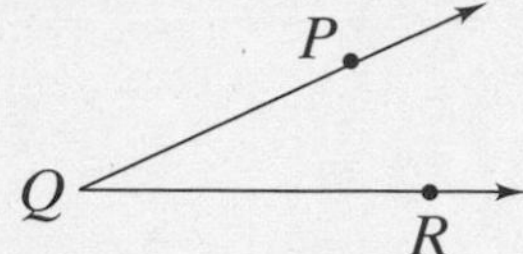

■ **SOLUTION**

Step 1 Open the compass and place it on $\overrightarrow{QR}$ so that the point and and the pencil tip coincide with Q and R, respectively. Draw an arc passing through both sides of $\angle PQR$. Mark Z where the arc meets $\overrightarrow{QP}$.

Step 2 Draw $\overrightarrow{YX}$ such that $YX = QR$. Using the compass, construct part of a circle with center Y and passing through X.

Step 3 Place the compass tip at R and the pencil tip at Z. With the same compass setting, place the compass tip at X and mark the point T where the pencil tip intersects the arc.

Step 4 Use a straightedge to construct $\overrightarrow{YT}$.

Step 1 **Step 2** **Step 3** **Step 4**

As a result of this construction, $\angle TYX \cong \angle PQR$.

EXAMPLE 5 **Constructing an angle whose measure is a specified sum**

5 Given $\angle A$ and $\angle B$, construct $\angle C$ such that $m\angle C = m\angle A + \angle B$.

■ **SOLUTION**

Step 1 Copy $\angle A$. Call the vertex of the copy point C.

Step 2 Copy $\angle B$ so that point C is the vertex of the copy of $\angle B$, the copy shares a side with one side of the copy of $\angle A$, and the copy of $\angle B$ does not lie inside the copy of $\angle A$.

The copies of $\angle A$ and $\angle B$ together become adjacent angles.

copy of $\angle B$

copy of $\angle A$

As a result of this construction, $m\angle C = m\angle A + m\angle B$.

You can use a compass to construct the angle bisector of a given angle.

Go Online
PHSchool.com
Visit: PHSchool.com
Web Code: ayp-0091

EXAMPLE 6 **Constructing the angle bisector of a given angle**

6 Construct the angle bisector of $\angle P$.

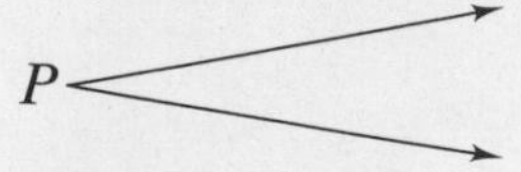

■ SOLUTION

Step 1 Construct an arc centered at P and intersecting both sides of $\angle P$. Label the points of intersection A and B.

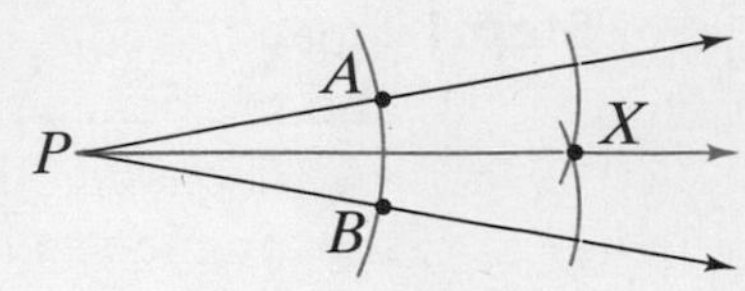

Step 2 Construct arcs with the same radius centered at A and at B. Make sure the arcs intersect in a point. Label the point of intersection X.

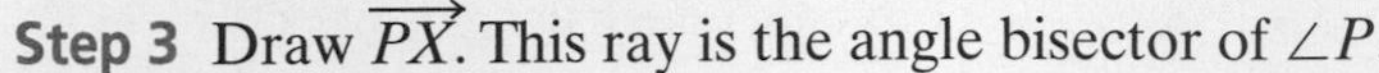
Step 3 Draw $\overrightarrow{PX}$. This ray is the angle bisector of $\angle P$.

If you are given a right angle, then you can construct an angle that measures 45°. The angle bisector of a right angle will give a 45° angle. As a result, you can now construct a 45°-45°-90° right triangle.

By definition, an equilateral triangle has three congruent sides. You can construct the triangle by constructing the three congruent segments. (If the sides of a triangle are congruent, then the angles opposite are also congruent.)

EXAMPLE 7 **Constructing an equilateral triangle**

7 Construct an equilateral triangle.

■ SOLUTION

Step 1 Starting at C, open the compass to D to measure the length of the segment CD.

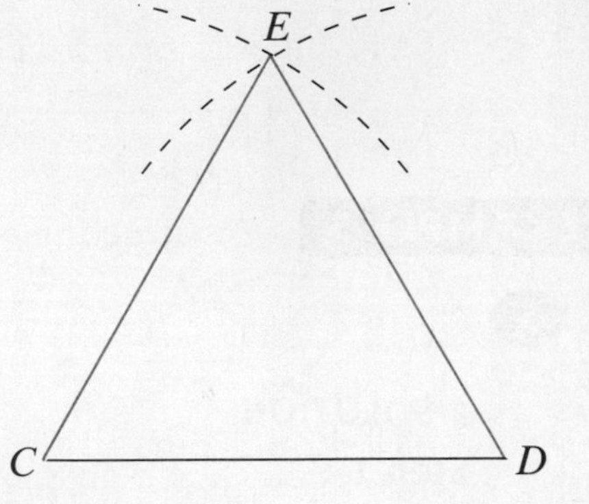

Step 2 With compass still at C, draw an arc.

Step 3 With compass at D, draw an arc.

Step 4 Label the intersection of the two arcs point E. Draw $\overline{CE}$ and $\overline{DE}$.

Since $\overline{CD} \cong \overline{CE} \cong \overline{DE}$, $\triangle CED$ is an equilateral triangle.

You can construct other types of triangles. For example, you can construct an isosceles triangle by copying two congruent segments and placing them onto a common base.

Practice

Choose the numeral preceding the word or expression that best completes the statement or answers the question.

1 Use a compass to determine which of the following statements about $\overline{AB}$ and $\overline{CD}$ is true.

(1) $AB = CD$ (3) $CD = 0.5(AB)$

(2) $2(AB) = CD$ (4) $5CD = 2(AB)$

2 Which of the following statements about $m\angle A$ and $m\angle B$ is not true?

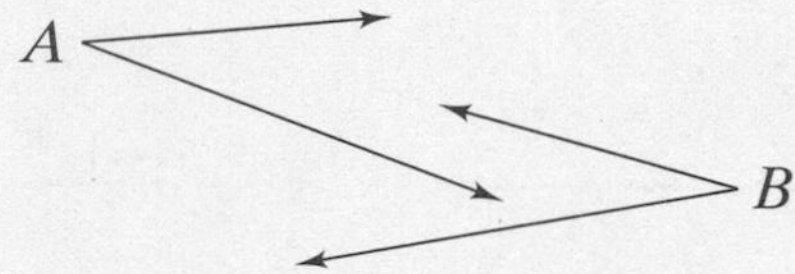

(1) $m\angle A = m\angle B$

(2) $m\angle A + m\angle B = 2(m\angle A)$

(3) $m\angle A + m\angle B = 2(m\angle B)$

(4) $m\angle A = 0.5(m\angle B)$

3 Use a compass to decide which of the following statements is false.

(1) $PQ = 2(PS)$

(2) $PQ = 4(PR)$

(3) $PQ = PS + SQ$

(4) $PS = SQ + 2(PR)$

In Exercises 4–8, use the segments below. Use a compass and straightedge for each construction.

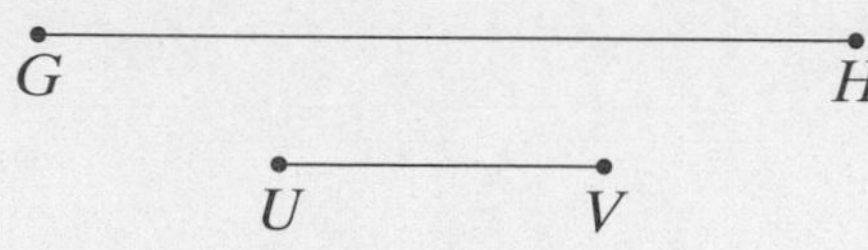

4 $\overline{AB}$ whose length is $2(UV)$

5 $\overline{AB}$ whose length is $GH - 2(UV)$

6 $\overline{AB}$ whose length is $3(UV)$

7 $\overline{AB}$ whose length is $UV + GH$

8 $\overline{AB}$ whose length is $GH - UV$

In Exercises 9–11, use the angles below. Use a compass and straightedge for each construction.

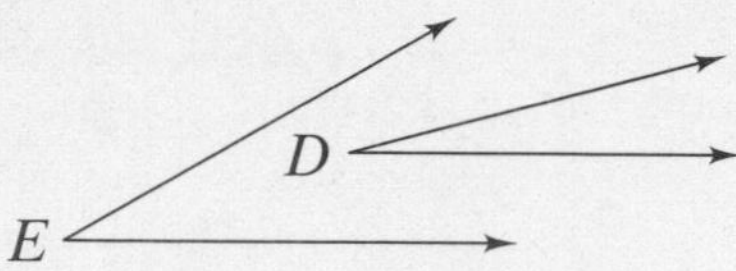

9 $\angle A$ whose measure is $2(m\angle D)$

10 $\angle A$ whose measure is $m\angle E + m\angle D$

11 $\angle A$ whose measure is $m\angle E - m\angle D$

12 Construct the angle bisector of $\angle Z$.

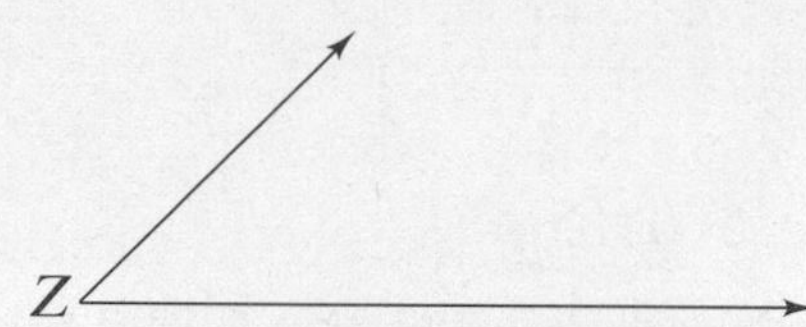

13 Construct the bisector of $\angle PTA$.

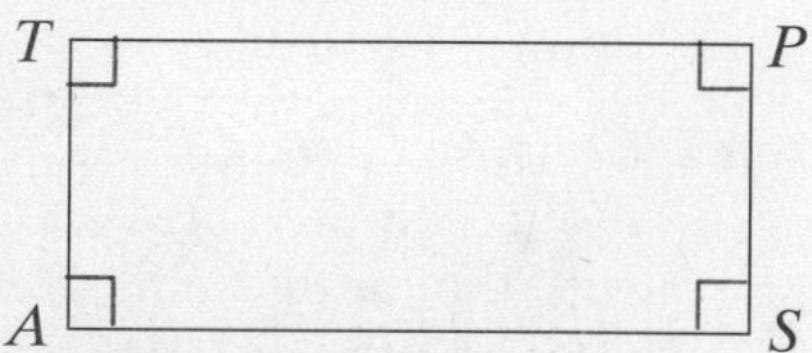

14 Construct an isosceles triangle using the segments below. (There are two constructions possible.)

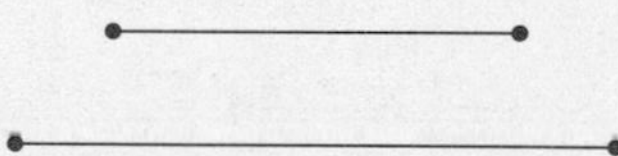

15 Construct an equilateral triangle using the segment below.

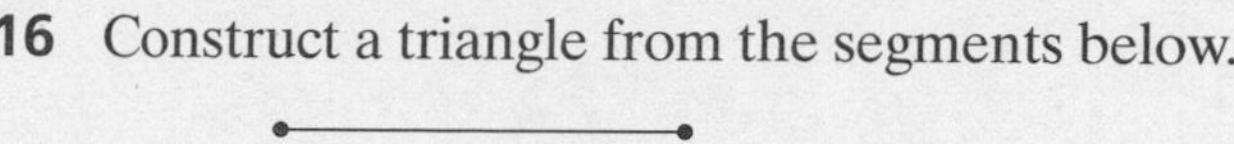

16 Construct a triangle from the segments below.

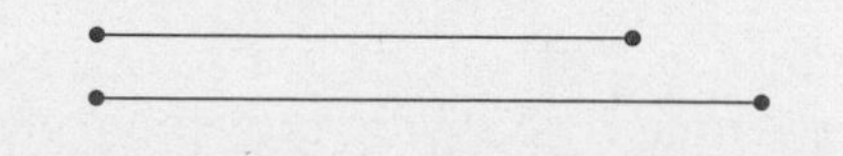

17 Construct $\overline{AB}$ whose length is $2(FD) - NY$.

F ——— D

N ——— Y

1.5 Constructing Perpendicular and Parallel Lines

New York Standards

G.G.18 Constructing perpendicular bisectors

G.G.19 Constructing parallel/perpendicular lines

Given any line m and any point P in the plane, there is exactly one line in the plane that contains P and that is perpendicular to m.

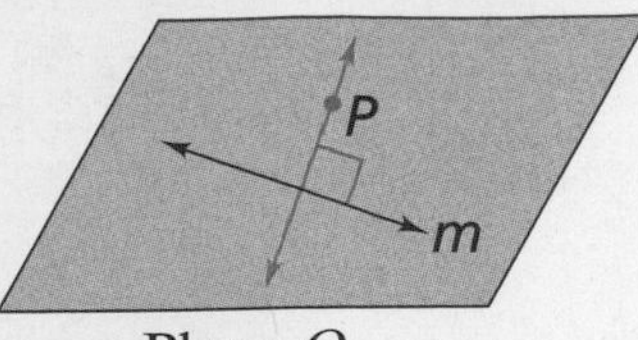

Plane Q

Visit: PHSchool.com
Web Code: ayp-0388

EXAMPLES 1 and 2 Constructing a line perpendicular to a given line

1 Construct the line containing P and perpendicular to line m.

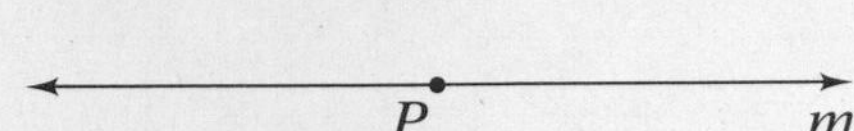

■ **SOLUTION**

Step 1 Construct arcs with the same radius centered at P and intersecting line m at two points, A and B.

Step 2 Construct arcs with the same radius centered at A and B, with the radius being greater than half the distance between A and B. Label the intersections X and Y.

Step 3 Draw line n through X and Y.

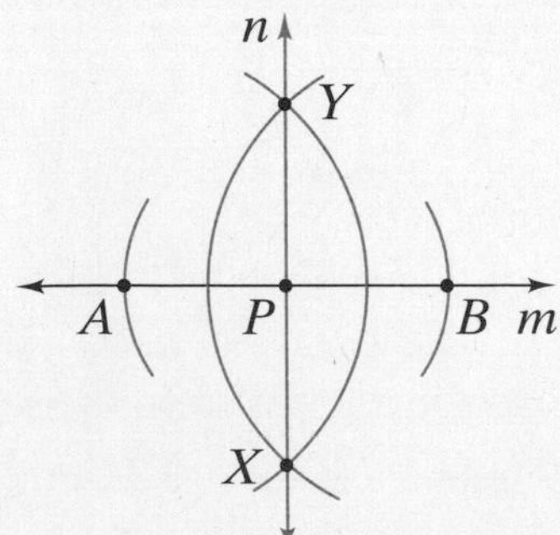

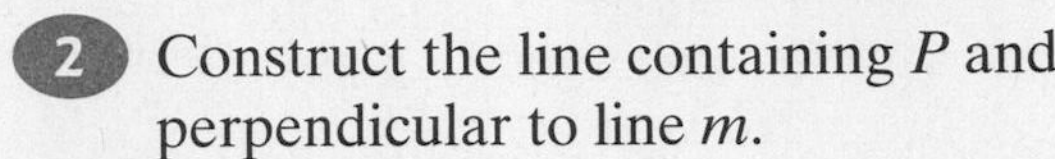

2 Construct the line containing P and perpendicular to line m.

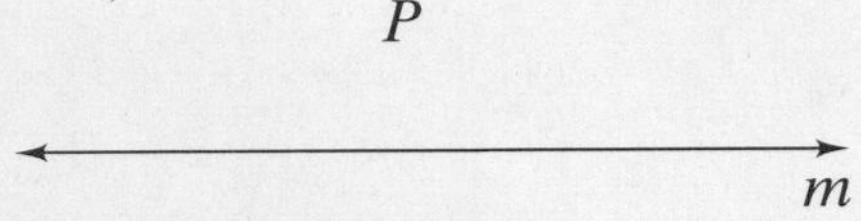

■ **SOLUTION**

Step 1 Construct an arc centered at P and intersecting line m at two points, A and B.

Step 2 Construct arcs with the same radius centered at A and B, with the radius being greater than half the distance between A and B. Label the intersections X and Y.

Step 3 Draw line n through X and Y.

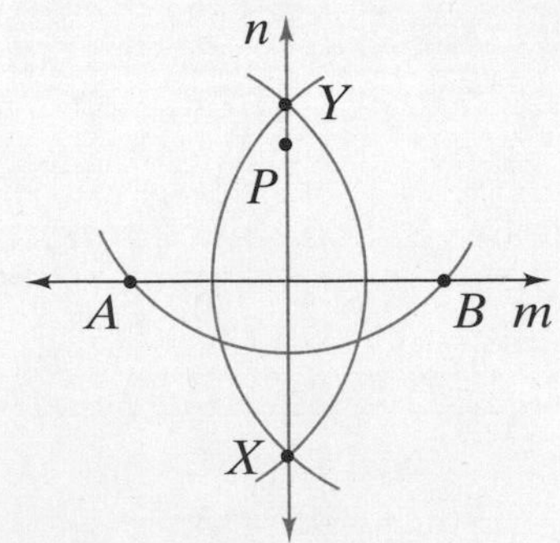

In each construction, line n contains P and is perpendicular to line m.

A **perpendicular bisector** of a segment is a line, ray, or segment that is perpendicular to the segment at its midpoint. Knowing how to construct a line perpendicular to a given line, as shown in Example 1, can help you construct the perpendicular bisector.

In Step 1 of Example 1, you drew arcs that made $\overline{AP}$ and $\overline{BP}$ congruent. That means P is the midpoint of $\overline{AB}$. By construction, line n is perpendicular to $\overline{AB}$ and passes through P. This makes n the perpendicular bisector of $\overline{AB}$.

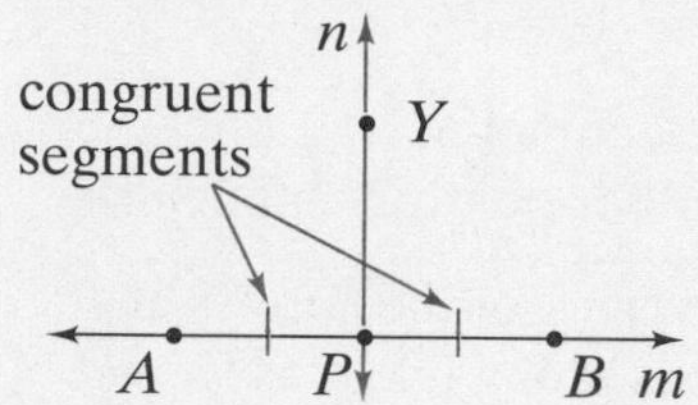

EXAMPLE 3 **Constructing the perpendicular bisector of a given segment**

Go Online
PHSchool.com
Visit: PHSchool.com
Web Code: ayp-0359

3 Construct the perpendicular bisector of $\overline{CD}$ shown here.

■ SOLUTION

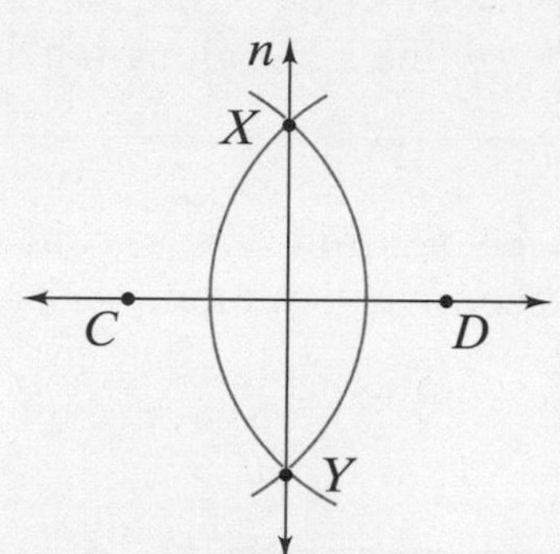

Step 1 Using a compass, construct arcs centered at C and at D and having the same radius. Be sure that the two arcs intersect at two points X and Y. (Make sure the radius used for both arcs is more than half the distance between C and D.)

Step 2 Draw line n through points X and Y. Line n is the perpendicular bisector of $\overline{CD}$.

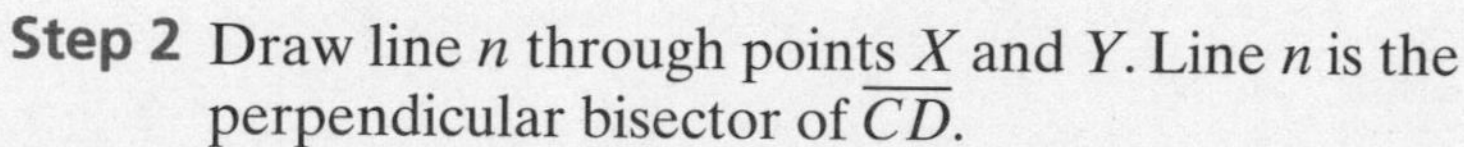

Recall that, if lines m and n in the figure below are parallel, then corresponding angles $\angle 1$ and $\angle 2$ are congruent. That is, $\angle 2$ is a copy of $\angle 1$.

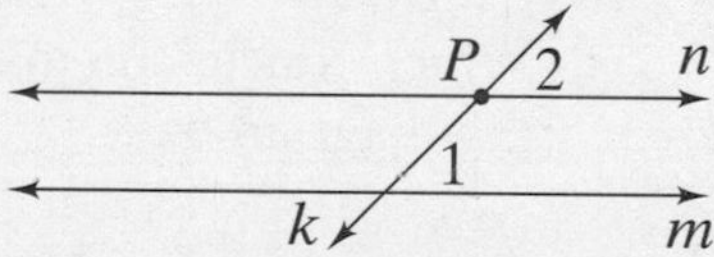

So, to construct a line through a given point P parallel to a given line m, you can draw a line through P and intersecting line m. Then construct a line such that corresponding angles $\angle 1$ and $\angle 2$ are congruent.

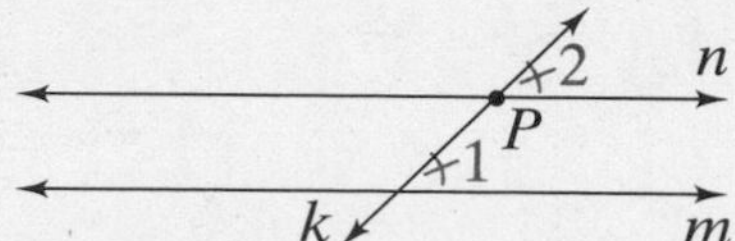

How does this construction tell you that line l is parallel to line m? By copying $\angle 2$, you created an angle that is congruent to $\angle 1$, as shown in the diagram to the right. By the Converse of the Alternate Interior Angles Theorem, you know that lines m and n are parallel.

EXAMPLE 4 **Constructing a line through a given point parallel to a given line**

4 Construct the line through P parallel to line m.

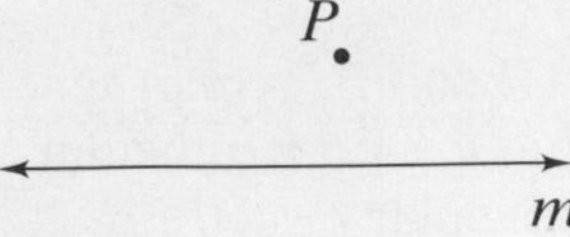

■ SOLUTION

Step 1 Draw any line k through P and intersecting line m. Label the intersection Q. Locate and mark another point R on line m.

Step 2 Copy $\angle PQR$ in such a way that the vertex of the copy is at P and one side of the copy of $\angle PQR$ lies along line k as shown.

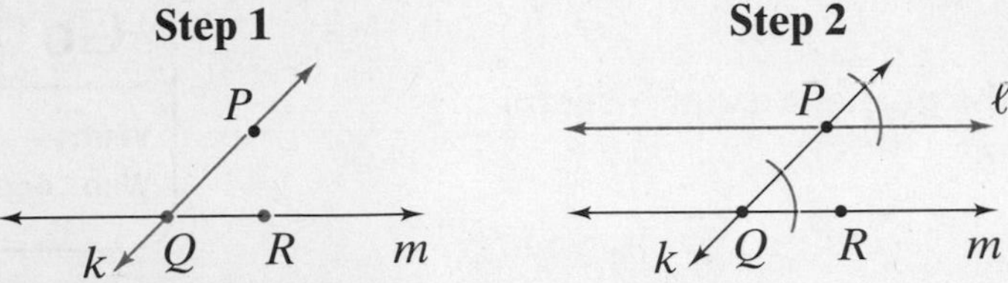

The side of the angle constructed in the second step not lying along line k lies along the line through P parallel to line m.

Once you know how to construct a line parallel to another line, you can use this construction along with others to construct the following:

parallelogram rhombus rectangle square trapezoid

Practice

Choose the numeral preceding the word or expression that best completes the statement or answers the question.

1 Centered at points B and C on $\overline{BC}$, arcs are made with the same compass setting and the arcs intersect in two points X and Y. Which statement is not always true?

(1) $\overline{BX} = \overline{CX}$
(2) $\overline{BY} = \overline{CY}$
(3) $\overline{BX} = \overline{CY}$
(4) $\overline{BX} = \overline{XY}$

2 Which conclusion may you not draw from the diagram below?

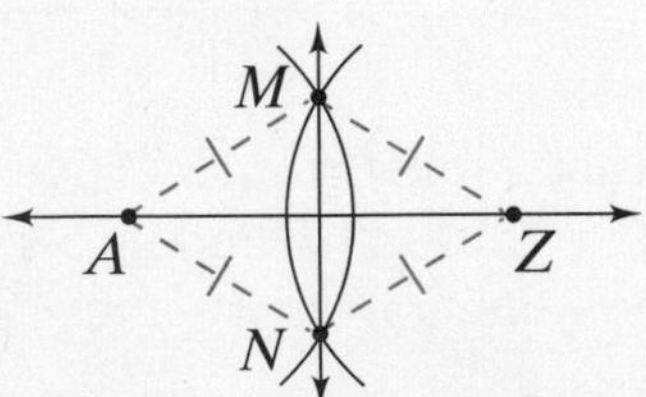

(1) $\overleftrightarrow{MN} \perp \overleftrightarrow{AZ}$
(2) $\overline{AM} \cong \overline{MN}$
(3) $\overline{AM} \cong \overline{MZ}$
(4) $\overline{AM} \parallel \overline{NZ}$

Use the following construction for Exercises 3 and 4.

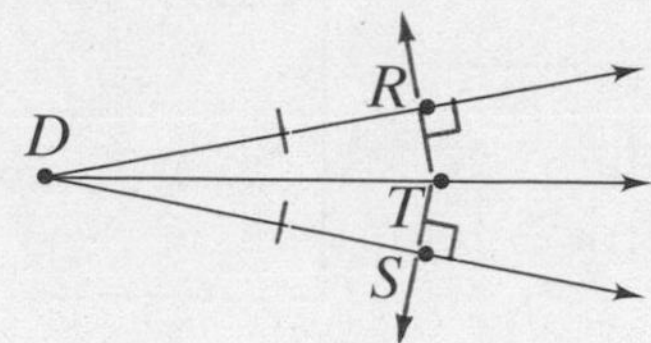

3 Which conclusion is false?

(1) $\angle RDT \cong \angle TDS$

(2) $\overline{TR} \cong \overline{ST}$

(3) $m\angle RDT = 0.5(m\angle RDS)$

(4) $\overline{RD} \cong \overline{TD} \cong \overline{SD}$

4 Which of the following best describes $\overrightarrow{DT}$?

(1) $\overrightarrow{DT}$ is perpendicular to $\overrightarrow{RT}$.

(2) $\overrightarrow{DT}$ is parallel to $\overrightarrow{DR}$.

(3) $\overrightarrow{DT}$ bisects $\angle RDS$.

(4) $\overrightarrow{DT}$ bisects $\overrightarrow{DS}$.

In Exercises 5–14, copy the given figure, then carry out the specified construction.

5 Construct the perpendicular bisector p of $\overline{MN}$.

6 Construct the line containing A and perpendicular to the line containing $\overline{BC}$.

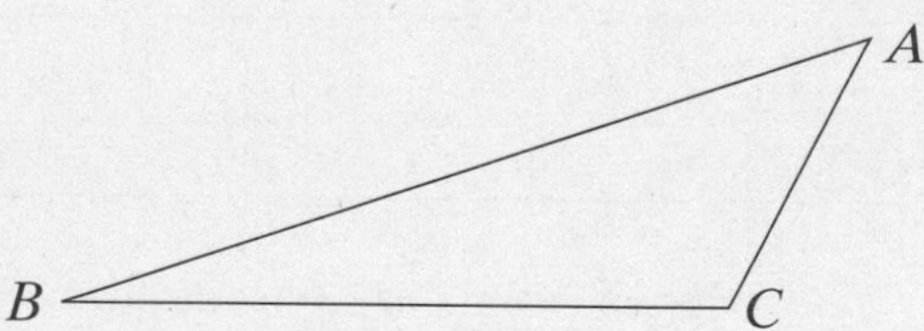

7 Construct the line through G perpendicular to $\overline{ST}$.

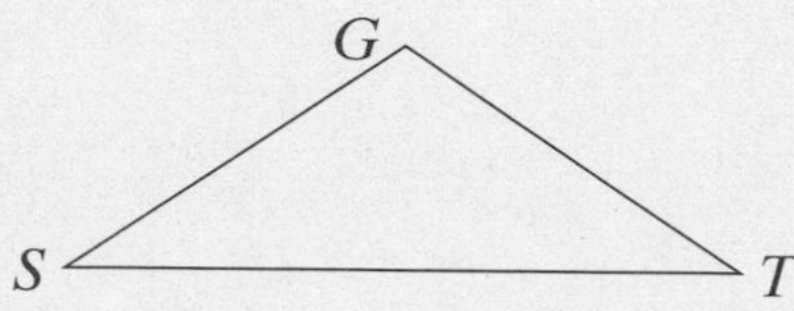

8 Construct the line containing B and parallel to $\overline{EF}$.

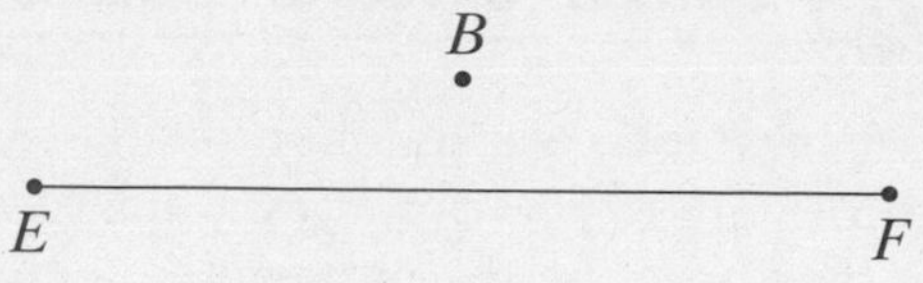

9 Construct the line containing U and perpendicular to $\overline{AW}$.

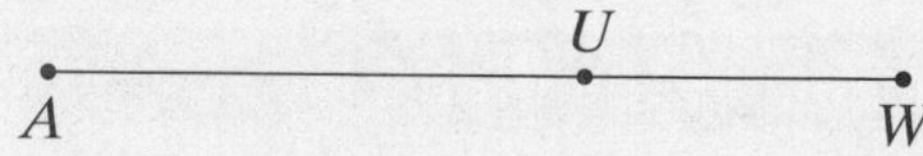

10 Construct a rhombus that is not a square and whose sides are congruent to $\overline{XY}$.

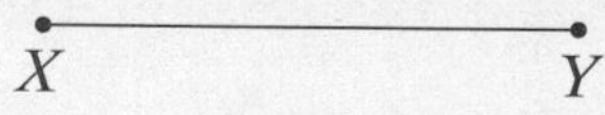

11 Construct a line perpendicular to line p at V and a line perpendicular to p through K.

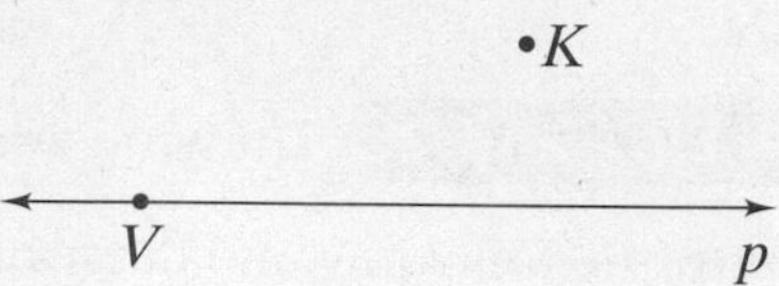

12 Construct the line parallel to $\overline{BZ}$ that contains the midpoint of $\overline{PW}$.

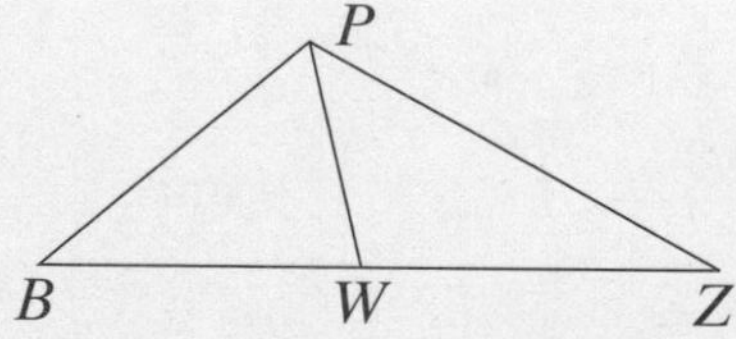

13 Construct the parallelogram whose adjacent sides are $\overline{AB}$ and $\overline{BC}$.

14 Construct the parallelogram whose adjacent sides are $\overline{CS}$ and $\overline{CT}$, where S and T are the midpoints of $\overline{CZ}$ and $\overline{CD}$, respectively.

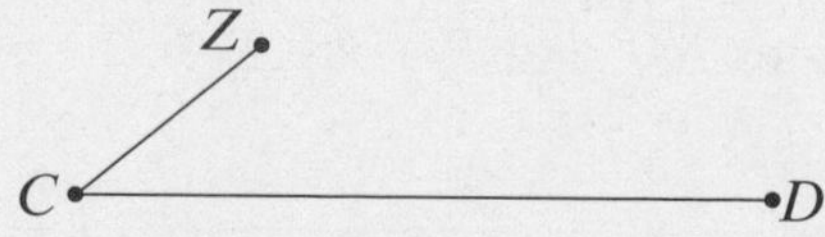

1.6 Locus: A Set of Points from a Fixed Distance or Line

New York Standards

G.G.22 Solve problems using compound loci

G.G.23 Graphing compound loci

A **locus** (plural **loci**) is a set of points that satisfies a specified condition. Given information, you can draw a diagram that satisfies the given condition. You can then describe the pattern that emerges.

There are 5 simple loci that you should know. The examples in this lesson describe these types of loci.

Basic Loci in the Plane

- The locus that is a fixed distance from a point.
- The locus that is a fixed distance from a line.
- The locus that is equidistant from 2 parallel lines.
- The locus that is equidistant from 2 intersecting lines.
- The locus that is equidistant from 2 points.

Go Online PHSchool.com
Visit: PHSchool.com
Web Code: ayp-0480

EXAMPLES 1 and 2 Drawing and describing a locus

Draw the following and describe each locus.

1 The set of all points 4 units from a given point C

SOLUTION

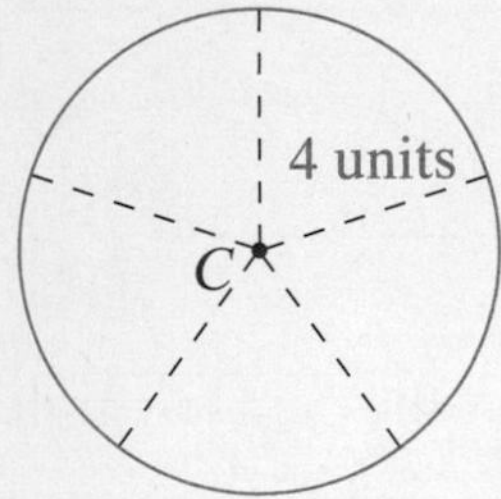

The locus of points is a circle with center C and a radius of 4.

2 The set of all points 3 cm from line l

SOLUTION

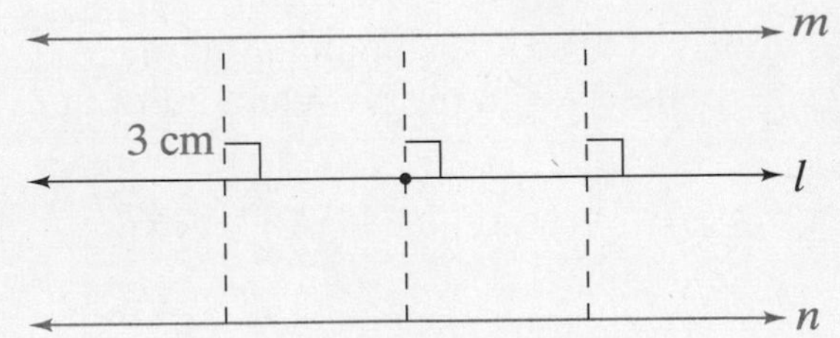

The locus of points is 2 parallel lines m and n, 3 cm above line l and 3 cm below line l.

EXAMPLE 3 Using a locus to describe a figure

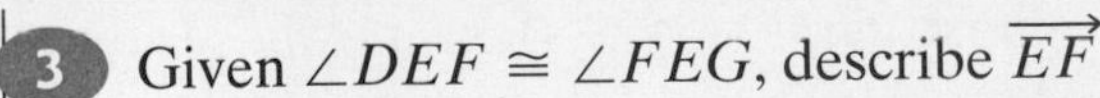

3 Given $\angle DEF \cong \angle FEG$, describe $\overrightarrow{EF}$.

SOLUTION

$\overrightarrow{EF}$ is the locus of points equidistant from sides $\overrightarrow{ED}$ and $\overrightarrow{EG}$ of $\angle DEG$.

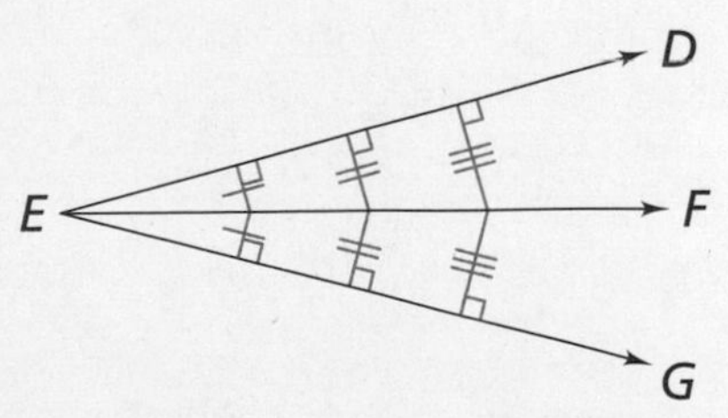

EXAMPLES 4 and 5 Finding the locus equidistant from two points

4 What is the locus of points equidistant from points M and N?

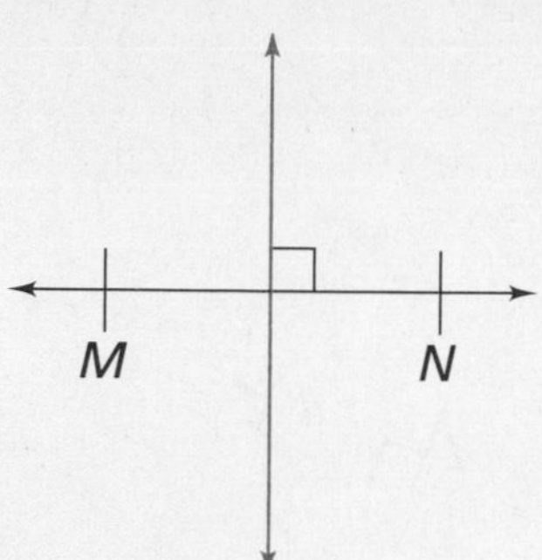

■ SOLUTION

The locus of points equidistant from 2 given points is the perpendicular bisector of the segment joining the 2 points.

5 Elena is planning a garden. Part of the boundary is a pair of large shrubs 50 feet apart. If she wants to build fountains each 25 feet from the two shrubs, how many fountains must she build? If she wants to build fountains each 30 feet from the two shrubs, how many fountains must she build?

■ SOLUTION

Since 25 ft is one half of 50 ft, locate the midpoint of the line segment joining the shrubs. The midpoint is the location for **one fountain.**

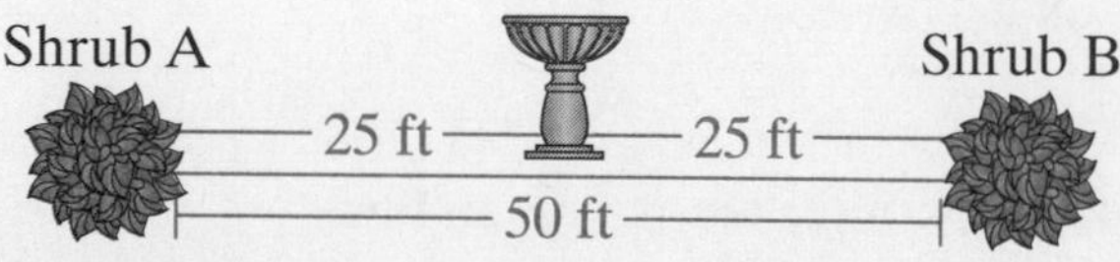

Draw arcs a little longer than half the distance between the shrubs. The intersections of the arcs are locations for **two fountains.**

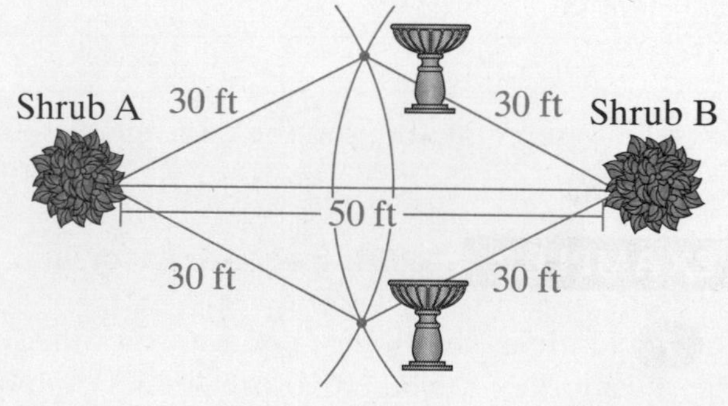

In the diagram below you can see that line z is the locus of points in the plane equidistant from lines m and n. Lines m and n are parallel. Sketch a line perpendicular to both m and n, and mark the points of intersection P and Q. Line z is parallel to m and n, and passes through M, the midpoint of $\overline{PQ}$.

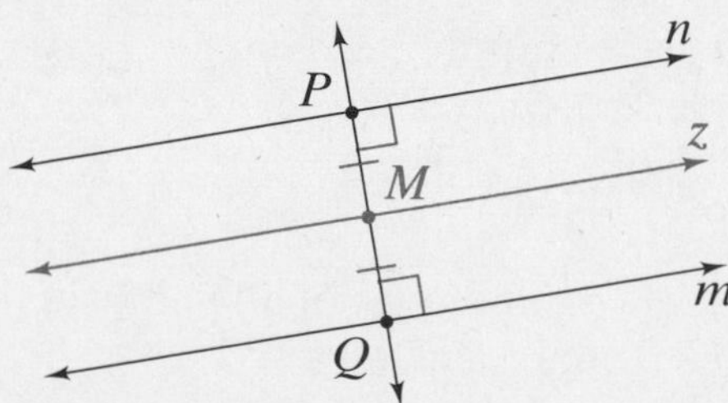

The **distance d between a point P not on line m and line m** is the length of the perpendicular segment from P to line m.

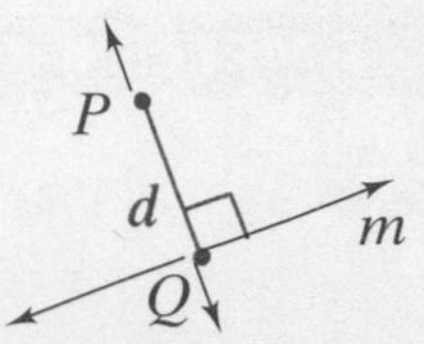

The **distance between two parallel lines** is the distance between any point on one of them and the other line. The set of all points containing P and the same distance from line m is the line containing P and parallel to line m.

parallel lines m and n
$d = d'$

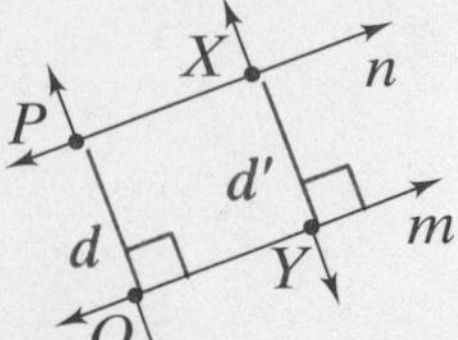

intersecting lines m and n
$d \neq d'$

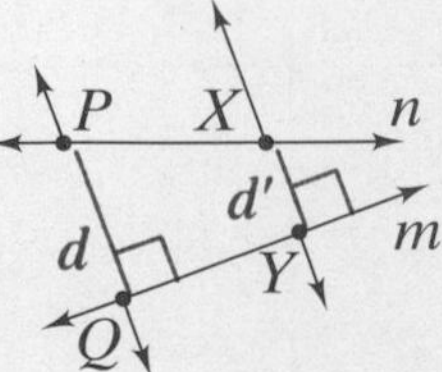

EXAMPLE 6 **Constructing lines in a plane a given distance from a given line**

6 Construct all lines in the plane that are the given distance d from line m.

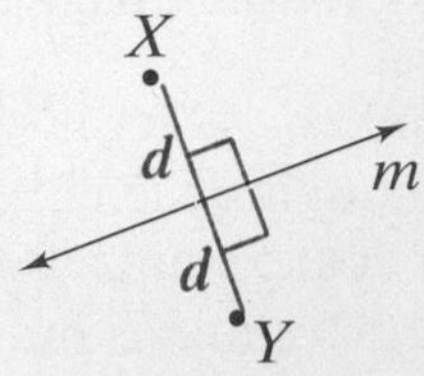

▪ SOLUTION

The required lines are line n containing X and parallel to line m together with line p containing Y and parallel to line m.

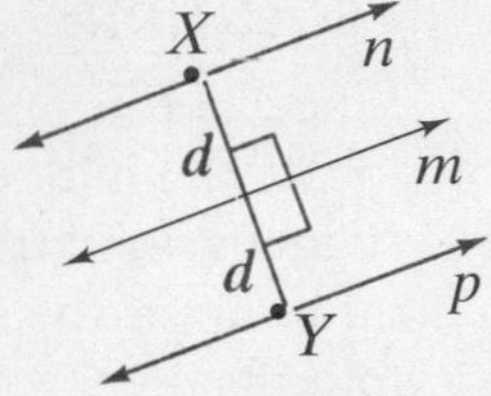

Step 1 Construct line n containing X and parallel to m.

Step 2 Construct line p containing Y and parallel to m.

Once you graph the locus in the coordinate plane, you can write its equation.

EXAMPLE 7 **Writing equations for lines a given distance from a given line**

 Find an equation or equations for the set of all points in the coordinate plane that are 3 units from the graph of $x = 2$.

▪ SOLUTION

Step 1 Sketch line m, the graph of $x = 2$.

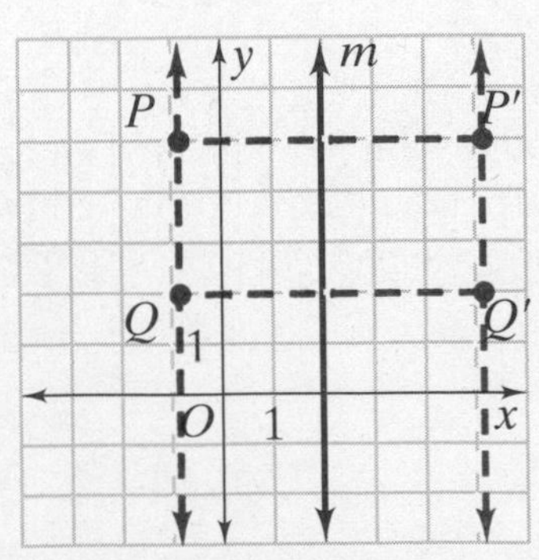

Step 2 Locate two points P and Q that are 3 units to the left of the graph of $x = 2$. For example, $P(-1, 5)$ and $Q(-1, 2)$ are 3 units to the left of the graph of $x = 2$. The line $x = -1$ is 3 units from line m.

Step 3 Locate two points P' and Q' that are 3 units to the right of the graph of $x = 2$. For example, $P(5, 5)$ and $Q(5, 2)$ are 3 units to the right of the graph of $x = 2$. The line $x = 5$ is 3 units from line m.

The pair of equations $x = -1$ and $x = 5$ represent the set of all points in the coordinate plane that are 3 units from line m, the graph of $x = 2$.

EXAMPLES 8 and 9 Sketching the set of all points equidistant from two horizontal or vertical lines

Sketch and write the equation of the locus of points equidistant from each pair of lines.

8 $x = -2$ and $x = 4$

■ **SOLUTION**

Sketch $x = -2$ and $x = 4$. Sketch the vertical line 3 units horizontally from each. The equation of the locus is $x = 1$.

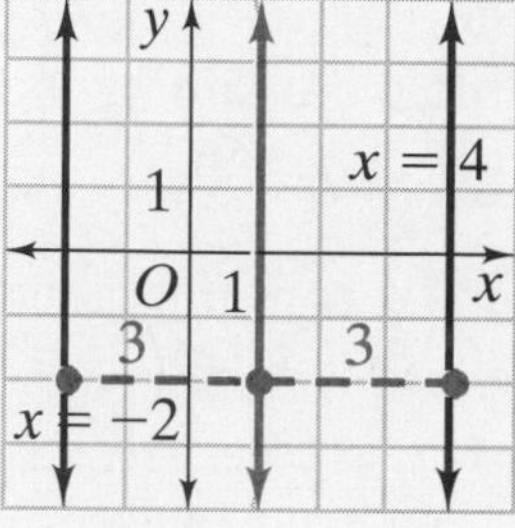

9 $y = -2$ and $y = 3$

■ **SOLUTION**

Sketch $y = -2$ and $y = 3$. Sketch the horizontal line 2.5 units vertically from each. The equation of the locus is $y = 0.5$.

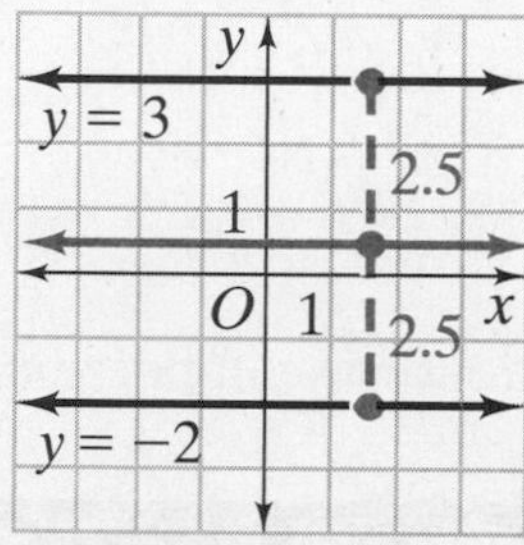

In Example 1, we showed that the locus of points that are a fixed distance from a given point forms a circle. You can graph this locus on the coordinate plane and write an equation to describe the locus.

EXAMPLE 10 Graphing a locus in the coordinate plane

10 Graph the locus of points 3 units from the origin and represent it as an equation.

■ **SOLUTION**

The equation of the locus of points 3 units from the origin would be a circle of radius 3. Recall that the equation of a circle is $x^2 + y^2 = r^2$. Therefore, the equation is $x^2 + y^2 = 3^2$ or $x^2 + y^2 = 9$.

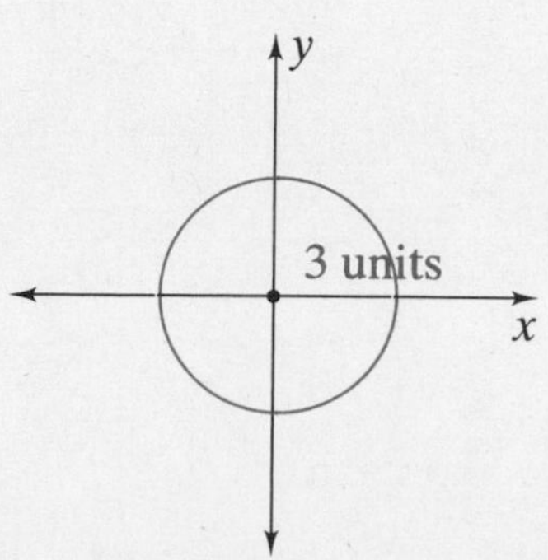

Note

The equation of a circle centered at the origin is $x^2 + y^2 = r^2$, where r is the radius of the circle.

You can use a compass and a straightedge to construct loci in the plane.

EXAMPLE 11 **Constructing the locus of points equidistant from intersecting lines**

11 Construct the locus of all points in the plane equidistant from intersecting lines m and n.

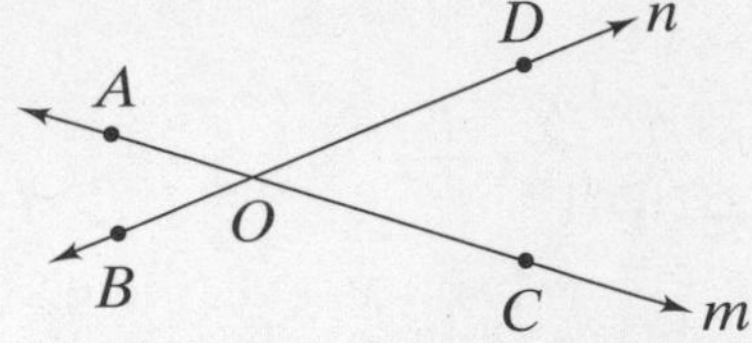

■ SOLUTION

Step 1 Construct line p containing the angle bisector of $\angle COD$.

Step 2 Construct line q containing the angle bisector of $\angle AOD$.

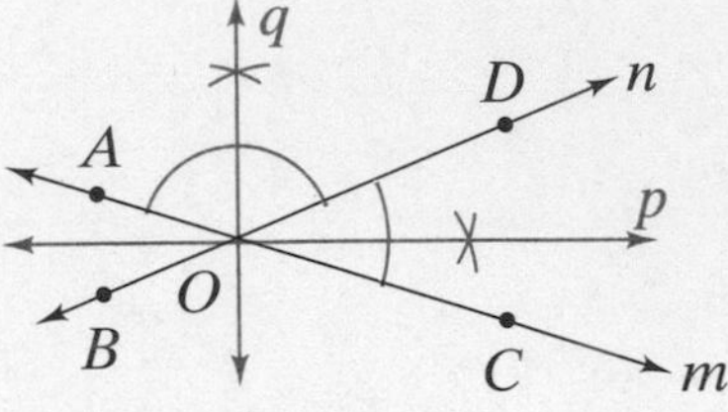

Lines p and q represent the set of all points in the plane equidistant from lines m and n.

Example 11 illustrates the following important fact.

Loci and Angle Bisectors

The set of all points in the plane that are equidistant from intersecting lines m and n consists of the bisectors of the four angles formed by the intersecting lines. The union of the four bisectors is a pair of perpendicular lines.

Practice

Choose the numeral preceding the word or expression that best completes the statement or answers the question.

1 Which represents the set of all points through which the tip of the minute hand on a clock passes during one hour?

(1) circle

(2) two concentric circles

(3) a segment

(4) a pair of parallel lines

2 Which equation represents all points in the coordinate plane 4 units below the x-axis?

(1) $y = -4$

(2) $x = 4$

(3) $x + y = 4$

(4) $y = 4 + x$

3 Which statement is true?

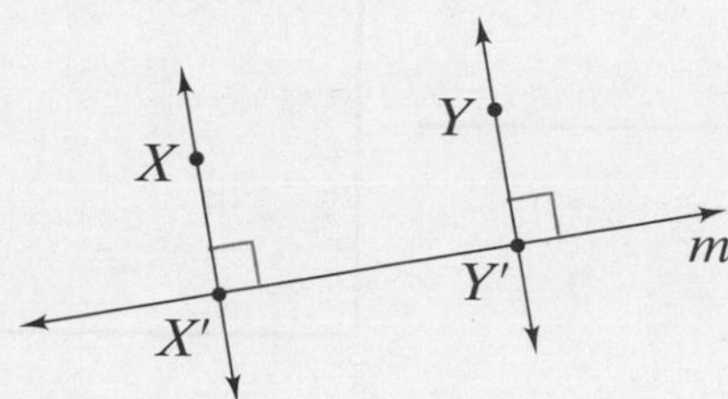

(1) $XX' = YY'$ for all X and Y on the same side of line m.

(2) $XX' = YY'$ if X and Y lie along a line parallel to line m.

(3) $XX' > YY'$ for all X and Y on the same side of line m.

(4) $XX' > YY'$ if X and Y lie on a line that intersects line m.

4 All points on the graph of $x = 4$ are equidistant from which two points?

(1) $A(4, 0)$ and $B(0, 4)$
(2) $A(0, 0)$ and $B(0, 8)$
(3) $A(0, 0)$ and $B(8, 0)$
(4) $A(4, 8)$ and $B(4, -8)$

5 Which equation(s) represents the set of all points equidistant from the x-axis and the y-axis?

(1) $y = x$ **(3)** $y = -x$
(2) $y = x$ and $y = -x$ **(4)** the origin

In Exercises 6–11, illustrate and describe each locus.

6 all points in the plane PQ units from Q

7 all points in the plane the given distance CD from C and also the given distance AB from point B

8 all points in the plane the same distance from line m as points A and B

9 all points in the plane the same distance from line m above as points A and B and at a distance $2(PB)$ from P

10 the location of a point equidistant from points U and V

11 the location of a point equidistant from lines r and s

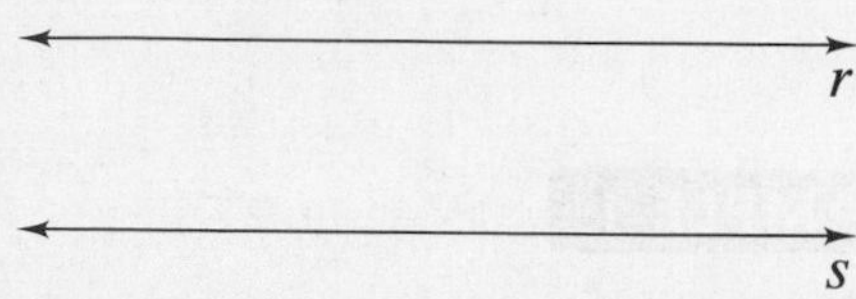

In Exercises 12–15, find an equation or equations to represent each locus in the coordinate plane.

12 the set of all points 2 units from $y = 2$

13 all points 4 units from the graph of $x = 3$

14 the set of all points equidistant from $X(2, 3)$ and $Y(5, 3)$

15 the set of all points equidistant from $P(2, 3)$ and $N(2, 6)$

In Exercises 16–20, find an equation for the set of all points in the plane for each locus.

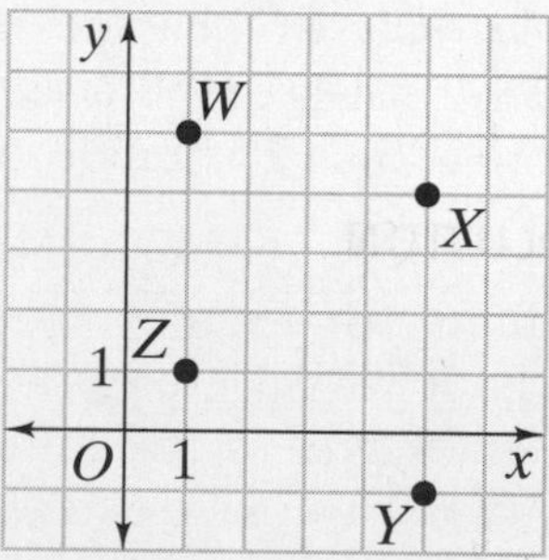

16 all points equidistant from W and Z

17 all points equidistant from W and Y

18 all points equidistant from X and Y

19 all points equidistant from X and Z

20 all points equidistant from $\overleftrightarrow{WZ}$ and $\overleftrightarrow{XY}$

In Exercises 21–23, describe each locus.

21 all points in the coordinate plane less than 3 units from the origin

22 all points in the coordinate plane less than or equal to 3 units from the origin

23 all points in the coordinate plane greater than or equal to 3 units from the graph of $x = 2$

1.7 Solving Problems with Compound Loci

New York Standards

G.G. 22 Solve problems using compound loci

G.G. 23 Graphing compound loci

In some problems, a locus must satisfy two or more conditions. To find the locus of points that satisfies these conditions, you must draw each condition using the same diagram. Then state the locus when both conditions have been satisfied.

EXAMPLE 1 **Solving problems involving multiple distances**

1 How many points in the plane are 3 units from a given line m and also 6 units from point A on m?

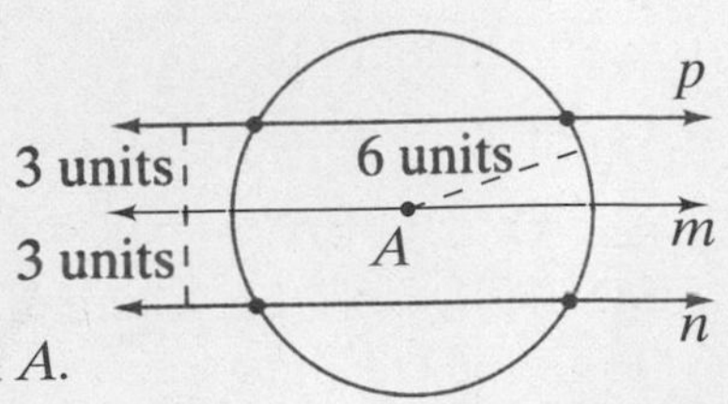

▪ **SOLUTION**

Step 1 Sketch m and lines n and p that are 3 units from m.

Step 2 Using A as center, sketch the circle whose radius is 6.

There are 4 points that are both 3 units from m and 6 units from A.

To solve problems with compound loci, you need to sketch each condition and identify the points where the sketches intersect.

EXAMPLES 2 and 3 **Choosing the correct number of points of intersection**

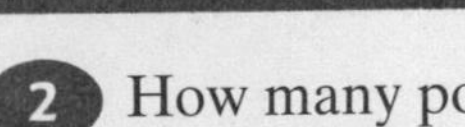

2 How many points in the plane are 5 units from line b and also 3 units from a point on line b?

(1) 0 (2) 1 (3) 2 (4) 4

not to scale

▪ **SOLUTION**

The minimum distance a point can be from line b is 5 units. Any circle with center on the line and radius 3 will not be large enough to intersect the points 5 units from the line. A sketch like this one can confirm this. The correct choice is (1).

3 Find the locus that is equidistant from 2 intersecting lines and 4 units from the point of intersection.

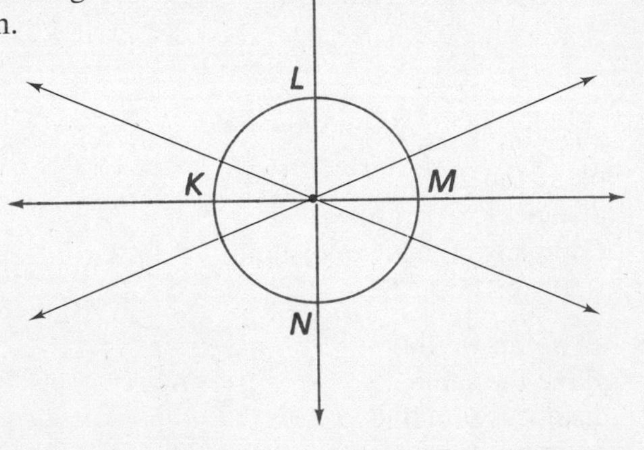

▪ **SOLUTION**

Step 1 The locus that is equidistant from 2 intersecting lines is shown by the lines that bisect the vertical angles.

Step 2 The locus that is 4 units from the intersection of the 2 lines is a circle with radius 4.

Therefore, the locus that satisfies both conditions is the set of 4 points K, L, M, N.

EXAMPLE 4 Choosing the correct number of points of intersection

 Given $\angle CAB$, how many points are equidistant from $\overrightarrow{AC}$ and $\overrightarrow{AB}$ and also 3 units from A?

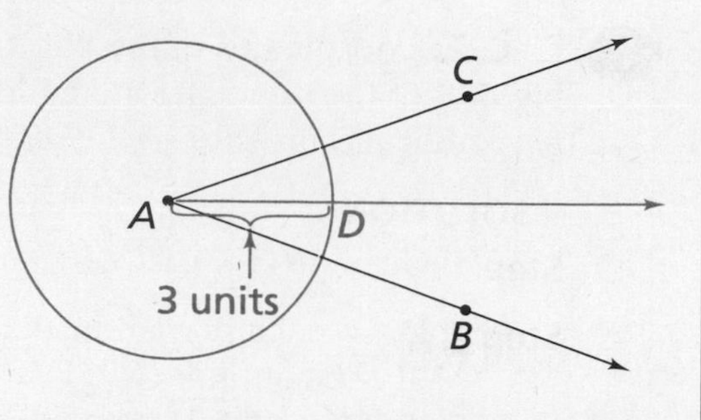

■ **SOLUTION**

Step 1 Draw $\overrightarrow{AB}$, the angle bisector of angle A.

Step 2 Draw the circle with its center at the vertex A and radius 3.

The intersection is at point D.

You can use a compass and straightedge to help you solve problems with compound loci.

EXAMPLE 5 Using perpendicular bisectors and constructions

 A landscape designer wants to place four bushes on a circle in such a way that they are equally spaced apart. Illustrate where they could be planted by using a diagram.

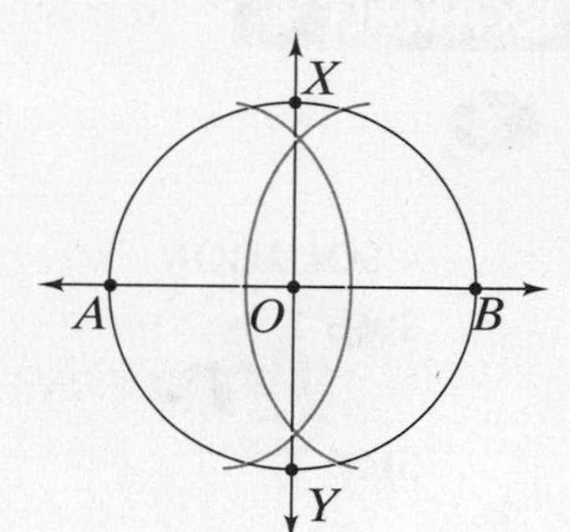

■ **SOLUTION**

Step 1 Draw a circle using a compass. Label the center O.

Step 2 Using a straightedge, draw a line containing O. Label the points where the line intersects the circle as A and B.

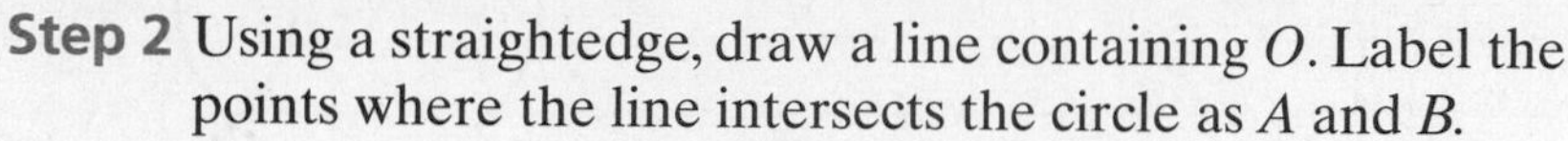

Step 3 Using compass and straightedge, construct the line perpendicular to $\overleftrightarrow{AB}$ and containing O. Label the points where this line intersects the circle as X and Y. The arcs show the construction of $\overleftrightarrow{XY}$.

The landscaper can plant the bushes at *A, B, X, and Y.*

Using the coordinate plane, you can solve a variety of locus problems.

EXAMPLE 6 Finding the coordinates of a point equidistant from four points

 Find the coordinates of any points in the plane equidistant from $A(1, 3)$, $B(7, 3)$, $C(4, 0)$, and $D(4, 6)$.

■ **SOLUTION**

Draw a sketch showing $A(1, 3)$, $B(7, 3)$, $C(4, 0)$, and $D(4, 6)$.

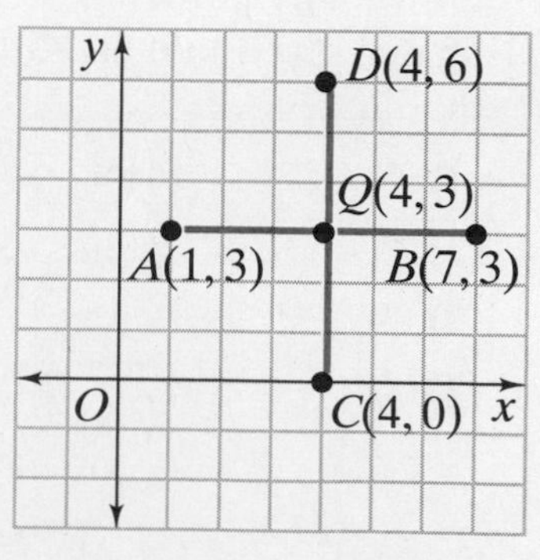

Any point meeting all the requirements must lie along the perpendicular bisector of $\overline{AB}$.

Any point meeting all the requirements must also lie along the perpendicular bisector of $\overline{CD}$.

The only point meeting all the requirements is $Q(4, 3)$, the point where the perpendicular bisectors of $\overline{AB}$ and $\overline{CD}$ intersect.

EXAMPLE 7 Finding the coordinates of the intersection of perpendicular bisectors

7 Find the coordinates of the point in the plane where the perpendicular bisector of the segment with endpoints $K(1,2)$ and $L(3,0)$ intersects the perpendicular bisector of the segment with endpoints $K(1,2)$ and $M(3,4)$.

▪ **SOLUTION**

Step 1 Graph $K(1,2)$, $L(3,0)$, and $M(3,4)$. Draw $\overline{KL}$ and $\overline{KM}$.

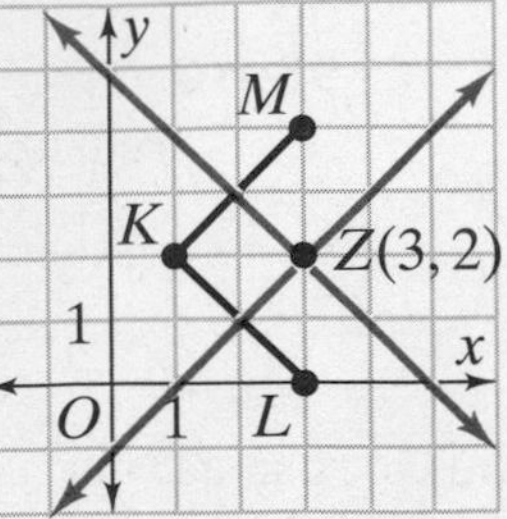

Step 2 Draw each perpendicular bisector. The perpendicular bisector of $\overline{KL}$ contains X(2, 1) and has slope 1. The perpendicular bisector of $\overline{KM}$ contains Y(2, 3) and has slope –1.

Step 3 Locate the point where the perpendicular bisectors intersect.

The perpendicular bisectors intersect in the point with coordinates $Z(3, 2)$.

EXAMPLE 8 Counting intersections of circles

8 In how many points in the plane will the circles with centers $C(-2, 4)$ and $C'(2, 4)$ intersect if each has radius 3?

▪ **SOLUTION**

Step 1 Set up a coordinate plane to graph the circles with given centers and radius.

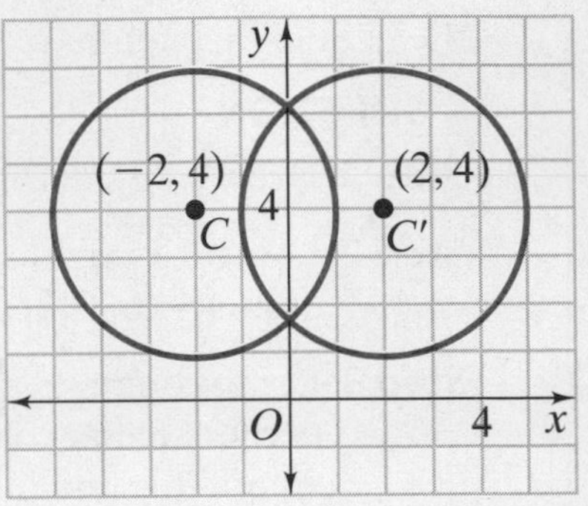

Step 2 Using a compass, graph the circle with center $C(-2, 4)$ and radius 3.

Step 3 Using a compass, graph the circle with center $C'(2, 4)$ and radius 3.

From the coordinate diagram, there are 2 points of intersection.

Practice

Choose the numeral preceding the word or expression that best completes the statement or answers the question.

1 How many points in the plane are 4 units from a given line and 5 units from a point on that line?

(1) 0
(2) 2
(3) 3
(4) 4

2 How many points in the plane are a given distance from line p and equidistant from two fixed points on line p?

(1) 0
(2) 2
(3) 3
(4) 4

3 How many points in the coordinate plane are 2 units from the y-axis and 1 unit from the origin?

(1) 0 **(3)** 2
(2) 1 **(4)** 4

4 How many points in the coordinate plane are 5 units from the line $x = 5$ and 5 units from the origin?

(1) 0 **(3)** 2
(2) 1 **(4)** 4

5 How many points in the coordinate plane are 3 units from the origin and 5 units from the point $(5, 0)$?

(1) 0 **(3)** 2
(2) 1 **(4)** 4

6 What are the coordinates of the point that is equidistant from the x- and y-axis and 2 units from the y-axis?

(1) $(2, 0)$ **(3)** $(0, 2)$
(2) $(2, 2)$ **(4)** $(0, 0)$

Use an illustration to answer Exercises 7–8.

7 How many points in the plane are equidistant from two given parallel lines and lie on a circle centered on one of the lines and having radius equal to the distance between the lines?

8 In how many points in the plane will two circles with equal radius intersect if the distance between the centers equals the diameter of either circle?

In Exercises 9–11, illustrate your response with a diagram on a coordinate plane.

9 How many points are equidistant from the coordinate axes and 3 units from the point $(1, 0)$?

10 How many points are equidistant from $y = 4$ and $y = -2$ and 2 units from $(1, 2)$?

11 How many points are equidistant from $(2, 4)$ and $(6, 4)$ and 3 units from $(4, 2)$?

In Exercises 12–15, find the coordinates of all points in the coordinate plane that satisfy all stated conditions.

12 all points 4 units from the x-axis and 5 units from the y-axis

13 all points 5 units from $(2, 1)$ that lie on the line $y = 6$

14 all points 5 units from $(2, 1)$ and also 5 units from $(12, 1)$

15 all points equidistant from $C(-3, 4)$ and $Q(5, 4)$ and equidistant from $X(1, 0)$ and $Y(1, 8)$

In Exercises 16–20, refer to the coordinate diagram below.

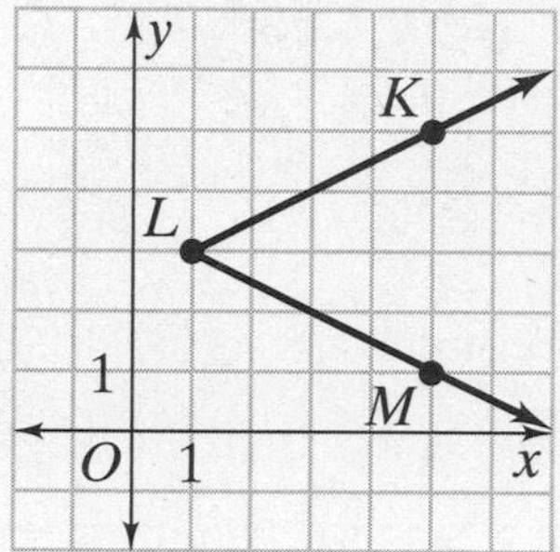

16 Write an equation for the line containing the angle bisector of $\angle KLM$. What are the coordinates of any point in which this line intersects the perpendicular bisector of $\overline{LK}$?

17 Find the coordinates of any point in which the perpendicular bisector of $\overline{LM}$ intersects the perpendicular bisector of $\overline{LK}$.

18 Describe the locus that is 8 units from L. At how many points will this locus intersect $\angle KLM$?

19 How many points are 3 units from K, L, and M?

20 Find the coordinates of the point that is 7 units from L and equidistant from K and M.

21 Describe the locus that is 1 unit from a circle centered at the origin with radius 5.

Chapter 1 Preparing for the New York Geometry Exam

Answer all questions in this part. For each question, select the numeral preceding the word or expression that best completes the statement or answers the question.

1 If two planes intersect, then they intersect in exactly

(1) one line **(3)** one point

(2) one plane **(4)** two points

2 Which three points determine plane B in the diagram below?

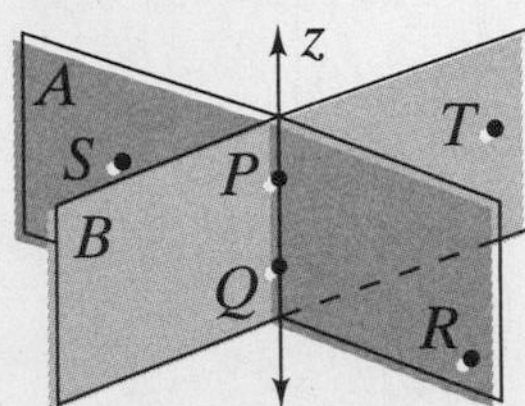

(1) P, Q, and R **(3)** R, S, and T

(2) P, Q, and T **(4)** Q, R, and S

3 Which is a possible relationship between two acute angles?

I vertical III complementary

II adjacent IV supplementary

(1) I and II only **(3)** I, II, and III only

(2) I and III only **(4)** I, II, III, and IV

4 Given that $\overrightarrow{KM}$ bisects $\angle JKL$, and $m\angle JKM = 74°$, then $m\angle JKL =$

(1) 26°. **(3)** 106°.

(2) 37°. **(4)** 148°.

5 In the figure below, $\ell \parallel m$ and $m\angle 1 = 48°$. Which other numbered angles have a measure of 48°?

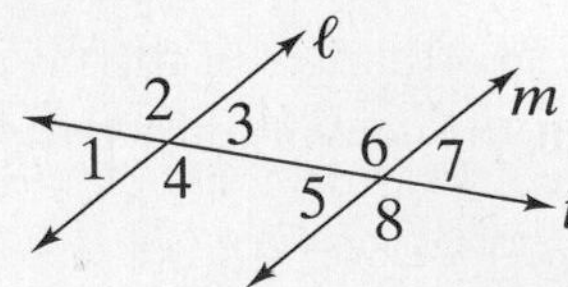

(1) $\angle 2$, $\angle 4$, and $\angle 8$

(2) $\angle 2$, $\angle 4$, $\angle 6$, and $\angle 8$

(3) $\angle 3$, $\angle 5$, and $\angle 7$

(4) $\angle 3$, $\angle 4$, $\angle 5$, and $\angle 6$

6 Which of the following statements must be true in order for p to be parallel to q in the diagram below?

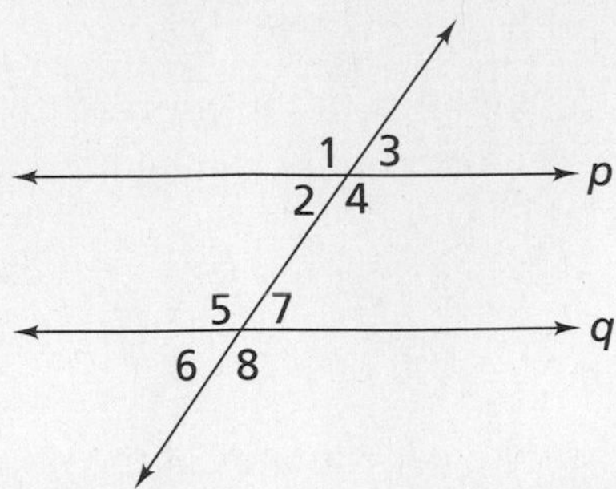

(1) $m\angle 1 = m\angle 2$ **(3)** $m\angle 1 = m\angle 6$

(2) $m\angle 1 = m\angle 5$ **(4)** $m\angle 1 = m\angle 7$

7 In the figure below, x is parallel to y. If the $m\angle 1 = 111°$, find $m\angle 6$.

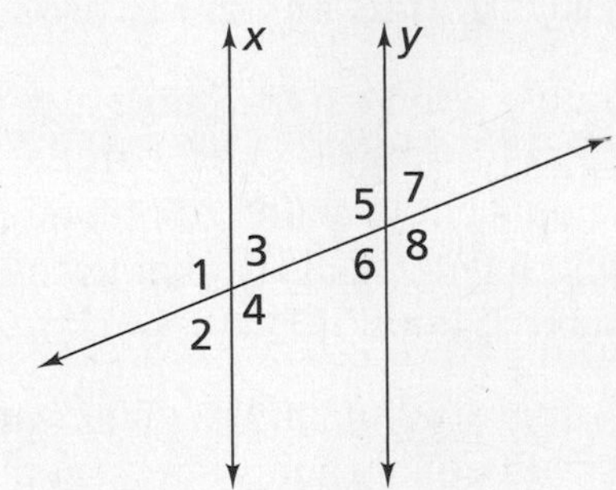

(1) 69° **(3)** 111°

(2) 90° **(4)** 180°

8 Use a compass to determine which of the following figures shows a line segment whose length is $PQ + XY$.

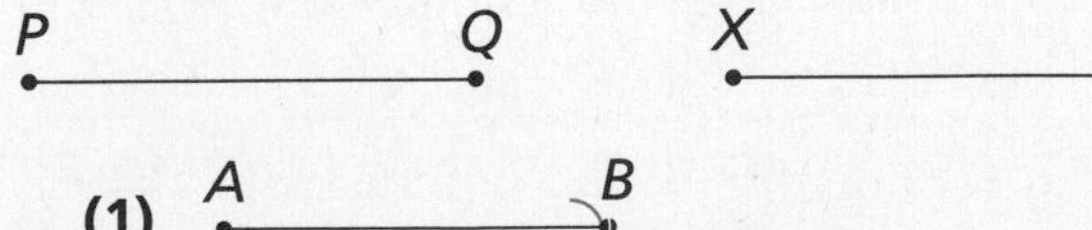

(1) 

(2) A B

(3) A B C

(4) A B C

9 In the figure below, lines k and l intersect at the point A. What is $m\angle 3$ when $m\angle 1 = 3n + 21$ and $m\angle 2 = 36n + 3$?

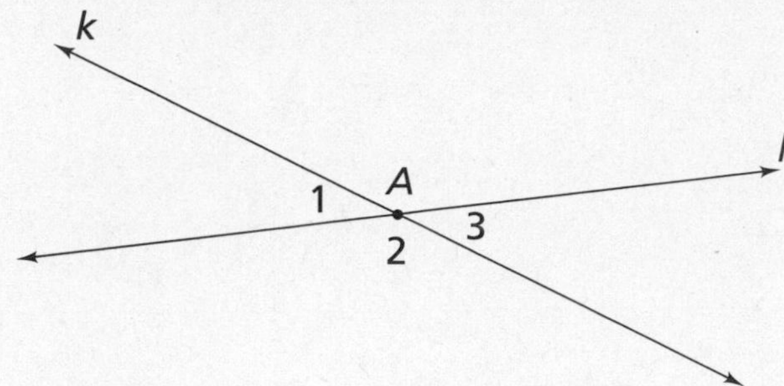

(1) 4
(2) 33
(3) 57
(4) 147

10 Use a compass to determine which of the following statements about $m\angle A$ and $m\angle B$ is true.

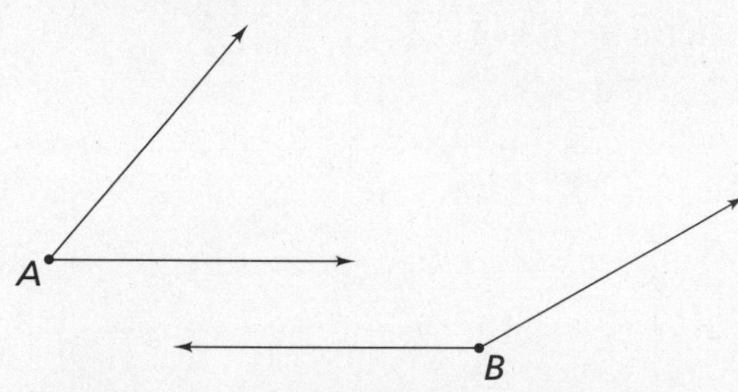

(1) $m\angle A = 2(m\angle B)$
(2) $m\angle B = 2(m\angle A)$
(3) $m\angle A = 3(m\angle B)$
(4) $m\angle B = 3(m\angle A)$

11 Which conclusion can you draw from the construction below?

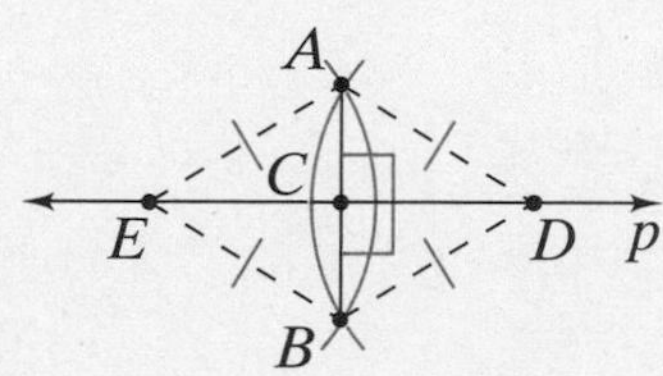

(1) $\overline{AE} \cong \overline{AB}$
(2) $\overline{AE} \cong \overline{EB}$
(3) $\overline{AE} \perp \overline{AD}$
(4) $\overline{AE} \perp \overline{EB}$

12 Which conclusion about the following construction is true?

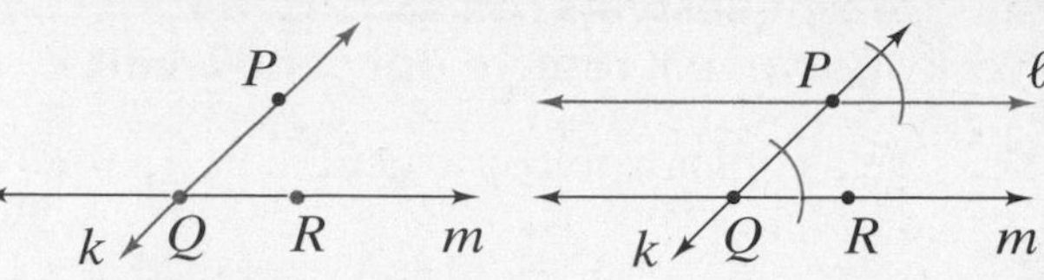

(1) l bisects $\angle PQR$
(2) $\overline{QR} \cong \overline{QP}$
(3) $k \perp m$
(4) $l \parallel m$

13 Which is an equation for the set of all points in the coordinate plane equidistant from the lines $y = \frac{3}{4}x - 2$ and $y = \frac{3}{4}x + 6$?

(1) $y = \frac{3}{4}x + 2$
(2) $y = -\frac{4}{3}x - 2$
(3) $y = \frac{3}{4}x + 4$
(4) $y = -\frac{4}{3}x + 2$

14 Which equation represents the set of all points in the coordinate plane equidistant from $P(0, 4)$ and $Q(4, 0)$?

(1) $y = x$
(2) $y = -x$
(3) $y = x + 4$
(4) $y = 0$

15 Which equation represents the set of all points equidistant from $y = -3$ and $y = 5$?

(1) $y = 2$
(2) $y = 1$
(3) $x = 1$
(4) $x = 2$

16 In how many points in the coordinate plane does the set of all points 5 units from $x = 5$ intersect the circle centered at the origin and having radius 5?

(1) 0 (2) 1 (3) 2 (4) 4

Answer all questions in this part. Clearly indicate the necessary steps, including appropriate formula substitutions, diagrams, graphs, charts, etc. For all questions in this part, a correct numerical answer with no work shown will receive only one credit.

17 Use a compass to construct the line perpendicular to $\overleftrightarrow{SA}$ and containing R.

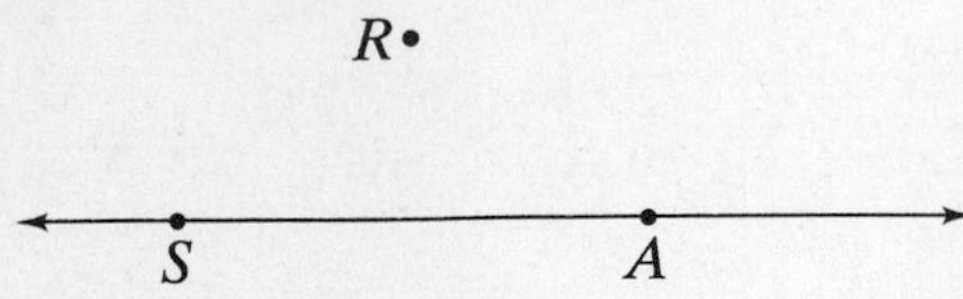

18 Write an equation for the set of all points equidistant from $\overleftrightarrow{RT}$ and $\overleftrightarrow{DZ}$.

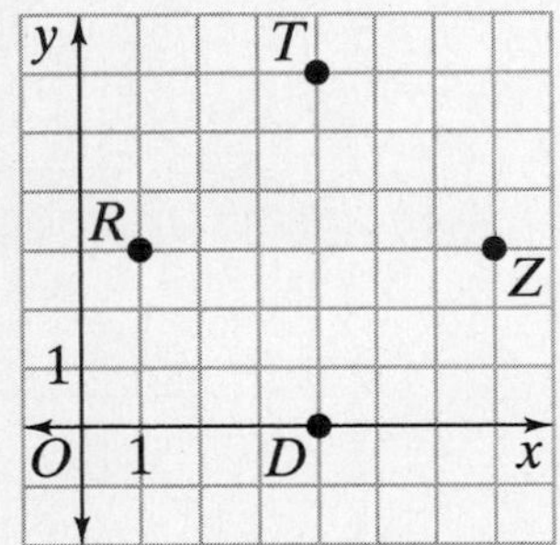

19 Describe the locus of all points in the coordinate plane that are equidistant from $x = -2$ and $x = 4$ that have y-coordinate between -3 and 3 inclusive.

2 Mathematical Statements

Discovering New York

Statue of Liberty

In 1855, France presented the Statue of Liberty to the people of the United States as a symbol of friendship. For the 12 million immigrants who entered this country through Ellis Island, the statue was their first glimpse of a new beginning. Standing more than 300 feet tall in New York Harbor, the Statue of Liberty has become an international symbol of freedom.

Nicknamed "Lady Liberty," the statue raises a lit torch with its right hand. In its left arm, it holds a tablet that reads "July 4, 1776," representing the Declaration of Independence. The seven points of the statue's crown represent the seven continents. When the 225-ton statue arrived in New York, it was in 350 separate pieces and took months to assemble.

2.1 Open and Closed Statements

New York Standards

G.G.24 Negation of a statement

A **statement** is any mathematical sentence. A statement is called an **open statement** if it cannot be determined whether or not the statement is true or false. The equation $x + 8 = 16$ is an example of an open statement. Until we know what the value of x is, the truth value of the statement cannot be determined.

Any statement that can be classified as true or false is called a **closed statement.** *A triangle is a four-sided figure* is an example of a closed statement. Its truth value is false.

EXAMPLE 1 **Determining the type and truth value of statements**

1 Classify each of the following statements as open or closed. If the statement is closed, determine its truth value.

Statement (Sentence)	Type	Truth Value
$5 + 2 = 7$	Closed	True
$n + 4 = 12$	Open	
If point C is between A and B, then $AC + CB = AB$.	Closed	True
Measures of supplementary angles add up to 90°.	Closed	False
The complement of a 50° angle is an angle of 40°.	Closed	True
Every segment has a unique perpendicular bisector.	Closed	True
$\sqrt{3}$ is a rational number.	Closed	False
$x + y = 6$	Open	

An unproven statement concerning an observation is called a **conjecture.** Much of geometry was developed by observation and formulating conjectures. To prove that a conjecture is true, you must show it is true for **all** cases. To prove that a conjecture is false, you need to find only one case where the statement is false. This case is called a **counterexample.**

EXAMPLE 2 **Working with counterexamples**

2 Is the following statement true or false?
No square has a perimeter numerically equal to its area.

■ **SOLUTION**

Side	1	3	5	4
Perimeter	$4(1) = 4$	$4(3) = 12$	$4(5) = 20$	$4(4) = 16$
Area	$1^2 = 1$	$3^2 = 9$	$5^2 = 25$	$4^2 = 16$

If a square has a side that is 4 units in length, then its perimeter and area are numerically equal. This counterexample shows that the statement is false.

EXAMPLE 3 Working with conjectures and counterexamples

Go Online
PHSchool.com
Visit: PHSchool.com
Web Code: ayp-0366

3 What is the truth value of the following conjecture?
For a given line segment there is one and only one bisector.

■ **SOLUTION**

This conjecture is false because the example to the right shows $\overline{AB}$ with more than one bisector. The segment, lines, and ray shown in the figure all pass through the midpoint of the segment and therefore are all bisectors of the segment. This drawing provides a **counterexample** to the conjecture.

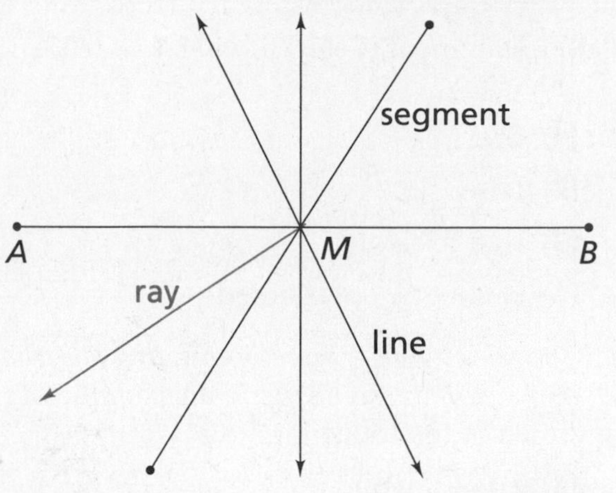

By inserting or removing the word *not* in a statement, the **negation** of the statement is formed.

Note

If a statement is true, its negation is false. If a statement is false, its negation is true.

Statement	Truth Value	Negation	Truth Value
All squares are rectangles.	T	All squares are *not* rectangles.	F
There are 8 days in a week.	F	There are *not* 8 days in a week.	T
All triangles are not right.	T	All triangles *are* right.	F

You can use symbols to represent statement. Let p represent a closed statement. You would write the negation of the statement p as $\sim p$. You would read $\sim p$ as "not p."

p	$\sim p$
T	F
F	T

EXAMPLE 4 Negations and their truth value

4 Determine the truth value of each statement. Then write its negation and the negation's truth value.

■ **SOLUTION**

Statement	Truth Value	Negation	Truth Value
All right angles measure 90°.	T	All right angles do not measure 90°.	F
Parallel lines intersect.	F	Parallel lines do not intersect.	T

Practice

Choose the numeral preceding the word or expression that best completes the statement or answers the question.

1 If a statement is closed, what is its truth value?

(1) true

(2) false

(3) true or false

(4) cannot be determined

2 The statement *If three points are collinear they lie on the same line* is an example of which of the following?

(1) open statement

(2) closed statement

(3) counterexample

(4) negation

3 Which figure provides a counterexample to the following statement?

If a quadrilateral has two pairs of equal sides, the quadrilateral is a parallelogram.

(1) rectangle

(2) kite

(3) trapezoid

(4) rhombus

4 If a statement is true, what is the truth value of its negation?

(1) true

(2) false

(3) neither

(4) cannot be determined

5 Which of the following is the negation of $5 + 6 = 11$?

(1) $5 + 6 \neq 11$

(2) $6 - 5 = 11$

(3) $11 - 6 = 5$

(4) $5 + 6 < 11$

6 What best describes the following statement?

All squares have four sides.

(1) true open

(2) open

(3) true closed

(4) false closed

7 Which of the following is the negation of the statement, *Vertical angles are congruent*?

(1) Vertical angles are congruent.

(2) Nonvertical angles are congruent.

(3) Vertical angles are not congruent.

(4) Congruent angles are vertical.

8 Which of the following is a counterexample to the statement, *If you are not a guitar player, then you are not a musician*?

(1) someone who can play only the guitar

(2) someone who cannot play any instrument

(3) someone who can play both the guitar and the piano

(4) someone who cannot play the guitar but can play the piano

9 If the negation of a statement is true, then the original statement is

(1) true.

(2) false.

(3) unknown.

(4) neither true nor false.

10 What is the truth value of the negation of the statement, *He wore a green shirt on Friday*?

(1) true

(2) false

(3) neither

(4) cannot be determined

In Exercises 11–21, complete the following table.

Statement	Truth Value	Negation	Truth Value
11 Perpendicular lines meet to form right angles.			
12 There are not 30 days in September.			
13 The supplement of an acute angle is an obtuse angle.			
14 Parallel lines do not intersect.			
15 The bisector of an angle is unique.			
16 Three noncollinear points do not determine a plane.			
17 The complement of an acute angle is an acute angle.			
18 A line contains at least two points.			
19 27 is a prime number.			
20 Two intersecting lines intersect at exactly one point.			
21 A straight angle does not measure 180°.			

In Exercises 22–37, find a counterexample for each of the statements.

22 Two angles are never congruent and supplementary.

23 Any three points determine a plane.

24 If two lines don't intersect, they are parallel.

25 The sum of two rational numbers is never an integer.

26 A point that is equidistant from the endpoints of a segment must be the midpoint of the segment.

27 The sum of two odd numbers is an odd number.

28 If $AM = \frac{1}{2}AB$ then M is the midpoint of AB.

29 The sum of two integers is greater than the larger integer.

30 All polygons have five sides.

31 All complementary angles are congruent.

32 The product of three negative integers is even.

33 The value of x^2 is greater than the value of x.

34 All real numbers are also rational numbers.

35 The area of a circle is always greater than its circumference.

36 All right triangles are isosceles.

37 $a^2 + b^2 = c^2$ for all integers a, b, and c.

2.2 Conjunction and Disjunction

New York Standards

G.G.25 Compound statements

A **compound statement** is formed by joining two statements. When the word *and* is used to join two statements, the new statement is called a **conjunction.**

A sample of a conjunction is *A square has equal angles, and a square has equal sides.* A conjunction is true only when both statements are true. Since a square has equal angles and equal sides, the conjunction above is true.

EXAMPLE 1 **Identifying conjunctions**

1 What is the truth value of the conjunction, *Acute angles measure less than 90° and supplementary angles add up to 90°?*

■ **SOLUTION**

Since the statement *acute angles measure less than 90°* is true and the statement *supplementary angles add up to 90°* is false, the conjunction is ***false.***

When a compound statement is formed by joining two statements with the word ***or,*** the new statement is known as a **disjunction.** A disjunction is true if at least one of its parts is true.

EXAMPLES 2 and 3 **Identifying disjunctions**

2 Form a disjunction from the following statement and determine its truth value.

Statement 1: *Supplementary angles add up to 180°.*

Statement 2: *Supplementary angles add up to 90°.*

■ **SOLUTION**

Disjunction: Supplementary angles add up to 180°, or supplementary angles add up to 90°.

Since the first statement is true and the second statement is false, the disjunction is ***true.***

3 Given that $\angle A = 90°$, determine the truth value of the following statement: $\angle A$ is an acute angle or $\angle A$ is a right angle.

■ **SOLUTION**

The first statement of this disjunction is false and the second statement is true. Therefore, the disjunction is ***true.***

A conjunction is represented by the symbol $\wedge$. A disjunction is represented by the symbol $\vee$. The following table shows the truth values of the conjunction and disjunction of statements p and q.

p	q	$p \wedge q$	$p \vee q$
T	T	T	T
T	F	F	T
F	T	F	T
F	F	F	F

The *TEST* feature of a graphing calculator can be used to verify the truth values of conjunctions and disjunctions. The calculator reports a 1 for a true statement and a 0 for a false statement.

Statement		Calculator	
$5 + 2 = 7$ and $4 + 3 = 7$	✓	5+2=7 and 4+3=7	1
$5 + 2 = 7$ and $4 + 4 = 7$	✗	5+2=7 and 4+4=7	0
$5 + 1 = 7$ and $4 + 3 = 7$	✗	5+1=7 and 4+3=7	0
$5 + 1 = 7$ and $4 + 4 = 7$	✗	5+1=7 and 4+4=7	0

Statement		Calculator	
$5 - 7 = -2$ or $5 \times 2 = 10$	✓	5−7=−2 or 5×2=10	1
$5 - 7 = 2$ or $5 \times 2 = 10$	✓	5−7=2 or 5×2=10	1
$5 - 7 = -2$ or $5 \times 2 = 7$	✓	5−7=−2 or 5×2=7	1
$5 - 7 = 2$ or $5 \times 2 = 7$	✗	5−7=2 or 5×2=7	0

EXAMPLES 4 and 5 Finding truth values involving conjunctions and disjunctions

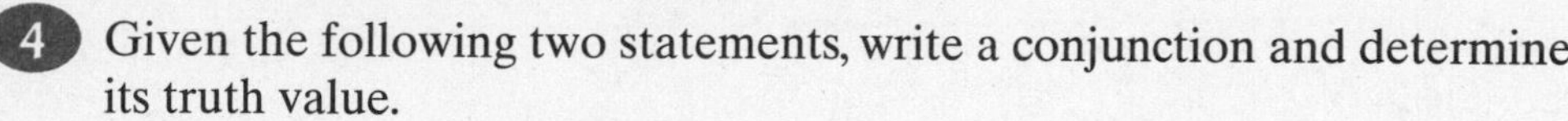

4 Given the following two statements, write a conjunction and determine its truth value.

Statement 1: All right angles measure 90°.

Statement 2: All squares are quadrilaterals.

■ SOLUTION

The conjunction: All right angles measure 90°, and all squares are quadrilaterals.

The conjunction is ***true*** because both statements are true.

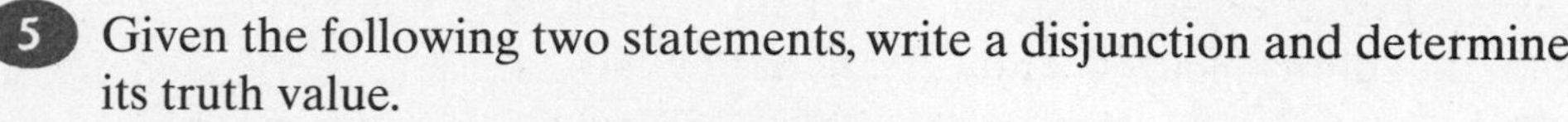

5 Given the following two statements, write a disjunction and determine its truth value.

Statement 1: All quadrilaterals are squares.

Statement 2: Complementary angles add up to 180°.

■ SOLUTION

The disjunction: All quadrilaterals are squares, or complementary angles add up to 180°.

Both of the original statements are false; therefore, the disjunction is ***false.***

EXAMPLE 6 Finding truth values of conjunctions and disjunctions with negations

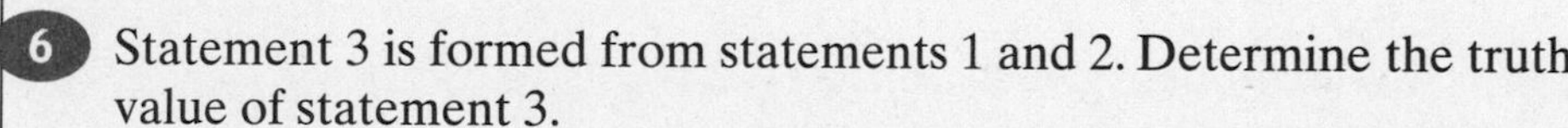

6 Statement 3 is formed from statements 1 and 2. Determine the truth value of statement 3.

Statement 1: Parallel lines do not intersect.

Statement 2: Perpendicular lines meet to form right angles.

Statement 3: Parallel lines intersect, or perpendicular lines meet to form right angles.

■ SOLUTION

Statement 3 is a disjunction formed by the negation of statement 1 and statement 2. Statement 1 is true; therefore, its negation is false. Statement 2 is a true statement. This results in a ***true*** disjunction.

To find the negation of a conjunction, you need to negate each statement and write the disjunction of the negations. Similarly, to find the negation of a disjunction, you need to negate each statement and write the conjunction of the negations.

Negation of conjunctions and disjunctions

The **negation of a conjunction** is the disjunction of the negations.

The **negation of a disjunction** is the conjunction of the negations.

EXAMPLES 7 and 8 Negation of a conjunction

7 What is the negation of the following conjunction?
Mary had the lead in the play and Mr. Brown directed it.

SOLUTION

This statement is a conjunction. A conjunction is true when both parts are true. If Mary did not have the lead in the play *or* if Mr. Brown did not direct it, the conjunction would be false. Notice that the statement *Mary did not have the lead in the play* is the negation of *Mary had the lead in the play*. Similarly, *Mr. Brown did not direct it* is the negation of *Mr. Brown directed it.* The negation of the conjunction is ***Mary did not have the lead in the play or Mr. Brown did not direct it.***

8 Write the negation of the following disjunction and determine its truth value. *All triangles have three sides, or squares have four right angles.*

SOLUTION

The negation is ***All triangles do not have three sides, and squares do not have four right angles.*** Both statements are false; therefore, the conjunction is false. The original disjunction was true. The original disjunction and its negation have opposite truth values.

Practice

Choose the numeral preceding the word or expression that best completes the statement or answers the question.

1 To form a conjunction, two simple statements are connected with which of the following words?

(1) and

(2) or

(3) not

(4) maybe

2 Which value of x makes the statement *x is prime or x is odd* false?

(1) 2

(2) 3

(3) 6

(4) 9

3 If a given statement is true, which of the following must be false?

(1) the conjunction containing the statement

(2) the disjunction containing the statement

(3) the negation of the disjunction

(4) the negation of the statement

4 Which statement about the figure below is true?

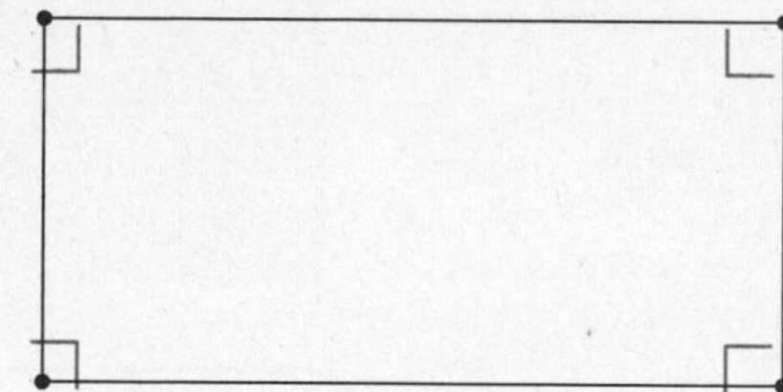

(1) The figure is a rectangle or a square.

(2) The figure is a rectangle and a square.

(3) The figure is a rectangle and a trapezoid.

(4) The figure is a square or a trapezoid.

5 Which statement represents the negation of the following statement? *A square is a rectangle, and a square is a parallelogram.*

(1) A square is not a rectangle, and a square is not a parallelogram.

(2) A square is a rectangle, and a square is not a parallelogram.

(3) A square is a rectangle, or a square is a parallelogram.

(4) A square is not a rectangle, or a square is not a parallelogram.

6 A disjunction is false when which condition holds?

(1) Both parts are false.

(2) Both parts are true.

(3) The first part is true and the second is false.

(4) The first part is false and the second is true.

7 The statement $x > 4$ *and x is irrational* is true when x is equal to

(1) π.

(2) 5.5.

(3) 7.

(4) $\sqrt{23}$.

8 The statement *Doohickeys are green and doodads are blue* is true. What is the truth value of the statement *Doohickeys are green or triangles have four sides*? Explain your answer.

In Exercises 9–15, determine the truth value of the statement and justify your answer.

9 Every square has four sides, and every pentagon has five sides.

10 George Washington was the first president of the United States, or Rochester is the capital of New York.

11 $5^2 = 10$ or $3 + 5 = 8$.

12 Triangles do not have three sides, or trapezoids are parallelograms.

13 $x^2 + x - 6 = (x + 3)(x - 2)$ or $2 + 3 = 2(3)$

14 Supplementary angles add up to 180°, and complementary angles add up to 90°.

15 Right triangles contain one right angle, and squares contain at least one right angle.

16 Write the negation of the statement *Acute angles are not equal to* 90°, *and parallel lines do not intersect.*

17 Write the negation of the statement *All right angles are equal, or squares have all sides equal.* Determine the truth value of this new statement and explain your reasoning.

18 Given the statement *Squares are quadrilaterals* and the statement *Right angles measure* 180°, write a true conjunction.

2.3 Conditional and Biconditional Statements

New York Standards

G.G.25 Compound statements

G.G.26 Conditional statements

If you study hard, then you will earn good grades. Statements like this are common. This type of statement is called a **conditional** statement. In a conditional statement, the words *if* and *then* are used to join two mathematical statements.

The *if* part of a conditional statement is called the **hypothesis.** The *then* part is called the **conclusion.**

Note

If hypothesis, then conclusion.

EXAMPLE 1 **Writing conditionals and identifying the hypothesis and conclusion**

Write each statement as a conditional in *if . . . then* form and identify the hypothesis and conclusion.

1 You can go to the movies if you finish your homework.

■ **SOLUTION**

If you finish your homework, then you can go to the movies.

Hypothesis: you finish your homework
Conclusion: you can go to the movies

Visit: PHSchool.com
Web Code: ayp-0365

Suppose someone says, "If you pass the test, you will be rewarded."

If you pass the test and receive a reward, the hypothesis is fulfilled and the promise kept.

If you fail the test and are still rewarded, the hypothesis is not fulfilled yet the promise is kept.

If you pass the test and are not rewarded, the hypothesis is fulfilled and the promise is not kept.

If you fail the test and you are not rewarded, the hypothesis is not fulfilled and the promise is not kept.

Only if you pass the test and you do not receive a reward has the speaker spoken falsely.

Note

A conditional statement is false only when the hypothesis is true and the conclusion is false.

EXAMPLE 2 **Determine the truth value of conditional statements**

2 What is the truth value of the statement *Triangles have four angles if parallel lines intersect*?

■ **SOLUTION**

Rewrite the statement in *if . . . then* form: *If parallel lines intersect, then triangles have four angles.*

Both the hypothesis and conclusion are false. Therefore, the conditional statement is true.

One way to show that a conditional statement is false is to find a counterexample.

EXAMPLE 3 **Finding a counterexample**

Show that this conditional statement is false by finding a counterexample:

If a quadrilateral has two pairs of equal sides, then the quadrilateral is a parallelogram.

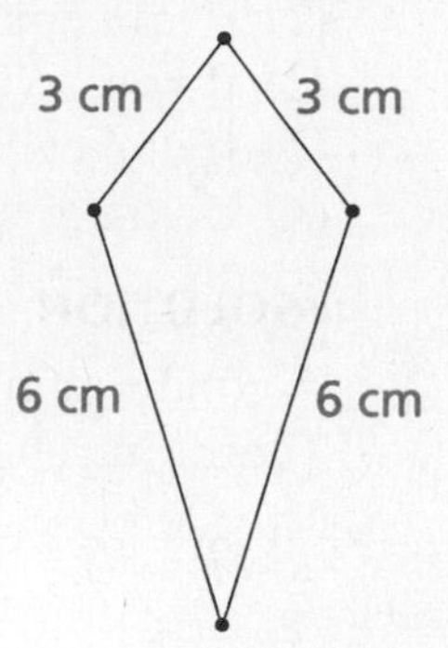

SOLUTION

To show that this conditional is false, it is necessary to find a quadrilateral that makes the hypothesis true and the conclusion false.

In the figure to the right, the quadrilateral has two pairs of equal sides. Therefore, the hypothesis is true. However, this quadrilateral is not a parallelogram. The conclusion is false. The original conditional statement is false because a counterexample has been found.

Three other types of conditional statements can be formed by changing the original conditional statement.

Inverse, Converse, and Contrapositive Statements

Original statement: *If a quadrilateral is a rectangle, then its diagonals are equal.*

Negating the hypothesis and the conclusion forms a new statement called the **inverse.**

Inverse: *If a quadrilateral is not a rectangle, then its diagonals are not equal.*

Interchanging the hypothesis and the conclusion forms a new statement called the **converse.**

Converse: *If the diagonals of a quadrilateral are equal, then it is a rectangle.*

If the hypothesis and conclusion are both interchanged and negated, a new statement called the **contrapositive** is formed.

Contrapositive: *If the diagonals of a quadrilateral are not equal, then it is not a rectangle.*

The original statement and its contrapositive are true. An isosceles trapezoid is a counterexample that shows that the inverse and converse are false.

Two statements that have the same truth value are said to be **logically equivalent.**

A conditional statement and its contrapositive always have the same truth value. Therefore, they are logically equivalent.

The inverse and converse always have the same truth value and are therefore logically equivalent.

Knowing the truth value of a conditional, however, does not give information about the truth value of the inverse or the converse.

Visit: PHSchool.com
Web Code: ayp-0367

EXAMPLE 4 Logical equivalence

Which statement is equivalent to the statement *If you study hard, then you will earn good grades*?

(1) If you don't study hard, then you will not earn good grades.
(2) If you do not earn good grades, then you did not study hard.
(3) If you earn good grades, then you studied hard.
(4) If you don't study hard, you will earn good grades.

■ SOLUTION

A conditional statement is logically equivalent to its contrapositive. Therefore, choice (2) is the correct answer.

Another compound statement can be formed using the conditional and the conjunction. An example of such a statement is shown below.

If a polygon has four sides then it is a quadrilateral, and if a polygon is a quadrilateral then it has four sides.

A **biconditional statement** is the conjunction of a conditional statement and its converse. A biconditional can be abbreviated using the words *if and only if:*

A polygon is a quadrilateral if and only if it has four sides.

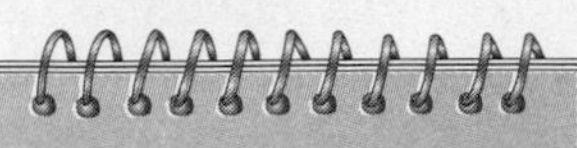

NOTE

All definitions can be written as biconditional statements.

EXAMPLE 5 Writing biconditionals

Go Online PHSchool.com

Visit: PHSchool.com
Web Code: ayp-0368

Write the biconditional for *If you like music, then you watch music videos.*

■ SOLUTION

The converse of this statement is *If you watch music videos, then you like music.* The biconditional is the conjunction of the original statement and its converse: *If you like music videos, then you watch music videos* and *if you watch music videos, then you like music.* The more common and simpler form of the biconditional is *You like music if and only if you watch music videos.*

Biconditional	Truth value of parts	Biconditional truth value
$3 + 2 = 5$ if and only if $5 > 2$.	Both parts true	True
2 is irrational if and only if $2 < 9$	First part false, second part true	False
3 is prime if and only if $2 + 3 = 6$	First part true, second part false	False
4 is odd if and only if $7 < 3$	Both parts false	True

NOTE

A biconditional is true when each statement has the same truth value. If the statements have different truth values, then the biconditional is false.

Practice

Choose the numeral preceding the word or expression that best completes the statement or answers the question.

1 A conditional statement is false when

(1) both the hypothesis and conclusion are true.

(2) the hypothesis is true and the conclusion is false.

(3) the hypothesis is false and the conclusion is true.

(4) both the hypothesis and conclusion are false.

2 Which statement is logically equivalent to a conditional?

(1) inverse

(2) converse

(3) contrapostitive

(4) biconditional

3 Which of the following is the inverse of the statement *If an angle measure* 95° *then it is obtuse*?

(1) If an angle is obtuse, then it measures 95°.

(2) If an angle does not measure 95°, then it is not obtuse.

(3) If an angle is not obtuse, then it does not measure 95°.

(4) If an angle measures 95°, then it is obtuse.

4 Is the statement *If a square has equal diagonals, then the square has four right angles* true or false?

5 Write the following statement as a conditional in *if . . . then* form and identify the hypothesis and conclusion.

A good job implies a good salary.

In Exercises 6–10, underline the hypothesis, double underline the conclusion, determine the truth value of the statement, and write the inverse, converse, and contrapositive of each statement.

6 If two planes are parallel, then they have no points in common.

7 Two angles of a triangle are equal if it is an isosceles triangle.

8 A ray cuts an angle into two equal angles if it is an angle bisector.

9 If you want lower taxes, elect Harris.

10 A figure has four equal angles if the figure is a square.

11 Write the following biconditional as a conditional and its converse: *Two angles are supplementary if and only if the sum of their measures is 180°.*

12 If a conditional statement is true, what can be said about its contrapositive?

13 Given the conditional statement *If two lines in a plane intersect, then they are not parallel*, write its converse and determine its truth value.

14 Give a counterexample to show that the following statement is not always true: *If a parallelogram has four right angles, then all the sides are equal.*

15 Rewrite the true statement *Two circles have the same area if they have the same radius* in *if . . . then* form and then write its converse. If the converse is true, combine the statements to form a biconditional.

16 Write a statement that is logically equivalent to *If it rains it pours.*

2.4 Thinking, Reasoning, Conjecturing, and Verifying

New York Standards

G.G.27 Writing proofs

Go Online PHSchool.com

Visit: PHSchool.com
Web Code: ayp-0346

When you reach a conclusion based upon observation, you use **inductive reasoning.** Inductive reasoning assumes that what you have observed will continue to occur. The conclusion you draw based upon your reasoning is called a **conjecture.**

EXAMPLE 1 Making a conjecture

Make a conjecture about the next two elements in the sequence: *George, John, Thomas, James, . . .*

■ **SOLUTION**

These appear to be the first names of the first four presidents of the United States. Based upon this conjecture, the next two elements would be *James* and *John.*

Inductive reasoning involves a certain amount of guessing. Therefore, the process will not necessarily lead to correct results every time.

EXAMPLE 2 Verifying a conjecture

Is the following conjecture true? *When a circle is cut with a straight line, the number of pieces is twice the number of lines.*

# Lines	# Pieces
1	2
2	4
3	6
4	7

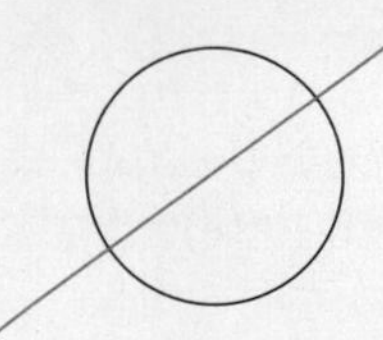

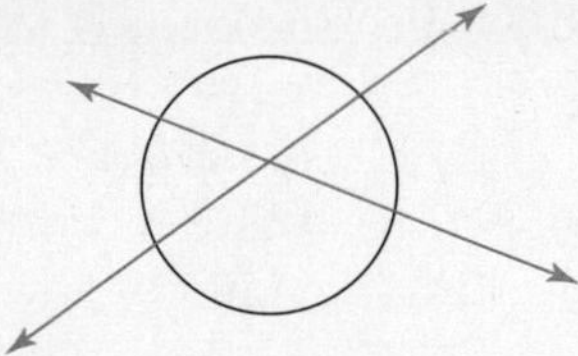

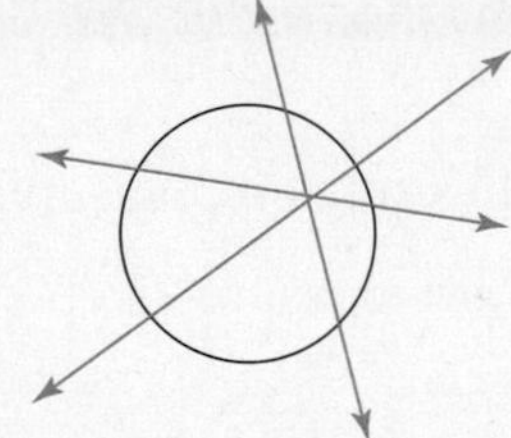

■ **SOLUTION**

Based upon these examples, this conjecture seems true. However, the figure to the right shows three lines cutting the circle into seven pieces. This counterexample proves the conjecture is false.

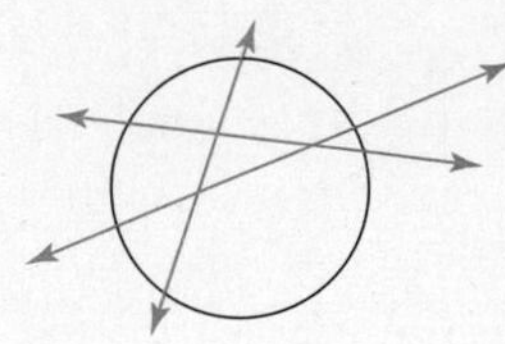

When you reach a conclusion from a true statement using known facts, you are using **deductive reasoning.**

EXAMPLE 3 Using deductive reasoning to draw a conclusion

Given the equation $2x - 3 = 11$, solve for x.

■ **SOLUTION**

Step 1 $2x - 3 = 11$ Given

Step 2 $2x = 14$ **Addition property of equality**

Step 3 $x = 7$ **Division property of equality**

Deductive reasoning is used to verify the results of conjectures and theorems.

EXAMPLE 4 **Verifying a conjecture using deductive reasoning**

Verify the conjecture *If two angles are supplementary to the same angle, then they are equal to each other.*

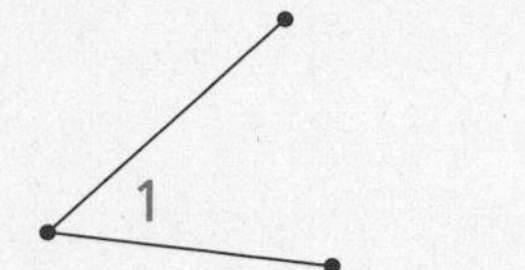

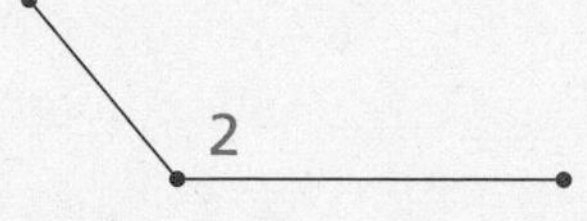

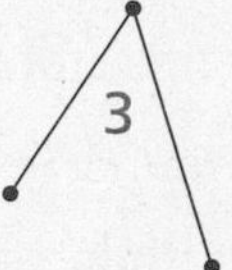

SOLUTION

Step 1 State the hypothesis: $\angle 1$ and $\angle 2$ are supplementary and $\angle 2$ and $\angle 3$ are supplementary.

Step 2 $m\angle 1 + m\angle 2 = 180$ and $m\angle 2 + m\angle 3 = 180$ — **Definition of supplementary angles**

Step 3 $m\angle 1 + m\angle 2 = m\angle 3 + m\angle 2$ — **Transitive property of equality**

Step 4 $m\angle 1 = m\angle 3$ — **Subtraction property of equality**

You have **deduced** the true result that $m\angle 1 = m\angle 3$.

Practice

In Exercises 1–5, tell whether inductive or deductive thinking is involved.

1 You examine ten rocks and determine that all rocks are hard.

2 If $3x + 4 = 25$, then $x = 7$.

3 Two intersecting lines form equal vertical angles.

4 After tasting a grapefruit and a lemon, you conclude that fruit is sour.

5 If two lines are perpendicular to the same line, they are parallel to each other.

6 What is the next element in the sequence? Justify your answer.

0, 2, 2, 4, 6, 10, . . .

7 Use a logical argument to verify that if two lines intersect, the vertical angles formed by the intersection are equal.

8 In the diagram below, $\overline{AB}$ is a straight line. Fill in the justification for each of the following steps.

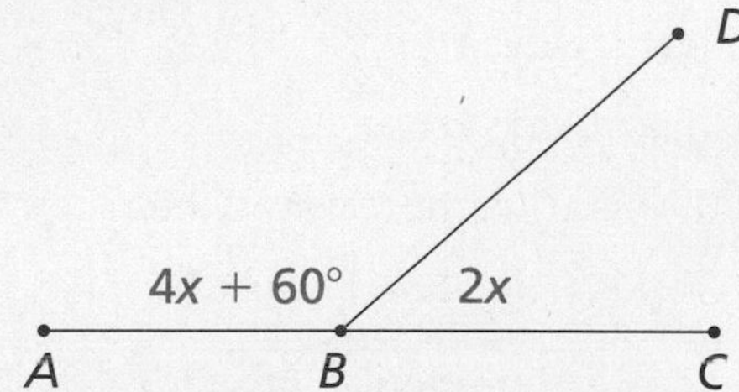

$\angle ABD$ and $\angle DBC$ are supplementary	
$m\angle ABD + m\angle DBC = 180°$	
$2x + 4x + 60° = 180°$	
$6x + 60° = 180°$	
$6x = 120°$	
$x = 20°$	

Chapter 2 Preparing for the New York Geometry Exam

Answer all questions in this part. For each question, select the numeral preceding the word or expression that best completes the statement or answers the question.

1 Which is the inverse of this statement?

You are smart if you like geometry.

(1) If you like geometry, then you are smart.

(2) If you do not like geometry, then you are not smart.

(3) If you are smart, then you like geometry.

(4) If you are not smart, then you do not like geometry.

2 Which best describes the statement *All rhombi are parallelograms*?

(1) true closed **(3)** open

(2) true open **(4)** false closed

3 If a conditional statement is true, which statement is also true?

(1) inverse **(3)** contrapositive

(2) converse **(4)** negation

4 If the contrapositive of the statement, *If* p *then* q is true, then which of the following is correct?

(1) p is always true.

(2) q is always true.

(3) If p is true, then q must be true.

(4) If p is true, then q must be false.

5 When is a conjunction false?

(1) when both statements are true

(2) when the first statement is true and the second is false

(3) when the first statement is false and the second is true

(4) both (2) and (3)

6 Which of the following is a negation of the statement *A trapezoid is not a parallelogram*?

(1) A parallelogram is not a trapezoid.

(2) A trapezoid is a parallelogram.

(3) No trapezoid is a parallelogram.

(4) No parallelograms are trapezoids.

7 When is a disjunction true?

(1) when at least one part is true

(2) when all of the parts are true

(3) when at least one part is false

(4) when all of the parts are false

8 Which of the following best explains the truth value of the statement *If triangles have three sides, then quadrilaterals have five sides*?

(1) true, because the antecedent is true and the consequent is false

(2) true, because both the antecedent and consequent are false

(3) false, because the antecedent is true and the consequent is false

(4) false, because both the antecedent and consequent are false

9 Which of the following is the negation of the statement *Right angles measure 90°, and parallel lines intersect*?

(1) Right angles do not measure 90°, and parallel lines do not intersect.

(2) Right angles do not measure 90°, or parallel lines do not intersect.

(3) Right angles do not measure 90°, or parallel lines intersect.

(4) Right angles measure 90°, or parallel lines do not intersect.

10 Which of the following statements is the converse of the statement *If you study, then you will earn good grades*?

(1) You will earn good grades if you study.

(2) If you earn good grades, then you studied.

(3) If you do not earn good grades, then you did not study.

(4) If you do not study, then you will not earn good grades.

11 Which of the following statements is logically equivalent to the statement *If I eat lunch, then I am hungry*?

(1) If I am not hungry, then I will not eat lunch.

(2) If I will not eat lunch, then I am not hungry.

(3) I will eat lunch if and only if I am hungry.

(4) If I am hungry, then I will eat lunch.

12 In the conditional statement *If you like giraffes, then you like horses*, the phrase *If you like giraffes* is called the

(1) disjunct. **(3)** conclusion.

(2) consequent. **(4)** hypothesis.

13 What are possible values for the next two elements of the sequence 1, 2, 4, 8, 16, . . . ?

(1) 18, 32 **(3)** 32, 64

(2) 24, 32 **(4)** 64, 128

14 What type of reasoning do you use to find the next elements of the sequence $1, \frac{1}{2}, \frac{1}{4}, \frac{1}{8}, \frac{1}{32}, \ldots$?

(1) hypothesis

(2) conjecture

(3) deductive

(4) inductive

15 Given the statement *If the measure of an angle is 125°, then the angle is obtuse*, which of the following is correct?

(1) The contrapositive of the statement is true.

(2) The contrapositive of the statement is false.

(3) The converse of the statement is true.

(4) The original statement is false.

For Exercises 16–18, *p* and *q* represent closed mathematical statements.

16 If the negation of the disjunction of statements p and q is true, which of the following is correct?

(1) p is true and q is false.

(2) p is false and q is true.

(3) Both p and q are true.

(4) Both p and q are false.

17 If p is true and q is false, which of the following is logically equivalent to the conjunction "p and q"?

(1) not p and not q

(2) not p or not q

(3) if q, then p

(4) if not p, then not q

18 Under what condition would the converse of the statement "If p then q" be false?

(1) p is true and q is false.

(2) p is true and q is true.

(3) p is false and q is true.

(4) p is false and q is false.

Answer all questions in this part. Clearly indicate the necessary steps, including appropriate formula substitutions, diagrams, graphs, charts, etc. For all questions in this part, a correct numerical answer with no work shown will receive only one credit.

19 $\overline{RT} = 42$. Fill in the justification for each of the following steps.

$x + 7$ $3x - 5$

R S T

$RT = 42$	
$RS + ST = RT$	
$x + 7 + 3x - 5 = 42$	
$4x + 2 = 42$	
$4x = 40$	
$x = 10$	

20 $\angle AOB$ and $\angle BOC$ are adjacent angles. $\angle BOC$ is ten more than twice $\angle AOB$. The measure of $\angle AOC$ is 139°. Use deductive reasoning to determine the value of x. Justify each step of your solution.

21 A geometry drawing program is used to create the figure shown in the accompanying diagram. Line BC has been constructed to be parallel to line DE. As point E is moved, what would you expect to happen to the measures of the angles shown in the figure? Justify your answer.

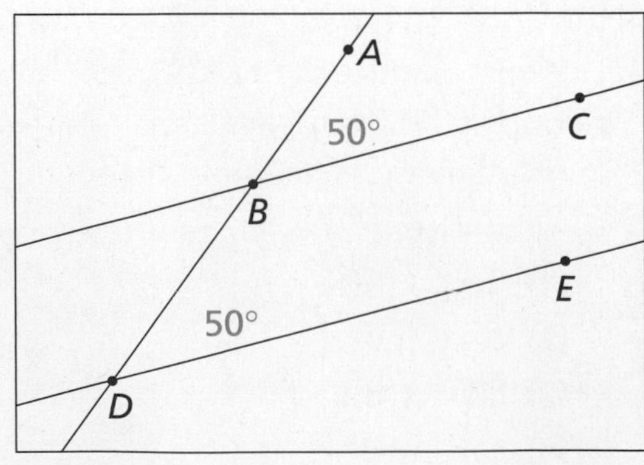

3 Triangles

Discovering New York

Jackie Robinson

Jackie Robinson made history on April 15, 1947, by becoming the first African American Major League Baseball player, as a member of the Brooklyn Dodgers. Prior to then, African Americans played in a separate league.

During his first year, Robinson overcame prejudice from baseball players, fans, and even his own teammates to become Rookie of the Year. Robinson was named the National League's Most Valuable Player in 1948 and helped the Dodgers win the World Series in 1955. Robinson retired in 1957 with a batting average of .311 and 137 home runs.

Robinson opened the door to professional sports for African American athletes.

3.1 Classifying Triangles and Angles of a Triangle

New York Standards

G.G.27 Writing proofs
G.G.30 Theorems about triangle angle measures
G.G.31 Isosceles triangle theorem
G.G.32 Exterior angle theorem

A triangle is a polygon with three sides. We name a triangle by its three vertices, and name its sides by the endpoints of the segments.

In the accompanying figure $\triangle ABC$ has sides $\overline{AB}$, $\overline{AC}$, and $\overline{BC}$.

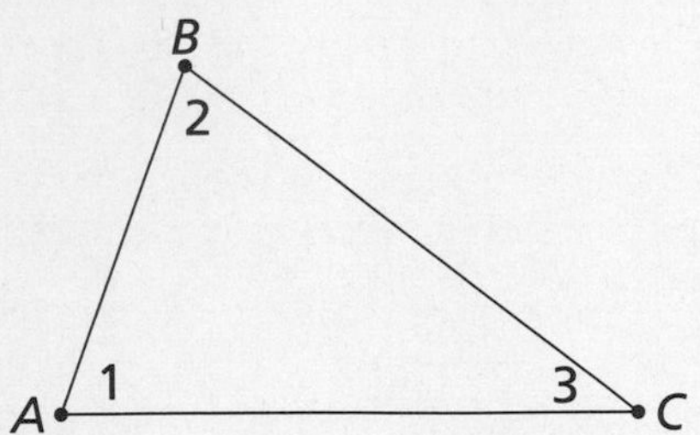

The three angles are the **interior angles** and can be named in the following ways:

$\angle A$ or $\angle BAC$ or $\angle CAB$ or $\angle 1$
$\angle B$ or $\angle ABC$ or $\angle CBA$ or $\angle 2$
$\angle C$ or $\angle BCA$ or $\angle ACB$ or $\angle 3$

Triangle Angle-Sum Theorem

The sum of the measures of the angles of a triangle is 180°.

In our triangle this means $m\angle 1 + m\angle 2 + m\angle 3 = 180°$.

Visit: PHSchool.com
Web Code: ayp-0383

EXAMPLE 1 **Verify the Angle-Sum Theorem**

1 Verify that the sum of the measures of the angles of a triangle is 180°.

■ SOLUTION

To verify the **Angle-Sum Theorem,** draw a triangle on a piece of paper, number each angle, and then tear off each angle. Now arrange the angles adjacent to each other and observe that they form a straight angle, 180°.

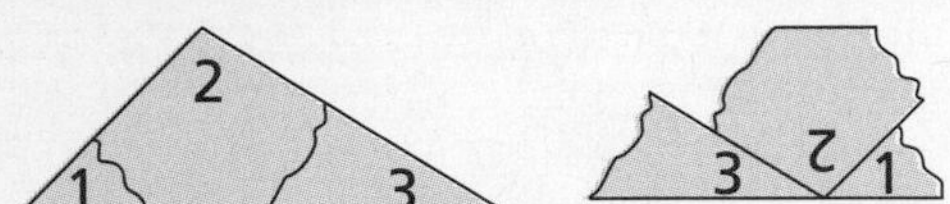

Example 1 does not prove that the sum of the angles of a triangle is 180°. One popular form of proof is the two-column form. In the first column you list each statement, and in the second column you list the reason that supports it.

Notice that each statement proceeds logically from the statement before it. The **hypothesis** is listed as **given,** and the **consequent** is listed as what we want to **prove.**

The truth of the Angle-Sum Theorem can be established more formally by the following proof.

EXAMPLE 2 Proving the Angle-Sum Theorem

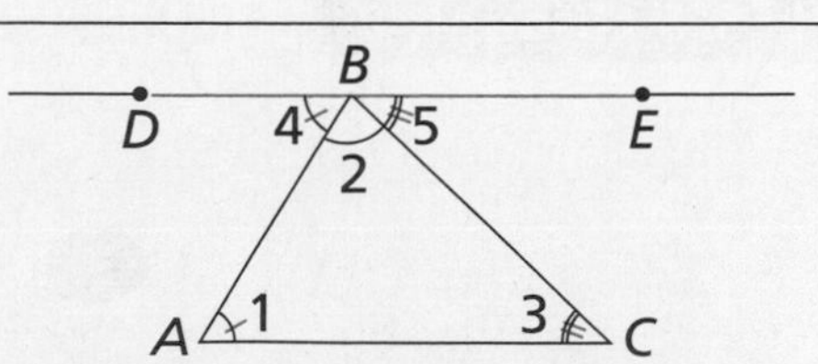

Given: $\triangle ABC$
Prove: $m\angle 1 + m\angle 2 + m\angle 3 = 180°$

■ SOLUTION

Statements	Reasons
1. Construct $\overline{DE}$ parallel to $\overline{AC}$ through B.	1. One and only one line can be constructed parallel to a given line through a given point.
2. $\angle DBC$ and $\angle 5$ are supplementary.	2. Two adjacent angles whose exterior angles form a straight line are supplementary.
3. $m\angle DBC = m\angle 4 + m\angle 2$	3. Angle addition axiom
4. $m\angle 4 + m\angle 2 + m\angle 5 = 180°$	4. Substitution
5. $m\angle 4 = m\angle 1; m\angle 5 = m\angle 3$	5. If two parallel lines are cut by a transversal the alternate interior angles are congruent.
6. $m\angle 1 + m\angle 2 + m\angle 3 = 180°$	6. Substitution

You can use the Angle-Sum Theorem to find the measure of angles in a triangle.

EXAMPLES 3 through 5 Finding the measures of interior angles

Find the measure of the interior angles.

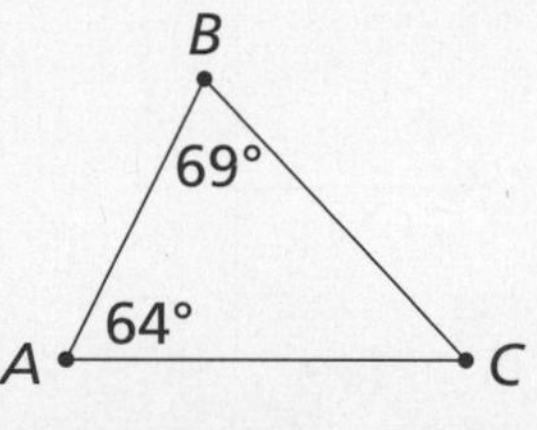

■ SOLUTION

$m\angle C + 69° + 64° = 180°$
$m\angle C + 133° = 180°$
$m\angle C = 47°$

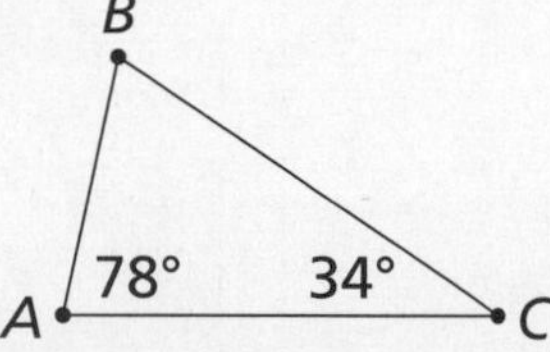

■ SOLUTION

$m\angle B + 78° + 34° = 180°$
$m\angle B + 112° = 180°$
$m\angle B = 68°$

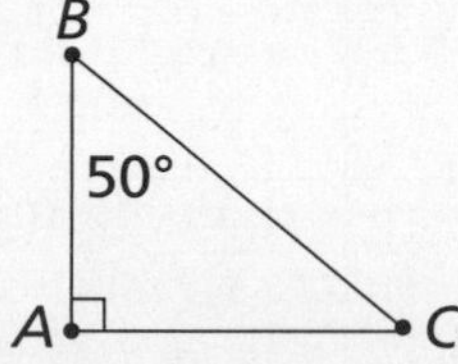

■ SOLUTION

$m\angle C + 50° + 90° = 180°$
$m\angle C + 140° = 180°$
$m\angle C = 40°$

When the side of a triangle is extended, the angle formed outside the triangle is called an **exterior angle.** A triangle has six exterior angles.

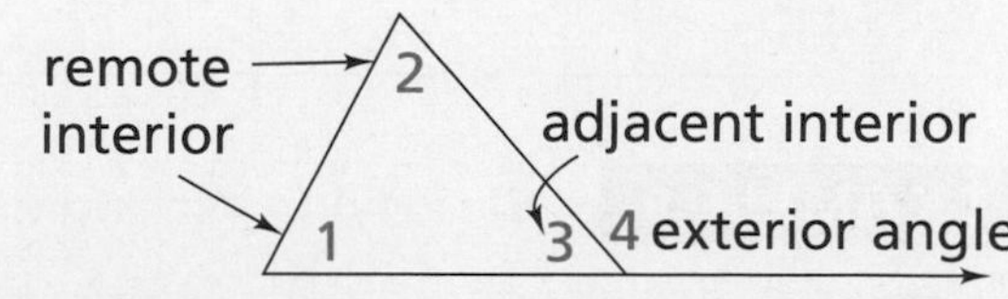

$$m\angle 1 + m\angle 2 + m\angle 3 = 180°$$
$$m\angle 3 + m\angle 4 = 180°$$
$$m\angle 1 + m\angle 2 = m\angle 4$$

Exterior Angle Theorem

The remote interior angles are the nonadjacent angles to the exterior angle. The measure of an exterior angle of a triangle is equal to the sum of the **remote interior angles.**

Visit: PHSchool.com
Web Code: ayp-0384

EXAMPLES 6 through 8 Finding the measures of exterior angles

Find the measure of the numbered angles.

6

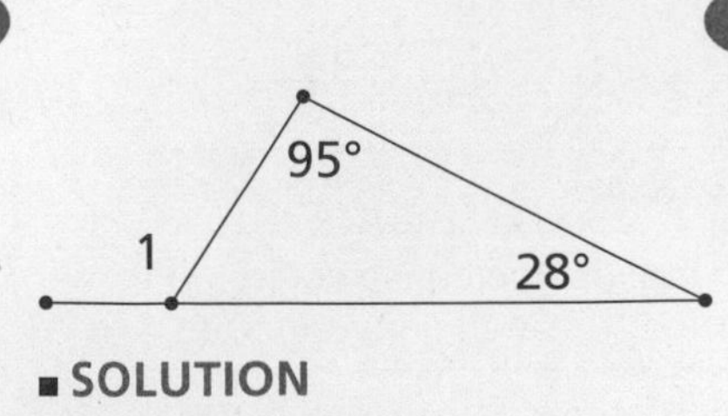

■ **SOLUTION**

$m\angle 1 = 95° + 28°$
$m\angle 1 = 123°$

7

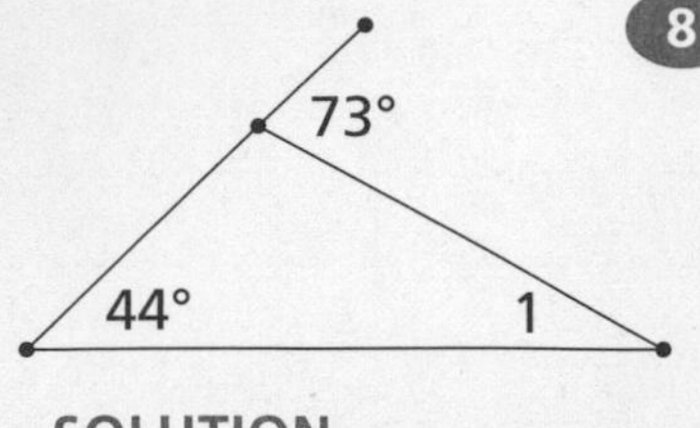

■ **SOLUTION**

$73° = 44° + m\angle 1$
$29° = m\angle 1$

8

1
2
34°
123°

■ **SOLUTION**

$123° = m\angle 1 + 34°$
$89° = m\angle 1$

$123° + m\angle 2 = 180°$
$m\angle 2 = 57°$

Triangles can be classified by their sides and their angles.

Classification by Sides		
Triangle	**Description of Sides**	**Angle Properties**
Equilateral Triangle	All three sides are congruent.	All three angles are congruent and measure 60°.
Isosceles Triangle	Two sides are congruent.	The angles opposite the congruent sides are congruent.
Scalene Triangle	No sides are congruent.	No angles are congruent.

Classification by Angles	
Triangle	**Description of Angles**
Acute Triangle	All angles are acute.
Right Triangle	One angle is a right angle and the other two are acute.
Obtuse Triangle	One angle is obtuse and the other two are acute.

EXAMPLE 9 Classifying a triangle

9 Classify the accompanying triangle by using its sides and angles.

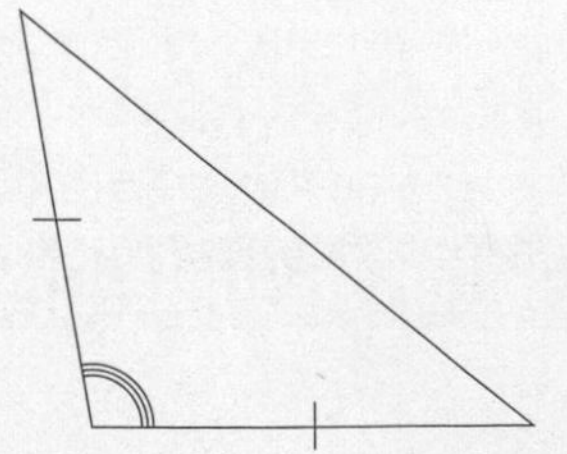

■ **SOLUTION**

Two sides of this triangle are equal and one angle is obtuse. This is an **obtuse isosceles triangle.**

Isosceles Triangle Theorem

If two sides of a triangle are congruent, then the angles opposite those sides are congruent.

The converse is also true:

If two angles of a triangle are equal, then the sides opposite the angles are also equal.

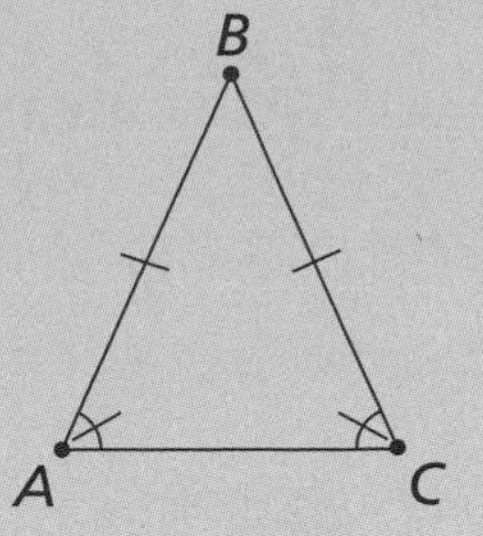

Verifying the Isosceles Triangle Theorem and its converse

10 Describe how to verify the Isosceles Triangle Theorem and its converse.

■ **SOLUTION**

Begin with an isosceles triangle and construct the perpendicular bisector of the base. The base is the non-equal side. Note that this bisector passes through the vertex of the isosceles triangle. Now fold the figure over $\overline{BD}$. $\triangle ABD$ lies on top of $\triangle CBD$. This also confirms that the bisector of the base is the bisector of the vertex angle.

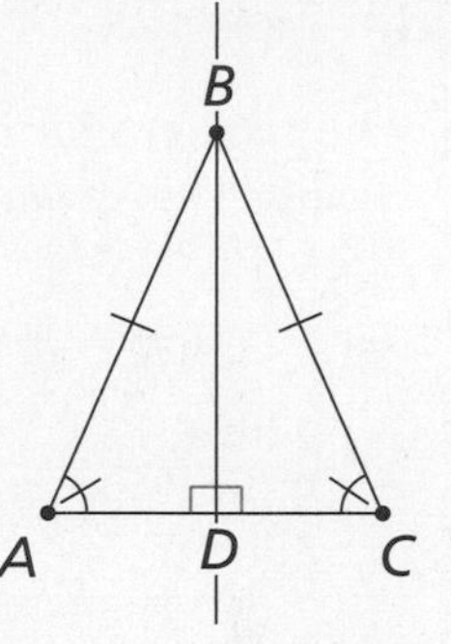

Equilateral Triangle Corollaries

If a triangle is equilateral, then it is equiangular.

If $AB = BC = AC$, then $m\angle A = m\angle B = m\angle C$.

If a triangle is equiangular, then it is equilateral.

If $m\angle A = m\angle B = m\angle C$, then $AB = BC = AC$.

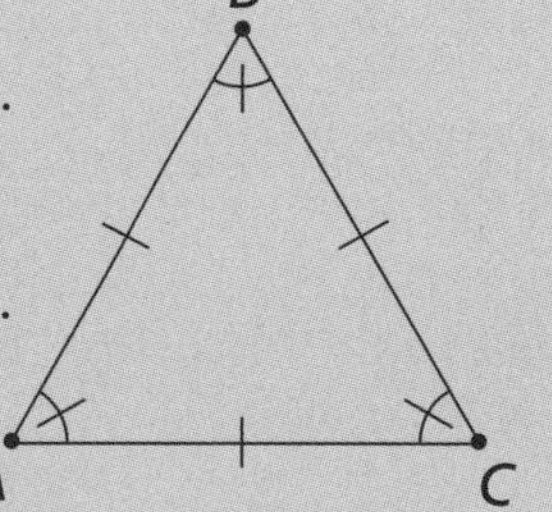

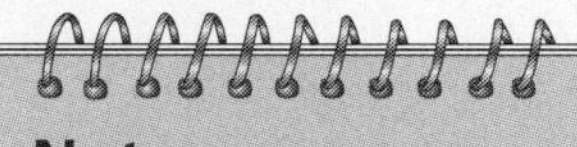

Note

A **corollary** is a theorem that follows directly from a previously proved theorem.

Additional Theorems About Angles in Triangles

- If a triangle is a right triangle, then the acute angles are complementary.
- All right angles are congruent.
- If two angles are both congruent and supplementary, then they are right angles.
- If two angles of one triangle are congruent to two angles of another, the third angles are congruent.

Practice

Choose the numeral preceding the word or expression that best completes the statement or answers the question.

1 If two angles of a triangle measure 55° and 25°, then the triangle is

(1) right.

(2) acute.

(3) obtuse.

(4) isosceles.

2 The triangle in the accompanying figure can best be described as

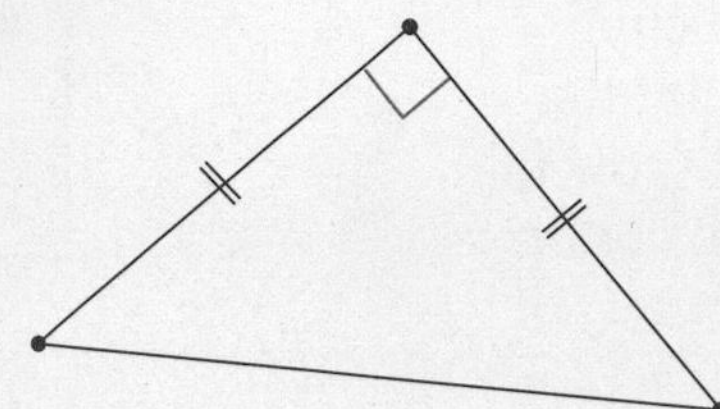

(1) acute, scalene.

(2) right, isosceles.

(3) right, scalene.

(4) acute, isosceles.

3 The exterior angle of a triangle is represented by $5x - 15$, and the two remote interior angles are represented by $2x$ and $x + 5$, respectively. What are the measures of the interior angles of this triangle?

(1) 10°, 15°, 20°

(2) 15°, 25°, 35°

(3) 10°, 35°, 145°

(4) 15°, 20°, 145°

4 Which of the following types of triangles **cannot** be a right triangle?

(1) equilateral

(2) scalene

(3) isosceles

(4) all of the above

5 Which term best describes the acute angles of a right triangle?

(1) equal

(2) supplementary

(3) complementary

(4) obtuse

6 If the exterior angle of a right triangle is 160°, then the measure of the remote interior angle is

(1) 20°. **(3)** 90°.

(2) 70°. **(4)** 110°.

7 The roof lines of the building in the accompanying figure form triangles. Determine the measure of the angle that is labeled with a question mark.

8 In triangle CAT the measure of $\angle A$ is 50° and the measure of $\angle T$ is 30°. Classify triangle CAT by both its sides and its angles.

9 $\triangle MNO$ is isosceles with $\overline{MO} \cong \overline{NO}$. If MO is represented by $3x + 11$, NO is represented by $5x - 9$, and MN is represented by $7x + 3$, determine the perimeter of $\triangle MNO$.

10 Justify (prove) that the acute angles of a right triangle are complementary.

Use the accompanying figure to answer Exercises 11–16.

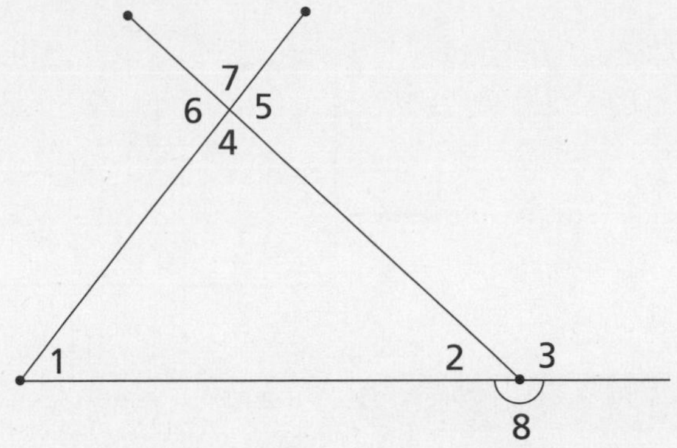

11 Name the remote interior angles for angle 5.

12 How are angles 4 and 7 related?

13 $m\angle 1 + m\angle 4 = m\angle ?$

14 What kind of angle is represented by angle 8?

15 $m\angle 1 + m\angle 7 + m\angle ? = m\angle 8$.

16 Name the exterior angles at the vertex of angle 4.

Use the following figure to answer Exercises 17–18.

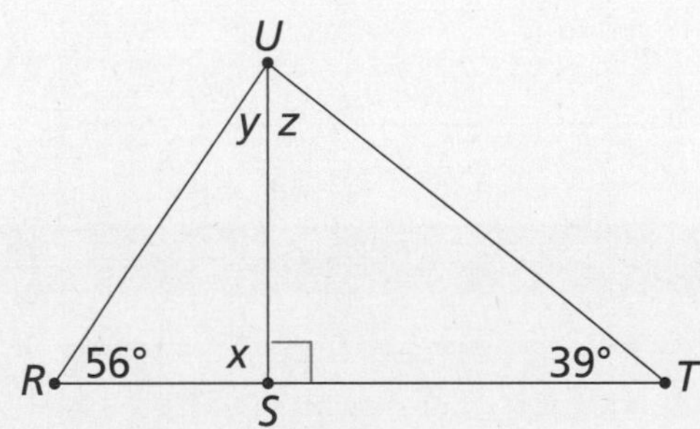

17 Determine the values of x, y, and z. Classify triangle RTU.

18 If TR is extended through R to a point V, what is the measure of angle URV?

19 Draw an obtuse, isosceles triangle.

20 The angles of a triangle are in the ratio of 3:4:5. Determine the measure of each angle.

21 Determine the value of s in the accompanying figure.

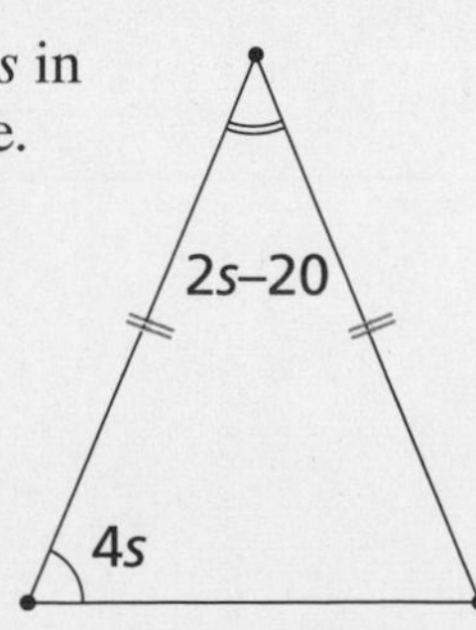

22 Determine the values of x, y, and z in the accompanying figure.

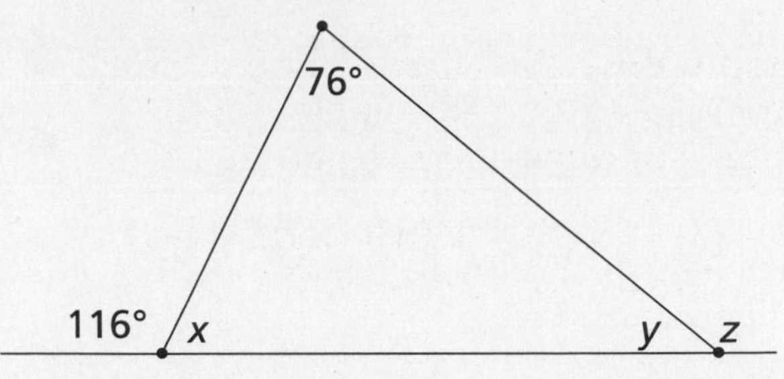

23 Determine the values of a and b in the accompanying figure.

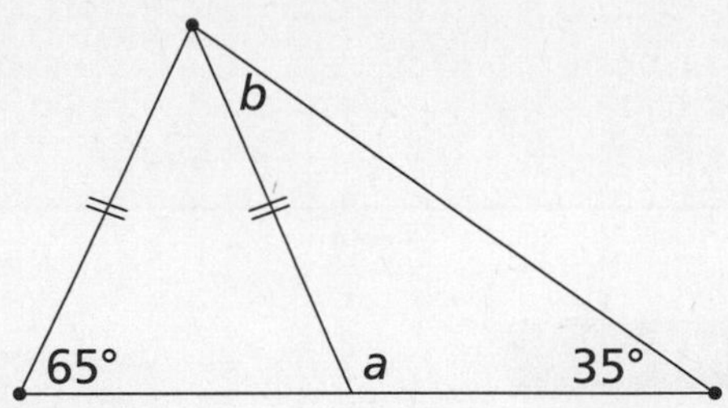

In Exercises 24–26, determine the value of *x*.

24

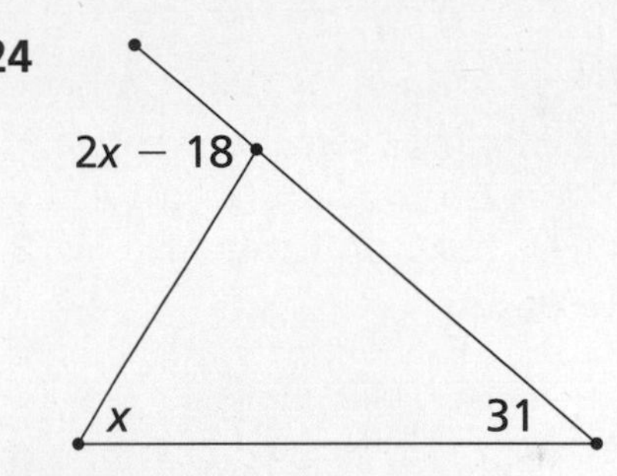

25

26

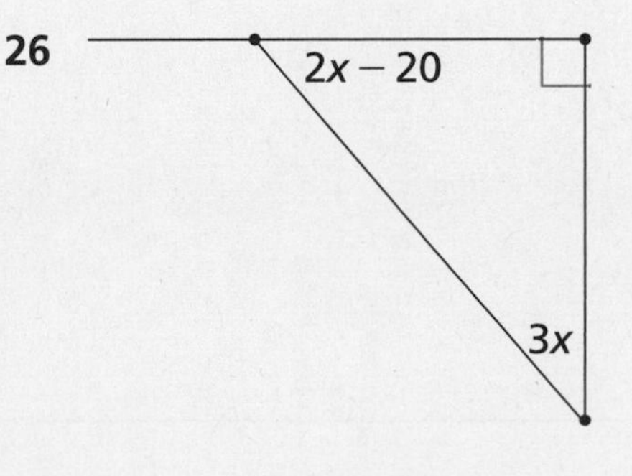

3.2 Triangle Inequalities

An exterior angle is greater than either remote interior angle. Using the Exterior Angle Theorem, you know that $m\angle 1 = m\angle 2 + m\angle 3$. The measure of both $\angle 2$ and $\angle 3$ are greater than zero. By the comparison property of inequality, you can conclude that $m\angle 1 > m\angle 2$ and $m\angle 1 > m\angle 3$.

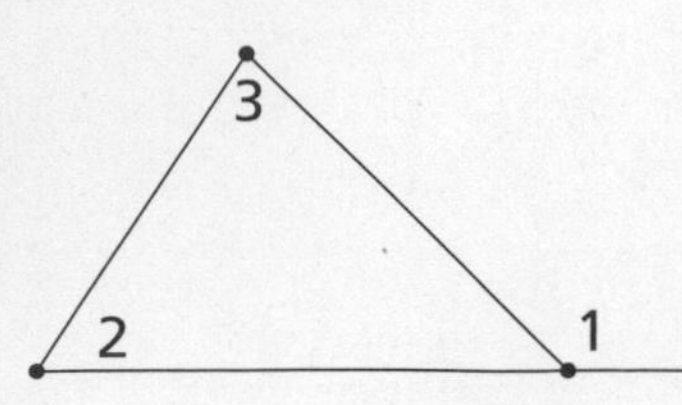

New York Standards

G.G.32 Exterior angle theorem

G.G.33 Triangle inequality theorem

G.G.34 Longest side/largest angle of triangle

Exterior Angle Corollary

The measure of an exterior angle of a triangle is greater than the measure of each of its remote interior angles.

$$m\angle 1 > m\angle 2 \text{ and } m\angle 1 > m\angle 3$$

Note

Comparison Property of Inequality

If $a = b + c$ and $c > 0$, then $a > b$.

EXAMPLE 1 **Using the exterior angle corollary**

In the accompanying figure $QT = ST$. Explain why $m\angle 1 > m\angle 3$.

SOLUTION

$m\angle 1 = m\angle 2$ by the Isosceles Triangle Theorem, and $m\angle 2 > m\angle 3$ by the Exterior Angle Corollary. By substituting $m\angle 1$ for $m\angle 2$, you get $m\angle 1 > m\angle 3$.

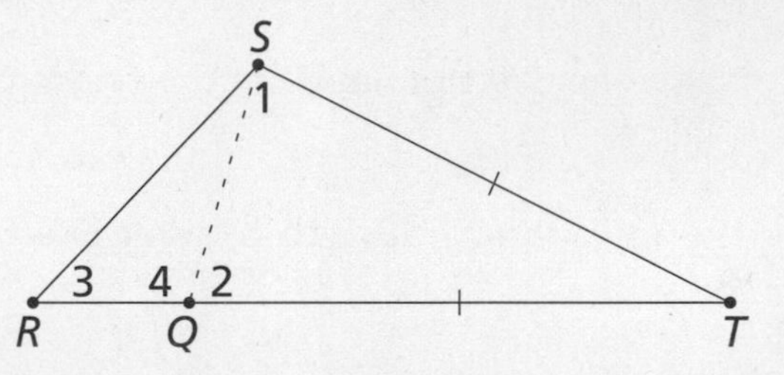

Largest Side Theorem and Its Converse

Largest Side Theorem If one side of a triangle is larger than another, then the angle opposite the larger side is the larger angle.

$$m\angle A > m\angle C$$

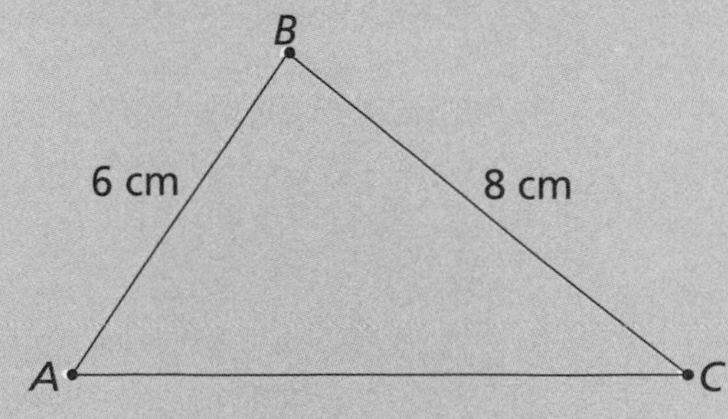

Converse of the Largest Side Theorem If one angle of a triangle is larger than another, then the side opposite the larger angle is the larger side.

$$AC > AB$$

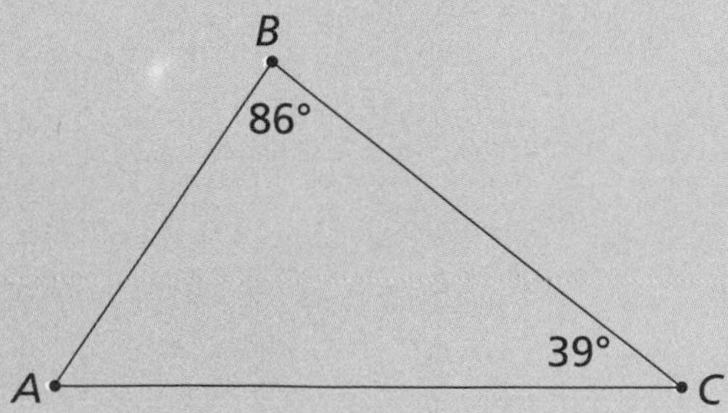

EXAMPLE 2 Ordering the parts of a triangle

Order the measurements of the parts of the accompanying triangle from least to greatest.

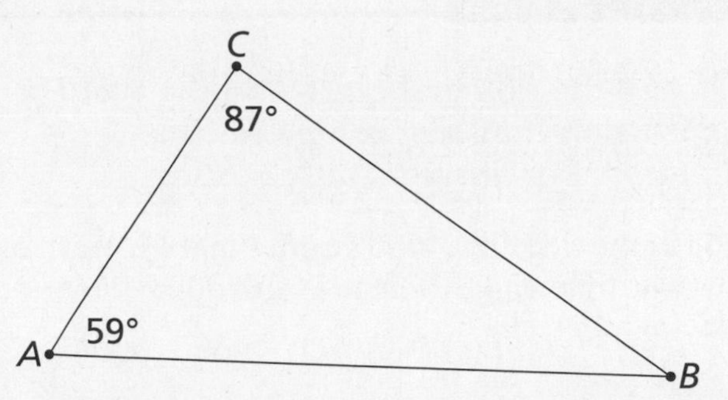

■ **SOLUTION**

$m\angle B = 34°$, therefore $m\angle B < m\angle A < m\angle C$ and $AC < BC < AB$

Imagine that you have a pack of straws of different lengths. If three straws are selected, will they form a triangle? Not every group of three straws will form a triangle. The lengths of the straws must fit a certain relationship. In Figure A, the three straws do not meet to form a triangle. In Figure B, the straws do form a triangle.

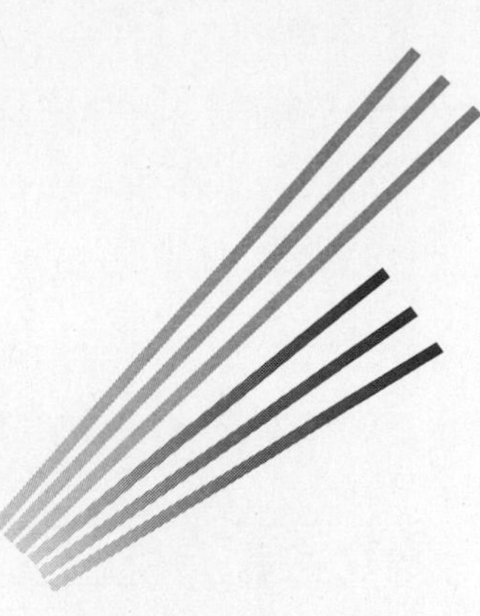

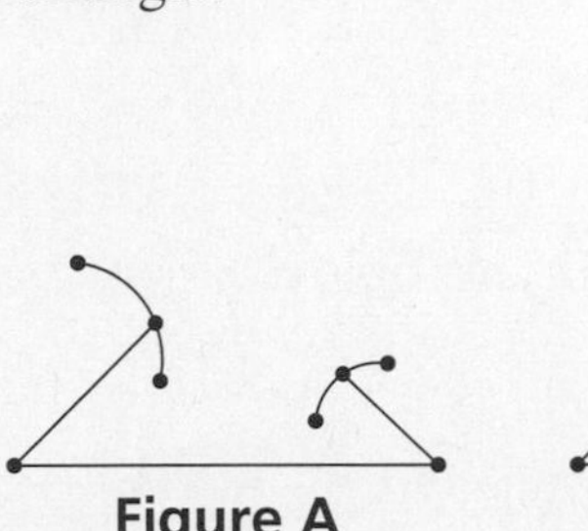

Figure A

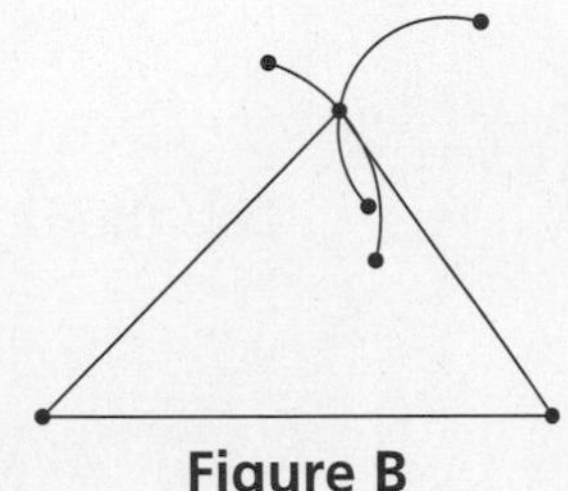

Figure B

Triangle Inequality Theorem

The sum of the lengths of any two sides of a triangle is greater than the length of the third side.

$$AB + BC > AC$$
$$AC + BC > AB$$
$$AB + AC > BC$$

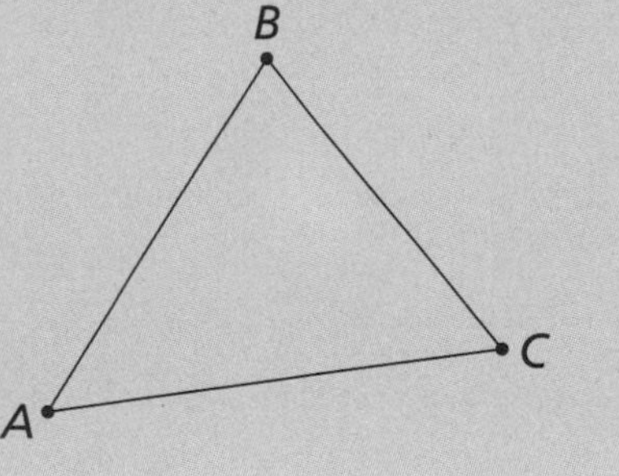

Visit: PHSchool.com
Web Code: ayp-0410

EXAMPLE 3 Determine possible lengths for the side of a triangle

A triangle has sides of length 9 and 16. What are possible lengths for the missing side?

■ **SOLUTION**

Call the missing side n. Using the Triangle Inequality Theorem, you know that the following inequalities must be true:

$9 + 16 > n$	$9 + n > 16$	$16 + n > 9$
$15 > n$	$n > 7$	True for any value of n

Therefore $7 < n < 15$. The missing side must have a length between 7 and 15.

Note

When two sides of a triangle are known, the length of the missing side is less than the sum of the two known sides and greater than their difference.

Practice

Choose the numeral preceding the word or expression that best completes the statement or answers the question.

1 If the sides of a triangle are 8 and 14, which of the following is *not* the length of the third side?

(1) 17.5 **(2)** 12 **(3)** 10.5 **(4)** 6

2 Which of the following are *not* sides of a triangle?

(1) 11 cm, 12 cm, 15 cm

(2) 1 cm, 15 cm, 15 cm

(3) 2 in., 3 in., 6 in.

(4) 2 yd, 9 yd, 10 yd

3 In $\triangle ABC, m\angle A = 35°, m\angle B = 75°, m\angle C = 70°$. Which is the longest side?

(1) AB

(2) AC

(3) BC

(4) cannot be determined

4 Which statement is true about the accompanying figure?

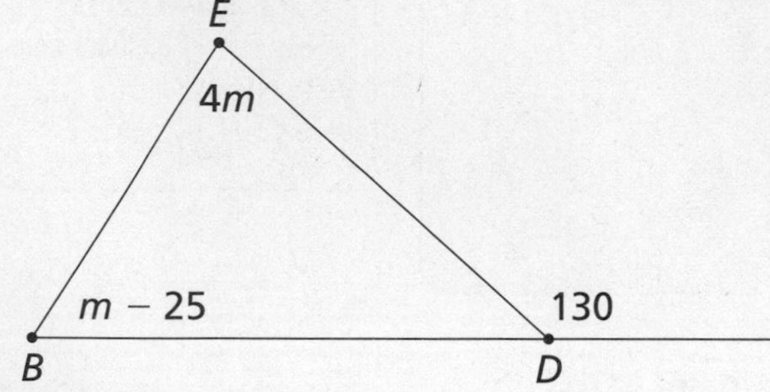

(1) $ED > EB$

(2) $ED > BD$

(3) BE is the shortest side.

(4) BD is the longest side.

5 Suppose you know the distance from Saint Paul to Nashville is 690 mi and the distance from Denver to Nashville is 1023 mi. What is the possible range of distances from St. Paul to Denver?

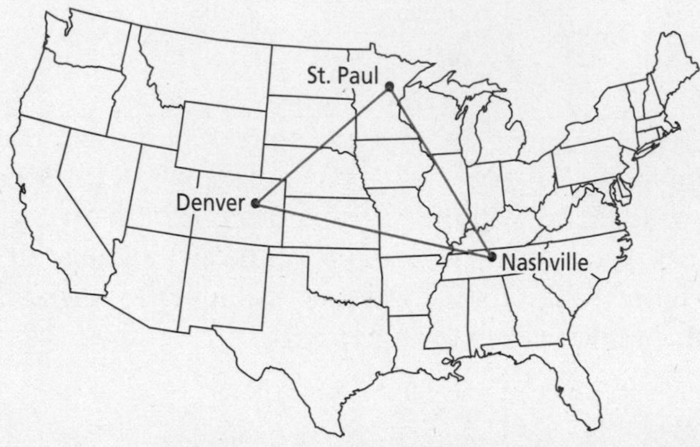

Use the figure below to answer Exercises 6–7.

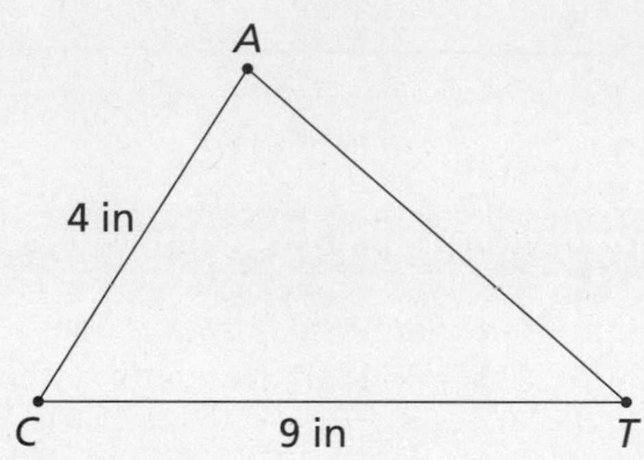

6 What are the possible integer values for the length of side AT?

7 Which angle has the smallest measure?

8 Is the statement $x < 8$ true or false? Explain your answer.

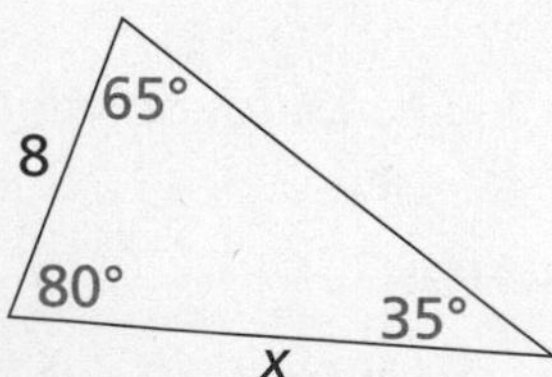

9 Fill in the reasons for each step of the following argument, which proves the following theorem: *If two sides of a triangle are not congruent, then the larger angle lies opposite the larger side.*

Given: $\triangle TOP$, $PO > PT$
Prove: $m\angle OTP > m\angle 3$

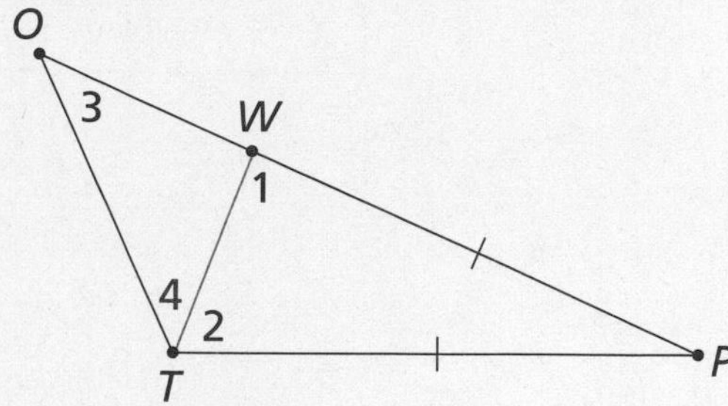

Statements	Reasons
1. Construct $\overline{TW}$ such that $TP = WP$	
2. ΔTPW is isosceles	
3. $m\angle 1 = m\angle 2$	
4. $m\angle OTP = m\angle 4 + m\angle 2$	
5. $m\angle OTP > m\angle 2$	
6. $m\angle OTP > m\angle 1$	
7. $m\angle 1 > m\angle 3$	
8. $m\angle OTP > m\angle 3$	

10 Which part of the chair is longer, $\overline{AB}$ or $\overline{BC}$? Explain you answer.

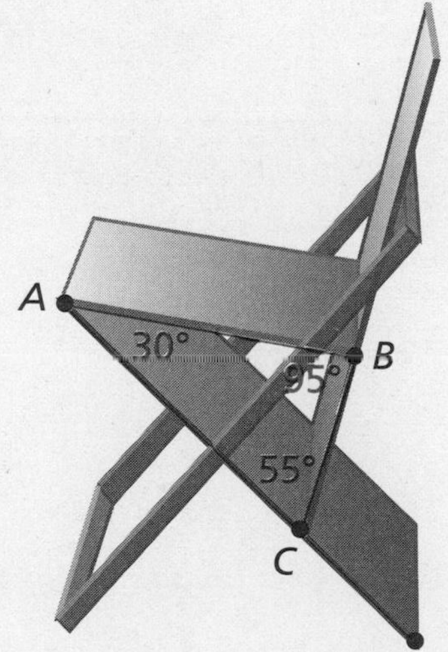

In Exercises 11–14, list the sides from smallest to largest.

11

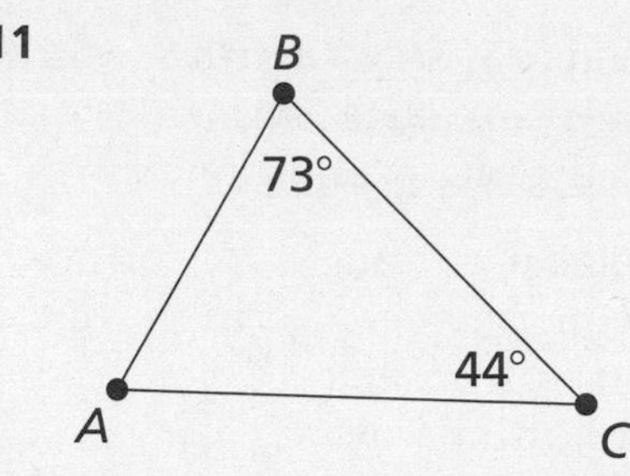

12

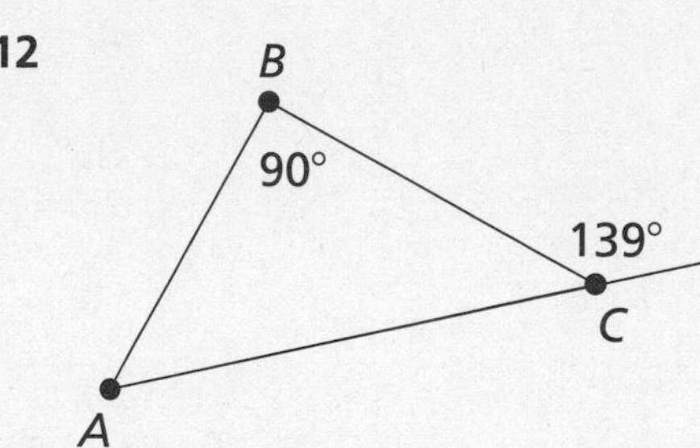

13

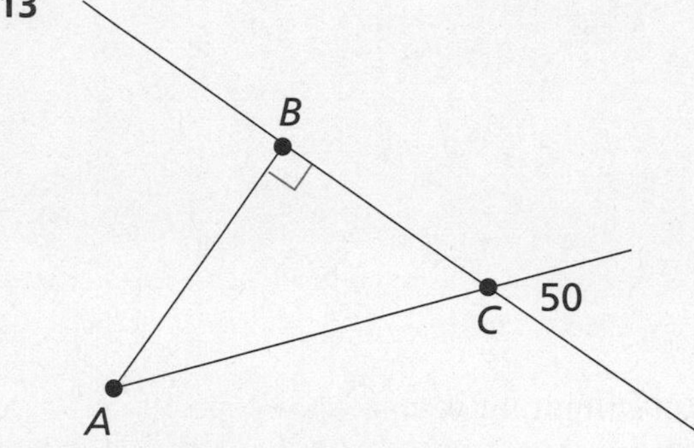

14

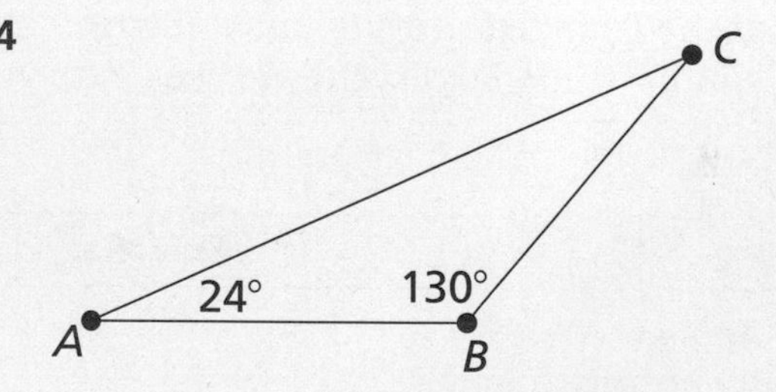

15 List three lengths that can *not* be sides of a triangle.

16 Can you construct the triangle sketched below? Explain why or why not.

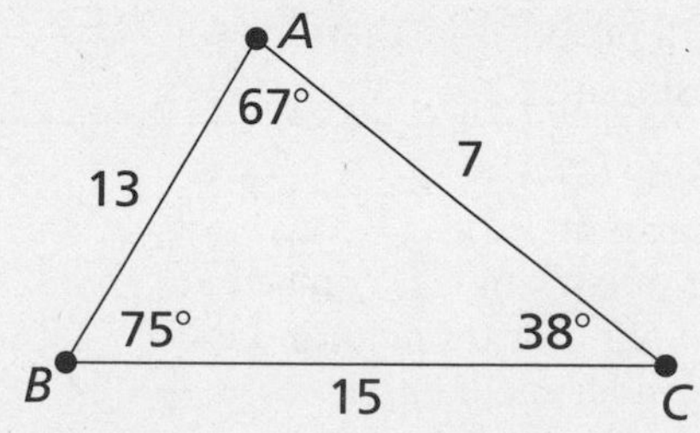

3.3 Triangle Similarity

New York Standards

G.G.27 Writing proofs
G.G.44 Similarity of triangles
G.G.45 Theorems about similar triangles
G.G.46 Proportional relationships of triangles

Two triangles are similar if they have the same shape but different size. **Similar triangles** have corresponding angles that are equal in measure and corresponding sides that are proportional.

Corresponding angles in a triangle are congruent, and the **corresponding sides** are opposite congruent angles. In the figure below, $\angle A$ corresponds to $\angle D$, $\angle B$ corresponds to $\angle E$, and $\angle C$ corresponds to $\angle F$. The sides correspond in the following way:

$\overline{AB}$ corresponds to $\overline{DE}$.
$\overline{BC}$ corresponds to $\overline{EF}$.
$\overline{CA}$ corresponds to $\overline{FD}$.

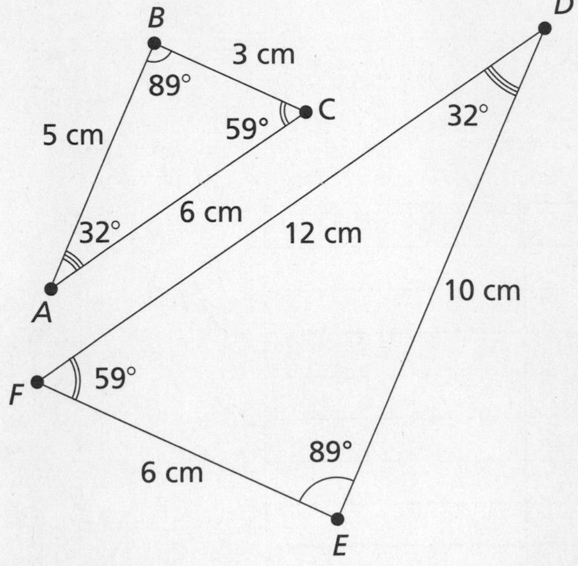

The ratio of the lengths of corresponding sides is called the **similarity ratio,** or the **scale factor.** In the triangles above, the similarity ratio is $\frac{1}{2}$ or 1:2. To show that the triangles are similar, you write $\triangle ABC \sim \triangle DEF$. When naming similar triangles, list the vertices in the order of the corresponding angles.

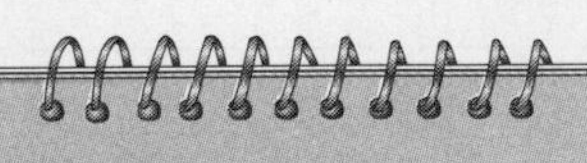

Note

The symbol to show similarity is ~.

Proving That Triangles Are Similar	
Angle-Angle (AA) Similarity Postulate If two angles of one triangle are congruent to two angles of another triangle, then the triangles are similar.	$\triangle ABC \sim \triangle ZXY$
Side-Side-Side (SSS) Similarity Theorem If corresponding sides of two triangles are in proportion, then the triangles are similar.	$\frac{AB}{XZ} = \frac{BC}{ZY} = \frac{CA}{YX}$ $\triangle ABC \sim \triangle XZY$
Side-Angle-Side (SAS) Similarity Theorem If an angle of one triangle is congruent to an angle of another triangle, and the lengths of the sides including these angles are in proportion, then the triangles are similar.	$\frac{AB}{YZ} = \frac{BC}{ZX}$ $\triangle ABC \sim \triangle YZX$

EXAMPLE 1 Using the AA Postulate

 In the accompanying figure $\overline{RS} \| \overline{VU}$. Explain whether the triangles are similar.

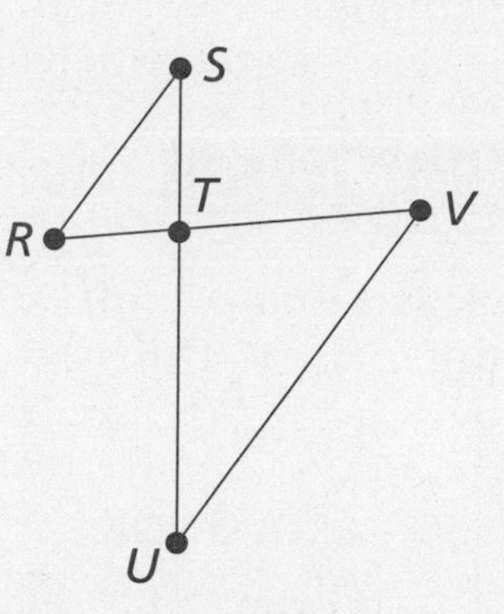

■ SOLUTION

Because $\overline{RS} \| \overline{VU}$, we know $\angle R \cong \angle V$ and $\angle S \cong \angle U$ by the Alternate Interior Angles Theorem. The triangles are similar by AA, and $\triangle RST \sim \triangle VUT$.

When lengths are difficult to measure, similar triangles often can be used to find missing distances. This is referred to as **indirect measurement.**

Go Online PHSchool.com
Visit: PHSchool.com
Web Code: ayp-0427

EXAMPLE 2 Using indirect measurement

 A tree casts a shadow 30 m long, and a 2 m stick casts one that is 3 m long. How tall is the tree?

■ SOLUTION

These two triangles are similar because they are both right triangles and share $\angle A$. Therefore, their corresponding sides are in the same ratio. This results in the proportion $\frac{2}{h} = \frac{3}{30}$. Solving, we find that $h = 20$ m.

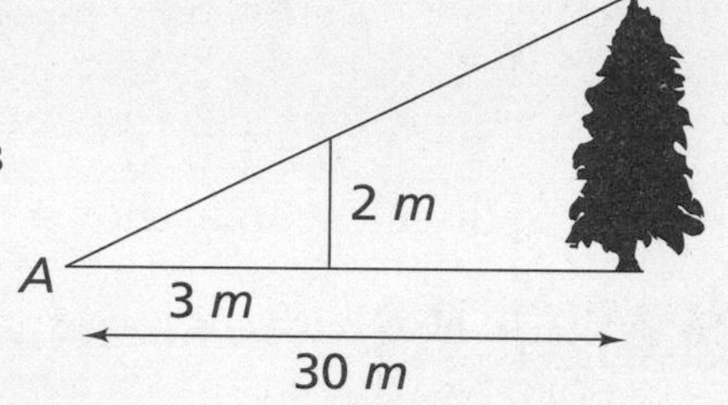

You can use the similarity postulates and theorems to formally prove that two triangles are similar.

EXAMPLE 3 Proving triangles are similar

 **Given:** $\angle N \cong \angle P$ and $\overline{MO} \perp \overline{NP}$
Prove: $\triangle MNO \sim \triangle QPO$

■ SOLUTION

Statements	Reasons
1. $\overline{MO} \perp \overline{NP}$	1. Given
2. $\angle MON \cong \angle MOP$	2. Perpendiculars form right angles, and all right angles are equal.
3. $\angle N \cong \angle P$	3. Given
4. $\Delta MNO \sim \Delta QPO$	4. Angle-Angle Similarity Postulate

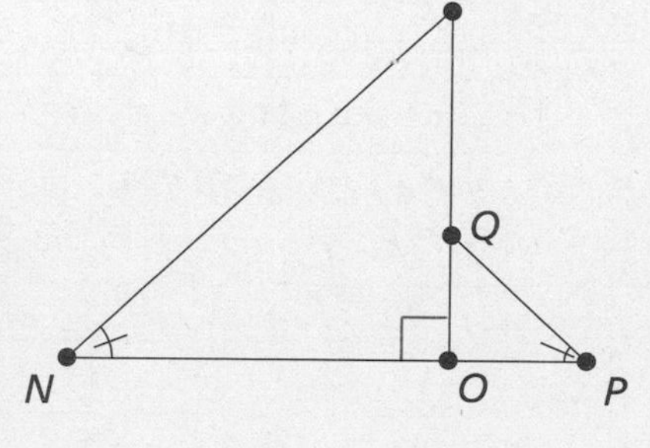

In the above example, a two-column proof was used to show that two triangles are similar. A **paragraph proof** is a proof where the statements and reasons are written as sentences in a paragraph.

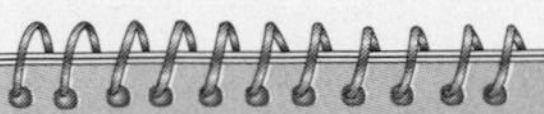

Note

Remember that a **ratio** is a comparison of two numbers by division. A **proportion** is a statement that two ratios are equal.

EXAMPLE 4 Proving a proportion

Given: $\triangle ABC$ is an isosceles triangle with $\overline{AB} \cong \overline{AC}$ and altitudes $\overline{AE}$ and $\overline{CD}$.

Prove: $\frac{AC}{EC} = \frac{CB}{DB}$

▪ **SOLUTION**

Given $\overline{AB} \cong \overline{AC}$ implies $\angle B \cong \angle ACB$ because base angles of an isosceles triangle are congruent. $\overline{CD} \perp \overline{AB}$ *and* $\overline{AE} \perp \overline{BC}$ by the definition of altitudes. Therefore, $\angle AEC \cong \angle CDB$, as perpendicular lines form right angles and all right angles are congruent. This leads to $\triangle AEC \sim \triangle CDB$ by AA. Now, $\frac{AC}{EC} = \frac{CB}{DB}$ because corresponding sides of similar triangles are proportional.

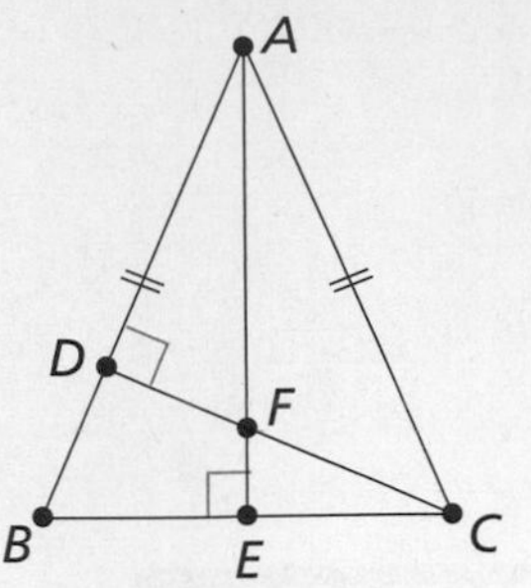

Side-Splitter Theorem

If a line is parallel to a side of a triangle and intersects the other two sides, then it splits those sides proportionally.

The Side-Splitter Theorem shows that overlapping triangles are similar.

EXAMPLE 5 Proving that overlapping triangles are similar

Given: $\triangle ABC$ with $\overline{DE} \parallel \overline{AC}$

Prove: $\frac{AD}{DB} = \frac{CE}{EB}$

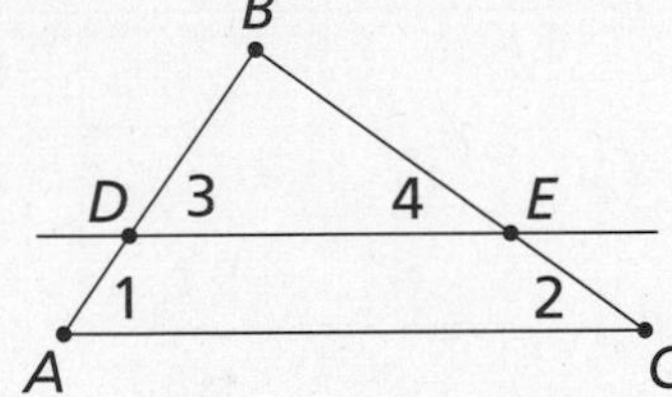

▪ **SOLUTION**

Statements	Reasons
1. ΔABC with $\overline{DE} \parallel \overline{AC}$	1. Given
2. $\angle 1 \cong \angle 3$ and $\angle 2 \cong \angle 4$	2. Corresponding angles are congruent.
3. $\triangle ABC \sim \triangle DBE$	3. AA
4. $\frac{AB}{DB} = \frac{CB}{EB}$	4. Corresponding sides of similar triangles are proportional.
5. $AB = AD + DB$ and $CB = CE + EB$	5. Segment Addition Postulate
6. $\frac{AD + DB}{DB} = \frac{CE + EB}{EB}$	6. Substitution
7. $\frac{AD}{DB} + \frac{DB}{DB} = \frac{CE}{EB} + \frac{EB}{EB} \Rightarrow \frac{AD}{DB} + 1 = \frac{CE}{EB} + 1$	7. Algebra and simplification
8. $\frac{AD}{DB} = \frac{CE}{EB}$	8. Subtraction Property of Equality

Additional Theorems About Similarity and Proportions

- If three parallel lines intersect two transversals, they divide them proportionally.
- The perimeters of similar triangles are proportional to the measures of the corresponding sides.
- Similarity of triangles is reflexive, symmetric, and transitive.
- If a ray bisects an angle of a triangle, then it divides the opposite side into two segments that are proportional to the other two sides of the triangle.
- If two triangles are similar, the lengths of corresponding altitudes are proportional to the measures of the corresponding sides.

Triangle similarity theorems allow you to solve a wide range of problems involving similar triangles.

EXAMPLES 6 through 8 Using triangle similarity theorems

6 Use a graphing calculator or geometry software to investigate the theorem concerning the angle bisector of a triangle. Verify that the relationship stated in the theorem holds for many cases by dragging the vertices of the triangle and observing the results of the calculated ratios.

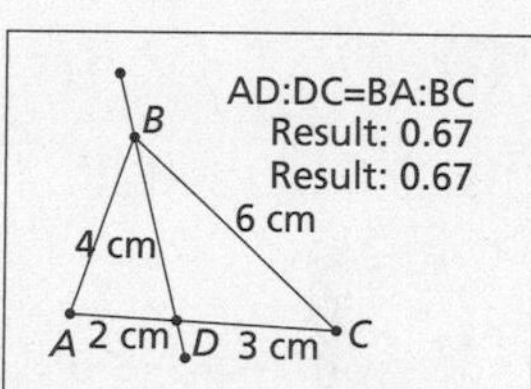

■ SOLUTION

In the accompanying figure we can see one case where the proportion is true, accurate to two decimal places.

7 In the accompanying figure, M is the midpoint of side $\overline{JK}$, and N is the midpoint of side $\overline{JL}$. Prove that $\triangle JKL \sim \triangle JMN$.

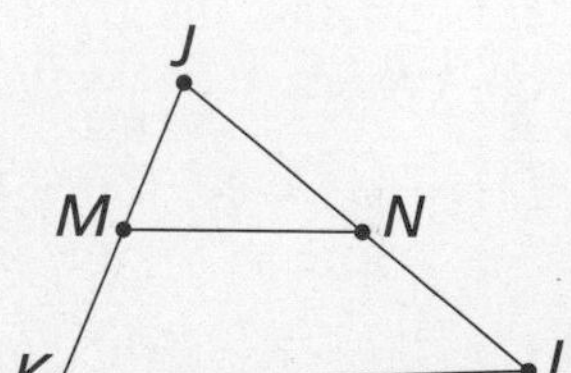

■ SOLUTION

$\frac{JM}{JK} = \frac{JN}{JL} = \frac{1}{2}$ by the definition of midpoint. $\angle J$ is in both triangles and is included between the proportional sides. Therefore, $\triangle JKL \sim \triangle JMN$ by the SAS Similarity Theorem.

8 Hazelwood Ave., Fernwood Ave., and Pinehurst St. run parallel to each other. The distance along Golden Glow Dr. between Hazelwood and Fernwood is 1,320 ft. Between Fernwood and Pinehurst, the distance is 540 ft. The distance along Alvord Dr. between Pinehurst and Fernwood is 620 ft. What is the distance between Pinehurst and Hazelwood along Alvord Dr.?

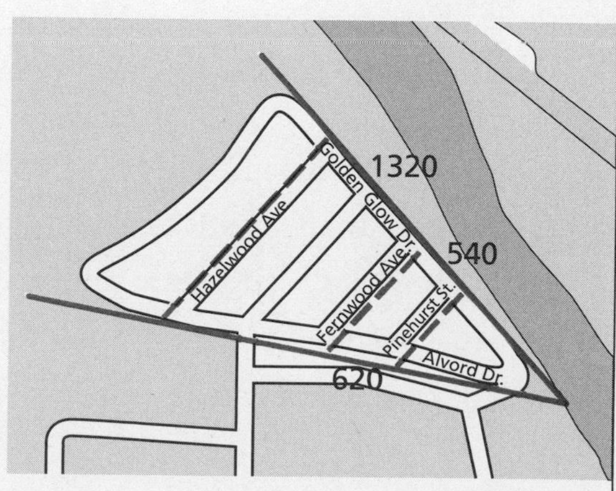

■ SOLUTION

$$\frac{620}{n} = \frac{540}{1860} \Rightarrow 1153200 = 540\,n \Rightarrow n \approx 2135.56 \text{ ft}$$

Practice

Choose the numeral preceding the word or expression that best completes the statement or answers the question.

1 Based upon the accompanying figure, which is the correct expression of the similarity?

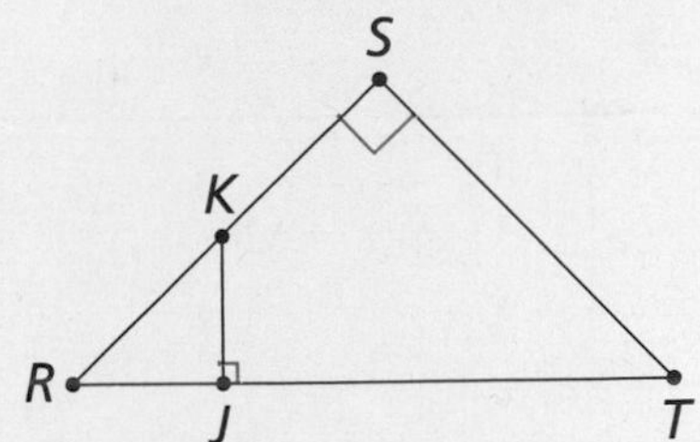

(1) $\triangle RST \sim \triangle RKJ$ (3) $\triangle RST \sim \triangle JKR$

(2) $\triangle RST \sim \triangle RJK$ (4) $\triangle RST \sim \triangle JRK$

2 Which of the following is true for similar triangles?

(1) Corresponding sides are congruent.

(2) Corresponding angles are proportional.

(3) Corresponding sides are proportional.

(4) All of the above

3 If two triangles are similar but not congruent, what is true about them?

(1) They have the same size and same shape.

(2) They have the same size but different shapes.

(3) They have different sizes and different shapes.

(4) They have the same shape but different sizes.

4 Which of the following is true?

(1) All right triangles are similar.

(2) All isosceles triangles are similar.

(3) All equilateral triangles are similar.

(4) All scalene triangles are similar.

In the figure below, $MN \parallel AC$. Use this figure for Exercises 5–11.

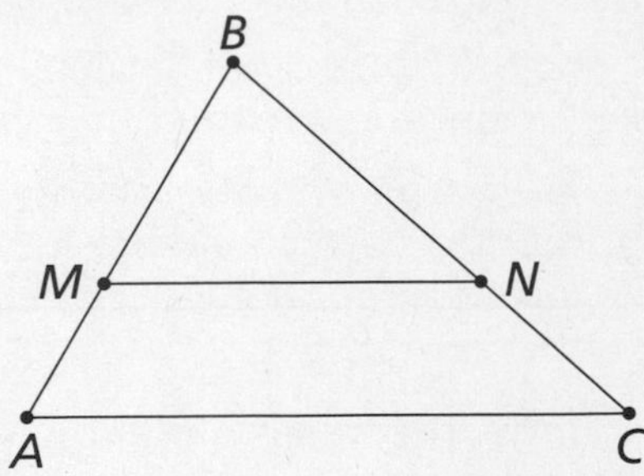

5 Write a similarity statement and justify your answer.

6 If $AM = 4$, $MB = 8$, and $BC = 36$, find BN.

7 If $AB = 9$, $AC = 15$, and $MB = 6$, find MN.

8 If $MB = 7$, $MA = 5$, and $BN = 10$, find NC.

9 If $AM = 4$, $AB = 12$, and the perimeter of $\triangle ABC$ is 32, find the perimeter of $\triangle MBN$.

10 If $MN = 10$, $AC = 15$, and $MB = 4$, find MA.

11 If $MB = 4$, $BN = 5$, and $NC = 10$, find MA.

12 Determine whether the triangles in the accompanying figure are similar. If they are, write a similarity statement and list the six pairs of corresponding parts.

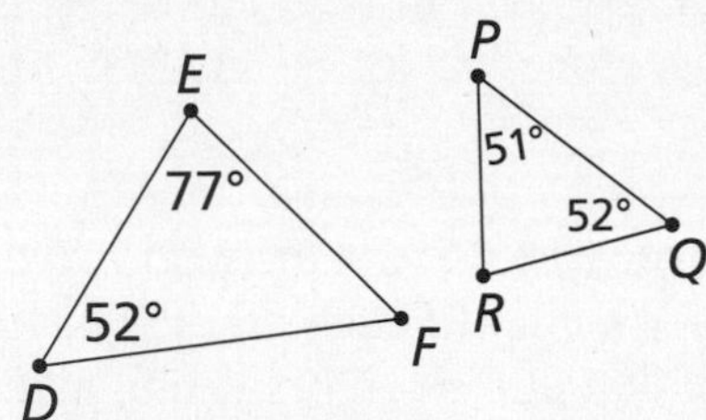

13 A meter stick casts a shadow that is 90 cm long. At the same time a tree has a shadow that is 4.3 m long. Determine the height of the tree.

In Exercises 14–16, write a similarity statement and identify the postulate or theorem that justifies the similarity.

14

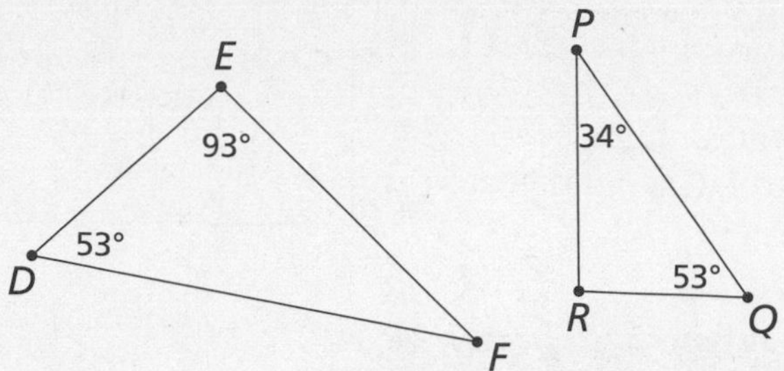

15

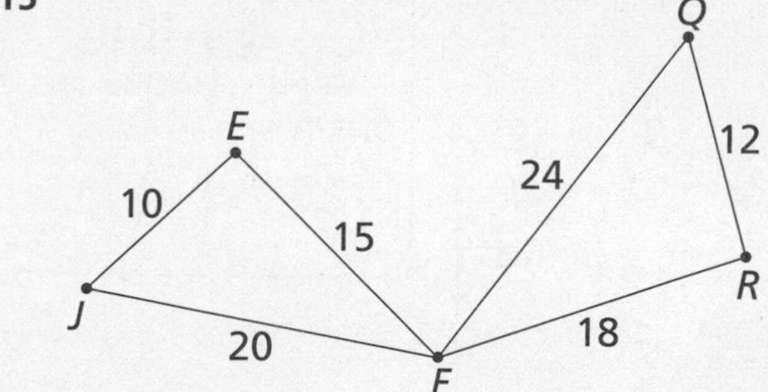

16

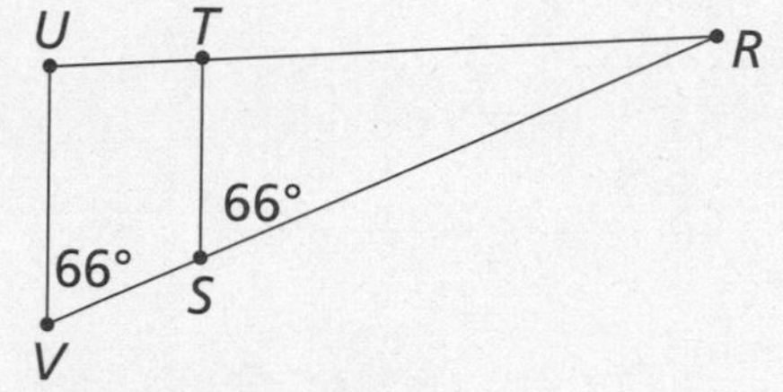

17 In the accompanying figure $\angle 1 \cong \angle 2$. Write a paragraph proof to show $\triangle ACB \sim \triangle DCE$.

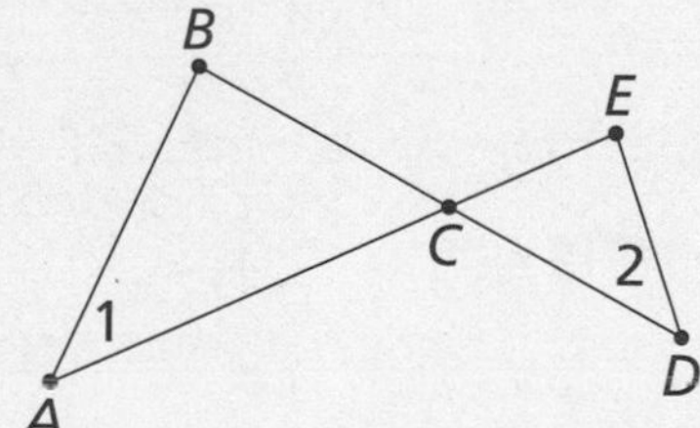

18 Given $\triangle ABC$ with altitudes $\overline{CD}$ and $\overline{AE}$, write a two column proof that $\frac{BC}{AB} = \frac{DC}{AE}$.

19 Complete the following proof of the converse of the Side-Splitter Theorem.

Given: $\frac{XR}{RQ} = \frac{YS}{SQ}$

Prove: $\overline{RS} \parallel \overline{XY}$

Statements	Reasons
1. $\frac{XR}{RQ} = \frac{YS}{SQ}$	1.
2. $\frac{XR+RQ}{RQ} = \frac{YS+SQ}{SQ}$	2.
3. $\frac{XQ}{RQ} = \frac{YQ}{SQ}$	3.
4. $\angle Q \cong \angle Q$	4.
5. $\triangle XQY \sim \triangle RQS$	5.
6. $\angle QXY \cong \angle QRS$	6.
7. $\overline{RS} \parallel \overline{XY}$	7.

20 The sides of a triangle are 6 cm, 12 cm, and 15 cm long. Determine the lengths, to the nearest tenth, of the segments formed when each angle bisector divides the opposite side.

21 To determine the width of Small Lake, the measurements of two similar right triangles are taken as shown in the accompanying figure. What is the width of Small Lake?

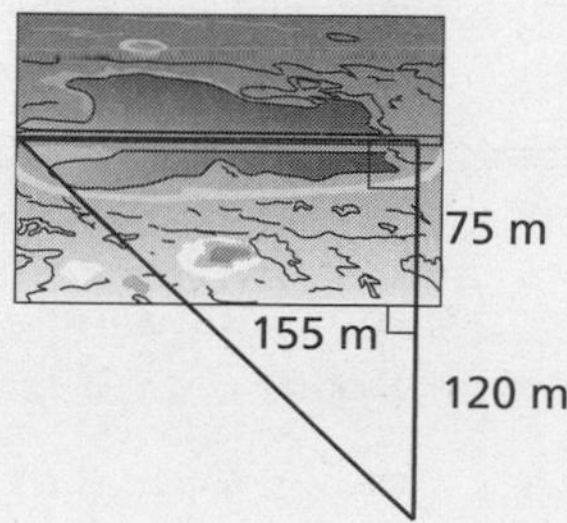

3.4 Triangle Congruence

New York Standards

G.G.27 Writing proofs
G.G.28 Congruence techniques
G.G.29 Corresponding parts of congruent triangles

Congruent triangles are triangles that are the same size and the same shape. Congruent triangles have three pairs of **corresponding angles congruent** and three pairs of **corresponding sides congruent**.

You do not need all six pairs of congruent sides and congruent angles to prove that two triangles are congruent. You can use postulates and theorems presented in this lesson to show that triangles are congruent.

Side-Side-Side Postulate (SSS)

If the three sides of one triangle are congruent to the three corresponding sides of another triangle, then the two triangles are congruent.

$\triangle ABC \cong \triangle DEF$

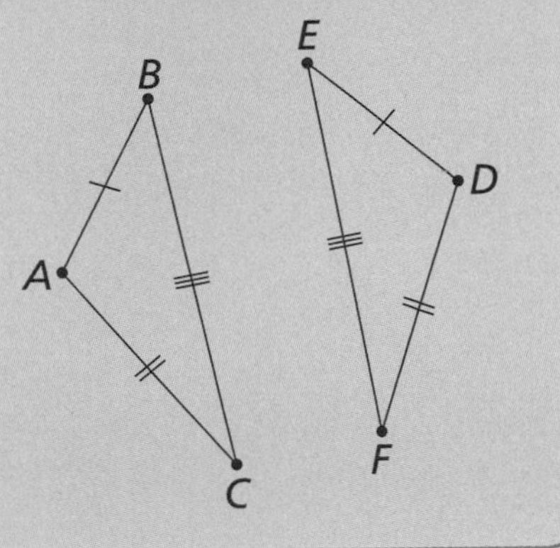

Go Online
PHSchool.com
Visit: PHSchool.com
Web Codes: ayp-0393
ayp-0401

EXAMPLE 1 **Matching corresponding parts**

1 List the pairs of corresponding parts for the triangles shown in the postulate above.

■ **SOLUTION**

$\angle A \cong \angle D$ $\overline{AB} \cong \overline{DE}$
$\angle B \cong \angle E$ $\overline{AC} \cong \overline{DF}$
$\angle C \cong \angle F$ $\overline{BC} \cong \overline{EF}$

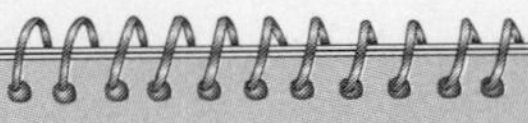

Note

Since $\overline{AB} \cong \overline{CD}$ if and only if $AB = CD$, and $\angle A \cong \angle B$ if and only if $m\angle A = m\angle B$, these congruence and equality statements will be used interchangeably.

Recall that postulates are statements accepted without proof. This particular postulate is one of the most self-evident.

Side-Angle-Side Postulate (SAS)

If two sides and the included angle of one triangle are congruent to the corresponding parts of another triangle, the triangles are congruent.

$\triangle ABC \cong \triangle DEF$

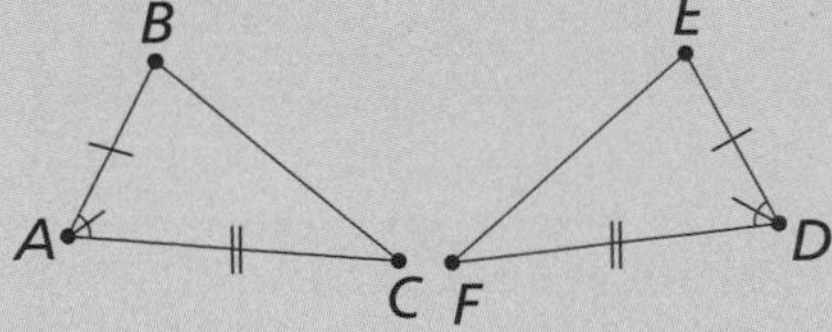

Go Online
PHSchool.com
Visit: PHSchool.com
Web Code: ayp-0394

Included angles and included sides are often used when showing that triangles are congruent. An included side is the common side of two angles of a triangle. An included angle is the angle formed by two sides of the triangle.

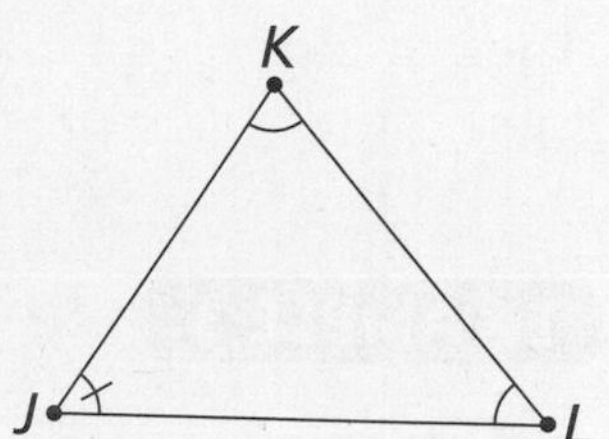

In the accompanying figure, $\angle J$ is included between $\overline{KJ}$ and $\overline{LJ}$ and side $\overline{KL}$ is included between $\angle K$ and $\angle L$.

EXAMPLE 2 **Proving that triangles are congruent**

Given: Segments AB and CD bisect each other at M.
Prove: $\triangle ACM \cong \triangle BDM$

■ **SOLUTION**

Statements	Reasons
1. Segments AB and CD bisect each other.	1. Given
2. $\overline{AM} \cong \overline{BM}$; $\overline{CM} \cong \overline{DM}$	2. Definition of bisector
3. $\angle 1 \cong \angle 2$	3. If two lines intersect, the vertical angles are ≅.
4. $\triangle ACM \cong \triangle BDM$	4. SAS Postulate

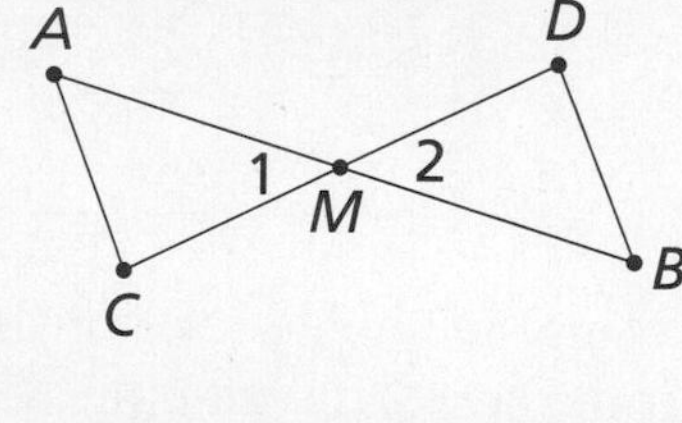

Given two angles and a side, you can show that triangles are congruent.

Angle-Side-Angle Postulate (ASA)

If two angles and the included side of one triangle are congruent to the corresponding parts of another triangle, the triangles are congruent.

$\triangle RST \cong \triangle GHI$

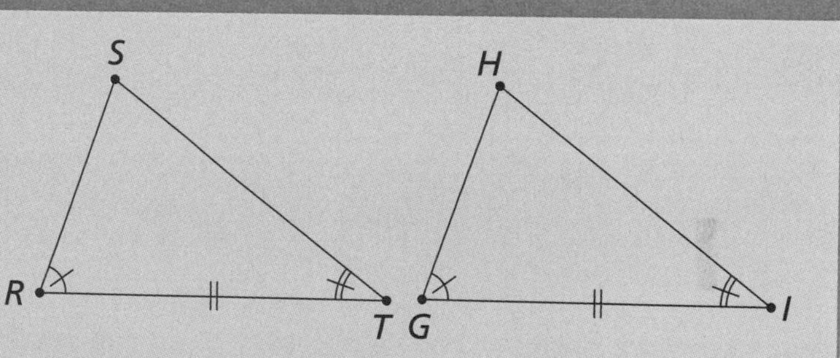

Angle-Angle-Side Theorem (AAS)

If two angles and the nonincluded side of one triangle are congruent to the corresponding parts of another triangle, the triangles are congruent.

$\triangle DEF \cong \triangle XYZ$

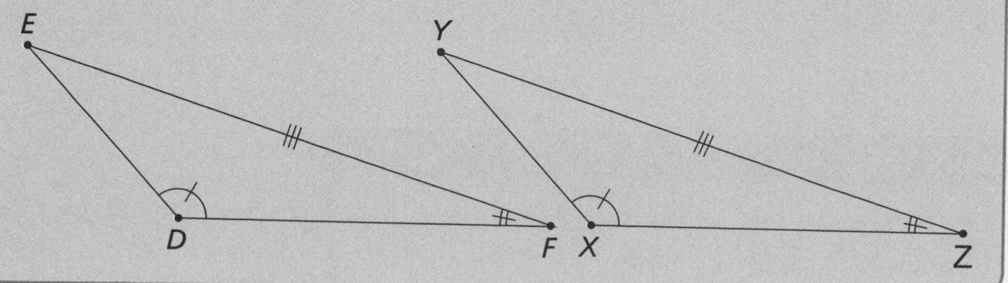

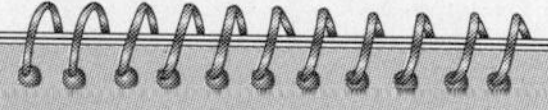

Note

The AAS is a theorem and not a postulate because it can be proved from known facts.

Another type of proof known as a **flow proof** uses arrows to show the logical connection between statements. The reasons are usually written below the statements.

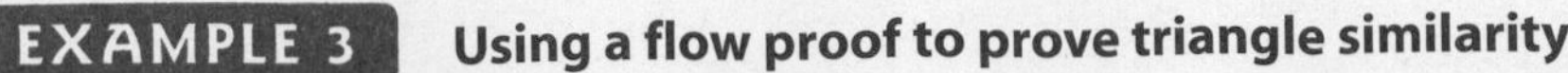

EXAMPLE 3 Using a flow proof to prove triangle similarity

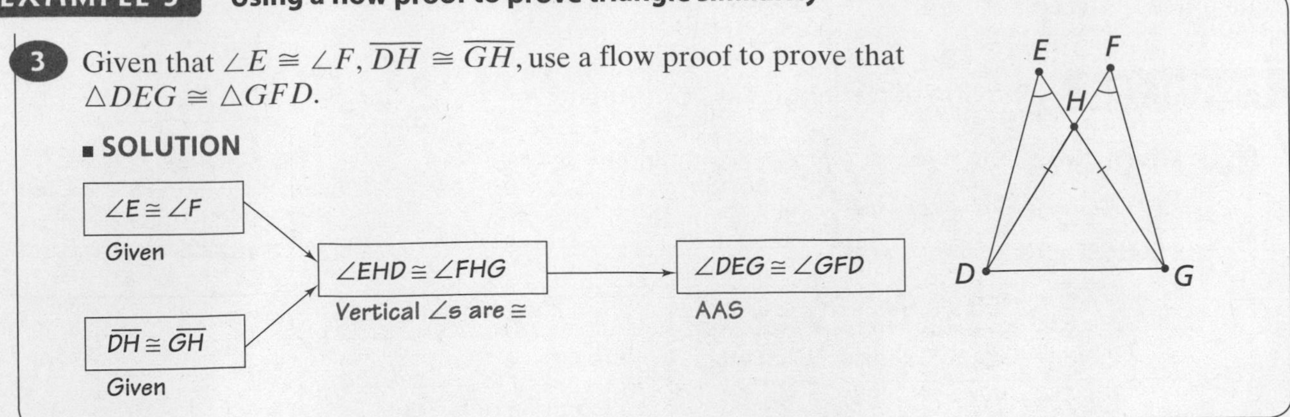

Some side-angle relationships cannot be used to show that triangles are congruent. For example, SSA cannot be used to show congruence. In the figure below, $\angle ACD$ was constructed to be congruent to the given angle and $DC \cong b$. Notice that there are two possible triangles that can now be completed; $\triangle ADC$ and $\triangle BDC$ are not congruent.

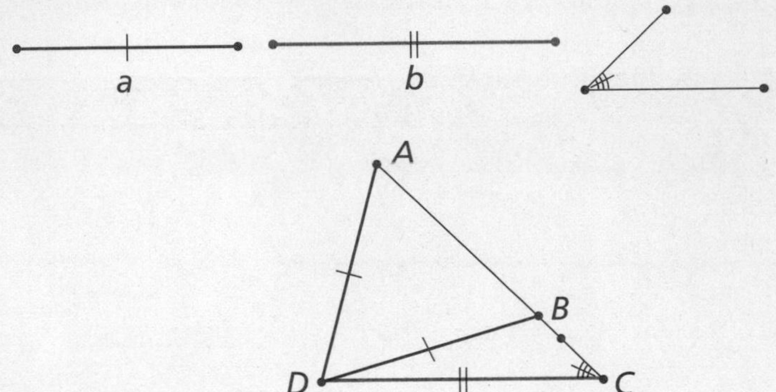

AAA cannot be used to show congruence of triangles. For example, equilateral triangles have three 60° angles; yet they are not all congruent.

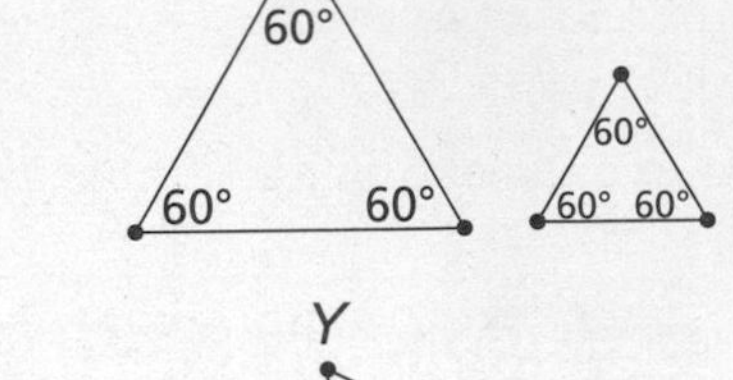

If $\triangle ABC$ and $\triangle XYZ$ are right triangles, with $\overline{BC} \cong \overline{YZ}$ and $\overline{BA} \cong \overline{YX}$, then $\triangle ABC \cong \triangle XYZ$. Extend $\overline{ZX}$ to a point W such that $XW \cong AC$. $\triangle ABC \cong \triangle YXW$ by SAS. Because these triangles are congruent, their hypotenuses are congruent. That is, $\overline{BC} \cong \overline{YW}$. Since we were given $\overline{BC} \cong \overline{YZ}$, we know that $\overline{YW} \cong \overline{YZ}$ by the transitive property of congruence. $\angle W \cong \angle Z$ by the Isosceles Triangle Theorem. So, $\triangle YXW \cong \triangle YXZ$ by AAS. Therefore, $\triangle ABC \cong \triangle XYZ$ by the transitive property of congruence. This result is known as the **Hypotenuse-Leg Theorem.**

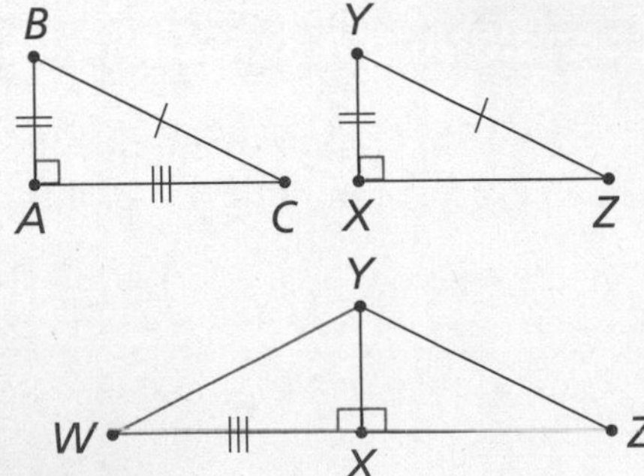

Hypotenuse-Leg Theorem (HL)

If the hypotenuse and a leg of one right triangle are congruent to the hypotenuse and corresponding leg of another, then the right triangles are congruent.

EXAMPLES 4 and 5 Different methods of proof

4 **Given:** $\overline{BE} \perp$ bisector of $\overline{AD}$, $\overline{AB} \cong \overline{DE}$
Prove: $\triangle ABC \cong \triangle DEC$ using a two-column proof

▪ **SOLUTION**

Statements	Reasons
1. $\overline{BE} \perp$ bisector of $\overline{AD}$	1. Given
2. $\overline{AC} \cong \overline{DC}$	2. Definition of bisector
3. $\angle 1$ & $\angle 2$ are right $\angle$s	3. $\perp$s form right $\angle$s
4. $\triangle ABC$ and $\triangle DEC$ are right $\triangle$s	4. Definition of right $\triangle$
5. $\overline{AB} \cong \overline{DE}$	5. Given
6. $\triangle ABC \cong \triangle DEC$	6. HL

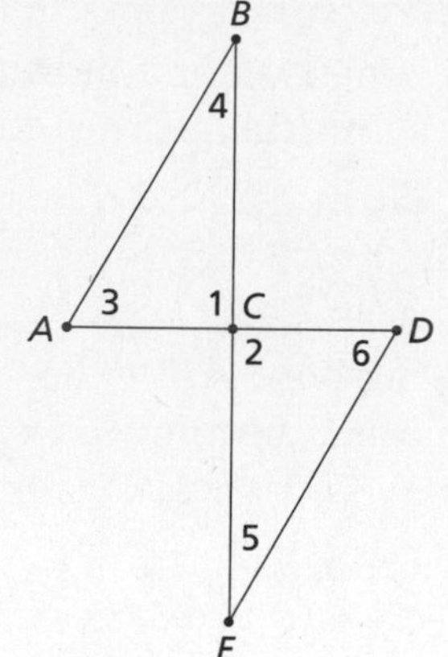

5 Prove the same result as Example 5, using a flow proof.

▪ **SOLUTION**

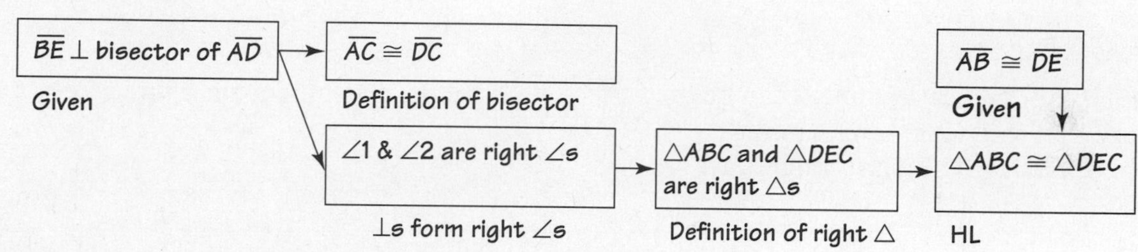

Showing That Triangles Are Congruent		
Side-Side-Side (SSS) Congruence Postulate If three sides of one triangle are congruent to three sides of another triangle, then the triangles are congruent.	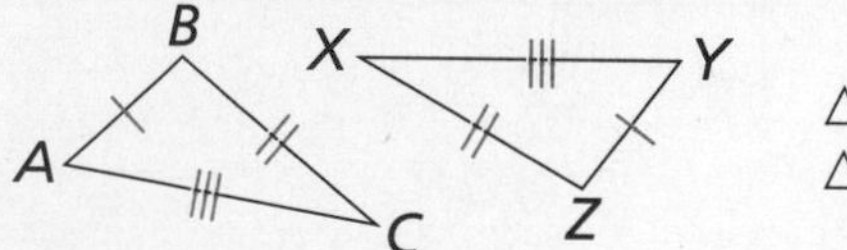	$\triangle ABC \cong \triangle YZX$
Side-Angle-Side (SAS) Congruence Postulate If two sides and the included angle of one triangle are congruent to two sides and the included angle of another triangle, then the triangles are congruent.	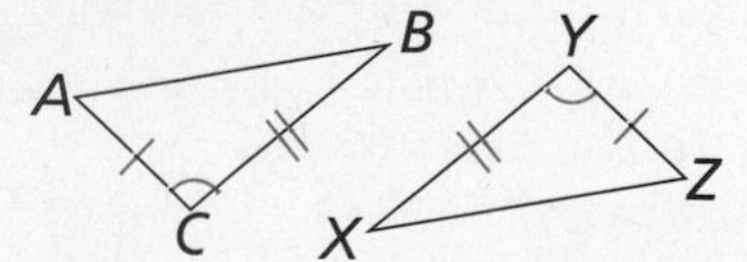	$\triangle ABC \cong \triangle ZXY$
Angle-Side-Angle (ASA) Congruence Postulate If two angles and the included side of one triangle are congruent to two angles and the included side of another triangle, then the triangles are congruent.	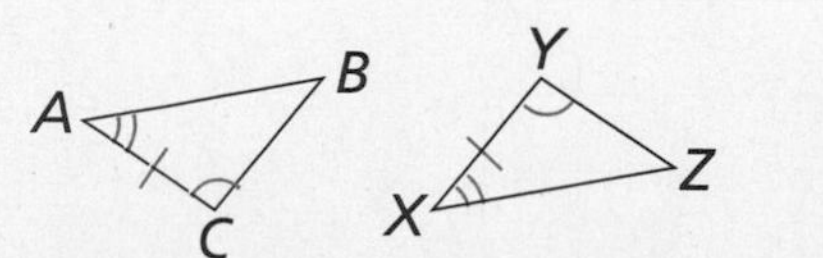	$\triangle ABC \cong \triangle XZY$
Angle-Angle-Side (AAS) Congruence Theorem If two angles and the nonincluded side of one triangle are congruent to two angles and the nonincluded side of another triangle, then the triangles are congruent.	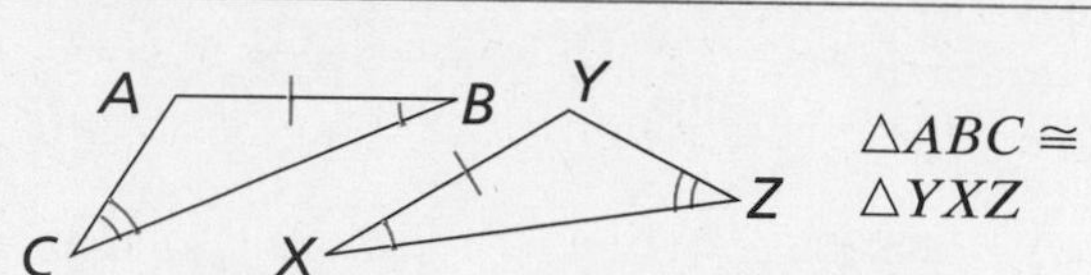	$\triangle ABC \cong \triangle YXZ$
Hypotenuse-Leg (HL) Congruence Theorem If the hypotenuse and one leg of a right triangle are congruent to the hypotenuse and one leg of another right triangle, then the triangles are congruent.	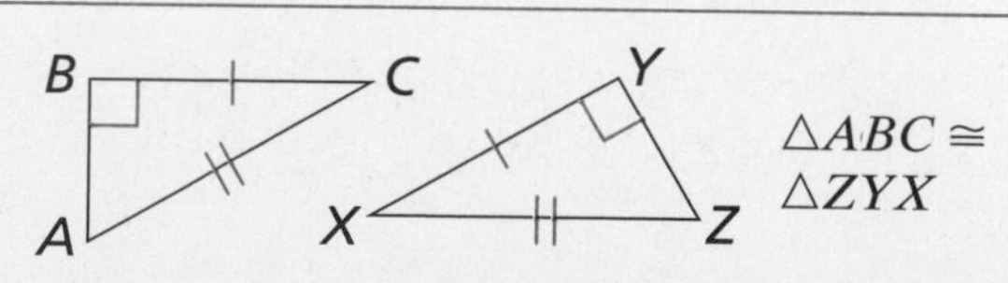	$\triangle ABC \cong \triangle ZYX$

Practice

Choose the numeral preceding the word or expression that best completes the statement or answers the question.

1 Which of the following can *not* be used to show triangles are congruent?

(1) AAA (3) SAS

(2) SSS (4) ASA

2 Suppose $AB = RS$ and $\angle A = \angle R$. What other information is needed to prove that $\triangle ABC \cong \triangle RST$ by ASA?

(1) $\angle C = \angle T$

(2) $AC = RT$

(3) $\angle B = \angle S$

(4) $\angle A = \angle B$

3 Which congruence statement can be used to prove that the two triangles in the accompanying figure are congruent?

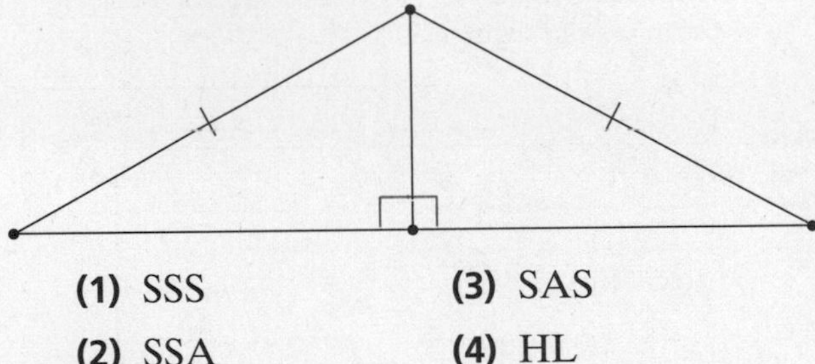

(1) SSS (3) SAS

(2) SSA (4) HL

In Exercises 4–7, determine if there is enough information to prove the triangles congruent. If so, write the statement; otherwise, write "not possible."

4

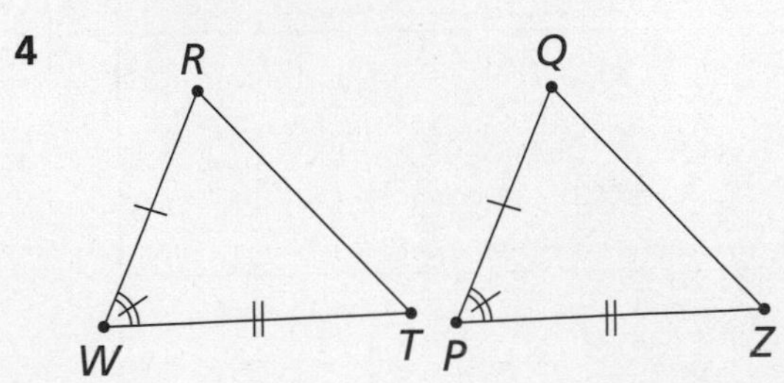

5

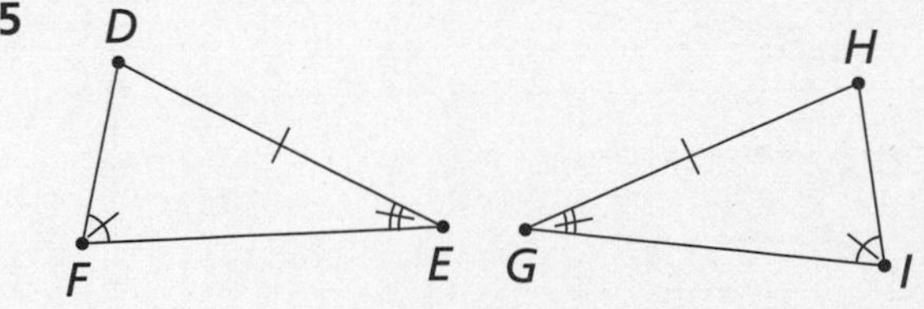

6

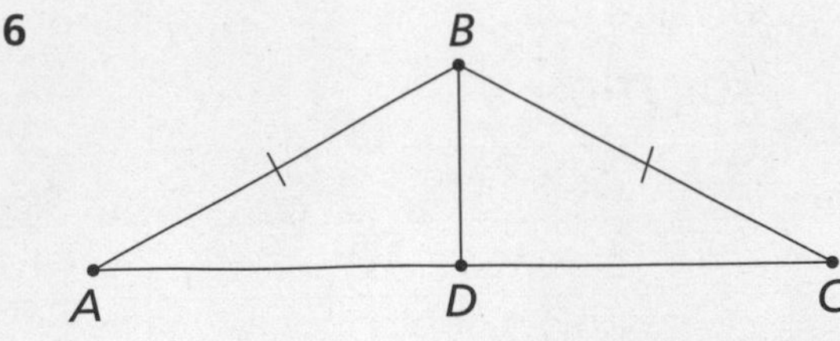

7

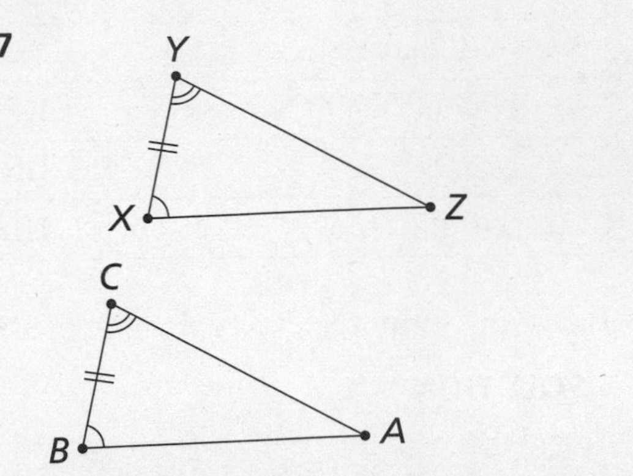

8 In the accompanying figure $\angle S \cong \angle T$ and $\overline{ST} \cong \overline{TU}$.

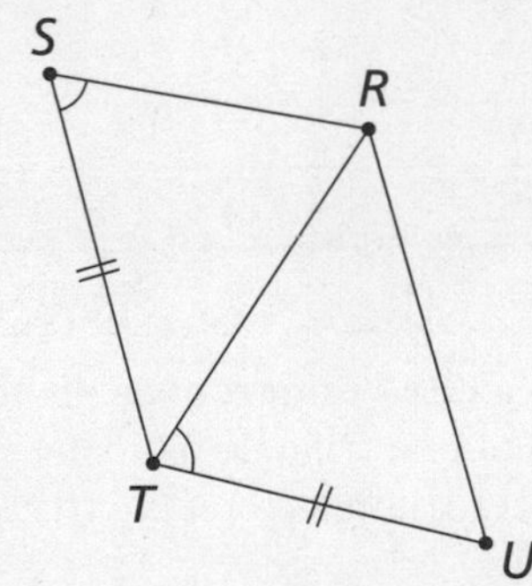

a. Can you identify any other congruent parts in these triangles? If so, state them and the property that justifies your conclusion.

b. Based upon what you know, are these two triangles congruent? Justify your answer.

9 Construct 2 triangles with two sides and a nonincluded angle congruent. Verify that this construction demonstrates that SSA is not a valid argument for congruence.

10 Prove the AAS Theorem: *If two angles and the nonincluded side of one triangle are congruent to the corresponding parts of another triangle, the triangles are congruent.*

Given the congruent triangles in Exercises 11–13, name the corresponding parts of the two triangles.

11 $\triangle ABC \cong \triangle CDA$

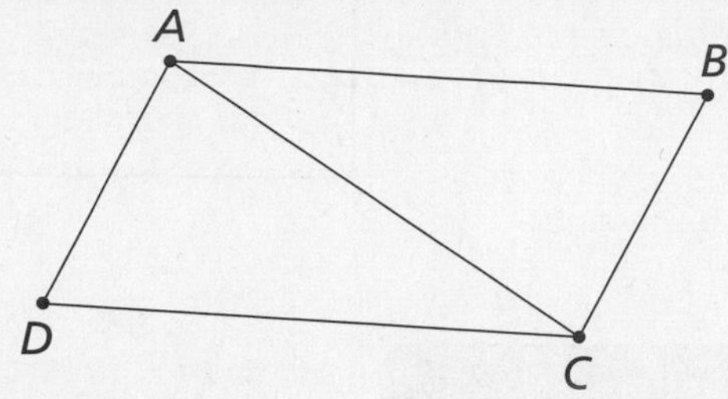

12 $\triangle ACB \cong \triangle ECD$

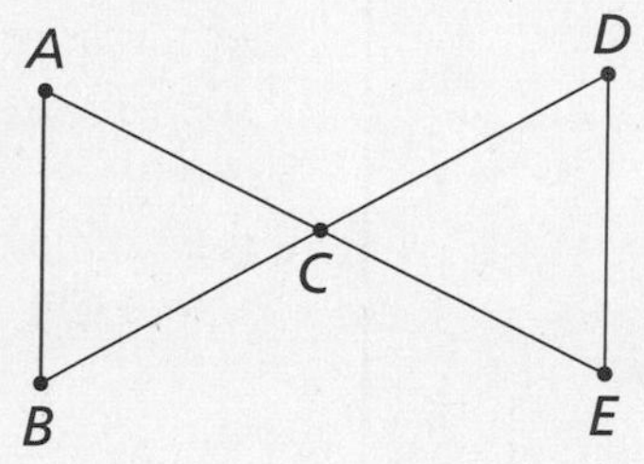

13 $\triangle ABC \cong \triangle ADC$

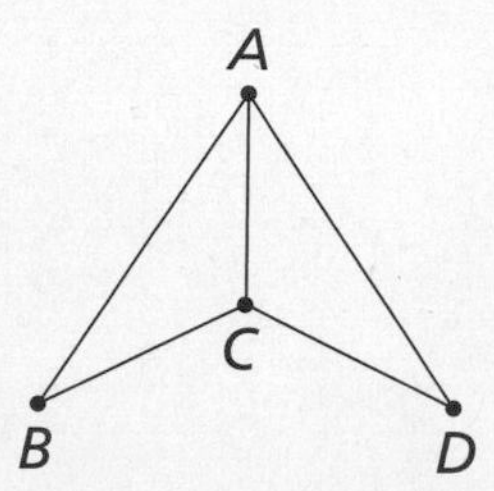

14 **Given:** $\overline{AB} \cong \overline{CB}$, $\overrightarrow{BD}$ bisects $\angle B$
Prove: $\triangle ABD \cong \triangle CBD$

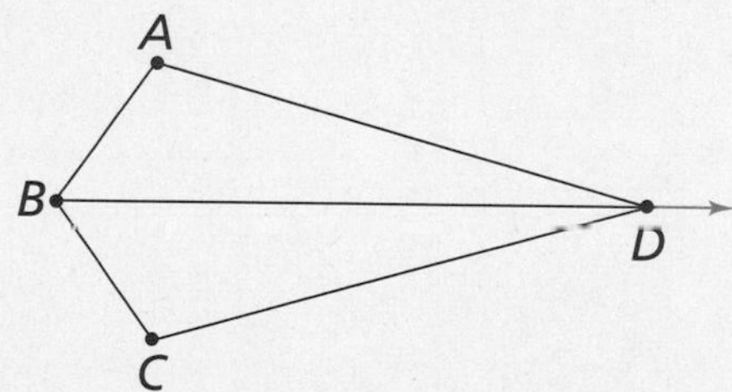

15 **Given:** $\angle ABC \cong \angle DCB$, $\angle DBC \cong \angle ACB$
Prove: $\triangle ABC \cong \triangle DCB$

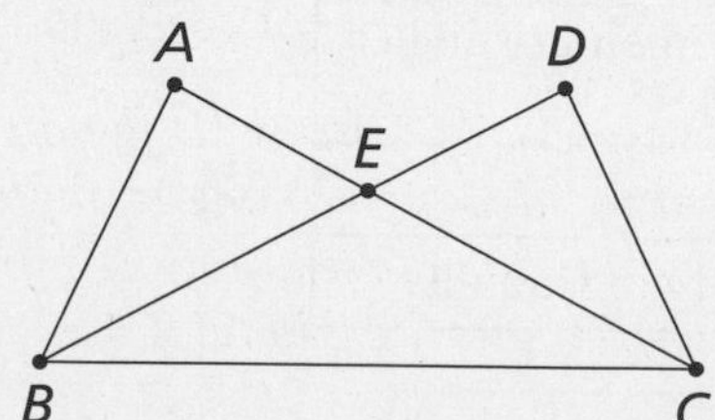

16 **Given:** $\overline{SW}$ is the $\perp$ bisector of $\overline{RT}$
$\overline{RS} \cong \overline{TS}$
Prove: $\triangle RWS \cong \triangle TWS$

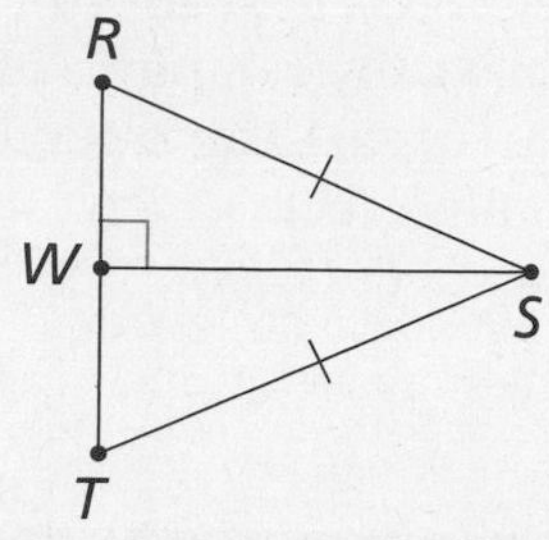

17 **Given:** $\angle G \cong \angle E$, $\angle 2 \cong \angle 3$, $\overline{AB} \cong \overline{DC}$
Prove: $\triangle GAC \cong \triangle EDB$

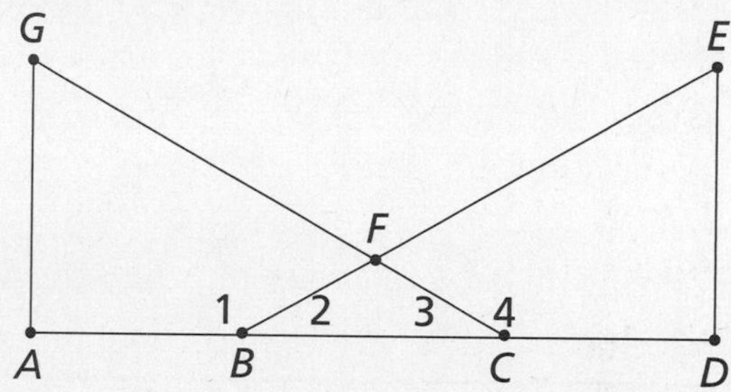

18 Roberta says, "If the hypotenuse and an acute angle of one right triangle are congruent to the hypotenuse and an acute angle of another right triangle, then the triangles are congruent." Is she correct? Justify your answer.

19 The diagonal legs of this chair have equal lengths and are joined at their midpoints. Is this enough information to prove that $\triangle ABE \cong \triangle DCE$? Justify your answer.

20 Is it sufficient to say that two quadrilaterals are congruent if four sides of one are congruent to the four sides of the other? Explain.

3.5 More Formal Proofs Involving Triangles

New York Standards

G.G.27 Writing proofs

G.G.28 Congruence techniques

G.G.29 Corresponding parts of congruent triangles

The first step in writing a proof is analyzing what is given and what needs to be proved. Next, develop an argument that leads from the hypothesis to the conclusion. Finally, decide which form—two-column, paragraph, or flow—you should use to write the proof.

The steps to writing a good proof are summarized in the following box:

Writing a Proof

1. Draw and label a figure that represents the situation.
2. State the given conditions, expressing them in terms of letters and symbols used in the figure.
3. State the conclusion that you want to prove, using the letters and symbols in the figure.
4. Present an argument that leads from the given conditions to the conclusion. Present statements and the reasons that justify each statement.

Note

Remember, only given information, definitions, axioms, and proven theorems can be used as reasons in your proof.

EXAMPLE 1 Writing a proof

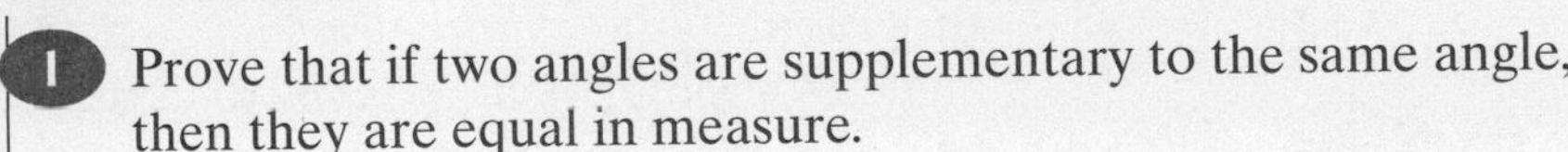

1. Prove that if two angles are supplementary to the same angle, then they are equal in measure.

SOLUTION

Analysis: Supplementary means that the angles total 180°. Draw a figure that represents the problem.

Figure

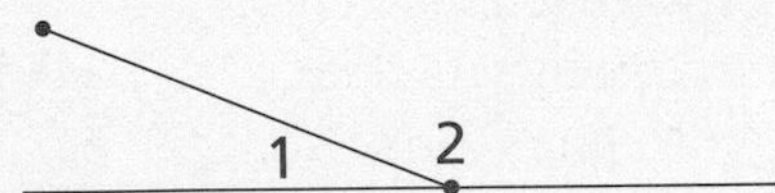

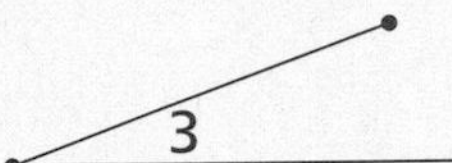

Given: $\angle 1$ and $\angle 2$ are supplementary
$\angle 3$ and $\angle 2$ are supplementary

Prove: $m\angle 1 = m\angle 3$

Statements	Reasons
1. $m\angle 1$ and $m\angle 2$ are supplementary $m\angle 3$ and $m\angle 2$ are supplementary	1. Given
2. $m\angle 1 + m\angle 2 = 180°$ $m\angle 3 + m\angle 2 = 180°$	2. Definition of supplementary angles
3. $m\angle 1 + m\angle 2 = m\angle 3 + m\angle 2$	3. Substitution
4. $m\angle 1 = m\angle 3$	4. Subtraction Property of Equality

When triangles are congruent, their corresponding parts are congruent. In other words, **corresponding parts of congruent triangles are congruent (CPCTC).** You will often use this fact when writing proofs.

EXAMPLES 2 and 3 Proving corresponding parts of congruent triangles are congruent

2 Prove that in an isosceles triangle, the segment joining the vertex angle to the midpoint of the opposite side bisects the vertex angle and is perpendicular to the opposite side.

■ **SOLUTION**

Given: $\triangle ABC$; $\overline{AB} \cong \overline{CB}$; D is the midpoint of $\overline{AC}$.

Prove: $\angle 1 \cong \angle 2$; $\overline{BD} \perp \overline{AC}$

Statements	Reasons
1. $\overline{AB} \cong \overline{CB}$; D is the midpoint of $\overline{AC}$	1. Given
2. $\overline{AD} \cong \overline{CD}$	2. Definition of midpoint
3. $\overline{BD} \cong \overline{BD}$	3. Reflexive Property of Congruence
4. $\triangle ABD \cong \triangle CBD$	4. SSS
5. $\angle 1 \cong \angle 2$	5. Corresponding part of $\cong$ $\triangle$s are $\cong$.
6. $\overline{BD}$ bisects $\angle ABC$	6. Definition of angle bisector
7. $\angle 3 \cong \angle 4$	7. Corresponding part of $\cong$ $\triangle$s are $\cong$.
8. $\overline{BD} \perp \overline{AC}$	8. If two lines intersect to form $\cong$ adjacent $\angle$s, the lines are $\perp$.

3 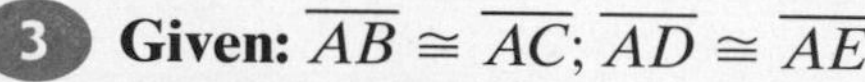
Given: $\overline{AB} \cong \overline{AC}$; $\overline{AD} \cong \overline{AE}$

Prove: $\angle 1 \cong \angle 2$

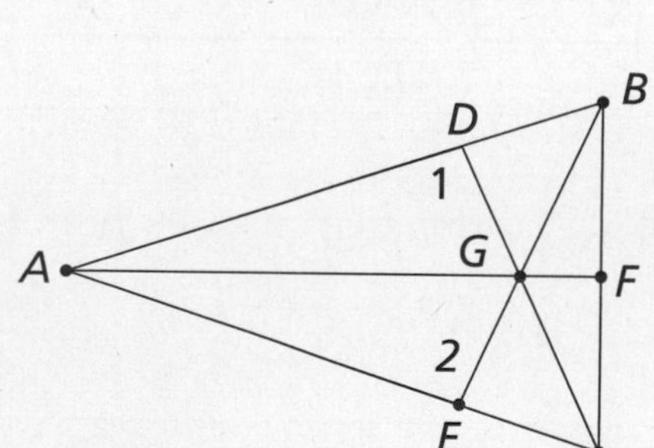

■ **SOLUTION**

Analysis: Begin by analyzing the figure to see the corresponding parts. If $\angle 1$ and $\angle 2$ are corresponding parts of congruent triangles, then the proof is done. $\overline{AB}$ and $\overline{AE}$ are sides of $\triangle AEB$. $\overline{AC}$ and $\overline{AD}$ are sides of $\triangle ADC$. $\angle A$ is included between both pairs of sides, so the triangles are congruent by SAS.

Statements	Reasons
1. $\overline{AB} \cong \overline{AC}$; $\overline{AD} \cong \overline{AE}$	1. Given
2. $\angle DAC \cong \angle EAB$	2. Reflexive Property
3. $\triangle ABE \cong \triangle ACD$	3. SAS
4. $\angle 1 \cong \angle 2$	4. CPCTC

Go Online
PHSchool.com
Visit: PHSchool.com
Web Code: ayp-0397

EXAMPLES 4 and 5 Proving more than one pair of triangles congruent

Given: $\angle N \cong \angle P, \overline{MO} \cong \overline{QO}$
Prove: $\overline{MP} \cong \overline{QN}$

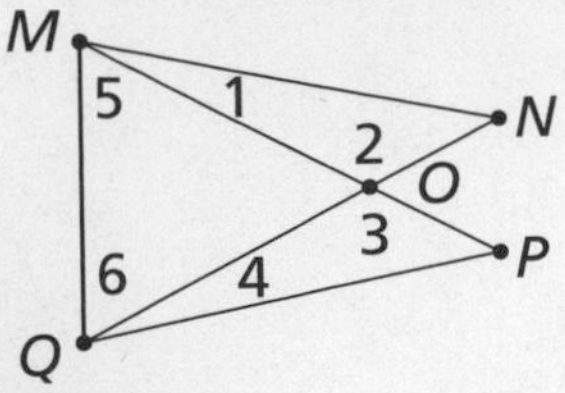

■ **SOLUTION**

Analysis: To prove $\overline{MP} \cong \overline{QN}$ it might seem necessary to show that the black and blue triangles are congruent. However, only one angle of one triangle is congruent to one angle of the other. That is, $\angle N \cong \angle P$.

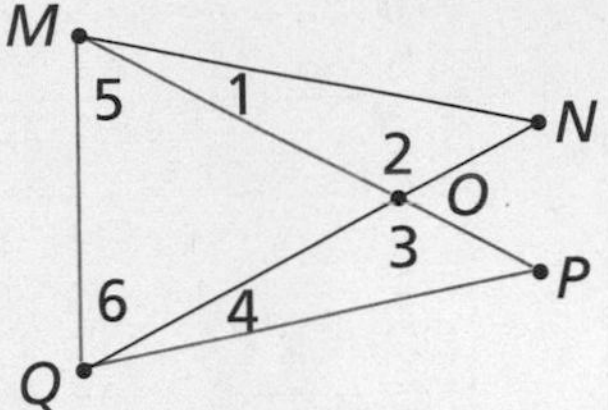

Statements	Reasons
1. $\angle N \cong \angle P$, $\overline{MO} \cong \overline{QO}$	1. Given
2. $\angle 2 \cong \angle 3$	2. Two intersecting lines form $\cong$ vertical $\angle$s.
3. $\triangle MON \cong \triangle QOP$	3. AAS
4. $\overline{MN} \cong \overline{QP}$	4. CPCTC
5. $\angle 5 \cong \angle 6$	5. If two sides of a triangle are congruent, the angles opposite those sides are congruent. ($\triangle MOQ$)
6. $\triangle QNM \cong \triangle MPQ$	6. AAS
7. $\overline{MP} \cong \overline{QN}$	7. CPCTC

Visit: PHSchool.com
Web Code: ayp-0392

5 Prove Example 4 by showing that only one pair of triangles is congruent.

■ **SOLUTION**

Statements	Reasons
1. $\angle N \cong \angle P$, $\overline{MO} \cong \overline{QO}$	1. Given
2. $\overline{MQ} \cong \overline{MQ}$	2. Reflexive Property
3. $\angle 5 \cong \angle 6$	3. If two sides of a triangle are congruent, the angles opposite those sides are congruent. ($\triangle MOQ$)
4. $\triangle QNM \cong \triangle MPQ$	4. AAS
5. $\overline{MP} \cong \overline{QN}$	5. CPCTC

As shown in the above examples, there is often more than one way of doing a proof. Use the type of proof that you recognize and can complete.

If a valid argument from a statement leads to a false conclusion (a contradiction), then the statement is false.

An **indirect proof** is one that involves the use of indirect reasoning. In this type of proof, a statement and its negation are often the only possibilities.

Writing an Indirect Proof

1. Assume the opposite of what you want to prove.
2. Use logical reasoning to show a contradiction.
3. Conclude that your assumption must be false and that what you wanted to prove must be true.

EXAMPLES 6 through 8 Writing indirect proofs

6 Prove that $3(4x + 3) \neq 6(2x + 4)$.

■ SOLUTION

Assume that $3(4x + 3) = 6(2x + 4)$ is true.

$12x + 9 = 12x + 24$ ← **Distributive property**

$9 = 24$ ← **Subtraction property of equality**

This is false. Therefore, the original statement must be false: $3(4x + 3)$ does not equal $6(2x + 4)$.

7 **Given:** $\triangle ABC$ with $m\angle 1 \neq m\angle 2$

Prove: $AB \neq CB$

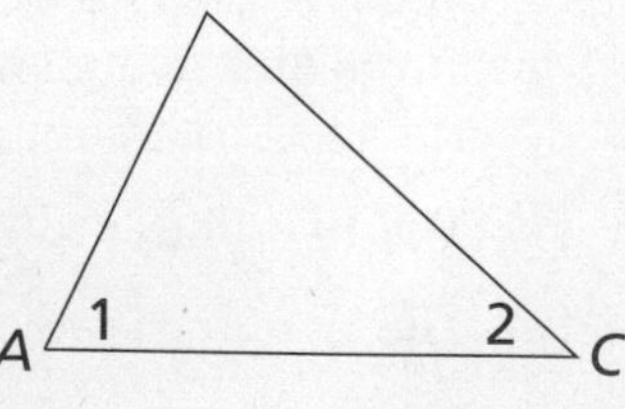

■ SOLUTION

Assume that $AB = CB$. If two sides of a triangle are equal, then the angles that are opposite those sides are equal. Therefore, $m\angle 1 = m\angle 2$. But this contradicts what is given, that $m\angle 1 \neq m\angle 2$. The assumption must be false. This means its negation is true: $AB \neq CB$.

8 **Given:** $\triangle ABC$

Prove: $\triangle ABC$ has at most one right angle.

■ SOLUTION

Assume that $\triangle ABC$ has more than one right angle. That is, assume $\angle A$ and $\angle B$ are both right angles. Then

$$m\angle A + m\angle B + m\angle C = 90^\circ + 90^\circ + m\angle C = 180^\circ + m\angle C$$

This conclusion contradicts what we were given: $\triangle ABC$. Since the sum of the measures of the interior angles of a triangle is 180°, the assumption must be false. Therefore, **$\triangle ABC$ has at most one right angle.**

Practice

Choose the numeral preceding the word or expression that best completes the statement or answers the question.

1 Which of the following can *not* be used when writing a proof?

(1) axioms

(2) definition

(3) theorems that are yet to be proven

(4) theorems that have been proven

2 Which of the following statements contradict each other?

I l and m are coplanar lines.
II l and m are parallel lines.
III l and m are intersecting lines.

(1) I and II

(2) II and III

(3) I and III

(4) None of the statements contradict each other.

3 If you wanted to prove that two lines are perpendicular using an indirect proof, what do you need to assume?

(1) The two lines are parallel.

(2) The two lines are congruent.

(3) The two lines are not perpendicular.

(4) The angle formed by the two lines is 90°.

4 If two triangles are congruent, which of the following allows you to conclude that their corresponding angles have the same measure?

(1) AAS

(2) CPCTC

(3) Reflexive Property

(4) All right angles are congruent.

For Exercises 5–10, fill in the blanks in the following flow proof.

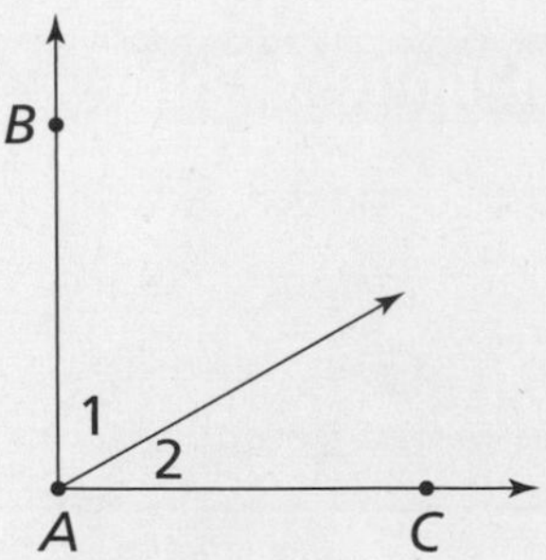

Given: $\angle 1$ and $\angle 2$ are complementary
Prove: $\overrightarrow{AB} \perp \overrightarrow{AC}$

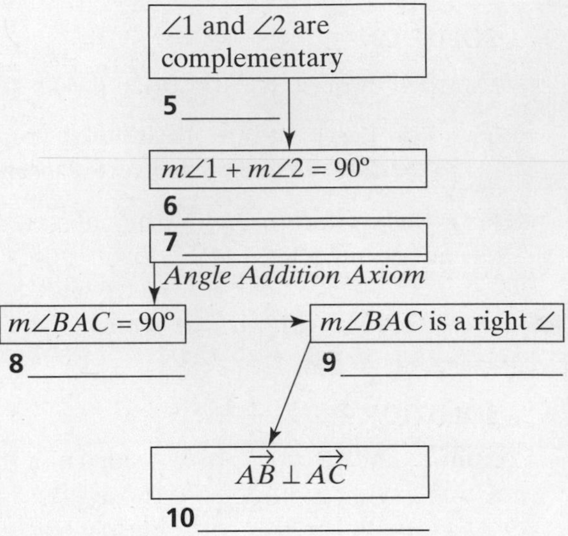

11 **Given:** $\overline{AD} \cong \overline{CE}$, $\angle DAC \cong \angle ECA$
Prove: $\triangle CED \cong \triangle ADE$

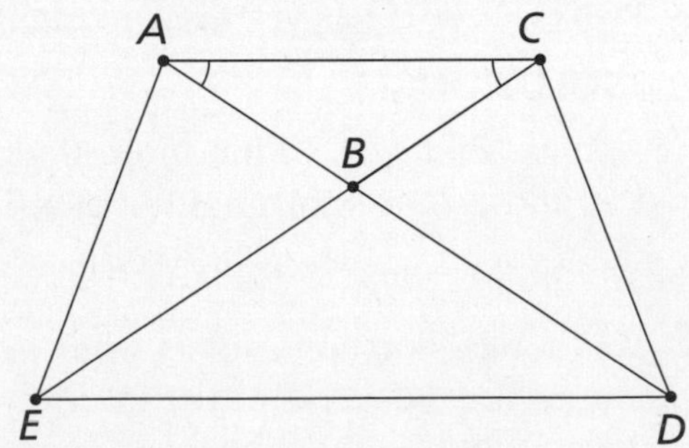

12 **Prove:** If $m\angle 1 \neq m\angle 2$, then $\angle 1$ and $\angle 2$ are not vertical angles. Hint: Use an indirect proof.

13 Complete the following proof.

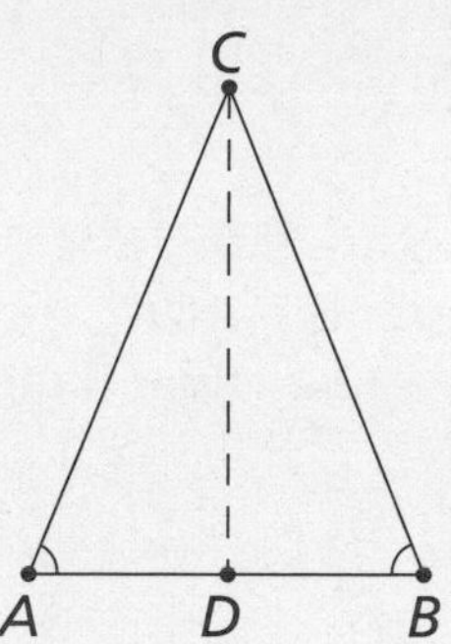

Given: $\triangle ABC$, $\angle A \cong \angle B$
Prove: $\overline{AC} \cong \overline{BC}$

Statements	Reasons
1. Construct the angle bisector of $\angle C$ and let D be the point where it intersects side AB.	1.
2. $\angle ACD \cong \angle BCD$	2.
3. $\angle A \cong \angle B$	3.
4. $\overline{CD} \cong \overline{CD}$	4.
5. $\triangle ACD \cong \triangle BCD$	5.
6. $\overline{AC} \cong \overline{BC}$	6.

14 Prove that the median drawn from the vertex of an isosceles triangle bisects the vertex angle.

15 **Given:** $\overline{AD} \cong \overline{BE}$, $\angle DAB \cong \angle EBA$
Prove: $\overline{BD} \cong \overline{AE}$

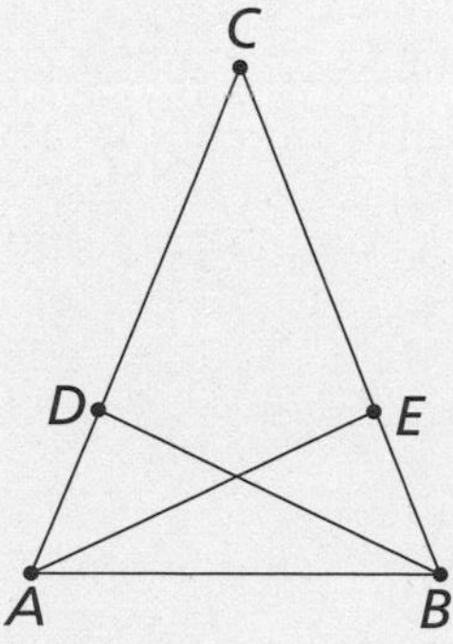

16 **Given:** $\overline{AD} \cong \overline{BE}$, $\overline{CD} \cong \overline{CE}$
Prove: $\overline{AE} \cong \overline{BD}$

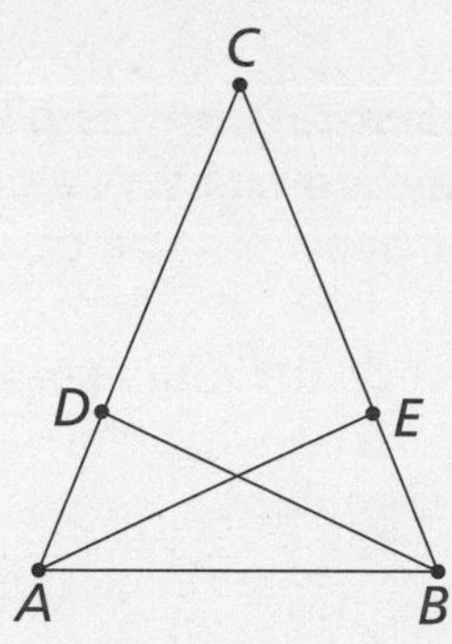

17 **Given:** $\angle 2 \cong \angle 3$, $\angle 4 \cong \angle 5$
Prove: $\overline{BA} \cong \overline{BC}$

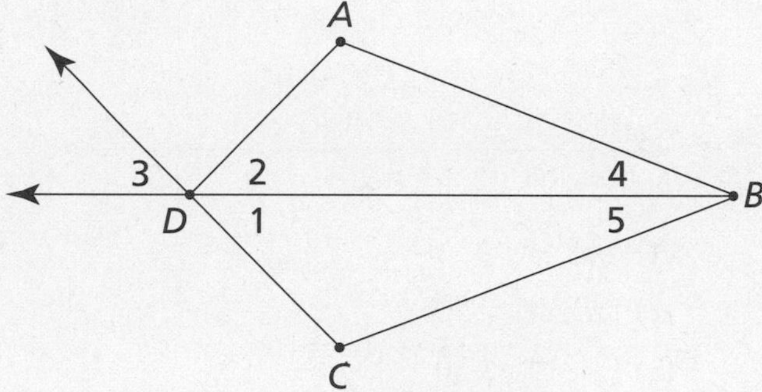

18 **Given:** $\overline{AD} \cong \overline{CD}$ and $\overline{BD}$ bisects $\angle ADC$
Prove: $\angle 2 \cong \angle 3$

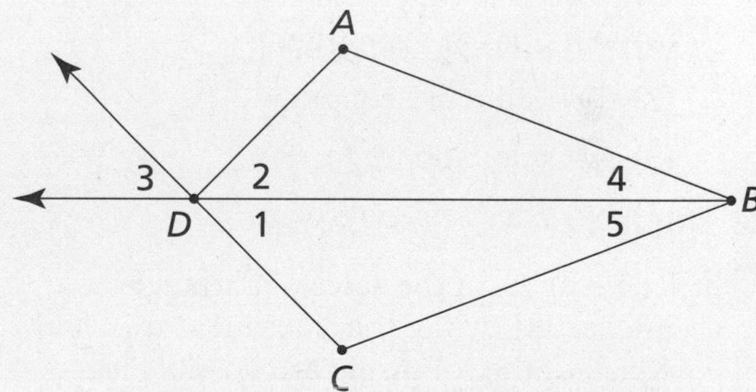

19 **Prove:** Any point on the perpendicular bisector of a line segment is equidistant from the endpoints of the segment.

20 **Prove:** The altitude drawn to the base of an isosceles triangle bisects the vertex angle.

Chapter 3 Preparing for the New York Geometry Exam

Answer all questions in this part. For each question, select the numeral preceding the word or expression that best completes the statements or answers the questions.

1 If B, C, and D are collinear, and $m\angle ACD = 50°$, what can you say about the measure of angle A?

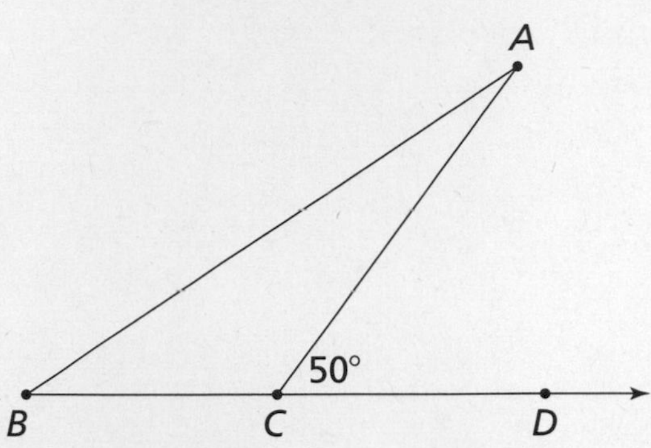

(1) $m\angle A > 50°$

(2) $m\angle A = 50°$

(3) $m\angle A < 50°$

(4) $m\angle A = 40°$

2 What is true about the sides of a scalene triangle?

(1) All sides are congruent.

(2) Two sides are congruent.

(3) All sides add up to 180°.

(4) No sides are congruent.

3 The lengths of the sides of a triangle are integers. If two of the sides measure 4 and 7, which of the following are possible lengths of the third side?

(1) 6, 7, 8, 9, 10, 11, 12

(2) 3, 4, 5, 6, 7, 8

(3) 5, 6, 7, 8

(4) 4, 5, 6, 7, 8, 9, 10

4 $\triangle ABC \cong \triangle EFD$, $\triangle EFD \cong \triangle GIH$, $m\angle A = 90°$, and $m\angle F = 20°$. What is the $m\angle H$?

(1) 20° **(3)** 90°

(2) 70° **(4)** 110°

In the following diagram, K is the midpoint of $\overline{JM}$, L is the midpoint of $\overline{JN}$, and $\overline{KL} \parallel \overline{MN}$. Use this information to answer Exercises 5 and 6.

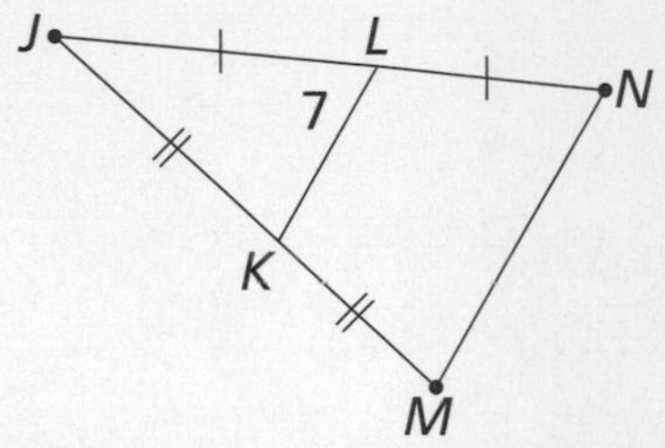

5 What is the length of $\overline{NM}$?

(1) 3.5 **(2)** 7 **(3)** 10.5 **(4)** 14

6 If the perimeter of $\triangle JMN$ is x, which of the following represents the perimeter of $\triangle JKL$?

(1) $\frac{x}{2}$ **(2)** x **(3)** $2x$ **(4)** $7x$

7 Classify $\triangle RST$.

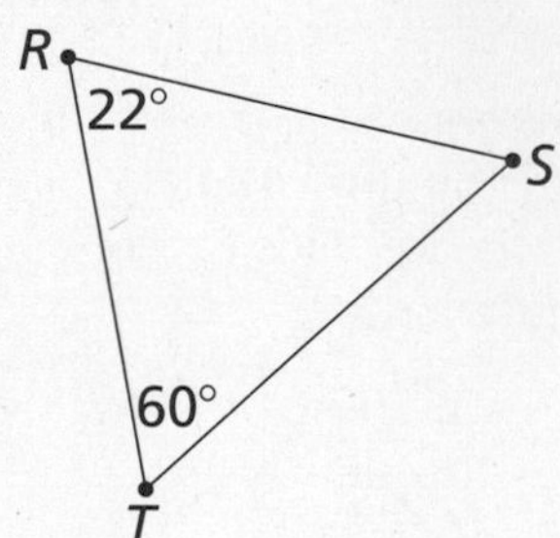

(1) isosceles **(3)** obtuse

(2) equilateral **(4)** acute

8 Using the accompanying figure, determine the value of x.

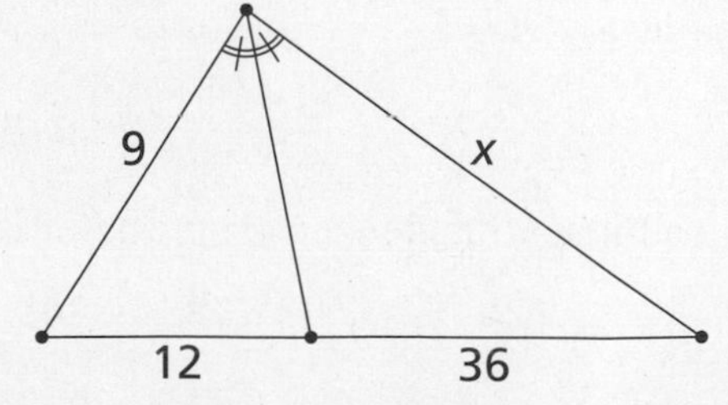

(1) 18 **(2)** 27 **(3)** 45 **(4)** 48

9 What is the value of x?

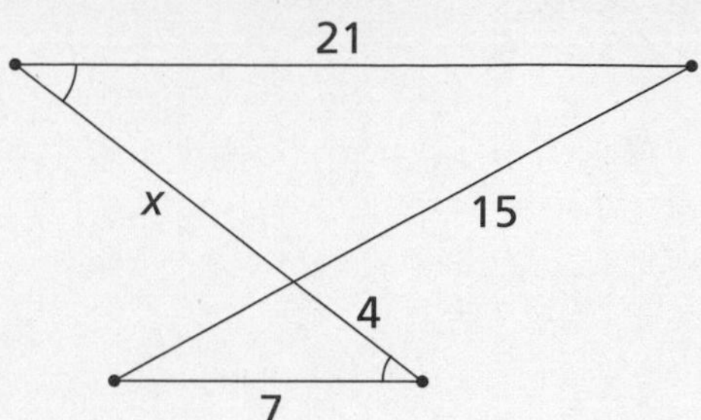

(1) 5 **(2)** 10 **(3)** 12 **(4)** 16

10 What is the value of x?

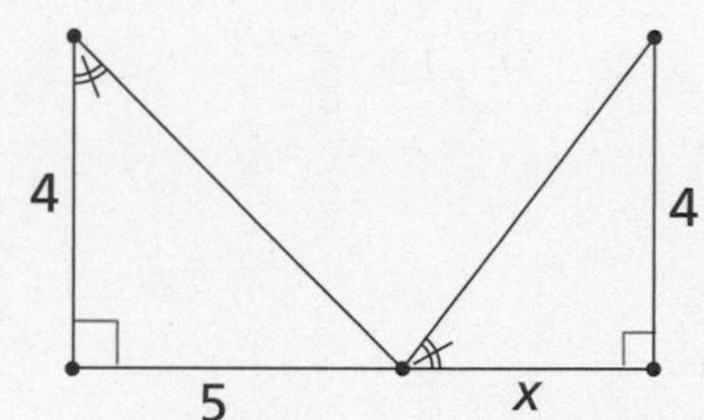

(1) 2 **(2)** $2\frac{1}{2}$ **(3)** $3\frac{1}{5}$ **(4)** 5

11 What is the value of x?

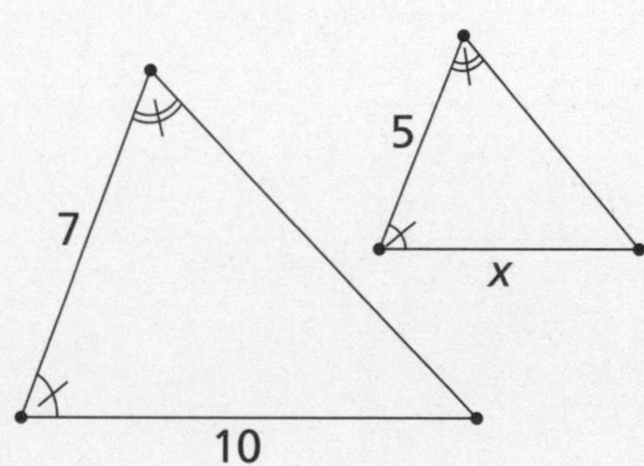

(1) 5 **(2)** 6 **(3)** $7\frac{1}{7}$ **(4)** 9

12 If the angle measures of a triangle are 60°, 60°, and 60°, what type of triangle is it?

(1) scalene **(3)** right
(2) equiangular **(4)** obtuse

13 The measures of the sides of a triangle are 4, 6, and 8. Find the measure of the shortest side of a similar triangle whose perimeter is 54.

(1) 8 **(2)** 12 **(3)** 18 **(4)** 24

14 The ratio of the sides of two similar triangles is 3:2. The smaller triangle has an altitude of 5. What is the altitude of the larger triangle?

(1) $7\frac{1}{2}$ **(2)** 10 **(3)** 12 **(4)** 15

15 Using similar triangles to measure the height of a tree is known as

(1) indirect measurement.

(2) direct measurement.

(3) proportional.

(4) similar measurement.

16 The measures of two angles of a triangle are 60° and 10°. Classify the type of triangle.

(1) acute

(2) isosceles

(3) obtuse

(4) right

17 If the side lengths of a triangle are 6 m, 3 m, and 6 m, what type of triangle is it?

(1) equilateral

(2) isosceles

(3) right

(4) scalene

18 Which is not a possible length for the third side of a triangle whose other two sides are 12 and 20?

(1) 10 **(2)** 16 **(3)** 24 **(4)** 40

19 If the angles of a triangle are $x°$, $3x°$, and 60°, what type of triangle is it?

(1) acute

(2) isosceles

(3) obtuse

(4) right

Answer all questions in this part. Clearly indicate the necessary steps, including appropriate formula substitutions, diagrams, graphs, charts, etc. For all questions in this part, a correct numerical answer with no work shown will receive only one credit.

20 **Given:** $\angle RSQ \cong \angle RQT$

Prove: $\triangle QSR \sim \triangle TQR$

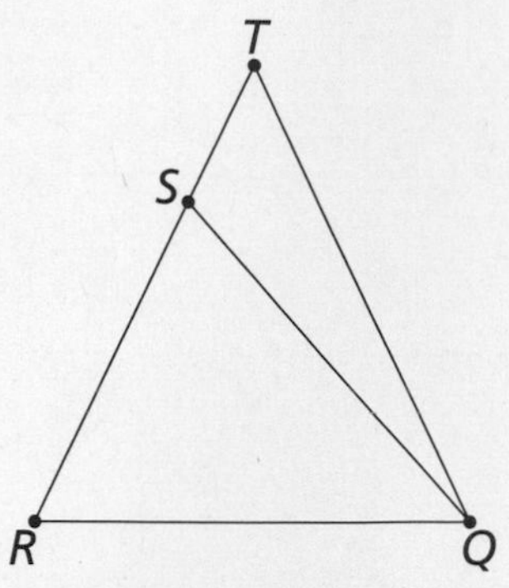

21 **Given:** $\overline{AB} \cong \overline{CB}$, $\overline{AE} \cong \overline{CD}$,

$\angle AED \cong \angle CDE$

Prove: $\triangle ABE \cong \triangle CBD$

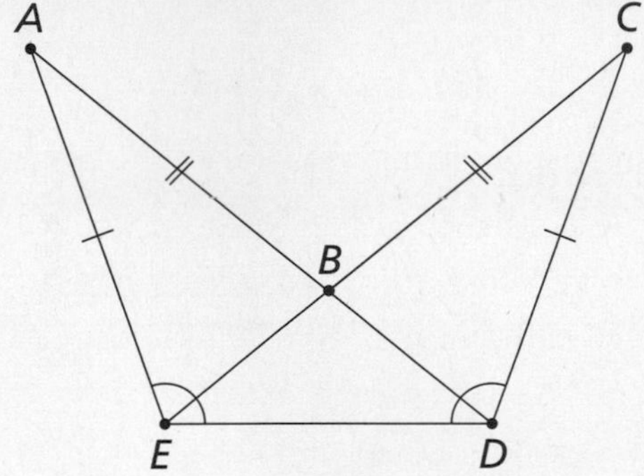

22 **Given:** $\triangle ABC$ is scalene,

$m\angle ABD = m\angle CBD = 36$.

Prove: $\overline{BD}$ is not perpendicular to $\overline{AC}$.

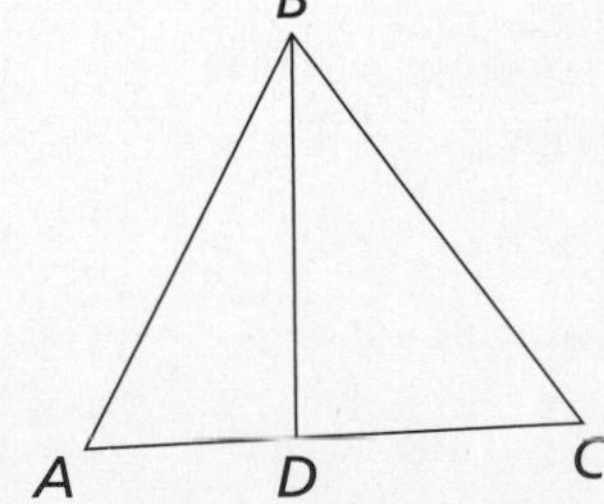

4 Relationships with Triangles

Discovering New York

West Point

New York is home to the oldest military academy in the United States, West Point. Also known as the United States Military Academy, West Point was founded in 1802. The academy's huge campus is located on the Hudson River about 50 miles north of New York City.

Admission is highly competitive. Applicants must have a letter of recommendation from a member of Congress or the Department of the Army. Students, known as "cadets," learn basic military training through a rigorous four-year program. Each year, approximately 900 students graduate from West Point as officers, making up about 25% of new lieutenants in the Army.

4.1 Midsegments in Triangles

New York Standards
G.G.42 Theorems about geometric relationships

A **midsegment of a triangle** is a segment that connects the midpoints of two sides of a triangle.

Triangle Midsegment Theorem

If a segment joins the midpoints of two sides of a triangle, then it is parallel to the third side and equal to one half its length. That is, in $\triangle ABC$ with D the midpoint of $\overline{AB}$ and E the midpoint of $\overline{AC}$, then $\overline{DE} \parallel \overline{BC}$ and $DE = \frac{1}{2}BC$.

Visit: PHSchool.com
Web Code: ayp-0402

EXAMPLE 1 Proving the Triangle Midsegment Theorem

Given: $\triangle ABC$ with D and E midpoints of $\overline{AB}$ and $\overline{AC}$, respectively.
Prove: $\overline{DE} \parallel \overline{BC}$ and $DE = \frac{1}{2}BC$

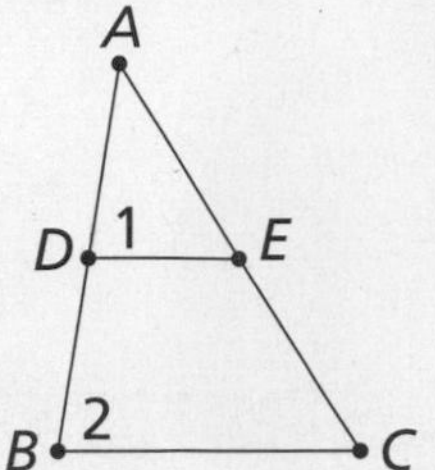

■ **SOLUTION**

Statements	Reasons
1. $\triangle ABC$ with D and E midpoints of $\overline{AB}$ and, $\overline{AC}$, respectively	1. Given
2. $\frac{AD}{AB} = \frac{AE}{AC} = \frac{1}{2}$	2. Definition of midpoint
3. $\angle A \cong \angle A$	3. Reflexive Property
4. $\triangle ABC \sim \triangle ADE$	4. SAS Similarity Theorem
5. $\angle 1 \cong \angle 2$	5. Corresponding $\angle$s of similar $\triangle$s are $\cong$.
6. $\overline{DE} \parallel \overline{BC}$	6. Two lines cut by a transversal such that corresponding $\angle$s are $\cong$ the lines are parallel.
7. $\frac{AD}{AB} = \frac{DE}{BC}$	7. Corresponding sides of similar $\triangle$s are proportional.
8. $\frac{DE}{BC} = \frac{1}{2}$	8. Substitution
9. $DE = \frac{1}{2}BC$	9. Multiplication Property of Equality

If the midpoints of the sides of a triangle are connected consecutively, another triangle is formed. This triangle is called the **medial triangle.** In the figure to the right, $\triangle DEF$ is the medial triangle of $\triangle ABC$.

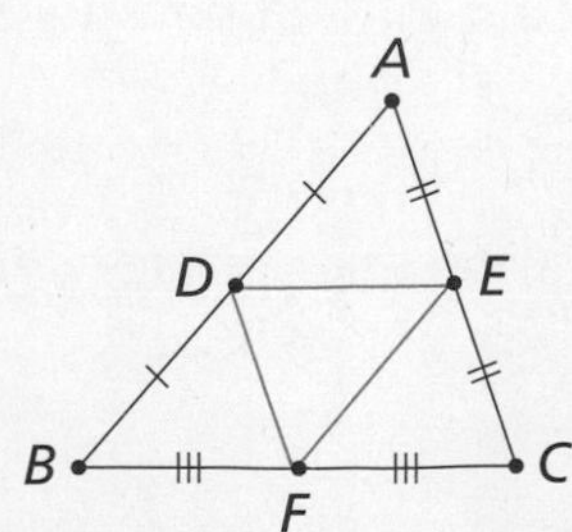

Properties of Medial Triangles

$\triangle DEF$ is the medial triangle of $\triangle DEF$. The following statements are true:

- $\triangle ADE \cong \triangle DBF \cong \triangle EFC \cong \triangle FED$
- $\triangle ABC \sim \triangle ADE \sim \triangle DBF \sim \triangle EFC \sim \triangle FED$

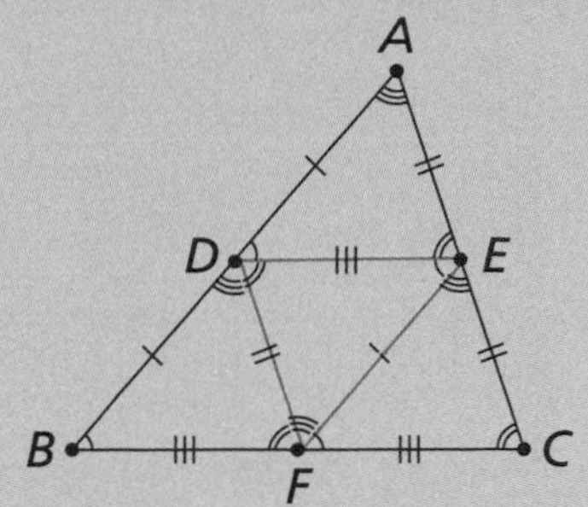

You can use the Triangle Midsegment Theorem and the properties of medial triangles to find the various measurements of triangles.

EXAMPLES 2 through 4 Working with medial triangles

2 In the accompanying figure, $\overline{DE}$, $\overline{EF}$, and $\overline{DF}$ are midsegments of $\triangle ABC$, $AB = 12$, $BC = 8$, and $DF = 5$. What are the following lengths?

$DE =$ $EF =$ $AC =$ $AE =$

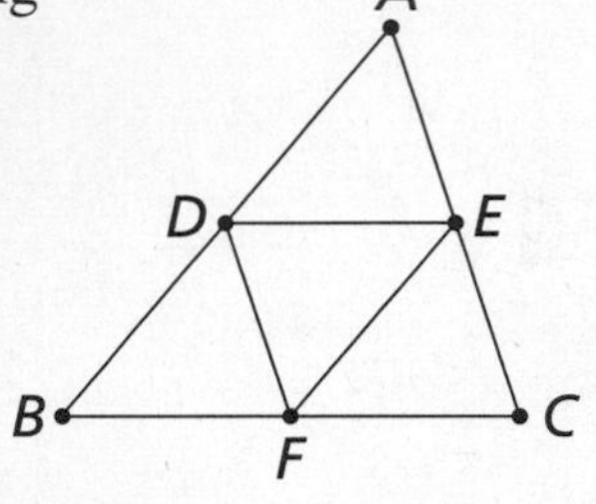

■ SOLUTION

$DE = 4$ $EF = 6$ $AC = 10$ $AE = 5$

3 Determine the ratio of the areas of $\triangle ADE$ to $\triangle ABC$.

■ SOLUTION

Because the four small triangles are all congruent, their areas are equal. Therefore, the area of $\triangle ADE$ is $\frac{1}{4}$ the area of $\triangle ABC$.

4 In the accompanying figure, $\overline{MN}$ and $\overline{PN}$ are midsegments. If $RS = 14$, $NT = 8$, and $PN = 10$, find MN and RT and the perimeter of the medial triangle.

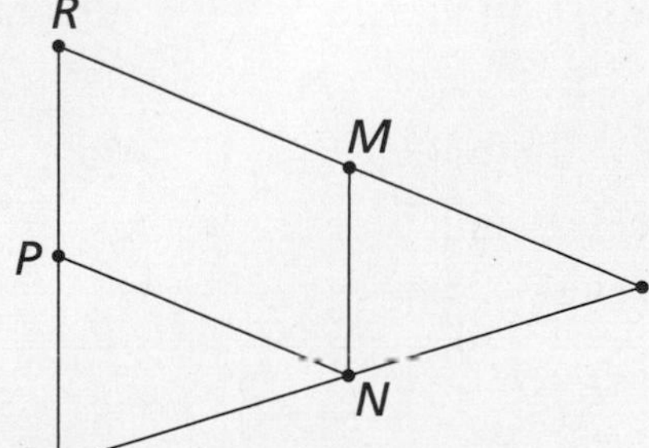

■ SOLUTION

$MN = \frac{1}{2}RS = \frac{1}{2}(14) = 7$

$RT = 2(PN) = 2(10) = 20$

$PM = NT = 8$

Perimeter $PMN = PN + NM + MP$
$= 10 + 7 + 8 = 25$

The above examples illustrate some two properties of medial triangles. If $\triangle DEF$ is the medial triangle of $\triangle ABC$, then the perimeter $\triangle DEF$ is one-half the perimeter of $\triangle ABC$ and the area of $\triangle DEF$ is one-quarter the area of $\triangle ABC$.

Practice

Choose the numeral preceding the word or expression that best completes the statement or answers the question.

1 What triangle is formed by joining the midpoints of the sides of a triangle?

(1) middle triangle

(2) average triangle

(3) medial triangle

(4) center triangle

2 In the accompanying diagram $\overline{JK}$ is a midsegment of $\triangle MNO$. What is true about $\overline{JK}$?

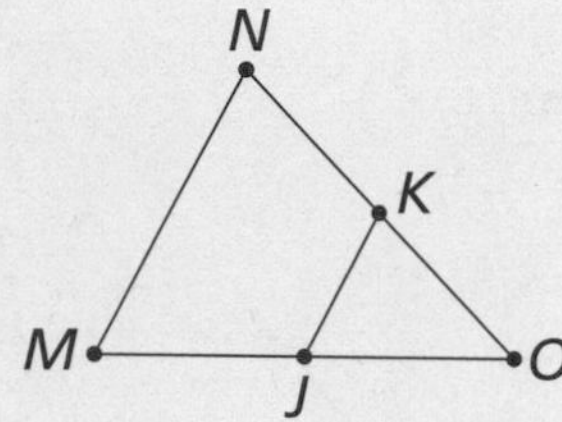

(1) $\overline{JK} \perp \overline{NO}$

(2) $JK = JO$

(3) $JK = 0.5NO$

(4) $\overline{JK} \parallel \overline{MN}$

3 If the area of a triangle $\triangle HIJ$ is 40 unit^2, what is the area of the medial triangle of $\triangle HIJ$?

(1) 10 unit^2

(2) 20 unit^2

(3) 80 unit^2

(4) 160 unit^2

4 How many congruent triangles are formed when you create a medial triangle?

(1) 1 **(2)** 2 **(3)** 4 **(4)** 5

Use the following figure to answer Exercises 5 and 6.

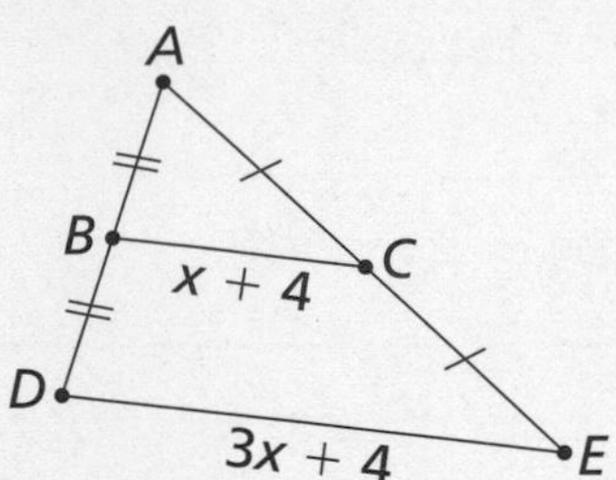

5 What is the value of x?

(1) 2 **(2)** 6 **(3)** 4 **(4)** 8

6 What is the perimeter of $\triangle ADE$ if the perimeter of $\triangle ABC$ is 28?

(1) 14 **(2)** 32 **(3)** 28 **(4)** 56

7 What is the ratio of the area of $\triangle RST$ to $\triangle ABC$ knowing that $\triangle JKL$ and $\triangle RST$ are medial triangles?

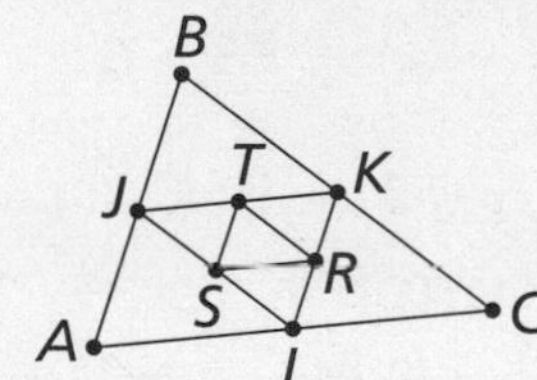

(1) $\frac{1}{2}$ **(2)** $\frac{1}{3}$ **(3)** $\frac{1}{4}$ **(4)** $\frac{1}{16}$

8 The top of a 10-ft pole is halfway between you and a tree. How tall is the tree shown in the diagram?

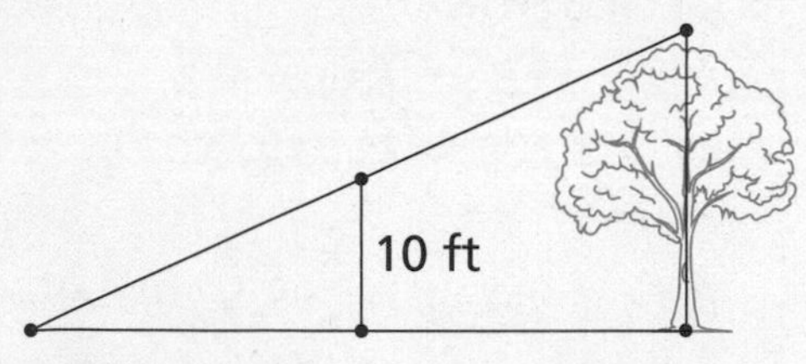

(1) 10 ft **(2)** 20 ft **(3)** 30 ft **(4)** 40 ft

9 In the accompanying diagram, D, E, and F are midpoints of sides $\overline{AC}$, $\overline{AB}$, and $\overline{CB}$, respectively. Name three pairs of parallel segments.

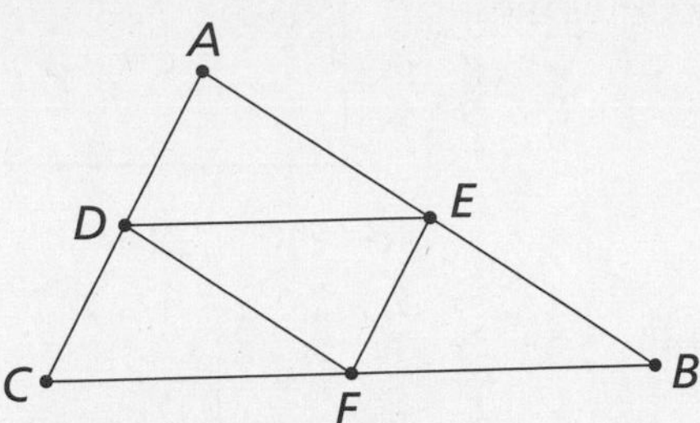

10 In $\triangle HIJ$, M is the midpoint of $\overline{HI}$ and N is the midpoint of $\overline{IJ}$. If $MN = 5x + 3$ and $HJ = 4x + 18$, what is the value of x?

11 In the figure below, each medial triangle was shaded. If the sum of the perimeter of the original triangle is 1, what is the perimeter of all the shaded triangles in the figure?

12 The midsegment of a triangle is represented by $3x + 7$. The third side of the original triangle is parallel to the midsegment represented by $7x + 6$. Determine the length of this midsegment.

13 **Given:** $\triangle DEF$ is a medial triangle of $\triangle ABC$.
Prove: $\triangle DEF \cong \triangle ADE$.

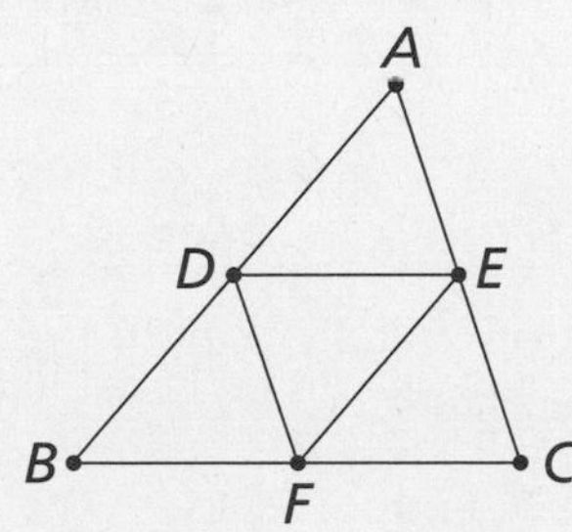

Use the accompanying figure for Exercises 14–16. In the figure, *J* and *K* are midpoints.

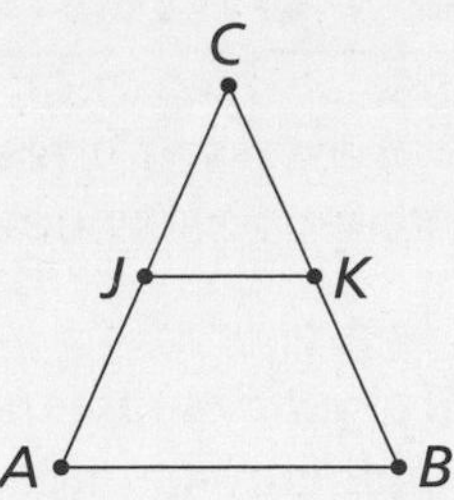

14 **Given:** Isosceles $\triangle ABC$ with $\overline{AC} \cong \overline{BC}$, and midsegment $\overline{JK}$
Prove: $\triangle CJK$ is isosceles.

15 If $\overline{JK}$ is 7 inches long and $AC = BC = 20$ in., what is the perimeter of $\triangle CJK$?

16 If $m\angle AJK = 113°$, what is $m\angle ABC$?

Use the accompanying figure for Exercises 17–21. In the figure *S, T,* and *U* are midpoints.

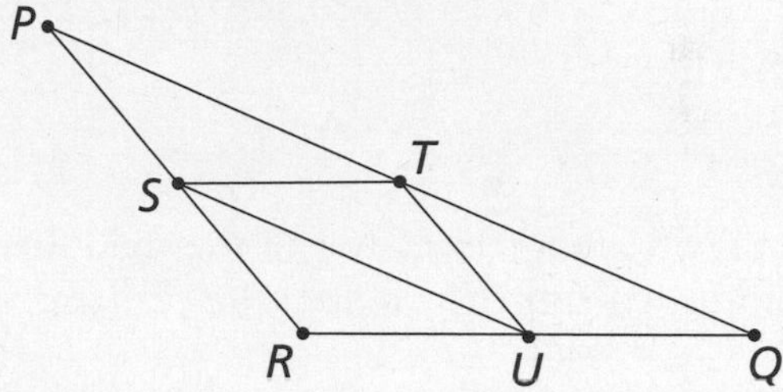

17 If $PR = 10$ and $RQ = 17$, find $TU + ST$.

18 Find the perimeter of $\triangle TSU$ given the following values. $PR = 8$, $RQ = 12$, and $PQ = 18$

19 If $PS = 3x + 5$ and $TU = 21 + x$, find SR.

20 If $RU = x^2$ and $ST = 6x + 16$, find UQ.

21 If $PR = z^2$ and $TU = 10(z - 5)$, find PR and TU.

22 The segment joining the midpoints of two adjacent sides of a rectangle is 55 in. Determine the length of the diagonal of the rectangle.

4.2 Special Segments, Lines, and Points

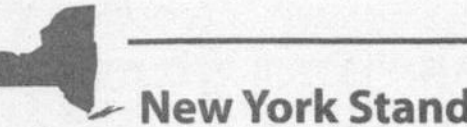

New York Standards

G.G.21 Triangle concurrence theorems

G.G.43 Theorems about centroid of a triangle

When three or more lines intersect at a unique point, we say the lines are **concurrent.** The point at which they intersect is called the **point of concurrency.**

The point of concurrency of the perpendicular bisectors of each side of the triangle is equidistant from the three vertices of the triangle. This point is the center of a circle that passes through the three vertices of the triangle. This point of concurrency is called the **circumcenter** of the triangle and labeled *O*.

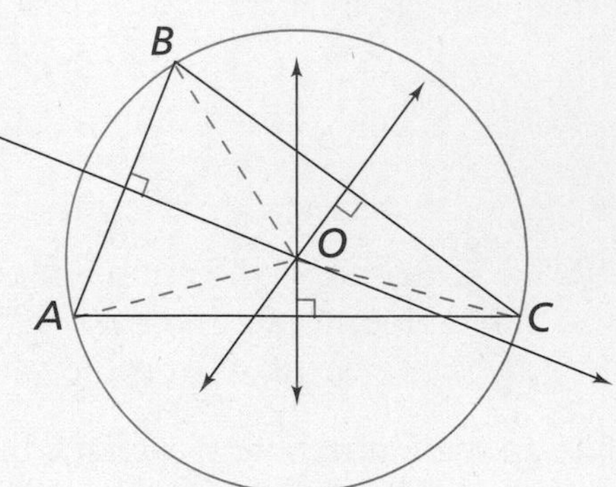

$BO = AO = CD$

The 3 angle bisectors of a triangle are also concurrent. Their point of concurrency is called the **incenter** of the triangle. The incenter is also the center of the circle inscribed in the triangle. The incenter is labeled *I*.

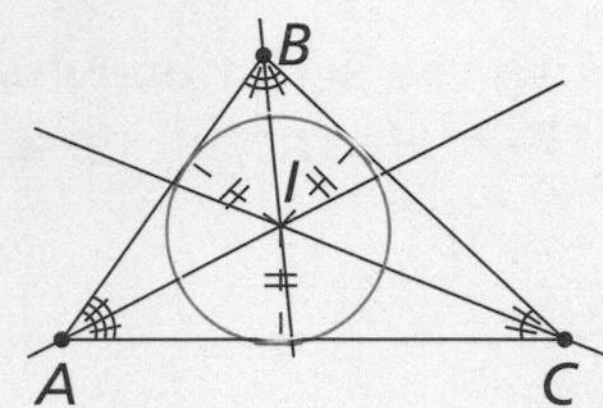

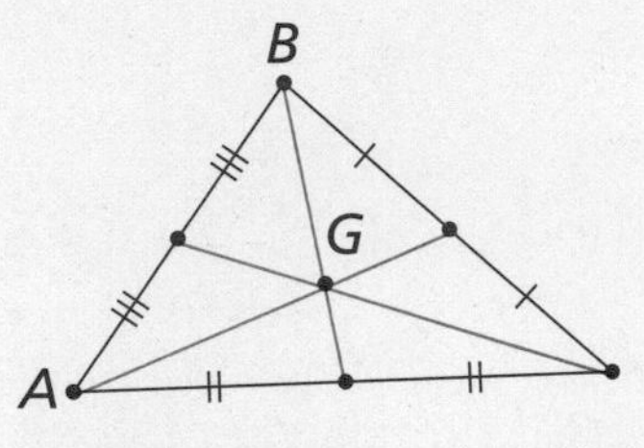

The point of concurrency for all the medians in a triangle is called the **centroid,** or **center of gravity.** The centroid is labeled *G*.

The three altitudes of a triangle are concurrent. This point of concurrency is called the **orthocenter** and labeled *H*.

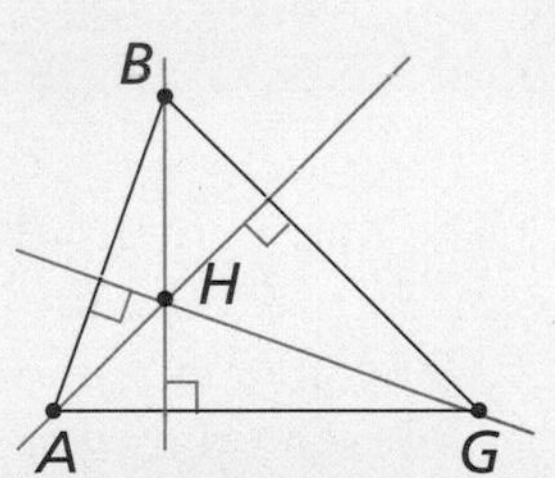

Summary of the Centers of a Triangle

Circumcenter (O)	Center of the circumscribed circle	Point of concurrency of the perpendicular bisectors of the sides of a triangle.
Incenter (I)	Center of the inscribed circle	Point of concurrency of the angle bisectors of the triangle.
Centroid (G)	Center of gravity or balancing point	Point of concurrency of the medians of the triangle.
Orthocenter (H)		Point of concurrency of the altitudes of the triangle.

If you construct the four centers of a triangle using interactive geometry software, you should make some interesting observations. If the triangle is isosceles, all four centers are collinear. In an equilateral triangle, the four centers are all the same point.

These centers do not always fall inside the triangle, as shown below.

Acute Triangle	**Obtuse Triangle**	**Right Triangle**
Four centers interior	Two interior, two exterior	Two interior, two on the triangle

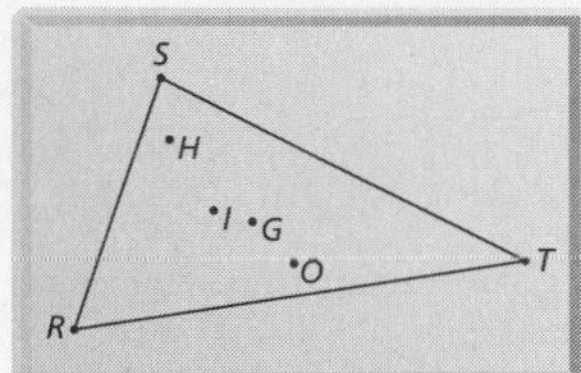

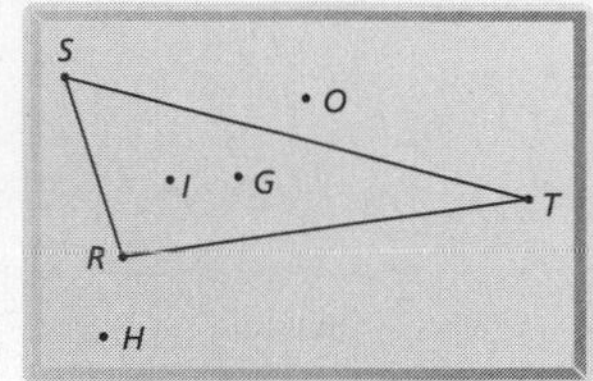

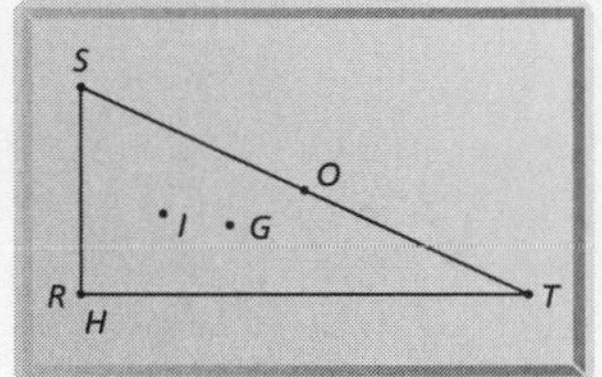

The line passing through the orthocenter, the centroid, and the circumcenter is called the **Euler line.**

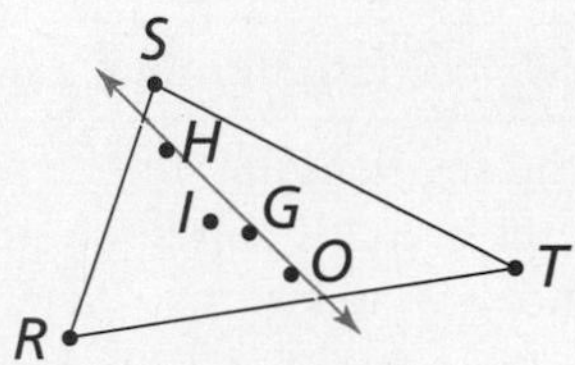

EXAMPLE 1 Proving the concurrency of the altitudes of a triangle

Given: $\triangle ABC$ with altitudes $\overline{BD}$, $\overline{AE}$, and $\overline{CF}$

Prove: The altitudes are concurrent.

SOLUTION

Draw a line that is parallel to side $\overline{AD}$ of the triangle and passes through the vertex opposite $\overline{AD}$. Repeat this construction for the remaining two sides of the triangle. These lines intersect at the points R, S, and T. $\overline{TB} \parallel \overline{AC}$ and $\overline{TA} \parallel \overline{BC}$. The quadrilateral $TBCA$ is a parallelogram. Similarly, the quadrilateral $ABRC$ is a parallelogram. Because opposite sides of a parallelogram are congruent, $TB = AC$ and $BR = AC$. By substitution, $TB = BR$.

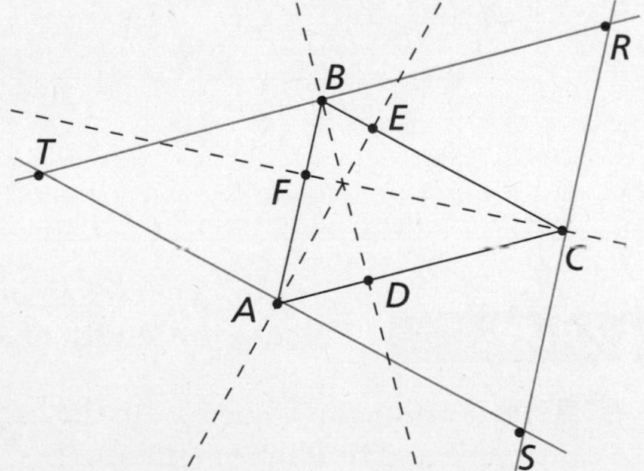

By the definition of midpoint, B is the midpoint of $\overline{TR}$. $\overline{BD} \perp \overline{TR}$ because a line perpendicular to one parallel line is perpendicular to the other. So $\overline{BD}$ is the perpendicular bisector of $\overline{TR}$. Likewise, $\overline{FC}$ is the perpendicular bisector of $\overline{RS}$, and $\overline{AE}$ is the perpendicular bisector of $\overline{TS}$. Therefore, the **altitudes of $\triangle ABC$ are the perpendicular bisectors of the sides of $\triangle TRS$,** which we know are concurrent.

The Median Measure Theorem

The centroid is located $\frac{2}{3}$ of the distance from the vertex to the opposite side and divides the median into segments whose lengths are in the ratio of 2:1.

EXAMPLE 2 **Proving the Median Measure Theorem**

Given: $\triangle ABC$ with medians BN and AM

Prove: $\frac{BG}{GN} = \frac{2}{1}$

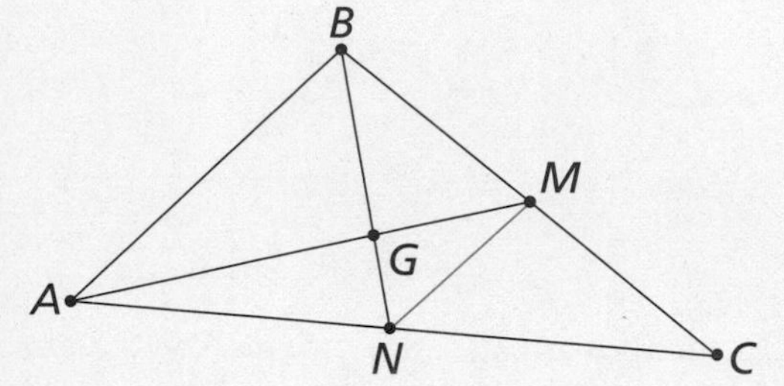

■ **SOLUTION**

Statements	Reasons
1. $\triangle ABC$ with medians $\overline{BN}$ and $\overline{AM}$	1. Given
2. Draw NM	2. Two points determine a line segment.
3. $NM \parallel AB$ and $NM = \frac{1}{2}AB$	3. The segment joining the midpoints of two sides of a $\triangle$ is parallel to the third side and $\frac{1}{2}$ its measure.
4. $\frac{AB}{MN} = \frac{2}{1}$	4. By algebra
5. $\angle AMN = \angle MAB$ and $\angle MNB = \angle ABN$	5. If two parallel lines cut by a transversal, the alternate interior $\angle$s are =.
6. $\triangle GMN \sim \triangle GAB$	6. AA
7. $\frac{BG}{GN} = \frac{AB}{MN}$	7. Corresponding sides of $\sim\triangle$s are proportional.
8. $\frac{BG}{GN} = \frac{2}{1}$	8. Substitution

You can apply the Median Measure Theorem to find missing lengths of triangles.

EXAMPLE 3 **Finding the length of a side**

Determine the value of x in the accompanying figure and find the length of BD.

■ **SOLUTION**

$BF = 2FD$

$BF = 2(7) = 14$

$BD = 14 + 7 = 21$

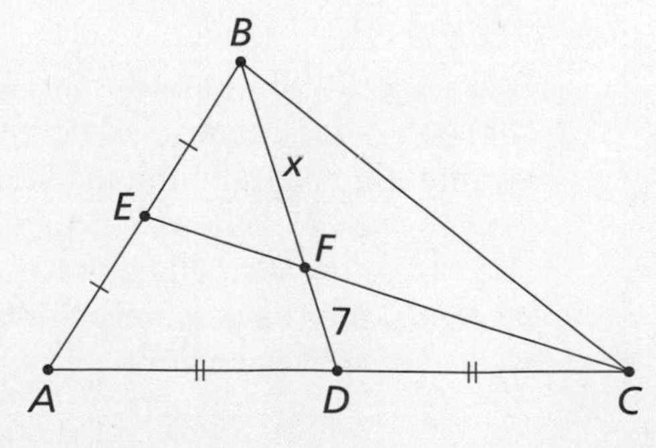

Practice

Choose the numeral preceding the word or expression that best completes the statement or answers the question.

1 Which triangle center is *never* outside the triangle?

(1) orthocenter only

(2) incenter only

(3) both orthocenter and circumcenter

(4) both incenter and centroid

2 In a right triangle, which center is the midpoint of the hypotenuse?

(1) orthocenter **(3)** incenter

(2) circumcenter **(4)** centroid

3 In the accompanying diagram $\overline{RN}$ and $\overline{TM}$ are medians of $\triangle RST$. If $TM = 12z^2 - 9k$, which expression represents TW?

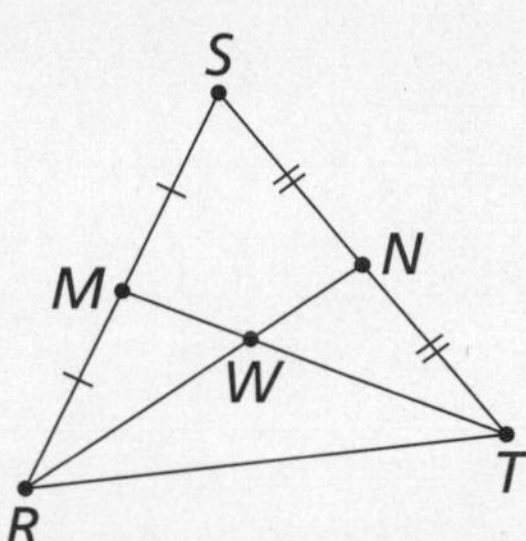

(1) $4z^2 - 3k$ **(3)** $6z^2 - 3k$

(2) $4z^2 - 9k$ **(4)** $8z^2 - 6k$

4 $\overline{AK}$ is a median of a triangle. The length of $\overline{AK}$ is 15. What is the distance from the vertex A to the centroid?

(1) 5 **(2)** 10 **(3)** 15 **(4)** 30

5 In $\triangle ABC$, $\overline{AM}$, $\overline{BN}$, and $\overline{CW}$ are medians with a point of intersection P. If $AM = 12$, what is the length of PM?

(1) 4 **(2)** 8 **(3)** 12 **(4)** 16

Use the accompanying figure to answer Exercises 6–11. In $\triangle RST$, M and N are midpoints.

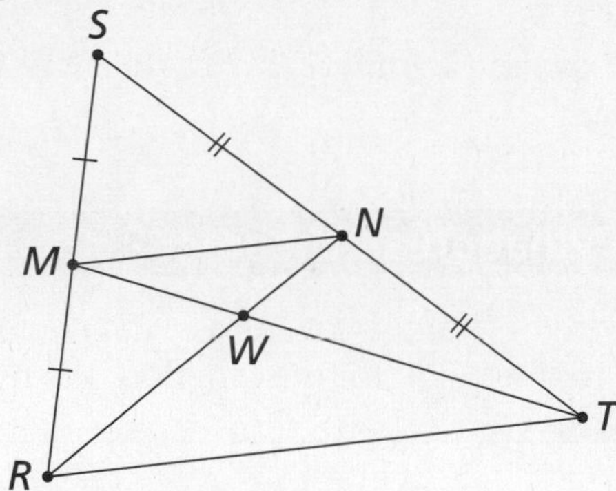

6 If $MN = 3x + 4$ and $RT = 8x - 15$, determine the value of x.

7 Prove $\triangle MNW \sim \triangle TRW$

8 If a line is drawn through S and W, where will it cut $\overline{RT}$? Explain your answer.

9 If $WN = 5$, determine WR.

10 If $MT = 18$, determine WT.

11 What is point W called?

12 Use a compass and straight edge to circumscribe a circle around $\triangle ABC$.

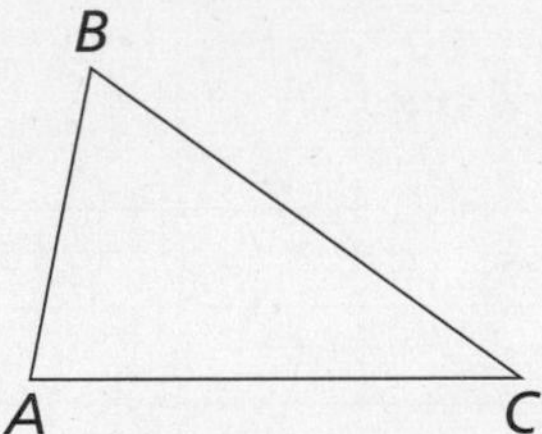

13 Draw a triangle on a piece of paper. Construct an equilateral triangle on each side of the triangle. Connect each vertex of the original triangle to the vertex of the equilateral triangle constructed on the opposite side with a segment. What do you notice about these three segments?

4.3 Pythagorean Theorem and Its Converse

New York Standards
G.G.48 Pythagorean Theorem

The figure shown is a right triangle with sides a, b, and c. The side opposite the right angle, called the **hypotenuse,** is the longest side. Each of the sides, a and b, that form the right angle, is called a **leg** of the right triangle.

You can use the Pythagorean Theorem to find an unknown side length of a right triangle.

The Pythagorean Theorem

In any right triangle, the sum of the squares of the lengths of the legs is equal to the square of the length of the hypotenuse. That is, $a^2 + b^2 = c^2$.

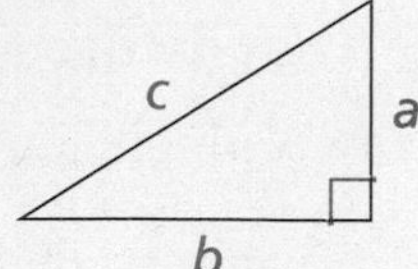

Two different proofs are presented below.

EXAMPLES 1 and 2 Proving the Pythagorean Theorem

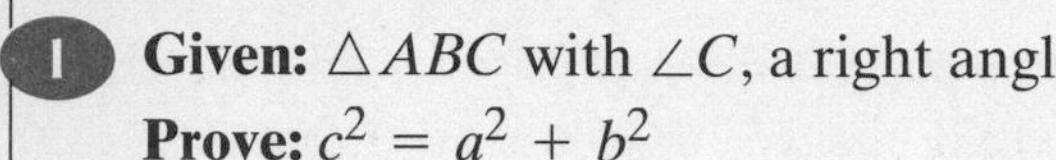

1 **Given:** $\triangle ABC$ with $\angle C$, a right angle
Prove: $c^2 = a^2 + b^2$

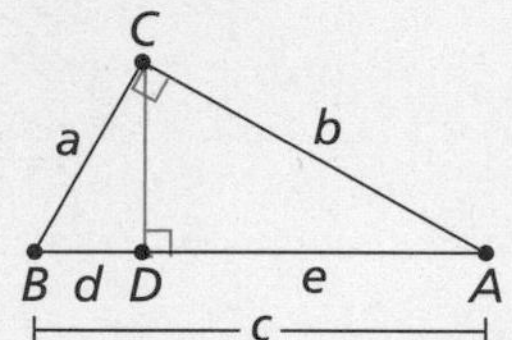

■ **SOLUTION**

Statements	Reasons
1. Construct a perpendicular from C to $\overline{AB}$	1. By construction
2. $\frac{c}{a} = \frac{a}{d}$ and $\frac{c}{b} = \frac{b}{e}$	2. In a right triangle, the leg is the mean proportional between the hypotenuse and the segment of the hypotenuse connected to the leg.
3. $a^2 = cd$ and $b^2 = ce$	3. Product of the means equals the product of the extremes.
4. $cd + ce = a^2 + b^2$	4. Addition Property of Equality
5. $c(d + e) = a^2 + b^2$	5. Distributive Property
6. $c = d + e$	6. Segment addition axiom
7. $c^2 = a^2 + b^2$	7. Substitution

2 Explain how the accompanying figure could be used to prove the Pythagorean Theorem.

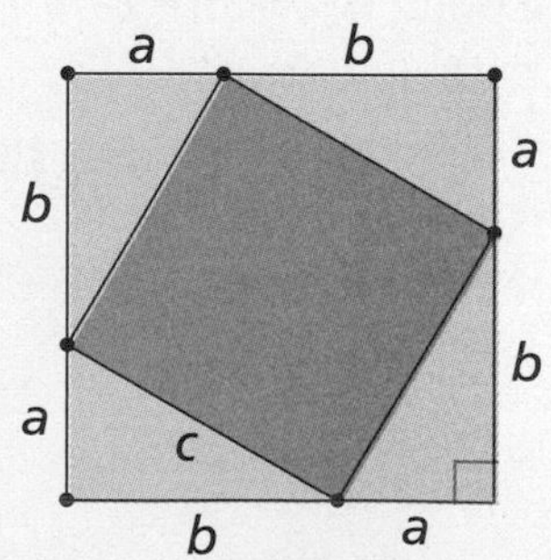

■ **SOLUTION**

The area of the large square is $(a + b)^2$. This area is also the area of the four triangles plus the area of the inner square or $4\left(\frac{1}{2}ab\right) + c^2$. This leads to $a^2 + 2ab + b^2 = 2ab + c^2$. Subtracting $2ab$ from both sides yields $a^2 + b^2 = c^2$.

EXAMPLES 3 and 4 Finding lengths of sides in a right triangle by using the Pythagorean Theorem

3 Find n in the right triangle below.

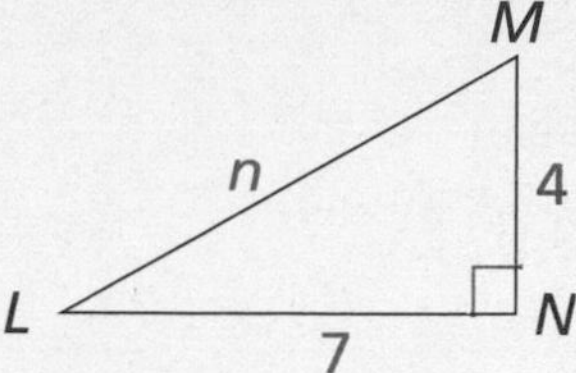

■ **SOLUTION**

The unknown n is the length of the hypotenuse.

$n^2 = 7^2 + 4^2$

$n^2 = 65$

$n = \pm\sqrt{65} \approx \pm 8.06$

$n = \sqrt{65}$ units, or about 8.06 units

4 Find z in the right triangle below.

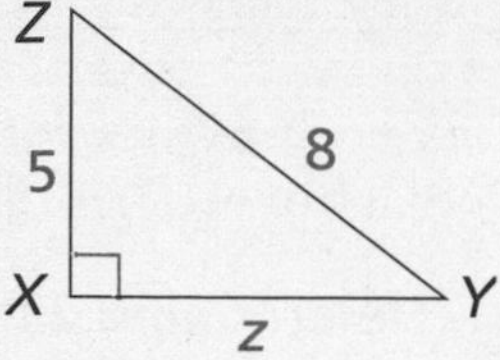

■ **SOLUTION**

The unknown z is the length of a leg.

$8^2 = z^2 + 5^2$

$39 = z^2$

$z = \pm\sqrt{39} \approx \pm 6.24$

$z = \sqrt{39}$ units, or about 6.24 units

If the lengths of all three sides of a right triangle are counting numbers, they form a **Pythagorean Triple.** The following are some examples of side lengths that form Pythagorean Triples.

a) 3, 4, 5 b) 5, 12, 13 c) 8, 15, 17 d) 7, 24, 25

EXAMPLE 5 Proving Pythagorean Triples

5 Determine if 3, 4, 5 and 4, 6, 8 are sets of Pythagorean Triples.

■ **SOLUTION**

Apply the Pythagorean Theorem to each set of numbers and determine if the resulting equation is true.

$3^2 + 4^2 = 5^2$	$4^2 + 6^2 = 8^2$
$9 + 16 = 25$	$16 + 36 = 64$
$25 = 25$	$52 = 64$
True	**False**

3, 4, 5 are Pythagorean Triples; 4, 6, and 8 are not.

Multiples of Pythagorean Triples are also Pythagorean Triples.

EXAMPLE 6 Using Pythagorean Triples ratios

6 Find the hypotenuse of a right triangle whose legs are 60 and 144.

■ **SOLUTION**

$\frac{60}{144} = \frac{12(5)}{12(12)} = \frac{5}{12}$ **60 and 144 are in the ratio of 5 to 12.**

Therefore, the hypotenuse = 12(13) or 156.

The Converse of the Pythagorean Theorem

If a, b, and c are the lengths of the sides of a triangle such that $a^2 + b^2 = c^2$, then the triangle is a right triangle with hypotenuse of length c.

Since the hypotenuse is always the longest side of a right triangle, you can use the Converse of the Pythagorean Theorem to find out if a triangle is a right triangle.

EXAMPLE 7 **Determining if three positive numbers determine a right triangle**

7 Do 5, 12, and 14 determine a right triangle?

■ **SOLUTION**

Since the hypotenuse of a right triangle must be the longest side, check to see if $5^2 + 12^2$ equals 14^2.

$$5^2 + 12^2 = 169 \qquad 14^2 = 196$$

Since $169 \neq 196$, these numbers **do not determine a right triangle.**

The next example shows how you can use the Pythagorean Theorem to solve problems.

EXAMPLE 8 **Solving problems involving the Pythagorean Theorem**

8 A ladder is placed against the side of a building. To climb the ladder safely, the ladder must be placed against the building at a height that is three times the distance from the foot of the ladder to the base of the building. To the nearest tenth of a foot, how far from the base of a building should the foot of a 24-foot ladder be placed to meet safety recommendations?

■ **SOLUTION**

Step 1 Draw a sketch. Let x represent the distance from the foot of the ladder to the base of the building.

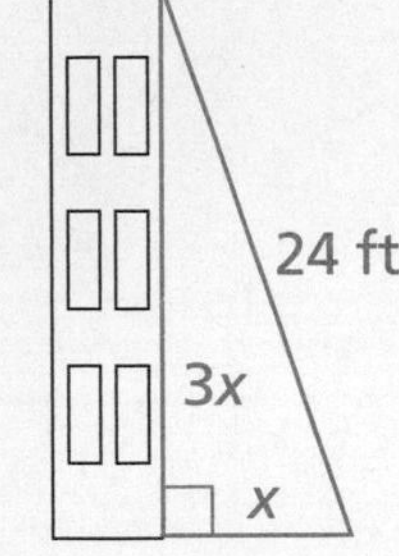

Step 2 Use the Pythagorean Theorem to solve for x.

$$x^2 + (3x)^2 = 24^2$$
$$10x^2 = 576$$
$$x^2 = 57.6$$
$$x = \sqrt{57.6} \approx 7.6$$

The foot of the ladder should be placed about 7.6 feet from the base of the building.

To apply the Pythagorean Theorem, you must know the lengths of two sides of a right triangle. However, if you are given only the length of one side of a right triangle, you can find the other side by knowing the values of its complementary angles.

Certain right triangles have special properties that make it easier to find the length of a side. You can use formulas based on these special properties to find the leg and hypotenuse of triangles with angle measures 45°-45°-90° and 30°-60°-90°.

An isosceles right triangle with each base angle of 45° is called a 45°-45°-90° triangle. Since both of its base angles are congruent, both of its legs are also congruent.

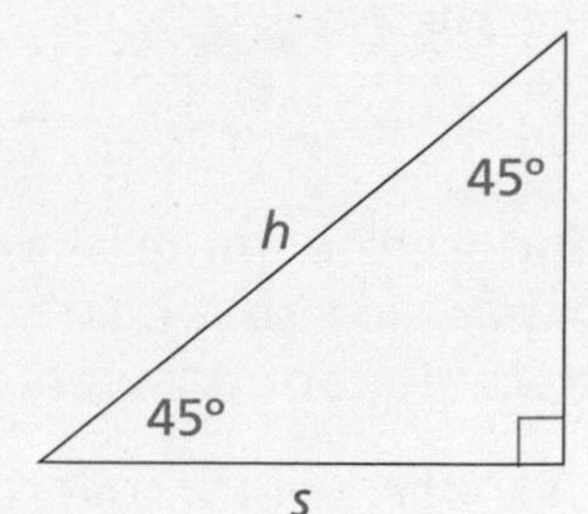

Let each leg $= s$.

Then $h^2 = s^2 + s^2$

$$h^2 = 2s^2$$

$$\sqrt{h^2} = \sqrt{2s^2}$$

$$h = s\sqrt{2}$$

In a 45°-45°-90° triangle, the length of the hypotenuse is the length of the leg times $\sqrt{2}$. **Hypotenuse = leg** $\cdot \sqrt{2}$; $h = s \cdot \sqrt{2}$. If you know the hypotenuse, solving for s gives $s = \frac{1}{2}h\sqrt{2}$.

EXAMPLE 9 **Finding lengths in a 45°-45°-90° triangle**

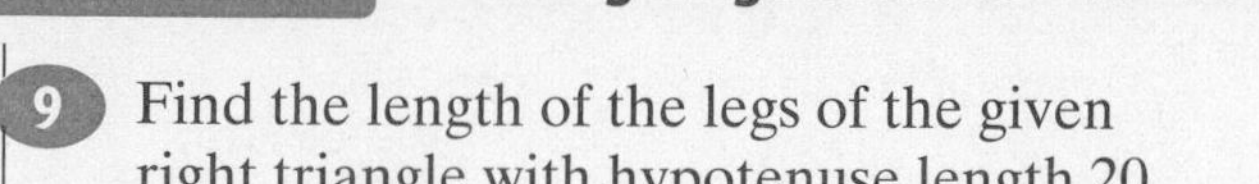

9 Find the length of the legs of the given right triangle with hypotenuse length 20.

▪ **SOLUTION**

Since $s = \frac{1}{2}h\sqrt{2}$, then $s = \frac{20}{2}\sqrt{2} = 10\sqrt{2} \approx 14.1$.

An easy way to work with a 30°-60°-90° right triangle is to make it a part of an equilateral triangle with sides $2x$ and altitude a. The altitude a bisects the vertex angle and the base. Therefore, the side opposite the 30° angle $= \frac{1}{2}(2x) = x$. The length of the hypotenuse is twice the length of the side opposite the 30° angle (the shorter side): $h = 2x$. The length of the side opposite the 60° angle (the longer side) is $\sqrt{3}$ times the length of the side opposite the 30° angle: $a = x\sqrt{3}$.

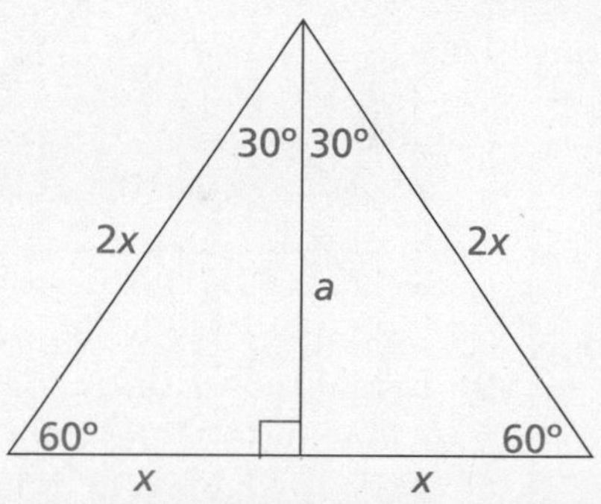

EXAMPLE 10 **Finding lengths in a 30°-60°-90° triangle**

10 Find the missing lengths in the given right triangle with hypotenuse 14 units.

▪ **SOLUTION**

x = length of shorter leg $= \frac{1}{2}h$

$x = \frac{1}{2}(14) = 7$

y = length of longer leg = length of shorter leg $\sqrt{3}$

$y = 7\sqrt{3} \approx 12.1$ units

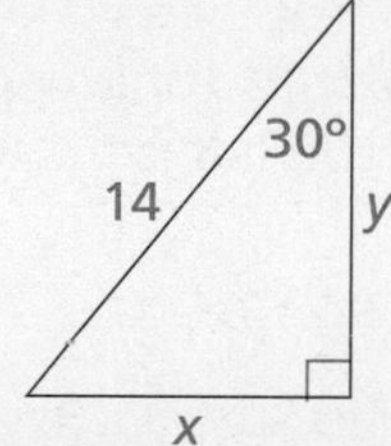

Right Triangle Theorems

45°-45°-90° Triangles

The hypotenuse of a 45°-45°-90° triangle with side length s and hypotenuse h is given by $h = s\sqrt{2}$.

30°-60°-90° Triangles

The side opposite the 30° angle (the shorter side) $= \frac{1}{2}$ hypotenuse, or the hypotenuse = 2 times the shorter leg. The side opposite the 60° angle is $\frac{1}{2}$ hypotenuse times $\sqrt{3}$, or the longer leg = shorter leg times $\sqrt{3}$.

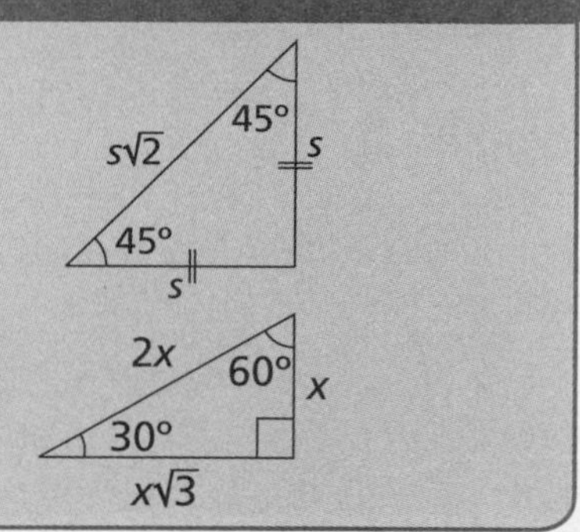

Practice

Choose the numeral preceding the word or expression that best completes the statement or answers the question.

1 Which of the following is the measure of the side of a square whose diagonal is 14?

(1) 7 **(2)** $7\sqrt{2}$ **(3)** $7\sqrt{3}$ **(4)** 14

2 Which of the following is not a Pythagorean Triple?

(1) 15, 20, 25 **(3)** 5, 12, 13
(2) 7, 24, 25 **(4)** 12, 16, 30

3 The distance from home plate to first base on a baseball field is 90 feet. How far is it from home plate to second base?

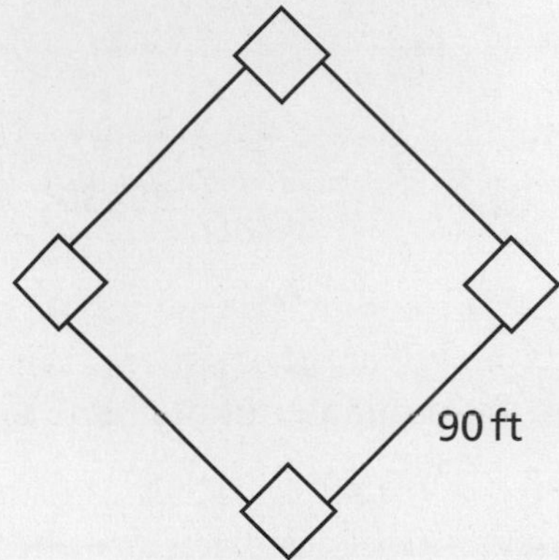

(1) $\sqrt{90}$ ft **(3)** $90\sqrt{2}$ ft
(2) 90 ft **(4)** $90\sqrt{3}$ ft

4 The length of the hypotenuse of an isosceles right triangle is $10\sqrt{6}$ ft. What is the length of the leg?

(1) $5\sqrt{3}$ ft **(3)** $10\sqrt{3}$ ft
(2) $5\sqrt{6}$ ft **(4)** $10\sqrt{12}$ ft

5 The hypotenuse of a right triangle measures 20 in. and one of its legs measures 8 in. Determine the length of the other leg in simplest radical form.

(1) $\sqrt{336}$ in. **(3)** $2\sqrt{42}$ in.
(2) $\sqrt{168}$ in. **(4)** $4\sqrt{21}$ in.

6 Determine the area of the triangle in the accompanying figure.

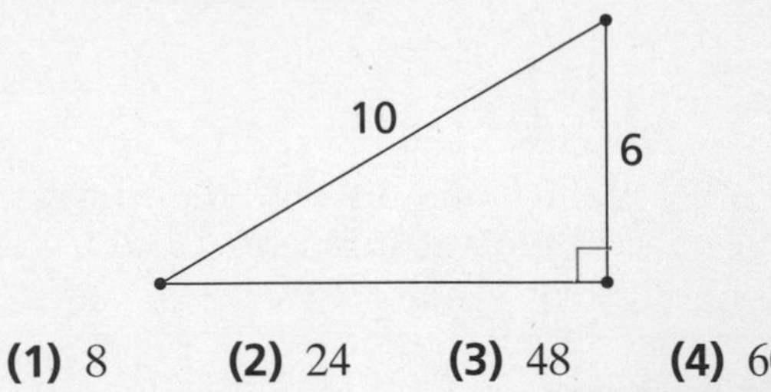

(1) 8 **(2)** 24 **(3)** 48 **(4)** 60

7 Determine the area of the shaded region in the accompanying figure.

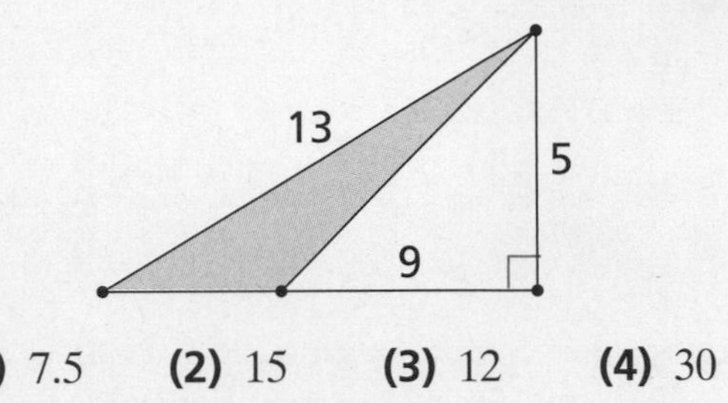

(1) 7.5 **(2)** 15 **(3)** 12 **(4)** 30

8 Determine the value of a such that a, 13, and 85 form a Pythagorean Triple.

(1) $7\sqrt{2}$
(2) 84
(3) $\sqrt{7394}$
(4) 98

9 The longer leg of a 30°-60°-90° triangle is 6. What is the length of the hypotenuse?

(1) 12
(2) $4\sqrt{3}$
(3) $3\sqrt{2}$
(4) $2\sqrt{3}$

10 The lengths of the sides of a 45°-45°-90° right triangle is 8. What is the length of the hypotenuse?

(1) 4 **(3)** $8\sqrt{2}$
(2) $4\sqrt{2}$ **(4)** 16

11 A raised truck bed is shown in the accompanying figure. The base of the right triangle shown is 6 ft and the length of the bed is 10 ft. How high does the bed rise?

12 An isosceles triangle has legs that measure 20 cm and a base that measures 16 cm. Determine the length of the altitude drawn to the base of the triangle. Write your answer in simplest radical form.

13 A contractor leans a 30-ft ladder against a house. The base of the ladder is 6 ft from the house. How high will the ladder reach on the side of the house? Round your answer to the nearest tenth of a foot.

14 A rectangular prism that measures $3 \times 4 \times 12$ has a straw placed from the corner of one face to the corner diagonally opposite on the parallel face as shown in the accompanying figure. What is the length of the straw?

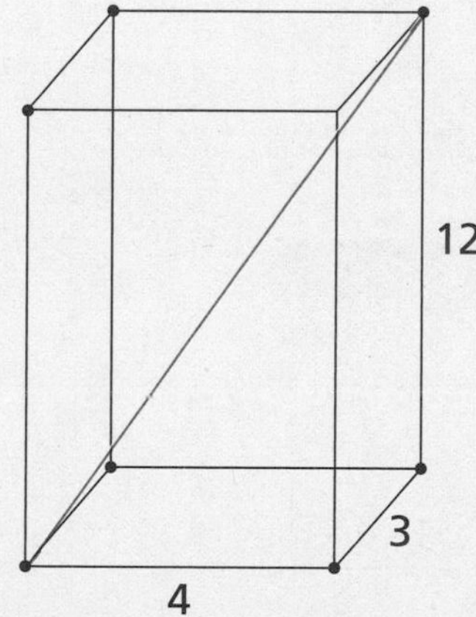

15 The length of the altitude of an equilateral triangle is 1 m. Determine the length of the side of the triangle. Write your answer in simplest radical form.

16 Determine all of the missing lengths in triangle ABC.

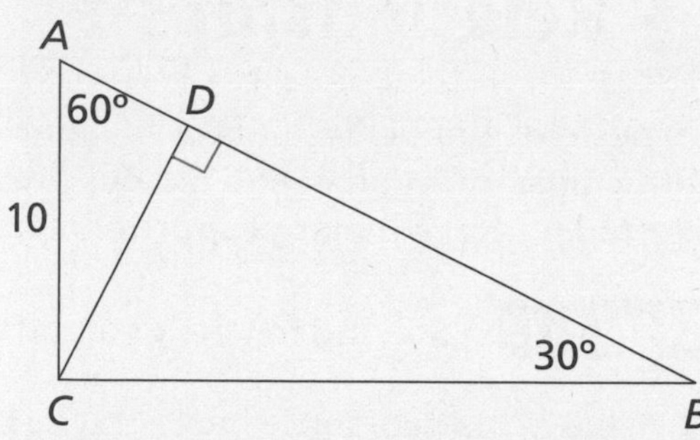

17 Determine the length of the diagonal of a cube if its side has a length of 4 units. Write your answer in simplest radical form.

18 Do the numbers 11, 20, and 23 form a Pythagorean Triple?

19 Determine the length of the diagonal of a square if its area is 256 units^2. Write your answer in simplest radical form.

20 A person travels 5 miles north, 2 miles east, 1 mile north, and finally 4 miles east. How far is the person from the starting point?

21 The side of a square is equal to the length of the diagonal of another square. What is the ratio of the perimeter of the large square to the smaller square?

22 One leg of a right triangle is 7 inches longer than the other. The length of the hypotenuse is 13 inches. Find the lengths of the 2 legs algebraically.

23 The length of the hypotenuse of a 30°-60°-90° triangle is $4\sqrt{3}$. What is the area of this triangle?

24 The lengths of the side of a triangle are $\sqrt{50}$, 5, and 5. Classify the triangle as right, acute, or obtuse.

25 The lengths of the legs of a right triangle measure x and $x + 2$ in. The hypotenuse of the triangle measures $2\sqrt{5}$ in. Find x.

4.4 Special Right Triangle Relationships

New York Standards

G.G.47 Theorems about mean proportionality

For two positive numbers a and b, the number x such that $\frac{a}{x} = \frac{x}{b}$ is called the **geometric mean** of a and b. Solving this proportion leads to $x = \sqrt{ab}$. x is also referred to as the **mean proportional** between a and b.

EXAMPLE I **Solving for the geometric mean**

What is the geometric mean (mean proportional) of 2 and 8?

■ **SOLUTION**

$\frac{2}{x} = \frac{x}{8}$

$x^2 = 16$

$x = \sqrt{16}$

$x = 4$

or

$x = \sqrt{(2)(8)}$

$x = \sqrt{16}$

$x = 4$

Consider the accompanying figure in which right triangle ABC has an altitude drawn from the right angle to the hypotenuse ($\overline{BD}$). This altitude divides the triangle into two right triangles, $\triangle ADB$ and $\triangle BDC$.

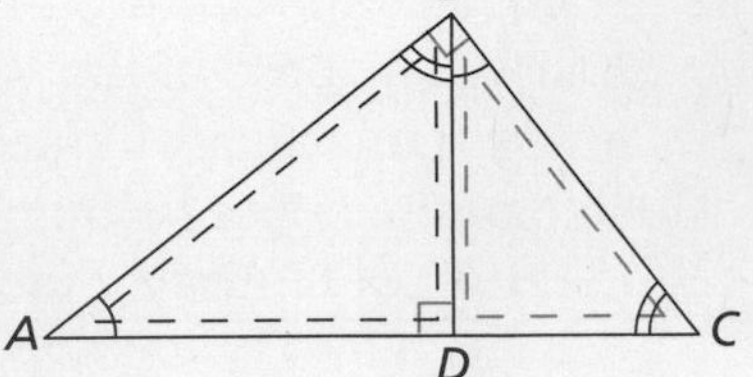

Altitude Drawn to Hypotenuse Theorem

The altitude drawn to the hypotenuse of a right triangle divides the triangle into two triangles that are similar to the original and to each other.

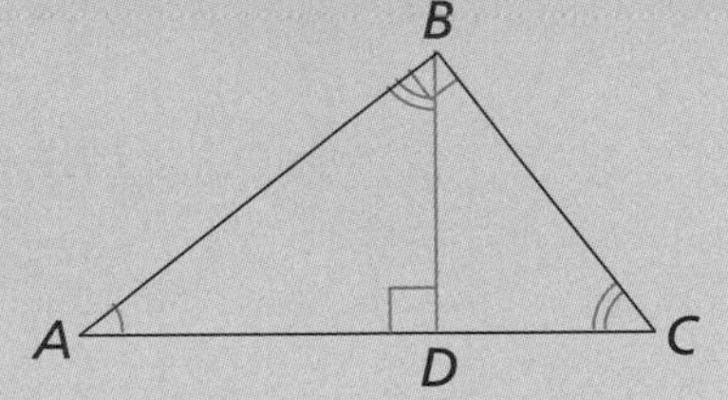

Corollary 1

The altitude drawn to the hypotenuse of a right triangle is the mean proportional between the segments of the hypotenuse.

That is, $\frac{AD}{BD} = \frac{BD}{DC}$.

Corollary 2

When the altitude is drawn to the hypotenuse of a right triangle, each leg of the triangle is the geometric mean between the whole hypotenuse and the segment of the hypotenuse attached to the leg.

That is, $\frac{AC}{AB} = \frac{AB}{AD}$ and $\frac{AC}{BC} = \frac{BC}{DC}$.

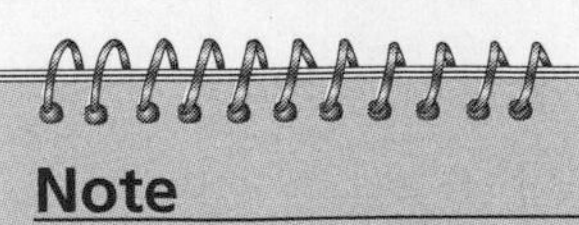

Note

Altitude · Hypotenuse = Leg 1 · Leg 2

EXAMPLE 2 Verifying the Altitude Drawn to Hypotenuse Theorem

2 Verify that $\triangle ABC \sim \triangle ADB \sim \triangle BDC$.

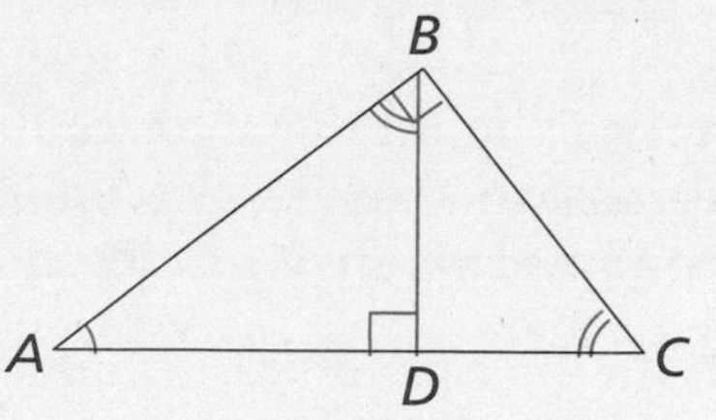

SOLUTION

$\triangle ABC \sim \triangle ADB$ because $\angle A$ is in both triangles and both contain a right angle. Therefore, the angles are similar by the AA Theorem. Likewise, $\triangle ABC \sim \triangle BDC$ because $\angle C$ is in both triangles and both contain a right angle. Again, the AA Theorem applies. By the transitive property, $\triangle ABC \sim \triangle ADB \sim \triangle BDC$.

You can use the geometric mean and the Altitude Drawn to Hypotenuse Theorem to solve a variety of real-world problems.

EXAMPLES 3 and 4 Applying proportions

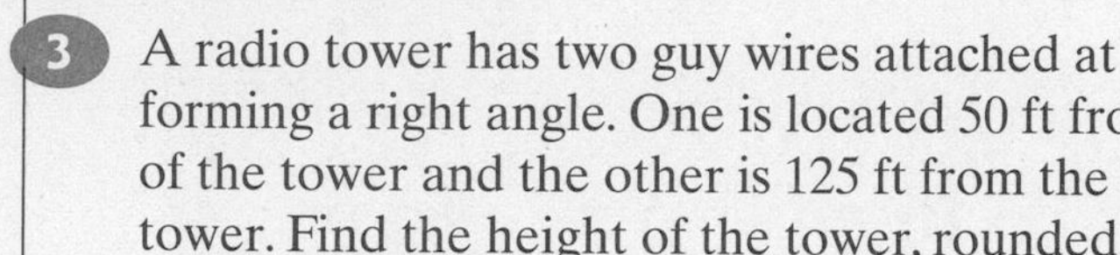

3 A radio tower has two guy wires attached at the top forming a right angle. One is located 50 ft from the base of the tower and the other is 125 ft from the base of the tower. Find the height of the tower, rounded to the nearest foot.

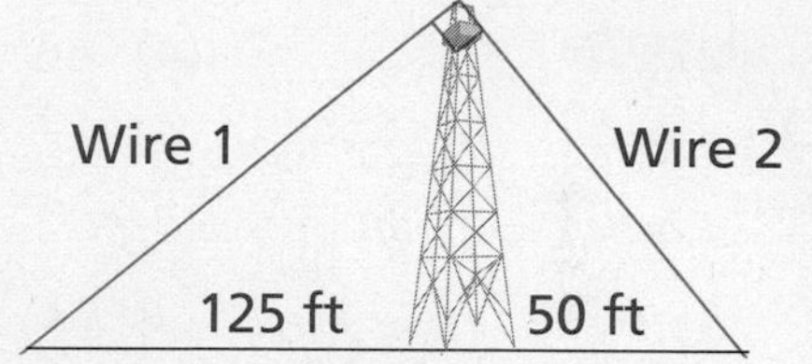

SOLUTION

Let h represent the height of the tower. The tower is the altitude to the hypotenuse of a right triangle, which establishes the following proportion.

$$\frac{125}{h} = \frac{h}{50} \Rightarrow h^2 = 6250$$

$$h = \sqrt{6250} = 25\sqrt{10} \approx 79 \text{ ft}$$

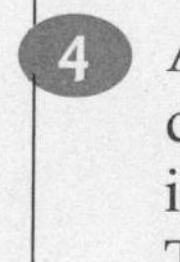

4 At Panguitch Lake, the first-aid station is located directly across the lake from the lodge. The beach is 200 yards directly east of the first-aid station. The paths from the lodge to the beach and from the lodge to the campground form a right angle. If the distance from the lodge to the beach is 450 yards, what is the distance from the beach to the campground?

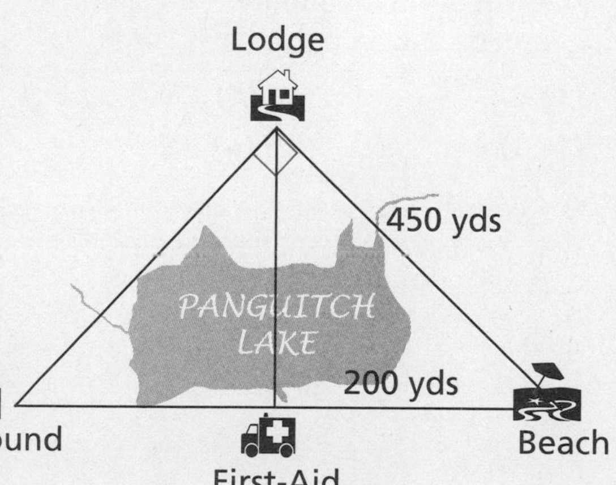

SOLUTION

Let x = the distance from the beach to the campground.

$$\frac{x}{450} = \frac{450}{200}$$

$$200x = 202500$$

$$x = \frac{202500}{200} = 1012.5 \text{ yds}$$

Practice

Choose the numeral preceding the word or expression that best completes the statement or answers the question.

1 In the accompanying diagram $AD = a$ and $DC = b$. Which segment represents the geometric mean of a and b?

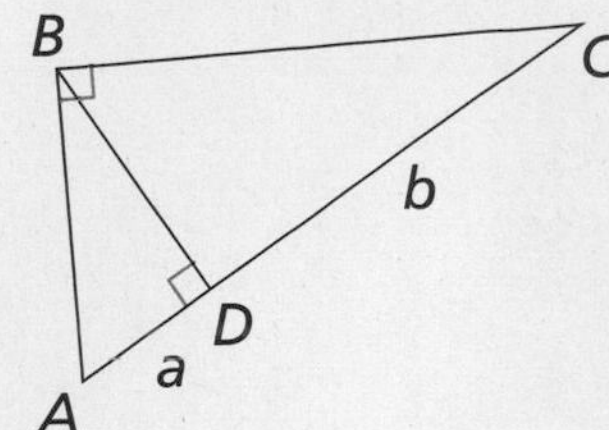

(1) $\overline{AB}$ (3) $\overline{BC}$
(2) $\overline{BD}$ (4) $\overline{AC}$

2 Which of the following represents the geometric mean of 4 and 9?

(1) 6 (3) 18
(2) 6.5 (4) 36

3 8 is the geometric mean between 4 and which of the following values?

(1) 64 (3) 16
(2) 24 (4) 4

4 If k is a positive number, what is the geometric mean between $4k$ and k?

(1) $2k$ (3) $2k^2$
(2) $4k^2$ (4) $4k$

5 What is the value of x in the accompanying figure?

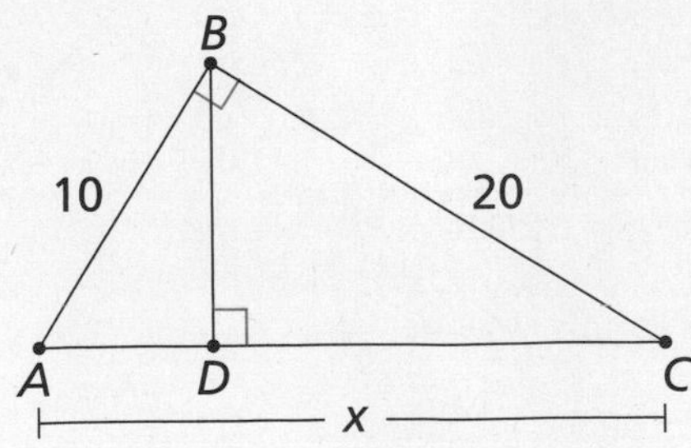

(1) $10\sqrt{5}$ (3) $5\sqrt{2}$
(2) $5\sqrt{10}$ (4) $2\sqrt{5}$

6 Which of the following expressions represents the geometric mean of the positive numbers x and y?

(1) $x + y$ (3) $\frac{x + y}{2}$
(2) xy (4) $\sqrt{xy}$

Use the accompanying figure to complete the proportions in Exercises 7–9.

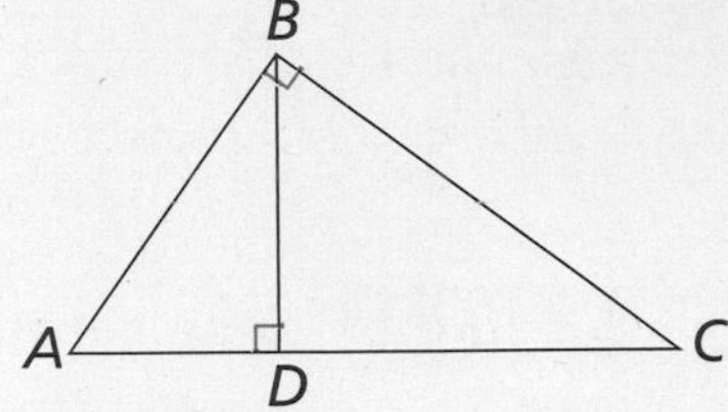

7 $\frac{AC}{?} = \frac{?}{AD}$

(1) BD (3) DC
(2) AB (4) BC

8 $\frac{DC}{?} = \frac{?}{AD}$

(1) BD (3) DC
(2) AB (4) BC

9 $\frac{AC}{BC} = \frac{BC}{?}$

(1) BD (3) DC
(2) AB (4) BC

10 Determine the geometric mean of $2\sqrt{3}$ and $3\sqrt{3}$.

(1) $5\sqrt{3}$ (3) $3\sqrt{2}$
(2) $2\sqrt{3}$ (4) $3\sqrt{6}$

11 Let a and b be positive real numbers. If the geometric mean between a and b is 3, which of the following is true?

(1) $a = \sqrt{3}, b = \sqrt{3}$
(2) $a = \sqrt{3}, b = 3\sqrt{3}$
(3) $a = \sqrt{3}, b = 3$
(4) $a = 9, b = 9$

Use the accompanying figure to complete each proportion in Exercises 12–17.

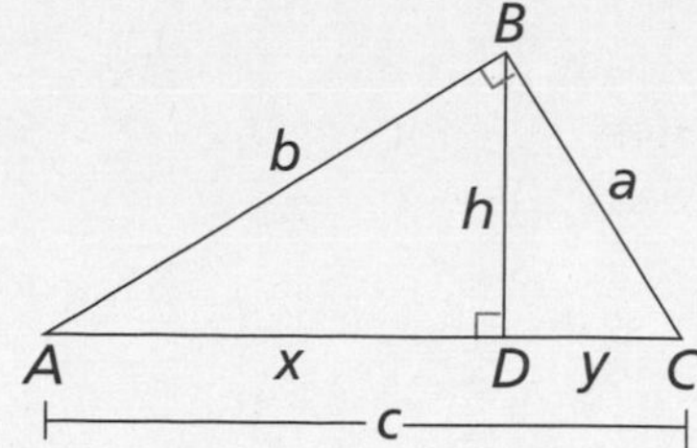

12 $\frac{x}{h} = \frac{?}{y}$

13 $\frac{a}{b} = \frac{?}{h}$

14 $\frac{a}{b} = \frac{h}{?}$

15 $\frac{a}{c} = \frac{y}{?}$

16 $\frac{a}{c} = \frac{h}{?}$

17 $\frac{b}{x} = \frac{?}{b}$

18 The main sail on a sailboat is shaped like the right triangle below. What is the value of h?

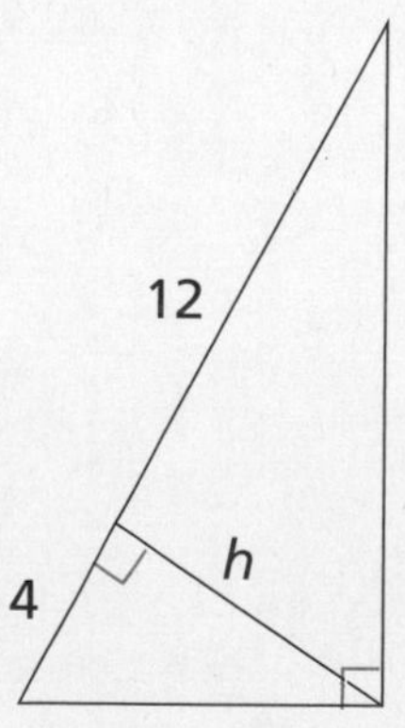

In Exercises 19–24, determine the value of the variables.

19

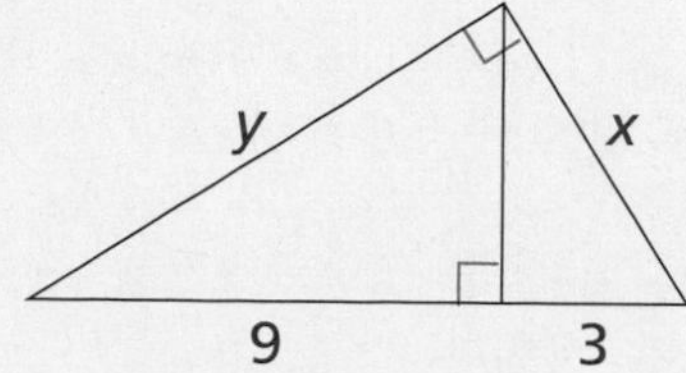

20

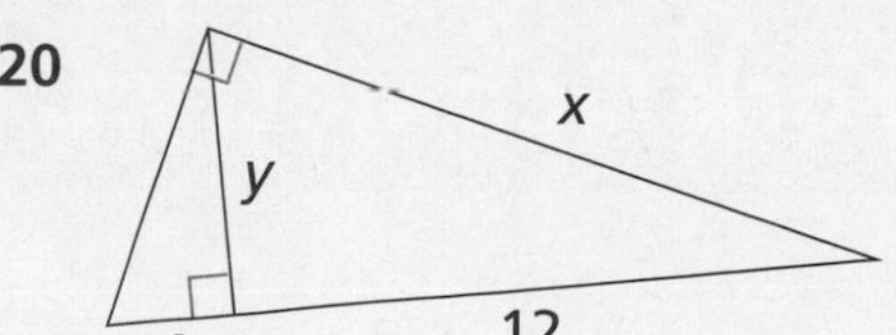

21

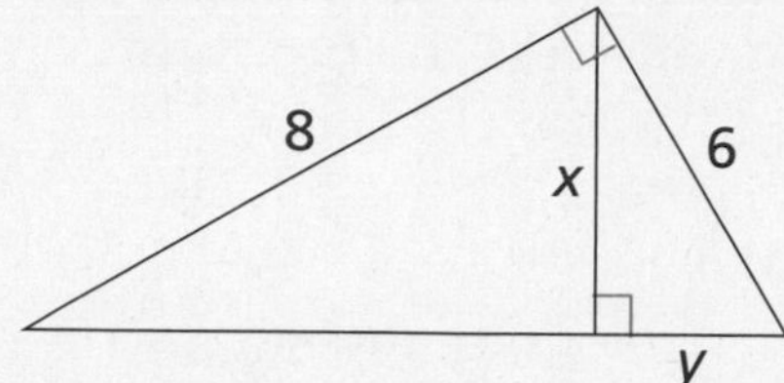

22

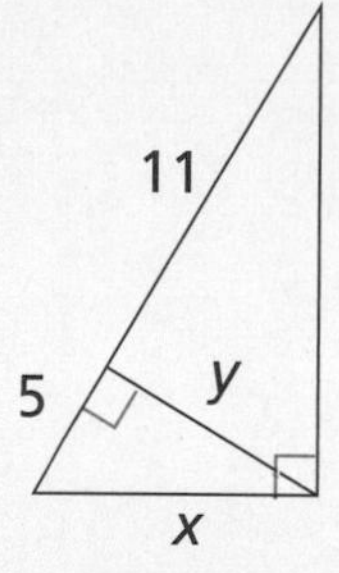

23

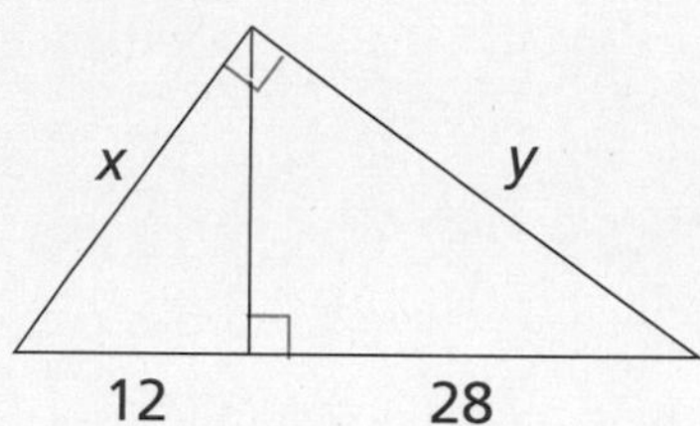

24

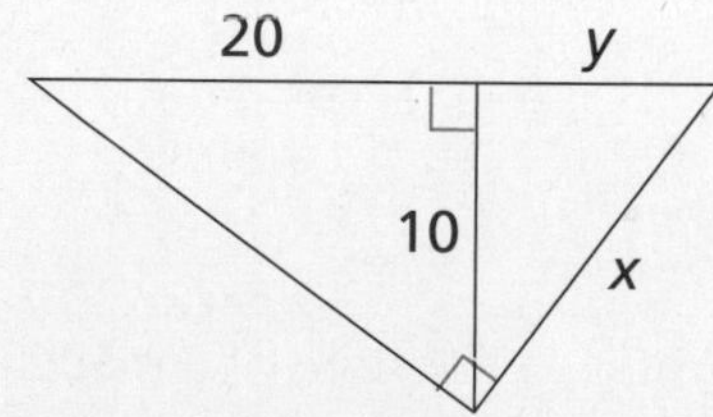

25 The face of the building in the accompanying figure is shaped like a right triangle. The height of the building is 300 ft and the width at the base is 200 ft. If d is perpendicular to the hypotenuse, what is the value of d?

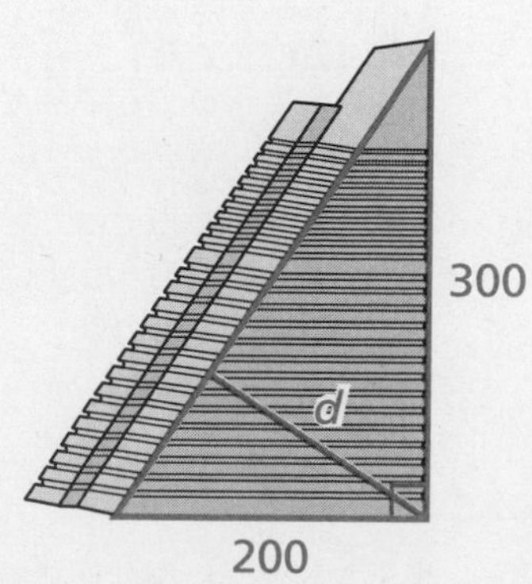

Chapter 4 Preparing for the New York Geometry Exam

Answer all questions in this part. For each question, select the numeral preceding the word or expression that best completes the statements or answers the questions.

1 The Pythagorean Theorem holds for which type of triangle?

(1) acute **(3)** obtuse
(2) right **(4)** left

2 In the accompanying figure M and N are midpoints. What is true about $\overline{MN}$?

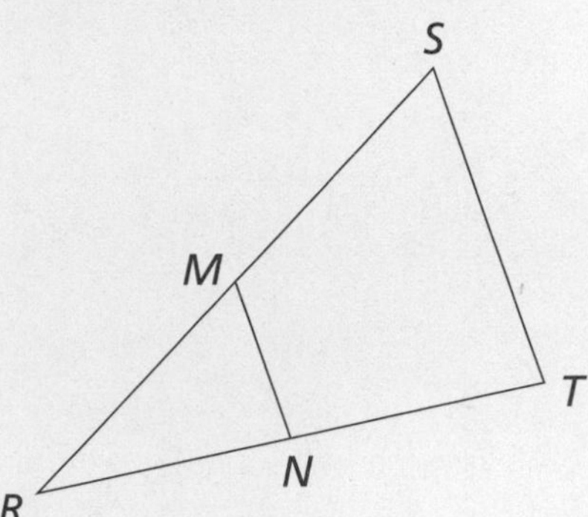

(1) $\overline{MN} \perp \overline{RT}$
(2) $MN = \frac{1}{2}RT$
(3) $MN = RN$
(4) $MN = \frac{1}{2}ST$

3 What is the ratio of the area of a medial triangle to the area of the original triangle?

(1) 1:1 **(3)** 1:4
(2) 1:2 **(4)** 1:8

4 The length of the hypotenuse of an isosceles right triangle is 12. Which of the following represents the length of the leg?

(1) $6\sqrt{2}$ **(3)** $2\sqrt{6}$
(2) $2\sqrt{3}$ **(4)** 6

5 The circumcenter is the point of concurrency of which lines or segments in a triangle?

(1) medians
(2) altitudes
(3) bisectors of the sides
(4) perpendicular bisectors of the sides

6 In the accompanying figure J and K are midpoints of sides of triangle ABC. The length of $\overline{JK}$ is represented by $2x + 5$ and the length of $\overline{AC}$ is $6x - 8$. Determine the value of x.

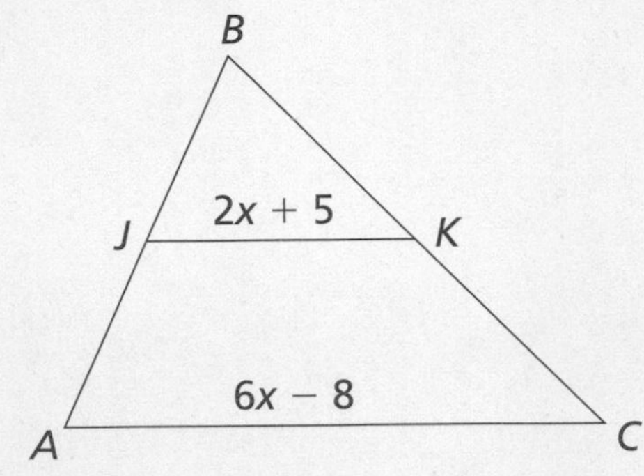

(1) 2 **(3)** 3
(2) 5 **(4)** 9

7 Which point can be a vertex of a triangle?

(1) circumcenter
(2) orthocenter
(3) centroid
(4) incenter

8 $\overline{RS}$ is the median of a triangle. The length of $\overline{RS}$ is 21. What is the distance from vertex R to the centroid of the triangle?

(1) 7 **(3)** 14
(2) 10.5 **(4)** 31.5

9 The area of a square is 49 cm^2. What is the length of the diagonal of the square?

(1) 7 **(2)** $2\sqrt{7}$ **(3)** $7\sqrt{2}$ **(4)** $7\sqrt{3}$

10 The diagonal of a rectangle divides the angle of the rectangle into two angles that are in the ratio of 1 to 2. If the length of the diagonal is 12 in., determine the area of the rectangle.

(1) $6\sqrt{2}$ in.^{2} **(3)** $72\sqrt{3}$ in.^{2}
(2) $36\sqrt{3}$ in.^{2} **(4)** 72 in.^{2}

Use the following figure to answer Exercises 11 and 12.

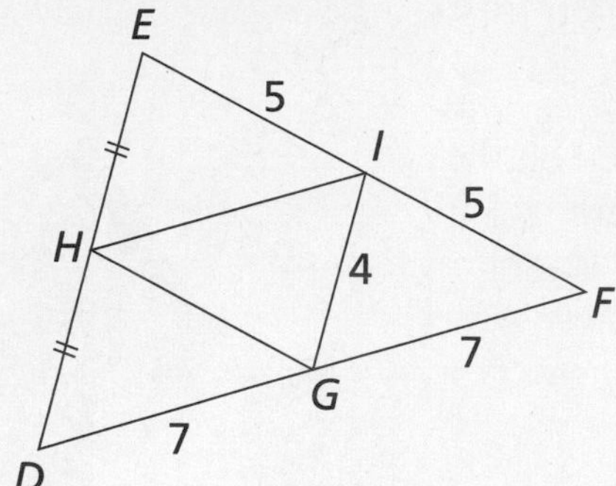

11 Determine the length of $\overline{HG}$ in the accompanying figure.

(1) 4 **(2)** 5 **(3)** 7 **(4)** 9

12 Determine the length of $\overline{HD}$ in the accompanying figure.

(1) 4 **(2)** 5 **(3)** 7 **(4)** 8

13 The vertices of $\triangle DEF$ are $D(2, 5)$, $E(4, 9)$, and $F(6, 1)$. Which ordered pair gives the coordinates of the centroid P of $\triangle DEF$?

(1) $(4, 3)$ **(3)** $(5, 5)$

(2) $(4, 5)$ **(4)** $(6, 5)$

14 Which group of side lengths can be used to construct a right triangle?

(1) 3, 4, 5 **(3)** 11, 16, 27

(2) 3, 5, 7 **(4)** 12, 14, 26

Use the following figure to answer Exercises 15 and 16.

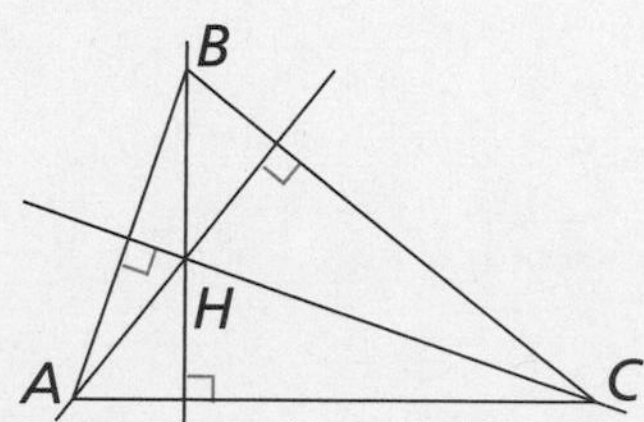

15 If H is on the interior of $\triangle ABC$, the $\triangle ABC$ must be what type of triangle?

(1) acute **(3)** obtuse

(2) scalene **(4)** right

16 If point H is outside $\triangle ABC$, what type of triangle is it?

(1) right **(3)** obtuse

(2) acute **(4)** equilateral

17 What is the height of $\triangle XYZ$?

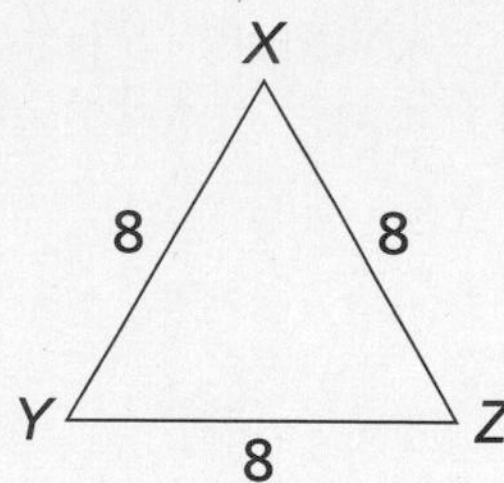

(1) 4

(2) $4\sqrt{3}$

(3) 8

(4) $8\sqrt{3}$

18 What is the geometric mean of 4 and 6?

(1) $3\sqrt{4}$

(2) $4\sqrt{3}$

(3) $2\sqrt{6}$

(4) $3\sqrt{6}$

19 What is the length of the hypotenuse of a right triangle with leg lengths of 9 in. and 12 in.?

(1) 10

(2) 15

(3) 21

(4) 25

20 The centroid is the point of concurrency of which lines and segments?

(1) altitudes

(2) medians

(3) bisectors of the sides

(4) perpendicular bisectors of the sides

Answer all questions in this part. Clearly indicate the necessary steps, including appropriate formula substitutions, diagrams, graphs, charts, etc. For all questions in this part, a correct numerical answer with no work shown will receive only one credit.

21 In the accompanying figure, squares have been constructed on the sides of a right triangle. How do the areas of the squares relate to each other? Would this relationship be true for any other shapes constructed on the sides of the right triangle?

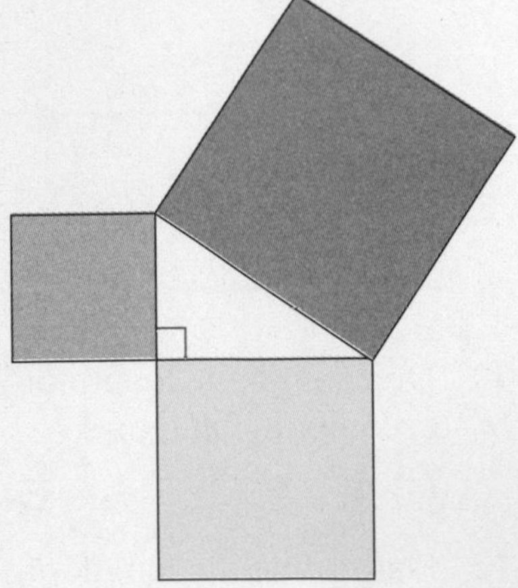

22 Determine the area and perimeter of *ABCD*.

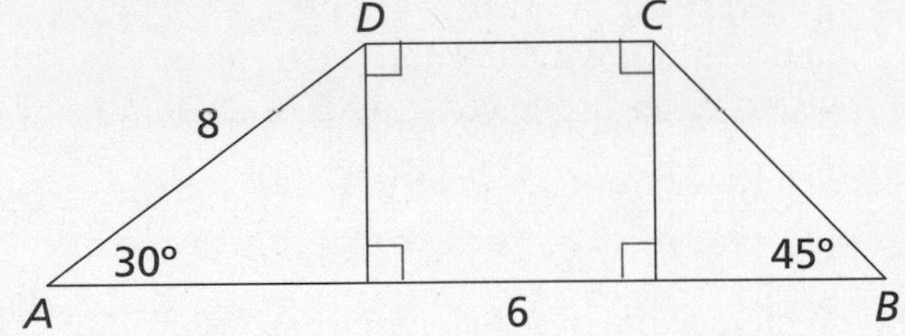

23 A regular hexagon is equilateral and equiangular. *ABCDEF* is a regular hexagon. Determine the area of rectangle *FBCE* if $AB = 8$.

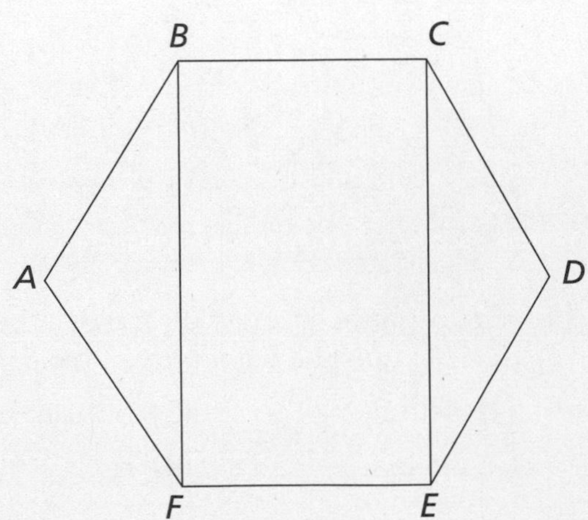

5 Quadrilaterals and Other Polygons

Discovering New York

Adirondack Park

Created by the state of New York in 1892, Adirondack Park is the largest area protected by any U.S. state. The park, located in northeast New York, covers approximately 6 million acres (about the size of Vermont). This protected wilderness includes private land; about 130,000 people live in the park's villages.

Adirondack Park attracts more than 8 million visitors every year. It contains 2,000 miles of hiking trails, 1,500 miles of rivers, and nearly 100 campgrounds. The two highest mountain peaks in the park, Marcy and Algonquin, reach heights of more than 5,000 feet. Many species of wildlife can be found in the park, including black bears, moose, deer, and loons.

5.1 Polygons

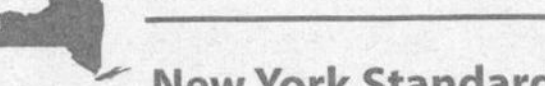

New York Standards

G.G.36 Sum of measures of a polygon's angles

G.G.37 Measures of angles of regular polygons

Recall that a **polygon** is a closed plane figure with at least three sides.

All closed plane figures can be classified as either *convex* or *concave*. In a **convex polygon,** no point on any diagonal lies outside the figure. In a **concave polygon,** at least one diagonal will contain points that lie outside the figure.

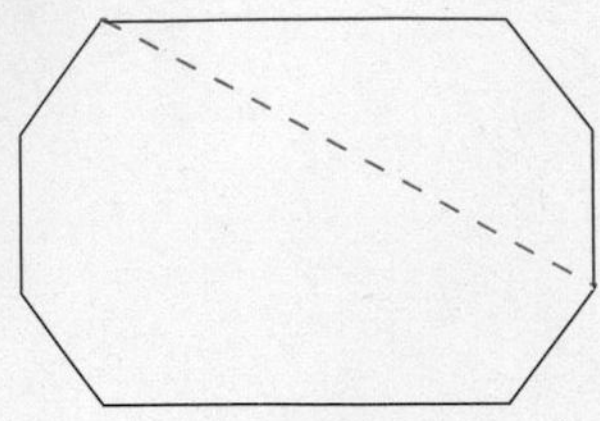

Convex Polygon

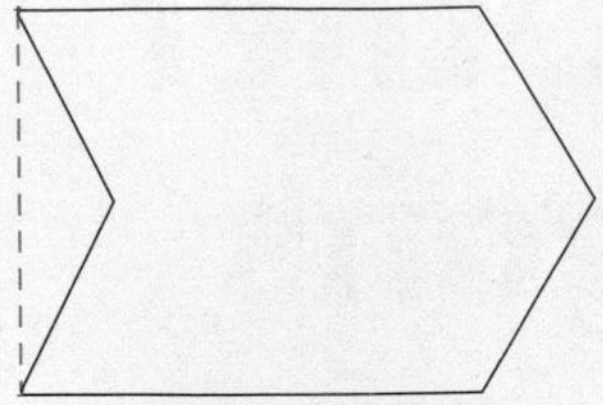

Concave Polygon

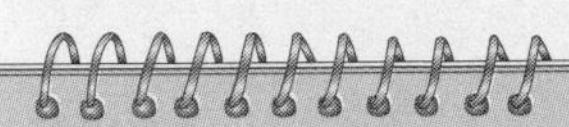

Note

A **diagonal** of a polygon is any line segment whose endpoints lie on non-consecutive vertices.

The properties, theorems, and postulates discussed in this lesson will pertain to convex polygons.

You can classify any polygon by its number of sides. The following table lists names for the most common polygons.

Classifying a Polygon by the Number of Sides	
Number of Sides	**Name**
3	triangle
4	quadrilateral
5	pentagon
6	hexagon
8	octagon
9	nonagon
10	decagon
12	dodecagon

Note

If a polygon has n sides, you call it an n-gon. For example, a 16-sided polygon is called a 16-gon.

The following table shows how you can find the sum of the interior angles of a convex polygon by drawing all the diagonals from one vertex.

Interior Angles of a Polygon			
Polygon	**Number of Sides**	**Number of Triangles Formed**	**Sum of the Measures of the Interior Angles**
	3	$3 - 2 = 1$	$1 \cdot 180° = 180°$
	4	$4 - 2 = 2$	$2 \cdot 180° = 360°$
	5	$5 - 2 = 3$	$3 \cdot 180° = 540°$
	8	$8 - 2 = 6$	$6 \cdot 180° = 1080°$

Note

The number of triangles found in the interior of any polygon is always two fewer than the number of sides.

The relationship between the number of sides and the number of interior triangles of any polygon leads to the following theorem.

Polygon Interior Angle-Sum Theorem

The sum of the measures of the interior angles of a convex polygon with n sides is $(n - 2)180°$.

Go Online PHSchool.com
Visit: PHSchool.com
Web Code: ayp-0385

EXAMPLE 1 **Using the Polygon Interior Angle-Sum Theorem**

1 Find the sum of the measures of the interior angles of a dodecagon.

▪ **SOLUTION**

A dodecagon is a polygon that has 12 sides. Use the Polygon Interior Angle-Sum Theorem with $n = 12$.

$$\text{sum of measures of interior angles} = (n - 2)180° = (12 - 2)180° = (10)180° = 1800°$$

Note

An **exterior angle of a convex polygon** is an angle that forms a linear pair with one of its interior angles.

The sum of the exterior angles of a polygon is consistent, regardless of the number of sides of a given figure.

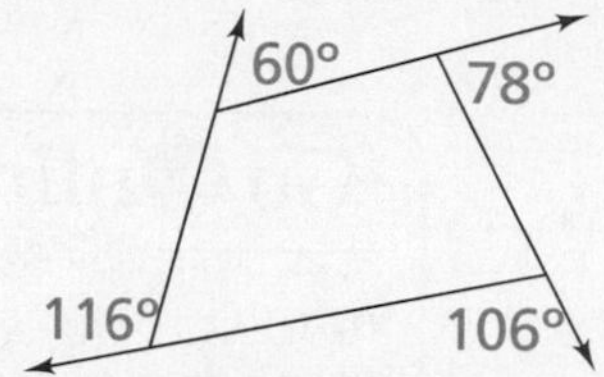

$116° + 60° + 78° + 106° = 360°$

$120° + 120° + 120° = 360°$

Polygon Exterior Angle-Sum Theorem

The sum of the measures of the exterior angles of a convex polygon, one at each vertex, is 360°.

EXAMPLE 2 **Using the Polygon Exterior Angle-Sum Theorem**

2 Find the $m\angle A$.

▪ **SOLUTION**

$m\angle A + m\angle B + m\angle C + m\angle D + 87° = 360°$ ← Use the Polygon Exterior Angle-Sum Theorem.

$m\angle B + 126° = 180°$ ← Linear pair

$m\angle B = 54°$

$m\angle C = 90°$

$m\angle D + 112° = 180°$

$m\angle D = 68°$

$m\angle A + 54° + 90° + 68° + 87° = 360°$ ← Substitute.

$m\angle A + 299° = 360°$ ← Solve.

Therefore, $m\angle A = 61°$.

An **equilateral polygon** is a polygon in which all sides are congruent. An **equiangular polygon** is a polygon in which all angles are congruent. A **regular polygon** is both equilateral and equiangular. There is a relationship between the number of sides and the angle measure of regular polygons.

Corollaries for Regular Polygons

The measure of each interior angle of a regular n-gon is $\frac{(n-2)180°}{n}$.

The measure of each exterior angle of a regular n-gon is $\frac{360°}{n}$.

EXAMPLES 3 and 4 Using the corollaries for regular polygons

3 Find the measure of each interior angle of the polygon shown at the right.

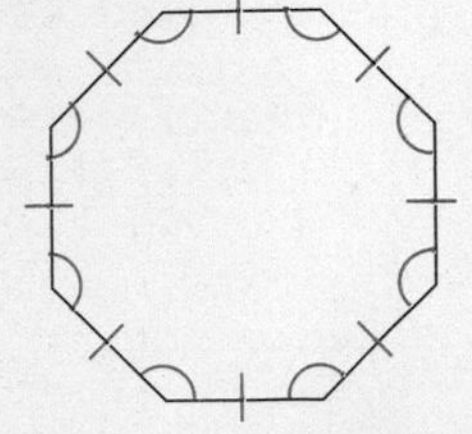

All sides are congruent and all angles are congruent, so the figure is a regular polygon. Use the first corollary with $n = 8$.

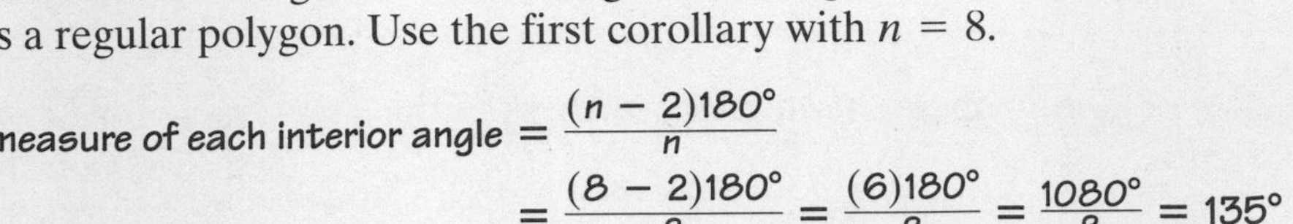

$$\text{measure of each interior angle} = \frac{(n-2)180°}{n}$$
$$= \frac{(8-2)180°}{8} = \frac{(6)180°}{8} = \frac{1080°}{8} = 135°$$

4 The measure of each exterior angle of a regular polygon is 40°. Find the number of sides.

SOLUTION

$$\text{measure of each exterior angle} = \frac{360°}{n}$$
$$40° = \frac{360°}{n}$$
$$n = 9$$

The polygon has 9 sides.

Practice

Choose the numeral preceding the word or expression that best completes the statement or answers the question.

1 Four interior angles of a pentagon each measure 110°. What is the measure of the fifth interior angle?

(1) 72°

(2) 100°

(3) 108°

(4) 110°

2 What is the measure of each exterior angle of a regular decagon?

(1) 30°

(2) 36°

(3) 72°

(4) 144°

3 Which expression represents the measure of each interior angle of a regular n-gon?

(1) $(180n)°$ **(3)** $(n - 2)180°$

(2) $\frac{360°}{n}$ **(4)** $\frac{(n - 2)180°}{n}$

4 The measure of each interior angle of a regular polygon is 144°. How many sides does the polygon have?

(1) 6 **(2)** 7 **(3)** 8 **(4)** 10

5 In the figure below, one side of polygon $RSTU$ has been extended as shown. What is $m\angle S$?

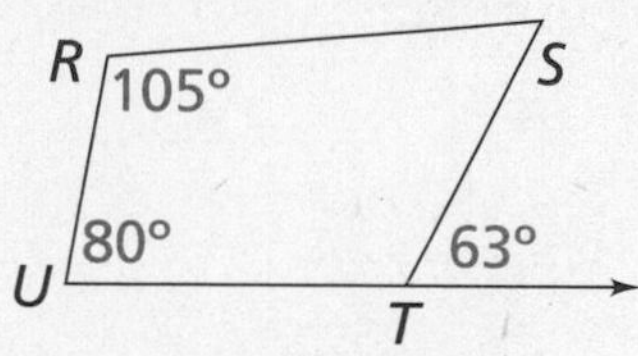

(1) 58° **(3)** 75°

(2) 63° **(4)** 112°

In Exercises 6–9, find the values for each regular polygon.

6

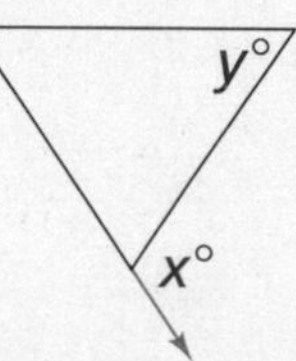

7

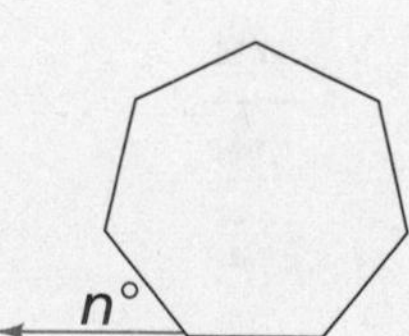

8

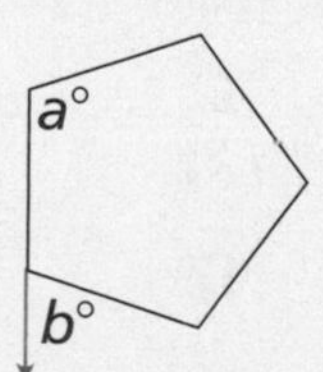

9

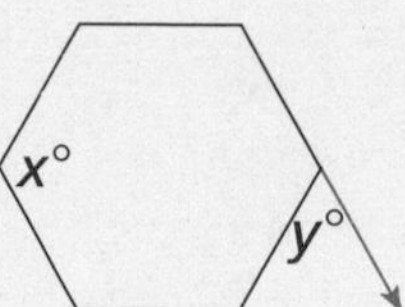

10 The measures of four interior angles of a pentagon are 115°, 92°, 107°, and 83°. Find the measure of the fifth interior angle.

In Exercises 11–13, the sum of the measures of the interior angles of a polygon is given. Find the number of sides.

11 180° **12** 900° **13** 2700°

In Exercises 14–16, the measure of an exterior angle of a regular polygon is given. Find the number of sides.

14 120° **15** 72° **16** 18°

In Exercises 17–19, the measure of an interior angle of a regular polygon is given. Find the number of sides. Then name the figure.

17 120 **18** 108 **19** 135

In Exercises 20–21, classify the polygon by its number of sides. Then find the value of a.

20

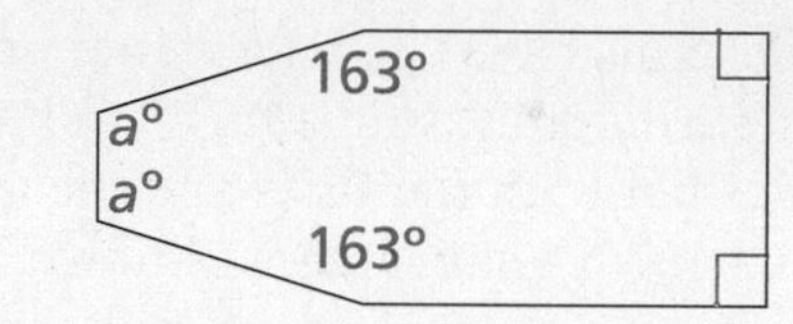

21

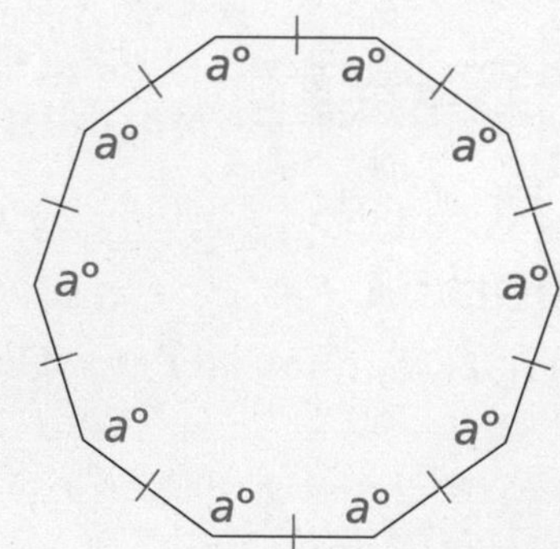

22 Find $m\angle B$.

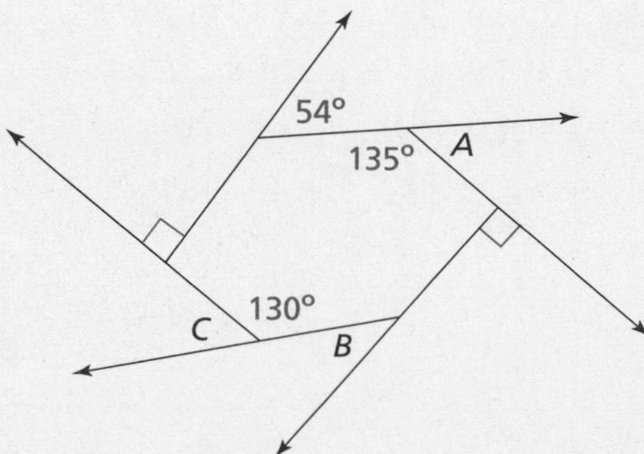

5.2 Properties of Special Quadrilaterals

New York Standards

G.G.38 Theorems about parallelograms

G.G.41 Classify quadrilaterals

A **quadrilateral** is a 4-sided polygon. To name a quadrilateral, start at any vertex and list the other **vertices** consecutively. **Consecutive** vertices are next to each other and form the consecutive angles of the quadrilateral. You can name these vertices either clockwise or counterclockwise.

Note

Nonconsecutive vertices of a quadrilateral are opposite angles.

EXAMPLES 1 and 2 **Naming quadrilaterals**

Use the diagram at the right for Examples 1 and 2.

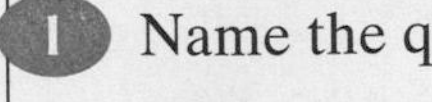

1 Name the quadrilateral.

■ **SOLUTION**

ABCD, BCDA, CDAB, or *DABC*

2 Name each angle of the quadrilateral.

■ **SOLUTION**

$\angle A, \angle B, \angle C, \angle D$ or $\angle DAB, \angle ABC, \angle BCD, \angle CDA$ or $\angle BAD, \angle CBA, \angle DCB, \angle ADC$

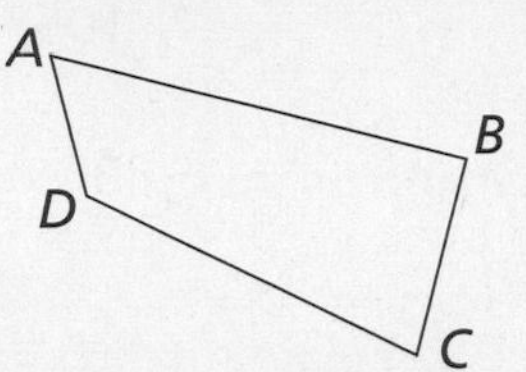

All quadrilaterals have four sides, four angles, and a sum of the angles equal to 360°. Quadrilaterals can be further classified according to specific unique relationships between the sides and the angles of a figure. These unique relationships form a subcategory known as **special quadrilaterals.**

EXAMPLES 3 and 4 **Finding the measure of a missing angle in a quadrilateral**

3 Find the value of x.

■ **SOLUTION**

In a quadrilateral, all the angles add up to 360°.

$x = 360 - (131 + 66 + 112)$
$x = 360 - 309$
$x = 51$

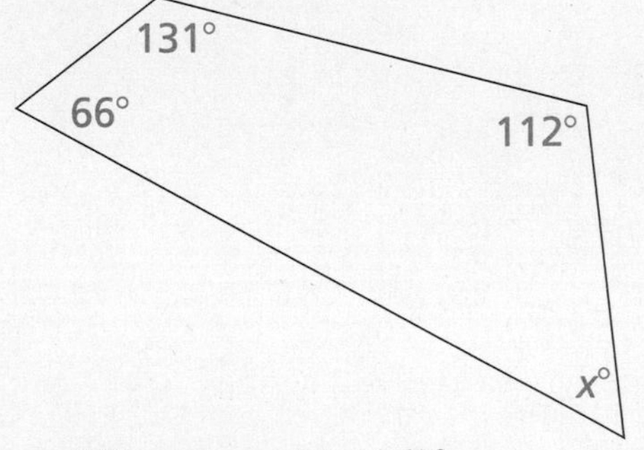

4 In the quadrilateral $JKLM$, $\angle J \cong \angle K$, $m\angle L = 54°$, and $m\angle M = 60°$. What is the measure of $\angle J$?

■ **SOLUTION**

$$m\angle J + m\angle K + m\angle L + m\angle M = 360°$$
$$m\angle J + m\angle K + 54° + 60° = 360°$$
$$m\angle J + m\angle K = 360° - 114°$$
$$2m\angle J = 246° \quad \leftarrow m\angle J + m\angle K = 2m\angle J$$
$$m\angle J = 123°$$

The following table lists seven major **special quadrilaterals.**

Special Quadrilaterals	
Definition	**Properties**
A **parallelogram** is a quadrilateral with two pairs of parallel sides.	If a quadrilateral is a parallelogram, then • its opposite sides are congruent; • its opposite angles are congruent; • its consecutive angles are supplementary; and • its diagonals bisect each other.
A **rhombus** is a parallelogram with four congruent sides.	If a quadrilateral is a rhombus, then it has all the properties of a parallelogram, plus • each diagonal bisects a pair of opposite angles; and • its diagonals are perpendicular.
A **rectangle** is a parallelogram with four right angles.	If a quadrilateral is a rectangle, then it has all the properties of a parallelogram, plus • its diagonals are congruent.
A **square** is a parallelogram with four congruent sides and four right angles.	If a quadrilateral is a square, then it has all the properties of a parallelogram, plus • each diagonal bisects a pair of opposite angles; • its diagonals are perpendicular; and • its diagonals are congruent.
A **trapezoid** is a quadrilateral with exactly one pair of parallel sides.	The parallel sides of a trapezoid are called its **bases.** Two angles whose vertices are the endpoints of a single base form a pair of **base angles.** The nonparallel sides of a trapezoid are its **legs.** The **midsegment** of a trapezoid is the segment that joins the midpoints of the legs. If a quadrilateral is a trapezoid, then • two consecutive angles whose vertices are endpoints of different bases are supplementary.
An **isosceles trapezoid** is a trapezoid whose nonparallel opposite sides are congruent.	If a quadrilateral is an isosceles trapezoid, then it has all the properties of a trapezoid, plus • its base angles are congruent; and • its diagonals are congruent.
A **kite** is a quadrilateral with two pairs of congruent adjacent sides and no opposite sides congruent.	In a kite, the common endpoint of a pair of congruent sides is called an **endpoint of the kite.** If a quadrilateral is a kite, then • its diagonals are perpendicular; and • one diagonal bisects the angles whose vertices are the endpoints of the kite.

You can use these properties to solve problems involving quadrilaterals. If you know a quadrilateral is of a given type, you can use the properties of the quadrilateral to find the lengths of missing angles and sides.

Go Online PHSchool.com
Visit: PHSchool.com
Web Code: ayp-0413

EXAMPLES 5 through 8 **Using the properties of quadrilaterals**

5 In the figure at the right, $WXYZ$ is a parallelogram. Find $m\angle X$.

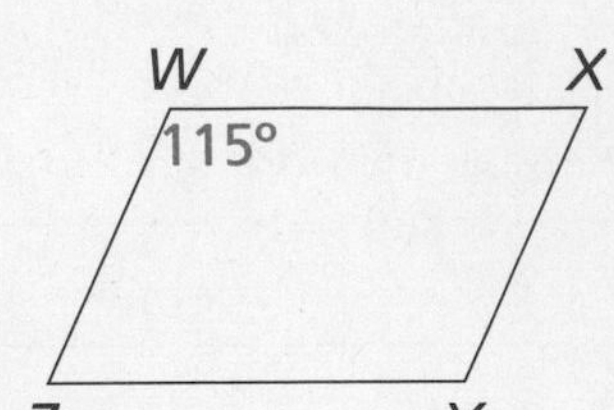

■ **SOLUTION**

Consecutive angles of a parallelogram are supplementary.
Therefore: $m\angle X = 180° - 115° = 65°$

6 Given that $ABCD$ is an isosceles trapezoid, find $m\angle D$.

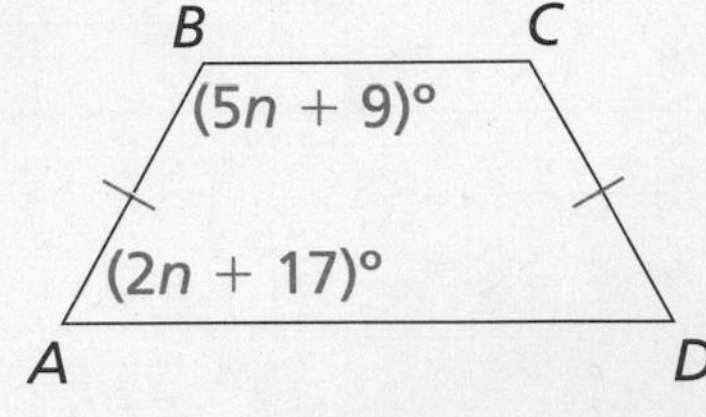

■ **SOLUTION**

In a trapezoid, two consecutive angles whose vertices are endpoints of different bases are supplementary.
Therefore:
$$m\angle A + m\angle B = 180°$$
$$(2n + 17°) + (5n + 9)° = 180°$$
$$7n + 26 = 180$$
$$n = 22$$

Base angles of an isosceles trapezoid are congruent.
Therefore: $m\angle D = m\angle A = (2n + 17)° \rightarrow m\angle D = (2[22] + 17)° = 61°$

7 In the figure at the right, $EFGH$ is a kite with congruent sides as marked. Find $m\angle FEH$.

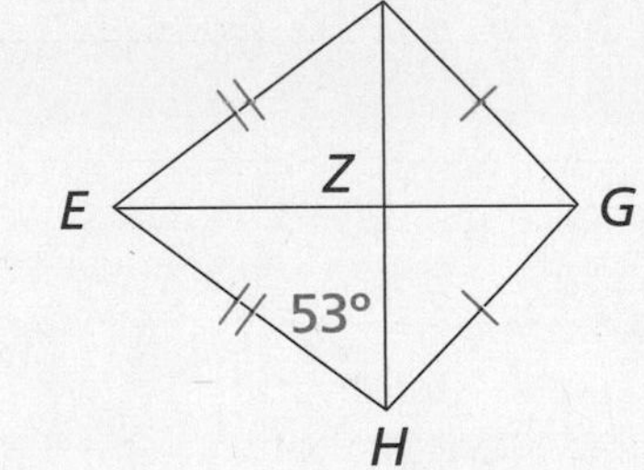

■ **SOLUTION**

The diagonals of a kite are perpendicular.
Therefore, in $\triangle EZH$: $m\angle EZH = 90°$

The sum of the measures of the angles of a triangle is 180°.
Therefore, in $\triangle EZH$: $m\angle ZEH = 180° - (53° + 90°) = 37°$

In a kite, one diagonal bisects the angles whose vertices are the endpoints of the kite.
Therefore, in kite $EFGH$: $m\angle FEH = 2(m\angle ZEH) = 2(37°) = 74°$

8 In the figure at the right, $PQRS$ is a rectangle with diagonals $\overline{PR}$ and $\overline{QS}$. Find PR and QS.

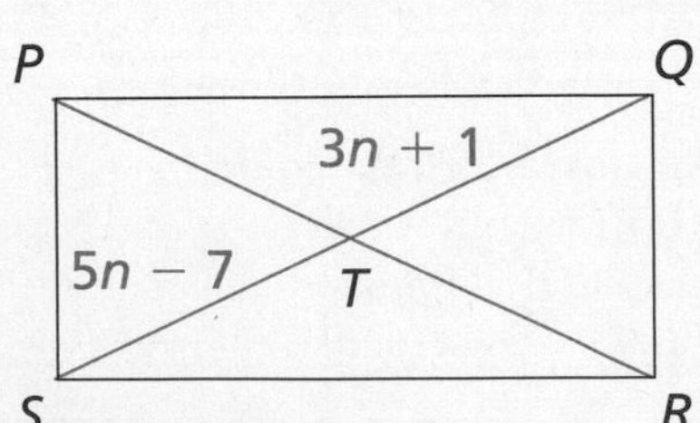

■ **SOLUTION**

A rectangle is a type of parallelogram.

The diagonals of a parallelogram bisect each other.
Therefore: $5n - 7 = 3n + 1 \rightarrow n = 4$
$$QS = (5n - 7) + (3n + 1)$$
$$= (5[4] - 7) + (3[4] + 1) = 26$$

The diagonals of a rectangle are congruent.
Therefore: $PR = QS = 26$

The diagram below shows how the special quadrilaterals are related.

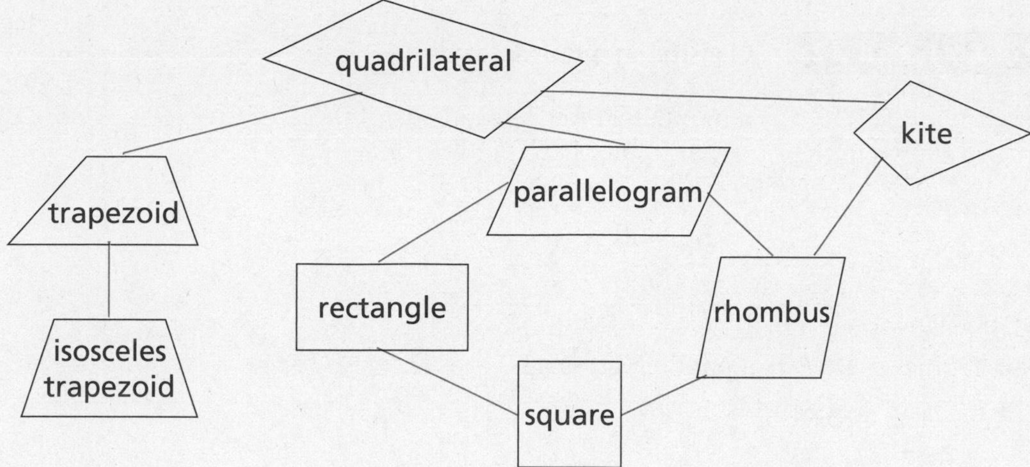

You can see from the diagram why statements such as the following are true.

All squares are rectangles.

Some parallelograms are squares.

No trapezoid is a kite.

Similarly, you can see why statements like these are false.

All rectangles are squares.

Some rectangles are trapezoids.

No square is a rhombus.

EXAMPLES 9 and 10 Classifying quadrilaterals

9 Is the following statement true or false? Explain your reasoning.

All kites are parallelograms.

SOLUTION

The statement is false.

For a quadrilateral to be a parallelogram, its opposite sides must be congruent and parallel to each other. Unlike a parallelogram, a kite does not have parallel sides, and consecutive sides are congruent, not opposite sides.

10 Is the following statement true or false? Explain your reasoning.

All squares are parallelograms.

SOLUTION

The statement is true.

In order for a quadrilateral to be a parallelogram, it must have two pairs of parallel sides. All squares have two pairs of parallel sides. Therefore, a square must also be a parallelogram.

You can use the properties of quadrilaterals to help you identify and classify figures.

EXAMPLES 11 and 12 Classifying quadrilaterals

11 Quadrilateral $ABCD$ is a parallelogram. The lengths of three of the legs are shown in the diagram to the right. Find the length of AB.

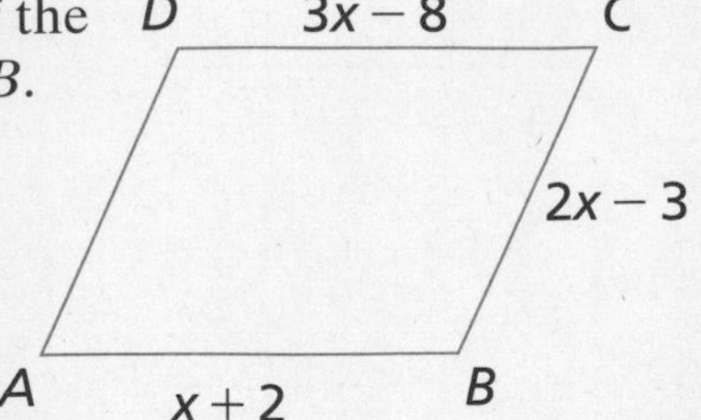

$AB = x + 2$
$BC = 2x - 3$
$CD = 3x - 8$

■ **SOLUTION**

Step 1 Since $ABCD$ is a parallelogram, $AB = CD$. Solve for x.

$x + 2 = 3x - 8$
$2x = 10$
$x = 5$

Step 2 Find the length of AB

$AB = x + 2$
$AB = 5 + 2$ ← **substitute $x = 5$**
$AB = 7$

12 Find the length of $\overline{DA}$ in the quadrilateral from Example 11.

■ **SOLUTION**

Since $ABCD$ is a parallelogram, opposite sides are congruent.

$DA = BC$
$DA = 2x - 3$
$DA = 2(5) - 3$ ← **substitute $x = 5$**
$DA = 7$

Practice

Choose the numeral preceding the word or expression that best completes the statement or answers the question.

1 In quadrilateral $ABCD$, $\angle A$ is a right angle, $m\angle B = 126°$, and $\angle C \cong \angle D$. What is the measure of $\angle D$?

(1) 36° **(3)** 72°

(2) 54° **(4)** 108°

2 In which type of quadrilateral are the diagonals not necessarily perpendicular?

(1) rectangle **(3)** kite

(2) square **(4)** rhombus

3 This figure is a trapezoid with congruent sides as marked. Which statement is false?

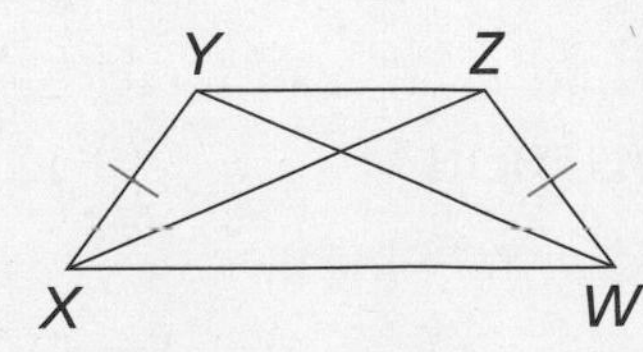

(1) $\overline{YZ} \cong \overline{XW}$

(2) $\overline{XZ} \cong \overline{WY}$

(3) $m\angle XYZ = m\angle WZY$

(4) $m\angle XYZ + m\angle YXW = 180°$

4 In the figure below, $EFGH$ is a parallelogram. What is $m\angle F$?

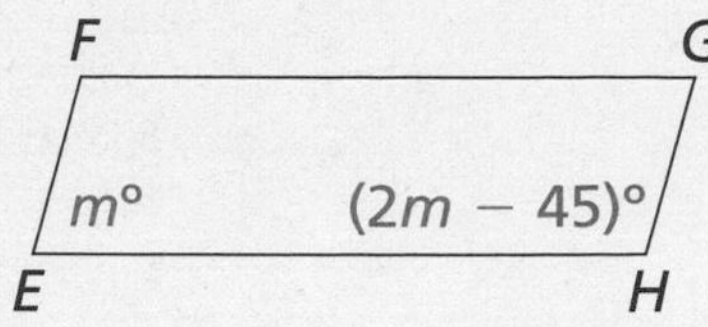

(1) 15° **(3)** 105°

(2) 75° **(4)** 255°

5 Which conditions will not guarantee that quadrilateral $QUAD$ is a parallelogram?

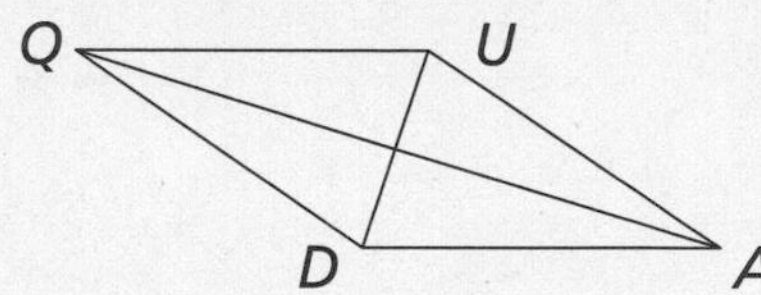

(1) $\overline{QD} \cong \overline{QU}$ and $\overline{AD} \cong \overline{AU}$

(2) $\overline{QD} \cong \overline{AU}$ and $\overline{QU} \cong \overline{AD}$

(3) $\overline{QD} \cong \overline{AU}$ and $\overline{QD} \parallel \overline{AU}$

(4) $\overline{QU} \parallel \overline{AD}$ and $\overline{QD} \parallel \overline{AU}$

6 In quadrilateral $PQRS$, find $m\angle P$, $m\angle Q$, and $m\angle R$.

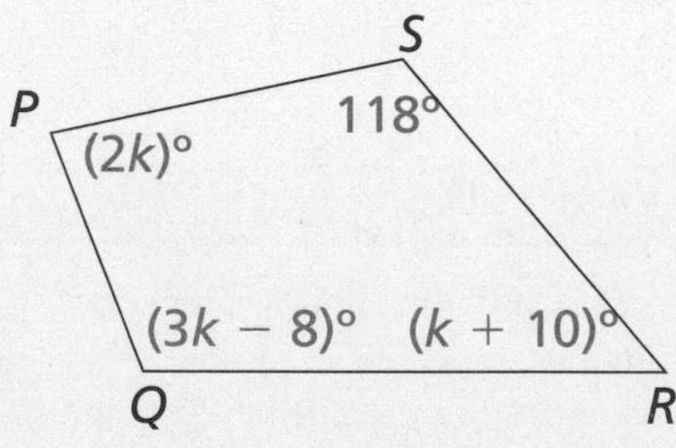

7 Given that $JKLM$ is a parallelogram, find $m\angle K$, $m\angle L$, and $m\angle M$.

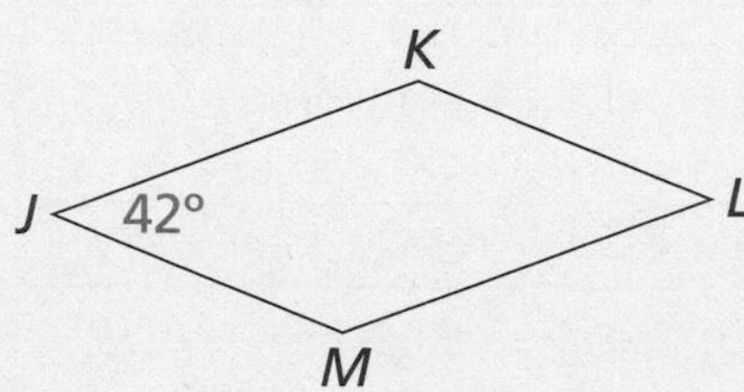

8 Given that $MATH$ is a rhombus, find MA, AT, TH, and HM.

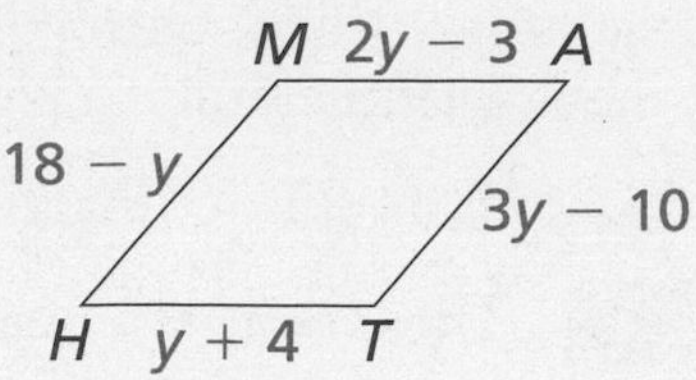

9 In quadrilateral $NOPQ$, $m\angle POQ = 70°$ and $m\angle PQN = 135°$. Find $m\angle ONQ$.

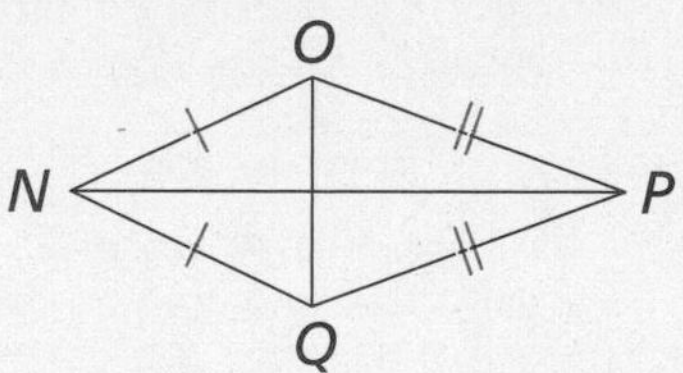

10 In quadrilateral $ABCD$, $\overline{AB} \parallel \overline{DC}$. $\overline{AD} \cong \overline{BC}$, $AC = 5z - 3$, and $BD = 4z$. Find AC and BD.

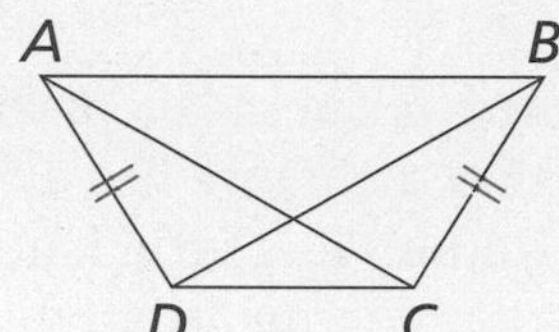

In Exercises 11–16, tell whether each statement is *always true, sometimes true,* or *never true.*

11 A rectangle is a square.

12 A trapezoid is a parallelogram.

13 A rhombus is a rectangle.

14 A rhombus is a square.

15 The diagonals of a square bisect each other.

16 The diagonals of a parallelogram are congruent.

17 Quadrilateral $ABCD$ is a parallelogram. Under what conditions will $ABCD$ also be a trapezoid, rhombus, kite, and square?

5.3 Proofs on Special Quadrilaterals

New York Standards

G.G.39 Theorems about special parallelograms

G.G.40 Theorems about trapezoids

You can use the properties of **special quadrilaterals** to algebraically demonstrate that a quadrilateral is a parallelogram.

EXAMPLE 1 **Showing that a quadrilateral is a parallelogram**

1 Find the values of x and y for which $PQRS$ is a parallelogram.

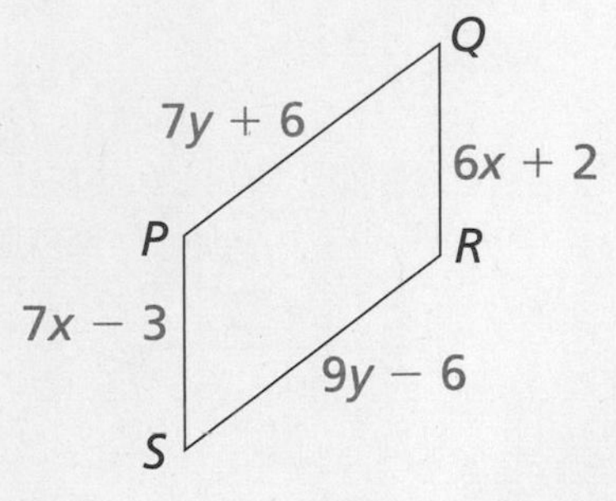

■ **SOLUTION**

A quadrilateral is a parallelogram if both pairs of opposite sides are congruent.

Therefore: $SP = QR$ and $PQ = RS$

$$7x - 3 = 6x + 2 \qquad 7y + 6 = 9y - 6$$
$$x - 3 = 2 \qquad 6 = 2y - 6$$
$$x = 5 \qquad 12 = 2y$$
$$6 = y$$

So $PQRS$ is a parallelogram when $x = 5$ and $y = 6$.

When proving that a figure is a particular type of quadrilateral, you do not need to prove that the figure has all the properties of that type of quadrilateral. Rather, it is sufficient to show the minimal properties required to be a specific type of quadrilateral.

The following table summarizes the minimal properties necessary to prove a quadrilateral is of a particular type:

A quadrilateral is a parallelogram if...	A quadrilateral is a rhombus if...
• both pairs of opposite sides are parallel. • both pairs of opposite sides are congruent. • both pairs of opposite angles are congruent. • consecutive angles are supplementary. • 1 pair of sides are parallel and congruent. • the diagonals bisect each other.	• it is parallelogram with perpendicular diagonals. • all 4 sides are congruent. • it is a parallelogram with 2 consecutive congruent sides.
A quadrilateral is a rectangle if...	**A quadrilateral is a trapezoid if...**
• it is a parallelogram with congruent diagonals. • it is a parallelogram with right angles.	• one pair of opposite sides are parallel.
A quadrilateral is a square if...	**A quadrilateral is an isosceles trapezoid if...**
• it is a rectangle with 2 congruent consecutive sides. • it is rhombus with 1 right angle.	• it is a trapezoid with congruent base angles. • it is a trapezoid with congruent diagonals. • it is a trapezoid with congruent nonparallel sides.

For example, in order to prove that a quadrilateral is a parallelogram, it is sufficient to show that both pairs of opposite angles are congruent. You do not need to show that the quadrilateral has all the properties of a parallelogram. To show that a quadrilateral is a rectangle, you must first show that it is a parallelogram, and then show that it has right angles.

Note that definitions are biconditional statements. For example, if both pairs of opposite sides are parallel, then the quadrilateral is a parallelogram. The converse is also true: If a quadrilateral is a parallelogram, then both pairs of opposite sides are parallel.

EXAMPLES 2 and 3 Proving a quadrilateral is a rectangle and parallelogram

2 Prove that a parallelogram containing one right angle is a rectangle.

Given: Parallelogram *KLMN* with right $\angle N$
Prove: *KLMN* is a rectangle

■ **SOLUTION**

Given *KLMN* is a parallelogram and $\angle N$ is a right angle, then $\angle L$ is also a right angle since opposite angles of a parallelogram are congruent. Since the sum of the four angles equals 360°, the other two angles add up to 180°. Since those angles are congruent, each one is also a right angle.

Therefore, by definition, if a parallelogram contains four right angles, the parallelogram is a rectangle.

3 If both pairs of opposite sides of a quadrilateral are congruent, prove that the quadrilateral is a parallelogram.

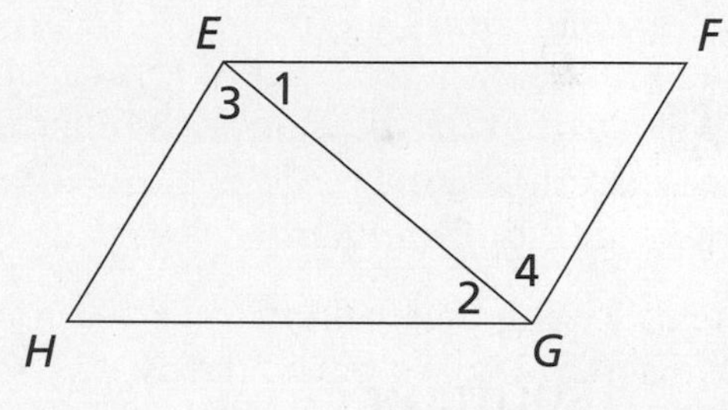

■ **SOLUTION**

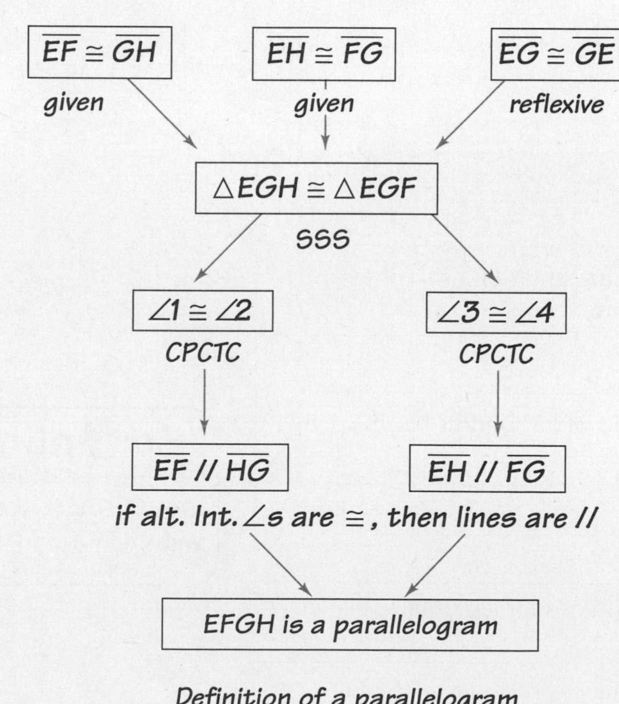

You can use the definitions of special types of quadrilaterals to prove their properties.

Go Online
PHSchool.com
Visit: PHSchool.com
Web Code: ayp-0417

EXAMPLES 4 and 5 Proving properties

Prove that the diagonals of an isosceles trapezoid are congruent.

Given: Isosceles trapezoid $PQRS$, with bases $\overline{QR}$ and $\overline{PS}$.
Prove: $\overline{PR} \cong \overline{QS}$

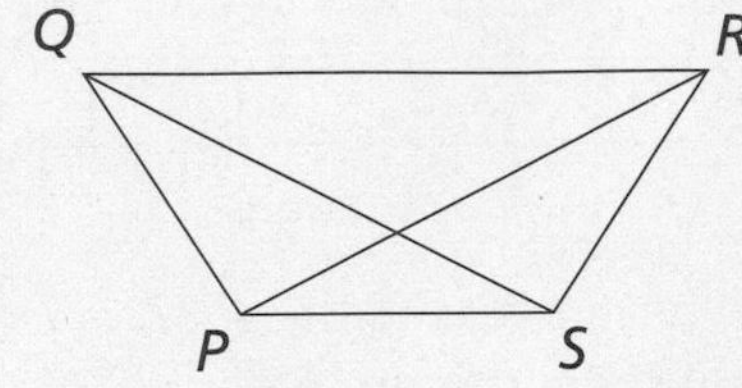

■ **SOLUTION**

Given $PQRS$ is an isosceles trapezoid then $\overline{PQ} \cong \overline{RS}$, and $\angle QPS \cong \angle RSP$. Opposite sides of an isosceles trapezoid are congruent, and the base angles are also congruent. We know $\overline{PS} \cong \overline{PS}$ by the reflexive property, so $\triangle PQS$ and $\triangle SRP$ are congruent by SAS. Therefore, the diagonals $\overline{PR}$ and $\overline{QS}$ are congruent by CPCTC.

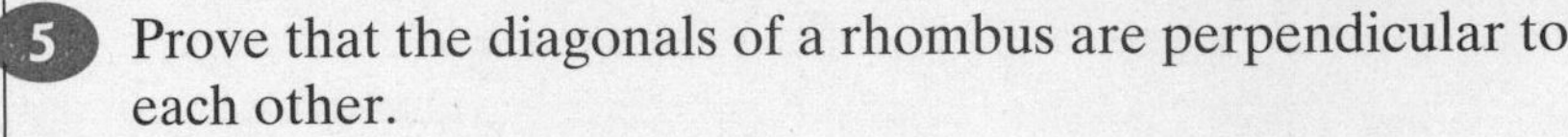

5 Prove that the diagonals of a rhombus are perpendicular to each other.

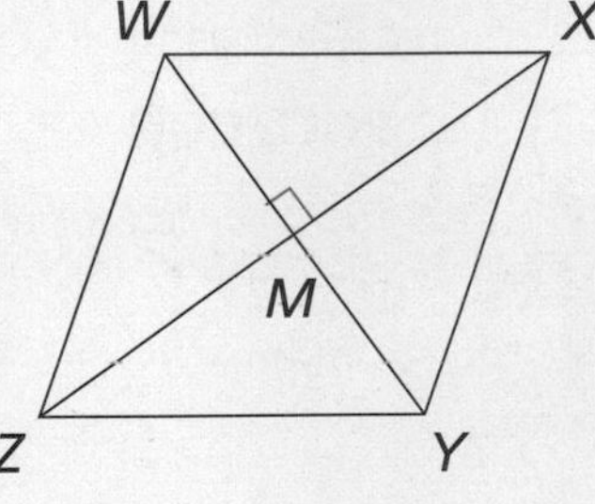

Given: $WXYZ$ is a rhombus.
Prove: $\overline{WY} \perp \overline{XZ}$

■ **SOLUTION**

Statements	Reasons
1. $WXYZ$ is a rhombus.	1. Given
2. $\overline{WZ} \cong \overline{ZY}$	2. Consecutive sides of a rhombus are congruent.
3. $\overline{ZM} \cong \overline{MZ}$	3. Reflexive property
4. $\overline{WM} \cong \overline{MY}$	4. Diagonals of a rhombus bisect each other.
5. $\Delta WMZ \cong \Delta YMZ$	5. SSS
6. $\angle WMZ \cong \angle YMZ$	6. CPCTC
7. $\angle WMZ$ *is the supplement* $\angle YMZ$	7. Definition of supplementary
8. $\angle WMZ$ *and* $\angle YMZ$ *are right* $\angle s$	8. If two angles are congruent and supplementary, they are right angles.
9. $\overline{WY} \perp \overline{XZ}$	9. If two angles are right angles, the lines that form them are perpendicular.

Practice

Choose the numeral preceding the word or expression that best completes the statement or answers the question.

1 Which of the following statements is *not* true?

(1) All quadrilaterals have four sides.

(2) A parallelogram with one right angle is a rectangle.

(3) A rhombus is always a square.

(4) The diagonals of a rhombus are perpendicular to each other.

2 If a parallelogram has four congruent sides, then it must be a

(1) square. **(3)** parallelogram.

(2) rhombus. **(4)** kite.

3 If a quadrilateral has both pairs of opposite angles congruent, then the figure is *at least* a

(1) square. **(3)** trapezoid.

(2) rhombus. **(4)** parallelogram.

4 If any two angles of a quadrilateral are supplementary and congruent, the quadrilateral can be which of the following?

(1) A square

(2) A rectangle

(3) A parallelogram

(4) All of the above

5 In quadrilateral $ABCD$, $\overline{BC} \cong \overline{AD}$, which of the following would make $ABCD$ a parallelogram?

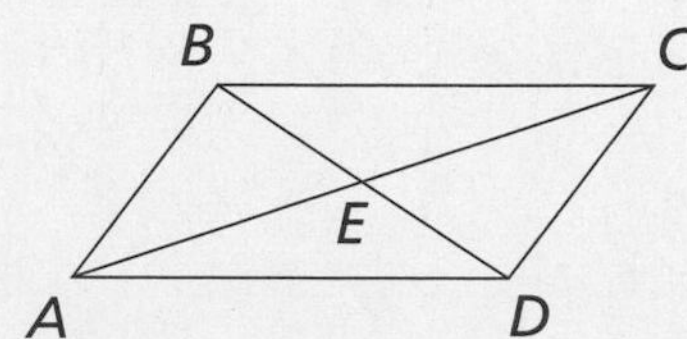

(1) $\overline{AC}$ bisects $\overline{BD}$

(2) $\angle CBD \cong \angle ADB$

(3) $\overline{BD} \cong \overline{AC}$

(4) $\overline{AB} \parallel \overline{DC}$

6 Which pairs of quadrilaterals are congruent?

I. Two squares whose corresponding diagonals are congruent

II. Two rectangles whose corresponding diagonals are congruent

III. Two rhombuses whose corresponding diagonals are congruent

(1) II only

(2) I and II

(3) I and III

(4) I, II, and III

7 Use a two-column proof to prove that given kite $DEFG$, with $\overline{EF} \cong \overline{GF}$, $\overline{DF}$ bisects $\overline{EG}$.

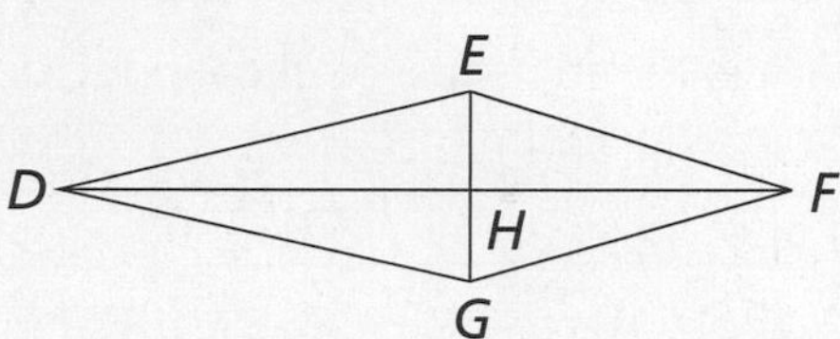

8 Use a flow proof to prove the following:

Given: $ABCD$ is a rhombus

Prove: $\triangle ACB = \triangle CAD$

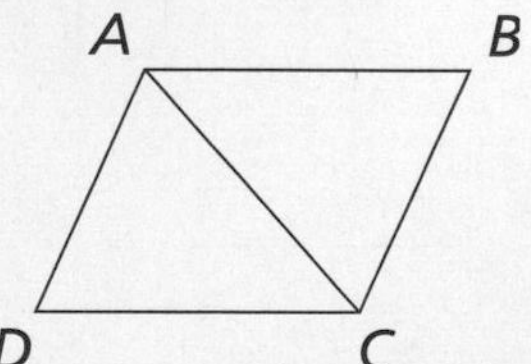

9 Write a paragraph proof showing that the diagonals of a rectangle are congruent.

10 **Given:** Quadrilateral $ABCD$
$\overline{AB} \parallel \overline{CD}$ and $\overline{AB} \cong \overline{CD}$

Prove: $ABCD$ is a parallelogram.

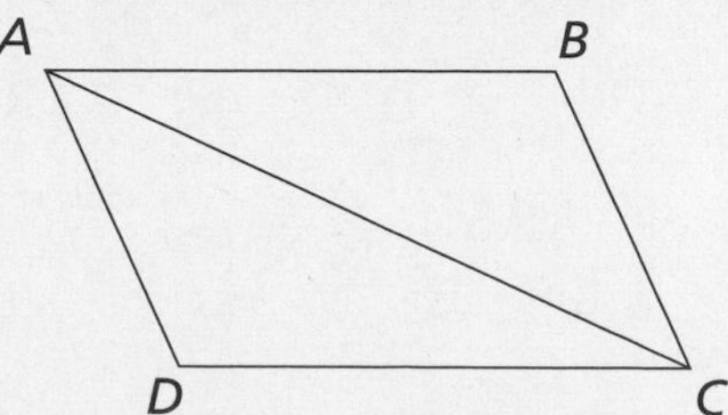

Chapter 5 Preparing for the New York Geometry Exam

Answer all questions in this part. For each question, select the numeral preceding the word or expression that best completes the statement or answers the question.

1 The sum of the exterior angles of any polygon is

(1) 180°. **(3)** $\frac{360°}{n}$.

(2) 360°. **(4)** $(n - 2)180°$.

2 The number of triangles found in the interior of any polygon is always

(1) the same as the number of sides.

(2) one less than the number of sides.

(3) two less than the number of sides.

(4) three less than the number of sides.

3 What is the measure of each exterior angle of a regular octagon?

(1) 45° **(3)** 360°

(2) 135° **(4)** 1080°

4 Find the measures of $\angle 1$, $\angle 2$, and $\angle 3$ in the parallelogram drawn below.

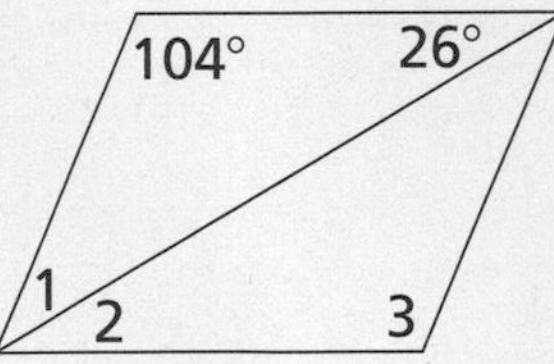

(1) $m\angle 1 = 13°, m\angle 2 = 52°; m\angle 3 = 154°$

(2) $m\angle 1 = 26°, m\angle 2 = 13°; m\angle 3 = 154°$

(3) $m\angle 1 = 26°, m\angle 2 = 50°; m\angle 3 = 104°$

(4) $m\angle 1 = 50°, m\angle 2 = 26°; m\angle 3 = 104°$

5 The figure $ABCD$ below is a rhombus, $m\angle ABC = 120°$, and the length of $\overline{EB}$ is 13. Find the length of $\overline{AB}$.

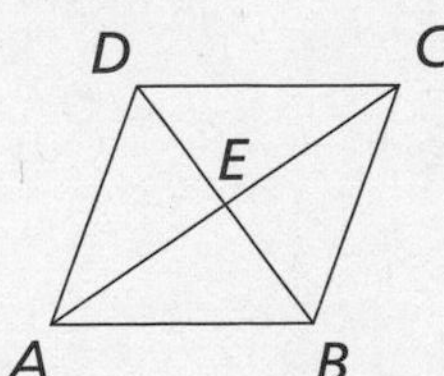

(1) 13 **(2)** 26 **(3)** 30 **(4)** 60

6 The figure below is a rhombus. Find the value of x, y, and z.

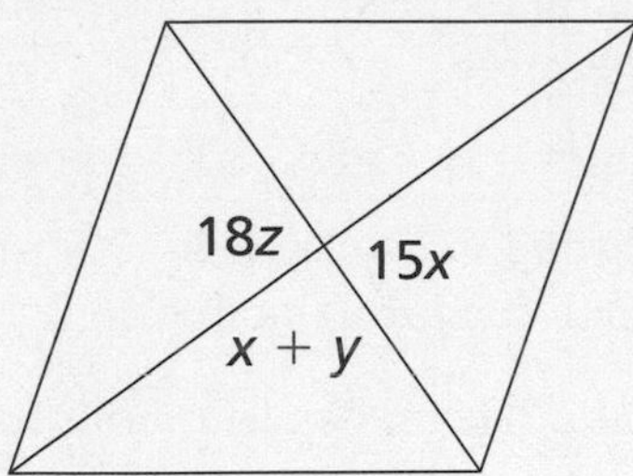

(1) $x = 6, y = 84, z = 5$

(2) $x = 6, y = 89, z = 0$

(3) $x = 12, y = 168, z = 10$

(4) $x = 12, y = 173, z = 5$

7 In an isosceles trapezoid, the length of the base is $10x - 4$, the length of one leg is $6x - 5$, and the length of the other leg is $4x + 7$. Find the value of x.

(1) 1

(2) $\frac{11}{6}$

(3) $\frac{9}{4}$

(4) 6

8 Determine the values of x and y for which the figure $ABCD$ is a parallelogram.

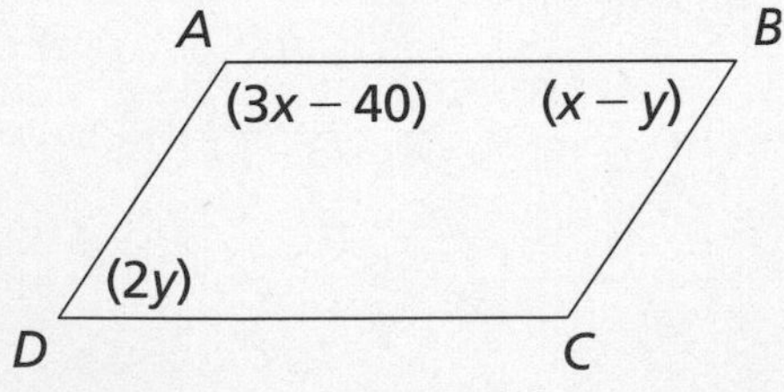

(1) $x = 20, y = 20$

(2) $x = 20, y = 60$

(3) $x = 60, y = 20$

(4) $x = 140, y = 40$

9 In the parallelogram below, if $m\angle 1 = m\angle 3 = 11x$, and $m\angle 2 = 3x - 30$, and $m\angle 4 = x$, find the value of x.

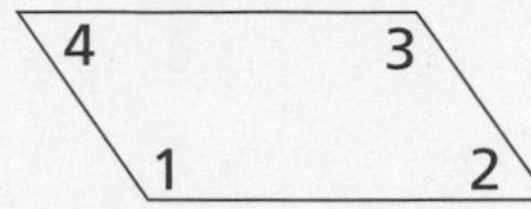

(1) 15 **(2)** 30 **(3)** 45 **(4)** 165

10 Find the value of x in the parallelogram $ABCD$.

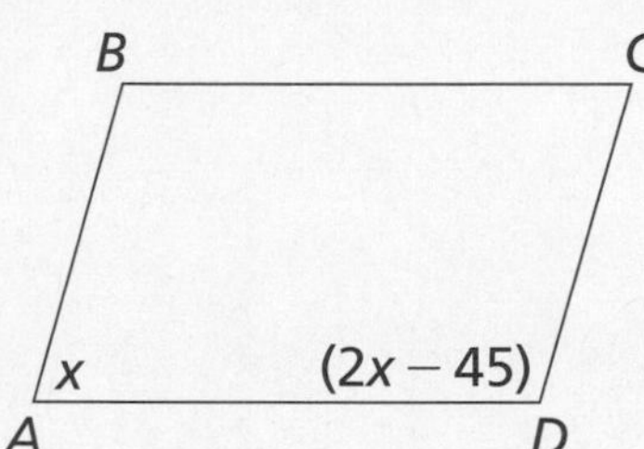

(1) 15 **(2)** 45 **(3)** 75 **(4)** 225

11 The figure below is an isosceles trapezoid with bases $\overline{BI}$ and $\overline{RD}$. Which of the following statements is true?

I. $m\angle BIR = m\angle DIB$
II. $m\angle BIR = 2m\angle BRD$
III. $m\angle BIR = 180 - m\angle IDR$

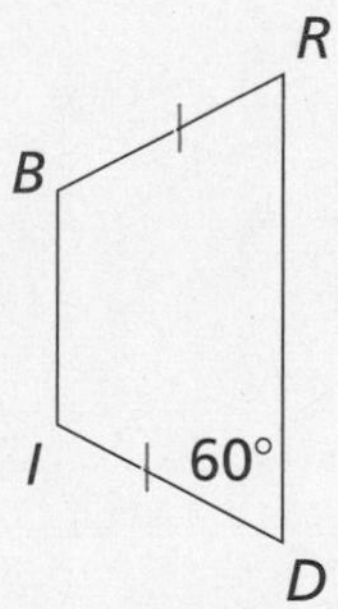

(1) I only **(3)** I and II
(2) II only **(4)** II and III

12 Which of the following do not have perpendicular diagonals?

I. Isosceles trapezoid
II. Kite
III. Rectangle
IV. Rhombus

(1) I only **(3)** I and III
(2) II only **(4)** II and III

13 Which property is sufficient to show that a quadrilateral is always a parallelogram?

(1) Both pairs of opposite sides are parallel and congruent.

(2) One pair of its opposite angles is congruent.

(3) One pair of its opposite sides is parallel.

(4) Three sides are congruent.

14 Which of the following conditions are sufficient to prove that a quadrilateral is a square?

(1) It has opposite sides that are parallel.

(2) It has opposite sides that are parallel and congruent.

(3) It has one pair of opposite angles that are right angles and all sides are congruent.

(4) It has one pair of opposite sides that are parallel and noncongruent.

15 The parallelogram $ABCD$ has diagonals $\overline{AC}$ and $\overline{BD}$. If $AC = 5x + 4$, $AE = 4x - 2y$, and $CE = 3x + 2y$, find the value of x.

(1) 1

(2) 2

(3) 3

(4) 4

16 What is the sum of the measures of the interior angles of an 18-gon?

(1) 20°

(2) 160°

(3) 360°

(4) 2880°

Answer all questions in this part. Clearly indicate the necessary steps, including appropriate formula substitutions, diagrams, graphs, charts, etc. For all questions in this part, a correct numerical answer with no work shown will receive only one credit.

17 Find the measure of angle x. Show your work.

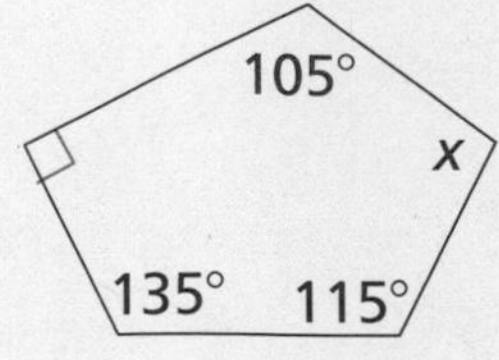

18 Draw a Venn diagram showing the relationship among the quadrilaterals: squares, rectangles, rhombuses, and parallelograms.

19 **Given:** $\triangle PUT \not\cong \triangle NTU$

Prove: *PUNT* is **not** a rectangle.

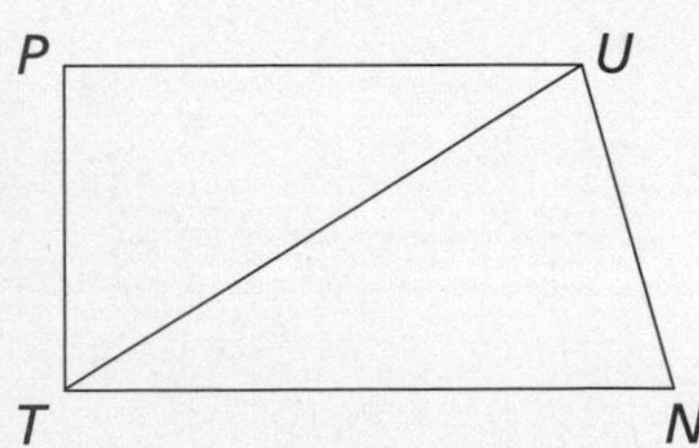

6 Coordinate Geometry

Discovering New York

The Empire State Building

Featured in many movies, including *King Kong* and *Sleepless in Seattle*, the Empire State Building is one of the most famous skyscrapers in the world. This historic New York landmark soars more than a quarter of a mile above Manhattan, extending 1,472 feet from its base to its antennae.

A pencil is said to have inspired the building's unique, art deco style. The top of the building is lit up at night in different colors to celebrate various holidays.

Construction of the Empire State Building began in 1930 and progressed rapidly, lasting only 18 months. The steel framework increased at an average of four and a half floors per week, with 3,000 workers working on the building at one time.

6.1 Slope of Parallel and Perpendicular Lines

New York Standards

G.G.62 Slope of perpendicular lines

G.G.63 Identify parallel/perpendicular lines

Given sufficient information about a line in the coordinate plane, you can write a linear equation in two variables to represent it. Stated below are important forms for an equation of a line.

Slope-Intercept and Point-Slope Forms

An equation of a line in **slope-intercept form,** $y = mx + b$ has slope m and y-intercept b.

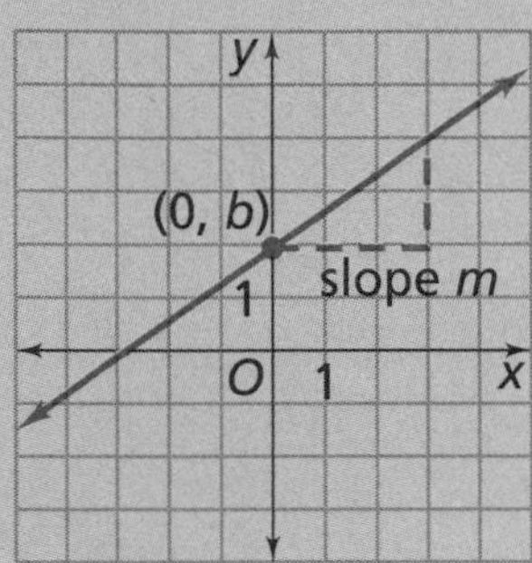

An equation of a line in **point-slope form,** $y - y_1 = m(x - x_1)$ has slope m and passes through (x_1, y_1).

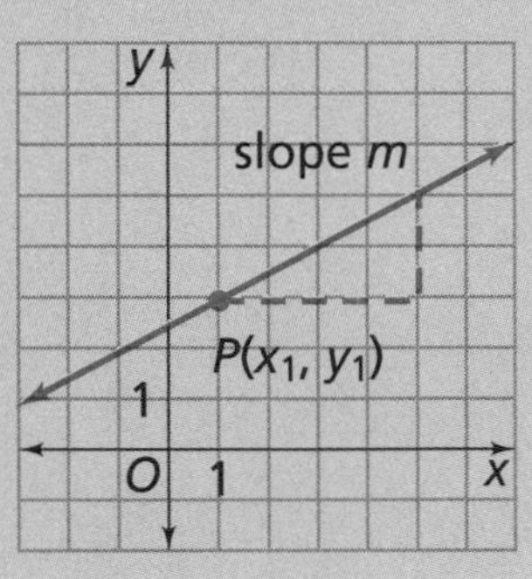

Note

The slope of a line passing through (x_1, y_1) and $(x_2, y_2) = \frac{(y_2 - y_1)}{(x_2 - x_1)}$. The slope of a horizontal line is 0. The slope of a vertical line is undefined.

Any vertical line containing $P(x_1, y_1)$ has equation $x = x_1$. For example, if a vertical line contains the point $(5, 2)$, an equation for that line is $x = 5$.

Any horizontal line containing $P(x_1, y_1)$ has equation $y = y_1$. For example, if a horizontal line contains the point $(4, -8)$, an equation for that line is $y = -8$.

Go Online
PHSchool.com

Visit: PHSchool.com

Web Codes: ayp-0208
ayp-0215

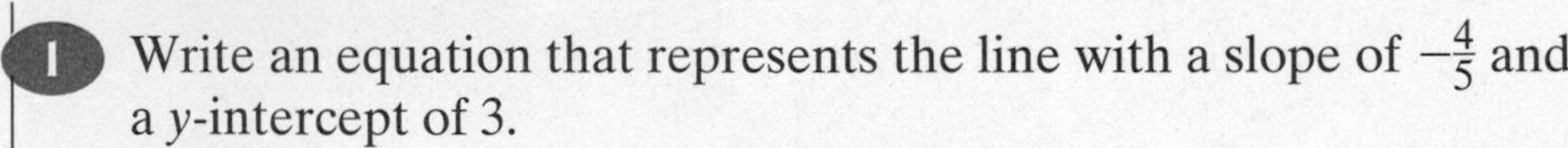

EXAMPLES 1 and 2 **Using slope and *y*-intercept to identify an equation for a line**

1 Write an equation that represents the line with a slope of $-\frac{4}{5}$ and a y-intercept of 3.

▪ SOLUTION

Use the slope-intercept form.

$$y = mx + b.$$

$$y = -\tfrac{4}{5}x + 3 \quad \leftarrow \text{Replace } m \text{ with } -\tfrac{4}{5} \text{ and } b \text{ with 3.}$$

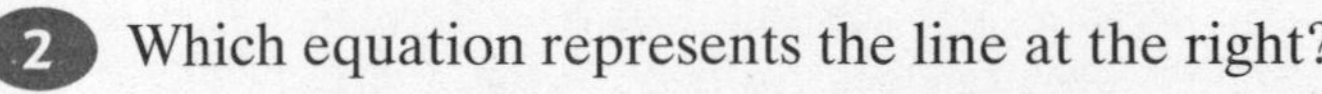

2 Which equation represents the line at the right?

(1) $y = \frac{1}{4}x + 3$ **(3)** $y = \frac{1}{4}x - 3$

(2) $y = -\frac{1}{4}x + 3$ **(4)** $y = -2x + 3$

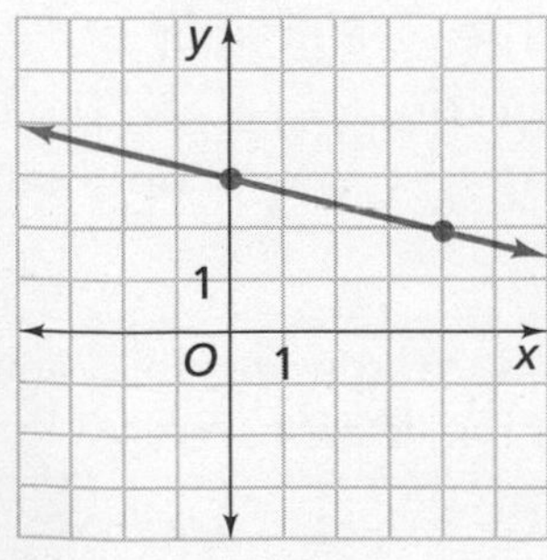

▪ SOLUTION

The y-intercept is 3. The slope of the line is $-\frac{1}{4}$. Using the slope-intercept form, the correct choice is **(2)**.

When you are given the slope and a point on a line, you can use the point-slope form to write an equation for that line.

Go Online
PHSchool.com
Visit: PHSchool.com
Web Code: ayp-0214

EXAMPLES 3 through 5 **Writing an equation for a line by using slope and a point on the line**

Write an equation in slope-intercept form for each line, if possible.

3 the line with slope $\frac{3}{4}$ and containing $P(2, -3)$

■ **SOLUTION**

$$y - (-3) = \frac{3}{4}(x - 2)$$
$$y = \frac{3}{4}x - 4.5$$

4 the line with slope 0 and containing $P(2, -3)$

■ **SOLUTION**

Because the slope is 0, the line is horizontal.

$$y = -3$$

5 the line with no slope and containing $P(2, -3)$

■ **SOLUTION**

Because there is no slope, the line is vertical.

$$x = 2$$

You can also use the point-slope form to find an equation of a line through two specific points. The point-slope form requires that you first find the slope. Recall that slope $= m = \frac{y_2 - y_1}{x_2 - x_1}$. You can write an equation of a line in slope-intercept or standard form.

EXAMPLES 6 through 9 **Writing an equation for a line given two points**

Write an equation for

6 the line containing $A(-5, -6)$ and $B(3, 8)$.

■ **SOLUTION**

First determine the slope.

$$m = \frac{y_2 - y_1}{x_2 - x_1} = \frac{-6 - 8}{-5 - 3}$$
$$= \frac{-14}{-8} = \frac{7}{4}$$

Using the point $B(3, 8)$ and the point-slope form results in:

$$y - 8 = \frac{7}{4}(x - 3)$$
$$y - \frac{32}{4} = \frac{7}{4}x - \frac{21}{4}$$
$$y = \frac{7}{4}x + 2.75$$

7 $\overleftrightarrow{DG}$ containing $D(2, 3)$ and $G(8, 11)$ in standard form.

■ **SOLUTION**

First determine the slope.

$$m = \frac{y_2 - y_1}{x_2 - x_1} = \frac{11 - 3}{8 - 2} = \frac{8}{6} = \frac{4}{3}$$

Using the point $D(2, 3)$ and the point-slope form results in:

$$y - 3 = \frac{4}{3}(x - 2)$$
$$3y - 9 = 4x - 8$$
$$-4x + 3y = 1$$

The standard form for the equation is $-4x + 3y = 1$.

8 the line containing $L(-5, -6)$ and $M(3, -6)$.

■ **SOLUTION**

The y-coordinates of L and M are equal. The line is horizontal.

$$y = -6$$

9 the line containing $R(4.2, -6)$ and $S(4.2, 9)$.

■ **SOLUTION**

The x-coordinates of R and S are equal. The line is vertical.

$$x = 4.2$$

Use what you know to solve problems involving points on a line.

EXAMPLES 10 and 11 Solving problems about points on a line

10 The point $Z(3, w)$ is on the graph of $y = 2x + 5$. The value of w is

(1) -1 **(2)** $w - 5$ **(3)** 11 **(4)** $2w + 5$

■ **SOLUTION**

If $x = 3$ and $y = w$, then $w = 2(3) + 5$; that is, $w = 11$.
The correct choice is (3).

11 Which point lies on the line containing $P(-3, -1)$ and $Q(5, 6)$?

(1) $A(-3, 0)$ **(2)** $B(21, 19)$ **(3)** $C(21, 20)$ **(4)** $D(-3, -2)$

■ **SOLUTION**

$m = \frac{6 - (-1)}{5 - (-3)} = \frac{7}{8}$ ← **Determine the slope.**

$y = \frac{7}{8}(x - 5) + 6$ ← **Write an equation for the line containing *P* and *Q*.**

Because $\frac{7}{8}(21 - 5) + 6 = 20$, the correct choice is *C*.

Two lines in a plane either intersect or do not intersect. If the lines never intersect, they are **parallel.** If the lines intersect at a right angle, the lines are **perpendicular.**

m: $y = \frac{1}{2}x + 3$ n: $y = \frac{1}{2}x - 1$

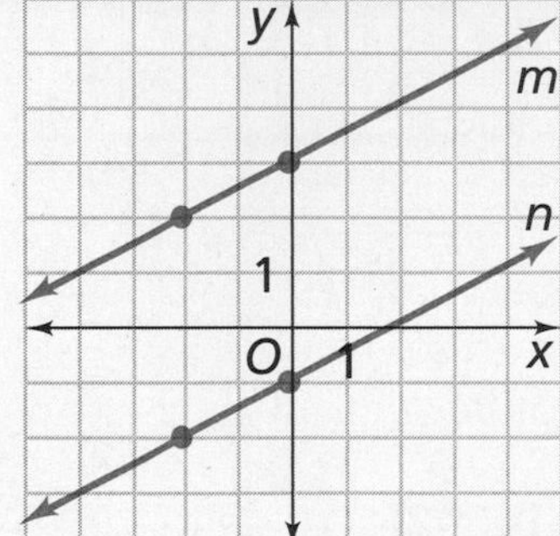

slope of m: $\frac{1}{2}$ slope of n: $\frac{1}{2}$

The lines are **parallel lines.**
The **slopes** of these lines are **equal.**

p: $y = -2x - 6$ q: $y = \frac{1}{2}x - 1$

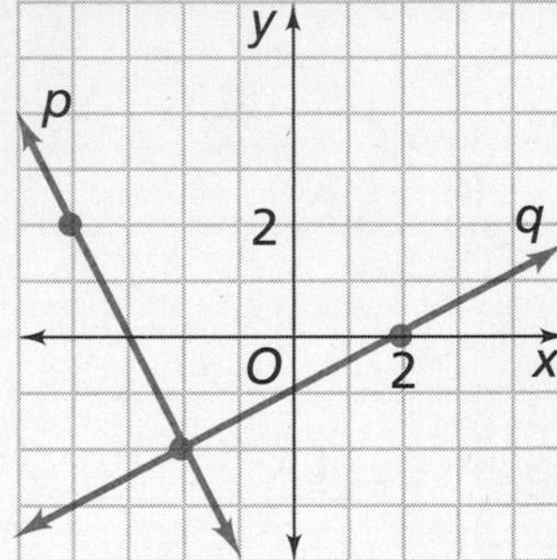

slope of p: -2 slope of q: $\frac{1}{2}$ Note: $-2 \cdot \frac{1}{2} = -1$

The lines are **perpendicular lines.**
The slopes are **negative reciprocals** of each other.

Parallel and Perpendicular Lines

- Two lines with slopes m_1 and m_2 are parallel if and only if $m_1 = m_2$.
(Any two vertical or horizontal lines are parallel.)
- Two lines with slopes m_1 and m_2 are perpendicular if and only if $m_1 m_2 = -1$.
(Every vertical line is perpendicular to every horizontal line.)

Practice

Choose the numeral preceding the word or expression that best completes the statement or answers the question.

1 What is the slope of a line parallel to a line with slope -2?

(1) 2 **(2)** -2 **(3)** $\frac{1}{2}$ **(4)** $-\frac{1}{2}$

2 What is the slope of a line perpendicular to a line with slope -2?

(1) 2 **(2)** -2 **(3)** 0.5 **(4)** -0.5

3 Which describes the relationship between two distinct nonvertical parallel lines?

(1) equal slopes; unequal y-intercepts

(2) unequal slopes; unequal y-intercepts

(3) equal slopes; equal y-intercepts

(4) unequal slopes; equal y-intercepts

4 The slope of a line perpendicular to line p is

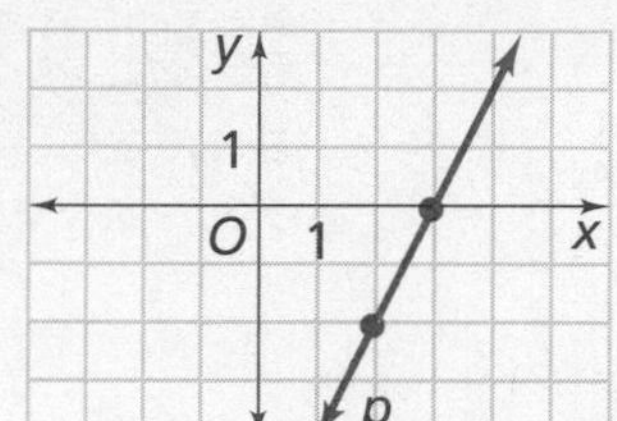

(1) 2. **(2)** 0.5. **(3)** -2. **(4)** -0.5.

5 Which equation represents the line with slope -3 and y-intercept -7?

(1) $y = -3x + 7$ **(3)** $y = -3x - 7$

(2) $y = -7x + 3$ **(4)** $y = 7x - 3$

6 What is the slope of a line parallel to m?

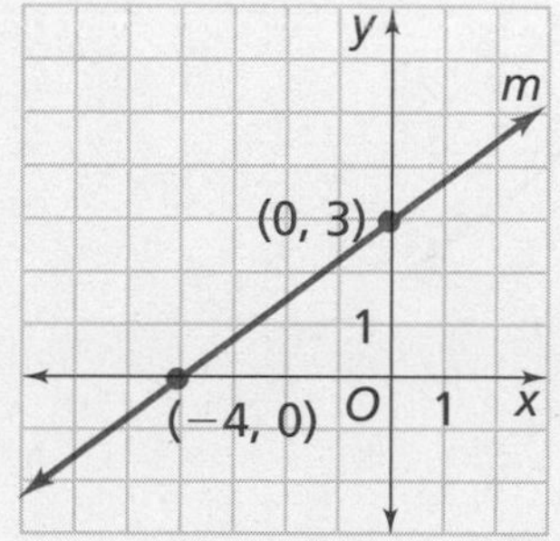

(1) $-\frac{4}{3}$

(2) $\frac{4}{3}$

(3) $-\frac{3}{4}$

(4) $\frac{3}{4}$

7 Which equation could not represent a line parallel to the graph of $y = -2.5x + 1$?

(1) $y = -2.5x + 3$ **(3)** $y = -2.5x - 1$

(2) $y = 2.5x + 1$ **(4)** $y = -2.5x$

In Exercises 8–17, write an equation in slope-intercept form for the specified line, where possible.

8 the line containing $A(0, 7)$ and $B(7, 0)$

9 the line containing $C(3, -7)$ and $D(-3, 5)$

10 slope: 2; containing $P(4, 5)$

11 slope: -0.6; containing $Z(-1, 1)$

12 slope: -0.2; y-intercept -3

13 slope: 0; y-intercept 7

14 slope: 0; y-intercept -7

15 no slope; x-intercept -11

16 no slope; containing $S(-1, -3)$

17 slope 0; containing $(0, 0)$

18 Is the suggested relationship between y and x linear? Explain your answer.

x	0	4	8	12
y	2	5	8	11

19 Write an equation in standard form for this graph.

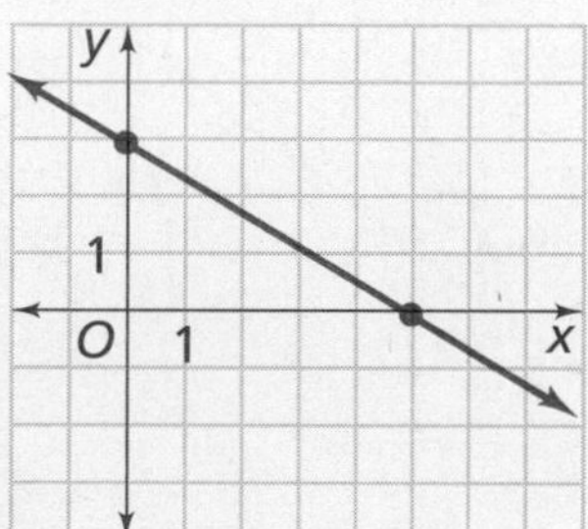

20 A student can work at a job that pays \$4 an hour for 25 hours to earn \$100 or can work at a second job that pays \$5 per hour for 20 hours to earn \$100. If the student spends time at each job, find two other amounts of time at each job needed to earn \$100. Show your work.

21 Is $S(93, 83)$ on the line containing $P(-3, -1)$ and $Q(5, 6)$? Justify your response.

22 Is $C(-102, 142)$ on the line that crosses the x-axis where $x = 17$ and crosses the y-axis where $y = 20$?

6.2 Equations of Parallel and Perpendicular Lines

New York Standards

G.G.64 Equations of perpendicular lines

G.G.65 Equations of parallel lines

You know that parallel lines have the same slope ($m_1 = m_2$) and different *y-intercepts*. You can use this to determine whether lines are parallel to each other.

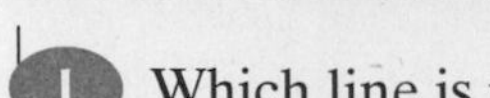

Identifying a line parallel to another line

1 Which line is parallel to the graph of $5x - 6y = 2$?

(1) the line with slope $-\frac{5}{6}$ and y-intercept $-\frac{1}{3}$

(2) the line with slope $\frac{5}{6}$ and y-intercept 3

(3) the line with slope $-\frac{6}{5}$ and y-intercept $-\frac{1}{3}$

(4) the line with slope $-\frac{6}{5}$ and y-intercept 3

■ SOLUTION

Write $5x - 6y = 2$ in slope-intercept form.

$$5x - 6y = 2$$
$$-6y = -5x + 2$$
$$y = \frac{5}{6}x - \frac{1}{3}$$

A line parallel to the graph of $5x - 6y = 2$ must have slope $\frac{5}{6}$. Therefore, eliminate choices **(1), (3),** and **(4).** The correct choice is (2).

Note

To see whether two distinct nonvertical lines are parallel, check to see whether:
- slopes are equal;
- y-intercepts are unequal.

2 Which line is parallel to $3x + 4y = 12$?

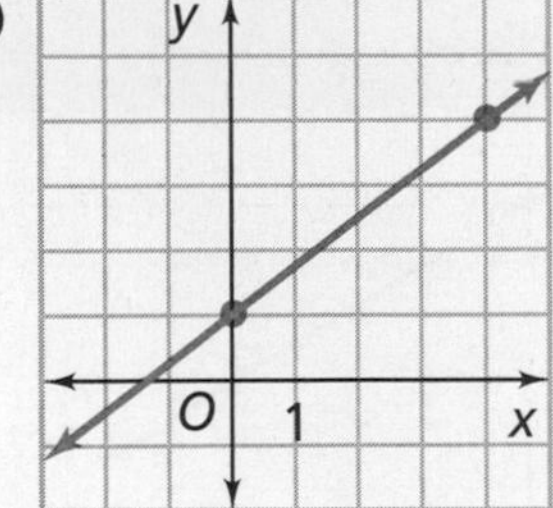

(3)

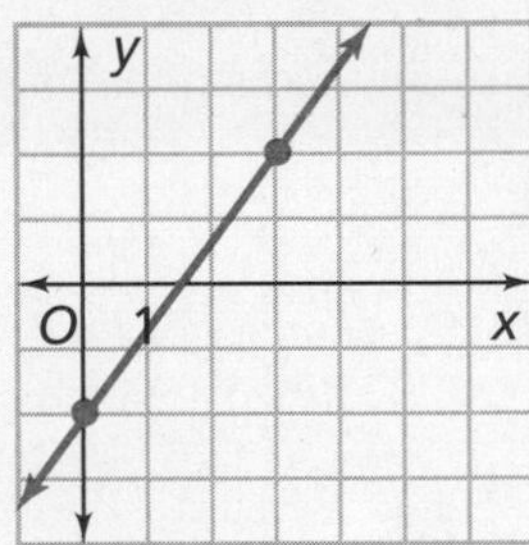

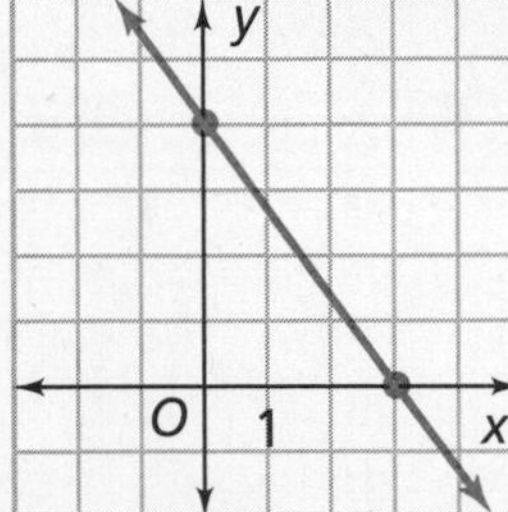

(4)

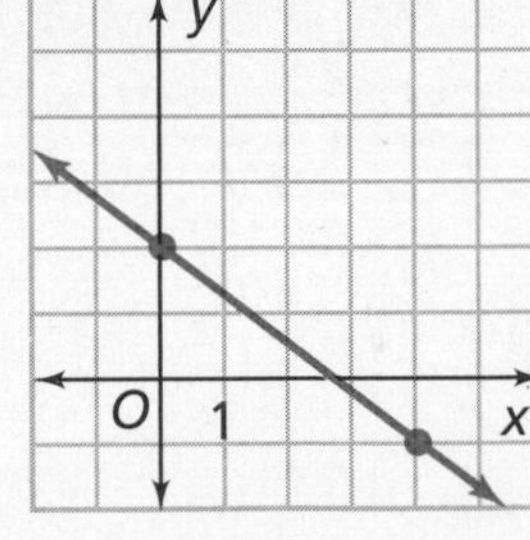

Go Online PHSchool.com

Visit: PHSchool.com

Web Codes: ayp-0219 ayp-0221

■ SOLUTION

Write $3x + 4y = 12$ in slope-intercept form.

$$y = -\frac{3}{4}x + 3$$

A line parallel to $3x + 4y = 12$ must have slope $-\frac{3}{4}$. You can eliminate choices **(1)** and **(3)** because the lines have positive slopes. The slope in line **(2)** is $-\frac{4}{3}$ and the slope in line **(4)** is $-\frac{3}{4}$. Therefore, (4) is the correct choice.

You can also use the slope to determine whether lines are perpendicular to each other. If two lines are perpendicular, then their slopes are negative reciprocals of each other ($m_1 \times m_2 = -1$).

EXAMPLES 3 and 4 Identifying a line perpendicular to a given line

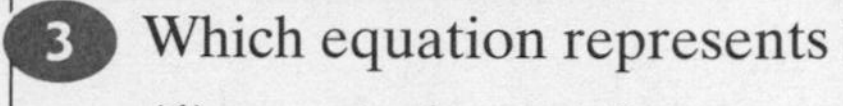

3 Which equation represents line q perpendicular to line p?

(1) $-x + 4y = -2$ **(3)** $-x + 4y = -7$

(2) $4x + y = 11$ **(4)** $4x + y = 2$

■ **SOLUTION**

Write the equation for each answer choice in slope-intercept form.

(1) $y = -\frac{1}{4}x - \frac{1}{2}$ **(3)** $y = \frac{1}{4}x - \frac{7}{4}$

(2) $y = -4x + 11$ **(4)** $y = -4x + 2$

Because the slope of p is $\frac{1}{4}$, the slope of q is -4. Eliminate choices **(1)** and **(3).** $C(3, -1)$ does not satisfy the equation in choice **(4).** The correct choice is **(2).**

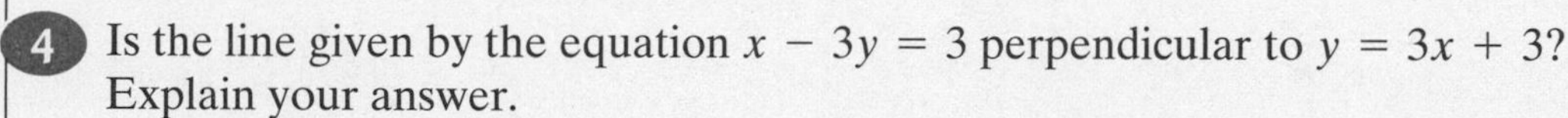

4 Is the line given by the equation $x - 3y = 3$ perpendicular to $y = 3x + 3$? Explain your answer.

■ **SOLUTION**

Write the equation of both lines in slope intercept form:

$y = \frac{1}{3}x - 1$

$y = 3x + 3$

Since their slopes are not negative reciprocals of each other, the lines are not perpendicular.

By comparing the slopes of two lines, you can determine whether they are perpendicular or parallel to each other.

EXAMPLE 5 Identifying if lines are parallel or perpendicular

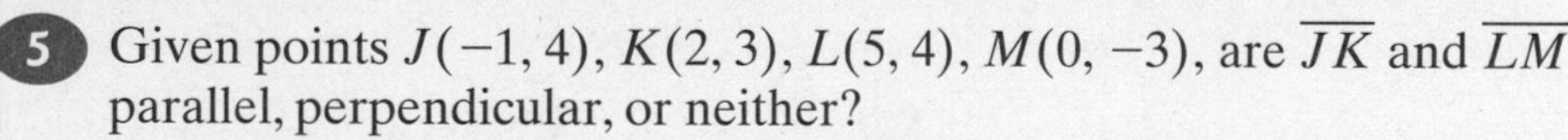

5 Given points $J(-1, 4)$, $K(2, 3)$, $L(5, 4)$, $M(0, -3)$, are $\overline{JK}$ and $\overline{LM}$ parallel, perpendicular, or neither?

■ **SOLUTION**

Slope of $\overline{JK} = \frac{3 - 4}{2 - (-1)} = -\frac{1}{3}$

Slope of $\overline{LM} = \frac{-3 - 4}{0 - (5)} = \frac{-7}{-5} = \frac{7}{5}$

Since their slopes are not equal, $\overline{JK}$ and $\overline{LM}$ are not parallel.

The product of their slopes is not -1.

$-\frac{1}{3} \times \frac{7}{5} = -\frac{7}{15}$

$\overline{JK}$ and $\overline{LM}$ are not perpendicular.

Therefore, they are neither parallel nor perpendicular.

Given a line containing a point, you can find the equation of a line parallel or perpendicular to it by using the slope-intercept method.

Go Online
PHSchool.com
Visit: PHSchool.com
Web Codes: ayp-0218
ayp-0220

EXAMPLES 6 and 7 **Finding equations for parallel or perpendicular lines**

Find an equation in slope-intercept form for the specified line.

 **6** line z containing $P(4, -3)$ and parallel to the graph of $y = \frac{1}{2}x + 3$

▪ SOLUTION

Because z is parallel to the graph of $y = \frac{1}{2}x + 3$, the slope of z is $\frac{1}{2}$. Also, z contains $P(4, -3)$.

$$y - (-3) = \frac{1}{2}(x - 4)$$
$$y = \frac{1}{2}x - 5$$

 **7** line n containing $Q(-2, 5)$ and perpendicular to the graph of $y = -\frac{1}{2}x + 5$

▪ SOLUTION

Because n is perpendicular to the graph of $y = -\frac{1}{2}x + 5$, the slope of n is 2. Also, n contains $Q(-2, 5)$.

$$y - 5 = 2(x - (-2))$$
$$y - 5 = 2(x + 2)$$
$$y = 2x + 9$$

Practice

Choose the numeral preceding the word or expression that best completes the statement or answers the question.

1 Which line is perpendicular to the graph of $3y + 2x = 12$?

(1) $y = -2x + 6$ **(3)** $2x - 3y = 6$

(2) $y = 3x - 2$ **(4)** $3x - 2y = 12$

2 If two lines have the same slope and the same y-intercept, they are

(1) parallel lines.

(2) the same line.

(3) undefined lines.

(4) perpendicular lines.

3 Which lines below are parallel?

I. $32y - 16x = 6$

II. $-16x - 32y = 6$

III. $-4y = 2x + 6$

(1) I and II

(2) I and III

(3) II and III

(4) None of the above

4 Which equation graphs a line that is *not* perpendicular to the graph of $2x + y = 8$?

(1) $x - 2y = 3$ **(3)** $y - \frac{x}{2} = 6$

(2) $2x - y = 4$ **(4)** $2y - x = 4$

5 Lines are perpendicular if

(1) one slope is the negative reciprocal of the other slope.

(2) one slope is the opposite sign of the other slope.

(3) one slope is the reciprocal of the other slope.

(4) one slope is identical to the other slope.

6 Which equation is perpendicular to the line given by the equation $3x - 5y = 15$ and passes through $(-2, 2)$?

(1) $3x + 5y = -4$

(2) $3x - 5y = -4$

(3) $5x + 3y = -4$

(4) $5x - 3y = -4$

In Exercises 7–14, write an equation in slope-intercept form for the specified line, where possible.

7 containing $H(2, 2)$ and parallel to the graph of $x - y = 3$

8 containing $A(-2, -2)$ and parallel to the graph of $y = 2x - 1$

9 containing $D(3, -5)$ and parallel to the graph of $y = -3x + 8$

10 containing $L(4, 7)$ and parallel to the graph of $x - 2y = 10$

11 containing $V(4, 0)$ and perpendicular to the graph of $y = -0.5x$

12 containing $B(0, 7)$ and perpendicular to the graph of $y = -0.6x$

13 containing $M(1, 4)$ and perpendicular to the graph of $y = -\frac{2}{3}x + 5$

14 What are the coordinates of the point where the line containing $K(-3, 5)$ and $L(5, -4)$ crosses the y-axis?

In Exercises 15–23, find the slope of $\overline{JK}$ and $\overline{LM}$, and tell if the lines are parallel, perpendicular, or neither.

15 $J(2, 0)$ $L(0, 4)$
$K(-1, 3)$ $M(-1, 5)$

16 $J(-4, -5)$ $L(6, 0)$
$K(5, 1)$ $M(4, 3)$

17 $J(-4, -4)$ $L(1, 3)$
$K(-1, 5)$ $M(5, 3)$

18 $J(0, 2)$ $L(3, 5)$
$K(4, 1)$ $M(5, 3)$

19

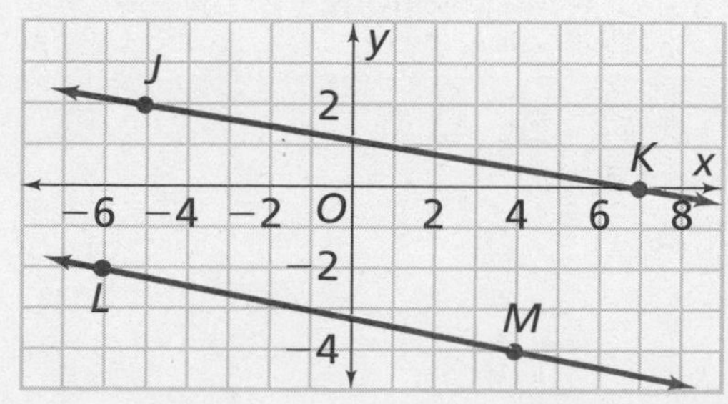

20

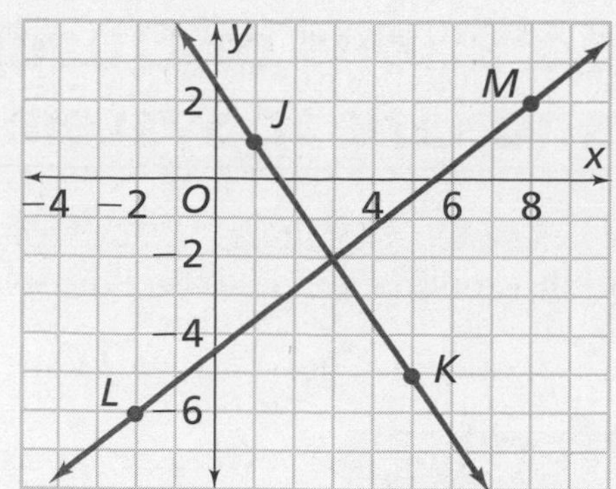

21

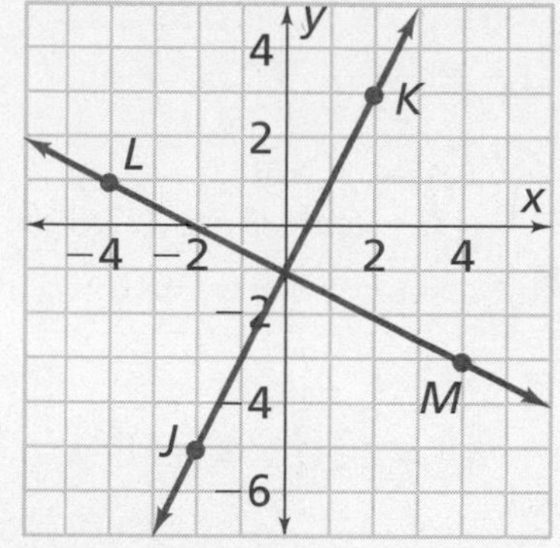

22 $\overline{JK}$: $y = \frac{1}{5}x + 8$
$\overline{LM}$: $y = 5x - \frac{1}{2}$

23 $\overline{JK}$: $2y + \frac{1}{2}x = -2$
$\overline{LM}$: $2x + 8y = 8$

24 Write the equation of a line in standard form that is parallel to the line drawn below and goes through the point P.

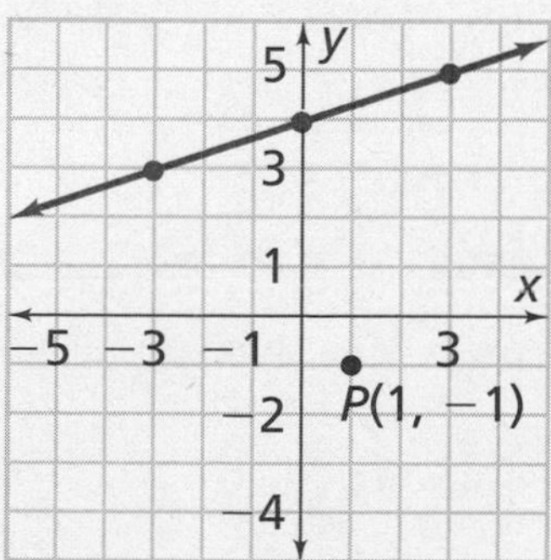

6.3 Solutions of Quadratic and Linear Systems

New York Standards

G.G.70 Systems of equations

You can solve a system of a linear and quadratic equations algebraically. You can use the substitution method to find the solution to a system of linear and quadratic equations.

EXAMPLES 1 and 2 **Solving systems of linear-quadratic equations algebraically**

Solve each system of equations algebraically.

1 $y = x^2$ and $y = 2x$

■ SOLUTION

$x^2 = 2x$ ← (substitute $2x$ for y)

$x^2 - 2x = 0$

$x(x - 2) = 0$

$x = 0$ or $x = 2$

If $x = 0$, then $y = 0$. If $x = 2$, then $y = 4$.

Check the solutions in each equation. The solutions are $(0, 0)$ and $(2, 4)$.

2 $y = x$ and $x^2 + y^2 = 50$

■ SOLUTION

$x^2 + x^2 = 50$ ← (substitute x for y)

$2x^2 = 50$

$x^2 = 25$

$x = 5$ or $x = -5$

If $x = 5$, then $y = 5$. If $x = -5$, then $y = -5$.

Check the solutions in each equation. The solutions are $(5, 5)$ and $(-5, -5)$

A linear-quadratic system can also be solved graphically. You will find that either there are two solutions, one solution, or no solutions. This is illustrated in the graphs below.

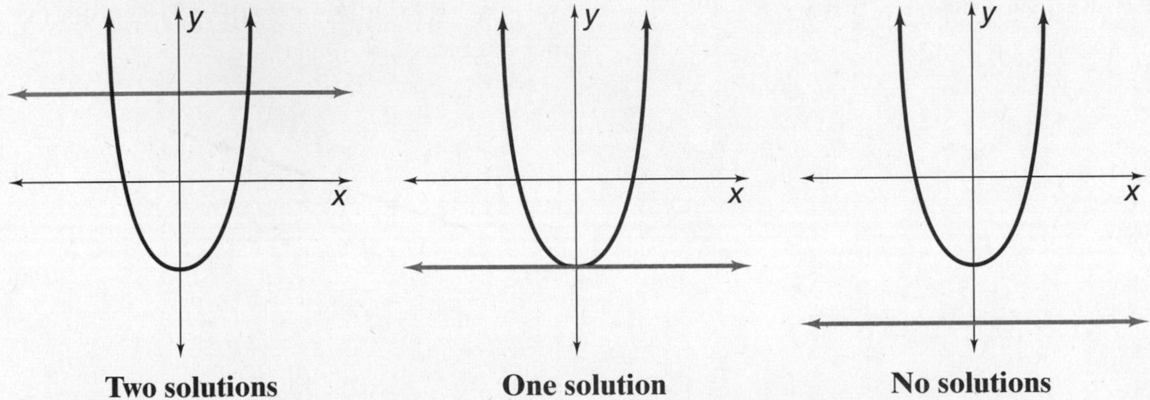

Two solutions **One solution** **No solutions**

You can find the number of solutions a system of equations has by looking at the number of points where the graphs of each equation intersect. If the graphs do not intersect, then the system has no solutions.

EXAMPLES 3 through 5 Finding the number of solutions to a system of equations graphically

How many solutions are there to the following systems of equations?

3 $y = 3$
$y = x^2 - 4x - 1$

■ **SOLUTION**

Step 1 Graph the parabola. The equation for the axis of symmetry is $x = 2$.

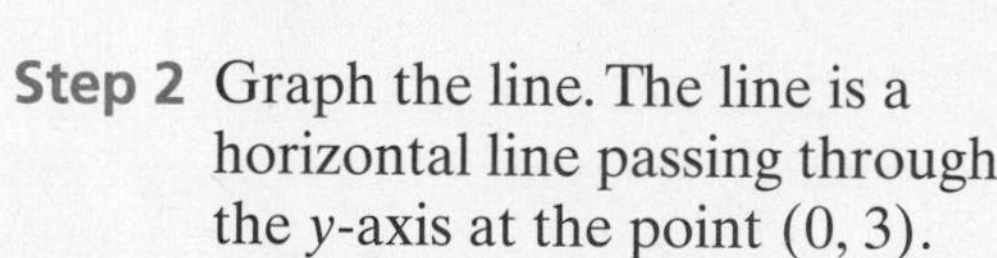

x	0	1	2	3	4
y	−1	−4	−5	−4	−1

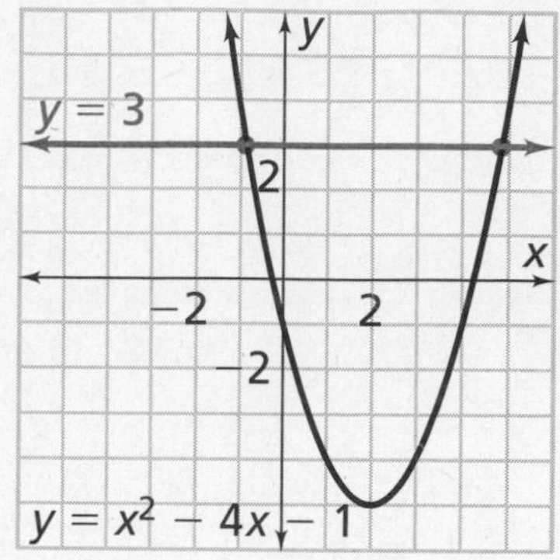

Step 2 Graph the line. The line is a horizontal line passing through the y-axis at the point (0, 3).

Step 3 Count the number of points where the two graphs intersect. The line crosses the parabola at two points.

The graphs intersect at two points, so this system has solutions.

4 $y = (x - 3)^2$
$2y + x = 2$

■ **SOLUTION**

Step 1 Graph both equations.

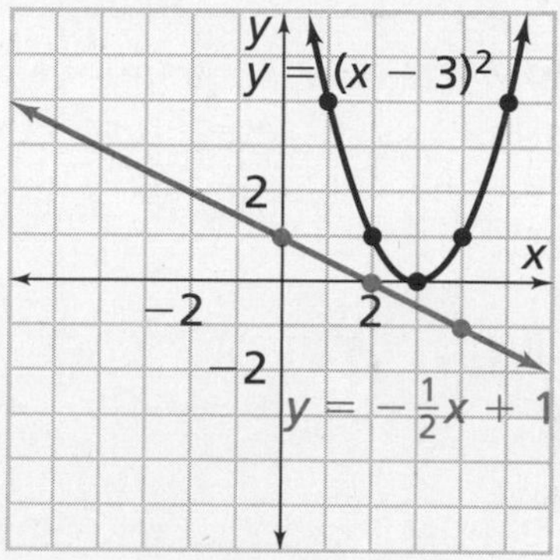

Step 2 Count the number of points where the two graphs intersect. The two graphs do not intersect.

Since the graphs of the equations do not intersect, this system has no solutions.

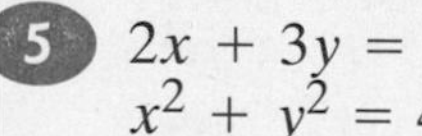

5 $2x + 3y = 5$
$x^2 + y^2 = 4$

■ **SOLUTION**

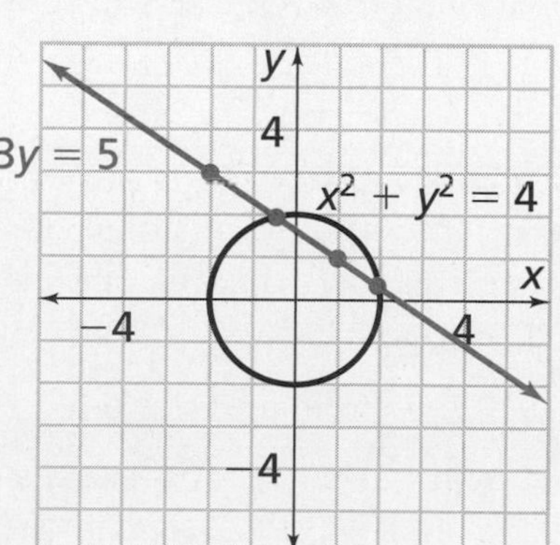

Step 1 Graph both equations.

The graph of the first equation is a line. The graph of the second equation is a circle centered at the origin and with a radius of 2.

Step 2 Count the number of points where the two graphs intersect. The line crosses the circle at two points.

Because the graphs intersect at two points, this system has two solutions.

Note

The graph of $y = ax^2 + bx + c$, where $a \neq 0$, has the line $x = -\frac{b}{2a}$ as its **axis of symmetry.** The vertex has coordinates $\left(-\frac{b}{2a}, f\left(-\frac{b}{2a}\right)\right)$

The equation $x^2 + y^2 = r^2$ describes a circle with its center at (0, 0) and a radius of r.

The coordinates of the points where the graphs intersect give the solutions to the system of equations.

EXAMPLES 6 and 7 Finding solutions to a system of equations

6 Solve the following system of equations by graphing.

$$y = -x + 1$$
$$y = x^2 + x - 2$$

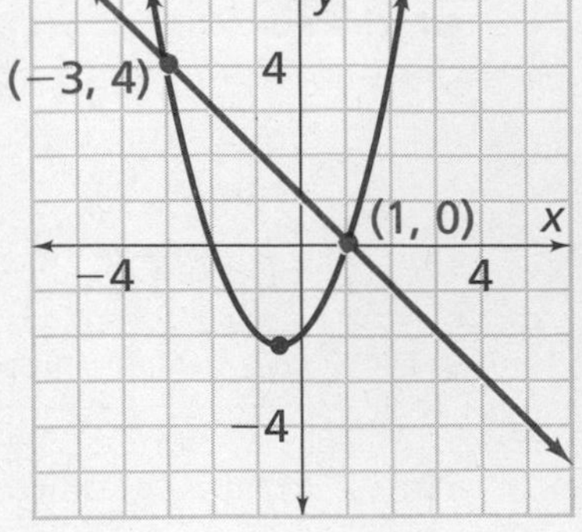

■ SOLUTION

Step 1 Graph the equations.

Step 3 Locate the points where the parabola and the line intersect.

The line intersects at the points $(-3, 4)$ and $(1, 0)$.

There are two solutions: **(−3, 4)** and **(1, 0)**.

7 Solve the following system of equations by graphing.

$$x^2 + y^2 = 16$$
$$y = 2x - 4$$

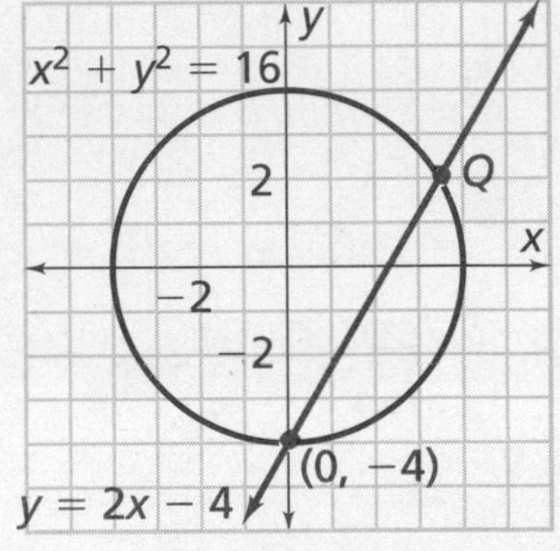

SOLUTION

Step 1 Graph both equations.

Step 2 Identify the points where the graphs intersect.

The graphs intersect at the point $(0, -4)$ and the point labeled Q, which is approximately at $(3, 2)$.

There are two solutions. One solution is **(0, −4)**. The other solution is approximately **(3, 2)**.

When you plot the above example on a coordinate grid, it's easy to find the coordinates of one of the points where the graphs intersect. However, the coordinates of the second point, Q, are not as easy to find just by looking at the graphs.

You can use a graphing calculator to find the exact coordinates of Q. The display below shows the graphs of $x^2 + y^2 = 16$ and $y = 2x - 4$. The calculator shows the coordinates of Q, which is $(3.2, 2.4)$.

Note

You can check your answers by substituting the values for x and y into the equations.

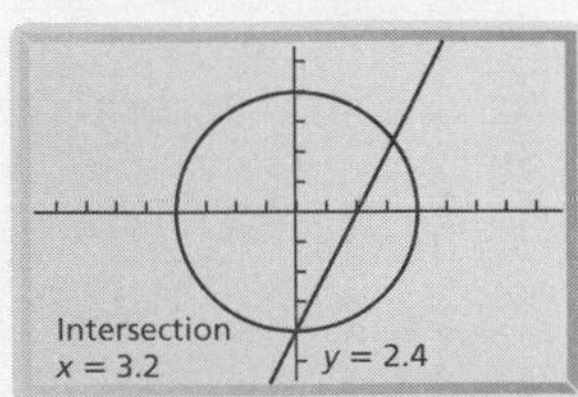

To find the points of intersection algebraically, substitute $y = 2x - 4$ into the equation of the circle and solve for x.

$$x^2 + (2x - 4)^2 = 16$$
$$x^2 + 4x^2 - 16x + 16 = 16$$
$$x(5x - 16) = 0$$

Solving for x, you get $x = 0$ and $x = 3.2$. Substituting these values into the equation $y = 2x - 4$, you see that the points of intersection are $(0, -4)$ and $(3.2, 2.4)$.

Practice

Choose the numeral preceding the word or expression that best completes the statement or answers the question.

1 In how many points does the graph of $y = (x - 3)(x + 5)$ intersect the x-axis?

(1) none **(3)** two

(2) one **(4)** three

2 A linear and a quadratic function are graphed on the same coordinate plane. Which are solution(s) to both equations?

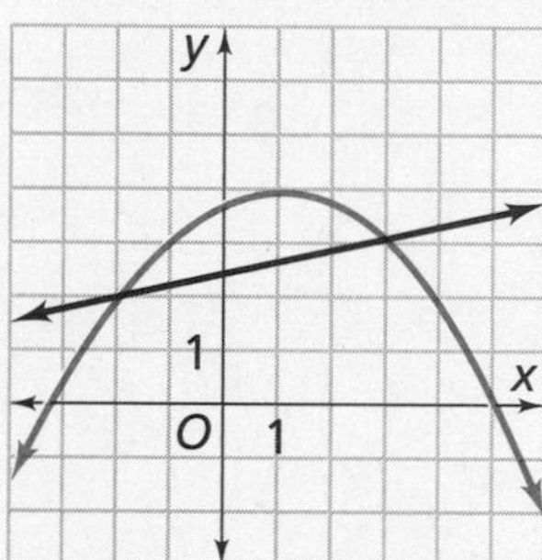

(1) $(-2, 2)$

(2) $(3, 3)$

(3) $(3, 3)$ and $(-2, 2)$

(4) $(-3, 3)$ and $(2, 2)$

3 A circle and a line lie in the same coordinate plane. Which situation is not possible?

(1) The graphs do not intersect.

(2) The graphs can intersect in one point.

(3) The graphs can intersect in two points.

(4) The graphs can intersect in three points.

4 A circle has radius 4 and center at the origin. For which equation will the circle and the line not intersect?

(1) $x = 2$ **(3)** $x = 4$

(2) $y = 2$ **(4)** $x = 5$

5 For which equation will the graph of $y = x^2 + 1$ and the line intersect in two points?

(1) $y = -2x$ **(3)** $y = 2$

(2) $x = 1$ **(4)** $y = 2x$

6 Which system of equations has two solutions?

(1) $x = 0; y = x^2$ **(3)** $y = -1; y = x^2$

(2) $y = 2; y = x^2$ **(4)** $y = 0; y = x^2$

In Exercises 7–13, graph the system of equations and name the intersecting points.

7 $y = 2x + 3$ and $y = x^2$

8 $y = x$ and $2y = x^2$

9 $y = x^2 - 4x + 8$ and $y + x = 1$

10 $x^2 + y^2 = 25$ and $x = y + 7$

11 $y = x^2 - 3x - 10$ and $y = 2x - 4$

12 $y = 5 - 4x - x^2$ and $y = 4x + 21$

13 $x^2 + y^2 = 25$ and $y - 3 = -(x + 4)$

In Exercises 14–15, use graphs to show that the pair of equations has no solution.

14 $x^2 + y^2 = 9$
$x^2 + y^2 = 4$

15 $y = x^2 + 1$
$y = -x^2 - 2$

In Exercises 16–20, determine the number of points of intersection of the specified graphs. Justify your response.

16 A parabola opens up and has vertex $P(-2, 3)$. A line has equation $y = 3$.

17 A parabola opens down and has vertex $P(-2, 3)$. A line has equation $y = 3$.

18 A circle has center at the origin and radius 3. A line has equation $y = 2x$.

19 A circle has equation $x^2 + y^2 = 9$. A line containing the points $(0, 6)$ and $(6, 0)$.

20 A parabola opens up and has vertex $\left(-\frac{1}{2}, \frac{3}{4}\right)$. A line containing the points $(0, -2)$ and $(2, 0)$.

21 For what value(s) of k does the system of equations have no solution? 1 solution? 2 solutions?

$$x^2 + y^2 = k$$
$$x = 4$$

6.4 Finding Distance, Midpoint, and the Perpendicular Bisector

New York Standards

G.G.66 Find midpoint of a segment

G.G.67 Find length of a segment

G.G.68 Equation of perpendicular bisector

You can use the Pythagorean Theorem to find the distance between any two points in the coordinate plane. If you graph any two points in the coordinate plane such that the line that connects them is not parallel to either axis, you can form a right triangle. The distance between the two points will be the length of the line segment joining those points.

In the figure below, you can see that if the coordinates of P are (x_1, y_1) and the coordinates of Q are (x_2, y_2), then the coordinates of R will be (x_2, y_1). With these coordinates known, you can determine the length of PR and QR by finding the difference in the x and y values.

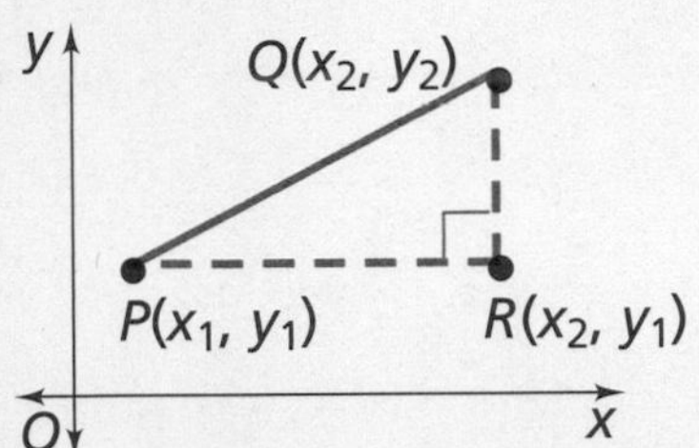

Using the Pythagorean Theorem, you can then find the distance between P and Q. This is called the *Distance Formula.*

The Distance Formula

The distance PQ between $P(x_1, y_1)$ and $Q(x_2, y_2)$ is given by the formula below.

$$PQ = \sqrt{(x_2 - x_1)^2 + (y_2 - y_1)^2}$$

Go Online PHSchool.com

Visit: PHSchool.com

Web Code: ayp-0360

EXAMPLE 1 Finding the distance between two points in the coordinate plane

Find the distance between $A(4, -1)$ and $B(-3, 5)$. Give an exact answer and an answer rounded to the nearest hundredth.

SOLUTION

$$AB = \sqrt{(-3 - 4)^2 + (5 - [-1])^2} = \sqrt{(-7)^2 + (6)^2} = \sqrt{85} \approx 9.22$$

The distance between A and B is $\sqrt{85}$, or about 9.22.

A midpoint of a segment in the coordinate plane is the point halfway between the endpoints of the segment. You can use the coordinates of the endpoints to find the midpoint. In the diagram at the right, the coordinates of P are (x_2, y_2), and the coordinates of Q are (x_1, y_1). The coordinates of the midpoint, M, are found by calculating the average of the x-values $\frac{x_1+x_2}{2}$ and the average of the y-values $\frac{y_1+y_2}{2}$.

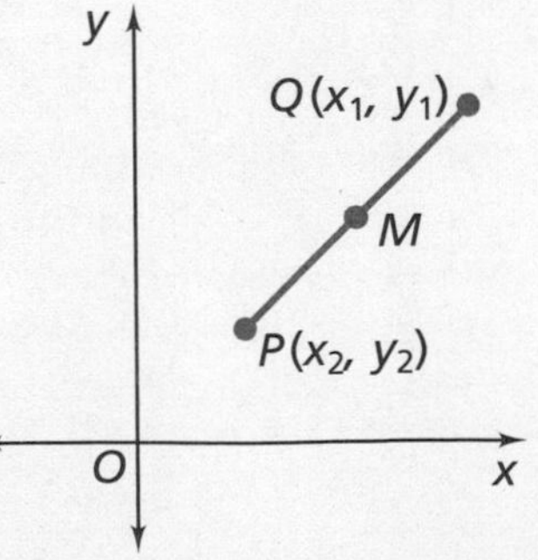

Therefore, to find the midpoint of a line segment in the coordinate plane, use the *Midpoint Formula.*

The Midpoint Formula

The coordinates of the midpoint (x_m, y_m) of the segment with endpoints $P(x_1, y_1)$ and $Q(x_2, y_2)$ are given by the following.

$$(x_m, y_m) = \left(\frac{x_1 + x_2}{2}, \frac{y_1 + y_2}{2}\right)$$

EXAMPLES 2 and 3 Using the Midpoint Formula

2 Find the coordinates of the midpoint of the segment whose endpoints are $A(-2, -3)$ and $B(5, 4)$.

■ **SOLUTION**

$$(x_m, y_m) = \left(\frac{x_1 + x_2}{2}, \frac{y_1 + y_2}{2}\right)$$

$$(x_m, y_m) = \left(\frac{-2 + 5}{2}, \frac{-3 + 4}{2}\right)$$

$$= \left(\frac{3}{2}, \frac{1}{2}\right)$$

3 The point $Z(3, -5)$ is the midpoint of the segment with endpoints $K(4, 6)$ and $P(x, y)$. Find x and y.

■ **SOLUTION**

$$(x_m, y_m) = \left(\frac{x_1 + x_2}{2}, \frac{y_1 + y_2}{2}\right)$$

$$(3, -5) = \left(\frac{4 + x}{2}, \frac{6 + y}{2}\right)$$

$$3 = \frac{4 + x}{2} \text{ and } -5 = \frac{6 + y}{2}$$

$$x = 2 \text{ and } y = -16$$

You can use the midpoint formula to help you find the perpendicular bisector of a given line segment.

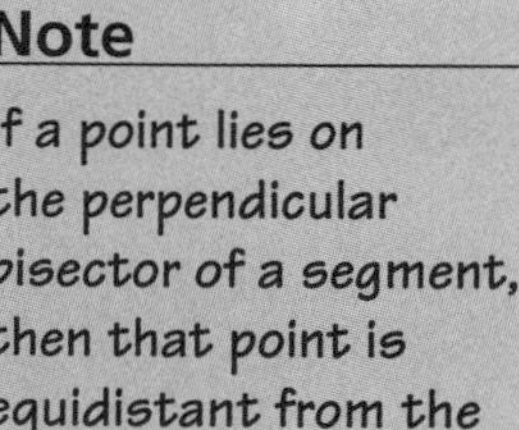

Note

If a point lies on the perpendicular bisector of a segment, then that point is equidistant from the endpoints.

EXAMPLE 4 Identifying the perpendicular bisector of a line segment

4 Which equation represents the set of all points in the coordinate plane equidistant from $A(4, -2)$ and $B(6, -2)$?

(1) $y = 5$

(2) $x = 5$

(3) $y = -5$

(4) $x = -5$

■ **SOLUTION**

If you look at the graph of the points, you can see $\overline{AB}$ is horizontal. Therefore, the set of all points equidistant from A and B is the perpendicular bisector, and it will be vertical to $\overline{AB}$.

You can eliminate choices (1) and (3) since they are also horizontal. The coordinates of the midpoint of $\overline{AB}$ are $\left(\frac{4 + 6}{2}, \frac{-2 + (-2)}{2}\right) = (5, -2)$. Since the x-value of $(5, -2)$ is 5, the vertical line $x = 5$ is the correct choice. This eliminates choice (4). Therefore, choice **(2)** is the correct answer.

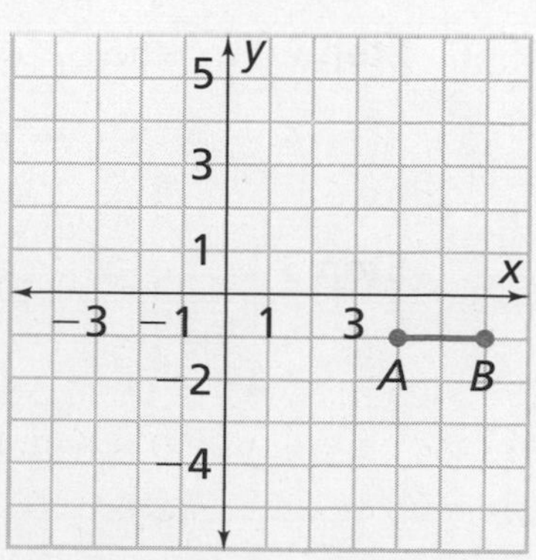

You can find the midpoint of a line segment with the midpoint formula. By using the midpoint of the segment and the slope of a line perpendicular to the given segment, you can write an equation for the perpendicular bisector of any line using the point-slope form.

Point-Slope Form

A line with slope m that goes through the point (x_1, y_1) can be written using the equation

$$(y - y_1) = m(x - x_1)$$

The steps for writing an equation for the perpendicular bisector of any given line segment are summarized below.

Finding the Perpendicular Bisector of a Line Segment

1 Find the coordinates of the midpoint using the midpoint formula.
2 Find the slope m of the given line segment.
3 Find the equation of the line containing the midpoint, having slope $= -\frac{1}{m}$ using the point-slope method.

The resulting equation is the perpendicular bisector of the given segment.

EXAMPLE 5 **Finding an equation for the perpendicular bisector of a segment**

5 Find an equation that represents the set of all points in the coordinate plane equidistant from $A(3, 8)$ and $B(-1, 2)$.

■ SOLUTION

The set of all points that are equidistant from A and B is the perpendicular bisector of $\overline{AB}$. So, you need to find the perpendicular bisector of $\overline{AB}$.

Step 1 Find the midpoint of $\overline{AB}$ using the midpoint formula.

$$\left(\frac{3 + (-1)}{2}, \frac{8 + 2}{2}\right) \text{ or } (1, 5)$$

Step 2 Find the slope of $\overline{AB}$. The slope of $\overline{AB}$ is $\frac{2 - 8}{-1 - 3} = \frac{-6}{-4} = \frac{3}{2}$.

If the slope of $\overline{AB}$ is $\frac{3}{2}$, the slope of the line perpendicular to $\overline{AB}$ is $-\frac{2}{3}$.

Step 3 Write the equation of the perpendicular bisector using the point-slope formula, $(y - y_1) + m(x - x_1)$. Remember to use the slope of the line perpendicular to $\overline{AB}$.

$$y - 5 = -\frac{2}{3}(x - 1) \quad \leftarrow \textbf{substitute } x_1 = 1, y_1 = 5, \textbf{ and } m = -\frac{2}{3}$$

$$y = -\frac{2}{3}x + 5$$

$$y = -\frac{2}{3}x + \frac{17}{3}$$

Therefore, an equation for the perpendicular bisector of $\overline{AB}$ is $y = -\frac{2}{3}x + \frac{17}{3}$.

Practice

Choose the numeral preceding the word or expression that best completes the statement or answers the question.

1 Find the midpoint of a segment with endpoints $(-1, 5)$ and $(6, -3)$.

(1) $\left(3\frac{1}{2}, 4\right)$ **(3)** $\left(-3\frac{1}{2}, -4\right)$

(2) $\left(2\frac{1}{2}, 1\right)$ **(4)** $\left(-2\frac{1}{2}, -1\right)$

2 If the midpoint of a segment is $(2, 8)$, and an endpoint is $(-4, 0)$, the other endpoint is

(1) $(-1, 4)$. **(3)** $(8, 16)$.

(2) $(4, 8)$. **(4)** $(3, 4)$.

3 Which pair of points has $(3.5, -9)$ as the midpoint of the segment joining them?

(1) $(6, -2)$ and $(10, 11)$

(2) $(0, -4)$ and $(-7, 5)$

(3) $(-2, -3)$ and $(9, 15)$

(4) $(-1, -7)$ and $(8, -11)$

4 Which represents the midpoint of the segment with endpoints $(4, 8)$ and $(-2, 1)$?

(1) $(3, 3.5)$ **(3)** $(6, -0.5)$

(2) $(3, 4.5)$ **(4)** $(1, 4.5)$

5 Which represents the length of the segment with endpoints $(1, 3)$ and $(4, 5)$?

(1) $\sqrt{13}$ **(2)** 5 **(3)** 13 **(4)** 25

In Exercises 6–9, find the coordinates of the midpoint and the length of the segment whose endpoints are given.

6 $A(3, -2)$ and $B(5, -4)$

7 $X(9, 15)$ and $Y(-6, -2)$

8 $P(1, 2)$ and $Q(4, 6)$

9 $M(3, -4)$ and $N(8, 6)$

In Exercises 10–15, give the distance between each pair of points. Round to the nearest hundredth as necessary.

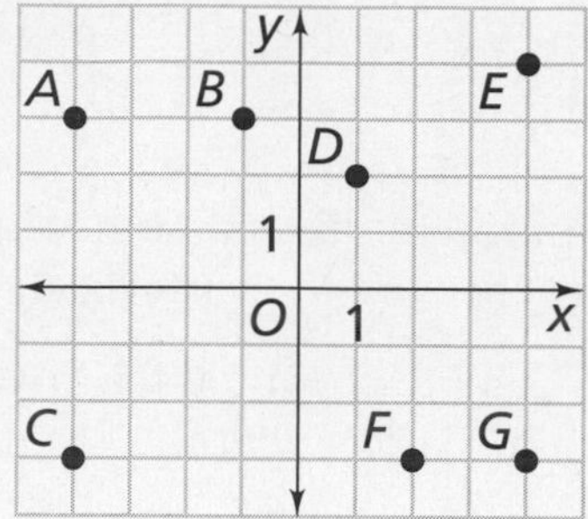

10 A and F

11 E and C

12 C and G

13 E and G

14 B and D

15 D and G

In Exercises 16–20, write an equation of the perpendicular bisector for the given line segment.

16 $\overline{CD}$ when $C = (2, 6)$ and $D = (4, 3)$

17 $\overline{XY}$ when $X = (3, 5)$ and $Y = (-3, -1)$

18 $\overline{AB}$ when $A = (-4, 1)$ and $B = (4, -3)$

19 $\overline{EF}$ when $E = (5, -5)$ and $F = (1, 1)$

20 $\overline{VW}$ when $V = (0, 3)$ and $W = (4, 4)$

21 Find the distance between the parallel lines given by the equations $y = x + 2$ and $y = x - 3$.

22 Find the distance between the line given by the equation $x + y = 2$ and a parallel line that passes through the origin.

6.5 Proof in the Coordinate Plane

New York Standards

G.G.69 Distance, midpoint, and slope formulas

Coordinate geometry is the study of geometric figures identified by their vertices on the coordinate plane. You can apply the definitions of triangles and quadrilaterals along with calculations of slope, midpoint, and distance to analyze and classify geometric figures in the coordinate plane.

You must show that all of the criteria in the definition of a specific geometric figure are met in order to prove its classification. If the definition of a geometric figure requires that the sides of the figure be parallel or perpendicular, you use slope. If the definition requires that the sides be congruent, you use the distance formula. You must prove these criteria algebraically.

You can use the distance formula to prove that two segments are congruent. If the distance formula shows that the segments have the same length, then they are congruent.

Note

Recall that parallel lines have equal slopes and that slopes of perpendicular lines multiply to −1.

EXAMPLE 1 **Proving a quadrilateral is a square**

Show that the quadrilateral at the right is a square.

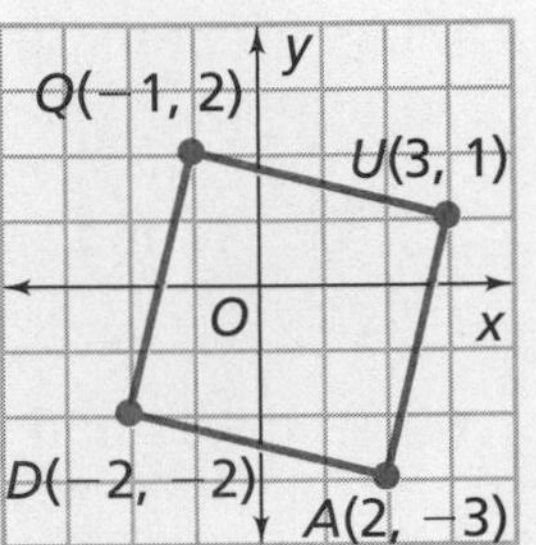

■ SOLUTION

To prove that a quadrilateral is a square, you need to show that it has one right angle and all its sides are congruent. You use slope to determine whether the sides form right angles (are perpendicular) and the distance formula to determine whether the sides are congruent.

Step 1 Calculate the slope of $\overline{QU}$ and $\overline{AU}$.

$$m\overline{QU} = \frac{y_2 - y_1}{x_2 - x_1} = \frac{1 - 2}{3 - (-1)} = \frac{-1}{4} \qquad m\overline{QD} = \frac{y_2 - y_1}{x_2 - x_1} = \frac{-2 - 2}{-2 - (-1)} = \frac{-4}{-1} = 4$$

Step 2 Calculate the length of each side of the quadrilateral.

$$QU = \sqrt{(x_2 - x_1)^2 + (y_2 - y_1)^2} = \sqrt{(3 - (-1))^2 + (1 - 2)^2} = \sqrt{(4)^2 + (-1)^2} = \sqrt{17}$$

$$AD = \sqrt{(x_2 - x_1)^2 + (y_2 - y_1)^2} = \sqrt{(-2 - 2)^2 + (-2 - (-3))^2} = \sqrt{(-4)^2 + (1)^2} = \sqrt{17}$$

$$QD = \sqrt{(x_2 - x_1)^2 + (y_2 - y_1)^2} = \sqrt{(-2 - (-1))^2 + (-2 - 2)^2} = \sqrt{(-1)^2 + (-4)^2} = \sqrt{17}$$

$$AU = \sqrt{(x_2 - x_1)^2 + (y_2 - y_1)^2} = \sqrt{(3 - 2)^2 + (1 - (-3))^2} = \sqrt{(1)^2 + (4)^2} = \sqrt{17}$$

Because $m\overline{QU} \cdot m\overline{AU} = -1$, $\overline{QU}$ and $\overline{AU}$ are perpendicular. Therefore, the quadrilateral has one right angle. All four sides are equal in measure. *QUAD* is a square because a quadrilateral with four congruent sides and 1 right angle is a square.

Visit: PHSchool.com
Web Code: ayp-0412

EXAMPLES 2 and 3 Prove the diagonals of a rectangle are congruent

2 Given $ABCD$ is a rectangle, prove that its diagonals are congruent.

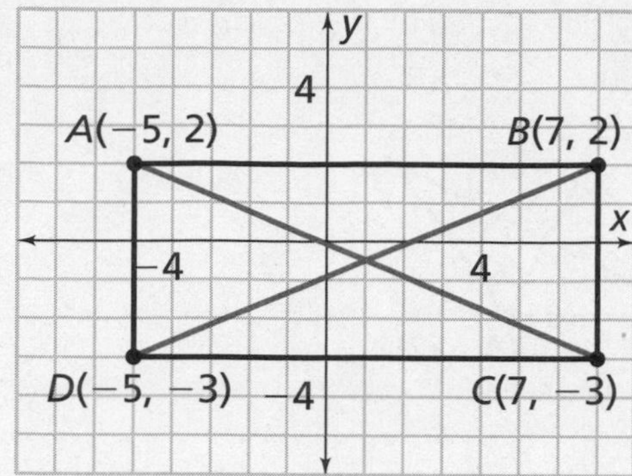

■ **SOLUTION**

Show $\overline{AC} \cong \overline{BD}$

$AC = \sqrt{(x_2 - x_1)^2 + (y_2 - y_1)^2}$

$= \sqrt{(7 - (-5))^2 + (-3 - 2)^2}$ **Apply the Distance Formula to $\overline{AC}$.**

$= \sqrt{(12)^2 + (5)^2}$

$= \sqrt{169}$

$= 13$

$BD = \sqrt{(x_2 - x_1)^2 + (y_2 - y_1)^2}$

$= \sqrt{((-5 - 7))^2 + (-3 - 2)^2}$ **Apply the Distance Formula to $\overline{BD}$.**

$= \sqrt{(-12)^2 + (-5)^2}$

$= \sqrt{169}$

$= 13$

The length of $\overline{AC}$ equals the length of $\overline{BD}$. Therefore $\overline{AC} \cong \overline{BD}$.

3 Explain how you would prove that a quadrilateral is a parallelogram using coordinate geometry.

■ **SOLUTION**

To prove that a quadrilateral is a parallelogram, you would need to show that its opposite sides are parallel. Using coordinate geometry, you could find the slopes of segments opposite each other. If the slopes of the opposite sides are equal, then the segments are parallel, and the quadrilateral is therefore a parallelogram.

To show that segments are perpendicular, you need to show that the slope of one segment is the negative reciprocal of the other segment.

EXAMPLE 4 **Prove a quadrilateral is a rhombus**

Use coordinate geometry to show that *EFGH* is a rhombus.

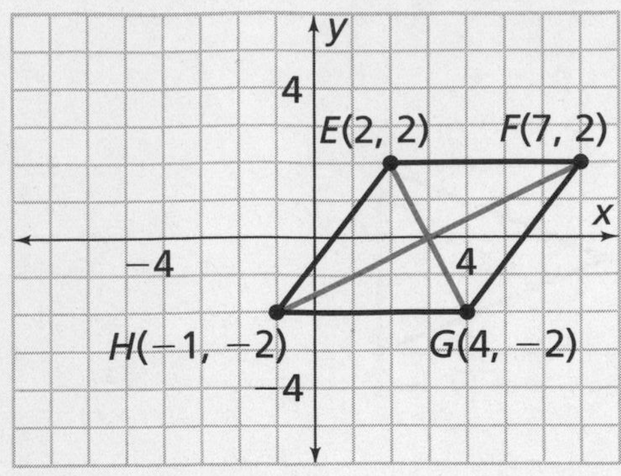

▪ SOLUTION

To prove that the quadrilateral *EFGH* is a rhombus, you need to show that two adjacent sides are congruent and that the diagonals are perpendicular to each other.

Step 1 Show that $\overline{EF} \cong \overline{EH}$.

$$EF = \sqrt{(7 - 2)^2 + (2 - 2)^2}$$
$$= \sqrt{5^2} = 5$$
$$EH = \sqrt{(2 - (-1))^2 + (2 - (-2))^2}$$
$$= \sqrt{3^3 + 4^2}$$
$$= \sqrt{25} = 5$$

Therefore $\overline{EF} \cong \overline{EH}$.

Step 2 Show that the slopes of $\overline{EG}$ and $\overline{FH}$ are negative reciprocals of each other.

$$\text{Slope of } \overline{EG} = \frac{2 - (-2)}{2 - 4} = \frac{4}{-2} = -2$$

$$\text{Slope of } \overline{FH} = \frac{2 - (-2)}{7 - (-1)} = \frac{4}{8} = \frac{1}{2}$$

The slopes are negative reciprocals of each other. Therefore, the diagonals are perpendicular to each other.

Since **two adjacent sides are congruent** and the **diagonals are perpendicular, EFGH is a rhombus.**

You can also analyze and classify triangles in a coordinate plane.

You can also prove other properties of triangles by using the midpoint and distance formulas.

EXAMPLE 5 Prove the triangle is isosceles

 Show that $\triangle RGV$ is isosceles.

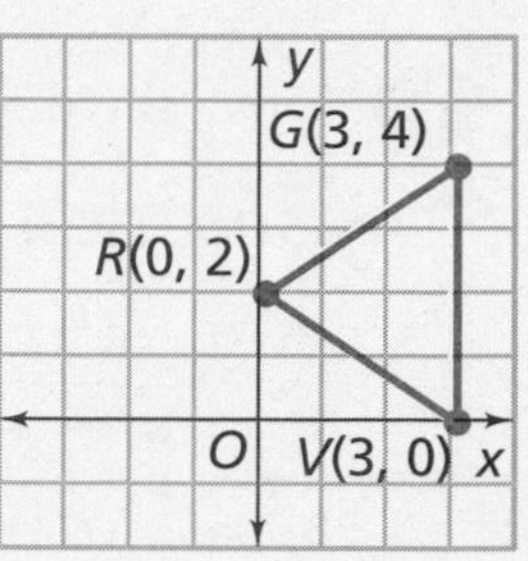

■ **SOLUTION**

An isosceles triangle must have at least two equal sides. You can use the distance formula to verify the side lengths.

$$RG = \sqrt{(x_2 - x_1)^2 + (y_2 - y_1)^2} = \sqrt{(3 - 0)^2 + (4 - 2)^2} = \sqrt{(3)^2 + (2)^2} = \sqrt{9 + 4} = \sqrt{13}$$

$$VR = \sqrt{(x_2 - x_1)^2 + (y_2 - y_1)^2} = \sqrt{(0 - 3)^2 + (2 - 0)^2} = \sqrt{(-3)^2 + (2)^2} = \sqrt{9 + 4} = \sqrt{13}$$

Because  $RG = VR$, $\triangle RGV$ is an isosceles triangle.

EXAMPLE 6 Prove the median to the hypotenuse of a right triangle is half the hypotenuse

 **Given:** $\triangle JKL$ with $\angle K = 90°$ and median $\overline{KM}$.

Prove: $KM = \frac{LJ}{2}$

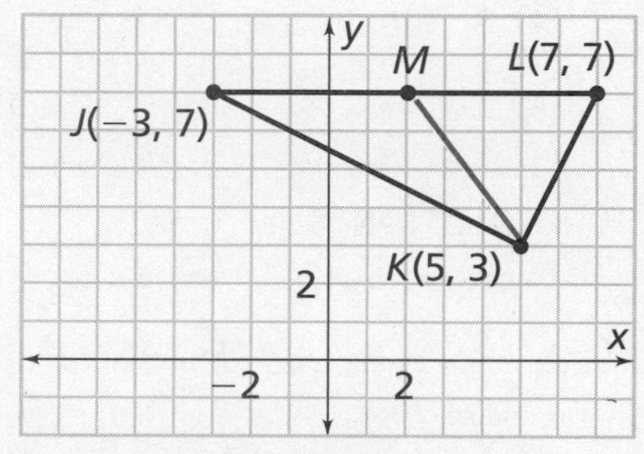

■ **SOLUTION**

Step 1 Find the coordinates of the midpoint M.

$$M = \left(\frac{7 + (-3)}{2}, \frac{7 + 7}{2}\right)$$

$$M = (2, 7)$$

Step 2 Find the length of $\overline{LJ}$ and $\overline{KM}$.

$$LJ = \sqrt{(7 - (-3)^2 + (7 - 7)^2} = \sqrt{10^2} = 10$$

$$KM = \sqrt{(5 - 2)^2 + (3 - 7)^2} = \sqrt{3^2 + (-4)^2} = \sqrt{5^2} = 5$$

Therefore, **the length of the median to the hypotenuse of a right triangle is half the length of the hypotenuse.**

You can also use the general coordinates for proving properties about geometric figures. Place the geometric figures on the coordinate plane and use variables to represent the coordinates of the vertices.

Coordinate Proofs Using General Coordinates

1. Begin by placing one of the vertices at the origin.
2. Place one of the sides of the figure on the x-axis.
3. Place the figure in the first quadrant.

The following examples show you how to use coordinate geometry to prove the properties of generic geometric figures.

EXAMPLES 7 through 10 Prove theorems and postulates using general coordinates

7 Prove the diagonals of a rectangle are congruent.

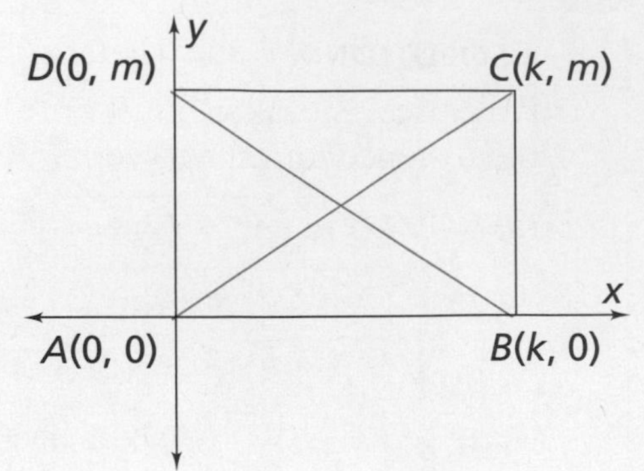

■ SOLUTION

$$AC = \sqrt{(k-0)^2 + (m-0)^2}$$
$$= \sqrt{k^2 + m^2}$$
$$BD = \sqrt{(0-k)^2 + (m-0)^2}$$
$$= \sqrt{(-k)^2 + m^2}$$
$$= \sqrt{k^2 + m^2}$$

Therefore $\overline{AC} \cong \overline{BD}$.

8 Which of the following statements must be true for rectangle *ABCD* in the above example to be a square?

(1) $k < m$
(2) $k > m$
(3) $k = m$
(4) $k \neq m$

■ SOLUTION

In order for *ABCD* to be a square, $AB = BC = CD = DA$.

$\sqrt{k^2} = \sqrt{m^2} = \sqrt{k^2} = \sqrt{m^2}$ ← **Apply the Distance Formula.**

$k = m$

Therefore, **(3)** is the correct answer choice.

9 Prove the line containing the midpoints of two sides of a triangle is parallel to the base.

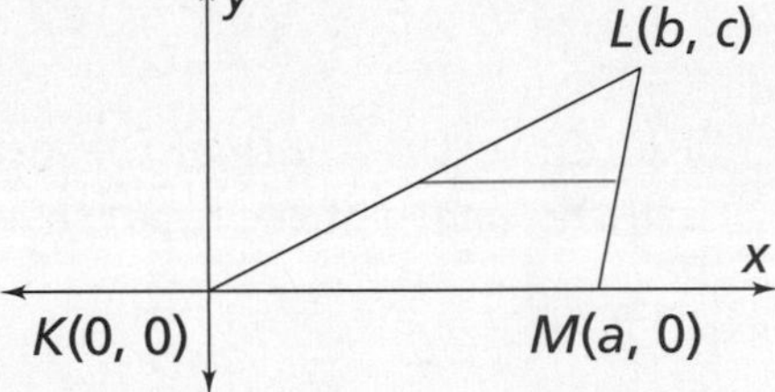

■ SOLUTION

Midpoint of $\overline{LM} = \left(\frac{b+a}{2}, \frac{c}{2}\right)$

Midpoint of $\overline{LK} = \left(\frac{b}{2}, \frac{c}{2}\right)$

The slope of the line containing the midpoints $= 0$, and therefore is parallel to the third side.

10 Prove the median, $\overline{BO}$, to the base of an isosceles triangle $\triangle ABC$ is the perpendicular bisector to the base.

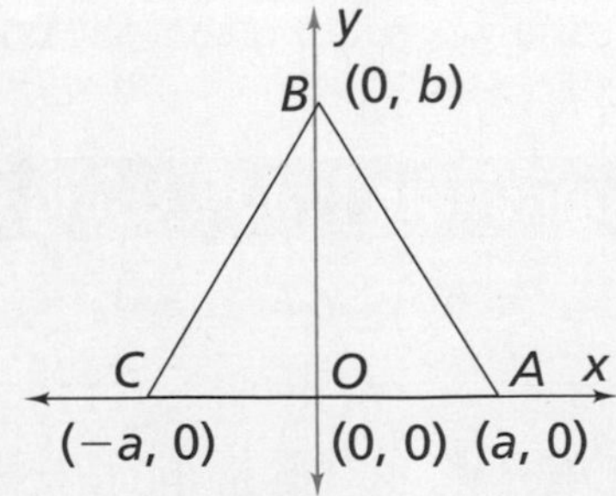

■ SOLUTION

The midpoint of the base is the origin (0, 0). Both lines are perpendicular as the median is the *y*-axis and the base is the *x*-axis. Therefore, the median to the base of an isosceles triangle is the perpendicular bisector of the base.

Practice

Choose the numeral preceding the word or expression that best completes the statement or answers the question.

1 If the diagonals of a quadrilateral are perpendicular, then the quadrilateral could be a

(1) rectangle. **(3)** square.

(2) parallelogram. **(4)** trapezoid.

2 If a quadrilateral has four congruent sides and one of the properties listed, it must be a square. Which property?

(1) opposite angles congruent **(3)** opposite sides parallel

(2) four right angles **(4)** four acute angles

3 Classify the quadrilateral with vertices $W(-3, 4)$, $X(6, 4)$, $Y(4, -5)$, and $Z(-5, -4)$.

(1) rhombus **(3)** parallelogram

(2) trapezoid **(4)** none of the above

In Exercises 4–6, solve each problem and clearly show all necessary work.

4 Show that the coordinates graphed below form a scalene triangle.

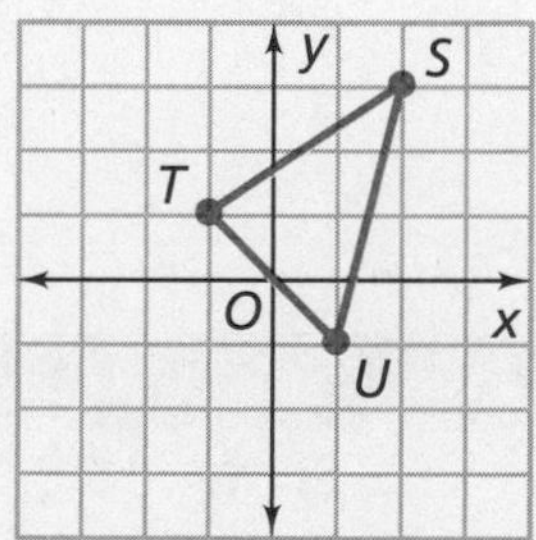

5 Show that the quadrilateral with vertices $A(1, 2)$, $B(3, 3)$, $C(5, 2)$, and $D(3, 1)$ is a rhombus.

6 Show that the quadrilateral below is a trapezoid.

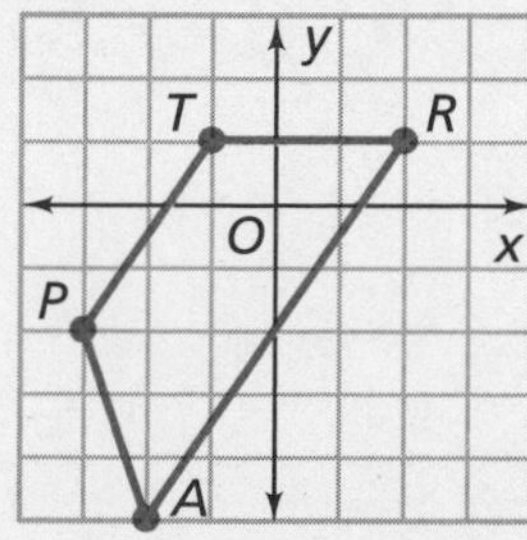

In Exercises 7–8, find the coordinates of the point described, given the points $K(-1, 0)$, $L(0, 3)$ and $M(3, 1)$.

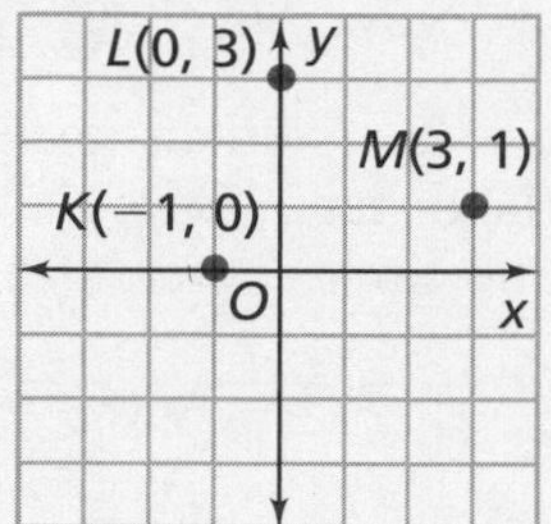

7 Determine point N so that $KLMN$ is a parallelogram.

8 Determine point P so that $KLPM$ is a parallelogram.

In Exercises 9–11, use coordinate geometry and the isosceles trapezoid below to prove each theorem.

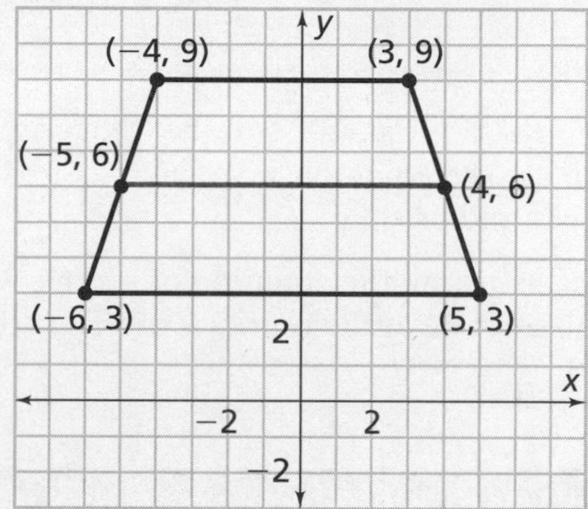

9 The line joining the midpoints is parallel to the base.

10 The line joining the midpoints is one-half the sum of the bases.

11 The diagonals of the isosceles trapezoid are congruent.

12 A quadrilateral has vertices $(a, 0)$, $(-a, 0)$, $(0, a)$ and $(0, -a)$. Show that it is a square.

13 A quadrilateral has vertices $(a, 0)$, $(0, a + 1)$, $(-a, 0)$, and $(0, -a - 1)$. Show that it is a rhombus.

6.6 Equations and Graphs of Circles

New York Standards

G.G.71 Find equation of circle from its radius
G.G.72 Find equation of circle from its graph
G.G.73 Find center and radius of a circle
G.G.74 Graphing a circle from its equation

Recall that a locus is a set of points that satisfy specified conditions. For example, we can define a circle as a locus of points equidistant from one point. It is the set of all points in the plane at a fixed distance, called the **radius,** from a fixed point, called the **center.** In the coordinate plane this locus can be represented as an equation.

Since the radius is the fixed distance of all points in a plane from the center, you can apply the distance formula to find the length of the radius, given the coordinates of the circle center, Q, and a point on the circle, P.

$$PQ = \sqrt{(x_2 - x_1)^2 + (y_2 - y_1)^2}$$

EXAMPLE 1 **Finding the equation of a circle with center at (0, 0)**

1 Find the equation of a circle with center $\boldsymbol{O}(0, 0)$ and radius $\boldsymbol{r}$ passing through the point (x, y).

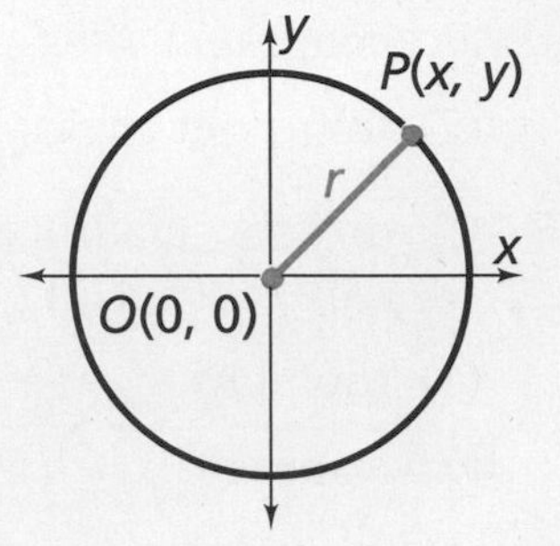

■ SOLUTION

$\sqrt{(x - 0)^2 + (y - 0)^2} = r$ ← **Apply the Distance Formula.**

$\sqrt{x^2 + y^2} = r$

$x^2 + y^2 = r^2$ ← **Square both sides.**

You can use the equation $x^2 + y^2 = r^2$ to describe a circle centered at the origin with radius r.

You can also write the equation of a circle whose center is not at the origin. Let the center be at the point (h, k). Then the formula will be $(x - h)^2 + (y - k)^2 = r^2$.

Equation of a Circle

The set of all points a fixed distance r from a fixed point $P(h, k)$ in the coordinate plane can be represented by the equation below, called the **standard form for an equation of a circle.**

$$(x - h)^2 + (y - k)^2 = r^2$$

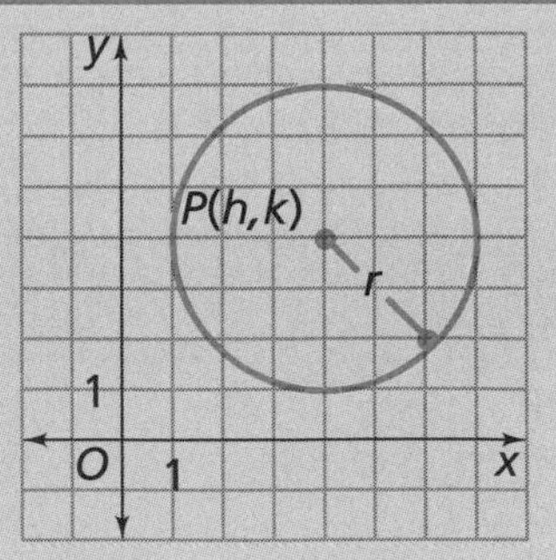

If the point $P(h, k)$ is the origin, then the equation becomes what is shown here.

$$x^2 + y^2 = r^2$$

EXAMPLE 2 Finding the equation of a circle with center (h, k)

2 Write the equation of the circle passing through the point $P(x, y)$ and three units from the center $C(4, 5)$.

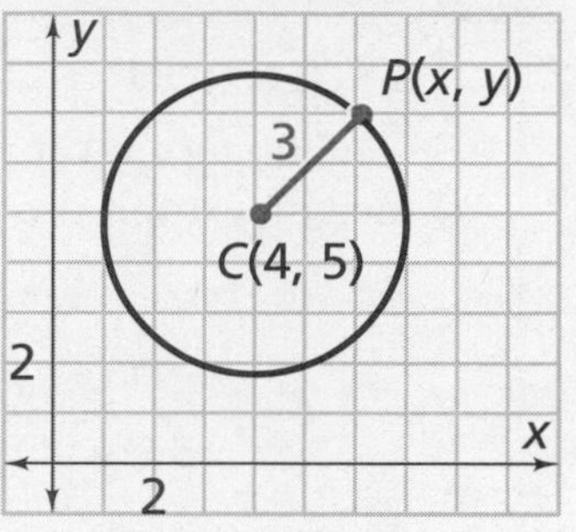

■ **SOLUTION**

Given: Center $C(4, 5)$, and $r = 3$

$$(x - h)^2 + (y - k)^2 = 3^2$$
$$(x - 4)^2 + (y - 5)^2 = 3^2 \quad \leftarrow \textbf{Substitute } h = 4 \textbf{ and } k = 5.$$

If you are given the equation of the circle, you can find its center and its radius.

Go Online
PHSchool.com
Visit:PHSchool.com
Web Codes:ayp-0479
ayp-0653

EXAMPLE 3 Finding the center and radius of a circle, given its equation

3 What is the center and radius of a circle whose equation is $(x - 4)^2 + (y + 5)^2 = 64$?

■ **SOLUTION**

Write $(x - 4)^2 + (y + 5)^2 = 64$ in the form $(x - h)^2 + (y - k)^2 = r^2$.

$$(x - h)^2 + (y - k)^2 = r^2$$
$$(x - 4)^2 + (y + 5)^2 = 64$$
$$(x - 4)^2 + (y - (-5))^2 = 8^2$$

$h = 4$, $k = -5$, and $r = 8$

The radius is 8 and the center is $(4, -5)$.

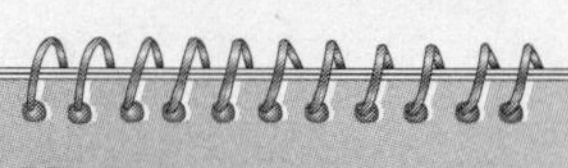

Note

If $-k = +5$, then $k = -5$.

You can determine whether a point lies on a circle by looking at the equation of the circle. A point lies on a circle. If the *x*- and *y*-coordinates of a point are a solution to the equation of a circle, then that point is a solution to the equation.

EXAMPLE 4 Determining whether points lie on a circle from its equation

4 Which points do not lie on the circle with equation $x^2 + y^2 = 5^2$?

(1) $(0, 5)$ and $(5, 0)$ **(2)** $(5, 5)$ and $(-5, 5)$ **(3)** $(0, -5)$ and $(-5, 0)$ **(4)** $(3, 4)$ and $(-4, 3)$

■ **SOLUTION**

A point lies on the circle if the ordered pair is a solution to the equation.

choice **(1)**	$(0, 5)$ and $(5, 0)$ are 5 units from O.	$(0, 5)$ and $(5, 0)$ are on the circle.
choice **(3)**	$(0, -5)$ and $(-5, 0)$ are 5 units from O.	$(0, -5)$ and $(-5, 0)$ are on the circle.
choice **(4)**	$3^2 + 4^2 = 5^2$ and $(-4)^2 + 3^2 = 5^2$.	$(3, 4)$ and $(-4, 3)$ are on the circle.

The correct choice is (2).

Once you have determined the center and radius of a circle, you can sketch its graph.

EXAMPLE 5 Sketching a circle from an equation

Graph $x^2 + y^2 = 4$.

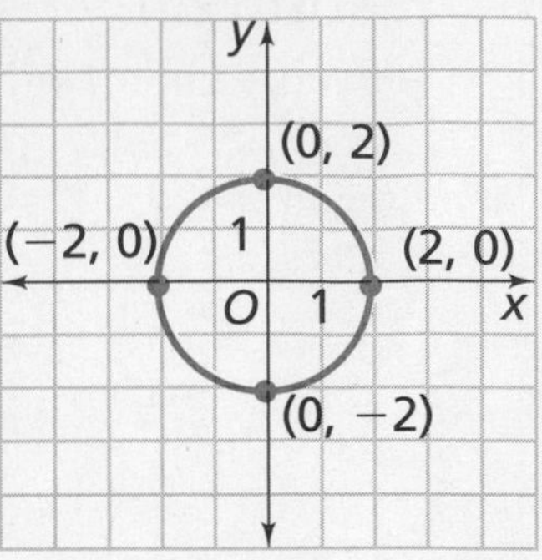

▪ SOLUTION

The equation represents a circle with radius 2 and center at the origin. Graph the points where the circle intersects each axis.

$x = 0$	$y = 0$
$0^2 + y^2 = 4$	$x^2 + 0^2 = 4$
So, $y = -2$ or 2.	So, $x = -2$ or 2.

Graph $(0, -2)$, $(0, 2)$, $(-2, 0)$, and $(2, 0)$. Sketch the circle as shown here.

You can also write the equation of a circle, given its graph.

EXAMPLES 6 and 7 Writing the equation of a circle given its graph

6 Find the equation of a circle with the endpoints of its diameter at $(-6, 0)$ and $(2, 0)$.

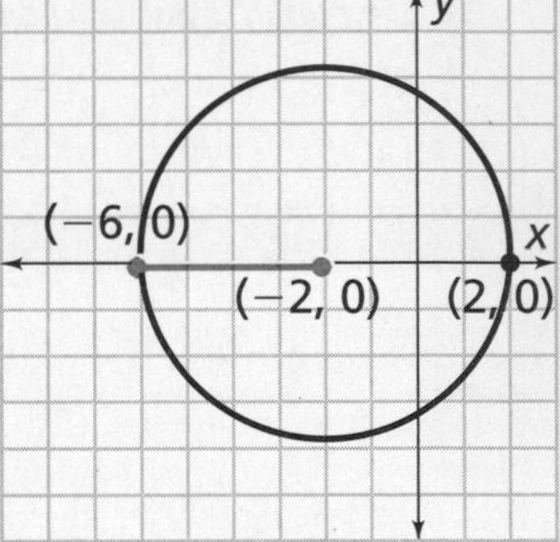

▪ SOLUTION

Step 1 You can use the midpoint formula to locate the midpoint of the diameter, which is the center of the circle, (h, k).

$$h = \frac{-6 + 2}{2} = \frac{-4}{2} = -2, k = \frac{0 + 0}{2} = 0$$

$$(h, k) = (-2, 0)$$

Step 2 Find the length of the radius, r, which is half the length of the diameter. Looking at the graph, you can see that $r = 4$.

$$(x - h)^2 + (y - k)^2 = r^2$$
$$(x - (-2))^2 + (y - 0)^2 = 4^2$$
$$(x + 2)^2 + y^2 = 16$$

Find the equation of the circle to the right.

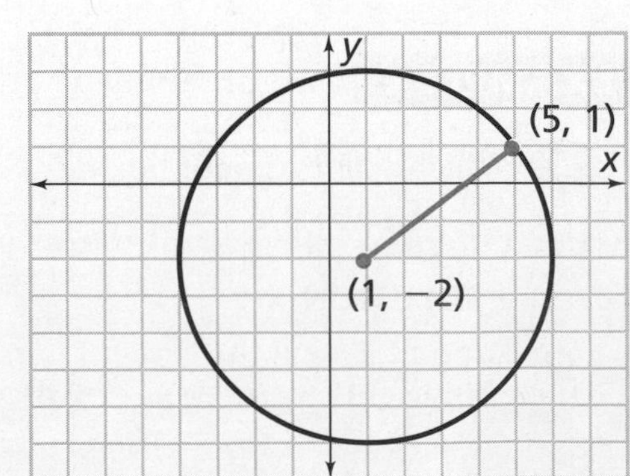

▪ SOLUTION

Step 1 Use the distance formula to find r.

$$r = \sqrt{(5 - 1)^2 + (1 - (-2)^2}$$
$$r = \sqrt{4^2 + 3^2}$$
$$r = \sqrt{25} = 5$$

Step 2 Substitute the values for h, k, and r.

$$(x - h)^2 + (y - k)^2 = r^2$$
$$(x - 1)^2 + (y - (-2))^2 = 5^2$$
$$(x - 1)^2 + (y + 2)^2 = 25$$

Practice

Choose the numeral preceding the word or expression that best completes the statement or answers the question.

1 The locus of points the tips of the minute and second hands of a clock will make in an hour is

(1) a line.

(2) a circle.

(3) two lines.

(4) two concentric circles.

2 Which equation represents a circle whose center is the origin and whose radius is 9?

(1) $x^2 - y^2 = 9$

(2) $x^2 + y^2 = 81$

(3) $x^2 + y^2 = 9$

(4) $3x^2 + 3y^2 = 3^2$

3 Which equation represents a circle with radius 3 and center (2, 3)?

(1) $9 = 2x^2 + 3y^2$

(2) $3^2 = (x - 2) + (y - 3)$

(3) $3^2 = (x - 2)^2 + (y - 3)^2$

(4) $9 = (x - 3)^2 + (y - 2)^2$

4 Which equation represents a circle with center $(-2, -2)$ passing through the point (2, 1)?

(1) $(x - 2)^2 + (y - 2)^2 = 25$

(2) $2x^2 + y^2 = 4$

(3) $x^2 + y^2 = 25$

(4) $(x + 2)^2 + (y + 2)^2 = 5^2$

5 Which of the following equations represents a circle with its center at the origin and with a radius of $\sqrt{5}$?

(1) $x^2 + y^2 = \sqrt{5}$

(2) $x^2 + y^2 = 5$

(3) $x^2 + y^2 = 25$

(4) $x^2 - y^2 = 5$

6 Which points are *not* on the circle given by the equation $x^2 + y^2 = 64$?

(1) (8, 0) and (0, 8)

(2) $(0, -8)$ and (8, 0)

(3) $(8, -8)$ and (8, 8)

(4) $(0, -8)$ and $(-8, 0)$

In Exercises 7–12, sketch each circle, then name its center, find the radius, and identify any point on the circle.

7 $x^2 + y^2 = 9$

8 $(x - 2)^2 + y^2 = 16$

9 $(x + 2)^2 + (y - 2)^2 = 4$

10 $x^2 + (y + 3)^2 = 16$

11 $(x - 2)^2 + (y - 1)^2 = 25$

12 $(x + 3)^2 + (y - 1)^2 = 1$

In Exercises 13–15, write the equation for each locus.

13 The set of all points that are in the coordinate plane and are 5 units from $P(-5, 2)$

14 The set of all points that are 5 units from the origin

15 The set of points 3 units from the point $(1, -3)$

16 Write the equation of a circle passing through the point (4, 3) and centered at the origin.

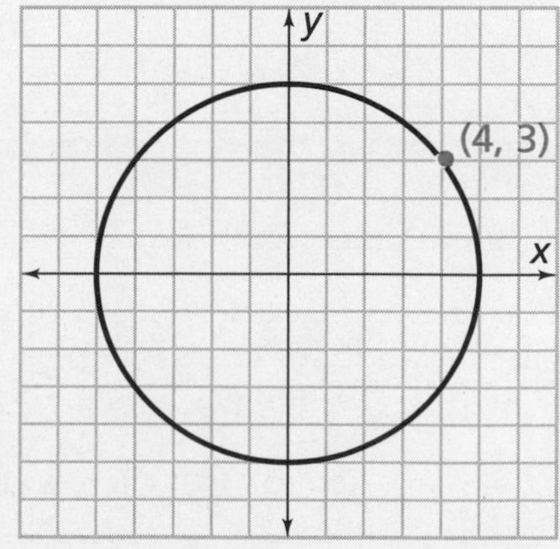

Chapter 6 Preparing for the New York Geometry Exam

Answer all questions in this part. For each question, select the numeral preceding the word or expression that best completes the statement or answers the question.

1 Which is the slope of a line perpendicular to the graph $y = \frac{5}{4}x + 8$?

(1) 1.25 **(3)** −0.8

(2) 0.8 **(4)** −1.25

2 Which of the following points is on the circle whose equation is $x^2 + y^2 = 25$?

(1) (0, 0) **(3)** (5, 5)

(2) (3, 4) **(4)** (25, 0)

3 The equation of a circle with center (−2, 2) and radius 4 is

(1) $x^2 + y^2 = 4$.

(2) $(x - 2)^2 + (y + 2)^2 = 4$.

(3) $(x - 2)^2 + (y + 2)^2 = 16$.

(4) $(x + 2)^2 + (y - 2)^2 = 16$.

4 The system pictured in the graph has how many solutions?

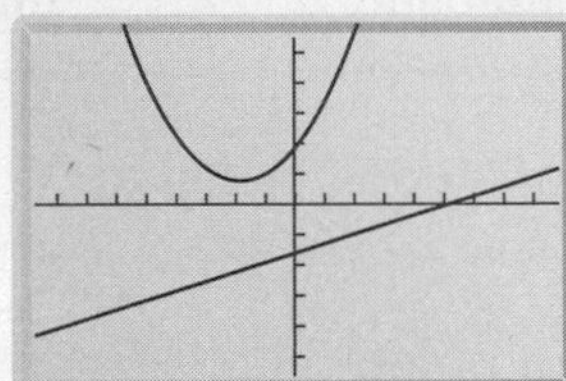

(1) 0 **(3)** 2

(2) 1 **(4)** Cannot determine

5 At how many points does the line $y = 3$ intersect the graph of $x^2 + y^2 = 9$?

(1) 0

(2) 1

(3) 2

(4) Cannot determine

6 The equation of a circle whose center is the origin and whose radius is $\sqrt{5}$ is

(1) $x^2 + y^2 = \sqrt{5}$. **(3)** $x^2 + y^2 = 5$.

(2) $x^2 - y^2 = 5$. **(4)** $x^2 + y^2 = 25$.

7 Which equation represents a line perpendicular to the line drawn below?

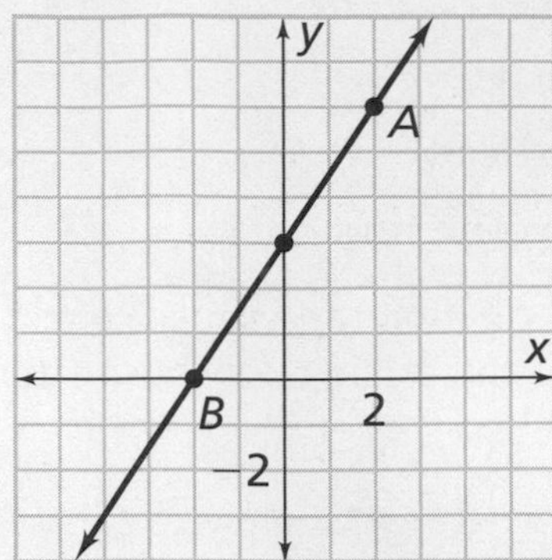

(1) $y = -\frac{3}{2}x + 3$ **(3)** $y = \frac{2}{3}x + 3$

(2) $y = -\frac{2}{3}x + 3$ **(4)** $y = \frac{3}{2}x + 3$

8 What is the slope of the line parallel to the line graphed by the equation $x + 4y = 7$?

(1) 4 **(3)** $-\frac{1}{4}$

(2) $\frac{7}{4}$ **(4)** −4

9 Which of the following points is the midpoint of a segment with the endpoints (−1, 1) and (4, 5)?

(1) $\left(\frac{3}{2}, 3\right)$

(2) $\left(\frac{5}{2}, 2\right)$

(3) $\left(3, \frac{3}{2}\right)$

(4) (5, 4)

10 What is the length of a segment with endpoints (−5, 1) and (2, 4)?

(1) $2\sqrt{6}$

(2) $\sqrt{34}$

(3) $\sqrt{58}$

(4) 58

11 Which of the following graphs represents a system of equations with one real solution?

(1)

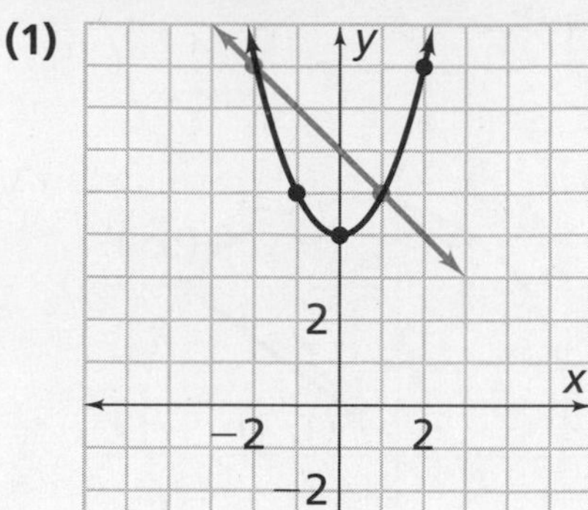

(2)

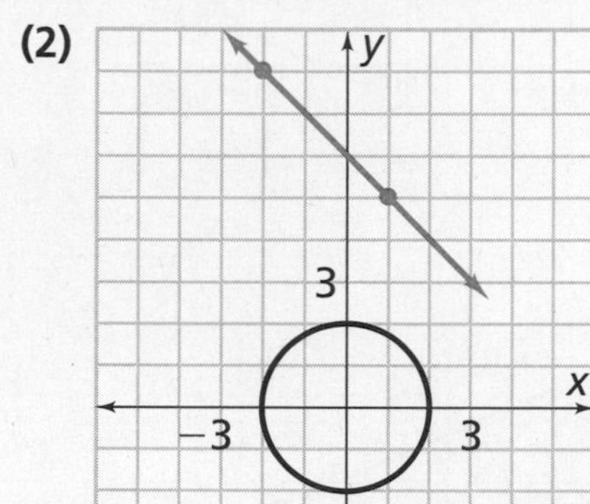

(3)

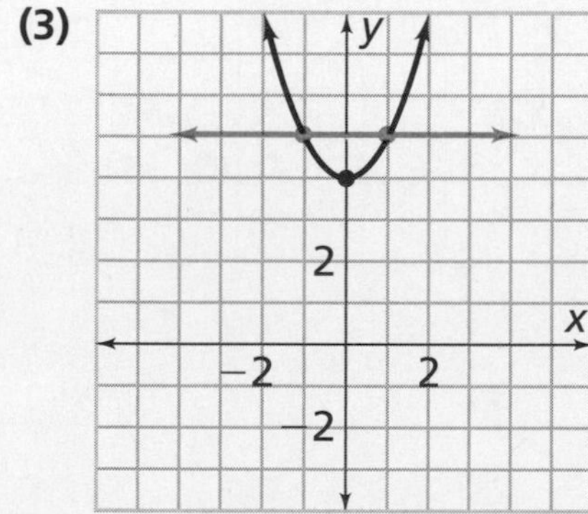

(4)

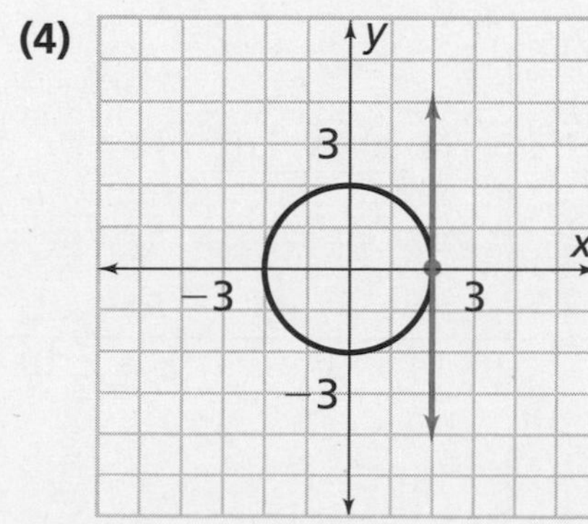

12 Which of the following is the equation to the perpendicular bisector of $\overline{AB}$?

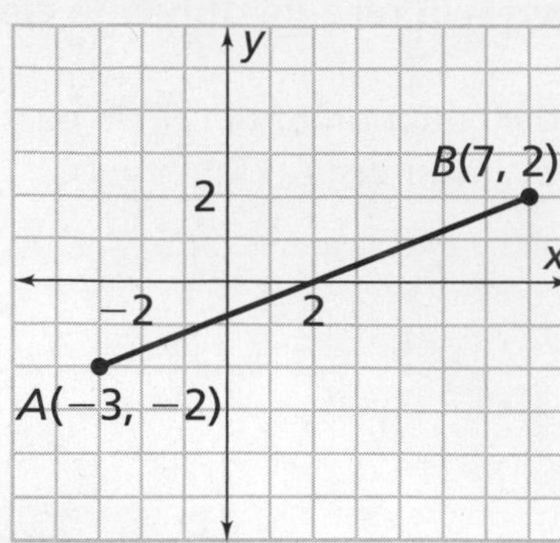

(1) $5x + 2y = 10$ **(3)** $2x + 5y = 24$

(2) $5x + 2y = -2$ **(4)** $2x + 5y = -4$

13 Which equation is perpendicular to the graph below?

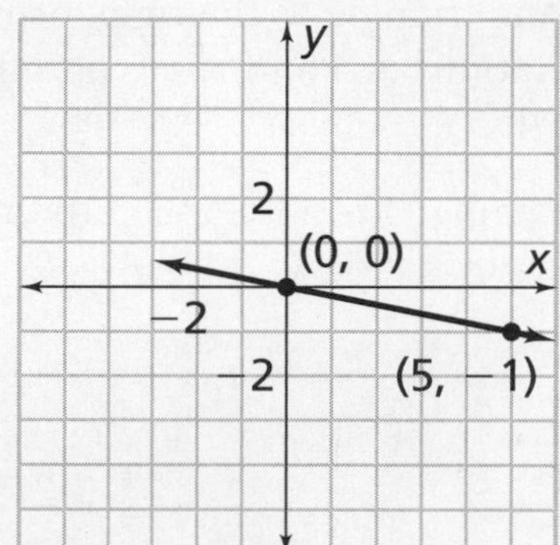

(1) $y = -5x + 3$

(2) $y = -\frac{1}{5}x - 3$

(3) $y = \frac{1}{5}x - 3$

(4) $y = 5x + 3$

14 A diameter of a circle has endpoints on the circle at $(-6, -6)$ and $(12, 8)$. What are the coordinates of the center of the circle?

(1) $(1, 3)$ **(3)** $(9, 1)$

(2) $(3, 1)$ **(4)** $(18, 14)$

Answer all questions in this part. Clearly indicate the necessary steps, including appropriate formula substitutions, diagrams, graphs, charts, etc. For all questions in this part, a correct numerical answer with no work shown will receive only one credit.

15 Write the equation of the circle passing through (5, 4) with center (1, 1).

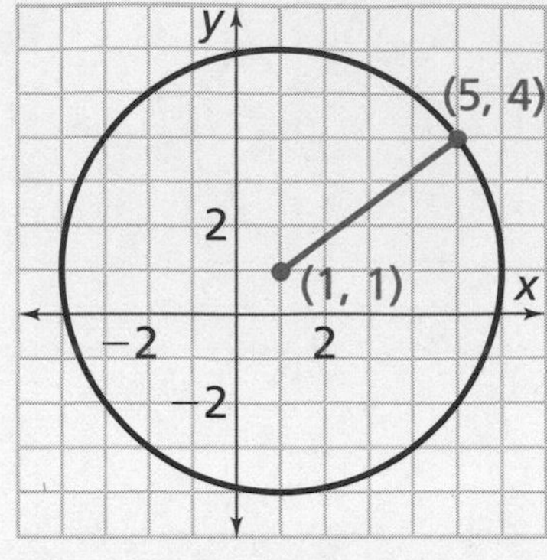

16 Given the triangle to the right, prove that the line joining the midpoints $\overline{AB}$ and $\overline{AC}$ is parallel to $\overline{BC}$ and one-half its length.

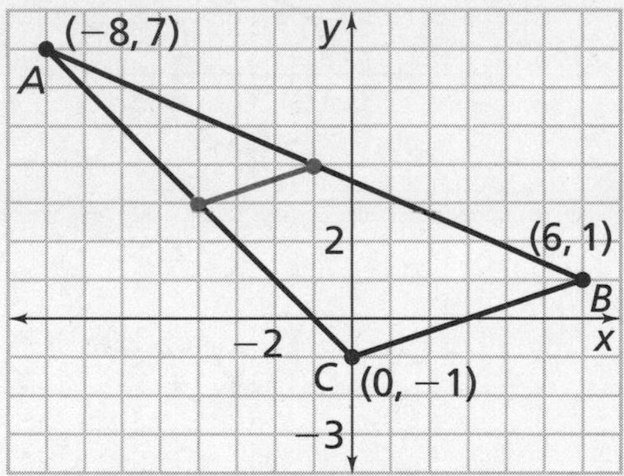

17 Prove that the figure is an isosceles trapezoid.

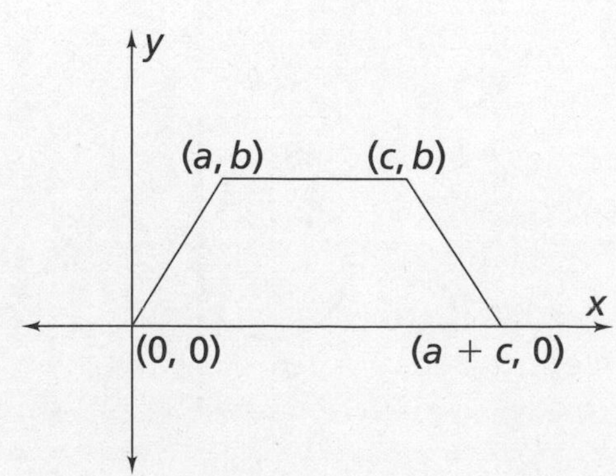

7 Transformational Geometry

Discovering New York

Central Park

Located in central Manhattan, Central Park is the most visited city park in the United States, with about 25 million visitors each year. Sprawling across 843 acres, Central Park is completely man-made. The park's design was decided by a landscape contest in 1858.

Central Park took more than 15 years to complete and cost $14 million, which is equivalent to about $200 million today. More than 500,000 trees, vines, and bushes were planted during the park's construction.

Today, Central Park contains 26,000 trees, 7 bodies of water, 58 miles of walking paths, and nearly 9,000 benches. The park also houses two ice-skating rinks, the Central Park Zoo, and the Central Park Conservatory Garden.

7.1 Reflections and Symmetry

New York Standards

G.G.54 Isometries in the plane

G.G.57 Justify transformations using relationships

In geometry, a transformation is a mapping of a figure, called the **preimage,** to a corresponding figure called its **image.** One type of transformation is a line reflection. If the image and preimage of a transformation are congruent, the transformation is called an **isometry.**

In the figure at the right, $\triangle ABC$, the preimage, is reflected across line m, which results in $\triangle A'B'C'$ (read A prime, B prime, C prime).

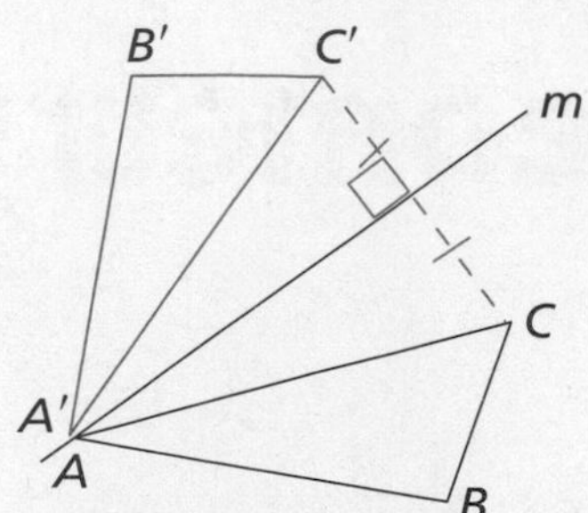

Line m is the line of reflection and acts like a mirror. For example, the image point C' must be the exact same distance from line m as its corresponding preimage point C. Further, the segment that connects the points C and C' must be perpendicular to line m. This reflection maps all of the points of $\triangle ABC$ onto $\triangle A'B'C'$.

Note that because point A lies directly on the line of reflection, it is its own image. A point that is its own image under a transformation is called a **fixed point.**

The preimage and image under a reflection are congruent; only their orientations change. You can use what you know about reflections to sketch an image of a figure under a reflection.

Go Online PHSchool.com

Visit: PHSchool.com
Web Code: ayp-0889

EXAMPLE 1 **Sketching the image of a polygon under a line reflection**

1 Sketch the image of a right triangle $\triangle ABC$ reflected across line p, where $\overline{BC}$ is parallel to p and $\overline{AC}$ is perpendicular to p.

SOLUTION

Step 1
Sketch a right triangle $\triangle ABC$ and line p not intersecting it.

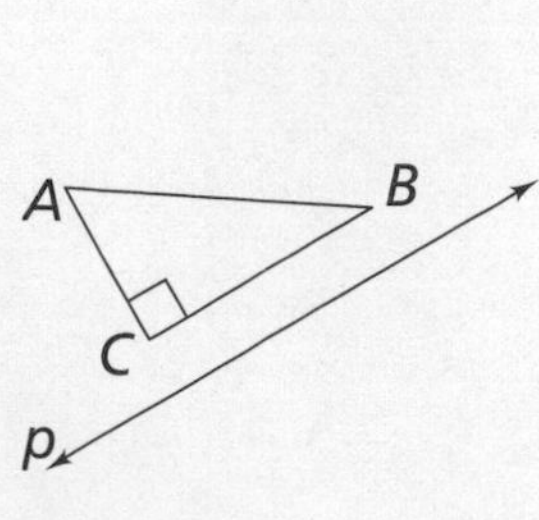

Step 2
Construct lines through A, B, and C that are perpendicular to p.

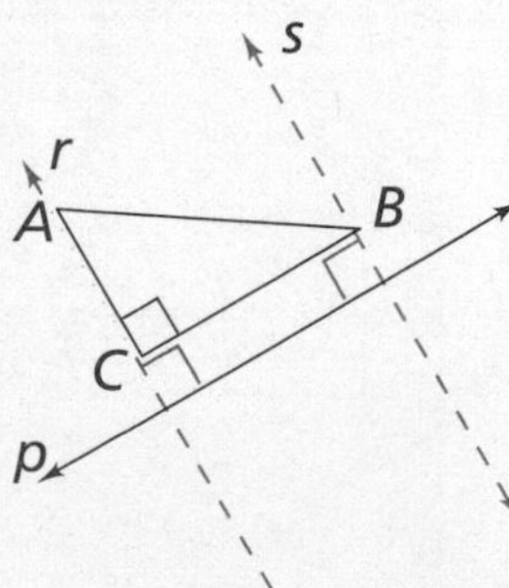

Step 3
Place points A', B', and C' the same distance from p as points A, B, and C are.

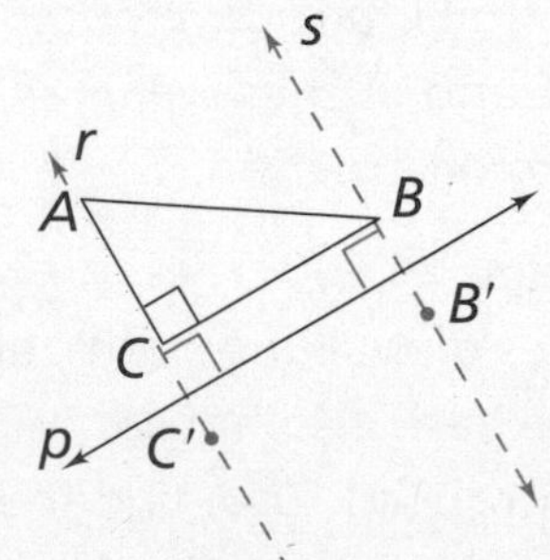

Step 4
Join points A', B', and C' to make $\triangle A'B'C'$, the image of $\triangle ABC$ under the reflection.

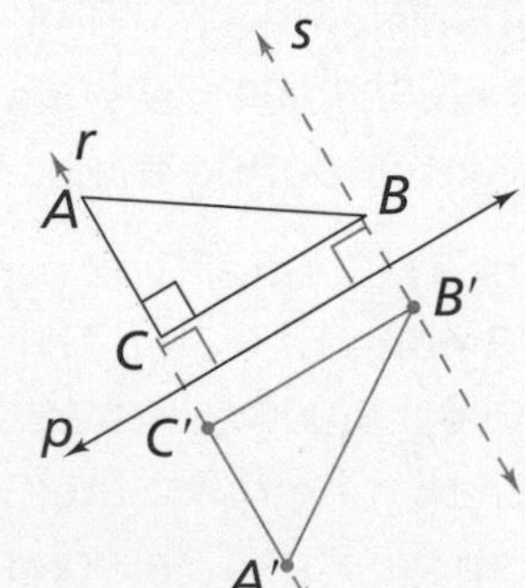

In the coordinate plane, there are three common line reflections. Reflections are isometries.

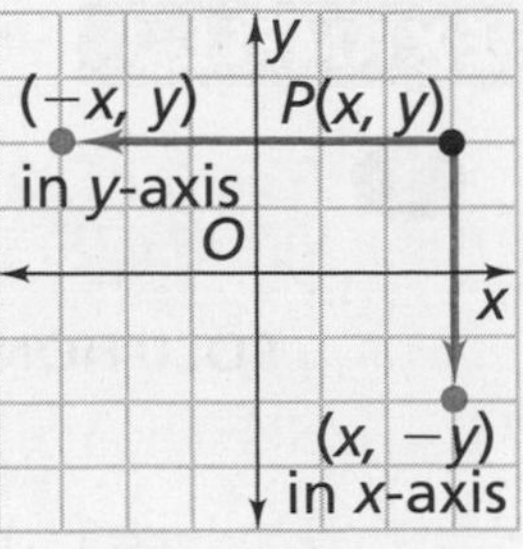

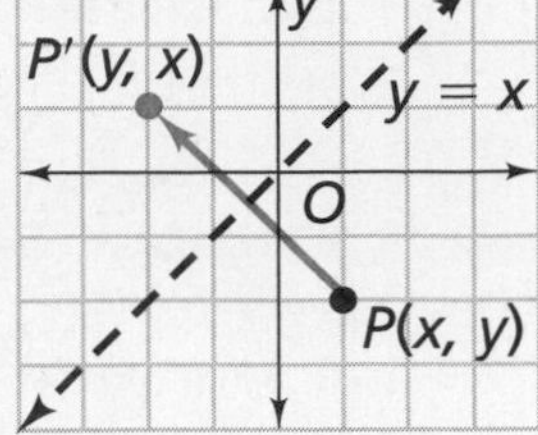

Special Reflections

The image of $P(x, y)$ under a **reflection across the *x*-axis** is the point $P'(x, -y)$.

$$r_{x\text{-axis}}(x, y) \rightarrow (x, -y)$$

The image of $P(x, y)$ under a **reflection across the *y*-axis** is the point $P'(-x, y)$.

$$r_{x\text{-axis}}(x, y) \rightarrow (-x, y)$$

The image of $P(x, y)$ under a **reflection across $y = x$** is the point $P'(y, x)$.

$$r_{x\text{-axis}}(x, y) \rightarrow (y, x)$$

EXAMPLE 2 **Sketching the image of a polygon under a reflection across an axis**

The vertices of $\triangle ABC$ are $A(-3, 3)$, $B(6, 6)$, and $C(4, 1)$. Sketch the image of this triangle after reflection across the *x*-axis and across the *y*-axis.

■ **SOLUTION**

Sketch $A(-3, 3)$, $B(6, 6)$, $C(4, 1)$, and $\triangle ABC$. Under a reflection across the *x*-axis, replace *y* with $-y$.

$r_{x\text{-axis}}(x, y) \rightarrow (x, -y)$
$r_{x\text{-axis}}(-3, 3) \rightarrow (-3, -3)$
$r_{x\text{-axis}}(6, 6) \rightarrow (6, -6)$
$r_{x\text{-axis}}(4, 1) \rightarrow (4, -1)$

Graph $A'(-3, -3)$, $B'(6, -6)$, and $C'(4, -1)$. Draw $\triangle A'B'C'$. The image is shown with solid blue segments.

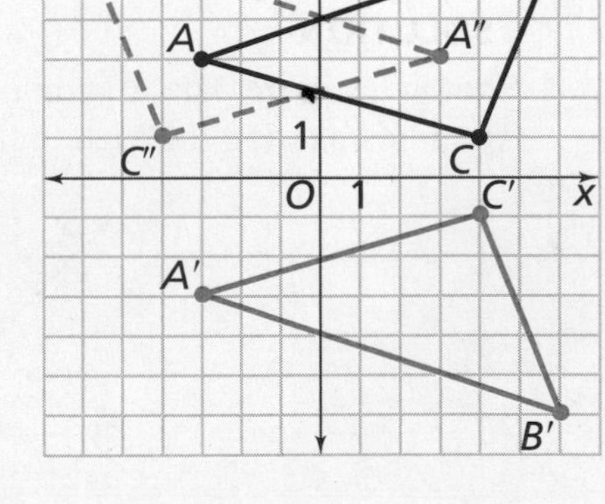

Under a reflection across the *y*-axis, replace *x* with $-x$.

$r_{x\text{-axis}}(x, y) \rightarrow (-x, y)$
$r_{x\text{-axis}}(-3, 3) \rightarrow (3, 3)$
$r_{x\text{-axis}}(6, 6) \rightarrow (-6, 6)$
$r_{x\text{-axis}}(4, 1) \rightarrow (-4, 1)$

Graph $A''(3, 3)$, $B''(-6, 6)$, and $C''(-4, 1)$. Draw $\triangle A''B''C''$. The image is shown with dashed blue segments.

A **reflection about a point** is another type of transformation. In the figure at the right, the image of point *P* is itself and the image of any other point *Q* is the point Q' where *P* is the midpoint of $\overline{QQ'}$. Point *P* is called the *point of reflection*. This diagram shows $\overline{QR}$ and its image $\overline{Q'R'}$ under a reflection in point *P*.

Now consider a special point of reflection in the coordinate plane. Suppose that the point of reflection is the origin. In that case, the coordinates (x, y) of any point in the preimage are reflected to $(-x, -y)$ in the image.

EXAMPLE 3 Sketching an image under reflection about the origin

3 The vertices of $\triangle ABC$ are $A(-3, 3)$, $B(6, 6)$, and $C(4, 1)$. Sketch the image of this triangle after reflection about the origin.

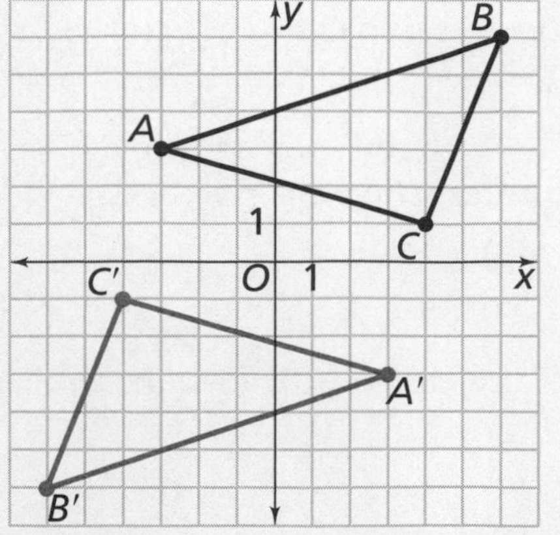

■ **SOLUTION**

Sketch $A(-3, 3)$, $B(6, 6)$, $C(4, 1)$, and $\triangle ABC$.

Under a reflection about the origin, replace x with $-x$ and y with $-y$.

$$r_{(0,0)}(x, y) \rightarrow (-x, -y)$$
$$r_{(0,0)}(-3, 3) \rightarrow (3, -3)$$
$$r_{(0,0)}(6, 6) \rightarrow (-6, -6)$$
$$r_{(0,0)}(4, 1) \rightarrow (-4, -1)$$

Graph $A'(-3, 3)$, $B'(-6, -6)$, and $C'(-4, -1)$. Draw $\triangle A'B'C'$. The image is shown with solid blue segments.

A figure may be its own image after reflection across a line. For example, if m is a line of reflection, then the image of the regular octagon $ABCDEFGH$ after reflection across line m is the octagon $ABCDEFGH$. A figure in the plane has **line symmetry** if it is its own image after reflection across some line in the plane. The line of reflection is called a **line of symmetry.**

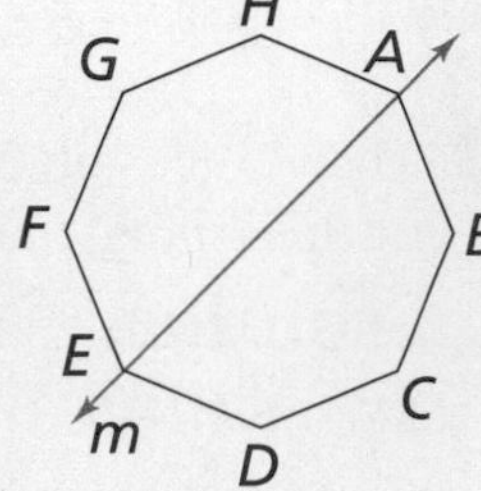

EXAMPLE 4 Drawing lines of symmetry

Sketch all lines of symmetry for a square.

■ **SOLUTION**

Sketch a square. The diagonals of the square are lines of symmetry. The lines passing through the midpoints of opposite sides are too.

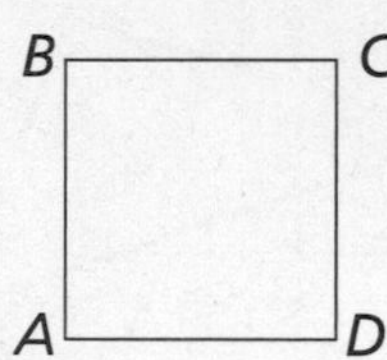

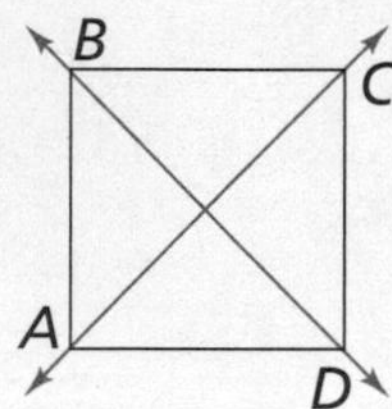

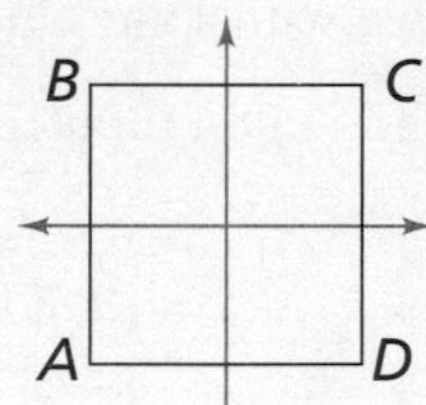

Lines of symmetry can be identified and specifically named when the figure is placed on a coordinate grid.

EXAMPLE 5 Identifying lines of symmetry

Does the figure at the right have line symmetry? Explain.

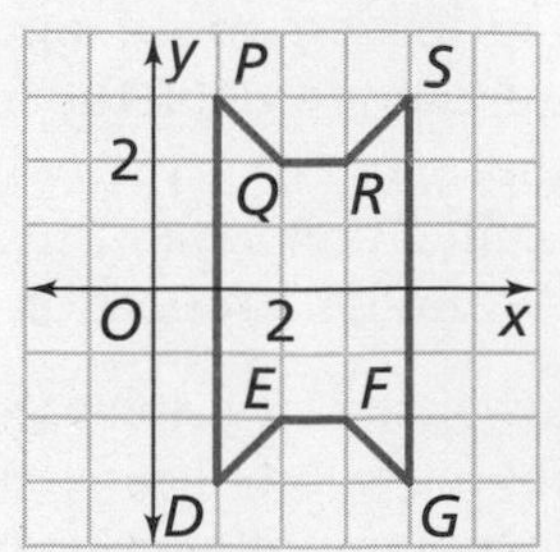

■ **SOLUTION**

The line $y = 0$ (the x-axis) and the line $x = 2.5$ are lines of symmetry. The figure is its own image after a reflection over either of those two lines.

Practice

Choose the numeral preceding the word or expression that best completes the statement or answers the question.

1 Which represents the image of $G(4, -3)$ after reflection in the x-axis?

(1) $G'(-4, -3)$ **(3)** $G'(-4, 3)$

(2) $G'(4, 3)$ **(4)** $G'(-3, 4)$

2 Which represents the image of $X(-3, -7)$ after reflection in the y-axis?

(1) $X'(-3, 7)$ **(3)** $X'(3, 7)$

(2) $X'(3, -7)$ **(4)** $X'(7, 3)$

3 If $r_{(x, y)}(4, 3) \rightarrow (8, -5)$, find x and y.

(1) $(-1, 6)$ **(3)** $(-2, 11)$

(2) $(6, -1)$ **(4)** $(12, -13)$

4 If $r_{(0,0)}(x, y) \rightarrow (9, -3)$, find (x, y).

(1) $(-9, -3)$ **(3)** $(-9, 3)$

(2) $(9, -3)$ **(4)** $(-3, 9)$

5 Which is the image of $K(3, 1)$ after reflection in the line $y = -1$?

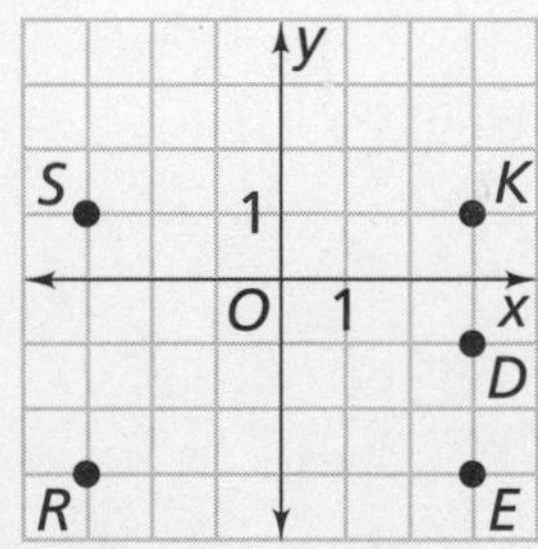

(1) D **(2)** E **(3)** R **(4)** S

6 Which of the following is the image of $r_{y=4}(x, y)$?

(1) $(x, 8 - y)$ **(3)** $(x, 4)$

(2) $(x, y + 4)$ **(4)** (x, y)

In Exercise 7, sketch the image of the given figure in the specified line.

7 $\triangle ABC$ in line z

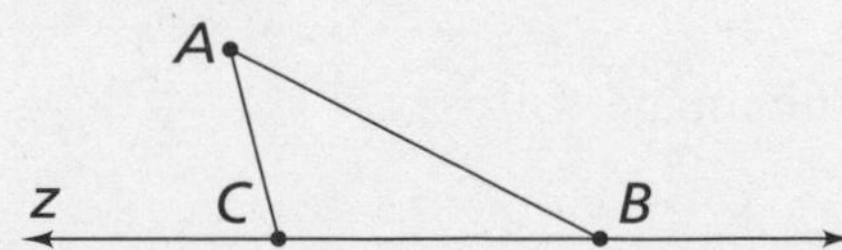

8 Copy this figure. Sketch all lines of symmetry.

In Exercises 9–11, write the coordinates of the image under the specified reflection.

9 $\triangle RST$ with vertices having coordinates $R(1, 1)$, $S(5, 1)$, and $T(5, 3)$ in the x-axis

10 $\triangle NBA$ with vertices having coordinates $N(1, 1)$, $B(5, 1)$, and $A(5, 3)$ in the y-axis

11 quadrilateral $EUDP$ with vertices having coordinates $E(3, 3)$, $U(5, 3)$, $D(1, -1)$, and $P(-1, -1)$ about $(2, 4)$

12 Under the reflection across line m, the image of $(0, 4)$ is $(2, 2)$. Write the equation of line m.

In Exercises 13–15, solve the problem. Clearly show all necessary work.

13 One vertex of a quadrilateral is $A(-3, -2)$. Find the coordinates of the other three vertices that complete a quadrilateral symmetric about the x-axis and the y-axis.

14 One vertex of a quadrilateral is $P(4, 2)$. Find the coordinates of the other three vertices that complete a quadrilateral symmetric about the lines $x = 1$ and $y = 1$.

15 Sketch the reflection of the parabola in the line $y = x$.

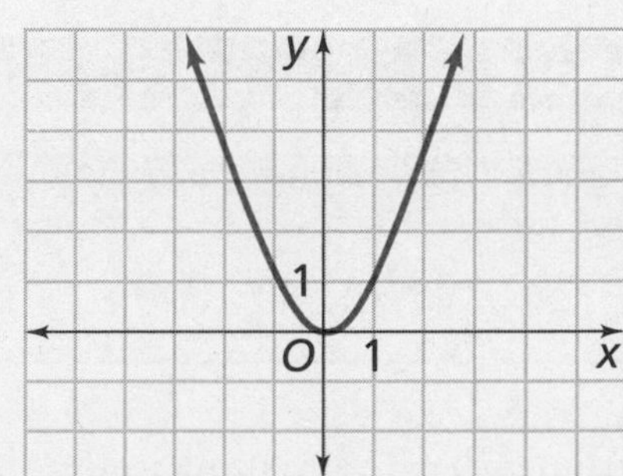

7.2 Translations and Rotations

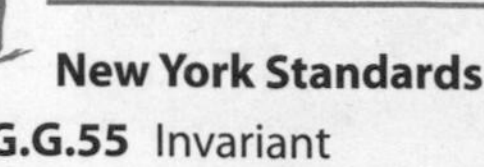

New York Standards

G.G.55 Invariant properties under transformations

A **translation** is a transformation of a figure in which each point is moved the same distance in the same direction. A translation is an isometry. The sketch at the right shows the translation of $\triangle ABC$ along the arrows shown in blue. The image of each vertex of $\triangle ABC$ is found by placing a point at the tip of the arrows shown. When you join the vertices, the image is $\triangle A'B'C'$.

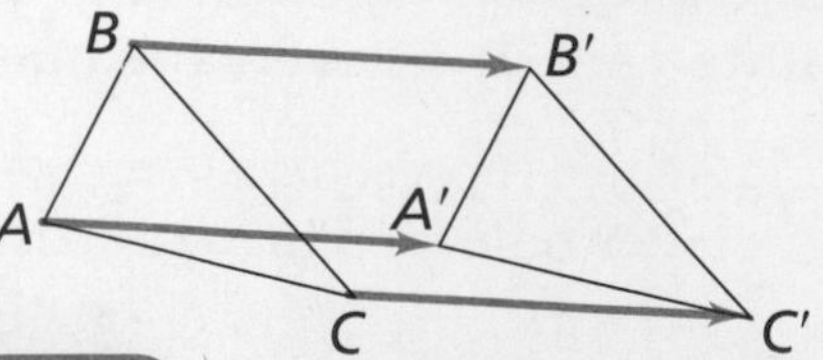

Invariant Characteristics of a Translation

If a line segment is translated, the image is a line segment congruent and parallel to the original line segment.

If an angle is translated, the image is an angle congruent to the original angle.

The orientation of the image is the same as that of the original object.

Note

A translation is also called a slide.

EXAMPLE 1 **Translating a polygon in the plane**

Draw the image of rectangle $WXYZ$ under the translation shown by the arrow.

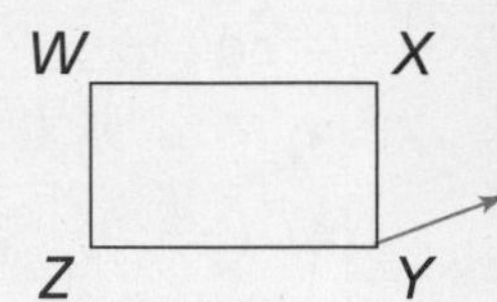

SOLUTION

Step 1 Draw an arrow from each of the three remaining vertices. Make sure that the arrows are the same length, point in the same direction, and are parallel to the original arrow.

Step 2 Draw the rectangle whose vertices are at the tips of the arrows.

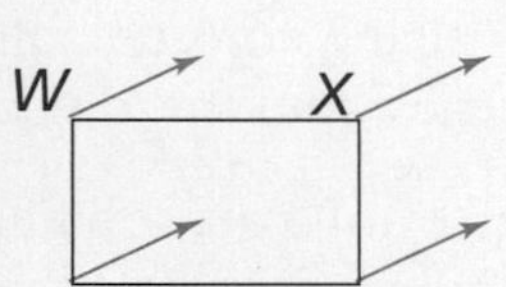

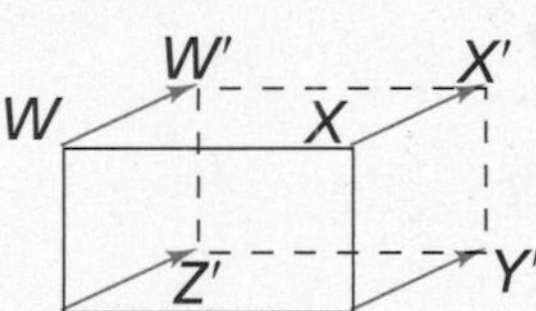

In the coordinate plane, you can represent a translation by specifying how far the object slides horizontally along the x-axis and how far the object slides vertically along the y-axis.

Translations

The image of $P(x, y)$ under a translation a units horizontally and b units vertically is given by:

$$T_{a,b}(x, y) \quad \rightarrow \quad (x + a, y + b)$$

If you translate $P(-2, 4)$ 5 units to the right and 3 units down, the image will be as follows:

$$T_{5,3}(-2, 4) \rightarrow P'(-2 + 5, 4 + (-3)) = P'(3, 1)$$

EXAMPLE 2 Describing translations

Visit: PHSchool.com
Web Code: ayp-0765

2 The point $A(6, 10)$ is translated to $Q(0, 3)$.
Which of the following is the correct translation?

(1) $T_{-6, 7}$ **(3)** $T_{-6, -7}$

(2) $T_{6, 7}$ **(4)** $T_{6, -7}$

■ SOLUTION

Let a be the horizontal distance and b be the vertical distance $A(6, 10)$ is translated.

$$0 = 6 + a \quad \text{and} \quad 3 = 10 + b$$
$$a = -6 \quad \text{and} \quad b = -7$$

The translation is $T_{-6, -7}$. Choose (3).

Note

If $a > 0$, slide right.
If $a < 0$, slide left.
If $b > 0$, slide up.
If $b < 0$, slide down.

You may need to find the coordinates of an image under a specific translation.

EXAMPLE 3 Finding the coordinates of the image under a translation

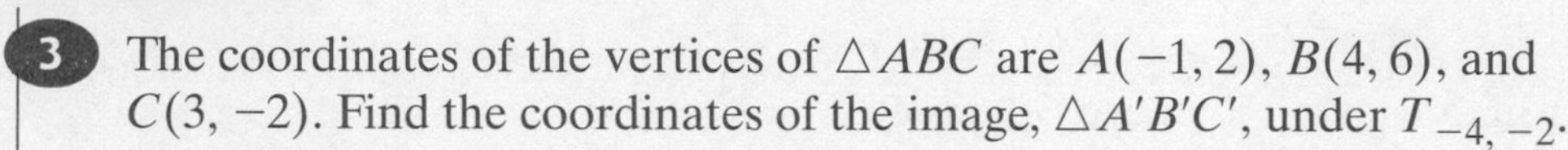

3 The coordinates of the vertices of $\triangle ABC$ are $A(-1, 2)$, $B(4, 6)$, and $C(3, -2)$. Find the coordinates of the image, $\triangle A'B'C'$, under $T_{-4, -2}$.

■ SOLUTION

$$A(-1, 2) \rightarrow A'(-1 + (-4), 2 + (-2)) = A'(-5, 0)$$
$$B(4, 6) \rightarrow B'(4 + (-4), 6 + (-2)) = B'(0, 4)$$
$$C(3, -2) \rightarrow C'(3 + (-4), -2 + (-2)) = C'(-1, -4)$$

A translation results when an object is reflected over two parallel lines.

EXAMPLE 4 Sketching the image of reflections in parallel lines

4 Sketch the image of $\triangle ABC$ after reflection across m and then n.

■ SOLUTION

Step 1 Copy the given figures.

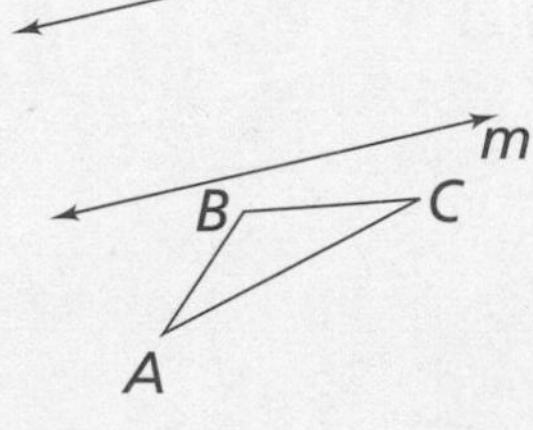

Step 2 Reflect $\triangle ABC$ across line m to get $\triangle A'B'C'$.

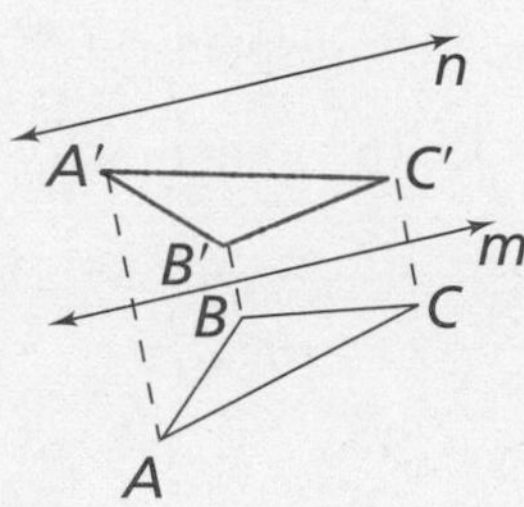

Step 3 Sketch the reflection of $\triangle A'B'C'$ across line n to get $\triangle A''B''C''$.

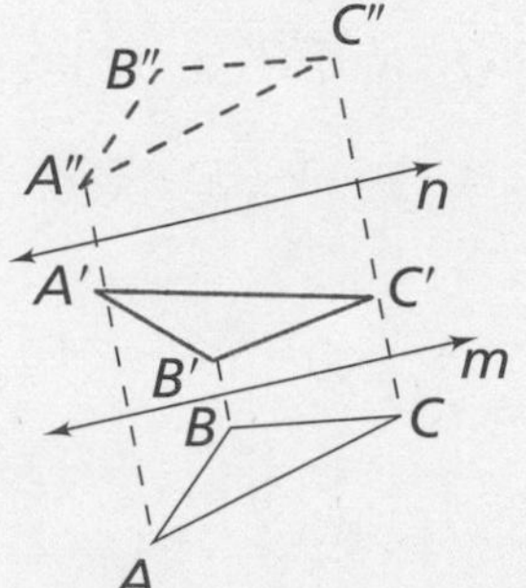

Translations Related to Reflections

If the reflection of A in line m is A' and the reflection of A' over line n parallel to m is A'', then A'' is a translation of A.

Given a translation and the coordinates of the image, you can use equations to find the coordinates of the preimage.

EXAMPLE 5 **Finding the coordinates of a point given its image under a translation**

5 After $G(x, y)$ is translated to the right 6 units and down 4 units, the coordinates of the image are $Z(-2, 7)$. Find the coordinates of $G(x, y)$.

■ **SOLUTION**

$$Z(-2, 7) = Z(x + 6, y + (-4)) \qquad a = 6 \text{ and } b = -4$$
$$-2 = x + 6 \quad \text{and} \quad 7 = y - 4$$
$$x = -8 \quad \text{and} \quad y = 11$$

Therefore, the coordinates of $G(x, y)$ are $G(-8, 11)$.

When you translate a figure, you slide it to another position in the plane. Under a **rotation** in the plane, you turn a figure using a fixed distance from a fixed point in the plane, called the **center of rotation.** The rotation may be clockwise or counterclockwise. In the diagram at the right, P is rotated counterclockwise 25° about point O to P'. A rotation is an isometry.

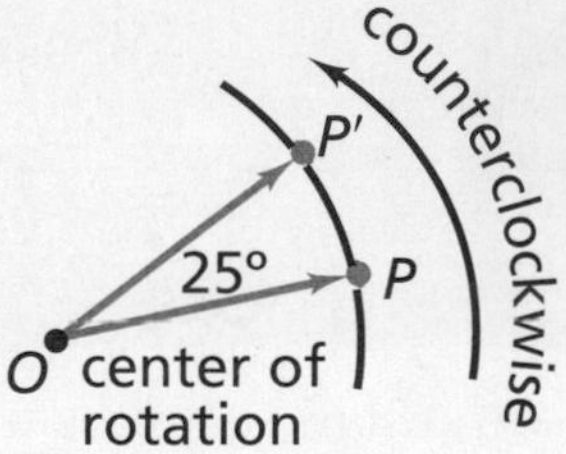

EXAMPLE 6 **Sketching the image of a figure under a rotation**

6 Sketch the image of $\triangle PQR$ under a rotation of 90° counterclockwise about O.

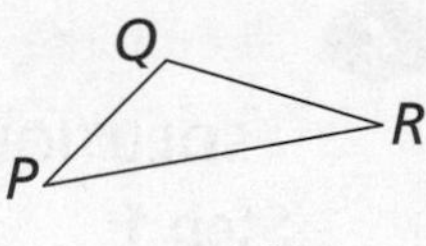

■ **SOLUTION**

Step 1 Copy the given figure. Draw segments joining O to P, Q, and R.

Step 2 Rotate $\overline{OR}$, $\overline{OQ}$, and $\overline{OP}$ counterclockwise 90°. Use a protractor to measure the 90° angle and a compass to draw $\overline{OR'}$, $\overline{OQ'}$, and $\overline{OP'}$ equal in length to $\overline{OR}$, $\overline{OQ}$, and $\overline{OP}$, respectively.

Step 3 Join P', Q', and R' to make $\triangle P'Q'R'$, the image of $\triangle PQR$.

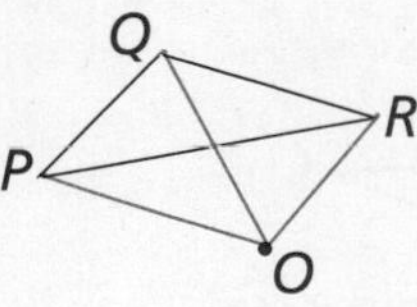

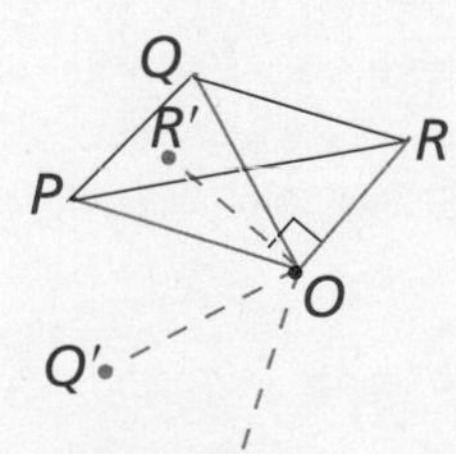

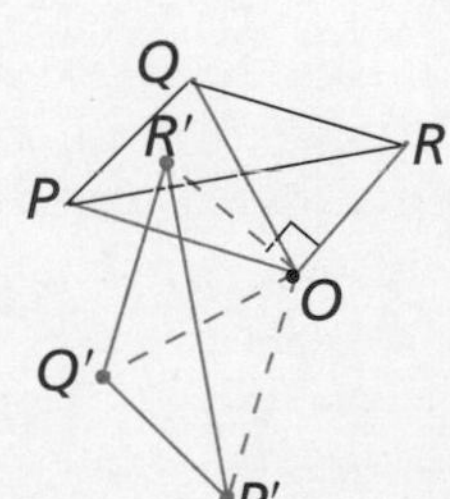

A rotation results when an object is reflected over two intersecting lines. The intersection point of the lines is the center of rotation.

Rotations Related to Reflections

If the reflection of A across line m is A' and the reflection of A' across line n intersecting line m is A'', then A'' is a rotation of A about the point where lines m and n intersect.

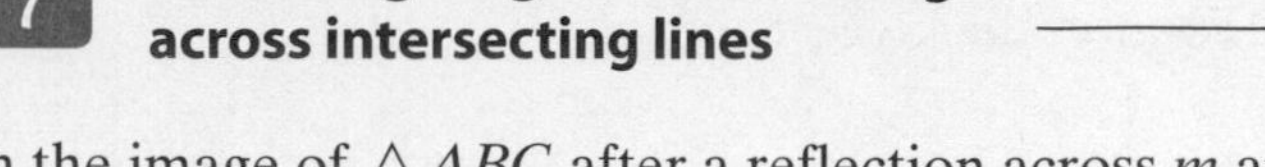

EXAMPLE 7 **Reflecting a figure and its image across intersecting lines**

Go Online PHSchool.com
Visit: PHSchool.com
Web Code: ayp-0443

7 Sketch the image of $\triangle ABC$ after a reflection across m and then across n.

▪ **SOLUTION**

Step 1 Copy the given figures.

Step 2 Reflect $\triangle ABC$ across line m to get $\triangle A'B'C'$.

Step 3 Sketch the reflection of $\triangle A'B'C'$ across line n to get $\triangle A''B''C''$.

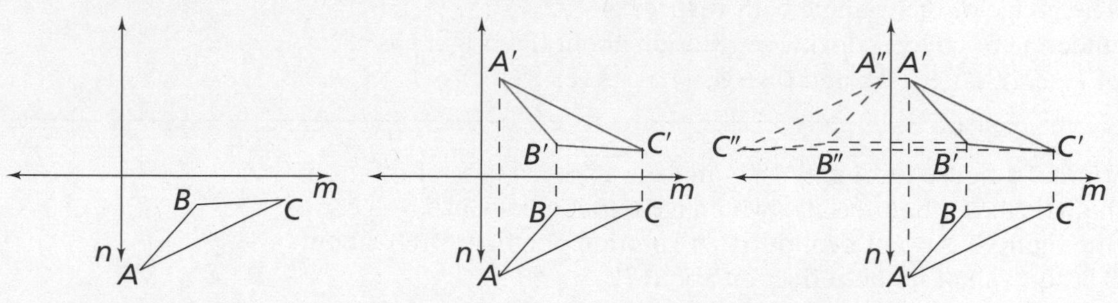

A figure in the plane has **rotational symmetry** if it is its own image after a rotation of 180° or less around some point in the plane. The point is called the **center of symmetry.**

EXAMPLE 8 **Recognizing and identifying rotational symmetry**

8 Which figure has rotational symmetry?

(1) square **(2)** letter T **(3)** isosceles trapezoid **(4)** ray

▪ **SOLUTION**

Sketch a square and its diagonals. If you rotate the square about the intersection of the diagonals 90° counterclockwise, the image will be the original square. Therefore, a square has rotational symmetry. (A rotation of 90° clockwise about O will also show rotational symmetry.) The correct choice is (1).

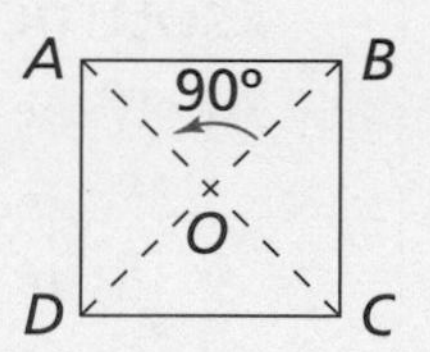

In the coordinate plane, you can rotate a figure 90° counterclockwise about the origin by using a transformation rule.

90° Counterclockwise Rotation About the Origin

The image of $P(x, y)$ under a 90° counterclockwise rotation about the origin, O, is given by the rule below.

$$R_{O, 90°}(x, y) \rightarrow (-y, x)$$

Go Online
PHSchool.com
Visit: PHSchool.com
Web Code: ayp-0866

EXAMPLE 9 **Sketching the image of a rotation in the coordinate plane**

9 Sketch the image of the triangle with vertices $A(1, 2)$, $B(5, 3)$, and $C(4, 6)$ under a 90° counterclockwise rotation about the origin.

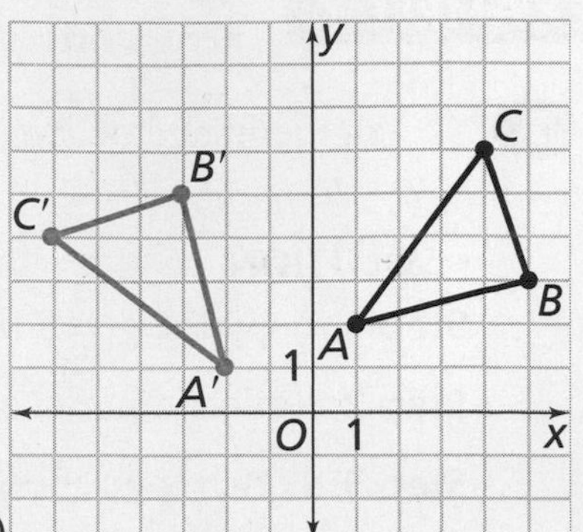

■ SOLUTION

Apply the rule for a 90° counterclockwise rotation about the origin.

$R_{O, 90°}(1, 2) \rightarrow (-2, 1)$
$R_{O, 90°}(5, 3) \rightarrow (-3, 5)$
$R_{O, 90°}(4, 6) \rightarrow (-6, 4)$

The image of the triangle with vertices $A(1, 2)$, $B(5, 3)$, $C(4, 6)$ under a 90° counterclockwise rotation about the origin has $A'(-2, 1)$, $B'(-3, 5)$, and $C'(-6, 4)$ as its vertices.

The rotation of a figure through a 180° angle is a special type of rotation called a **half-turn.** If a figure is its own image under a half-turn, you can say that the figure has **point symmetry.** A rotation of a figure 180° about a point P is equivalent to the reflection about P.

180° Rotation About the Origin

The image of $P(x, y)$ under a 180° rotation about the origin, O, is given by:

$$R_{O, 180°}(x, y) \rightarrow (-x, -y)$$

Visit: PHSchool.com
Web Code: ayp-0440

EXAMPLE 10 **Sketching the image of a half-turn in the coordinate plane**

10 Sketch the image of the triangle with vertices $X(2, 2)$, $Y(5, 3)$, and $Z(4, 5)$ under a half-turn about the origin.

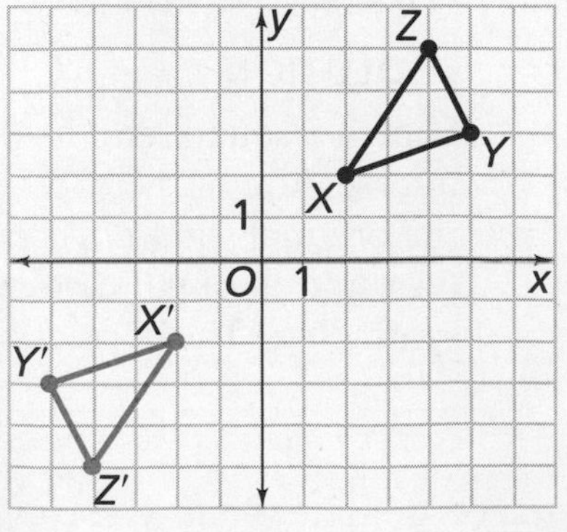

■ SOLUTION

Apply the rule for a 180° rotation about the origin.

$R_{O, 180°}(2, 2) \rightarrow (-2, -2)$
$R_{O, 180°}(5, 3) \rightarrow (-5, -3)$
$R_{O, 180°}(4, 5) \rightarrow (-4, -5)$

The coordinates of the image of $\triangle XYZ$ are $X'(-2, -2)$, $Y'(-5, -3)$, and $Z'(-4, -5)$.

Practice

Choose the numeral preceding the word or expression that best completes the statement or answers the question.

1 Under which transformation will $P'(2, -4)$ be the image of $P(1, 1)$?

(1) reflection in the x-axis
(2) translation 1 unit right and 5 units down
(3) rotation of 180° about the origin
(4) translation 1 unit right and 1 unit up

2 What are the coordinates of the image of $A(3, 5)$ under $T_{-5, -4}$?

(1) $A'(-2, 1)$ **(3)** $A'(8, 9)$
(2) $A'(-2, 9)$ **(4)** $A'(8, 1)$

3 Which transformation is illustrated below?

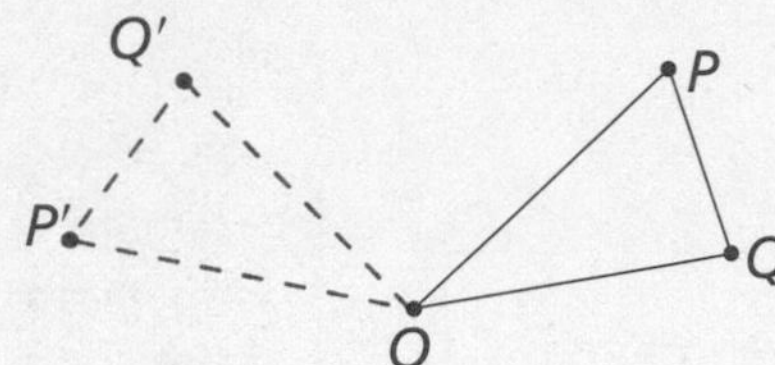

(1) rotation of $\triangle OPQ$ about O
(2) translation of $\triangle OPQ$ along $\overrightarrow{OQ}$
(3) translation of $\triangle OPQ$ along $\overrightarrow{OP}$
(4) reflection of $\triangle OPQ$ across $\overleftrightarrow{PQ}$

4 Which of the following are the coordinates of the image of $G(4, 6)$ under a $R_{O, 90°}$?

(1) $G'(4, -6)$ **(3)** $G'(-6, 4)$
(2) $G'(-4, 6)$ **(4)** $G'(-6, -4)$

5 Which represents the translation under which the image of $H(-3, -5)$ is $H'(7, 0)$?

(1) 10 units right and 5 units down
(2) 10 units right and 5 units up
(3) 10 units left and 5 units down
(4) 10 units left and 5 units up

6 If the length of $\overline{LM}$ is 10 units, what is the length of its image under a half-turn?

(1) 5 units **(3)** 20 units
(2) 10 units **(4)** −10 units

In Exercises 7–12, write the coordinates of the image of the given point under the specified transformation.

7 $A(4, 1)$; half-turn about the origin

8 $B(3, 4)$; 90° counterclockwise rotation about the origin

9 $C(-5, 4)$; translation 2 units left and 4 units up

10 $D(-5, 4)$; translation 4 units right and 4 units down

11 $E(3, 2)$; reflection in the x-axis followed by a reflection in the line $y = -3$

12 $F(3, 2)$; reflection in the x-axis followed by a reflection in the y-axis

In Exercises 13–15, graph the given points in the coordinate plane. In the same plane, sketch the image under the specified transformation.

13 quadrilateral $ABCD$ with vertices $A(1, 0)$, $B(4, 7)$, $C(6, 4)$, and $D(5, 0)$; translation 2 units left and 2 units up

14 $\triangle PQR$ with vertices $P(3, 0)$, $Q(0, 4)$, $R(0, 0)$; 90° counterclockwise rotation about the origin

15 $\triangle XYZ$ with vertices $X(4, 0)$, $Y(0, 4)$, and $Z(0, 0)$; half-turn about the origin

16 Under a translation, the image of $A(4, -3)$ is $A'(6, -7)$. Find the image of $B(-2, 7)$ under the same translation.

17 Sketch the 90° clockwise rotation of $\triangle LTY$ about T.

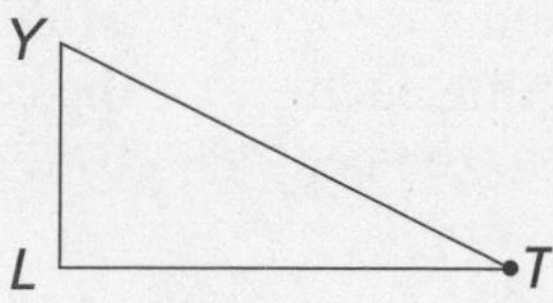

7.3 Dilations

New York Standards

G.G.56 Identifying isometries

G.G.58 Dilations and isometries

G.G.59 Invariant properties under similarities

G.G.60 Identify specific similarities

An **isometry** is a transformation under which the image and preimage are congruent. Reflections, translations, and rotations are all isometries. Properties that do not change under a transformation are said to be **invariant.**

A **dilation (similarity transformation)** with center O is a transformation in which a given figure is enlarged or reduced. The measures of the angles in the image equal the measures of the corresponding angles in the preimage. However, the dimensions of the image are n times those of the preimage. The **scale factor** n determines the *enlargement* or *reduction* of the preimage. Scale factors less than 1 result in a reduction of the preimage; scale factors greater than 1 result in an enlargement of the preimage.

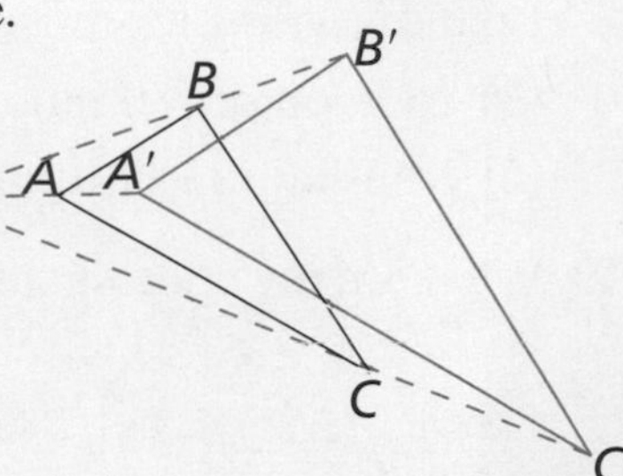

In the diagram at the right, you can see a dilation of $\triangle ABC$ with center O and scale factor 1.5. Notice $\triangle ABC \sim \triangle A'B'C'$.

$\frac{OA'}{OA} = \frac{OB'}{OB} = \frac{OC'}{OC} = 1.5$ and $\frac{A'B'}{AB} = \frac{B'C'}{BC} = \frac{A'C'}{AC} = 1.5$

EXAMPLE 1 **Identifying a scale factor for a dilation**

1 When $\triangle PQR$ is dilated, its image is $\triangle P'Q'R'$ and $PQ = 2P'Q'$. What is the scale factor?

(1) 2 **(2)** 1 **(3)** 0.5 **(4)** 0.25

■ **SOLUTION**

Under the dilation, the original figure is $\triangle PQR$ and the image is $\triangle P'Q'R'$. If $PQ = 2P'Q'$, then $P'Q' = 0.5(PQ)$. So, $\frac{P'Q'}{PQ} = 0.5$. The correct choice is (3).

Note

The scale factor is the ratio of side lengths in the image to the corresponding lengths in the preimage.

A dilation of any given scale factor can be sketched by multiplying the given scale factor by the distance from the center to any given point on the figure. A dilation is not an isometry.

EXAMPLE 2 **Sketching a dilation in the plane**

2 Sketch the image of square $WXYZ$ under a dilation with center O and scale factor 0.5.

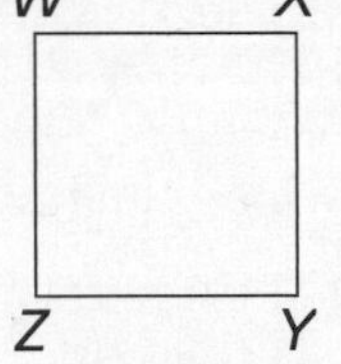

■ **SOLUTION**

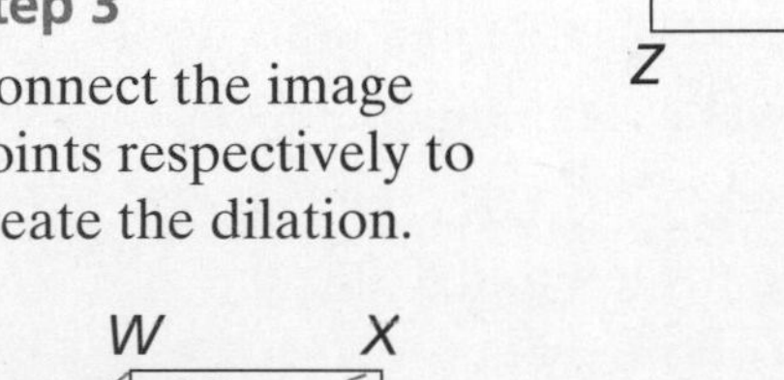

Step 1

Draw lines connecting each vertex to the center.

Step 2

Multiply the distance from the center to each vertex by the scale factor.

Step 3

Connect the image points respectively to create the dilation.

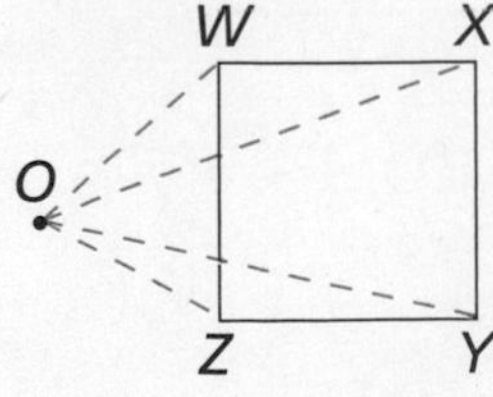

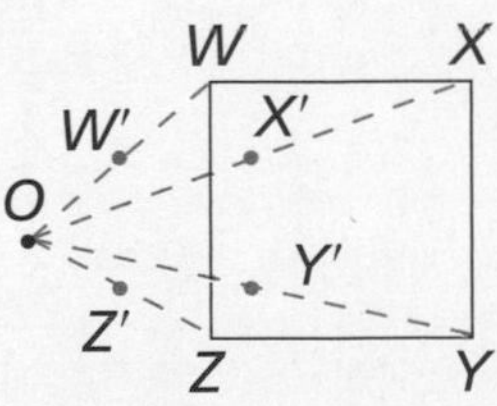

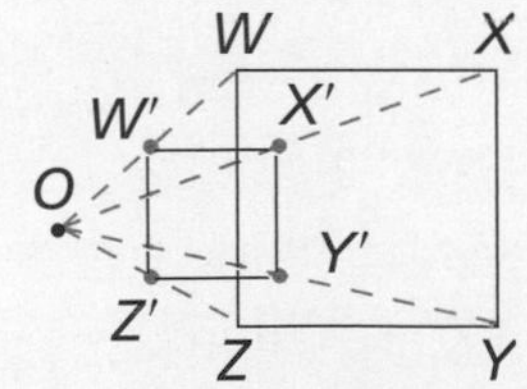

You can perform a dilation in the coordinate plane with the origin as the center of dilation by using a transformation rule.

Dilations in the Coordinate Plane

The image of $P(x, y)$ under a dilation in the coordinate plane with the origin as center of dilation and a scale factor k (k a nonzero real number) is $P'(kx, ky)$.

$$D_k(x, y) \rightarrow (kx, ky)$$

Note that the previous rule applies only when the dilation has center at the origin.

EXAMPLE 3 **Sketching a dilation in the coordinate plane**

A triangle has vertices $K(1, 2)$, $L(1, 4)$, and $M(4, 1)$. Sketch the image of $\triangle KLM$ under a dilation with center of dilation at the origin and scale factor 2.

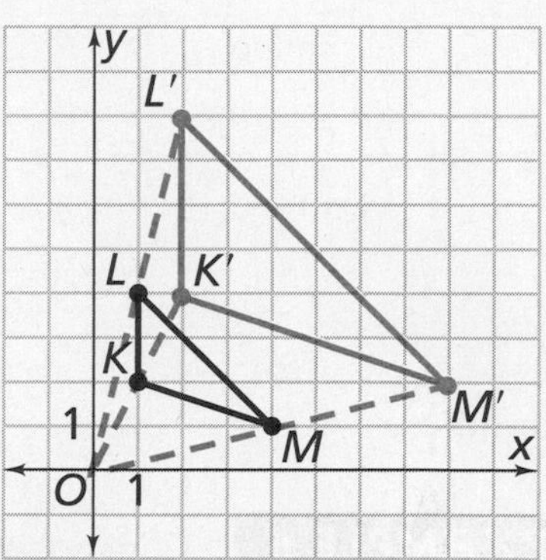

■ **SOLUTION**

Sketch $K(1, 2)$, $L(1, 4)$, and $M(4, 1)$ and $\triangle KLM$.
Under the dilation with the origin as center and scale factor 2:
$D_2(1, 2) \rightarrow (2, 4)$ $D_2(1, 4) \rightarrow (2, 8)$ $D_2(4, 1) \rightarrow (8, 2)$

Plot $K'(2, 4)$, $L'(2, 8)$, and $M'(8, 2)$ to form $\triangle K'L'M'$.

Characteristics of a Dilation

Let k represent a positive real number.

If a segment is dilated with a scale factor k, the image is a line segment whose length is k times that of the original.

If an angle is dilated with a scale factor k, the image is an angle congruent to the original angle.

You can use one pair of points to find the scale for the dilation of an entire figure.

EXAMPLE 4 **Finding unknown coordinates under a dilation**

Under a dilation with center at the origin, the image of $\triangle ABC$ is $\triangle A'B'C'$. Complete this table of coordinates.

preimage	image	preimage	image	preimage	image
$A(3, 6)$	$A'(4.5, 9)$	$B(-4, 0)$	$B'(\ ,\ )$	$C(\ ,\ )$	$C'(9, -3)$

■ **SOLUTION**

Find the scale. Because $\frac{4.5}{3} = \frac{9}{6} = 1.5$, the scale factor is 1.5.

coordinates of B': $B'(-4 \times 1.5, 0 \times 1.5) = B'(-6, 0)$ ← **Multiply to find the coordinates of the image.**

coordinates of C: $C'(9 \div 1.5, -3 \div 1.5) = C(6, -2)$ ← **Divide to find the coordinates of the original.**

If A is the area of the preimage, then the area of the image A' after a dilation with scale factor k is $A' = k^2A$.

EXAMPLE 5 **Relating areas of figures under a dilation**

5 A triangle has vertices $P(1, 5)$, $Q(6, 1)$, and $R(1, 1)$. Under a dilation with scale factor 2 and center at the origin, the image of the triangle is $\triangle P'Q'R'$. What is the area of $\triangle P'Q'R'$?

■ SOLUTION

Sketch a coordinate diagram and graph $P(1, 5)$, $Q(6, 1)$, and $R(1, 1)$. Find the area of $\triangle PQR$.

$$\text{Area of } \triangle PQR = \frac{1}{2}(RQ)(RP) = \frac{1}{2}(6 - 1)(5 - 1) = 10$$

The image $\triangle P'Q'R'$ is similar to $\triangle PQR$ and the similarity ratio is 2 : 1.

The area of $\triangle P'Q'R'$ is four times the area of $\triangle PQR$.

Therefore, the area of $\triangle P'Q'R'$ is 4(10) square units, or 40 square units.

You can perform two different transformations on the same object, one after the other.

EXAMPLE 6 **Composition of transformations**

6 $\triangle RST$ has vertices $R(1, 1)$, $S(0, 4)$, and $T(5, 2)$. Find the coordinates of $\triangle R'S'T'$ under a 90° counterclockwise rotation around the origin followed by a dilation scale factor 2 with the origin as the center.

■ SOLUTION

		90° counterclockwise rotation around the origin		Dilation scale factor 2
$P(x, y)$	→	$P'(-y', x')$	→	$P''(2(-y'), 2(x'))$
$R(1, 1)$	→	$R'(-1, 1)$	→	$R''(2(-1), 2(1)) = R''(-2, 2)$
$S(0, 4)$	→	$S'(-4, 0)$	→	$S''(2(-4), 2(0)) = S''(-8, 0)$
$T(5, 2)$	→	$T'(-2, 5)$	→	$T''(2(-2), 2(5)) = T''(-4, 10)$

The coordinates of the final image are $R''(-2, 2)$, $S''(-8, 0)$, and $T''(-4, 10)$.

Practice

Choose the numeral preceding the word or expression that best completes the statement or answers the question.

1 Under a dilation with center at $O(0, 0)$, the image of $A(-4, 2)$ is $A'(-2, 1)$. What is the scale factor for the dilation?

(1) 0.5 **(3)** 2

(2) 1 **(4)** −2

2 What is the image of $A(-4, 2)$, under $D_{0.25}$?

(1) $A'(-1, 8)$ **(3)** $A'(-1, 0.25)$

(2) $A'(-1, 0.5)$ **(4)** $A'(-100, 50)$

3 Identify the scale factor for this dilation. The image of $\overline{AB}$ is $\overline{A'B'}$.

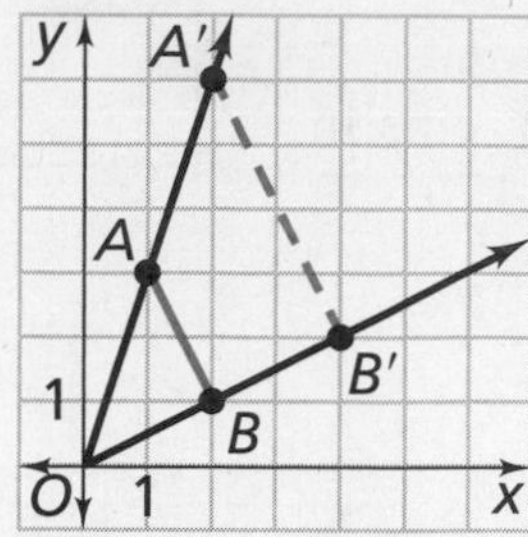

(1) 0.5 **(2)** 1 **(3)** 2 **(4)** 3

4 What are the coordinates of the image of a line segment with the endpoints $R(2, 2)$ and $S(5, 6)$ after a dilation with the origin as the center and a scale factor 2 followed by a dilation with the origin as center and a scale factor of 3?

(1) $R''(7, 7)$; $S''(11, 12)$

(2) $R''(10, 10)$; $S''(25, 30)$

(3) $R''(12, 12)$; $S''(30, 36)$

(4) $R''(6, 6)$; $S''(15, 18)$

5 What are the coordinates of parallelogram $C'D'E'F'$ after $C(-7, 2)$, $D(2, 2)$, $E(0, -2)$, and $F(-9, -2)$ are dilated with the origin as the center with scale factor 0.5?

(1) $C'(-3.5, 1)$, $D'(1, 1)$, $E'(0, -1)$, $F'(-4.5, -1)$

(2) $C'(-3.5, -1)$, $D'(1, 1)$, $E'(0, -1)$, $F'(4.5, 1)$

(3) $C'(-35, -10)$, $D'(10, 10)$, $E'(0, -10)$, $F'(45, 10)$

(4) $C'(-35, 10)$, $D'(10, 10)$, $E'(0, -10)$, $F'(-45, -10)$

6 Under D_4, the image of $\triangle ABC$ is $A'(3, 6)$, $B'(7, 1)$, $C'(6, 6)$. What are the coordinates of A, B, and C?

(1) $A(0.75, 1.5)$, $B(1.75, 0.25)$, $C(1.5, 1.5)$

(2) $A(7, 10)$, $B(11, 5)$, $C(10, 10)$

(3) $A(-1, 2)$, $B(3, -3)$, $C(2, 2)$

(4) $A(12, 24)$, $B(28, 4)$, $C(24, 24)$

7 If the coordinates of $\triangle XYZ$ are $X(-1, 5)$, $Y(3, -1)$, $Z(-2, -3)$, and the coordinates of $\triangle X'Y'Z'$ after a dilation with the origin as the center are $X'(-2.5, 12.5)$, $Y'(7.5, -2.5)$, $Z'(-5, -7.5)$, what is the scale factor?

(1) 1.5 **(2)** 4.5 **(3)** 2.5 **(4)** 4

In Exercises 8–10, sketch the image of each dilation.

8 The center of dilation is X and the scale factor is 0.5.

9 The center of dilation is O and the scale factor is 2.

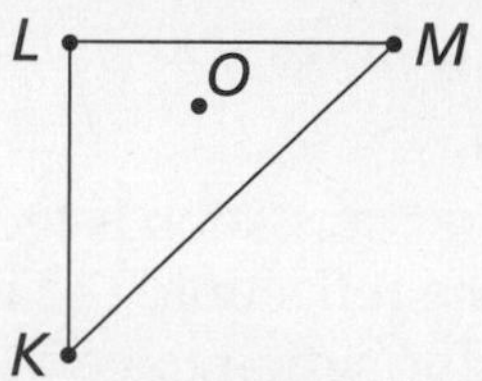

10 The vertices of a polygon are $A(-1, 1)$, $B(1, 2)$, $C(1, -2)$, and $D(-2, -1)$. Sketch the image of $ABCD$ under $D_{1.5}$.

In Exercises 11–12, write the coordinates of the vertices of the image of each polygon under the dilation with the given scale factor and the origin as center of dilation.

11 $\triangle ABC$ with vertices $A(-2, 1)$, $B(3, 1)$, and $C(-2, 5)$; scale factor 1.5

12 the square $WXYZ$ with vertices $W(-3, 3)$, $X(3, 3)$, $Y(3, -3)$, and $Z(-3, -3)$; scale factor 4

In Exercises 13–14, find the coordinates of the vertices of the image of the given figure after each pair of transformations.

13 the line segment with endpoints $X(-3, 1)$ and $Y(3, 4)$ after a translation 4 units right and 2 units down followed by a dilation with the origin as center and scale factor 3

14 the line segment with endpoints $A(0, -2)$ and $T(3, 5)$ after a dilation with the origin as center and scale factor 2 followed by a dilation with the origin as center and scale factor 0.5

7.4 Composite Transformations

> **New York Standards**
>
> **G.G.61** Analytic representations of translations

You know that multiple transformations can be applied to a figure one after the other. In the figure below, $\triangle ABC$ has been translated, resulting in $\triangle A'B'C'$, and then this image is reflected in line m, resulting in $\triangle A''B''C''$. This is called a **composition** of transformations.

The notation for such a combination of transformations—in this case, "a translation of $\triangle ABC$ to $\triangle A'B'C'$ and then a reflection of $\triangle A'B'C'$ over line m"—is $r_m \circ T_{a,b}$. r_m denotes the reflection over line m, and $T_{a,b}$ denotes the translation of a units on the x-axis and b units on the y-axis. Similarly, the notation that denotes a 90° rotation about point N is $R_{N,90°}$.

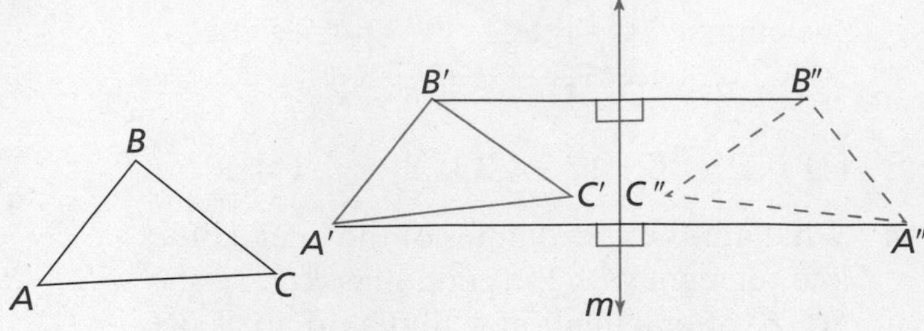

Notice that the translation listed last in the notation is performed first, followed by the reflection. The notation for composite transformations lists the first transformation to be performed last. For example, the notation $T_{a,b} \circ R_{Q,90°} \circ r_n$ denotes that first the object is to be reflected over line n, then rotated 90° about point Q, and finally translated a units on the x-axis and b units on the y-axis.

> **Note**
>
> When working with compositions, work right to left.

You can use transformation notation to determine which tranformations to perfom and in what order.

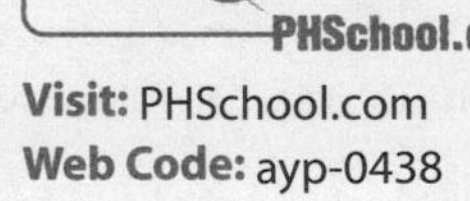

Visit: PHSchool.com
Web Code: ayp-0438

EXAMPLE 1 **Performing composite transformations**

1 Perform the composite transformation $r_m \circ R_{P,90°}$ on $\triangle ABC$.

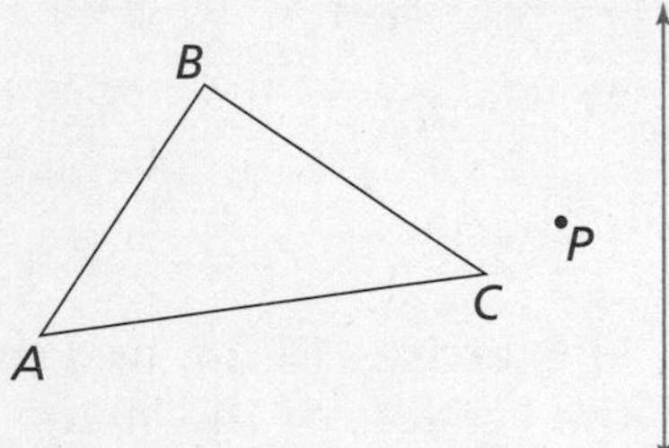

■ SOLUTION

Remember that the transformations are performed right to left. Therefore, the rotation is performed first, resulting in the dashed $\triangle A'B'C'$. Then the reflection over line m is performed, resulting in the image of this composite transformation, $\triangle A''B''C''$.

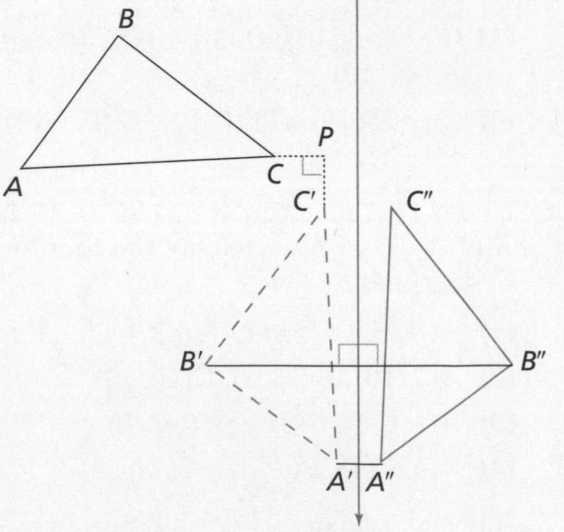

Practice

Choose the numeral preceding the word or expression that best completes the statement or answers the question.

1 Which of the following accurately denotes the composition transformation of pentagon ABC to pentagon $A''B''C''$ shown below?

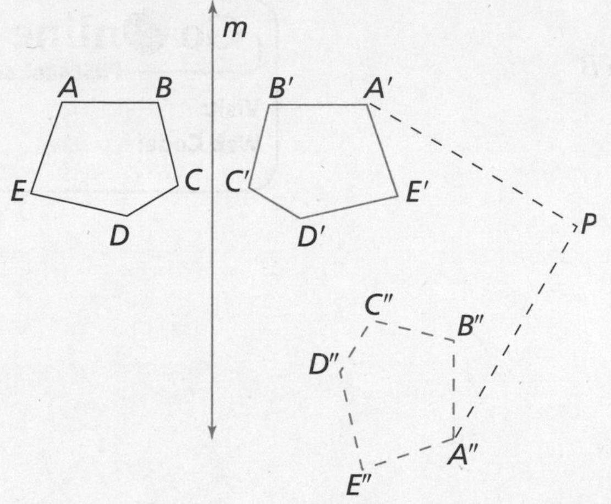

(1) $r_m \circ R_{P,90°}$

(2) $T_{a,b} \circ R_{P,90°}$

(3) $T_{a,b} \circ r_m$

(4) $R_{P,90°} \circ r_m$

2 What composite transformation is shown below?

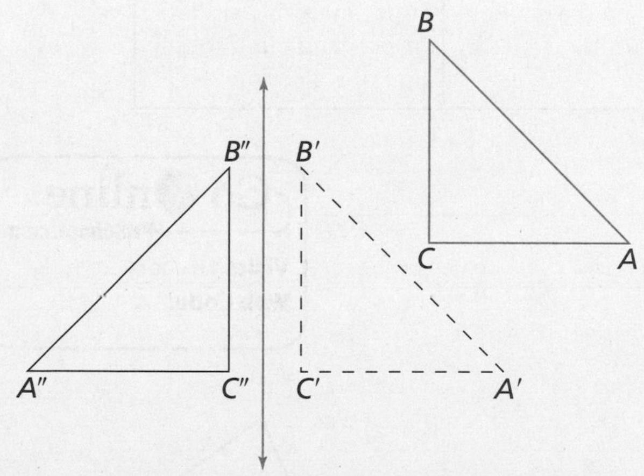

(1) a reflection followed by a translation

(2) a translation followed by a rotation

(3) a dilation followed by a reflection

(4) a translation followed by a reflection

3 Which composition is not an isometry?

(1) $r_{y\text{-axis}} \circ r_{(0,0)}$

(2) $T_{3,1} \circ R_{0,90°}$

(3) $D_{0.5} \circ r_{y=x}$

(4) $T_{3,8} \circ r_{(3,1)}$

In Exercises 4–5, use the following diagram.

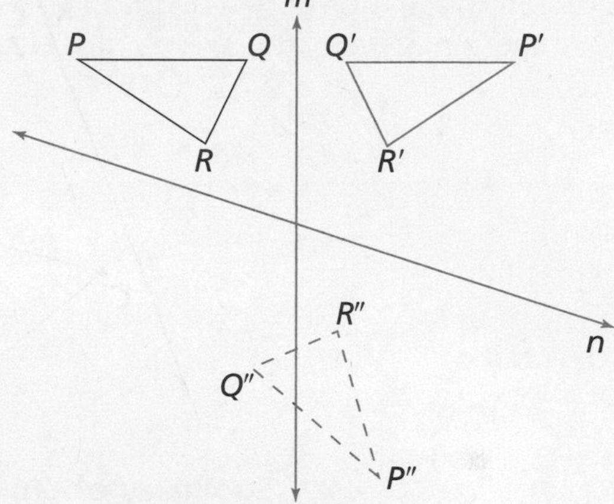

4 Which transformation is performed last in the composition?

(1) the reflection of $\triangle PQR$ over line m

(2) the reflection of $\triangle PQR$ over line n

(3) the reflection of $\triangle P'Q'R'$ over line m

(4) the reflection of $\triangle P'Q'R'$ over line n

5 Which denotes the composite transformation shown?

(1) $r_m \circ r_n$

(2) $r_m \circ R_{n,180°}$

(3) $r_n \circ r_m$

(4) $R_{n,180°} \circ r_m$

6 Find the image of $A(6, -2)$ under $r_{y=x} \circ T_{1,4}$.

7 Find the image of $B(-4, -3)$ under $T_{3,-2} \circ R_{(0,0),90°}$.

7.5 Proofs with Transformations

New year standards

G.G.27 Writing proofs
G.G.54 Isometries in the plane
G.G.55 Invariant properties under transformations
G.G.57 Justify transformations using relationships

You can use isometries to move geometric figures without changing their size or shape.

A **glide reflection** is the composition of a line reflection and a translation in a direction parallel to the line of reflection. In the accompanying figure $\triangle A''B''C''$ is the image of $\triangle ABC$ under the glide reflection $G_{C'C'',k}$. A glide reflection is an isometry. $G_{C'C'',k} = R_k \circ T_{C'C''}$. It makes no difference whether the translation or the reflection is performed first; the composition is the same glide reflection.

Visit: PHSchool.com
Web Code: ayp-0444

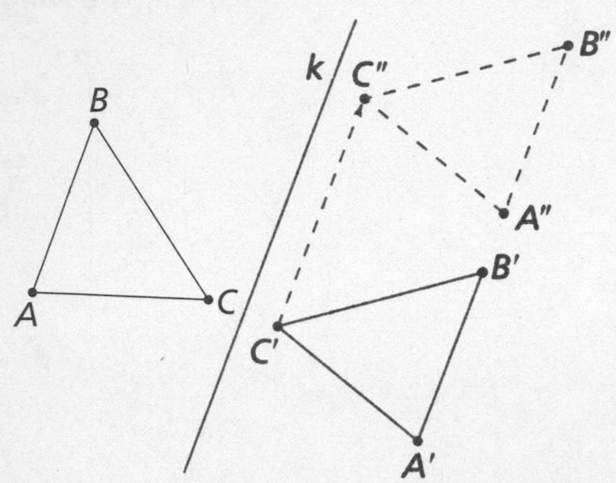

Summary of Characteristics of Isometries

	Reflections	Translations	Rotations	Glide Reflections
Fixed points	All points on line of reflection	None	One	None
Orientation	Mirror image	No change	No change	Mirror image
Line segment maps to parallel line segment	If preimage is parallel to line of reflection	Yes	When the angle of rotation is 180°	If preimage is parallel or perpendicular to the line of reflection

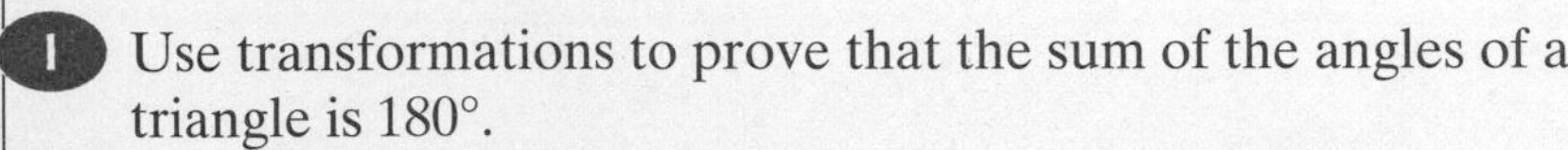

EXAMPLE 1 **Writing a transformational proof**

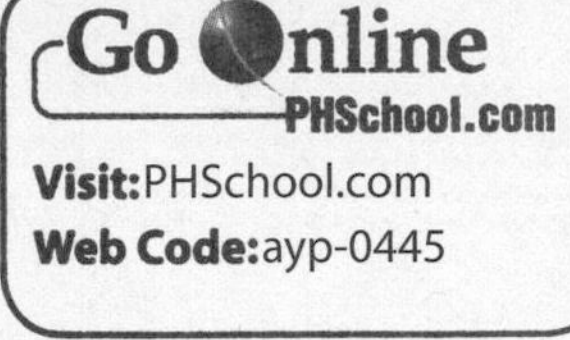

Visit: PHSchool.com
Web Code: ayp-0445

1 Use transformations to prove that the sum of the angles of a triangle is 180°.

■ SOLUTION

Given $\triangle ABC$, consider the $T_{\overline{AB}}$ where B is the image of A, B' is the image of B, and C' is the image of C under the translation. $\overline{AC} \parallel \overline{BC'}$ because a translation maps a line segment to a parallel line segment. $\measuredangle 3 \cong \measuredangle 4$ by the alternate interior angles theorem. $\measuredangle 1 \cong \measuredangle 5$ because a translation is an isometry and angle measure is preserved. $m\measuredangle 2 + m\measuredangle 4 + m\measuredangle 5 = 180°$ and by substitution $m\measuredangle 2 + m\measuredangle 3 + m\measuredangle 1 = 180°$.

You can use transformations to help you prove a theorem. A transformational proof can be used to confirm your proof.

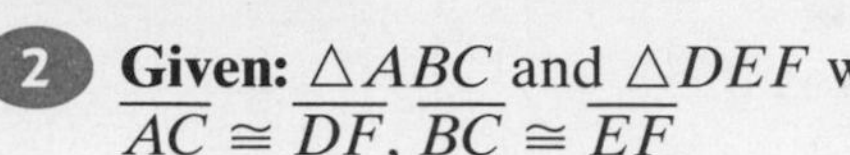

Confirming a proof using transformations

2 **Given:** $\triangle ABC$ and $\triangle DEF$ with $\overline{AB} \cong \overline{DE}$, $\overline{AC} \cong \overline{DF}$, $\overline{BC} \cong \overline{EF}$

Prove: $\triangle ABC \cong \triangle DEF$

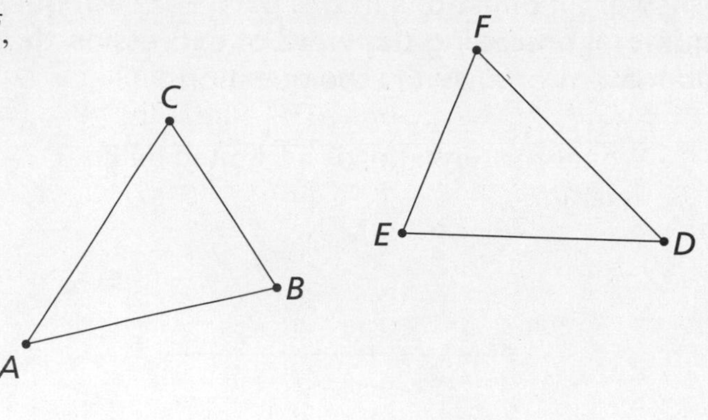

▪ SOLUTION

1. Since $\overline{AB} \cong \overline{DE}$ there is some isometry m such that $m(\overline{AB}) \rightarrow \overline{DE}$.
2. When $\overline{AB}$ is mapped to $\overline{DE}$ by the isometry m, the point C is mapped to C'. There are two possible locations for C'. It could be in either half plane of $\overleftrightarrow{DE}$.
3. If C' is in the same half plane of $\overleftrightarrow{DE}$ as F, reflect C' over $\overleftrightarrow{DE}$ so that the case in the accompanying diagram occurs. Thus $m(\triangle ABC) = \triangle DEC'$.
4. Since m is an isometry $\overline{AC} \cong \overline{DF} \cong \overline{A'C'}$ D lies on the $\perp$ bisector of $\overline{C'F}$.
   Similarly, $\overline{B'C'} \cong \overline{BC} \cong \overline{EF}$ and E lies on the $\perp$ bisector of $\overline{C'F}$.
   Therefore, $\overline{DE}$ is the $\perp$ bisector of $\overline{C'F}$.
   This establishes F as the image of C'; symbolically we write $r_{\overleftrightarrow{DE}}(C') = F$.
5. We now have $r_{\overleftrightarrow{DE}}(\triangle DEC') = \triangle DEF$
6. Since the composition of two isometries is an isometry, $R_{\overleftrightarrow{DE}} \circ m(\triangle ABC) = \triangle DEF$ and therefore $\triangle ABC \cong \triangle DEF$.

Practice

1 Use transformations to prove that the segment joining the midpoints of two sides of a triangle is parallel to the third side and equal to one-half its measure.

2 Prove the Isosceles Triangle Theorem using transformations.

3 In the accompanying diagram, T is on $\overline{RQ}$ and $\overline{PS} \perp \overline{RQ}$. If $\overline{PQ} \cong \overline{TQ}$ and $\overline{RQ} \cong \overline{QS}$, prove $\triangle PQR \cong \triangle TQS$.

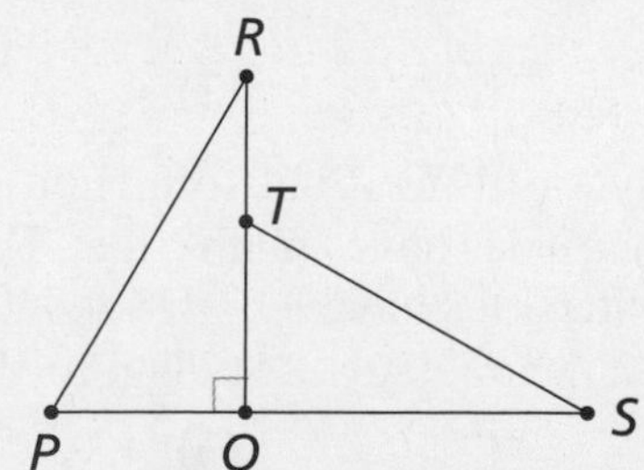

Chapter 7 Preparing for the New York Geometry Exam

Answer all questions in this part. For each question, select the numeral preceding the word or expression that best completes the statement or answers the question.

1 What transformation is illustrated in this diagram?

(1) line reflection **(3)** rotation
(2) translation **(4)** dilation

2 The vertices of $\triangle ABC$ are $A(0, 2)$, $B(0, 5)$, and $C(7, 2)$. Which point is inside the image of $\triangle ABC$ after it is reflected across the y-axis?

(1) $X(-1, -3)$ **(3)** $X(-1, 3)$
(2) $X(1, -3)$ **(4)** $X(1, 3)$

3 Which pair of points M and N could not be the images of the line segment with endpoints $A(3, 2)$ and $B(6, 4)$ under a translation?

(1) $M(4, 3)$ and $N(7, 5)$
(2) $M(2, 1)$ and $N(5, 3)$
(3) $M(7, 5)$ and $N(10, 8)$
(4) $M(-4, 8)$ and $N(-1, 10)$

4 How many lines of symmetry does the figure below have?

(1) 0 **(2)** 2 **(3)** 4 **(4)** 6

5 A polygon $WXYZ$ has four right angles. Two opposite sides have length 6 feet. The other two opposite sides have length 4 feet. How many lines of symmetry does polygon $WXYZ$ have?

(1) 0 **(2)** 2 **(3)** 4 **(4)** 6

6 The image of $A(5, -4)$ is $A'(-4, 5)$. By which transformation rule is A' the image of A?

(1) $r_{x\text{-axis}}$
(2) $r_{y\text{-axis}}$
(3) $r_{(0,0)}$
(4) $r_{y=x}$

7 Which points A' and B' are the images of the endpoints of $\overline{AB}$ under a 90° counterclockwise rotation about the origin?

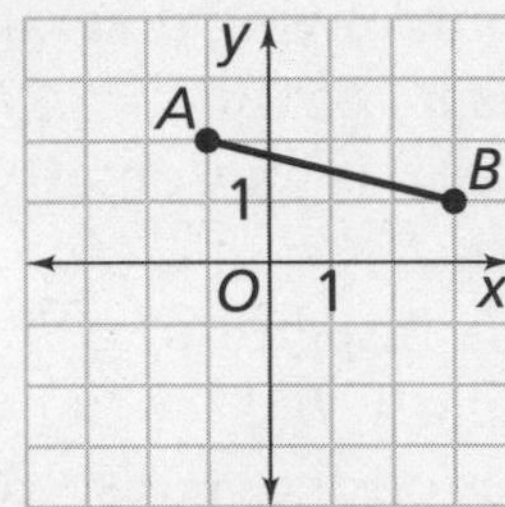

(1) $A'(-1, -2)$ and $B'(3, -4)$
(2) $A'(2, 1)$ and $B'(1, 3)$
(3) $A'(-2, -1)$ and $B'(-1, 3)$
(4) $A'(-2, 1)$ and $B'(1, -3)$

8 A figure in the plane has point symmetry if it is its own image under which transformation?

(1) 90° counterclockwise rotation about the origin
(2) half-turn
(3) reflection in a line
(4) some translation

9 $\triangle ABC$ has vertices $A(-3, 5)$, $B(2,1)$, and $C(5, 3)$. What are the coordinates of vertex B' under $T_{3,-2}$?

(1) $(0, 3)$ **(3)** $(3, 2)$
(2) $(5, -1)$ **(4)** $(8, 1)$

10 If quadrilateral $LMNP$ is reflected in the x-axis, which of the following statements is **not** true?

(1) MM' is perpendicular to line x.

(2) $MN = M'N'$

(3) The distance from P to line x is congruent to the distance from M to line x.

(4) $m\angle L = m\angle L'$

11 $\triangle ABC$ has coordinates of $A(1, 6)$, $B(5, 2)$, and $C(2, 1)$. What are the coordinates of $\triangle A'B'C'$ after a 90° counterclockwise rotation about the origin?

(1) $A'(-1, 6)$, B$'(-5, 2)$, and $C'(-2, 1)$

(2) $A'(1, -6)$, $B'(5, -2)$, and $C'(2, -1)$

(3) $A'(-6, 1)$, $B'(-2, 5)$, and $C'(-1, 2)$

(4) $A'(6, -1)$, $B'(2, -5)$, and $C'(1, -2)$

12 Which of the following characteristics of translations are true?

(1) A translated line segment is congruent to the original line segment.

(2) A translated angle is congruent to the original angle.

(3) The orientation of the image is the same as that of the original figure.

(4) All of the above.

13 Which figure has rotational symmetry?

(1) right triangle

(2) equilateral triangle

(3) isosceles triangle

(4) none of the above

14 A figure that is dilated with scale factor 1 will be

(1) larger than the preimage.

(2) smaller than the preimage.

(3) the same size as the preimage.

(4) none of the above.

15 Which of the following transformations is not an isometry?

(1) reflection **(3)** rotation

(2) translation **(4)** dilation

16 Parallelogram $WXYZ$ lies on the coordinate plane such that $W(-2, 2)$, $X(2, 1)$, $Y(2, -3)$, and $Z(-2, -2)$. What is the scale factor of the dilated image if $W'(-6, 6)$, $X'(6, 3)$, $Y'(6, -9)$, and $Z'(-6, -6)$?

(1) 2 **(2)** 3 **(3)** 0.5 **(4)** 5

17 Which two consecutive transformations does the figure illustrate?

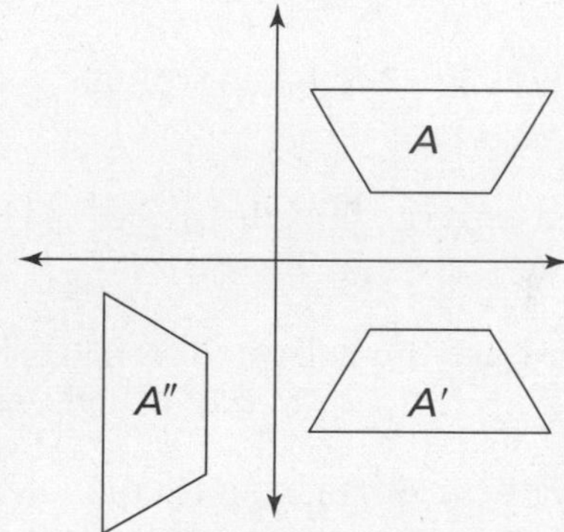

(1) translation and reflection

(2) rotation and translation

(3) reflection and rotation

(4) translation and tessellation

18 Find the coordinates of the image of the line segment with endpoints *G(5, 2)* and $H(7, 3)$ under $r_{x\text{-axis}} \cdot T_{4,-1}$.

(1) $G'(-1, 9)$ and $H'(-2, 11)$

(2) $G'(3, -6)$ and $H'(9, 1)$

(3) $G'(9, -1)$ and $H'(11, -2)$

(4) $G'(9, 1)$ and $H'(11, 2)$

Answer all the questions in this part. Clearly indicate the necessary steps, including appropriate formula substitutions, diagrams, graphs, charts, etc. For all questions in this part, a correct numerical answer with no work shown will receive only one credit.

19 The library is located at the origin on the coordinate grid. The locations of three houses are given in terms of blocks east or west and north or south of the library: $A(-4, 3)$, $B(1, 4)$, and $C(1, -2)$.

Locate and label the three houses on the coordinate grid.

Locate and label three other houses, A', B', and C', relative to the library if they are each 4 blocks east and 2 blocks north of houses A, B, and C.

Describe the transformation involved in solving this problem and the effect that the transformation has on the relative distance of A', B', and C' from the library.

20 $\triangle ABC$ lies on the coordinate plane such that $A(-3, 4)$, $B(2, 3)$, and $C(-2, 1)$.

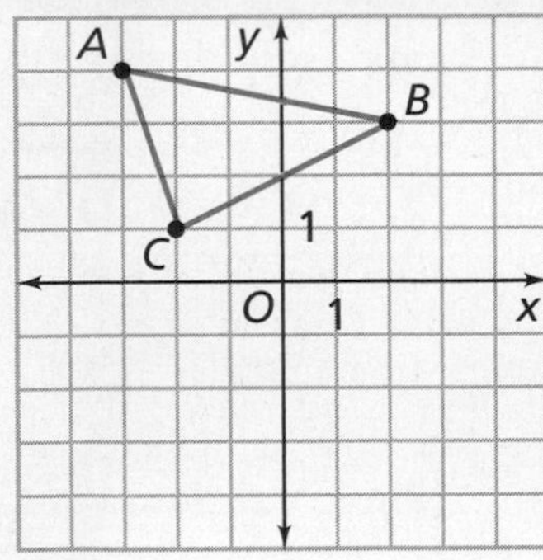

What are the coordinates of $\triangle A'B'C'$ when the figure is rotated 180° about the origin?

What are the coordinates of $\triangle A''B''C''$ of the image of $A'B'C'$ under a reflection about the x-axis?

What transformation is equivalent to $r_{x\text{-axis}} \cdot R_{(0,0),\,180°}$?

21 Draw a line segment $\overline{AB}$ and complete the following translations.

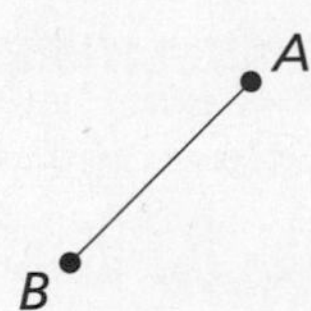

Translate AB a distance equal to and perpendicular to $\overline{AB}$. Label the image $\overline{A'B'}$.

Translate $\overline{A'B'}$ in the opposite direction, a distance equal to twice the length of $\overline{AB}$ and perpendicular to $\overline{AB}$.

8 Angles in Circles

Discovering New York

The Iroquois Confederacy

The Iroquois is a group of Native Americans who originally lived in the area that is now upstate New York. The group, also known as the Iroquois Confederacy, is made up of six nations, including the Mohawk, the Oneida, the Onondaga, the Cayuga, the Seneca, and the Tuscarora. The nations were bonded with a Constitution known as Gayanashagowa, which means "Great Law of Peace."

The Iroquois originally lived in longhouses, which were large houses that could hold up to 60 people. After the American Revolution in 1775, the Iroquois began to move across the country. Some moved into Canada, while others remained in cities such as Buffalo and Albany, New York.

8.1 Central Angles and Angles Formed by Chords, Secants, and Tangents

New York Standards

G.G.51 Theorems about arcs determined by rays

A **central angle** of a circle is an angle whose vertex is at the center of the circle. $\angle AOB$ is a central angle.

An arc is part of the circle. The arc formed by the endpoints of a diameter is a **semicircle.** In the accompanying figure $\overset{\frown}{RST}$ is one semicircle of circle O and $\overset{\frown}{RQT}$ is another.

A **minor arc** is smaller than a semicircle. A **major arc** is larger than a semicircle. Two letters are used to designate a minor arc. $\overset{\frown}{AB}$ is a minor arc of circle O. Three letters are used to designate a major arc. $\overset{\frown}{ANB}$ is a major arc of circle O.

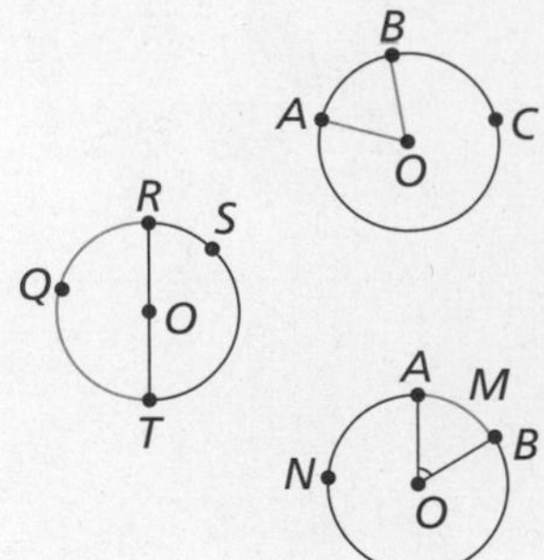

Arc Length and Measures

The **measure of a minor arc** is equal to the measure of its central angle.

$$m\overset{\frown}{AB} = m\angle AOB$$

The **measure of a major arc** is 360° minus the measure of its minor arc.

$$m\overset{\frown}{BCA} = 360° - m\overset{\frown}{AB}$$

The **measure of a semicircle** is 180°.

Note

1. All radii of a given circle are congruent.
2. Congruent circles have congruent radii.
3. Radii of congruent circles are congruent.

EXAMPLE 1 Finding the measure of an arc

In the accompanying figure, $m\angle JKL = 50°$. Find the $m\overset{\frown}{JL}$ and $m\overset{\frown}{JCL}$

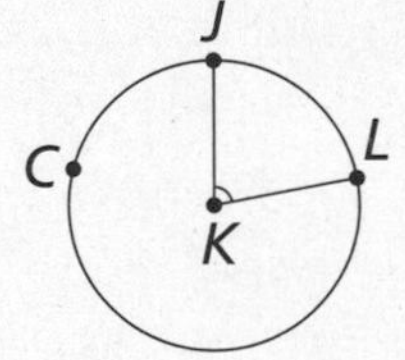

SOLUTION

$m\overset{\frown}{JL} = 50°$ and $m\overset{\frown}{JCL} = 360° - 50° = 310°$.

An angle whose vertex is a point on a circle is an **inscribed angle** of the circle. In the figure at the right, $\angle ABC$ and $\angle JKL$ are inscribed angles. $\overset{\frown}{AC}$ is the intercepted arc of $\angle ABC$ and $\overset{\frown}{JL}$ is the intercepted arc of $\angle JKL$.

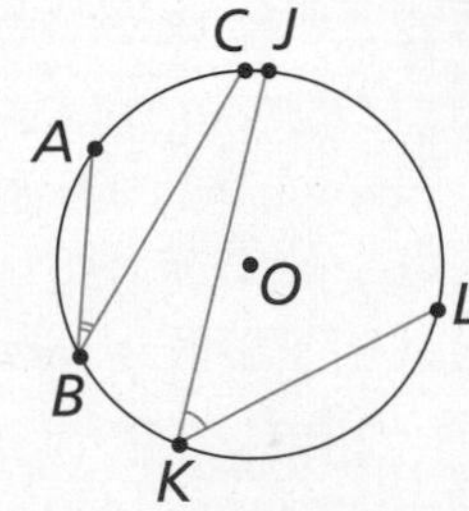

Inscribed Angle Theorem

The **measure of an inscribed angle** is half the measure of its intercepted arc.

$$m\angle BAC = \frac{m\overset{\frown}{BC}}{2}.$$

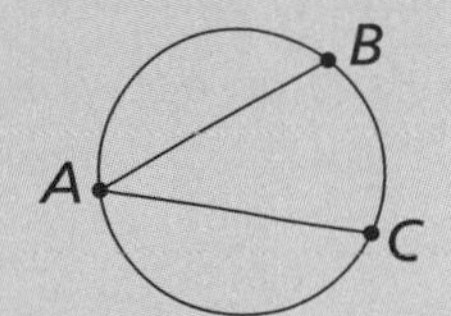

EXAMPLE 2 Using the Inscribed Angle Theorem

Find the measure of ∠1 and ∠2.

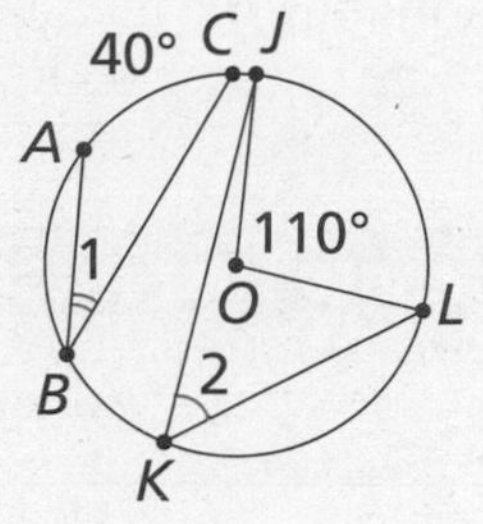

■ SOLUTION

$m\angle 1 = \frac{m\overset{\frown}{AC}}{2}$ $\qquad$ $m\angle 2 = \frac{m\overset{\frown}{JL}}{2}$

$\frac{40}{2} = 20°$ ← $m\overset{\frown}{AC} = 40°$ $\qquad$ $\frac{110}{2} = 55°$ ← $m\overset{\frown}{JL} = 110°$

Inscribed Angle Corollaries

1. An angle inscribed in a semicircle is a right angle.
2. If a quadrilateral is inscribed in a circle, the opposite angles are supplementary.
3. If two inscribed angles intercept congruent arcs, the angles are congruent.

Visit: PHSchool.com
Web Code: ayp-0473

A **chord** of a circle is a segment whose endpoints are on a circle. A **tangent to a circle** is a line, segment, or ray in the same plane of the circle that intersects the circle in exactly one point.

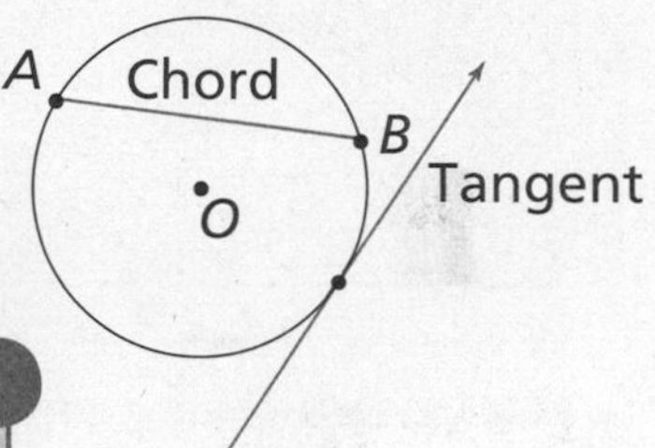

Angle Formed by a Chord and a Tangent Theorem

The measure of an angle formed by a chord and a tangent to an endpoint of the chord is equal to half the measure of the intercepted arc.

$$m\angle ACB = \tfrac{1}{2}m\overset{\frown}{BDC}$$

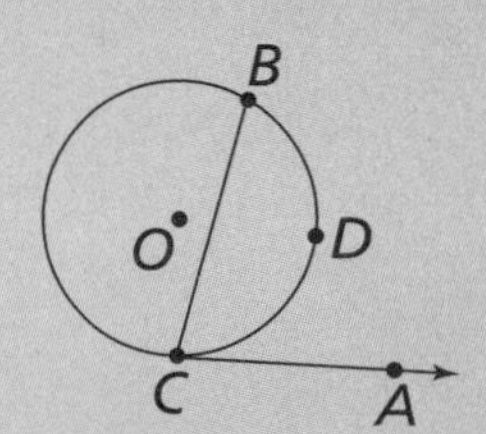

EXAMPLE 3 Finding the measure of an angle formed by a chord and a tangent

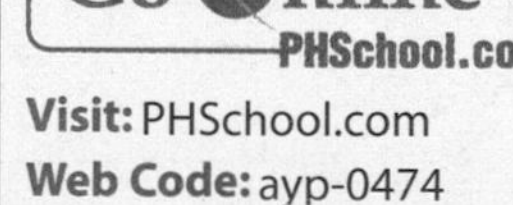

Visit: PHSchool.com
Web Code: ayp-0474

$m\overset{\frown}{CD} = 60°$ and $\overline{BC}$ is a diameter of circle O. Determine the $m\angle DBA$.

■ SOLUTION

$\overline{BC}$ is a diameter of O, so $m\overset{\frown}{CDB} = 180°$.

$m\overset{\frown}{BD} = m\overset{\frown}{CDB} - m\overset{\frown}{CD}$
$= 180° - 60° = 120°$

$m\angle DBA = \frac{1}{2}\overset{\frown}{BD}$ ← **Apply the Angle Formed by a Chord and a Tangent Theorem.**

$m\angle DBA = \frac{1}{2}(120°) = 60°$

A **secant** is a line, ray, or segment that intersects a circle at two points. Determining the measure of the angles formed by intersecting secants depends on where the secants intersect. Secants can intersect inside or outside the circle.

Secants That Intersect Inside a Circle

The measure of an angle formed by two chords or secants that intersect inside a circle is half the sum of the measures of its intercepted arcs.

$$m\angle 1 = \frac{m\overset{\frown}{AB} + m\overset{\frown}{CD}}{2}$$

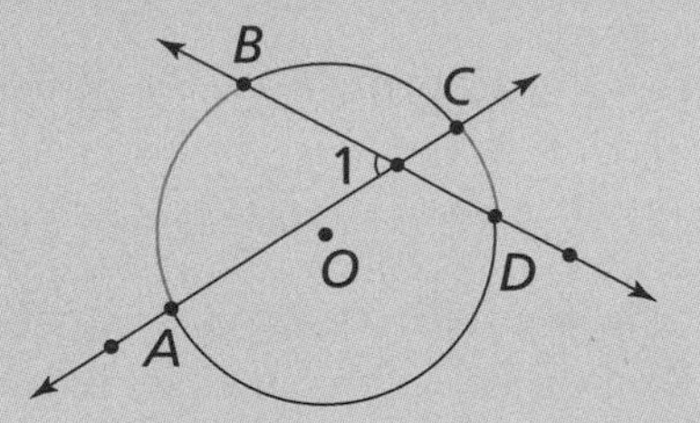

Secants That Intersect Outside a Circle

The measure of an angle formed by two secants that intersect outside a circle is half the difference of the measures of its intercepted arcs.

$$m\angle 2 = \frac{m\overset{\frown}{QR} - m\overset{\frown}{ST}}{2}$$

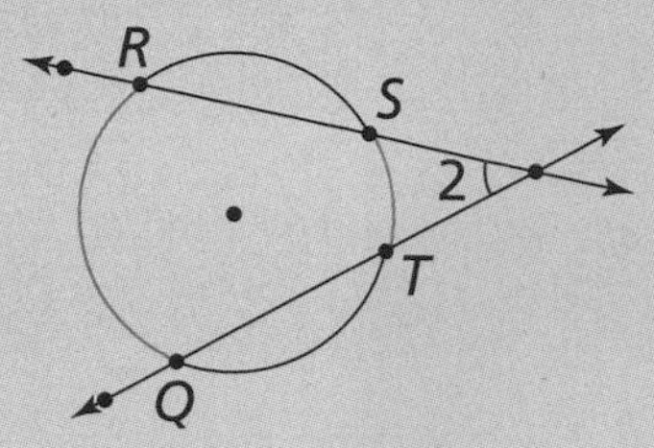

EXAMPLE 4 **Finding the measure of angles formed by secants**

In the figure to the right $m\overset{\frown}{RQ} = 100°$ and $m\overset{\frown}{ST} = 40°$. Find the measures of $\angle 1$ and $\angle 2$.

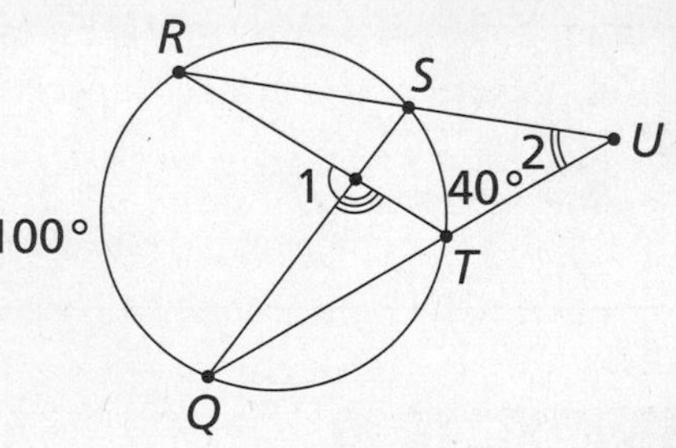

■ SOLUTION

$\angle 1$ is formed by the intersection of two secants, $\overline{RT}$ and $\overline{SQ}$, inside the circle.

$$m\angle 1 = \frac{m\overset{\frown}{RQ} + m\overset{\frown}{ST}}{2} = \frac{100° + 40°}{2} = \frac{140°}{2} = 70°$$

The measure of $\angle 1$ is 70°.

$\angle 2$ is formed by the intersection of two secants, $\overline{UR}$ and $\overline{UQ}$, outside the circle.

$$m\angle 2 = \frac{m\overset{\frown}{RQ} - m\overset{\frown}{ST}}{2} = \frac{100° - 40°}{2} = \frac{60°}{2} = 30°$$

The measure of $\angle 2$ is 30°.

You can prove the formulas for finding the measure of the angle formed by intersecting secants. Draw $\overline{AD}$. The measure of the exterior angles of a triangle equals the sum of the remote interior angles, so $m\angle 1 = m\angle 2 + m\angle 3$. The measure of an inscribed angle is half its intercepted arc. That is, $m\angle 2 = \frac{1}{2}m\overset{\frown}{BD}$ and $m\angle 3 = \frac{1}{2}m\overset{\frown}{AC}$. By substituting these values for $m\angle 2$ and $m\angle 3$, you get

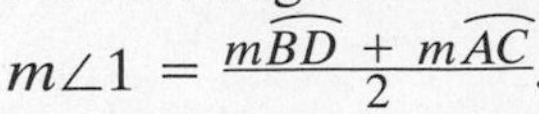
$m\angle 1 = \frac{m\overset{\frown}{BD} + m\overset{\frown}{AC}}{2}$.

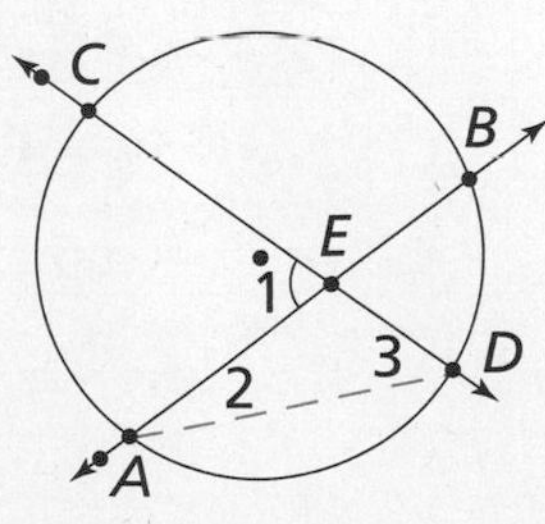

Practice

Choose the numeral preceding the word or expression that best completes the statement or answers the question.

Use the accompanying figure to answer Exercises 1–3.

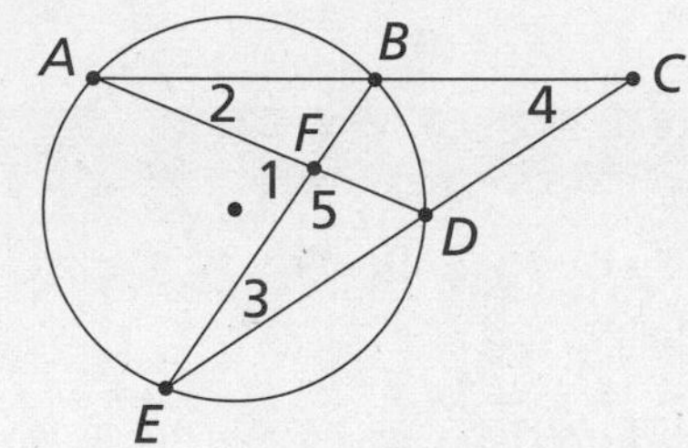

1 The measure of $\angle 1$ is half the ________ of the measures of $\overparen{AE}$ and $\overparen{BD}$.

(1) sum

(2) difference

(3) product

(4) quotient

2 The measure of $\angle 4$ is half the difference of the measures of which arcs?

(1) $\overparen{AE}$ and $\overparen{AB}$

(2) $\overparen{AED}$ and $\overparen{BDE}$

(3) $\overparen{AB}$ and $\overparen{ED}$

(4) $\overparen{AE}$ and $\overparen{BD}$

3 If $m\overparen{AE} = 90°$ and $m\overparen{BD} = 40°$, then

(1) $m\angle 1 = 130°$ and $m\angle 4 = 50°$.

(2) $m\angle 1 = 25°$ and $m\angle 4 = 65°$.

(3) $m\angle 1 = 65°$ and $m\angle 4 = 25°$.

(4) $m\angle 1 = 50°$ and $m\angle 4 = 130°$.

4 Use the accompanying figure to determine the measure of $\angle A$, $\angle B$, and $\overparen{ADC}$.

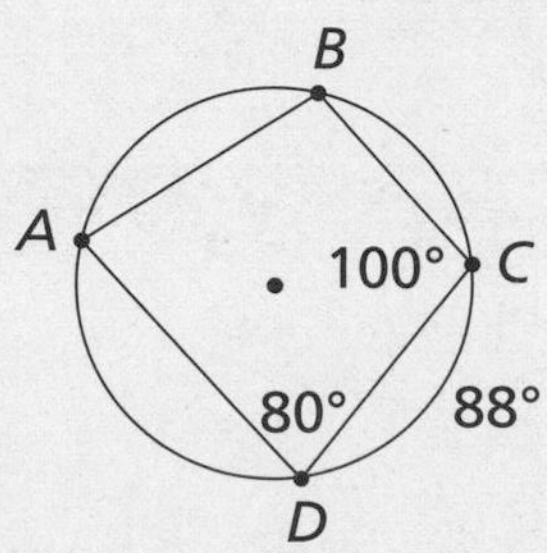

5 In the accompanying figure $\overline{AB}$, $\overline{BC}$, and $\overline{DE}$ are chords of the circle.

Given: $\overline{BG} \cong \overline{BF}$; $\overparen{DB} \cong \overparen{BE}$
Prove: $\overparen{DA} \cong \overparen{CE}$

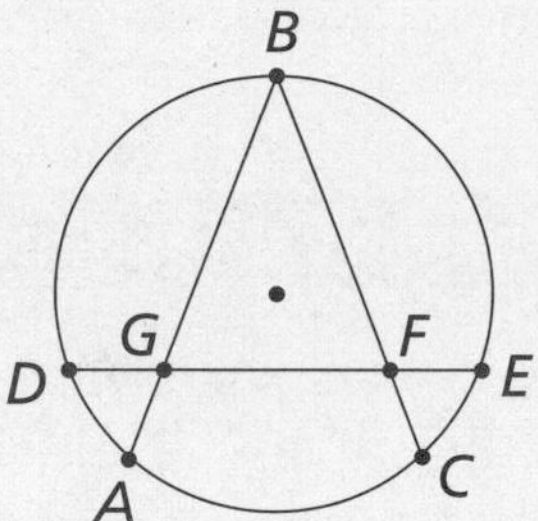

6 Use the accompanying figure to determine the measures of $\angle 1$, $\angle 2$, $\angle 3$, and $\angle 4$.

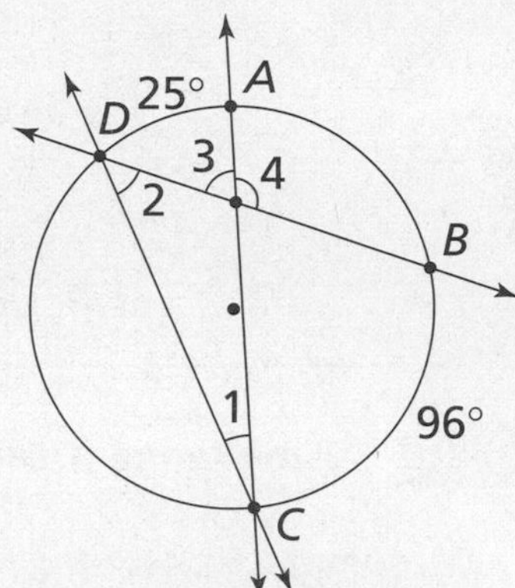

7 **Given:** Circle O with $\overparen{AC} \cong \overparen{BD}$
Prove: $\overline{AB} \parallel \overline{CD}$

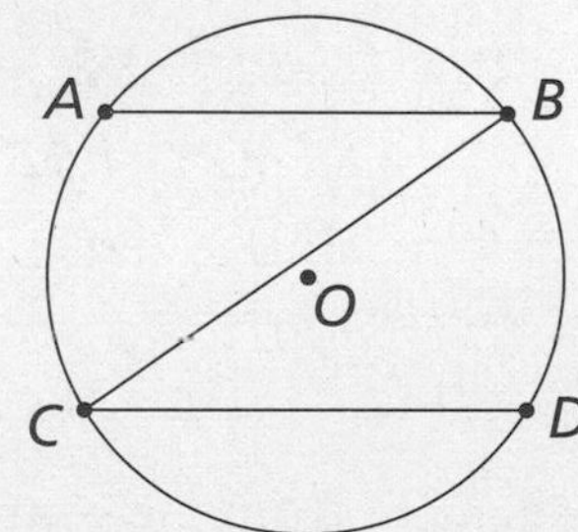

8 Prove the converse of Exercise 7.

8.2 Angles and Segments Formed by Secants and Tangents

New York Standards

G.G.50 Theorems about tangents to circles

G.G.51 Theorems about arcs determined by rays

A **secant** is a line, ray, or segment in the plane of the circle that intersects a circle at two points. A **tangent** to a circle is a line, segment, or ray in the plane of the circle that intersects the circle at exactly one point. The point of intersection is called the **point of tangency.**

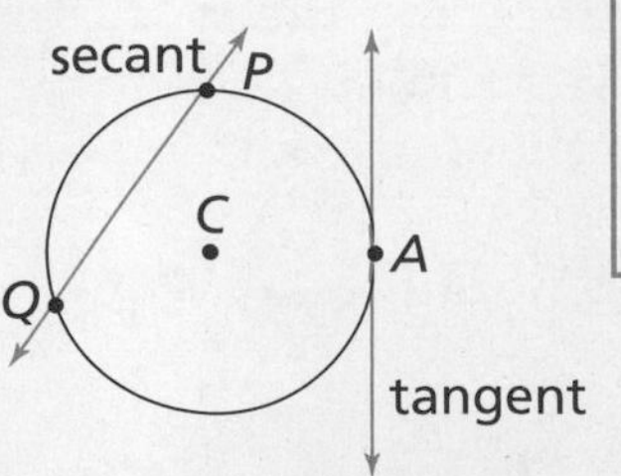

Angles Formed by a Tangent and a Secant

The measure of an angle formed by a tangent and secant or by two tangents with a common endpoint is equal to half the difference of the measures of the intercepted arcs.

$m\angle ACB = \frac{1}{2}(m\widehat{ADB} - m\widehat{AEB})$

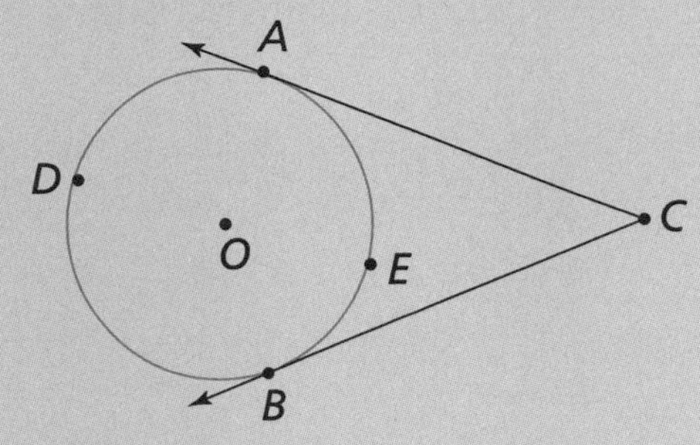

$m\angle RSU = \frac{1}{2}(m\widehat{RVU} - m\widehat{RWT})$

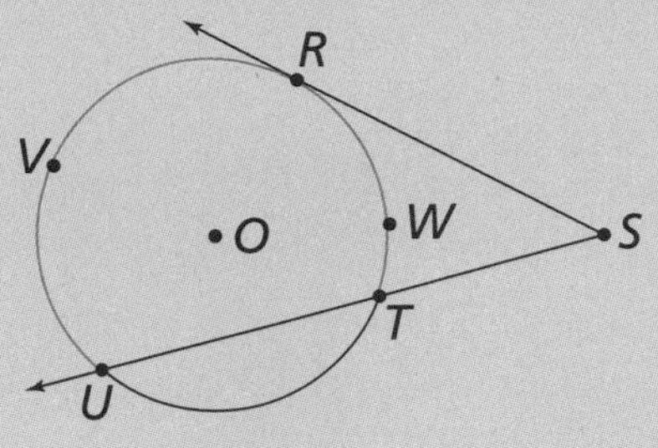

EXAMPLE 1 **Using tangent/secant relationships**

Go Online
PHSchool.com
Visit: PHSchool.com
Web Code: ayp-0475

In the accompanying figure, $m\angle RSU = 42°$ and $m\widehat{RT} = 82°$. Find $m\widehat{RU}$.

■ SOLUTION

$m\angle RSU = \frac{1}{2}(m\widehat{RU} - m\widehat{RT})$

$42° = \frac{1}{2}(m\widehat{RU} - 82°)$ ← $m\angle RSU = 42°$ and $m\widehat{RT} = 82°$

$84° = m\widehat{RU} - 82°$

$166° = m\widehat{RU}$

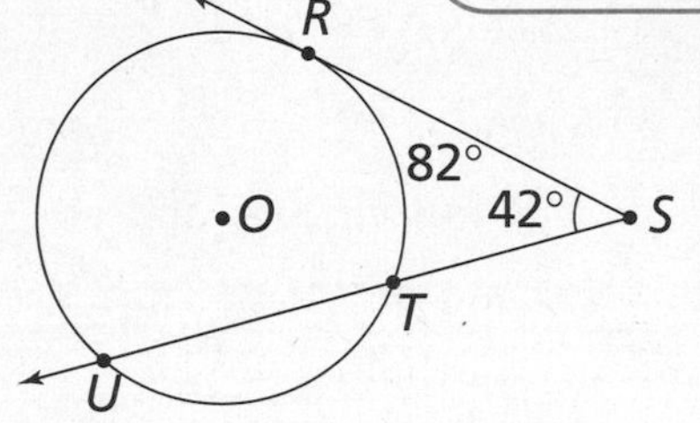

A radius is a segment from the center of the circle to any point on the circle. Through any given point on a segment, one, and only one, line can be drawn perpendicular to that segment at that point. This fact leads to the following relationships.

Radius-Tangent Relationships

If a line is tangent to a circle, then the line is perpendicular to the radius drawn to the point of tangency. That is, $\overleftrightarrow{AB} \perp \overline{OP}$.

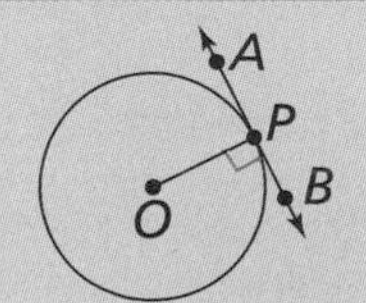

The converse is also true. If a line is perpendicular to the radius at its endpoint on the circle, then the line is tangent to the circle.

EXAMPLE 2 **Using radius-tangent relationships**

In the accompanying figure, is $\overline{KL}$ tangent to circle J?

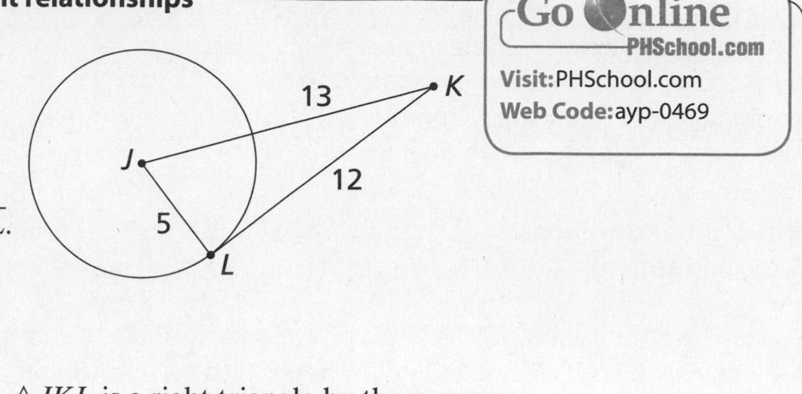

▪ SOLUTION

You can use the Pythagorean Theorem to show that $\overline{KL} \perp \overline{JL}$.

$$5^2 + 12^2 = 13^2$$
$$25 + 144 = 169$$
$$169 = 169$$

Since the above equation is true, $\triangle JKL$ is a right triangle by the converse of the Pythagorean Theorem with $\angle L$ a right angle. So, $\overline{KL} \perp \overline{JL}$.

If a line m is tangent to two or more circles, then m is called a common tangent. If two circles share a common tangent, then you can use the radius-tangent relationship to prove that the circles have parallel radii.

EXAMPLE 3 **Writing a proof using the radius-tangent relationship**

Given: $\overleftrightarrow{AB}$ is tangent to circle O and circle P at points A and B.

Prove: $\overline{OA} \parallel \overline{PB}$

▪ SOLUTION

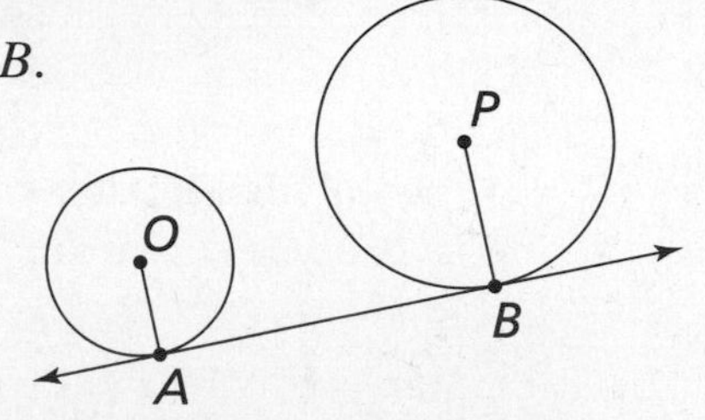

$\overline{OA}$ and $\overline{PB}$ are radii of circles O and P, respecitively that are perpendicular to $\overleftrightarrow{AB}$ because a line tangent to a circle is perpendicular to the radius at the point of tangency. Therefore, because two segments perpendicular to the same segment are parallel to each other, $\overline{OA} \parallel \overline{PB}$.

Two intersecting lines, segments, or rays that are tangent to the same circle have a special relationship that is formalized as the following theorem.

Two-Tangent Theorem

The two segments of tangents drawn to a circle from a point outside the circle are congruent.

$$\overline{AB} \cong \overline{BC}$$

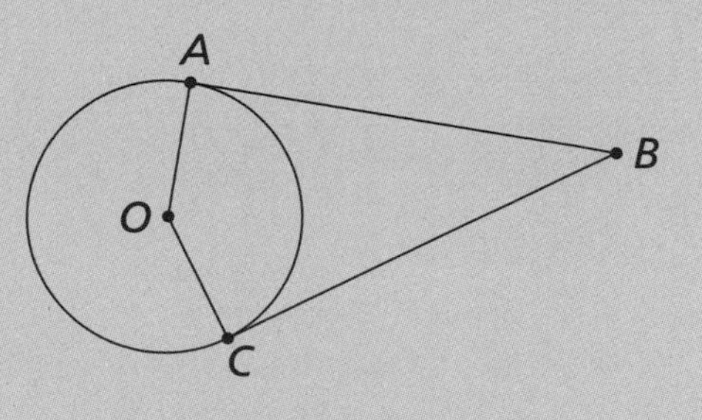

There are several types of common tangents, which can be classified on the basis of how the common tangents intersect the circles.

If a common tangent intersects the segment joining the centers of two circles, it is a **common internal tangent.**

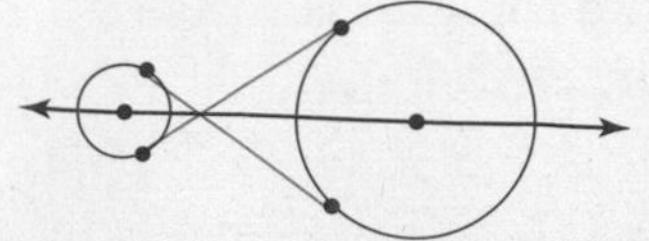

Two circles are **internally tangent** if their centers lie on the same side of the common tangent.

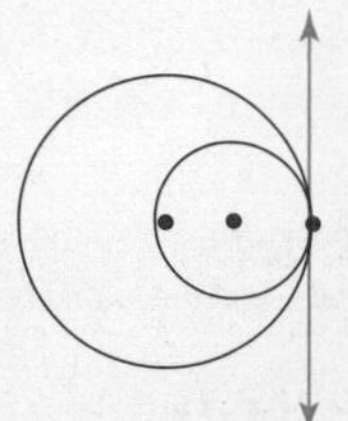

If a common tangent does not intersect the segment joining the centers of two circles, it is a **common external tangent.**

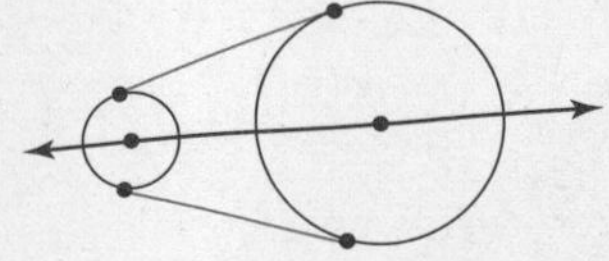

Two circles are **externally tangent** if their centers lie on opposite sides of the common tangent.

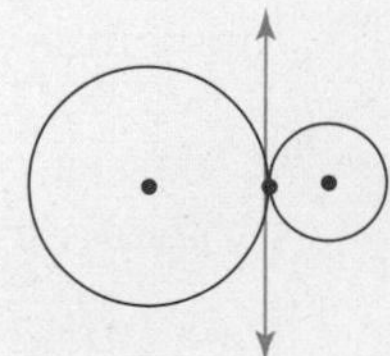

You can use the relationships between the radius of a circle and the tangent, as well as the Two-Tangent Theorem to solve problems involving common tangents.

EXAMPLES 4 and 5 Applying properties of tangents

4 Use the accompanying figure to determine the value of x.

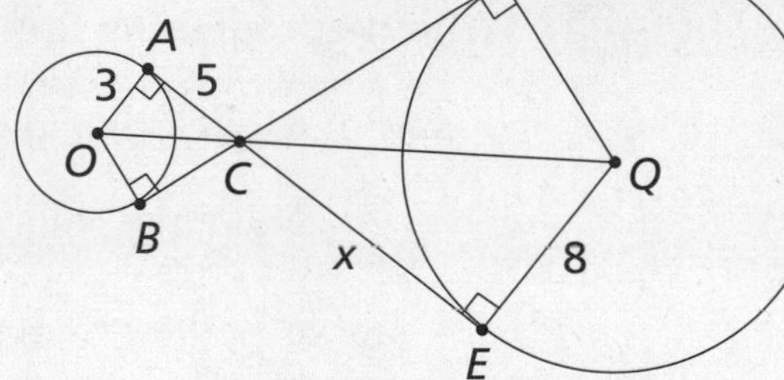

■ SOLUTION

$\angle QCE \cong \angle ACO$ because they are vertical angles. $\angle A \cong \angle E$ because all right angles are congruent. Therefore, $\triangle CQE \sim \triangle COA$ by the A.A. postulatc. Bccause corresponding sides of similar triangles are proportional,

$$\frac{3}{5} = \frac{8}{x}$$

$$3x = 40$$

$$x = \frac{40}{3} = 13\frac{1}{3}$$

5 **Given:** $\overline{AB}$ and $\overline{BC}$ are tangent to circle O.
Prove: $\overline{AB} \cong \overline{BC}$

■ SOLUTION

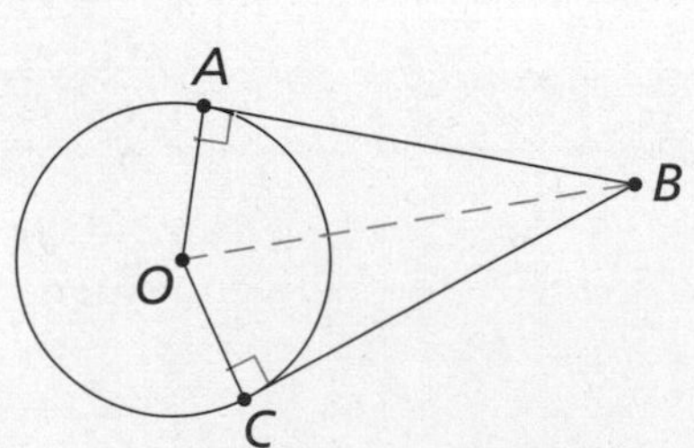

Draw OB. $\overline{AB}$ and $\overline{BC}$ are tangent to circle O is given. Therefore, $\overline{AB} \perp \overline{AO}$ and $\overline{BC} \perp \overline{OC}$, because a line tangent to a circle is perpendicular to the radius drawn to the point of tangency. By the definition of a right triangle, $\triangle BAO$ and $\triangle BCO$ are right triangles. All radii of a circle are congruent, so $\overline{OA} \cong \overline{OC}$.

By the Reflexive Property, $\overline{OB} \cong \overline{OB}$. $\triangle BAO \cong \triangle BCO$ by the Hypotenuse-Leg Theorem. Since congruent parts of congruent triangles are congruent, $\overline{AB} \cong \overline{BC}$.

Practice

Choose the numeral preceding the word or expression that best completes the statement or answers the question.

1 $\overline{RT}$ and $\overline{ST}$ are tangent to circle O. What is the value of x?

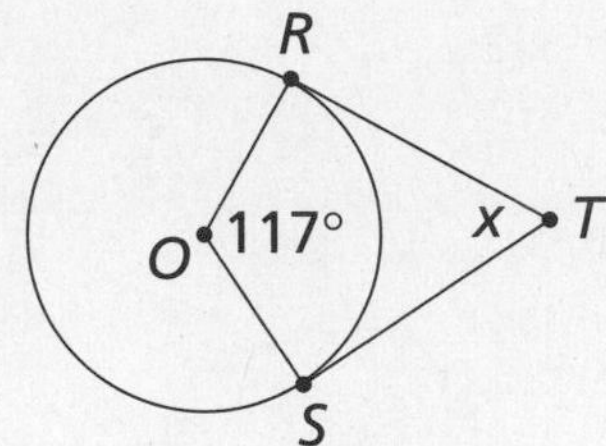

(1) 58° **(2)** 63° **(3)** 90° **(4)** 117°

2 Two circles share a common tangent and the centers of the circles lie on the same side of the tangent. These circles are said to be

(1) literally tangent.

(2) internally tangent.

(3) externally tangent.

(4) commonly tangent.

3 A radius drawn to a tangent at the point of tangency in a circle forms which kind of angle?

(1) acute **(3)** right

(2) obtuse **(4)** reflex

4 In which of the following figures is $\overline{AB}$ tangent to the circle?

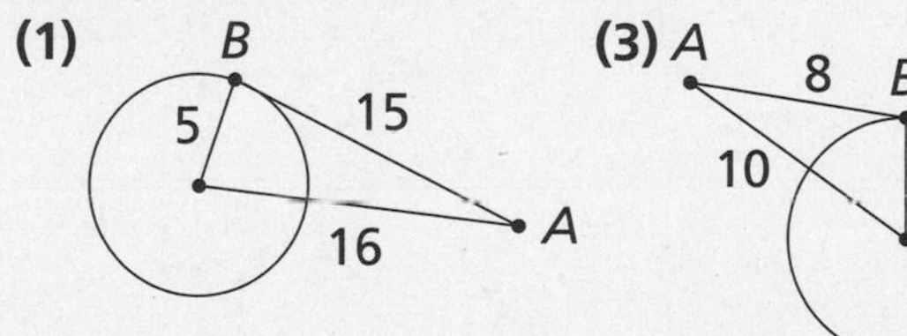

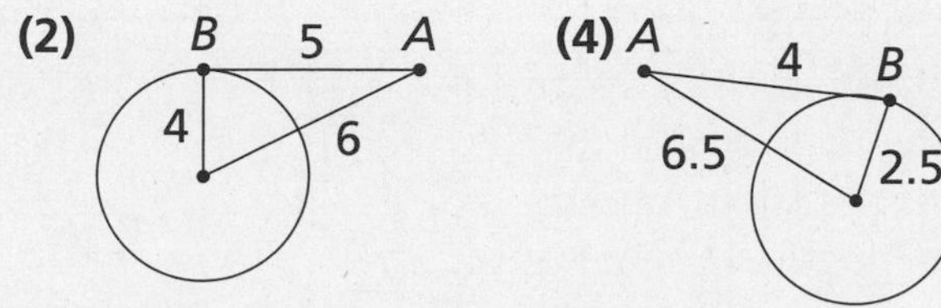

5 In the accompanying diagram, $m\overset{\frown}{RQ} = 166°$ and $m\overset{\frown}{QT} = 92°$. What is the measure of $\angle RSQ$?

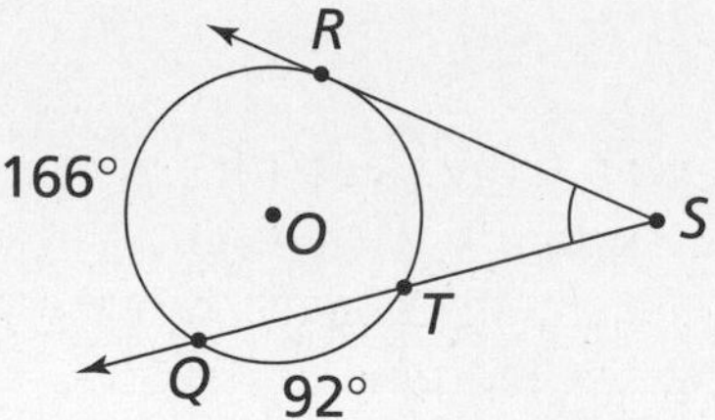

(1) 32° **(2)** 51° **(3)** 83° **(4)** 102°

6 **Given:** $\overline{LM}$ and $\overline{LN}$ are tangent to circle O.
Prove: $\triangle LMN$ is isosceles.

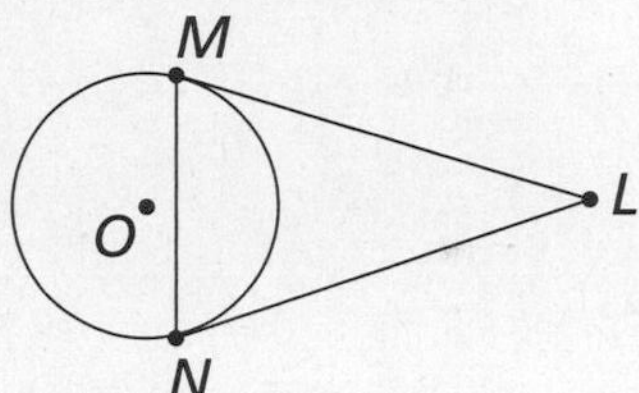

Use the following figure to answer Exercises 7–12.

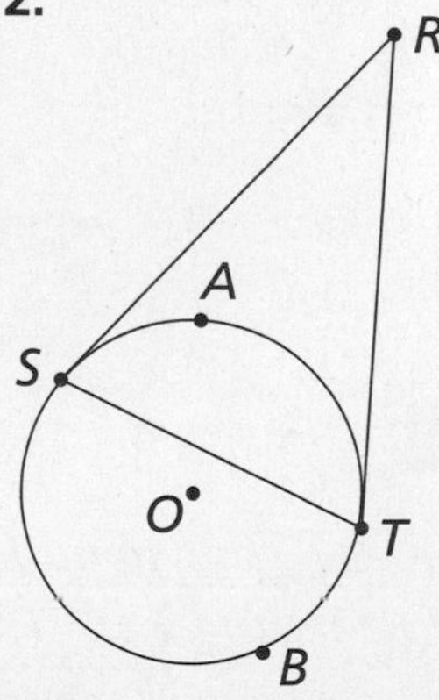

$\overline{SR}$ and $\overline{TR}$ are tangent to circle O

7 $m\overset{\frown}{SAT} = 100°$. Find $m\angle SRT$.

8 $m\overset{\frown}{SBT} = 204°$. Find $m\angle SRT$.

9 $m\angle SRT = 60°$. Find $m\overset{\frown}{SAT}$.

10 $m\angle SRT = k$. Find $m\overset{\frown}{SAT}$.

11 $m\angle RST = 70°$. Find $m\overset{\frown}{SBT}$.

12 $m\angle SRT = 50°$. Find $m\angle RST$.

8.3 Chords of a Circle and Segments Intersected by a Circle

New York Standards

G.G.49 Theorems about chords of a circle

G.G.52 Theorems about arcs of a circle

G.G.53 Theorems about segments intersected by a circle

A **chord** is a segment whose endpoints are on a circle. In the figure to the right, $\overline{AB}$ is a chord and its related arc is $\overset{\frown}{AB}$.

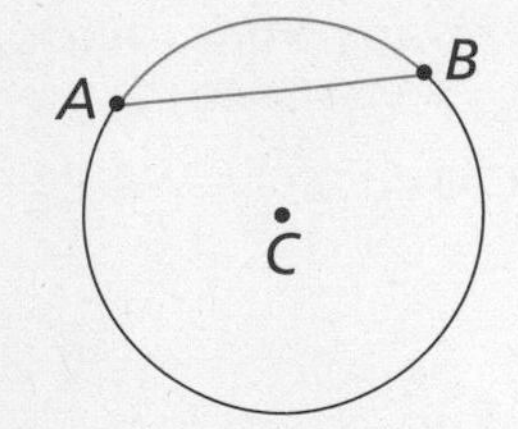

You should note that the diameter of a circle is a chord. In fact, the diameter is the longest chord of a circle, and its related arc forms a semicircle.

If you use a graphing calculator (or other interactive geometry software) to construct the figure to the right. You may notice that the product of the length of the segments of each chord is constant. This result is summarized by the following theorems.

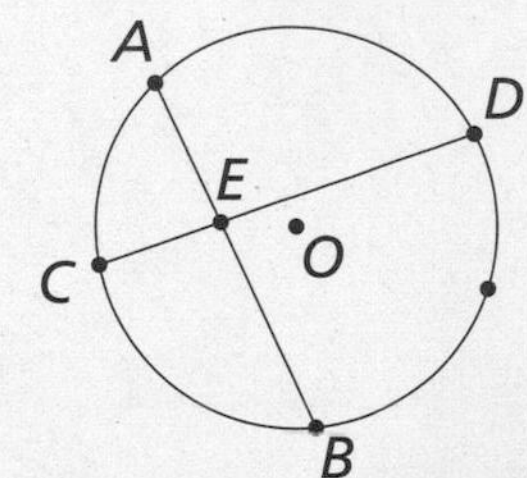

Segment Product Theorems

For a given circle and point E not on the circle, the product of the lengths of the two segments from E to a point on the circle is constant.

$AE \cdot EB = CE \cdot ED$

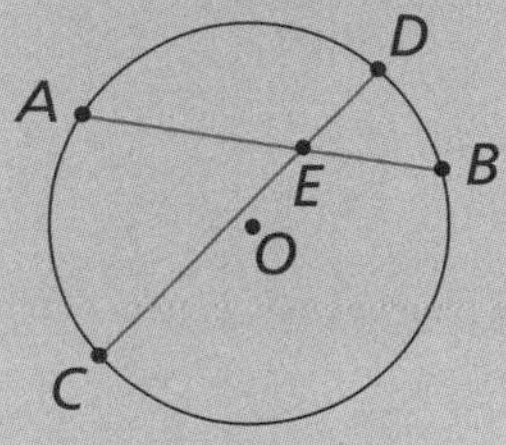

$EP \cdot EQ = ET \cdot ES$

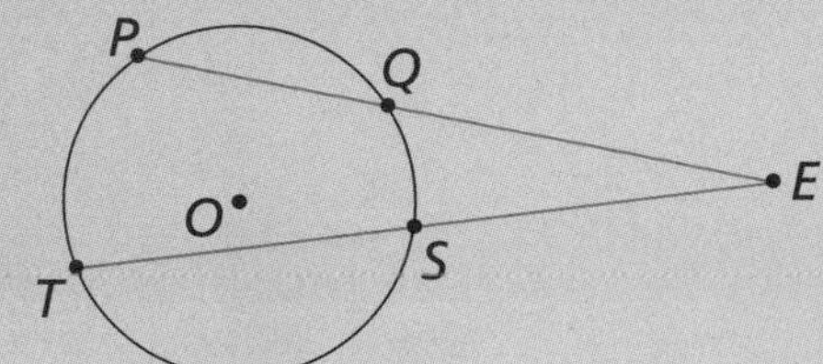

$EP \cdot EQ = ES \cdot ES$
$EP \cdot EQ = ES^2$

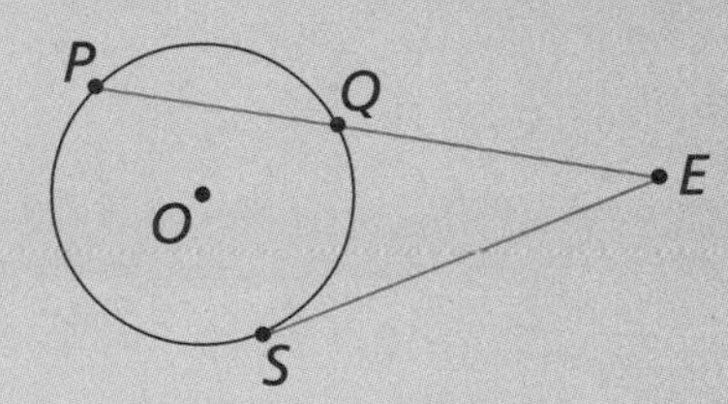

A proof of the first case of the segment Product Theorem is given in the following example.

EXAMPLE 1 Proving the Segment Product Theorem

1 **Given:** Circle O and point E not on the circle.
Prove: $AE \cdot EB = EC \cdot DE$

SOLUTION

Draw $\overline{AC}$ and $\overline{BD}$. $m\angle C = \frac{1}{2}\, m\overset{\frown}{AD}$ and $m\angle B = \frac{1}{2}\, m\overset{\frown}{AD}$ because the inscribed angles equal half their intercepted arc. Similarly, $m\angle A = \frac{1}{2}\, m\overset{\frown}{BC}$ and $m\angle D = \frac{1}{2}\, m\overset{\frown}{BC}$. By substitution, $m\angle A = m\angle D$ and $m\angle C = m\angle B$. Now $\triangle AEC \sim \triangle DEB$ by the A.A. postulate. Because corresponding parts of similar triangles are proportional, $\frac{AE}{EC} = \frac{DE}{EB}$. Since the product of the means is equal to the product of the extremes, we get $AE \cdot EB = EC \cdot DE$.

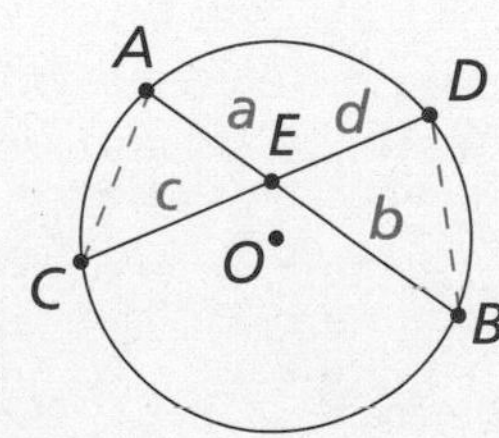

You can use the Segment Product Theorems to find missing lengths of tangents and secants.

EXAMPLES 2 through 4 **Applying the Segment Product Theorem**

Determine the value of x in each of the following figures.

2

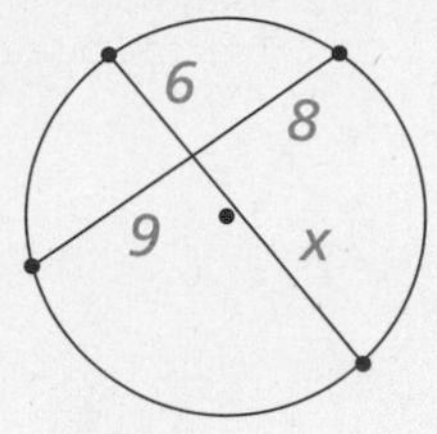

■ **SOLUTION**

$(6)(x) = (9)(8)$

$6x = 72$

$x = 12$

3

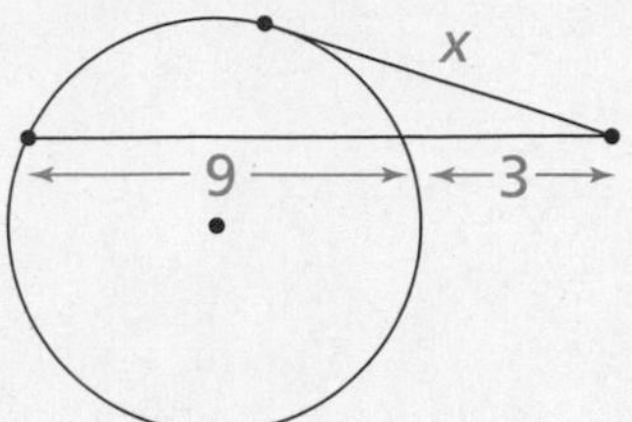

■ **SOLUTION**

$(x)(x) = 3(9 + 3)$

$x^2 = 36$

$x = 6$

4

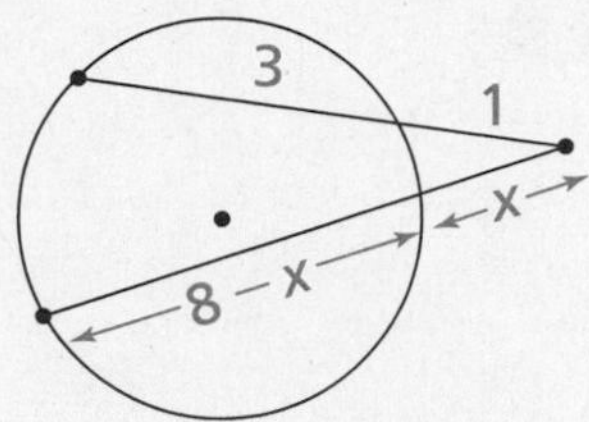

■ **SOLUTION**

$x(x + 8 - x) = (1)(4)$

$8x = 4$

$x = \frac{1}{2}$

The following table summarizes the remaining theorems about chords of a circle.

Theorems About Chords of a Circle		
In the same circle or in congruent circles, congruent chords have congruent arcs. The converse is also true: In the same circle or in congruent circles, congruent arcs have congruent chords.	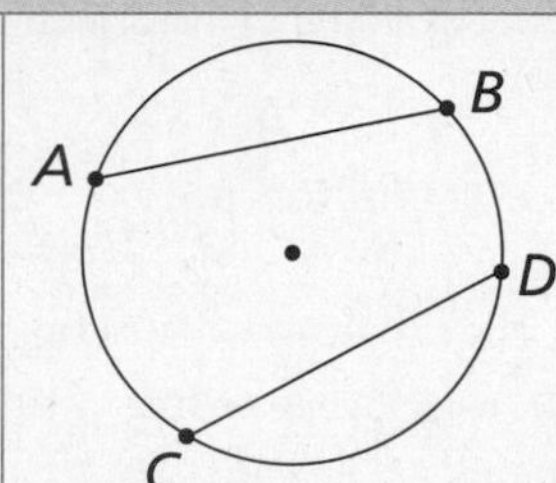	$\overline{AB} \cong \overline{CD} \rightarrow \overparen{AB} \cong \overparen{CD}$ $\overparen{AB} \cong \overparen{CD} \rightarrow \overline{AB} \cong \overline{CD}$
A diameter that is perpendicular to a chord bisects the chord and its two arcs. A diameter that bisects a chord is perpendicular to the chord.	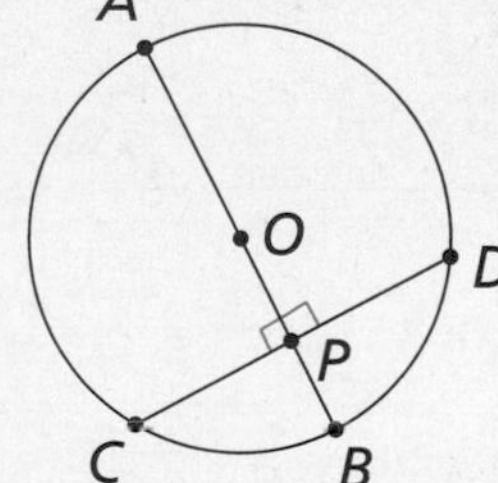	$\overline{AB} \perp \overline{CD} \rightarrow \overline{CP} \cong \overline{DP}$, $\overparen{CB} \cong \overparen{DB}$
In the same circle or in congruent circles, chords that are equidistant from the center are congruent. The converse is also true: In the same circle or in congruent circles, congruent chords are equidistant from the center of the circle.	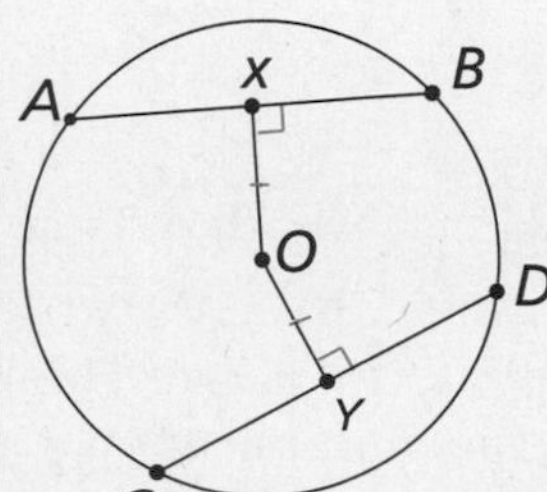	$\overline{AB} \perp \overline{OX}$, $\overline{CD} \perp \overline{OY}$, and $\overline{OX} \cong \overline{OY} \rightarrow \overline{AB} \cong \overline{CD}$ $\overline{AB} \cong \overline{CD} \rightarrow \overline{OX} \cong \overline{OY}$

You can use the theorems about chords of a circle to find the missing lengths of segments in a circle.

EXAMPLES 5 through 7 **Applying theorems about chords**

Determine the value of x in each of the following.

5

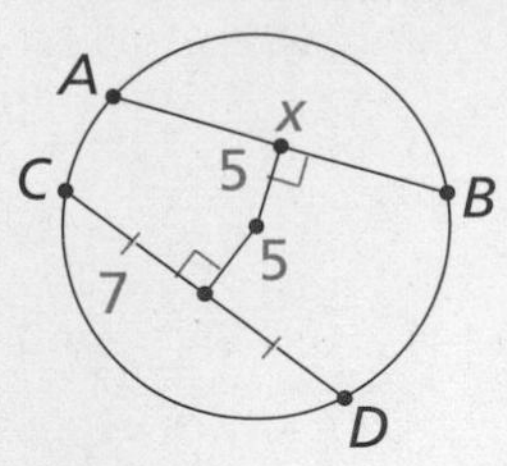

6

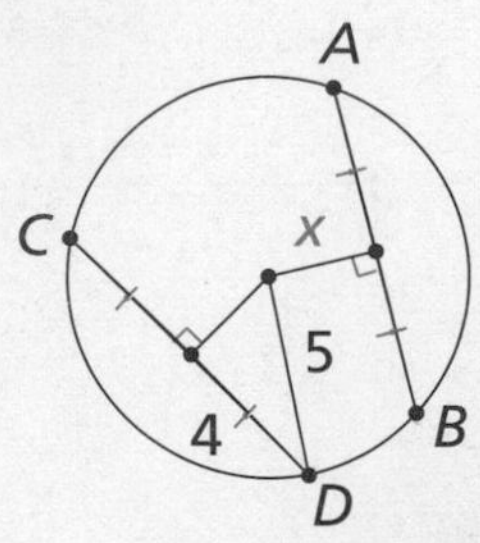

7

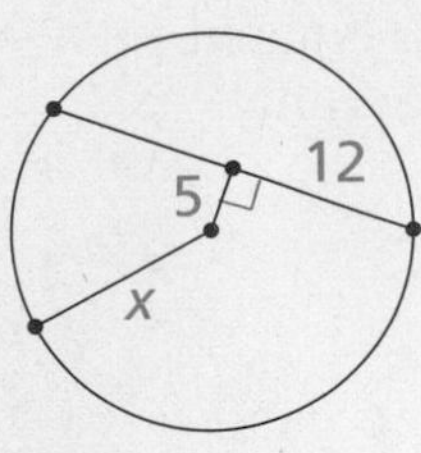

■ SOLUTION

$x = 14$

■ SOLUTION

$$x^2 + 4^2 = 5^2$$
$$x^2 = 9$$
$$x = 3$$

■ SOLUTION

$$12^2 + 5^2 = x^2$$
$$x^2 = 169$$
$$x = 13$$

Since congruent central angles intercept congruent arcs, and congruent arcs intercept congruent chords, you can conclude that congruent central angles also intercept congruent chords. Or, stated in another way, if two chords are congruent, then the central angles they intercept are congruent.

Suppose that a circle is cut by two parallel chords. What can you conclude about the arcs intercepted by them? You know that when two parallel lines are cut by a transversal, their alternate interior angles are congruent. Given two parallel chords, you can create a third chord that is the transversal between them. This fact can be used to prove the following theorem.

Parallel Chord Theorem

In a circle cut by parallel lines, the intercepted arcs are congruent.

EXAMPLE 8 **Proving the Parallel Chord Theorem**

Given: Circle O cut by $\overline{AB}$ and $\overline{CD}$, where $\overline{AB} \| \overline{CD}$.
Prove: $m\widehat{AB} = m\widehat{BD}$

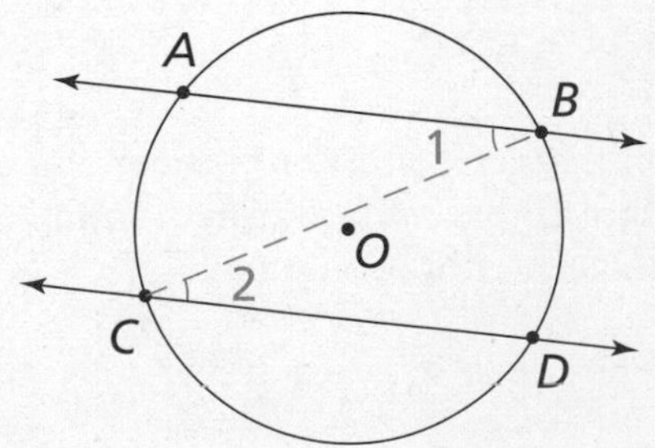

■ SOLUTION

Proof: Draw $\overline{BC}$. $m\angle 1 = \frac{1}{2}\widehat{AC}$ and $m\angle 2 = \frac{1}{2}\widehat{BD}$ because $\angle 1$ and $\angle 2$ are inscribed angles that equal half their intercepted arc. $\overline{BC}$ is a transversal that cuts two parallel segments. By the Aternate Interior Angle Theorem, $m\angle 1 = m\angle 2$ By substitution and the multiplication property of equality, we have $m\widehat{AB} = m\widehat{BD}$.

Practice

Choose the numeral preceding the word or expression that best completes the statement or answers the question.

1 $\overline{ST}$ is tangent to the circle at point T. Determine ST.

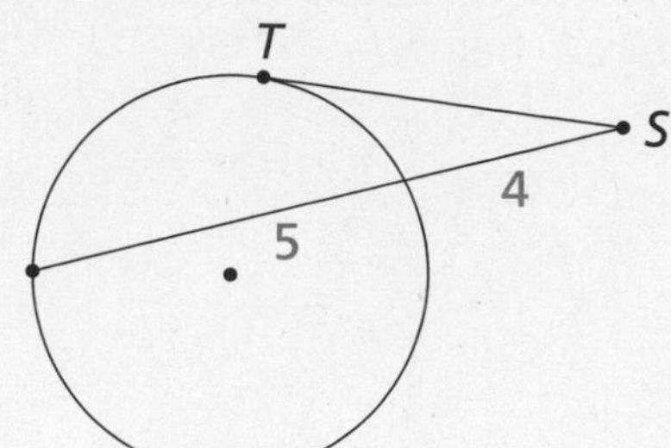

(1) 6 **(2)** $\sqrt{20}$ **(3)** 4.5 **(4)** 20

2 Find $m\angle BAC$.

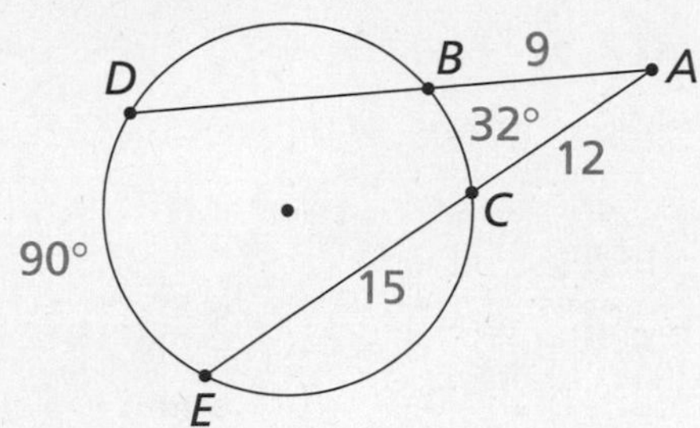

(1) 58° **(2)** 32° **(3)** 29° **(4)** 61°

In Exercises 3 and 4, determine the value of *x*.

3

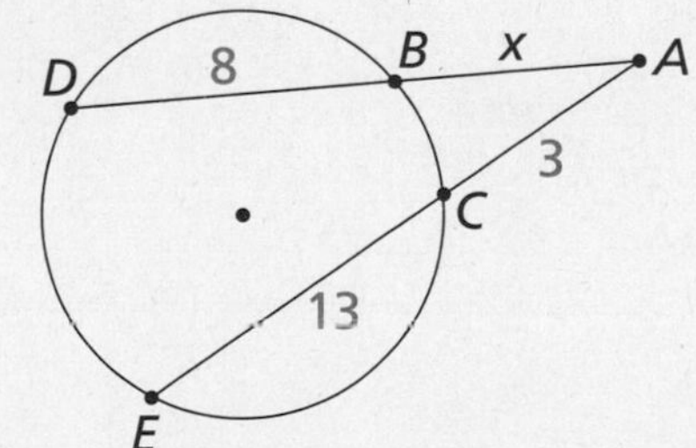

4 $\overline{AD}$ is tangent to the circle at D and $\overline{AE}$ is tangent to the circle at E.

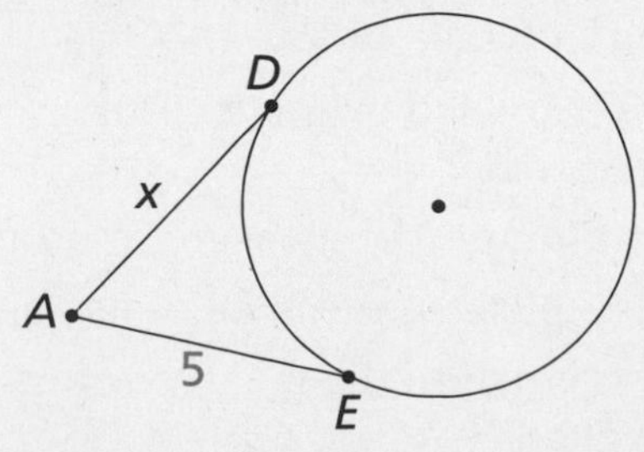

5 **Given:** $\overline{AEB}$ and $\overline{CED}$ are common internal tangents of circles O and Q.

Prove: $\overline{AB} \cong \overline{CD}$

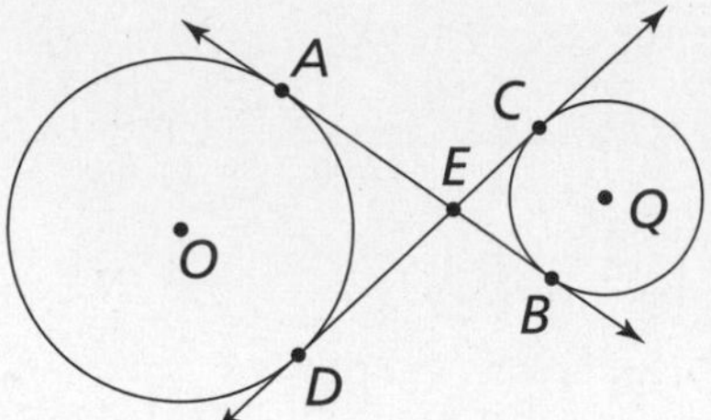

6 Find the value of x and y.

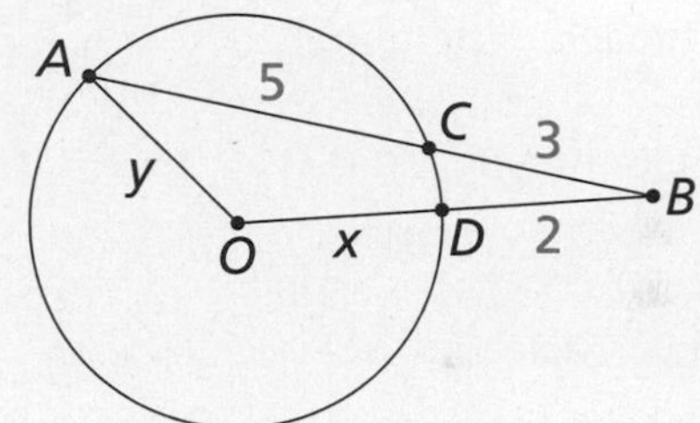

7 Find the value of x.

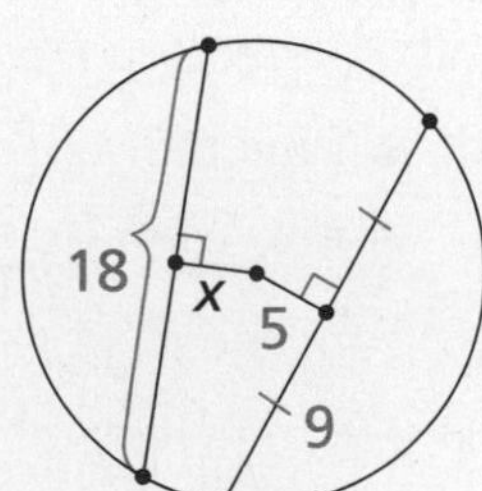

8 Find the value of x and y.

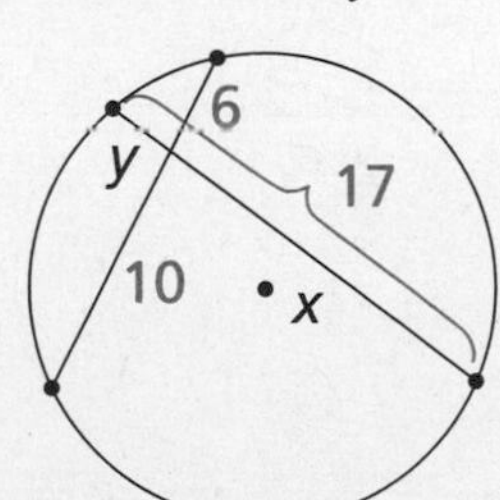

Chapter 8 Preparing for the New York Geometry Exam

Answer all the questions in this part. For each question, select the numeral preceding the word or expression that best completes the statement or answers the question.

1 What can you conclude from the diagram of circle O?

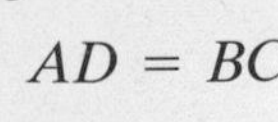

(1) $AD = BC$

(2) $m\angle A = m\angle D$

(3) $\overline{AC}$ and $\overline{BD}$ bisect each other

(4) all of the above

A B O D C

2 Determine the value of x in the accompanying figure.

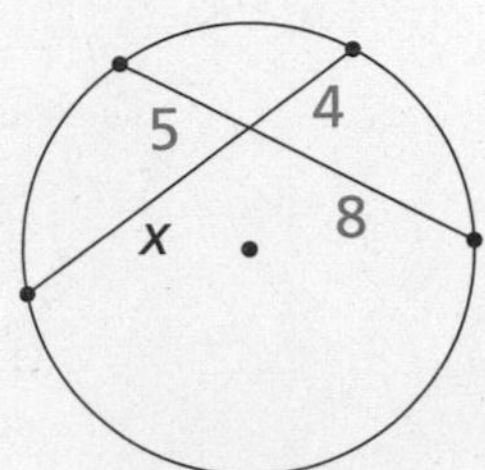

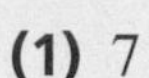

(1) 7

(2) 8

(3) 9

(4) 10

3 What is true about the opposite angles of a quadrilateral inscribed in a circle?

(1) They are complementary.

(2) They are supplementary.

(3) They are congruent.

(4) They are right.

4 Which equation could be used to determine the value of the radius in the circle below?

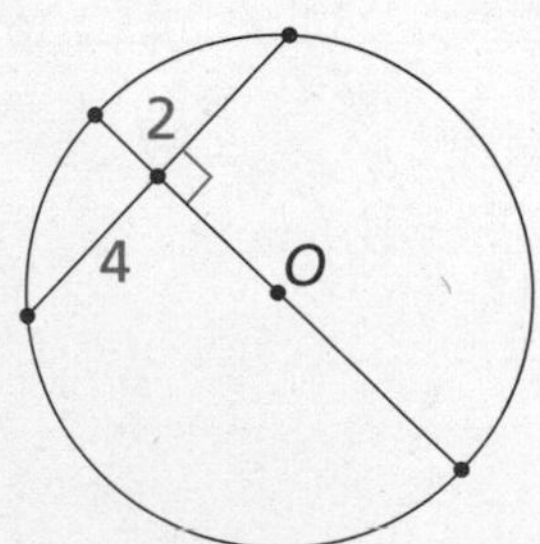

(1) $2^2 + 4^2 = r^2$

(2) $r^2 = (r - 2)^2 + 4^2$

(3) $r^2 + (r - 2)^2 = 4^2$

(4) $r^2 = (r + 2)^2 + 4^2$

5 Which statement is true about $\angle 1$ and $\angle 2$ in the figure below?

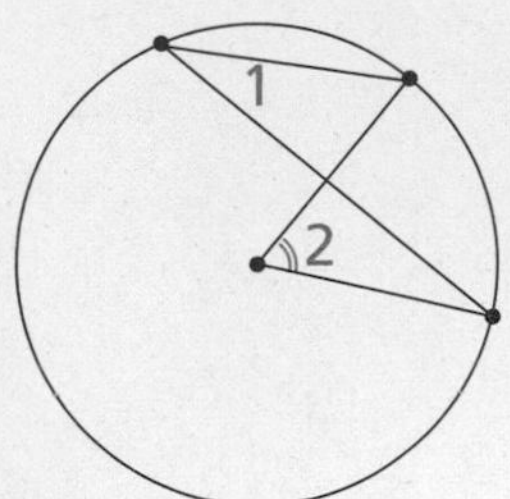

(1) $m\angle 1 = m\angle 2$

(2) $m\angle 1 = 2 \cdot m\angle 2$

(3) $m\angle 1 = \frac{1}{2} \cdot m\angle 2$

(4) $m\angle 1 \geq m\angle 2$

6 What is the measure of an angle inscribed in a semicircle?

(1) less than 90° **(3)** equal to 90°

(2) more than 90° **(4)** equal to 180°

7 The angle formed by a tangent to a circle and a radius to the point of tangency will have what measure?

(1) less than 90° **(3)** more than 90°

(2) equal to 90° **(4)** equal to 45°

8 In the accompanying figure, the $m\angle 2 = 115°$. Find the $m\angle 1$.

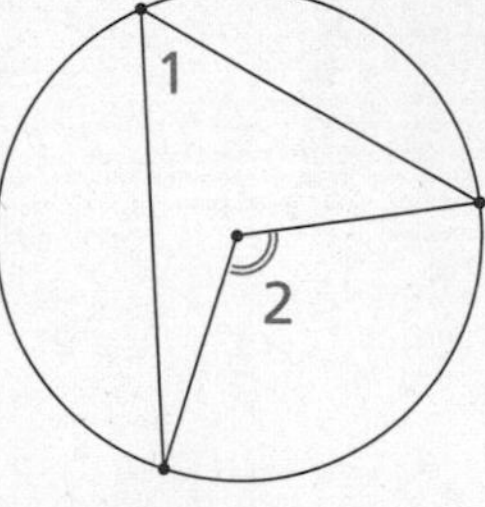

(1) 57.5°

(2) 60°

(3) 90°

(4) 245°

9 Which of the following describes the measure of a major arc?

(1) 360° divided by the measure of a semicircle.

(2) 360° minus the measure of its minor arc.

(3) 360° plus the measure of its minor arc.

(4) It is equal to the measure of its central angle.

10 An inflated tire has a diameter of 30 in. The tire is mounted on a wheel with a diameter of 18 in. When the tire goes flat, the flat part is tangent to the wheel at the center of the tire. The center of the tire is located on the perpendicular bisector of the flat part. Determine the length of the flat part of the tire.

(1) 6 in. **(2)** 12 in. **(3)** 24 in. **(4)** 48 in.

$\overline{AB}$ and $\overline{CD}$ are chords of the circle shown below. $m\angle 1 = 7x + 11$, $m\widehat{AC} = 2x$, and $m\widehat{DB} = x + 88$. Use this information to answer Exercises 11–12.

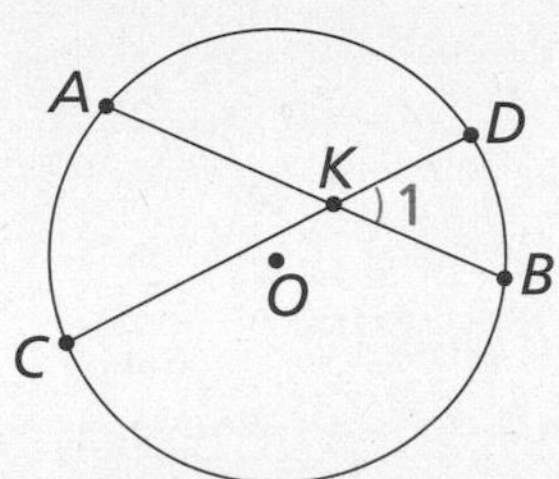

11 Find the value of x.

(1) 5 **(2)** 6 **(3)** 8 **(4)** 12

12 Find length of $\overline{KD}$ if $AK = 6$, $KB = 5$, and $CD = 13$.

(1) 3 **(2)** 5 **(3)** 6 **(4)** 8

13 Which of the following is true about the measure of an inscribed angle?

(1) The measure of an inscribed angle is double the measure of its intercepted arc.

(2) The measure of an inscribed angle is one half the measure of its intercepted arc.

(3) The measure of an inscribed angle is equal to the measure of its intercepted arc.

(4) The measure of an inscribed angle is the sum of 180° and the measure of its intercepted arc.

Use the following figure for Exercises 14–15.

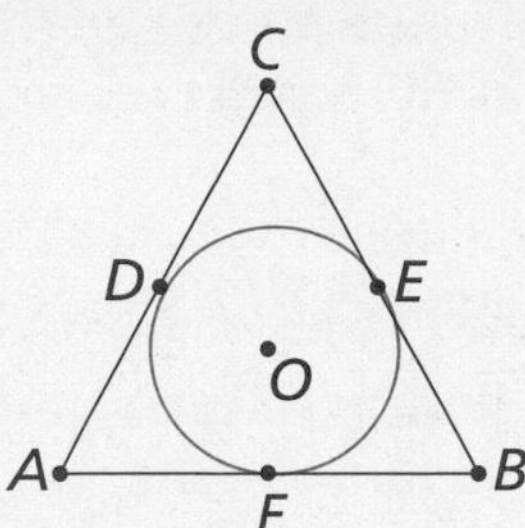

14 The sides of triangle ABC are tangent to circle O at points D, E, and F. $m\widehat{DE} = 100°$, and $AF = FB = 10$. Triangle ABC is an isosceles triangle. Find $m\angle A$.

(1) 40° **(2)** 50° **(3)** 60° **(4)** 80°

15 Find the length of side AB.

(1) 10 **(2)** 15 **(3)** 20 **(4)** 30

16 Which of the following is true about secants?

(1) The measure of an angle formed by two secants that intersect outside a circle is half the difference of the measures of its intercepted arcs.

(2) The measure of an angle formed by two secants that intersect inside a circle is half the sum of the measures of its intercepted arcs.

(3) The measure of an angle formed by two secants that intersect inside a circle is double the sum of the measures of its intercepted arcs.

(4) The measure of an angle formed by two secants that intersect outside a circle is double the difference of the measures of its intercepted arcs.

17 Two circles share a common tangent and the centers of the circles lie on the opposite sides of the common tangent. These circles are said to be

(1) externally tangent.

(2) internally tangent.

(3) commonly tangent.

(4) literally tangent.

Answer all the questions in this part. Clearly indicate the necessary steps, including appropriate formula substitutions, diagrams, graphs, charts, etc. For all questions in this part, a correct numerical answer with no work shown will receive only one credit.

18 Complete the following flow proof.

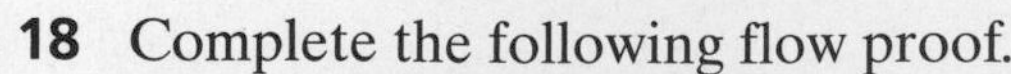

Given: Circle O with $\overline{AB} \cong \overline{CD}$

Prove: $m\widehat{AB} \cong m\widehat{CD}$

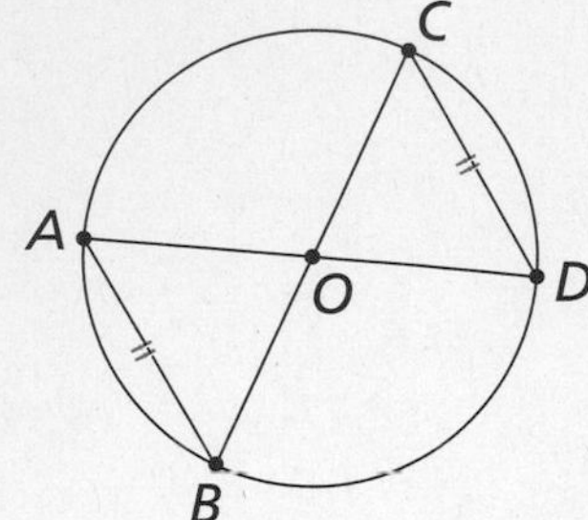

$\overline{AO} \cong \overline{BO} \cong \overline{CO} \cong \overline{DO}$

____

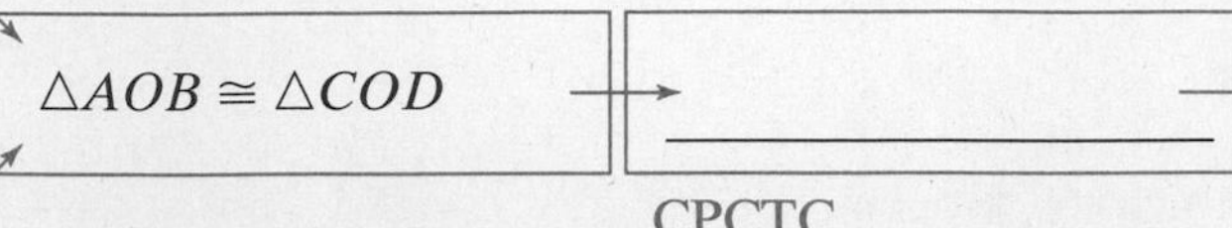

____

____

CPCTC

$m\widehat{AB} \cong m\widehat{CD}$

____

____

19 $\overline{PQ}$ and $\overline{PR}$ are chords of circle O. Prove that if O is on the bisector of $\angle QPR$, then $\overline{PQ} \cong \overline{PR}$.

20 Assume the radius of Earth is 3,960 mi and that there are no hills or obstructions on its surface. How far can you see from the top of the Eiffel Tower, which is 986 ft tall? How far can you see from the top of the CNN Tower, which is 1,815 ft tall?

9 Solid Geometry and Its Applications

Discovering New York

Niagara Falls

Niagara Falls, located on the border between New York state and Ontario, Canada, is the second largest waterfall in the world, behind Victoria Falls in South Africa. More than 1.5 million gallons of water flow over Niagara Falls every second.

Approximately 500 years ago, the flow of the Niagara River was shifted into two separate channels by the gradual formation of Goat Island. As a result, Horseshoe Falls is located on the western Canadian bank, while American Falls is located on the eastern bank.

Niagara Falls has been a major attraction for hundreds of years. About 12 million tourists visit Niagara Falls every year.

9.1 Points and Lines Perpendicular to the Plane

New York Standards

G.G.1 Line perpendicular to intersecting lines

G.G.2 Plane perpendicular to line at given point

G.G.3 Line perpendicular to a plane at point

G.G.4 Coplanar lines

G.G.5 Perpendicular planes

A line has only one dimension. A line has length (or distance). It has no width or depth.

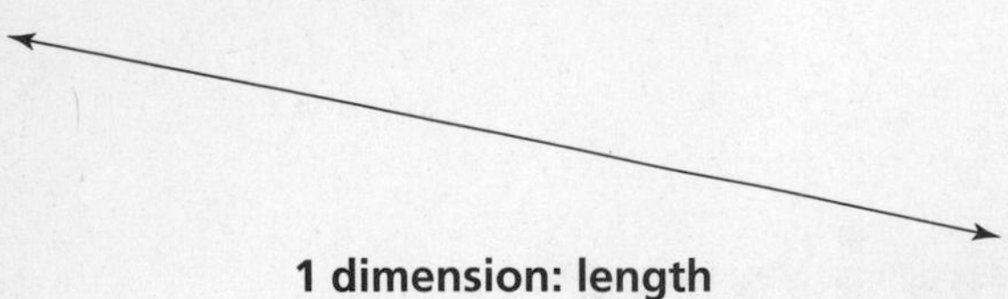

1 dimension: length

A plane exists in 2 dimensions. A plane has length and width, but no depth or thickness.

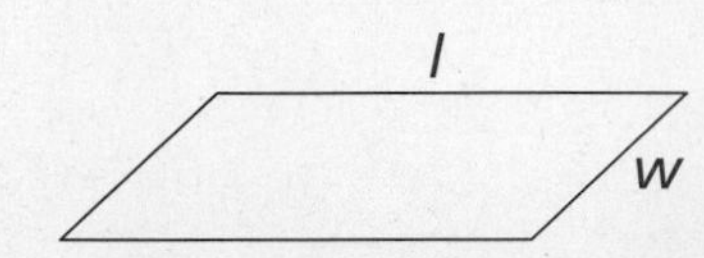

2 dimensions: length and width

Plane geometry deals with flat geometric figures that exist in a plane. You can find the perimeter and areas in plane geometry using length and width.

To consider all of the objects of our everyday existence, you have to include depth (or height). In order to understand 3-dimensional geometry, you have to consider points and lines that do not lie in the same plane.

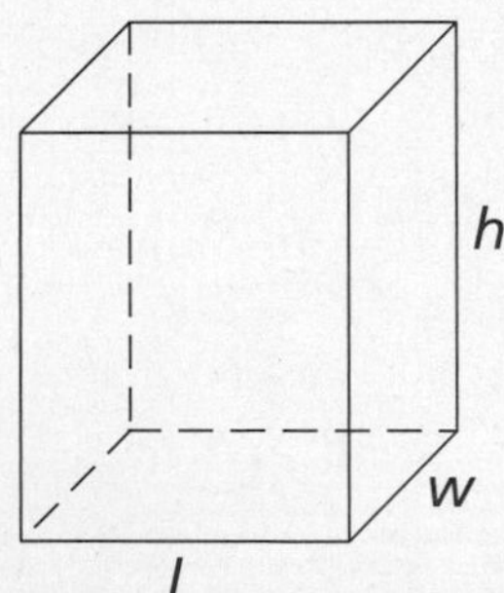

3 dimensions: length, width, and height

The postulates on the next page will help you analyze the characteristics and properties of perpendicular lines and planes. These postulates are essential to understanding 3-dimensional (or ***solid***) geometry.

For example, you can see that the walls in your classroom are perpendicular to each other, and that the walls intersect at the corners of the room. These postulates can be applied to large buildings as well as the construction of everyday objects.

Postulates About Perpendicular Lines and Planes	
1 Points and lines that lie in the same plane are coplanar. Collinear points are points that lie on the same line. If two lines intersect, then they are coplanar.	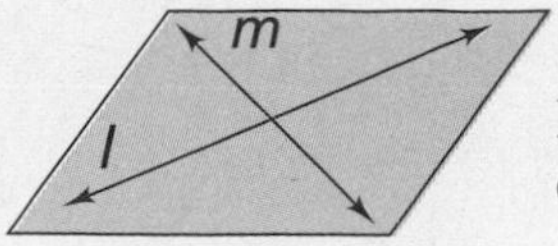 Lines *l* and *m* are coplanar.
2 Through any 3 noncollinear points, there is exactly one plane.	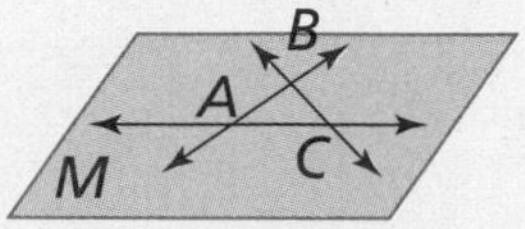 Plane *M* is determined by the points *A*, *B*, and *C*.
3 If a line intersects a plane, then it can intersect the plane at only one point.	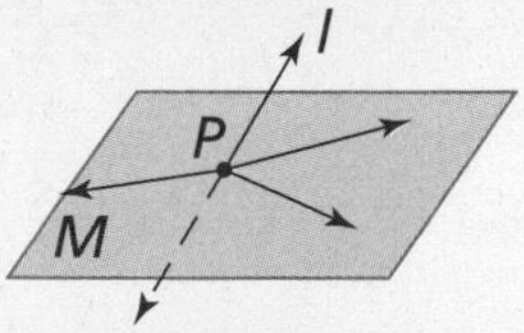 Line *l* intersects plane *M* at point *P*.
4 If a line is perpendicular to each of 2 intersecting lines at their intersection, then it is perpendicular to the plane that contains them.	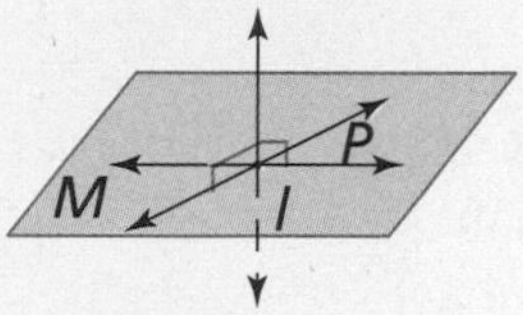 Line *l* is perpendicular to plane *M* at point *P*.
5 Through a given point not on a plane, there passes one and only one line perpendicular to the plane.	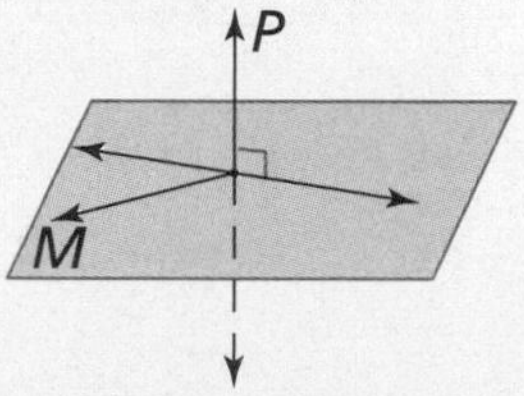 Point *P* can only be on one line that is perpendicular to plane *M*.
6 Through a given point there passes one and only one plane perpendicular to a line containing the point.	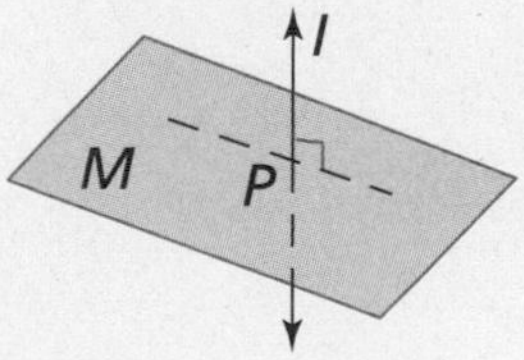 Plane *M* is the only plane that will be perpendicular to given line *l* through *P* on *l*.
7 If 2 lines are perpendicular to the same plane, they are coplanar.	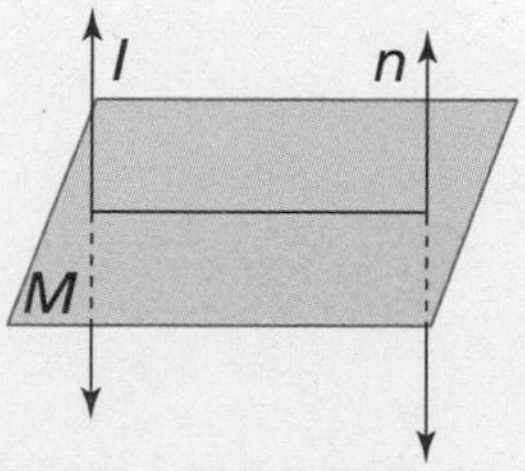 Line *l* and line *n* are both perpendicular to plane *M*, Therefore, they are coplanar and parallel.
8 Two planes are perpendicular to each other if one plane contains a line perpendicular to the second plane.	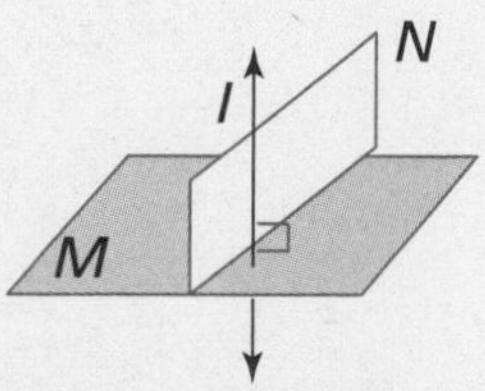 Line *l* is perpendicular to plane *M*. Therefore, plane *M* is perpendicular to plane *N*.

EXAMPLES 1 through 3 Working with planes

1 Explain why a 4-legged chair can be wobbly and a 3-legged stool is not.

■ **SOLUTION**

Recall that 3 noncollinear points form a plane. Therefore, the 3 legs of a stool (*A, B, C*) form a plane with the floor. If the end of the leg of the chair that ends at *D* is not in the same plane as *A, B,* and *C,* then the chair will wobble.

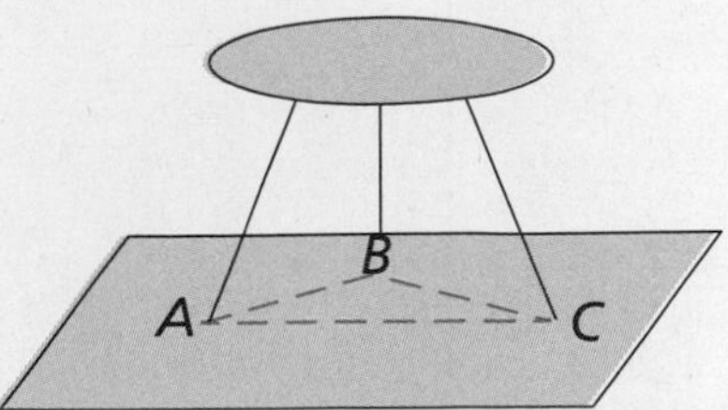

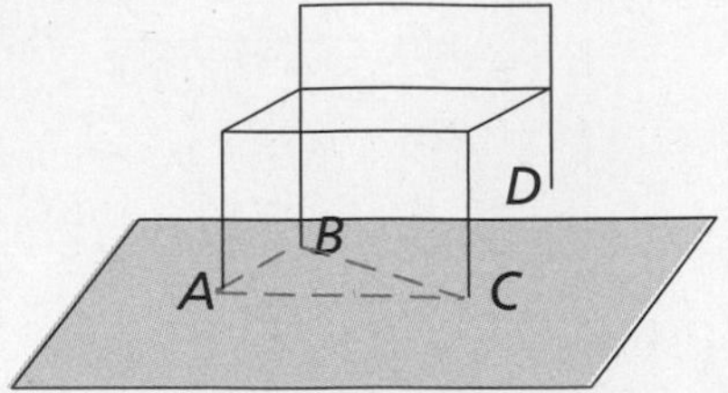

2 Draw a diagram to show why it is not sufficient to say that one and only one plane can pass through 2 points.

■ **SOLUTION**

The diagram shows that several planes include *A* and *B.* Two points will determine one and only one line. Note that the diagram illustrates that a single line lies in an infinite number of planes.

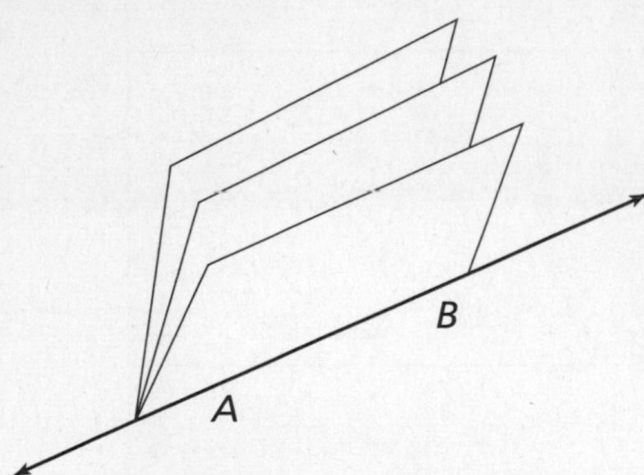

3 Using the rectangular solid to the right, name each of the following:

a. 2 segments perpendicular to *ABCD*
b. 2 planes perpendicular to each other
c. a plane that contains the diagonal *EC*
d. 2 planes that intersect each other, but are not perpendicular
e. the intersection of planes *CHE, CHG, EHG*

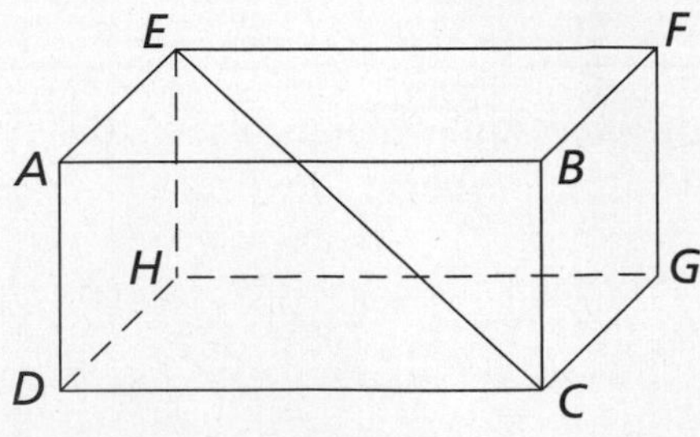

■ **SOLUTION**

a. $\overline{AE}$ and $\overline{BF}$ or $\overline{DH}$ and $\overline{CG}$
b. *CGH* and *GHE* (Answers will vary.)
c. *EHC*
d. *AEH* and *EHC* (Answers will vary.)
e. The 3 planes intersect at point *H*.

Practice

Choose the numeral preceding the word or expression that best completes the statement or answers the question.

1 Three noncollinear points determine a

(1) line.

(2) cube.

(3) point.

(4) plane.

2 The intersection of 2 planes is always a

(1) line.

(2) cube.

(3) point.

(4) plane.

3 At how many points does a line intersect a plane?

(1) 1

(2) 2

(3) 3

(4) infinite

Use the following diagram of a rectangular solid to answer Exercises 4–8.

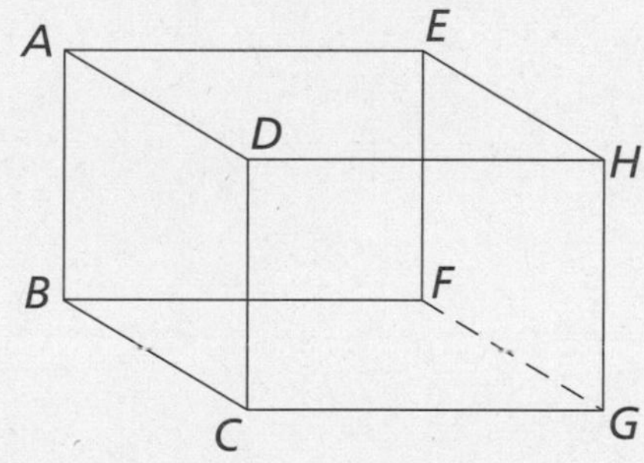

4 Name a set of collinear points.

5 Name a set of coplanar points.

6 Name a plane that contains the diagonal $\overline{AG}$.

7 Name a plane that contains the diagonal $\overline{EC}$.

8 Name each face of the cube.

Use the following diagram of a pyramid to answer Exercises 9–15.

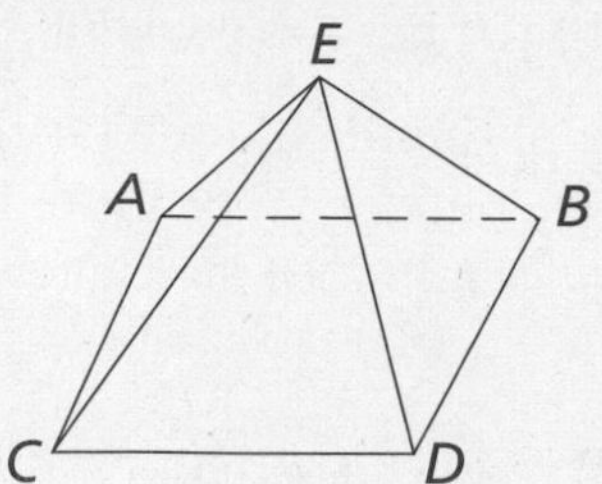

9 Name two intersecting planes.

10 Name a set of points that is not coplanar.

11 Name a set of collinear points.

12 Name a set of noncollinear points.

13 Name a line that is in the same plane as *EB*.

14 Name each face of the solid.

15 How many planes intersect at *E*?

In Exercises 16–22, state whether the statement is true or false.

16 If 5 points are coplanar, they are always collinear.

17 If 5 points are collinear, then they are coplanar.

18 Plane *P* contains the lines *m* and *n*, which intersect at point *Q*. Line *l* is not in plane *P*, but it is perpendicular to *m* and *n* at *Q*. Line *l* is perpendicular to plane *P*.

19 There is more than one line that can be perpendicular to a plane at the point of intersection.

20 If 2 lines are perpendicular to the same plane, they are coplanar.

21 For a given line and a point not on the line, there is exactly one plane that can contain them.

22 Given any 2 lines, there is only one plane that contains both of them.

9.2 Perpendicular and Parallel Planes

New York Standards

G.G.6 Line perpendicular to plane at point of intersection

G.G.7 Lines perpendicular to planes

G.G.8 Plane intersecting two parallel planes

G.G.9 Parallel planes

If 2 lines are perpendicular to the same plane, then they are coplanar, but are they parallel? If you can show that they are the same distance apart, then you know that the lines are parallel.

Recall that the perpendicular distance is the shortest distance between 2 or more lines, as shown in the diagram to the right.

In the diagram to the right, $d_1 \perp n$ and $d_1 = d_2$. Therefore $l \parallel n$. Therefore, if 2 lines are perpendicular to a plane, then they are parallel to each other.

EXAMPLE 1 Showing that 2 planes perpendicular to the same plane are not always parallel

If 2 planes are perpendicular to the same plane, are they parallel?

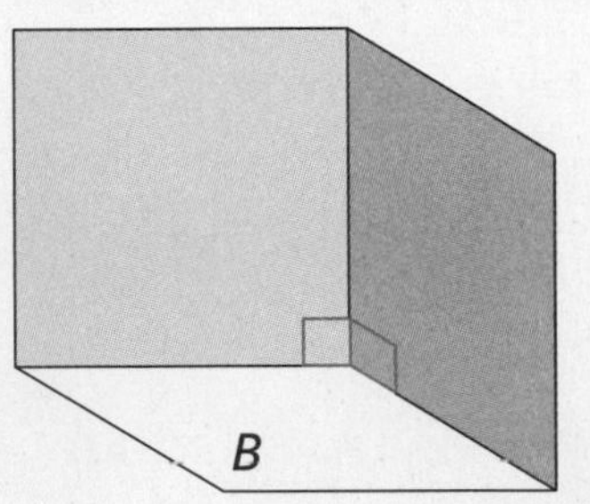

■ **SOLUTION**

In the figure to the right, you can see that the 2 shaded faces are both perpendicular to the plane B. They are also perpendicular to each other. This counterexample shows 2 planes that are perpendicular to a given plane are not always parallel to each other.

When 2 planes intersect, each plane is divided into a **half plane,** as shown in the figure to the right. The points W, X, Y, and Z each lie in a separate half plane.

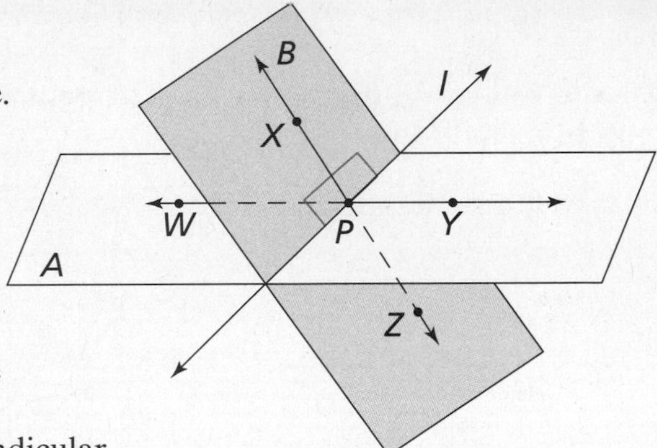

The angles formed when 2 planes intersect are called **dihedral angles.** Dihedral angles can be acute, obtuse, or right. You can find the measure of dihedral angles by measuring the plane angle formed by the rays in each half plane. For example, $\angle XPY$ is a plane angle.

When 2 planes intersect, their vertical dihedral angles are congruent. If the 2 planes intersect so that their dihedral angles form right plane angles, then the planes are perpendicular.

EXAMPLE 2 Identifying vertical dihedral angles

Identify a dihedral angle in the figure above that is congruent to $\angle XPY$.

■ **SOLUTION**

$\angle WPZ$ and $\angle XPY$ are vertical dihedral angles. Since vertical dihedral angles are congruent, $\angle XPY \cong \angle WPZ$.

This leads to the following postulates about perpendicular and parallel lines and planes.

Postulates About Perpendicular and Parallel Lines and Planes	
1 If a line is perpendicular to a plane, then any line perpendicular to the given line at its point of intersection with the given plane is in the given plane.	If $l \perp$ plane M at P and if lines a, b, and c are perpendicular to l, then a, b, and c all lie in plane M.
2 If a line is perpendicular to a plane, then every plane containing the line is perpendicular to the given plane.	If $l \perp$ plane M at P, then all the planes containing l are perpendicular to plane M.

You can use these postulates to describe the faces and properties of geometric solids.

EXAMPLES 3 and 4 Identifying perpendicular lines and planes

Use the rectangular prism to the right for Examples 3 and 4.

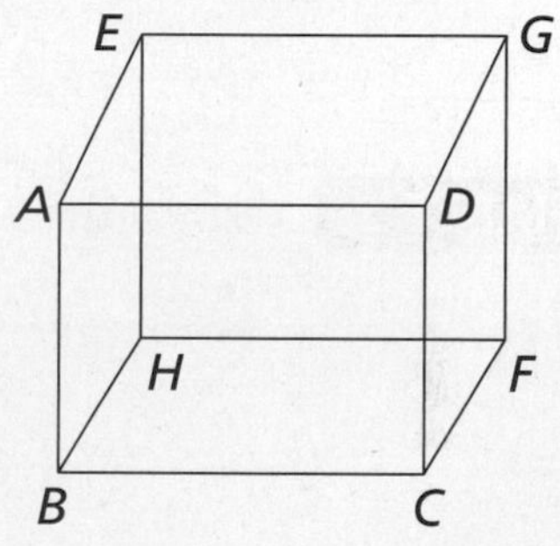

3 Name all the edges perpendicular to $\overline{AB}$.

■ **SOLUTION**

$\overline{AD}$, $\overline{AE}$, $\overline{BC}$, $\overline{BH}$

4 Name all the planes perpendicular to $\overline{AB}$.

■ **SOLUTION**

To find the planes perpendicular to $\overline{AB}$, name the planes that contain the lines perpendicular to $\overline{AB}$ from Example 3, but do not contain $\overline{AB}$ itself.

$$ADGE \text{ and } BCFH$$

When you look at geometric solids, you may see that many of their faces are parallel and lie in different planes. Just as lines that have no points in common are parallel, planes that have no points in common are parallel.

Parallel planes are planes that do not intersect. If two planes are parallel, then none of the lines contained in one plane will intersect with any of the lines contained in the other plane. If a line and a plane do not intersect, then they are also parallel.

In fact, many postulates about parallel and perpendicular lines can be extended to parallel and perpendicular planes.

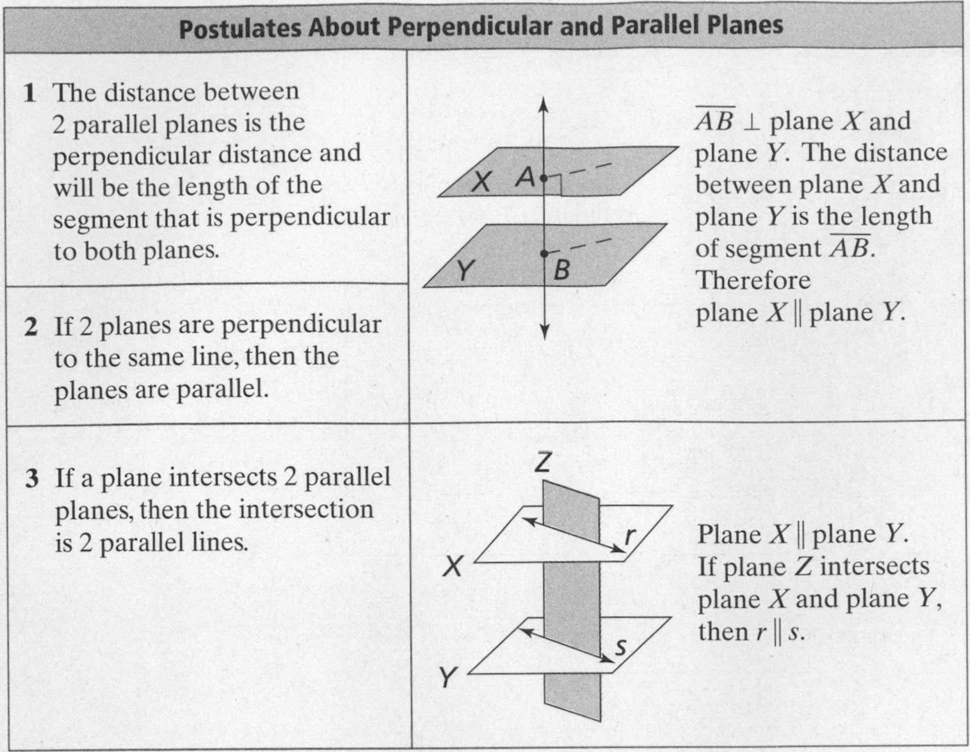

Postulates About Perpendicular and Parallel Planes	
1 The distance between 2 parallel planes is the perpendicular distance and will be the length of the segment that is perpendicular to both planes. **2** If 2 planes are perpendicular to the same line, then the planes are parallel.	$\overline{AB} \perp$ plane X and plane Y. The distance between plane X and plane Y is the length of segment $\overline{AB}$. Therefore plane $X \parallel$ plane Y.
3 If a plane intersects 2 parallel planes, then the intersection is 2 parallel lines.	Plane $X \parallel$ plane Y. If plane Z intersects plane X and plane Y, then $r \parallel s$.

If a plane intersects a 3-dimensional figure so that one half of the figure is identical to the other half, then the plane is called a **symmetry plane.**

EXAMPLE 5 **Exploring symmetry planes**

5 Draw a symmetry plane parallel to the bases of the solids below.

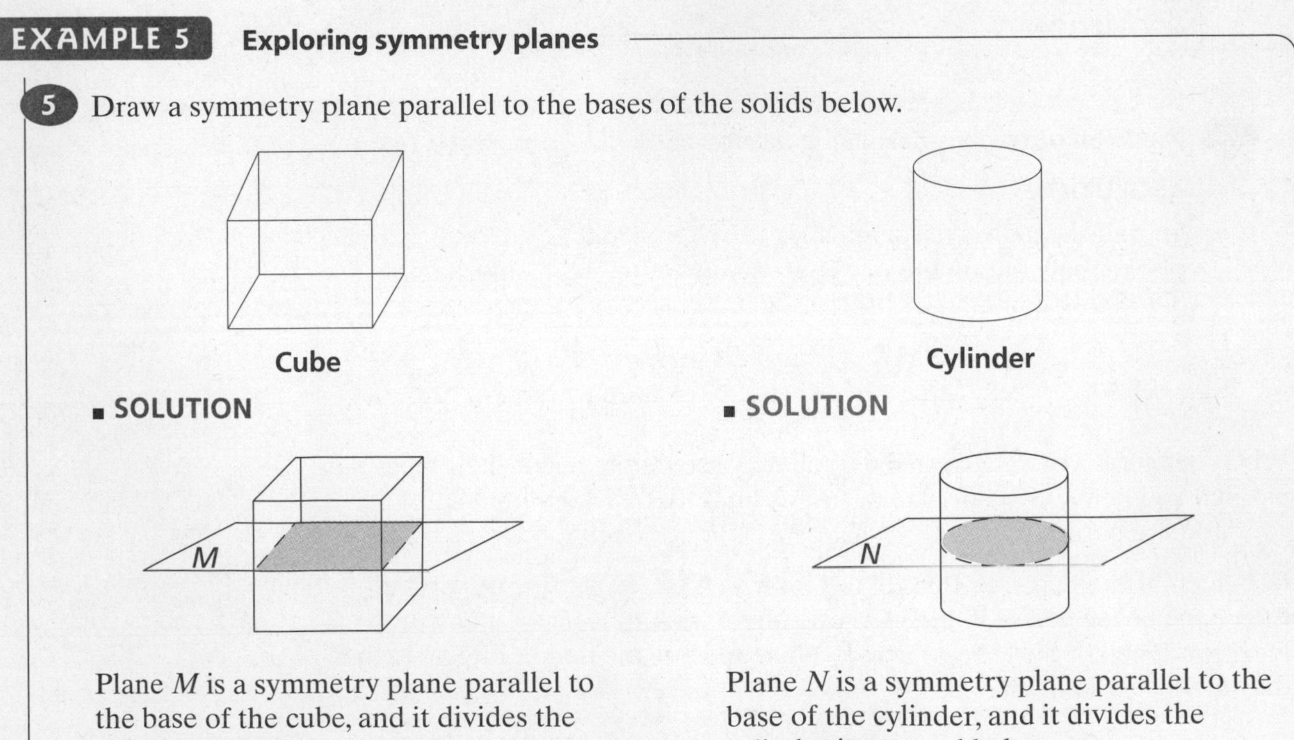

Cube

Cylinder

■ **SOLUTION**

Plane M is a symmetry plane parallel to the base of the cube, and it divides the cube into equal halves.

■ **SOLUTION**

Plane N is a symmetry plane parallel to the base of the cylinder, and it divides the cylinder into equal halves.

EXAMPLES 6 and 7 Exploring symmetry planes

6 How many symmetry planes does the cube in Example 5 have?

■ **SOLUTION**

The cube has one symmetry plane parallel to the bases, as shown in the in the solution to Example 5, and one symmetry plane for each symmetry line of its base, as shown in the figure to the right. Therefore, a cube has 5 symmetry planes.

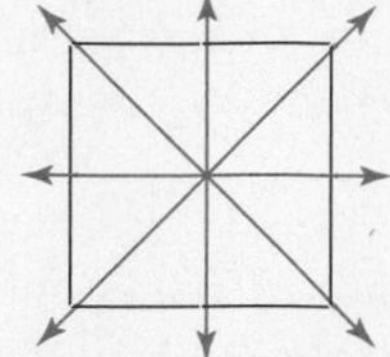

4 symmetry lines for the base

7 How many symmetry planes does the cylinder in Example 4 have?

■ **SOLUTION**

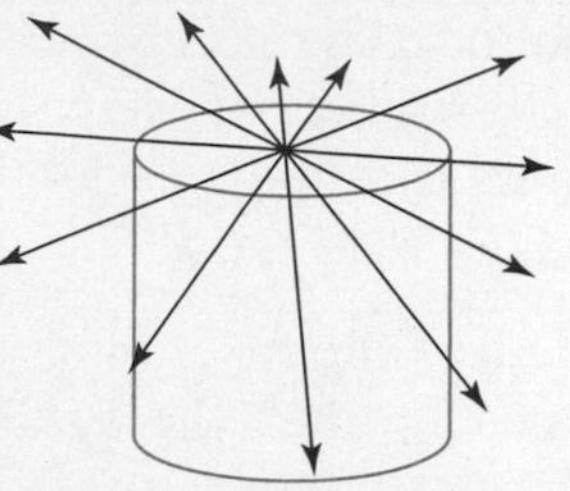

The cylinder has one symmetry plane parallel to its bases, as shown in the solution to Example 4. In the figure to the right, each of the lines passing through the diameter of the cylinder is in a unique symmetry plane. Therefore, there is an infinite amount of symmetry planes perpendicular to the cylinder's base.

Practice

Choose the numeral preceding the word or expression that best completes the statement or answers the question.

1 Two planes that are not parallel intersect at a

(1) line.
(2) plane.
(3) segment
(4) point.

2 How many symmetry planes are there in a rectangular solid that is not a cube?

(1) 4
(2) 3
(3) 2
(4) infinite

3 The corner of your classroom represents the intersection of

(1) 4 lines.
(2) 2 planes.
(3) 3 planes.
(4) 2 planes and a line.

In Exercises 4–12, state the postulate or definition that the statement represents.

4 a 4 legged table that is wobbly

5 a revolving door in a building

6 the goal posts on a football field

7 the floor and ceiling of a room

8 slicing an orange exactly in half

9 two adjacent faces of a cube

10 two opposite faces of a cube

11 measuring the intersection of 2 walls of a room to determine the height of the room

12 How many symmetry planes does the figure below have?

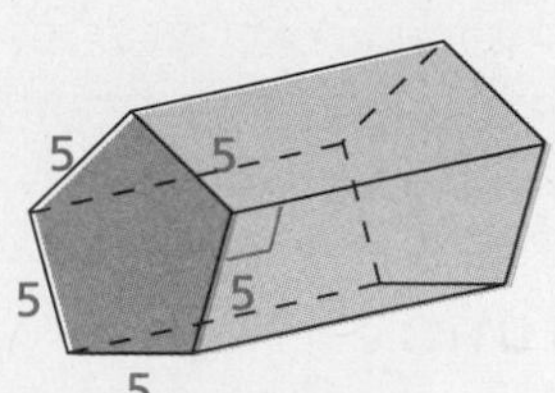

9.3 Lateral and Surface Areas of Prisms

New York Standards

G.G.10 Properties of lateral edges of a prism

G.G.13 Properties of a regular pyramid

A **polyhedron** is a three-dimensional figure formed by flat surfaces that are bounded by polygons joined along their sides. Each of the flat surfaces is called a **face** of the polyhedron. A segment that is the intersection of two faces is called an **edge.** A point that is the intersection of three or more edges is a **vertex.**

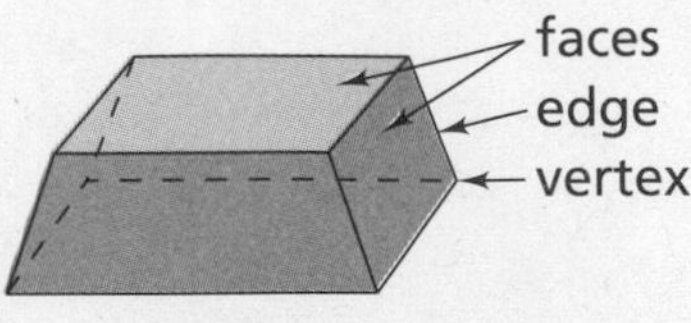

polyhedron

If all of the faces of a polyhedron are regular polygons that are congruent to each other, the figure is a **regular polyhedron.** In a regular polyhedron, the same number of faces meets at each vertex.

Regular Polyhedrons

- **Tetrahedron:** a polyhedron with 4 congruent faces that are triangles.
- **Hexahedron:** a polyhedron with 6 congruent faces that are squares. (A hexahedron is also called a **cube.**)
- **Octahedron:** a polyhedron with 8 congruent faces that are triangles.
- **Dodecahedron:** a polyhedron with 12 congruent faces that are pentagons.
- **Icosahedron:** a polyhedron with 20 congruent faces that are triangles.

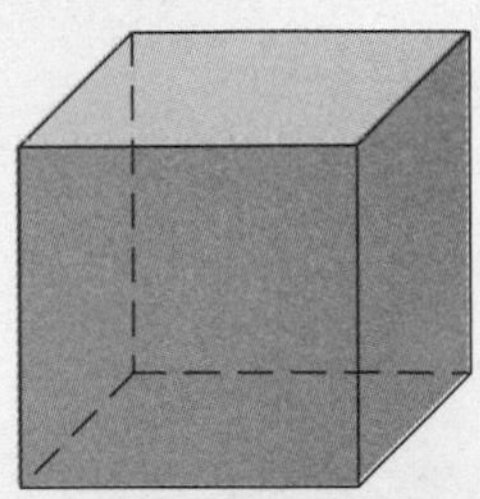
hexahedron

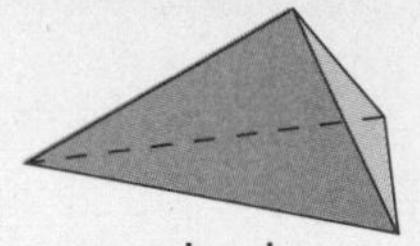
tetrahedron

A **prism** is a polyhedron with two parallel **bases** bounded by congruent polygons and with **lateral faces** bounded by parallelograms that connect corresponding sides of the bases. The **height** h of a prism is the length of any perpendicular segment drawn from a point on one base to the plane containing the other base.

A prism is a **right prism** if the segments that join corresponding vertices of the bases are perpendicular to the bases. Otherwise, the prism is called *oblique.* You can further classify a prism by the shape of its bases: triangular, square, rectangular, and so on.

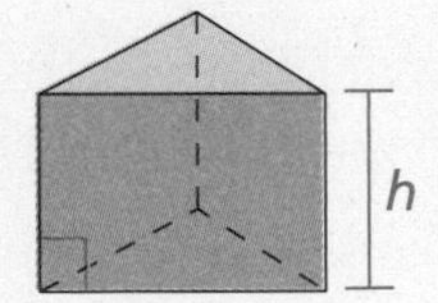

right triangular prism

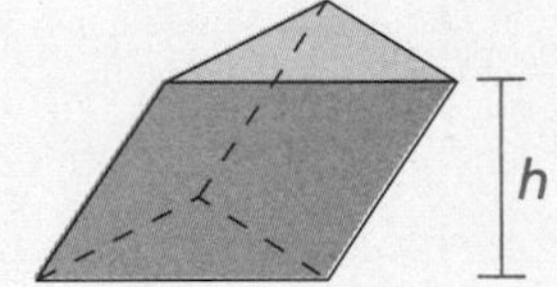

oblique triangular prism

EXAMPLE 1 **Classifying a prism**

Which best describes the prism at the right? The measure of each interior angle of a base is 108°.

(1) dodecahedron

(2) regular pentagonal prism

(3) right pentagonal prism

(4) oblique regular pentagonal prism

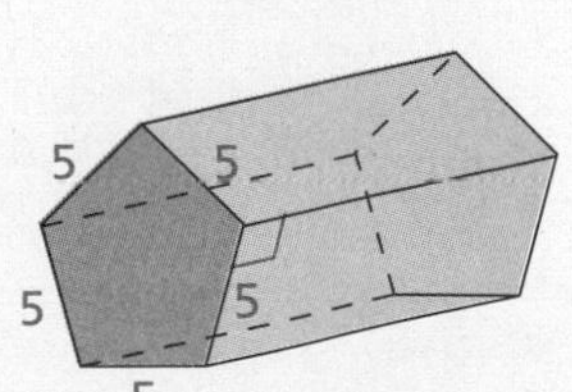

■ SOLUTION

The bases are regular pentagons. The right-angle symbol indicates that the segments joining corresponding vertices are perpendicular to the planes containing the bases. The correct choice is **(3).**

The **lateral area of a prism** is the sum of the areas of its lateral faces. If you look at a *net* of a rectangular prism you will see that it is made up of four rectangles laid side by side, all with the same height. The figure below is a **net** of the prism.

Note

The perimeter of the base of a rectangular prism is $2l + 2w$.

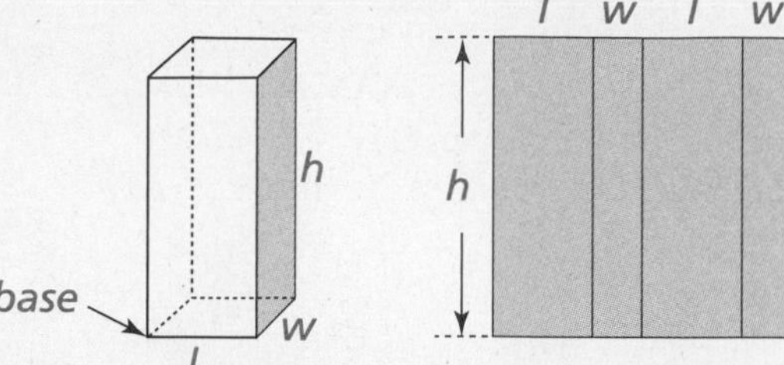

You can calculate the lateral area of a prism if you multiply the height of the figure by the perimeter of its base. The formula for lateral area is ph, where p is the perimeter of the base and h is the height of the figure.

Visit: PHSchool.com
Web Code: ayp-0097

$$\textbf{L.A.} = \mathbf{ph} \text{ or } \mathbf{h(2}\boldsymbol{l} + \mathbf{2}\boldsymbol{w}) \text{ or } \mathbf{2(}\boldsymbol{lh} + \boldsymbol{hw})$$

To find the total **surface area of a prism** you add the lateral area and the areas of the two congruent bases. The formula is **Surface Area = L.A. + 2*B***, where ***B*** is the area of the base.

Note

The base of a prism is not always the bottom of the drawing.

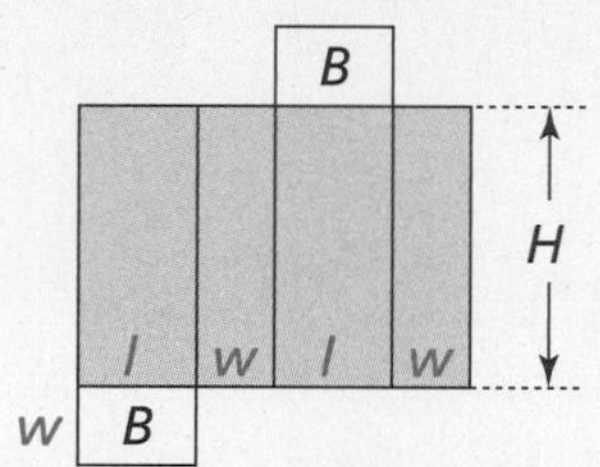

S.A. = L.A. + 2*B*

Since the L.A. $= 2(lh + hw)$ added to the area of the two bases, $2B = 2lw$, another formula for the surface area can be $\mathbf{S.A.} = \mathbf{2(}\boldsymbol{lh} + \boldsymbol{hw} + \boldsymbol{lw})$.

EXAMPLES 2 and 3 Finding lateral and total surface area of a right prism

2 Find the lateral and surface area of the right triangular prism below.

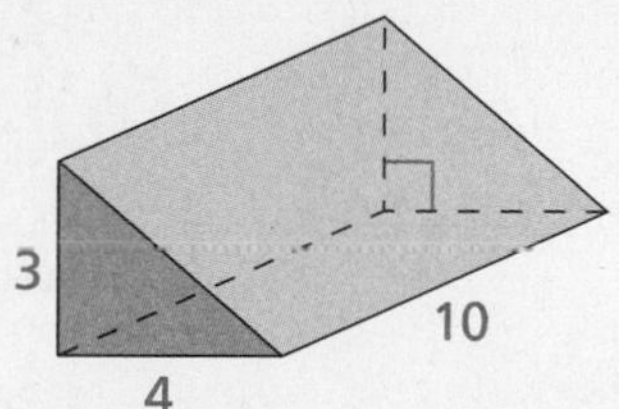

■ SOLUTION

The bases are right triangles. The length of the hypotenuse is 5 by the Pythagorean Theorem.

L.A. $= 5 \times 10 + 3 \times 10 + 4 \times 10$

$= 120$ square units

S.A. $= 120 + 2\left(\frac{1}{2} \times 3 \times 4\right)$

$= 132$ square units

3 Find the lateral and surface area of the right rectangular prism below.

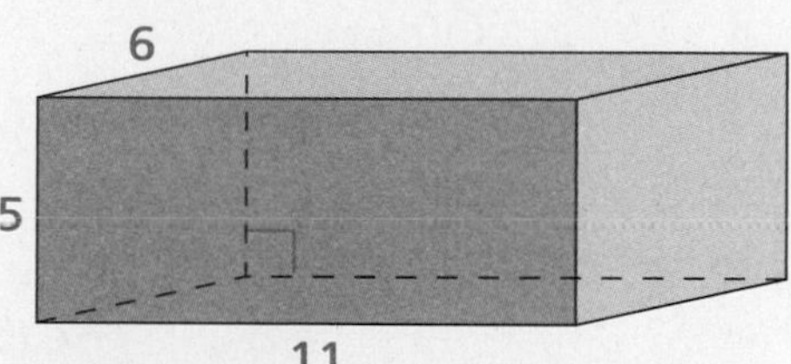

■ SOLUTION

Consider the top and the bottom as the bases of the prism.

L.A. $= 2(5 \times 11) + 2(6 \times 5)$

$= 170$ square units

S.A. $= 170 + 2(6 \times 11)$

$= 302$ square units

A **pyramid** is a polyhedron with one base that is bounded by a polygon, a point outside the plane of the base called the **vertex**, and lateral faces that are bounded by triangles connecting the vertex to each side of the base. The **height** h of a pyramid is the length of the perpendicular segment drawn from the vertex to the plane containing the base. Like a prism, a pyramid can be classified by the shape of its base.

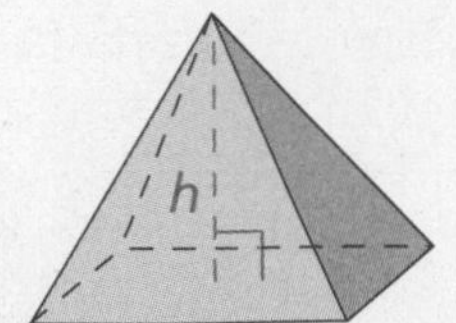

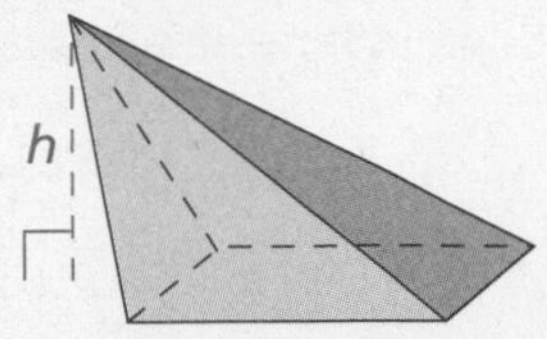

rectangular pyramids

A pyramid is a **regular pyramid** if its base is bounded by a regular polygon and the segment joining the center of this polygon to the vertex is perpendicular to the plane of the base. Its lateral faces are congruent isosceles triangles. The height of one of these triangles is called the **slant height** ℓ of the pyramid.

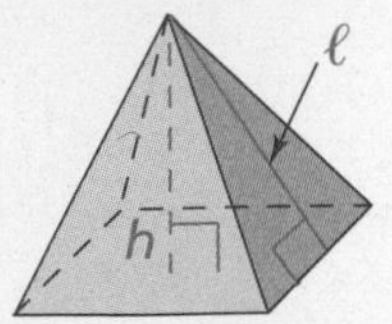

regular square pyramid

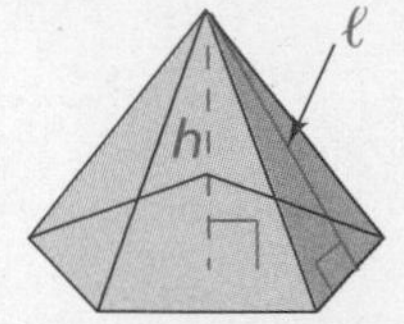

regular pentagonal pyramid

The **lateral area** of a pyramid is the sum of the areas of its lateral faces. The surface area of a pyramid is the sum of the area of the base and the lateral area.

Area Formulas for a Regular Pyramid

If the base of a regular pyramid has n sides each having length s and slant height ℓ, then the lateral area L.A. is given by this formula.

$$\text{L.A.} = n\left[\tfrac{1}{2}s\ell\right] = \tfrac{1}{2}ns\ell$$

The surface area S.A. is given by the following formula.

$\text{S.A.} = \text{L.A.} + B = \frac{1}{2}ns\ell + B$, where B is the area of the base

EXAMPLE 4 **Finding areas of a regular pyramid given height and slant height**

Go Online PHSchool.com
Visit: PHSchool.com
Web Code: ayp-0911

4 Find the lateral and surface area of a regular square pyramid with a height of 4 in. and a slant height of 5 in.

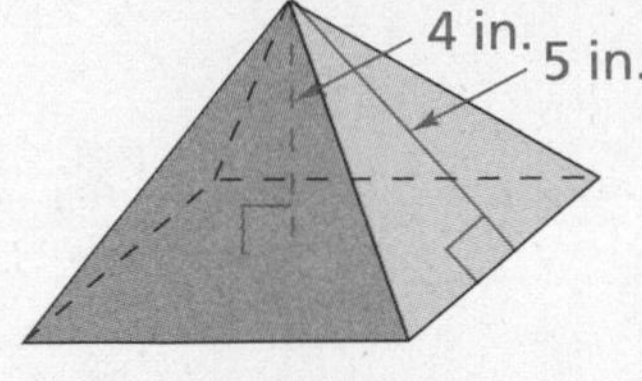

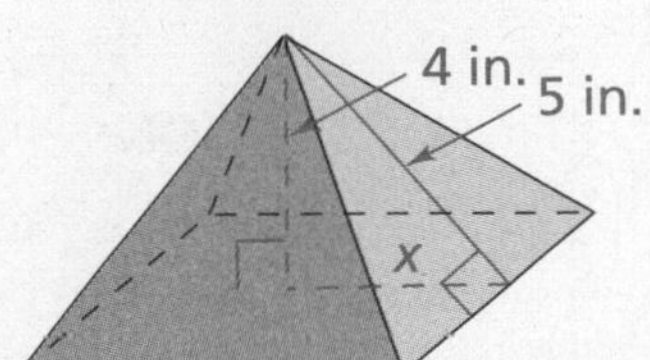

■ **SOLUTION**

Step 1 To find lateral area and surface area, you need to find the length of a side of the square base. The length of a side of the base is $2x$, where x represents the length shown in the second sketch at the right.

$4^2 + x^2 = 5^2$ ← **Use the Pythagorean Theorem.**
$x = 3$

The length of a side of the base is 2(3) in., or 6 in.

Step 2 Apply the formulas for lateral area and surface area.

$$\text{L.A.} = 4\left[\tfrac{1}{2}(6 \times 5)\right] = 60 \rightarrow 60 \text{ in.}^2$$

$$\text{S.A.} = 60 + 6^2 = 96 \rightarrow 96 \text{ in.}^2$$

You may need to find the slant height of a pyramid before finding the areas.

EXAMPLE 5 **Finding areas of a regular pyramid given height and length of one side of the base**

 Find the lateral and surface area of a regular square pyramid with a height of 6 in. and base with side length 8 in.

6 in.

8 in.

6 in.

y

4 in.

8 in.

■ **SOLUTION**

Step 1 To find lateral area and surface area, you need to find the slant height of the pyramid. This is represented by y in the second sketch at the right.

$4^2 + 6^2 = y^2$ ← **Use the Pythagorean Theorem.**

$y = \sqrt{52} = 2\sqrt{13}$

The slant height is $2\sqrt{13}$ in.

Step 2 Apply the formulas for lateral area and surface area.

$L.A. = 4[\frac{1}{2}(8 \times 2\sqrt{13})] = 32\sqrt{13} \rightarrow 32\sqrt{13}$ in.^{2}, or about 115.38 in.^{2}

$S.A. = 32\sqrt{13} + 8^2 = 64 + 32\sqrt{13} \rightarrow (64 + 32\sqrt{13})$ in.^{2}, or about 179.38 in.^{2}

Practice

Choose the numeral preceding the word or expression that best completes the statement or answers the question.

1 What is the surface area of a rectangular prism with length 20 m, width 6 m, and height 7 m?

(1) 604 m^2 **(3)** 564 m^2

(2) 456 m^2 **(4)** 744 m^2

2 Which is the lateral area of a regular square pyramid with base length 6 units and height 4 units?

(1) 12 units^2 **(3)** 84 units^2

(2) 60 units^2 **(4)** 96 units^2

In Exercises 3–4, find the surface area of each right prism. Round answers to the nearest tenth if necessary.

3

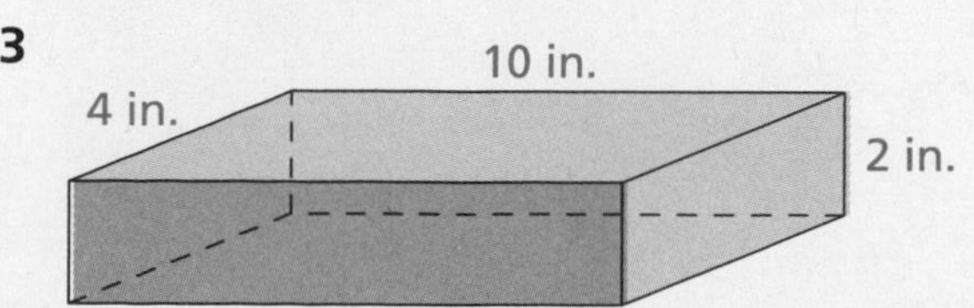

4

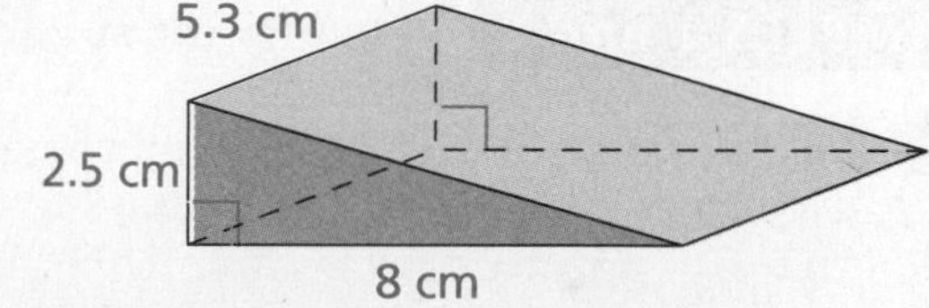

In Exercises 5–7, solve the problem. Clearly show all necessary work.

5 Find the lateral area of a regular pyramid whose base is a square, whose slant height is 5 m, and whose height is 3 m.

6 Find the lateral and surface area of the right rectangular prism whose length is 7.0 cm, width is 5.0 cm, and height is 1.5 cm.

7 Find the lateral and surface area of the regular square pyramid. Give exact answers.

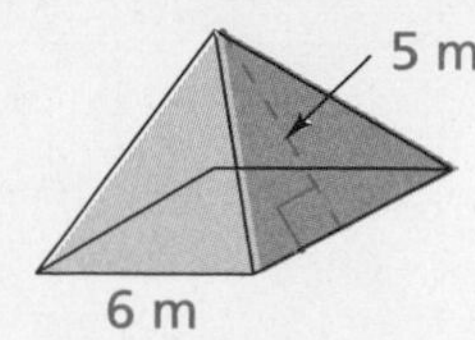

9.4 Lateral and Surface Areas of Cylinders and Cones

New York Standards

G.G.14 Properties of a cylinder

G.G.15 Properties of a right circular cone

A **cylinder** is a three-dimensional figure with two parallel **bases** bounded by congruent circles and a curved **lateral surface** that connects the circles. The **height** h of a cylinder is the length of any perpendicular segment drawn from a point on one base to the plane containing the other base. A cylinder is a **right cylinder** if the segment joining the centers of the bases is perpendicular to the planes of the bases. Otherwise, the cylinder is *oblique*.

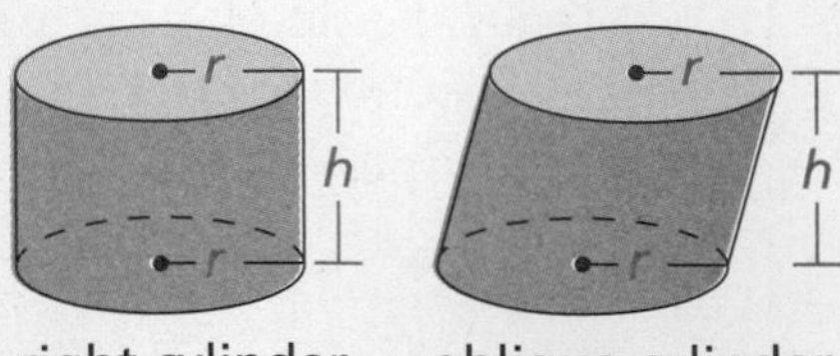

right cylinder   oblique cylinder

To derive area formulas for a right cylinder, imagine its net as shown at the right. Notice that the length of the lateral surface is equal to the circumference of a base.

Area Formulas for Cylinders

If a right cylinder has a height h and base with radius r, then the lateral area L.A. is given by this formula.

$$\text{L.A.} = 2\pi rh$$

The surface area S.A. is given by the following formula.

$$\text{S.A.} = \text{L.A.} + 2\pi r^2$$

EXAMPLES 1 and 2 Finding the surface area of a right cylinder

1 Find the surface area of a right cylinder with a radius of 4.5 ft and height 5 ft. Use $\pi = 3.14$.

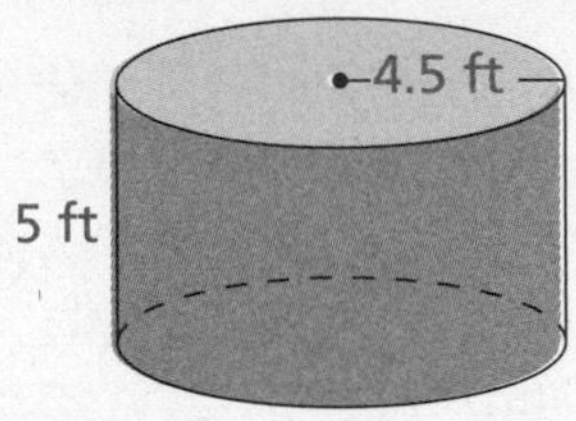

SOLUTION

$$\begin{aligned} \text{S.A.} &= 2\pi(4.5)(5) + 2\pi(4.5)^2 \\ &= 85.5\pi \\ &\approx 268.47 \end{aligned}$$

The surface area is 268.47 ft^2.

2 Find the surface area of a right cylinder with a diameter of 11 m and height 6 m. Use $\pi = 3.14$.

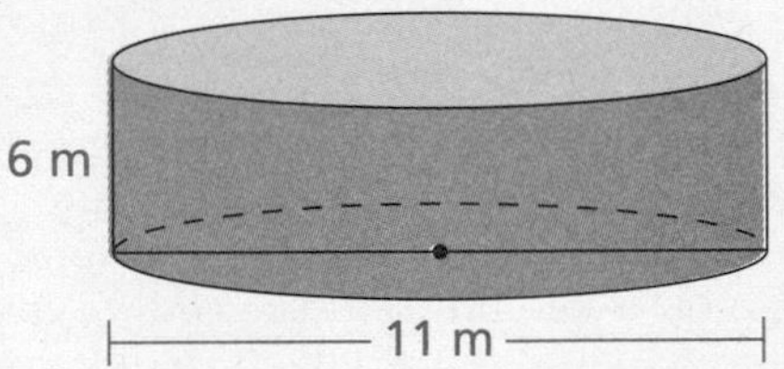

SOLUTION

$$\begin{aligned} \text{S.A.} &= 2\pi(5.5)(6) + 2\pi(5.5)^2 \leftarrow r = \tfrac{11}{2} \\ &= 126.5\pi \\ &\approx 397.21 \end{aligned}$$

The surface area is 397.21 m^2.

You can also use the formulas to solve problems that involve lateral and surface areas of a cylinder.

EXAMPLE 3 Finding the lateral and surface area of a cylinder

The can shown at the right is shaped like a right cylinder with no top base. It has a radius of 5 inches and a height of 7 inches. Estimate the lateral and total surface area of the outside of the can.

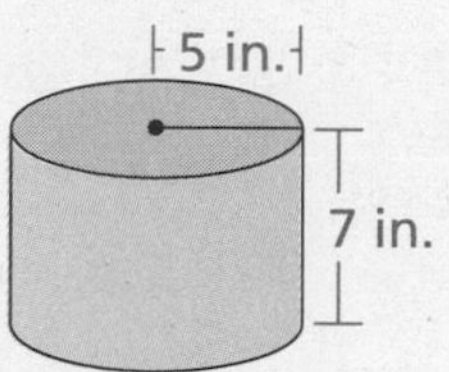

■ **SOLUTION**

Step 1 Estimate the lateral area of the can.

$$7(2 \times \pi \times 5) \approx 7(30) \approx 210$$

Step 2 Estimate the surface area of the can. Add the area of the bottom of the can.

$$210 + \pi \times 5^2 = 210 + 75$$
$$= 285$$

The lateral area $\approx$ 210 in.^{2} and the surface area $\approx$ 285 in.^{2}.

You can compare the properties of two different cylinders by evaluating their respective areas.

EXAMPLE 4 Comparing lateral areas

If the radius and height of a cylinder are doubled, then its lateral area

(1) stays the same.

(2) doubles.

(3) triples.

(4) quadruples.

■ **SOLUTION**

The lateral area of a cylinder is $2\pi rl$.

$$\text{L.A} = 2\pi rh$$

If you double the radius and height of the cylinder, you get

$$\text{L.A} = 2\pi(2r)(2h)$$
$$= 8\pi rh$$

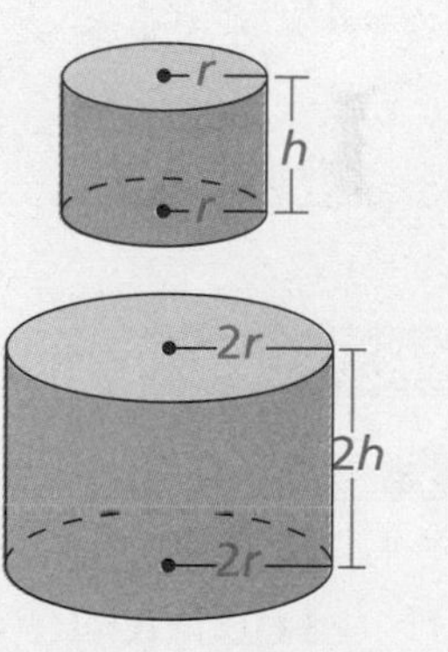

Notice that the lateral area is increased by a factor of 4. The lateral area is quadrupled, so the correct answer is (4).

A **cone** is a 3-dimensional figure with a circle as its base and a point outside the plane of the base called the **vertex.** The **lateral surface** is the curved surface that connects the vertex to each point on the boundary of the base. The **height** h of the cone is the perpendicular segment drawn from the vertex to the base of the cone.

A **right cone** is a cone whose height goes from the vertex to the center of the base. If a cone is not a right cone, it is called **oblique.**

The **slant height** *l* of the cone is the shortest line segment drawn from the vertex of the cone to any point on the circumference of the base.

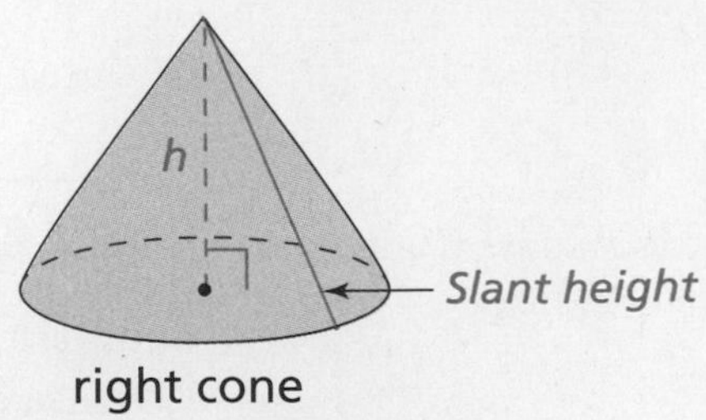

right cone

Note

You can generate a cone by rotating a right triangle around its height.

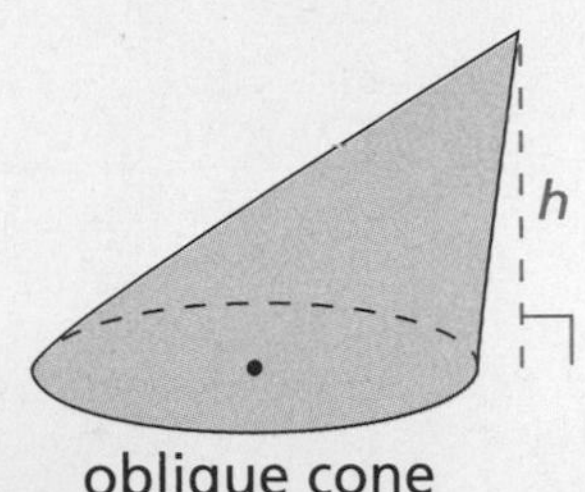

oblique cone

Lateral Area and Surface Area of a Right Cone

The lateral area L.A. of a right cone is half the product of the slant height (l) and the circumference of the base.

$$\text{L.A.} = \frac{1}{2}(2\pi r)l = \pi r l$$

The surface area S.A. is therefore L.A. + B where $B = \pi r^2$.

$$\text{S.A.} = \pi r l + \pi r^2 = \pi r(l + r)$$

EXAMPLE 5 **Finding lateral area and surface area of right cones**

5 Find the lateral and surface area of the cone to the right. (Answer may be left in terms of π.)

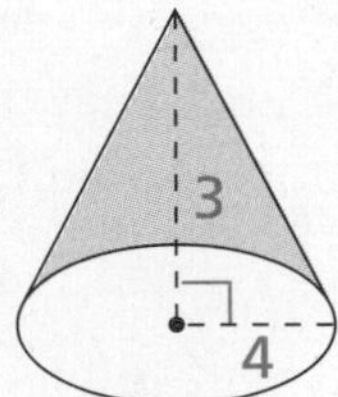

▪ SOLUTION

Notice that the radius of the base, the height, and the slant height are a Pythagorean triple. Therefore, the slant height $l = 5$.

$$\begin{aligned} \text{L.A.} &= \pi r l \\ &= \pi(4)(5) \\ &= 20\pi \text{ sq. units} \end{aligned}$$

$$\begin{aligned} \text{S.A.} &= \pi r l + \pi r^2 \\ &= (4)(5)\pi + 4^2\pi \\ &= 20\pi + 16\pi \\ &= 36\pi \text{ sq. units} \end{aligned}$$

Practice

Choose the numeral preceding the word or expression that best completes the statement or answers the question.

1 Find the lateral area of the cylinder below.

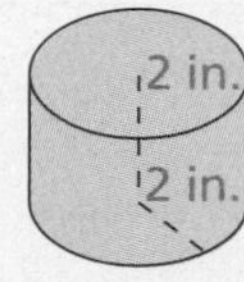

(1) 4π sq. in. (3) 8π sq. in.
(2) 6π sq. in. (4) 16π sq. in

2 A cone-shaped funnel has a height of 8 cm and a rim with a diameter of 12 cm. What is the lateral area of the funnel?

(1) 48π cm^2 (3) 96π cm^2
(2) 60π cm^2 (4) 120π cm^2

3 What is the lateral area of a cylinder with a height of 20 m and a radius of 7 m?

(1) 14π m^2 (3) 280π m^2
(2) 140π m^2 (4) 308π m^2

4 If the radius of a cylinder is doubled and the height remains constant, the lateral area is

(1) quadrupled.
(2) squared.
(3) doubled.
(4) tripled.

In Exercises 5–6, find the surface area of each right cylinder. Round your answer to the nearest tenth.

5

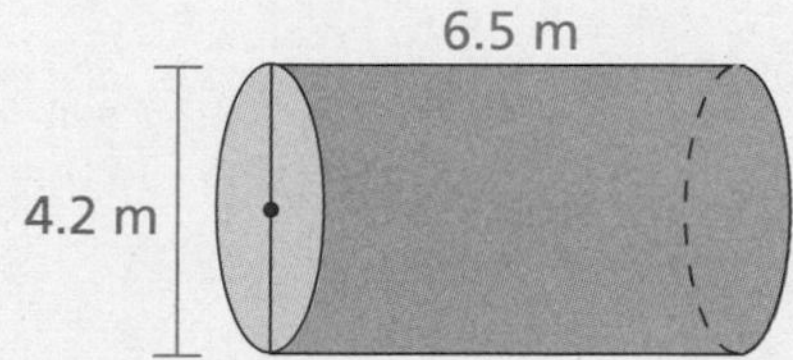

6

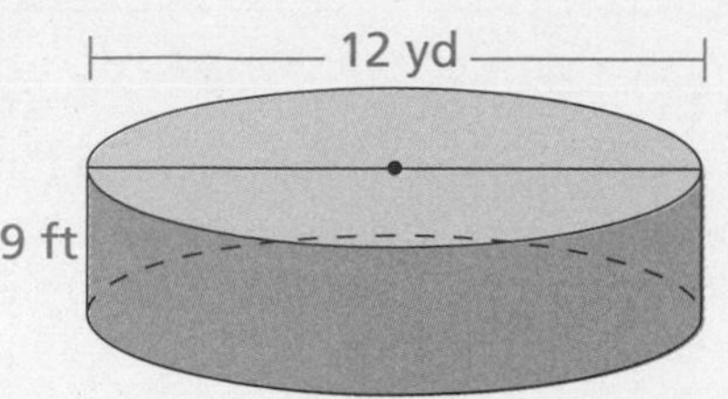

7 Find the lateral area of the cone below to the nearest tenth.

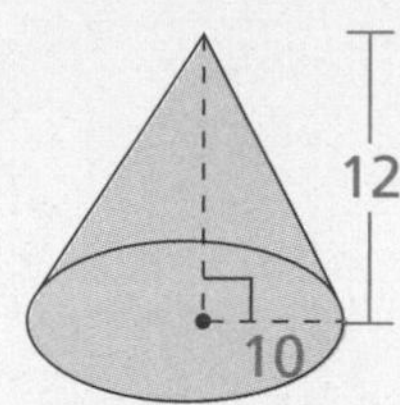

In Exercises 8–9, find the lateral or surface area as specified. Give exact answers.

8 the lateral area of a right cylinder with equal radius and height of 10 in.

9 the surface area of a right cylinder with radius 2.8 cm and height 6 cm.

10 One paint roller has length 11 in. and diameter 2 in. A second roller has length 7 in. and diameter 3 in. Which roller can spread more paint in one revolution?

11 One gallon of paint covers 250 ft^2. How many gallons of paint are needed to paint the top and lateral face of a right cylinder with radius 4.4 ft and height 9 ft? Give your answer to the nearest quarter of a gallon.

12 How does the lateral area of a cone with radius 6 and slant height of 12 compare to the lateral area of a cylinder with a height of 12 and a radius of 6?

13 A right cone has a base with radius of 6 cm and height of 8 cm. What are the dimensions of a cylinder that has the same surface area?

14 A right triangle with height of 5 cm and base of 3 cm is rotated about its height. What is the lateral area of the resulting figure, to the nearest square cm?

9.5 Volume of Selected Geometric Figures

New York Standards

G.G.11 Properties of prisms with equal volumes
G.G.12 Calculating the volume of a prism
G.G.13 Properties of a regular pyramid
G.G.14 Properties of a cylinder
G.G.15 Properties of a right circular cone

Consider the area of a rectangle, $A = lw$, and try to visualize the rectangle as the base of a 3-dimensional rectangle, with identical rectangles stacked on top to give it its *height*. This is known as a rectangular prism. It is easy to deduce that since the area of a rectangle is lw, the volume of a rectangular prism is $V = lwh$.

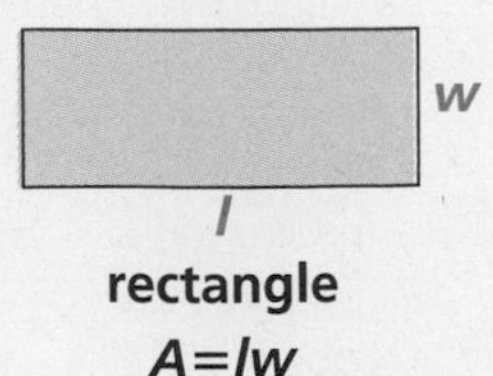

rectangle
A=lw

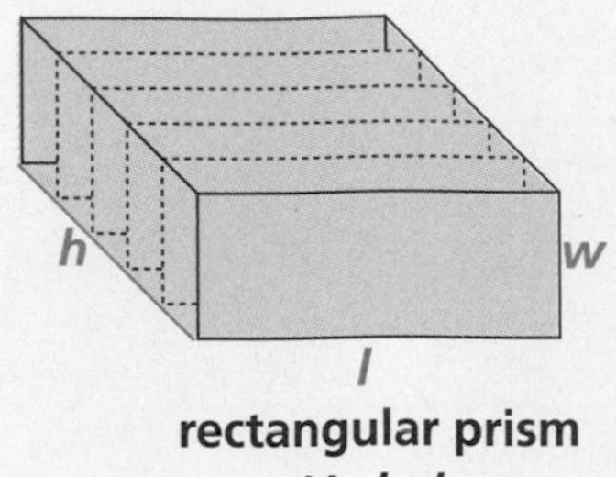

rectangular prism
V=lwh

The **volume** of a three-dimensional figure is the amount of space it encloses.

Note

Area is two-dimensional and is measured in square units. Since volume involves all three dimensions, it is measured in cubic units.

Volume of a Prism

The volume V of a prism is the product of the area B of a base and the height h of the prism.

$$V = Bh$$

Note

A **prism** is a polyhedron with two congruent and parallel faces, called *bases*. The *lateral faces* of a prism are parallelograms.

In the special case of a right rectangular prism with length l, width w, and height h, you can show that a formula for volume V is $V = (lw)h$, or simply $V = lwh$.

A **cube** is a prism whose faces are bounded by six congruent squares. The edges of a cube are all congruent to each other. For a cube with edges of length e, you can further refine the formula for volume as $V = (e^2)e$, or $V = e^3$.

EXAMPLES 1 and 2 **Finding the volume of a prism**

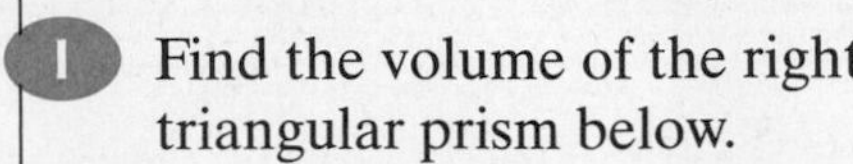

1 Find the volume of the right triangular prism below.

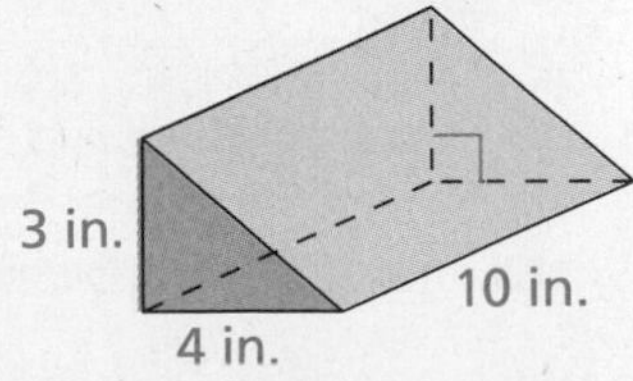

SOLUTION

$V = (\frac{1}{2} \times 4 \times 3) \times 10 = 60 \leftarrow V = Bh$

The volume is 60 in.^{3}.

2 Find the volume of the right rectangular prism below.

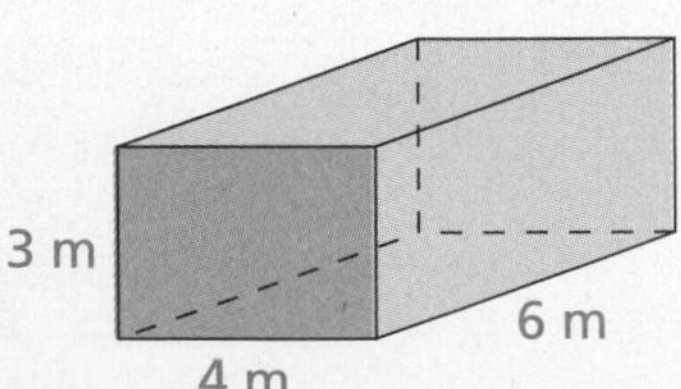

SOLUTION

$V = 3 \times 4 \times 6 = 72 \leftarrow V = lwh$

The volume is 72 m^3.

You can calculate the volume of prisms by multiplying the base by the height. That is, $V = Bh$. If 2 or more prisms have bases of equal area and equal heights, then their volumes will be equal.

EXAMPLE 3 **Comparing volumes of prisms**

3 Find the volume of the prisms below.

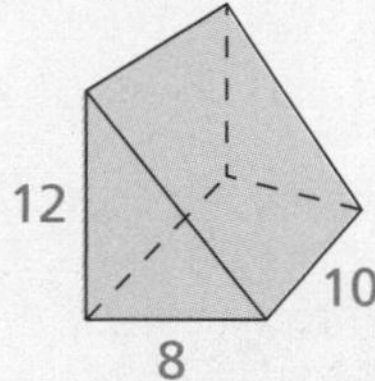

triangular prism

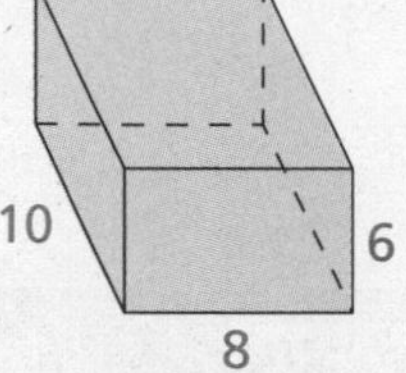

rectangular prism

SOLUTION

$V_{triangular\ prism} = (\frac{1}{2} \times 12 \times 8)(10) \leftarrow V = Bh$

$= 480$ cu. units

SOLUTION

$V_{rectangular\ prism} = (8 \times 6)(10) \leftarrow V = Bh$

$= 480$ cu. units

The volume of a cylinder is calculated by multiplying the area of the base of the cylinder by the height of the cylinder. The formula for the volume of a cylinder is similar to the formula for the volume of a prism.

Volume of a Cylinder

The volume V of a cylinder with base of radius r is the product of the area B of a base and the height h of the cylinder.

$$V = Bh, \text{ or } V = \pi r^2 h$$

You can find the volume of a cylinder by using its radius or diameter.

Go Online
PHSchool.com
Visit: PHSchool.com
Web Code: ayp-0463

EXAMPLES 4 and 5 **Finding the volume of a cylinder**

Find the volume of each cylinder. Round your answer to the nearest tenth.

4

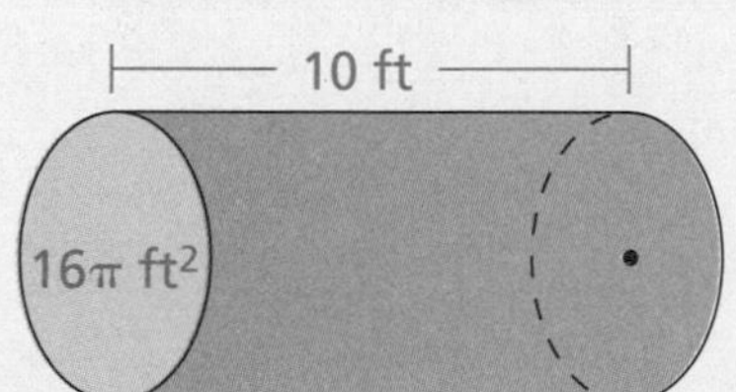

SOLUTION

$V = (16\pi)(10) \quad \leftarrow V = Bh$

$= 160\pi$

≈ 502.4

The volume is 502.4 ft^3.

5

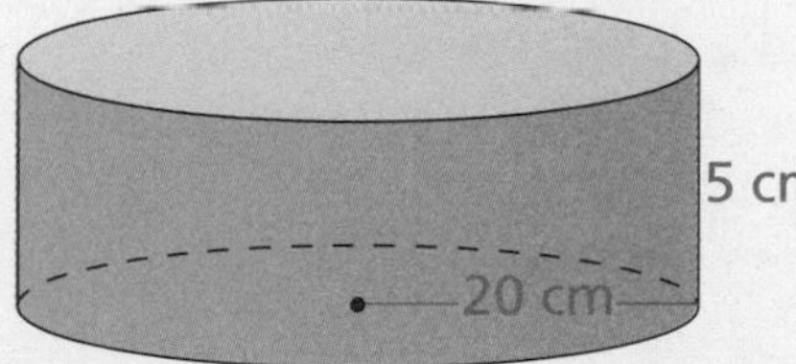

SOLUTION

$V = \pi(20)^2(5) \quad \leftarrow V = \pi r^2 h$

$= 2000\pi$

≈ 6283.2

The volume is 6283.2 cm^3.

If you compare a cone to a cylinder with the same base and height, you find that the cylinder is exactly three times the volume of the cone, or the cone is $\frac{1}{3}$ the volume of the cylinder.

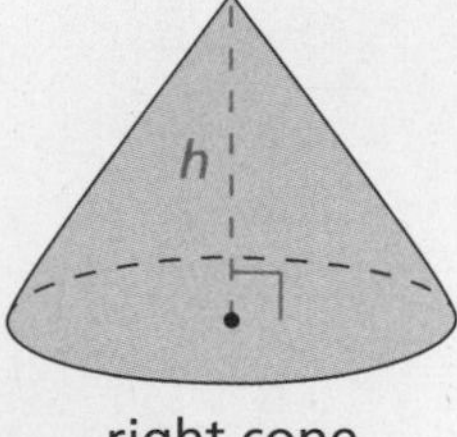

right cone

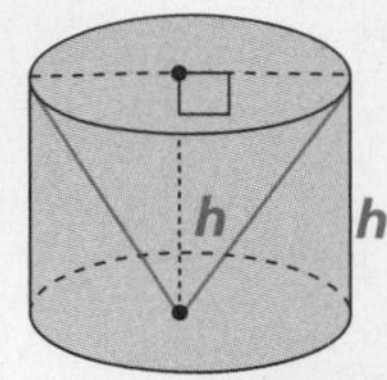

Volume of a Cone

The volume V of a right cone with radius of the base r and height h is given by $V = \frac{1}{3}\pi r^2 h$.

EXAMPLE 6 **Finding the volume of a right cone given radius of the base and slant height**

6 Find the volume of a right cone whose base has radius 6 cm and whose slant height is 10 cm. Round your answer to the nearest hundredth.

■ **SOLUTION**

To find the volume of a right cone, find its height h.

$$h^2 + 6^2 = 10^2 \leftarrow h^2 + r^2 = \ell^2$$

$$h = 8$$

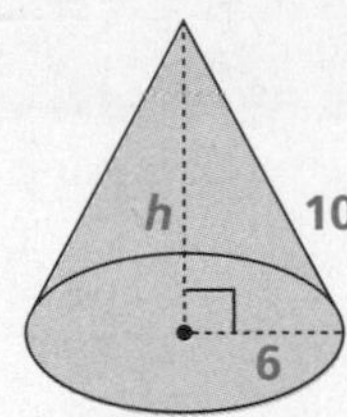

Apply the formula for volume.

$$V = \frac{1}{3}\pi(6)^2(8) = 96\pi = 301.44$$

The volume is 301.44 cm^3.

Volume of a Pyramid

The volume of a pyramid is $\frac{1}{3}$ the volume of a prism with the same base and height. Therefore, the $V_{\text{pyramid}} = \frac{1}{3}Bh$, where B is the area of the base.

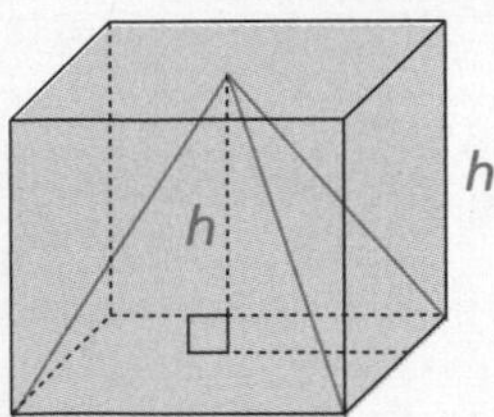

If you examine the two right rectangular prisms on the next page, you will see that the length, width, and height of figure B are all 1.5 times the corresponding dimensions of figure A. That is, the prisms are similar, with similarity ratio 1.5.

If you compare the volumes of the two figures, you will see a special relationship between them.

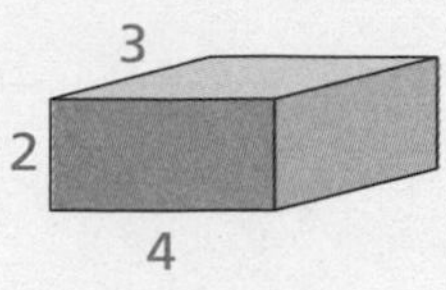

Figure *A*

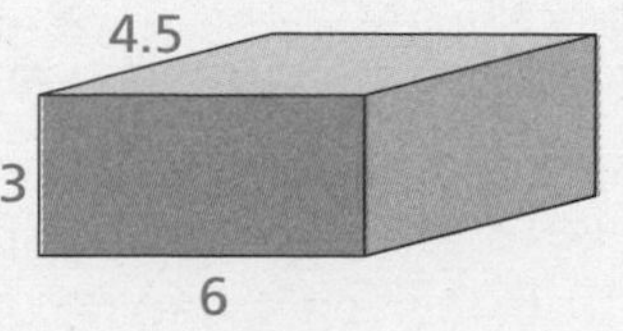

Figure *B*

Volume of Figure $A = 2 \times 3 \times 4 = 24$ cubic units

Volume of Figure $B = 2(1.5) \times 3(1.5) \times 4(1.5)$
$= 24 \times 1.5^3$ cubic units

Similarity and Volume

If figure B is similar to figure A, and the linear dimensions of figure B are s times the linear dimensions of figure A, then:

$$\text{volume of figure } B = s^3 \times \text{ volume of figure } A$$

Practice

Choose the numeral preceding the word or expression that best completes the statement or answers the question.

1 If the volume of a triangular prism is 256 in^3. and its height is 8 in., what is the area of the base of a rectangular prism of equal volume?

(1) 32 in.^{2} **(3)** 64 in.^{2}
(2) 32 in.^{3} **(4)** 64 in.^{3}

2 Find the volume of the figure at the right.

(1) $\frac{640\pi}{3}$ cm^3
(2) 1920π cm^3
(3) $\frac{6400\pi}{3}$ cm^3
(4) 2560π cm^3

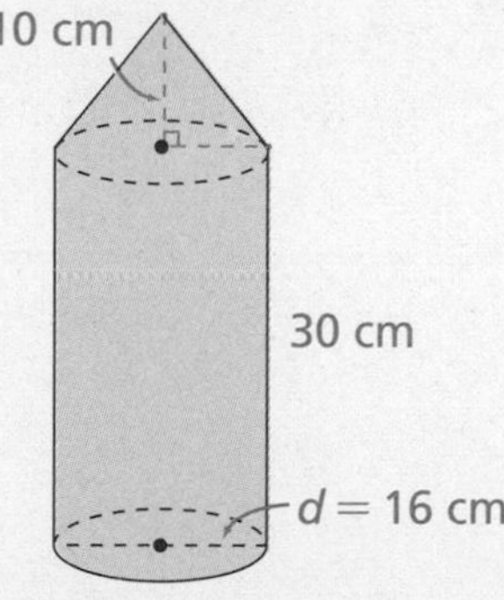

3 What is the volume of the figure at the right?

(1) 1062.3 cm^3
(2) 979.2 cm^3
(3) 538.9 cm^3
(4) 1931.2 cm^3

4 The volume of a right rectangular prism is 20 in.^{3} The linear dimensions of a larger prism are 2 times those of the original prism. Which is the volume of the larger prism?

(1) 40 in.^{3} **(3)** 160 in.^{3}
(2) 80 in.^{3} **(4)** 8000 in.^{3}

In Exercises 5–7, solve the problem. Clearly show all necessary work.

5 A small can of soup is shaped like a right cylinder with diameter 7 cm and height 12 cm. A family-size can of the soup has diameter 10 cm and height 15 cm. Which contains more soup, two small cans or one family-size can?

6 What is the volume of a right rectangular prism with length 12 ft, width 15 ft, and height 3 ft?

7 Find the weight of the contents of a right rectangular prism with length 13 ft, width 6 ft, and height 2.5 ft if the contents weigh 0.02 pounds per cubic inch.

9.6 Surface Area and Volume of Spheres

New York Standards

G.G.16 Properties of a sphere

If you rotated a circle around its center, you would produce a sphere. A **sphere** is the set of all points in 3-dimensional space that are a fixed distance r, the **radius,** from a given point, O, the **center.**

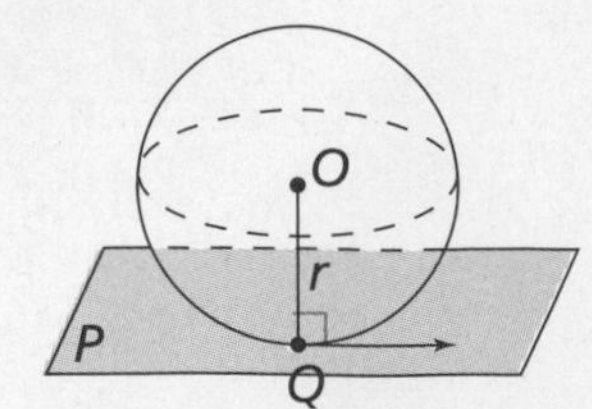

Plane P is tangent to the sphere at Q.

If a plane intersects a sphere at only one point, the plane is **tangent** to the sphere. A tangent plane is perpendicular to the radius of the sphere at the point of intersection.

A plane that intersects a sphere at more than one point will intersect it at an infinite number of points; the intersection will form a circle.

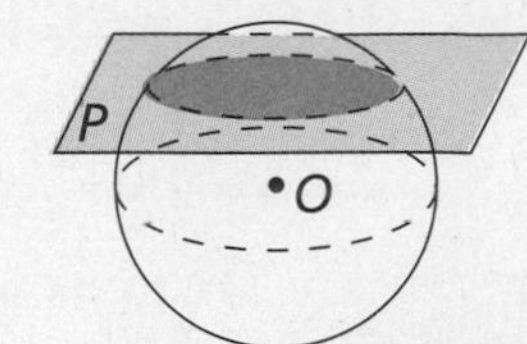

If the plane intersects a sphere and passes through the center of the sphere, the intersection is called the **great circle.** The great circle is the largest circle that can be drawn in a sphere.

The circumference of a sphere is the circumference of any great circle of the sphere. A great circle divides a sphere into 2 **hemispheres.**

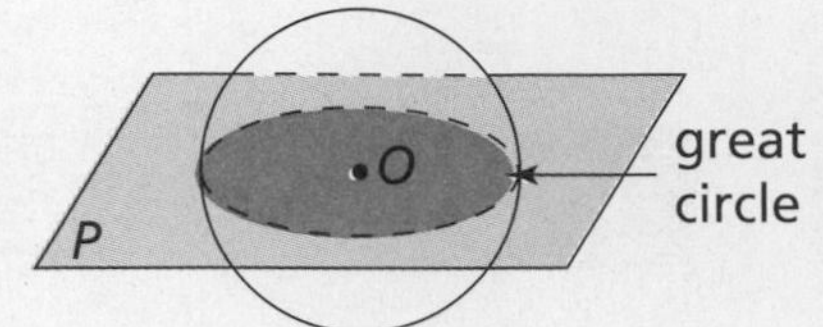

In the figure below, plane X and plane Y are parallel planes that intersect a sphere at 2 circles. If plane X and plane Y are also equidistant from the center of the sphere, then their intersection with the sphere results in 2 congruent circles.

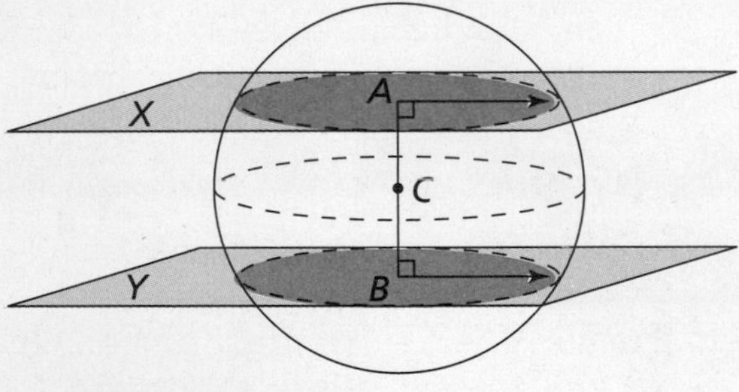

plane $X \parallel$ plane Y
$AC \cong CB$
circle $A \cong$ circle B

EXAMPLE 1 Applying the properties of spheres

If the circumference of a great circle of a sphere is 350 cm, find its radius to the nearest tenth.

SOLUTION

$C = 2\pi r$

$350 = 2\pi r \leftarrow$ Substitute $C = 350$

$\frac{350}{2\pi} = r$

$r = 55.7$ cm

You can use this formula to find the volume of a sphere. You can find the volume of a sphere if you are given indirect information about the radius, such as the diameter or the circumference of the sphere.

Volume of a Sphere

The volume V of a sphere with radius r is given by $V = \frac{4}{3}\pi r^3$.

Go Online PHSchool.com
Visit: PHSchool.com
Web Code: ayp-0465

EXAMPLES 2 through 4 **Finding the volume of a sphere**

2 Find the volume of a sphere with a radius of 12 ft. Round your answer to the nearest hundredth.

SOLUTION

$$V = \frac{4}{3}\pi r^3 \rightarrow \frac{4}{3}\pi(12)^3 = 2304\pi \approx 7234.56$$

The volume is 7234.56 ft^3.

3 Find the volume of a sphere with a diameter of 15 cm. Round your answer to the nearest hundredth.

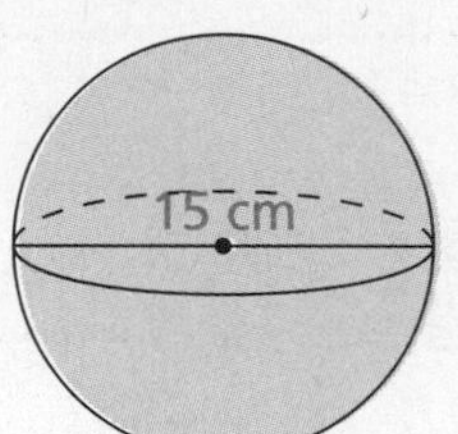

SOLUTION

The diameter is twice the radius, therefore $r = \frac{15}{2} = 7.5$.

$$V = \frac{4}{3}\pi r^3 \rightarrow \frac{4}{3}\pi(7.5)^3 = 562.5\pi \approx 1766.25 \text{ cm}^3$$

4 Find the volume of a sphere with a circumference of 6π m. Use 3.14 for π and round your answer to the nearest hundredth.

SOLUTION

The circumference is $6\pi = 2\pi r$, therefore $r = \frac{6\pi}{2\pi} = 3$.

$$V = \frac{4}{3}\pi r^3 \rightarrow \frac{4}{3}\pi(3)^3 = 36\pi \approx 113.04 \text{ m}^3$$

You can calculate the surface area of a sphere using the following formula.

Note
The area A of a circle with radius r is πr^2.

Surface Area of a Sphere

The surface area S.A. of a sphere with radius r is given by S.A. $= 4\pi r^2$.

Notice that the surface area of a sphere is 4 times the area of its great circle.

EXAMPLE 5 **Finding the surface area of a sphere**

5 Find the surface area of a sphere with a radius of 7 ft. Round your answer to the nearest hundredth.

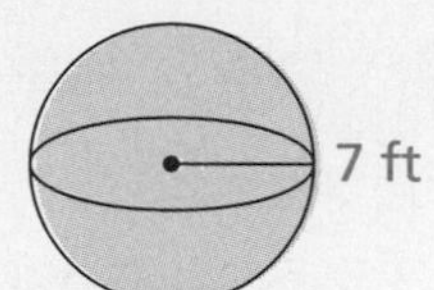

SOLUTION

$$\begin{aligned} \text{S.A.} &= 4\pi r^2 \\ &= 4\pi(7^2) && \leftarrow \text{Substitute } r = 7 \\ &= 4\pi(49) \\ &= 615.75 \text{ ft}^2 \end{aligned}$$

The volume of a sphere is completely determined by its radius. Suppose that sphere A has radius r and sphere B has radius $2r$. Then you can compare the volume V_B of sphere B to the volume V_A of sphere A as follows.

$$\frac{V_B}{V_A} = \frac{\frac{4}{3}\pi(2r)^3}{\frac{4}{3}\pi(r)^3} = \frac{(2r)^3}{r^3} = \frac{2^3r^3}{r^3} = 2^3$$

So, if the radius is doubled, then the volume is multiplied by 2^3.

Note

If the radius r of a sphere is multiplied by a, then the volume of the sphere with radius ra is a^3 times that of the sphere with radius r.

Similarity and Volume of a Sphere

If two spheres have radii of r_1 and r_2, then the ratio of their volumes is $\left(\frac{r_1}{r_2}\right)^3$.

Practice

Choose the numeral preceding the word or expression that best completes the statement or answers the question.

1 At how many points will a plane 5 units from the center of a sphere with radius 5 intersect the sphere?

(1) 0

(2) 1

(3) 2

(4) 3

2 If the intersection of 2 parallel planes with a sphere results in 2 congruent circles, then

(1) one plane is tangent to the sphere.

(2) both planes are tangent to the sphere

(3) both planes contain the center of the sphere

(4) the planes are equidistant from the center of the sphere.

3 The surface area of a sphere can be found by finding the area of a great circle and multiplying it by

(1) 1.

(2) 2.

(3) 3.

(4) 4.

4 What is the surface area of a sphere with $r = 2$m? Use 3.14 for π and round your answer to the nearest tenth.

(1) 12.6 m^2

(2) 33.5 m^2

(3) 50.2 m^2

(4) 100.5 m^2

5 Find the volume of the sphere shown below.

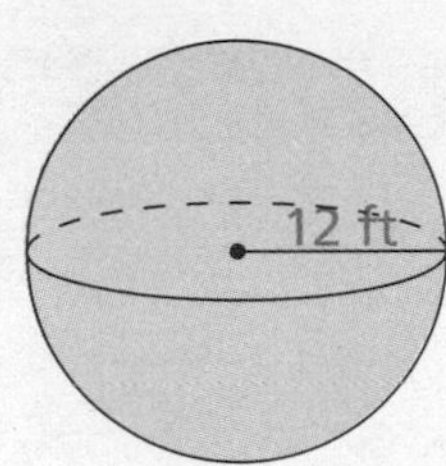

(1) 7238.23 ft^3

(2) 2412.74 ft^3

(3) 3619.11 ft^3

(4) 1809.56 ft^3

6 Which has the same volume as a sphere with radius 6?

(1) a cylinder with radius 4 and height 16

(2) a cone with radius 6 and height 24

(3) a cube whose edges are 6

(4) a pyramid with base area 36 units^2 and height 6

In Exercises 7–8, find the exact surface area and volume of each sphere.

7 a sphere whose diameter is 10 in.

8 a sphere with a circumference of 144π cm

In Exercises 9–12, solve the following problems. Clearly show all necessary work.

9 Find the volume of the sphere shown here. The circle contains the center of the sphere and its radius is the same as the radius of the sphere. Give an exact answer and an answer rounded to the nearest tenth.

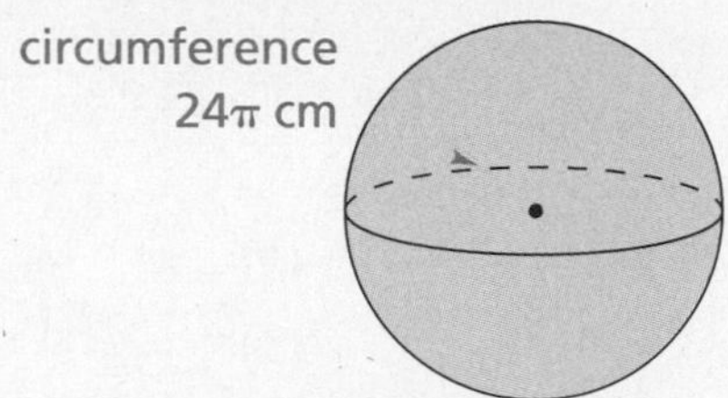

10 The sphere in the diagram below is tangent to the bases and lateral side of the cylinder. Find the volume of the space inside the cylinder but outside the sphere.

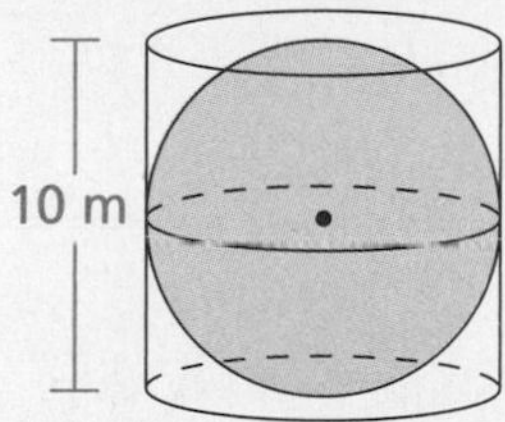

11 A sphere has a volume of 85.3π cm^3. What is the volume of a sphere with a radius that is 3 times longer?

12 The volume of a sphere is 8π ft^3. What is the radius of the sphere?

In the figure below, plane *X* intersects the sphere at point *P*. Use this information to answer Exercises 13–15.

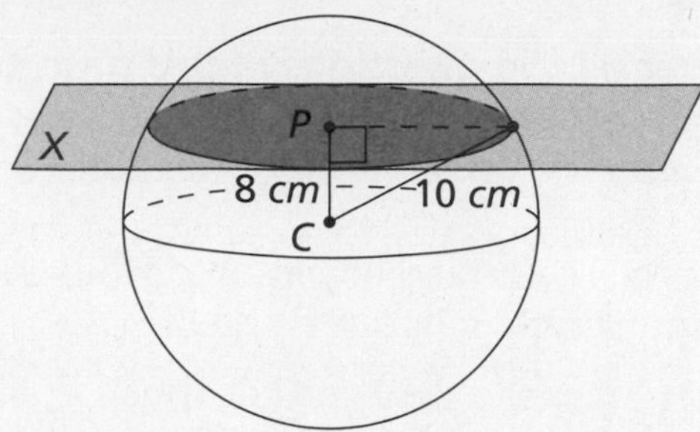

13 What is the circumference of the circle formed by the intersection of plane X with the sphere?

14 What is the circumference of the great circle of the sphere?

15 Plane Y is parallel to plane X. The area of the circle formed by the intersection of plane Y with the sphere is 36π cm^2. How far is plane Y from plane X?

16 The great circle of a sphere has an area of 25π in^2. What is the surface area of the sphere?

17 Find the area of the great circle of a sphere that has a volume of 36π cm^3.

18 The great circle of a sphere has a circumference of 18π. The circle formed by the intersection of a plane parallel to the great circle of the sphere is $\frac{1}{3}$ the circumference of the great circle. How far is this plane from the center of the sphere?

19 Lisa has a hoop that measures 9 inches in diameter. What is the volume of the largest ball that can fit through her hoop?

20 The volume of a spherical balloon is 36π ft^3. If the balloon expands so that the radius is doubled, what is the change in the balloon's surface area?

Chapter 9 Preparing for the New York Geometry Exam

Answer all the questions in this part. For each question, select the numeral preceding the word or expression that best completes the statement or answers the question.

1 If the radius and height of a cylinder are doubled then its lateral area

(1) stays the same. **(3)** triples.

(2) doubles. **(4)** quadruples.

2 Find the number of 3 ft × 2 ft × 1 ft boxes that can be packed in the prism below.

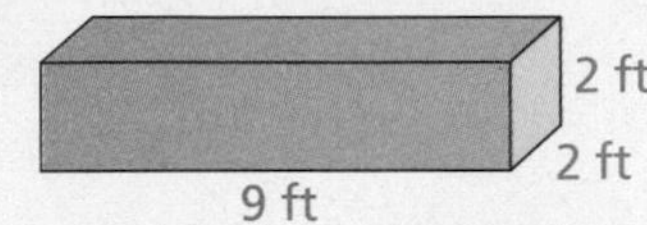

(1) 6 **(3)** 2

(2) 3 **(4)** 4

3 The volume of a right cylinder is 245 cm^3. If the radius of the cylinder is 5.5 cm, find its height to the nearest tenth.

(1) 2.1 cm **(3)** 2.4 cm

(2) 2.6 cm **(4)** 3.6 cm

4 If a plane intersects 2 parallel planes, the intersection is

(1) a line.

(2) a plane.

(3) 3 points.

(4) 2 parallel lines.

5 Find the surface area of the cone below.

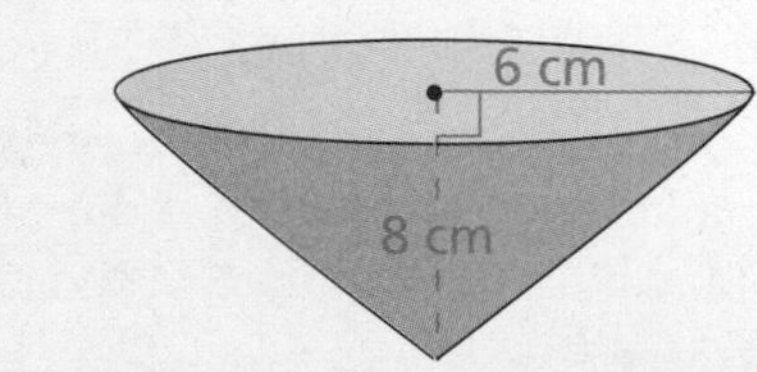

(1) 96π cm^3 **(3)** 60π cm^3

(2) 72π cm^3 **(4)** 36π cm^3

6 Which could be the dimensions of a right rectangular prism that has the same volume as a right rectangular prism with volume 132 cubic units?

(1) length 11, width 2, and height 5

(2) length 12, width 6, and height 2

(3) length 11, width 2, and height 6

(4) length 11, width 2, and height 12

7 Find the volume of the cylinder to the nearest tenth.

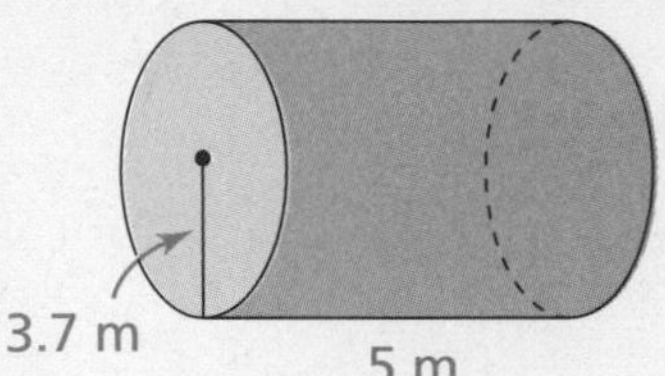

(1) 54.95 m^3 **(3)** 192.3 m^3

(2) 61.3 m^3 **(4)** 215.0 m^3

8 Find the weight of the contents of a right rectangular prism with length 15 ft, width 3 ft, and height 3.5 ft if the contents weigh 0.25 pounds per cubic ft.

(1) 39.375 pounds

(2) 630 pounds

(3) 33.75 pounds

(4) 540 pounds

9 The cone-shaped paper cup has a height 9 cm and a rim with circumference 12π cm. What is the approximate volume of the cup?

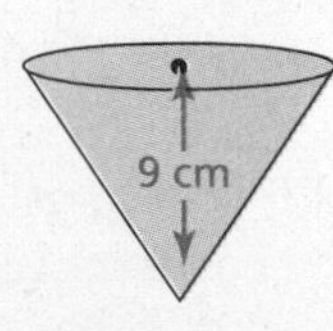

(1) 169.56 cm^3 **(3)** 508.68 cm^3

(2) 339.29 cm^3 **(4)** 1017.36 cm^3

10 Two lines perpendicular to the same plane must be

(1) skew.

(2) coplanar.

(3) intersecting.

(4) perpendicular.

11 A rectangular fish tank has dimensions 2.5 ft × 2 ft × 1.5 ft. It is packed in a 3 ft × 4 ft × 3 ft box. How much filler is needed to securely package the aquarium for shipping?

(1) 2.5 ft^3 **(3)** 42 ft^3

(2) 4 ft^3 **(4)** 28.5 ft^3

12 A can has a diameter of 3 inches and a height of 4.5 inches. Approximately how much paper will it take to create the label for the can?

(1) 84.78 $in.^2$

(2) 42.41 $in.^2$

(3) 31.79 $in.^2$

(4) 127.17 $in.^2$

13 The length of each side of the base of the Pyramid of Cheops originally measured 756 ft and its slant height was 482 ft. Find the lateral area of the pyramid when it was built.

(1) 926,100 ft^2

(2) 728,784 ft^2

(3) 927,315 ft^2

(4) 730,296 ft^2

14 If the lateral area of a right cylinder with a 1 ft radius is 9π ft^2, what is its height?

(1) 6 ft

(2) 2.9 ft

(3) 4.5 ft

(4) 0.9 ft

15 Which best describes the prism below?

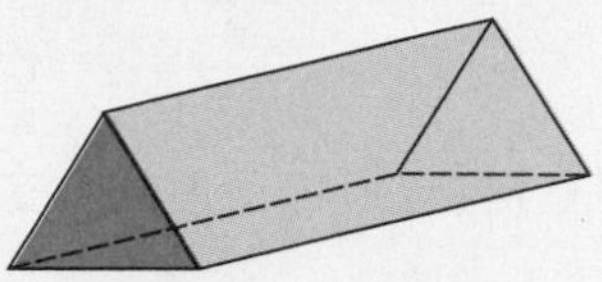

(1) triangular prism

(2) rectangular prism

(3) triangular pyramid

(4) rectangular pyramid

16 A cylinder has one lateral face. What is the shape of its face?

(1) circle

(2) square

(3) rectangle

(4) triangle

17 A right triangular prism has how many lateral faces?

(1) 1 **(3)** 3

(2) 2 **(4)** 4

18 Which solid is constructed from the net below?

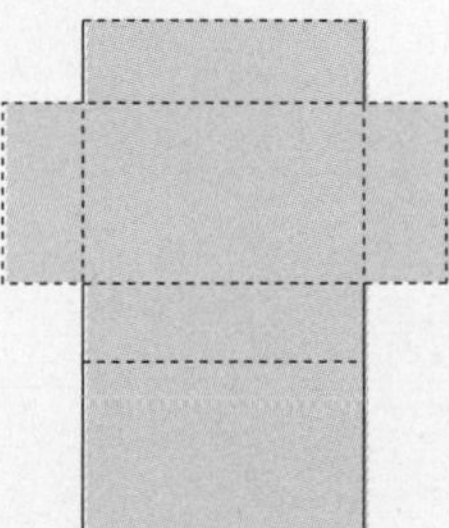

(1) rectangular prism

(2) triangular prism

(3) cylinder

(4) square pyramid

Answer all the questions in this part. Clearly indicate the necessary steps, including appropriate formula substitutions, diagrams, graphs, charts, etc. For all questions in this part, a correct numerical answer with no work shown will receive only one credit.

19 Find the volume of the entire figure below.

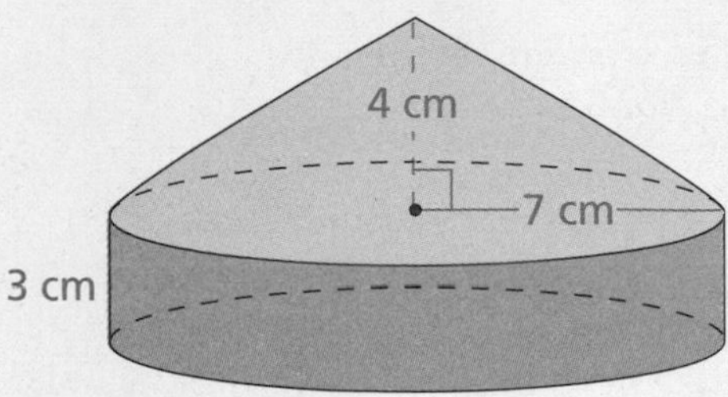

20 A rubber ball has a circumference of 22 in.

Find the radius of the rubber ball.

Find the surface area of the rubber ball.

Find the volume of the rubber ball.

Round your answers to the nearest tenth.

21 A circular water tank has a diameter of 8 ft and stands 5.5 ft high.

Find the lateral area of the water tank. (Round your answer to the nearest tenth.)

If a company charges $11 per square foot of surface area to install the water tank, how much will the installation cost?

If the pool is to be filled only to 75% of its maximum capacity, how much water can it hold?

COMMON CORE STATE STANDARDS

Common Core Standards in the New York Geometry Brief Review

***indicates modeling standards**

Number and Quantity

The Complex Number System N.CN

Represent complex numbers and their operations on the complex plane

N.CN.6 (+) Calculate the distance between numbers in the complex plane as the modulus of the difference, and the midpoint of a segment as the average of the numbers at its endpoints.

Algebra

Reasoning with Equations and Inequalities A.REI

Solve systems of equations

A.REI.7 Solve a simple system consisting of a linear equation and a quadratic equation in two variables algebraically and graphically. *For example, find the points of intersection between the line* $y = -3x$ *and the circle* $x^2 + y^2 = 3$.

Functions

Trigonometric Functions F.TF

Prove and apply trigonometric identities

F.TF.8 Prove the Pythagorean identity $\sin^2(\theta) + \cos^2(\theta) = 1$ and use it to find $\sin(\theta)$, $\cos(\theta)$, or $\tan(\theta)$ given $\sin(\theta)$, $\cos(\theta)$, or $\tan(\theta)$ and the quadrant of the angle.

Geometry

Congruence G.CO

Experiment with transformations in the plane

G.CO.4 Develop definitions of rotations, reflections, and translations in terms of angles, circles, perpendicular lines, parallel lines, and line segments.

G.CO.5 Given a geometric figure and a rotation, reflection, or translation, draw the transformed figure using, e.g., graph paper, tracing paper, or geometry software. Specify a sequence of transformations that will carry a given figure onto another.

Understand congruence in terms of rigid motions

G.CO.6 Use geometric descriptions of rigid motions to transform figures and to predict the effect of a given rigid motion on a given figure; given two figures, use the definition of congruence in terms of rigid motions to decide if they are congruent.

G.CO.8 Explain how the criteria for triangle congruence (ASA, SAS, and SSS) follow from the definition of congruence in terms of rigid motions.

Prove geometric theorems

G.CO.9 Prove theorems about lines and angles. *Theorems include: vertical angles are congruent; when a transversal crosses parallel lines, alternate interior angles are congruent and corresponding angles are congruent; points on a perpendicular bisector of a line segment are exactly those equidistant from the segment's endpoints.*

G.CO.10 Prove theorems about triangles. *Theorems include: measures of interior angles of a triangle sum to 180°; base angles of isosceles triangles are congruent; the segment joining midpoints of two sides of a triangle is parallel to the third side and half the length; the medians of a triangle meet at a point.*

G.CO.11 Prove theorems about parallelograms. *Theorems include: opposite sides are congruent, opposite angles are congruent, the diagonals of a parallelogram bisect each other, and conversely, rectangles are parallelograms with congruent diagonals.*

Make geometric constructions

G.CO.12 Make formal geometric constructions with a variety of tools and methods (compass and straightedge, string, reflective devices, paper folding, dynamic geometric software, etc.). *Copying a segment; copying an angle; bisecting a segment; bisecting an angle; constructing perpendicular lines, including the perpendicular bisector of a line segment; and constructing a line parallel to a given line through a point not on the line.*

G.CO.13 Construct an equilateral triangle, a square, and a regular hexagon inscribed in a circle.

Similarity, Right Triangles, and Trigonometry G.SRT

Understand similarity in terms of similarity transformations

G.SRT.1.b Verify experimentally the properties of dilations given by a center and a scale factor: The dilation of a line segment is longer or shorter in the ratio given by the scale factor.

Prove theorems involving similarity

G.SRT.4 Prove theorems about triangles. *Theorems include: a line parallel to one side of a triangle divides the other two proportionally, and conversely; the Pythagorean Theorem proved using triangle similarity.*

G.SRT.5 Use congruence and similarity criteria for triangles to solve problems and to prove relationships in geometric figures.

Define trigonometric ratios and solve problems involving right triangles

G.SRT.8 Use trigonometric ratios and the Pythagorean Theorem to solve right triangles in applied problems.*

Circles G.C

Understand and apply theorems about circles

G.C.2 Identify and describe relationships among inscribed angles, radii, and chords. *Include the relationship between central, inscribed, and circumscribed angles; inscribed angles on a diameter are right angles; the radius of a circle is perpendicular to the tangent where the radius intersects the circle.*

Find arc lengths and areas of sectors of circles

G.C.5 Derive using similarity the fact that the length of the arc intercepted by an angle is proportional to the radius, and define the radian measure of the angle as the constant of proportionality; derive the formula for the area of a sector.

Expressing Geometric Properties with Equations G.GPE

Translate between the geometric description and the equation for a conic section

G.GPE.1 Derive the equation of a circle of given center and radius using the Pythagorean Theorem; complete the square to find the center and radius of a circle given by an equation.

Use coordinates to prove simple geometric theorems algebraically

G.GPE.4 Use coordinates to prove simple geometric theorems algebraically. *For example, prove or disprove that a figure defined by four given points in the coordinate plane is a rectangle; prove or disprove that the point (1,* $\sqrt{3}$*) lies on the circle centered at the origin and containing the point (0, 2).*

G.GPE.5 Prove the slope criteria for parallel and perpendicular lines and use them to solve geometric problems (e.g., find the equation of a line parallel or perpendicular to a given line that passes through a given point).

G.GPE.7 Use coordinates to compute perimeters of polygons and areas of triangles and rectangles, e.g., using the distance formula.*

Geometric Measurement and Dimension G.GMD

Explain volume formulas and use them to solve problems

G.GMD.3 Use volume formulas for cylinders, pyramids, cones, and spheres to solve problems.*

Glossary

GLOSSARY

Acute angle An angle whose measure is greater than 0° and less than 90°.

Acute triangle A triangle that has three acute angles.

Adjacent angles Two coplanar angles that share a common side and a common vertex, but have no interior points in common.

Alternate exterior angles A pair of nonadjacent exterior angles on opposite sides of a transversal.

Alternate Exterior Angles Theorem If two parallel lines are cut by a transversal, then alternate exterior angles are congruent.

Alternate interior angles A pair of nonadjacent interior angles on opposite sides of a transversal.

Alternate Interior Angles Theorem If two parallel lines are cut by a transversal, then alternate interior angles are congruent.

Altitude of a triangle A perpendicular segment from a vertex to the line containing the opposite side.

Angle The figure formed by two rays with a common endpoint.

Angle Addition Postulate If point B is in the interior of $\angle AOC$, then $m\angle AOB + m\angle BOC = m\angle AOC$.

Angle-Angle-Side (AAS) Congruence Theorem If two angles and the nonincluded side of one triangle are congruent to two angles and the nonincluded side of another triangle, then the triangles are congruent.

Angle-Angle (AA) Similarity Postulate If two angles of one triangle are congruent to two angles of another triangle, then the triangles are similar.

Angle bisector The ray that divides a given angle into two congruent angles.

Angle of a convex polygon See *interior angle of a convex polygon.*

Angle of depression An angle whose vertex and horizontal side are level with an observer's eye and whose other side slopes downward from an observer's eye level to an object below.

Angle of elevation An angle whose vertex and horizontal side are level with an observer's eye and whose other side slopes upward from an observer's eye level to an object above.

Angle-Side-Angle (ASA) Congruence Postulate If two angles and the included side of one triangle are congruent to two angles and the included side of another triangle, then the triangles are congruent.

Angle-Sum Theorem The sum of the measures of the angles of a triangle is 180°.

Antecedent See *hypothesis.*

Apothem In a regular polygon, the segment, or the length of the segment, drawn from the center to the midpoint of a side.

Arc An unbroken part of a circle.

Area of a plane figure The number of nonoverlapping square units contained in its interior.

Axiom See *postulate.*

Base angles See *isosceles triangle, trapezoid.*

Base of an isosceles triangle See *isosceles triangle.*

Base of a plane figure See *triangle, trapezoid, parallelogram.*

Base of a three-dimensional figure See *prism, cylinder, pyramid, cone.*

Between On a number line, point C is between point A and point B if the coordinate of point C is between the coordinates of points A and B.

Biconditional statement The conjunction of a conditional statement and its converse. The biconditional *If p, then q and If q, then p* is written in abbreviated form as *p if, and only if, q.*

Boundary of a half-plane See *open half-plane.*

Center of a circle See *circle.*

Center of a regular polygon The point that is equidistant from all the vertices of the polygon.

Center of rotation See *rotation.*

Center of a sphere See *sphere.*

Center of symmetry See *rotational symmetry.*

Central angle of a circle An angle whose vertex is the center of the circle.

Centroid Point of concurrency of the medians of a triangle.

Chord of a circle Any line segment that has endpoints on the circle.

Circle The set of all points in a plane that are a fixed distance from a fixed point in the plane. The fixed point is called the *center of the circle.* The fixed distance is called the *radius of the circle.*

Circumcenter Point of concurrency of the perpendicular bisectors of the sides of a triangle.

Circumference of a circle The distance around the circle.

Closed half-plane The union of an open half-plane and its boundary.

Closed statement A statement that is either true or false.

Collinear points Points that lie on the same line. Points that do not lie on the same line are called *noncollinear points*.

Common external tangent A tangent that does not intersect the segment joining the centers of two circles.

Common internal tangent A tangent that intersects the segment joining the centers of two circles.

Compass A geometric tool used to draw circles and parts of circles, called *arcs*.

Complementary angles Two angles whose measures equal a sum of 90°. Each angle is the *complement* of the other.

Composition When multiple transformations are applied to a figure.

Compound statement A statement formed by linking two or more simple statements.

Concave polygon A polygon in which at least one diagonal contains a point in the exterior of the polygon.

Conclusion In a conditional statement, the part that follows *then*. Also called *consequent*.

Concurrent lines Three or more lines that intersect at a unique point.

Conditional statement A statement formed by connecting two statements with the words *if* and *then*.

Cone A three-dimensional figure that consists of a face bounded by a circle, called its *base*; a point called the *vertex* that is outside the plane of the base; and a *lateral surface* that connects the vertex to each point on the boundary of the base. The *height* of a cone is the length of a perpendicular segment drawn from the vertex to the plane of the base.

Congruent angles Angles that are equal in measure.

Congruent figures Figures that have the same shape and the same size.

Congruent polygons Polygons whose sides and angles can be placed in a correspondence so that corresponding sides are congruent and corresponding angles are congruent.

Congruent segments Segments that are equal in length.

Conjecture A conclusion based on deductive or inductive reasoning.

Conjunction A compound statement that is formed by linking simple statements with the word *and*.

Consecutive angles of a polygon Two angles whose vertices are consecutive vertices of the polygon.

Consecutive sides of a polygon Two sides that have a common endpoint.

Consecutive vertices of a polygon Two vertices that are endpoints of the same side.

Consequent See *conclusion*.

Contrapositive of a conditional statement The statement that results when the hypothesis and conclusion are interchanged, then both negated.

Converse of a conditional statement The statement that results when the hypothesis and conclusion are interchanged.

Conversion factor A ratio of two measurements that is equal to one.

Convex polygon A polygon in which no diagonal contains a point in the exterior of the polygon.

Coordinate plane A number plane formed by a horizontal number line and a vertical number line that intersect at their origins.

Coordinate(s) of a point The real number or numbers that correspond to the point. On a number line, the coordinate of each point is a single number. On a coordinate plane, each point has an ordered pair (x, y) of coordinates. The first number of the ordered pair is called the *x-coordinate* of the point, and the second is called the *y-coordinate*. See also *Ruler Postulate*.

Coplanar figures Figures that lie on the same plane. Figures that do not lie on the same plane are called *noncoplanar figures*.

Corollary A theorem that follows directly from a previously proved theorem.

Corresponding angles A pair of nonadjacent angles, one interior and one exterior, that are on the same side of a transversal.

Corresponding Angles Postulate If two parallel lines are cut by a transversal, then corresponding angles are congruent.

Corresponding Parts of Congruent Triangles Are Congruent Postulate If two triangles are congruent, then the corresponding sides and angles of the two triangles must also be congruent.

Counterexample A particular instance that shows a general statement is not true for all values in the replacement set.

Cube A prism whose faces are bounded by six congruent squares.

Cylinder A three-dimensional figure that consists of two parallel *bases* bounded by congruent circles and a *lateral surface* that connects the circles. The *height* of a cylinder is the length of any perpendicular segment drawn from a point on one base to the plane containing the other base.

D

Decagon A polygon that has exactly ten sides.

Deductive reasoning The process of reasoning logically from given facts to a conclusion.

Definition A statement of the meaning of a word or phrase.

Degree measure of an angle A unique real number from 0 to 180 that is paired with the angle.

GLOSSARY

Diagonal of a polygon A segment whose endpoints are nonconsecutive vertices of the polygon.

Diameter of a circle A segment, or the length of the segment, whose endpoints are points of the circle and that contains the center of the circle.

Dihedral angle The angle formed by two intersecting planes. Each plane is divided into two *half planes*.

Dilation A dilation with center O and *scale factor* n, where $n > 0$, is a transformation in which the image of a point A is a point A' such that point A' is on $\overrightarrow{OA}$ and $OA' = n \cdot OA$. The image of point O is point O. If $n > 1$, the dilation is an *enlargement*. If $0 < n < 1$, it is a *reduction*. A dilation is also called a *similarity transformation*. A dilation with scale factor n is denoted $D_n(x, y) \rightarrow (nx, ny)$.

Dimensional analysis A method for converting a measurement from one unit of measure to another by multiplying by a ratio representing the relationship between the units. The ratio is called a *conversion factor*.

Direct measurement See *indirect measurement*.

Direct variation A relationship described by an equation of the form $y = kx$, where k is a constant nonzero real number. The number k is called the *constant of variation*.

Disjunction A compound statement that is formed by linking simple statements with the word *or*.

Distance between a line and a point not on the line The length of the perpendicular segment from the line to the point.

Distance between two parallel lines The distance between one line and a point on the other line.

Distance between two points (number line) The absolute value of the difference of the coordinates of the points. See also *Ruler Postulate*.

Distance formula (coordinate plane) The distance PQ between $P(x_1, y_1)$ and $Q(x_2, y_2)$ is given by the formula $PQ = \sqrt{(x_2 - x_1)^2 + (y_2 - y_1)^2}$.

Dodecagon A polygon with exactly twelve sides.

Dodecahedron A polyhedron with 12 congruent faces that are pentagons.

Edge A line segment that joins two vertices.

Edge of a polyhedron A segment that is the intersection of two faces.

Endpoint See *segment* and *ray*.

Endpoint of a kite The common endpoint of a pair of congruent sides.

Enlargement See *dilation*.

Equiangular polygon A polygon whose angles are all congruent.

Equiangular triangle A triangle that has three congruent angles.

Equilateral polygon A polygon whose sides are all congruent.

Equilateral triangle A triangle that has three congruent sides.

Euler line The line passing through the orthocenter, the centroid, and the circumcenter of a triangle.

Exterior Angle Corollary The measure of an exterior angle of a triangle is greater than the measure of each of its remote interior angles.

Exterior angle of a convex polygon An angle that forms a linear pair with one of the polygon's interior angles.

External tangent A line, segment, or ray in the plane of the circle that intersects the circle at exactly one point.

Externally tangent Two circles are externally tangent if their centers lie on opposite sides of a common tangent.

Face of a polyhedron One of its flat surfaces.

Figure In geometry, any set of points.

Fixed point A point that is its own image under a transformation.

Formula A literal equation in which each variable represents a quantity.

Foundation or base drawing A drawing which shows the base of a structure and the height of each part.

Geometric construction A drawing that is made using only an unmarked *straightedge* and a *compass*. The straightedge is used to draw segments, rays, and lines. The compass is used to draw arcs and circles.

Geometric mean The number x such that $\frac{a}{x} = \frac{x}{b}$, where a, b, and x are positive numbers.

Given See *hypothesis*.

Graph of an inequality (number line) The set of the graphs of all solutions to the inequality.

Graph of a number The point that corresponds to the number on a number line.

Graph of an ordered pair The point that corresponds to the ordered pair on a coordinate plane.

Great circle Any circle in the plane that contains the center of the sphere. A great circle divides the sphere into 2 hemispheres.

Half plane See *dihedral angle*.

Half-turn A rotation of exactly 180°.

Height of a plane figure See *triangle*, *trapezoid*, *parallelogram*.

Height of a three-dimensional figure See *prism*, *cylinder*, *pyramid*, *cone*.

Hemisphere See *great circle*.

Hexagon A polygon that has exactly six sides.

Hexahedron A polyhedron with 6 congruent faces that are squares. See *cube*.

Hypotenuse The side of a right triangle that is opposite the right angle.

Hypotenuse-Leg (HL) Congruence Theorem If the hypotenuse and one leg of a right triangle are congruent to the hypotenuse and one leg of another right triangle, then the triangles are congruent.

Hypothesis In a conditional statement, the part that follows *if*. Also called the *antecedent*.

Icosahedron A polyhedron with 20 congruent faces that are triangles.

Image See *transformation*.

Incenter Point of concurrency of the angle bisectors of the triangle.

Indirect measurement Determining an unknown measurement by using mathematical relationships among known measurements rather than using a *direct measurement* tool such as a ruler or protractor.

Indirect reasoning A type of reasoning in which all possibilities are considered and then the unwanted ones are proved false. The remaining possibilities must be true.

Inductive reasoning A type of reasoning that draws conclusions based on a pattern of specific examples or observations.

Inscribed angle An angle inside a circle that is formed by three points that lie on the circle.

Intercepted arc The section of a circle that is between the endpoints of an inscribed angle.

Interior angle of a convex polygon An angle determined by two consecutive sides of the polygon. Also called an *angle of the polygon*.

Internally tangent Two circles are internally tangent if their centers lie on the same side of a common tangent.

Intersection of figures The set of all points common to two or more figures. The figures are said to *intersect* at these points.

Invariant property A property that does not change as a result of a transformation.

Inverse of a conditional statement The statement that results when the hypothesis and conclusion are both negated.

Isometry A transformation in which a figure and its image are congruent.

Isosceles trapezoid A trapezoid whose legs are congruent.

Isosceles triangle A triangle that has at least two congruent sides, called the *legs*. The third side is the *base*. The angles opposite the congruent sides are called the *base angles*. The third angle is the *vertex angle*.

Isosceles Triangle Bisectors Theorem The bisector of the vertex angle of an isosceles triangle is the perpendicular bisector of the base.

Isosceles Triangle Theorem If two sides of a triangle are congruent, then the angles opposite those sides are congruent. Also stated as: *Base angles of an isosceles triangle are congruent*.

Kite A convex quadrilateral in which two distinct pairs of consecutive sides are congruent.

Lateral area of a prism or pyramid The sum of the areas of the lateral faces.

Lateral face See *prism*, *pyramid*.

Lateral surface See *cylinder*, *cone*.

Legs of an isosceles triangle See *isosceles triangle*.

Legs of a right triangle The sides opposite the acute angles.

Legs of a trapezoid The nonparallel sides.

Length of a segment The distance between the endpoints of the segment.

Line A set of points that extends in two opposite directions without end. This is one of the basic *undefined terms* of geometry.

Line Intersection Postulate If two lines intersect, then they intersect in exactly one point.

Line segment See *segment*.

Line symmetry A plane figure that has line symmetry is its own image after reflection across some line in the plane. The line is called a *line of symmetry* for the figure.

Linear pair Adjacent angles whose noncommon sides are opposite rays.

Linear Pair Postulate If two angles form a linear pair, then they are supplementary.

Locus The set of all points that satisfy specified conditions. The plural of *locus* is *loci*.

Logically equivalent statements Statements that have the same truth values.

GLOSSARY

Major arc A major arc of a circle is an arc that is larger than a semicircle.

Medial triangle The triangle formed by connecting the midpoints of each side of a given triangle.

Median of a triangle A segment whose endpoints are a vertex of the triangle and the midpoint of the opposite side.

Midpoint of a segment The point that divides the segment into two congruent segments.

Midpoint formula The coordinates of the midpoint of the segment with endpoints $P(x_1, y_1)$ and $Q(x_2, y_2)$ are $\left(\frac{x_1 + x_2}{2}, \frac{y_1 + y_2}{2}\right)$.

Midsegment of a triangle A segment that connects the midpoints of two sides of a triangle.

Negation of a statement The statement formed when the word *not* is inserted into or removed from a statement. The negation of a true statement is always false. The negation of a false statement is always true.

Net A 2-dimensional model of a 3-dimensional figure.

Network See *Vertex-edge graph*.

***n*-gon** A polygon that has exactly *n* sides.

Nonagon A polygon that has exactly nine sides.

Noncollinear points Points that do not lie on the same line.

Number line A line whose points have been placed in one-to-one correspondence with the set of real numbers.

Oblique cylinder or prism A cylinder or prism where the segment joining the centers of the bases is not perpendicular to the planes containing the bases.

Obtuse angle An angle whose measure is greater than 90° and less than 180°.

Obtuse triangle A triangle that has one obtuse angle.

Octagon A polygon that has exactly eight sides.

Octahedron A polyhedron with 8 congruent faces that are triangles.

Open half-plane Either of two regions into which a line separates a coordinate plane. The line is called the *boundary* of each half-plane.

Open statement A statement that contains one or more variables.

Opposite angles of a quadrilateral Two angles that are not consecutive.

Opposite rays On a line, if point B is between points A and C, then $\overrightarrow{BA}$ and $\overrightarrow{BC}$ are opposite rays.

Opposite sides of a quadrilateral Two sides that are not consecutive.

Ordered pair In a coordinate plane, the pair of real numbers (x, y) that corresponds to a point.

Origin of a coordinate plane The point where the axes intersect.

Origin of a number line The point that corresponds to the number zero.

Orthocenter Point of concurrency of the altitudes of a triangle.

Orthographic drawing A drawing that shows a top view, a front view, and a right view.

Overlapping figures Figures that have interior points in common.

Parabola The U-shaped curve that is the graph of a quadratic function.

Parallel lines Coplanar lines that do not intersect. The symbol for *parallel* is $\parallel$.

Parallel Postulate Through a point not on a line, there is exactly one line parallel to the given line.

Parallelogram A quadrilateral that has two pairs of parallel sides. To calculate area, any of the sides may be considered the *base*, and the length of that side is also called the base. The *height* is then the length of any perpendicular segment drawn from a point on the side opposite the base to the line containing the base.

Path The sequence of connections between vertices.

Pentagon A polygon that has exactly five sides.

Perimeter of a plane figure The distance around the figure. The perimeter of a polygon is the sum of the lengths of its sides.

Perpendicular bisector of a segment Any line, ray, or segment that is perpendicular to the segment at its midpoint.

Perpendicular lines Lines that intersect to form right angles. The symbol for perpendicular is $\perp$.

Perpendicular Transversal Theorem If a transversal is perpendicular to one of two parallel lines, then it is perpendicular to the other.

Plane A set of points that extends along a flat surface in every direction without end. This is one of the basic *undefined terms* of geometry.

Plane figure A figure whose points all lie in the same plane.

Plane Intersection Postulate If two planes intersect, then they intersect in a line.

Point A location. This is one of the basic *undefined terms* of geometry.

Point of concurrency The unique point where concurrent lines intersect.

Point of tangency The point on a circle where a tangent intersects the circle.

Point-slope form of an equation of a line For an equation in the variables x and y, the point-slope form is $y - y_1 = m(x - x_1)$, where $P(x_1, y_1)$ is a point on the line and m is the slope of the line.

Point symmetry A plane figure that has point symmetry is its own image after a half-turn in the plane.

Polygon A plane figure formed by three or more segments such that each segment intersects exactly two others, one at each endpoint, and no two segments with a common endpoint are collinear. Each segment is a *side* of the polygon. The common endpoint of two sides is a *vertex* of the polygon. A polygon completely encloses a region of the plane, called its *interior*.

Polygon Exterior Angle-Sum Theorem The sum of the measures of the exterior angles of a convex polygon, one at each vertex, is 360°.

Polygon Interior Angle-Sum Theorem The sum of the measures of the interior angles of a convex polygon that has n sides is $(n - 2)180°$.

Polyhedron A three-dimensional figure formed by flat surfaces that are bounded by polygons joined in pairs along their sides.

Polynomial A monomial or a sum of monomials.

Population In a statistical study, the set of all individuals or objects being studied.

Postulate A statement whose truth is accepted without proof.

Preimage See *transformation*.

Prism A polyhedron with two parallel faces, called its *bases*, that are bounded by congruent polygons; and with *lateral faces* that are bounded by parallelograms connecting corresponding sides of the bases. The *height* of a prism is the length of any perpendicular segment drawn from a point on one base to the plane containing the other base.

Proof A convincing argument that uses deductive reasoning. In a *two-column proof*, the statements and reasons are aligned in columns. In a *paragraph proof*, the statements and reasons are connected in sentences. In a *flow proof*, arrows show the logical connections between the statements. In a *coordinate proof*, a figure is drawn on a coordinate plane and the formulas for slope, midpoint, and distance are used to prove properties of the figure. An *indirect proof* involves the use of indirect reasoning.

Proportion A statement that two ratios are equal. The proportion that equates the ratios "a to b" and "c to d" can be written in three ways:

a is to b as c is to d $\quad a:b = c:d \quad \frac{a}{b} = \frac{c}{d}$

Protractor Postulate Let $\overrightarrow{OA}$ and $\overrightarrow{OB}$ be opposite rays. Consider $\overrightarrow{OA}$, $\overrightarrow{OB}$, and all the rays with endpoint O that can be drawn in a plane on one side of $\overleftrightarrow{AB}$. These rays can be paired with the real numbers from 0 to 180, one-to-one, in such a way that:

- $\overrightarrow{OA}$ is paired with 0 and $\overrightarrow{OB}$ is paired with 180.
- If $\overrightarrow{OP}$ is paired with x and $\overrightarrow{OQ}$ is paired with y, then the number paired with $\angle POQ$ is $|x - y|$. This is called the *measure*, or the *degree measure*, of $\angle POQ$.

Pyramid A polyhedron that consists of a face bounded by a polygon, called its *base*; a point called the *vertex* that is outside the plane of the base; and triangular *lateral faces* that connect the vertex to each side of the base. The *height* of a pyramid is the length of the perpendicular segment drawn from the vertex to the plane of the base.

Pythagorean Theorem If a triangle is a right triangle with legs of lengths a and b and hypotenuse of length c, then $a^2 + b^2 = c^2$.

Pythagorean triple Any set of three positive integers that satisfy the relationship $a^2 + b^2 = c^2$.

Quadrant One of the four regions into which a coordinate plane is divided by the x- and y-axes.

Quadrilateral A polygon that has exactly four sides.

Quadrilateral Angle-Sum Theorem The sum of the measures of the interior angles of a quadrilateral is 360°.

Radius of a circle A segment, or the length of the segment, whose endpoints are the center of the circle and a point of the circle. See also *circle*.

Radius of a sphere See *sphere*.

Ratio A comparison of two numbers by division. *The ratio of a to b* can be written in three ways:

a to b $\quad a:b \quad \frac{a}{b}$

Ray Part of a line that begins at one point and extends without end in one direction. The point is called the *endpoint of the ray*.

Reciprocal Two numbers are reciprocals if their product is 1. See also *inverse property of multiplication*.

Rectangle A quadrilateral that has four right angles.

GLOSSARY

Reflection in a line A reflection across line m is a transformation such that, if point A is on line m, then the image of point A is point A; and if point B is not on line m, then its image B' is the point such that line m is the perpendicular bisector of $\overline{BB'}$. Line m is called the *line of reflection*. The reflection of point P across line m is denoted by $r_m P \rightarrow P'$.

Reflection in a point A reflection about point P is a transformation such that the image of point P is point P; and the image of any other point Q is the point Q' such that point P is the midpoint of $\overline{QQ'}$. Point P is called the *point of reflection*. The reflection of point Q about point P is denoted by $r_P Q \rightarrow Q'$.

Regular polygon A polygon that is both equilateral and equiangular.

Regular polyhedron All of the faces of a polyhedron are regular polygons that are congruent to each other.

Regular pyramid A pyramid whose base is bounded by a regular polygon and in which the segment joining the center of the base to the vertex is perpendicular to the plane of the base. The lateral faces of a regular pyramid are congruent isosceles triangles.

Remote interior angles For each exterior angle of a triangle, the two nonadjacent interior angles are called remote interior angles.

Rhombus A quadrilateral that has four congruent sides.

Right angle An angle whose measure is 90°.

Right cone A cone in which the segment joining the center of the base to the vertex is perpendicular to the plane of the base. If a cone is not a right cone, then it is called *oblique*.

Right cylinder A cylinder in which the segment joining the centers of the bases is perpendicular to the planes of the bases. If a cylinder is not a right cylinder, then it is called *oblique*.

Right prism A prism in which the segments that connect corresponding vertices of the bases are perpendicular to the planes of the bases. The lateral faces of a right prism are bounded by rectangles. If a prism is not a right prism, then it is called *oblique*.

Right triangle A triangle with one right angle.

Rotation A rotation of $x°$ about point O is a transformation such that the image of point O is point O; and for any other point P, its image is the point P' such that $\overline{OP} = \overline{OP'}$ and $m\angle POP' = x°$. Point O is called the *center of rotation*. The direction of rotation is specified as *clockwise* or *counterclockwise*. The rotation of $x°$ about point O is denoted $R_{O,\, x°} P \rightarrow P'$.

Rotational symmetry A plane figure that has rotational symmetry is its own image after a rotation of 180° or less around some point in the plane. The point is called the *center of symmetry* for the figure.

Ruler Postulate The points of a line can be paired with the real numbers, one-to-one, so that any point corresponds to 0 and any other point corresponds to 1. The real number that corresponds to a point is the *coordinate* of that point. The *distance* between two points is equal to the absolute value of the difference of their coordinates.

Same-Side Interior Angles Theorem If two parallel lines are cut by a transversal, then interior angles on the same side of the transversal are supplementary.

Scale drawing A two-dimensional drawing that is similar to the object it represents. The ratio of the size of the drawing to the actual size of the object is the *scale* of the drawing.

Scale factor See *similarity ratio, dilation*.

Scalene triangle A triangle that has no congruent sides.

Secant A line, ray, or segment that intersects a circle at 2 points.

Sector of a circle The part of a circle formed by two radii and the arc they intercept.

Segment Part of a line that begins at one point and ends at another. The points are called the *endpoints of the segment*. Also called *line segment*.

Segment Addition Postulate If point C is between point A and point B, then $AC + CB = AB$.

Segment bisector Any line, ray, or segment that intersects a given segment at its midpoint.

Semicircle Half of a circle.

Side of an angle One of the two rays that form the angle.

Side of a polygon See *polygon*.

Side-Angle-Side (SAS) Congruence Postulate If two sides and the included angle of one triangle are congruent to two sides and the included angle of another triangle, then the triangles are congruent.

Side-Angle-Side (SAS) Similarity Theorem If an angle of one triangle is congruent to an angle of another triangle, and the lengths of the sides including these angles are in proportion, then the triangles are similar.

Side-Side-Side (SSS) Congruence Postulate If three sides of one triangle are congruent to three sides of another triangle, then the triangles are congruent.

Side-Side-Side (SSS) Similarity Theorem If corresponding sides of two triangles are in proportion, then the triangles are similar.

Side-Splitter Theorem If a line is parallel to one side of a triangle and intersects the other two sides at distinct points, then it divides those two sides proportionally.

Similar figures Figures that have the same shape, but not necessarily the same size.

Similar polygons Polygons whose sides and angles can be placed in a correspondence so that corresponding angles are congruent and corresponding sides are in proportion.

Similarity ratio The ratio of the lengths of corresponding sides of similar polygons. Also called the *scale factor*.

Similarity transformation See *dilation*.

Skew lines Lines that are noncoplanar.

Slant height of a regular pyramid The height of a lateral face.

Slant height of a right cone The distance between the vertex of the cone and any point on the boundary of the base.

Slope On a coordinate plane, the steepness of a nonvertical line, described informally as $\frac{\text{rise}}{\text{run}}$. Formally, if $P(x_1, y_1)$ and $Q(x_2, y_2)$ lie on $\overleftrightarrow{PQ}$, and $x_1 \neq x_2$, then the slope m of $\overleftrightarrow{PQ}$ is defined by $m = \frac{y_2 - y_1}{x_2 - x_1}$.

Slope-intercept form of an equation of a line For an equation in the variables x and y, $y = mx + b$, where m is the slope of the graph and b is the y-intercept.

Solution to an equation or inequality in two variables For an equation or inequality in the variables x and y, any ordered pair of numbers (x, y) that together make the equation or inequality a true statement.

Solution to an open statement Any value of the variable(s) that makes the statement true.

Solution set of an open statement The set of all solutions to the open statement.

Solution to a system of equations or inequalities in two variables For a system in the variables x and y, any ordered pair (x, y) that is a solution to each equation or inequality in the system.

Space In geometry, the set of all points.

Space figure A figure whose points extend beyond a single plane into space. Also called a *three-dimensional figure*.

Sphere The set of all points in space that are a fixed distance from a fixed point. The fixed point is called the *center of the sphere*. The fixed distance is called the *radius of the sphere*.

Square A quadrilateral that has four congruent sides and four right angles.

Standard form of an equation of a circle For a circle with center $P(h, k)$ and radius r, the equation is $(x - h)^2 + (y - k^2) = r^2$. If P is the origin, the equation becomes $x^2 + y^2 = r^2$.

Statement Any mathematical sentence.

Straight angle An angle whose measure is 180°.

Straightedge A straightedge is a ruler with no markings on it.

Supplementary angles Two angles whose measures have a sum of 180°. Each angle is the *supplement* of the other.

Surface area The total area of all surfaces of a three-dimensional figure.

Tangent of an angle The tangent of an acute angle of a right triangle is the ratio of the length of the leg opposite the angle to the length of the leg adjacent to it. The symbol for the tangent of an angle A is tan A.

Tetrahedron A polyhedron with 4 congruent faces that are triangles.

Theorem A statement that can be proved true.

Three-dimensional figure See *space figure*.

Transformation A correspondence between one figure, called a *preimage*, and a second figure, called its *image*, such that each point of the image is paired with exactly one point of the preimage, and each point of the preimage is paired with exactly one point of the image.

Transitivity of Parallelism Theorem If two lines are parallel to a third line, then the lines are parallel to each other.

Translation A transformation in which the image is the figure that would result if each point of the preimage were moved the same distance and in the same direction. The translation of a point (x, y) in the coordinate plane a units horizontally and b units vertically is given by $\mathrm{T}_{a,b}(x, y) \rightarrow (x + a, y + b)$.

Transversal A line that intersects two or more coplanar lines at different points.

Trapezoid A quadrilateral that has exactly one pair of parallel sides. The parallel sides, and the lengths of the parallel sides, are called the *bases*. Two angles of the trapezoid whose vertices are the endpoints of a single base are a pair of *base angles*. The *height* is the length of any perpendicular segment drawn from a point on one base to the line containing the other base.

Triangle A polygon that has exactly three sides. To calculate area, any of the sides may be considered the *base*, and the length of that side is also called the base. The *height* is then the length of the altitude drawn to the base from the opposite vertex.

Triangle Angle-Sum Theorem The sum of the measures of the angles of a triangle is 180°.

Triangle Exterior-Angle Theorem The measure of each exterior angle of a triangle is equal to the sum of the measures of the remote interior angles.

Triangle Inequality Theorem The sum of the lengths of any two sides of a triangle is greater than the length of the third side.

Truth value A closed statement is either *true* or *false*. These are its possible truth values.

GLOSSARY

Two Perpendiculars Theorem If two coplanar lines are perpendicular to a third line, then the lines are parallel.

Two-point form of an equation of a line For an equation in the variables x and y, $y - y_1 = \frac{y_2 - y_1}{x_2 - x_1}(x - x_1)$ where $P(x_1, y_1)$ and $Q(x_2, y_2)$ lie on a nonvertical line.

Undefined term A term that is used without a specific mathematical definition. In geometry, the three undefined terms are *point*, *line*, and *plane*.

Unequal Angles Theorem If two angles of a triangle are not congruent, then the side opposite the larger of the two angles is longer than the side opposite the smaller angle.

Unequal Sides Theorem If two sides of a triangle are not congruent, then the angle opposite the longer of the two sides is larger than the angle opposite the shorter side.

Unique Line Postulate Through any two points there is exactly one line. Also stated as: *Two points determine a line.*

Unique Plane Postulate Through any three noncollinear points there is exactly one plane. Also stated as: *Three noncollinear points determine a plane.*

Venn diagram A diagram in which a rectangle represents all members of a set, with circles within it showing selected subsets and relationships among them.

Vertex angle of an isosceles triangle The angle opposite the base of an isosceles triangle. See *isosceles triangle*.

Vertex of an angle The common endpoint of the sides.

Vertex of a cone See *cone*.

Vertex-edge graph A graph in which the vertices are connected by edges to form a path.

Vertex of a polygon See *polygon*.

Vertex of a polyhedron A point that is the intersection of three or more edges.

Vertex of a pyramid See *pyramid*.

Vertical angles Two angles whose sides form two pairs of opposite rays.

Vertical Angles Theorem If two angles are vertical angles, then they are congruent.

Volume of a three-dimensional figure The amount of space the figure encloses, measured by the number of nonoverlapping cubic units in its interior.

***x*-axis** The horizontal number line in a coordinate plane.

***x*-coordinate** See *coordinate(s) of a point.*

***x*-intercept of a graph** The x-coordinate of any point where the graph intersects the x-axis.

***y*-axis** The vertical number line in a coordinate plane.

***y*-coordinate** See *coordinate(s) of a point.*

***y*-intercept of a graph** The y-coordinate of any point where the graph intersects the y-axis.

Sample

Geometry Examination

This sample exam has four parts with a total of 38 questions. Part I of this test contains 28 multiple-choice questions worth 2 points each. Parts II, III, and IV of the exam are open-response questions. There will be six 2-credit, three 4-credit, and one 6-credit open-response questions for these parts of the exam. You will need to solve the problems completely on a separate sheet of paper. You will have the use of a graphing calculator, ruler, and compass while taking the sample examination.

The following questions are actual test items released by the State of New York from the January 2005 Math A Exam: 2, 5, 6, 7, 8, 9.

The following questions are actual test items released by the State of New York from the August 2006 Math A Exam: 1, 3, 5.

Sample Geometry Examination

Part I

Use this space for computations.

Answer all questions in this part. Each correct answer will receive 2 credits. No partial credit will be allowed. For each question, write on the separate answer sheet the numeral preceding the word or expression that best completes the statement or answers the question.

1 Point $(k, -3)$ lies on the line whose equation is $x - 2y = -2$. What is the value of k?

(1) -8 **(2)** -6 **(3)** 6 **(4)** 8

2 What is the sum in degrees of the measures of the interior angle of a pentagon?

(1) 180° **(2)** 360° **(3)** 540° **(4)** 720°

3 What is the total number of points of intersection of the graphs of the equations $y = x^2 - 5$ and $y = x$?

(1) 1 **(2)** 2 **(3)** 3 **(4)** 4

4 Which line is perpendicular to the line whose equation is $5y + 6 = -3x$?

(1) $y = \frac{-5}{3}x + 7$ **(3)** $y = \frac{-3}{5}x + 7$

(2) $y = \frac{5}{3}x + 7$ **(4)** $y = \frac{3}{5}x + 7$

5 The coordinates of A are $(-3, 2)$ and the coordinates of B are $(4, 1)$. What is the length of $\overline{AB}$?

(1) $2\sqrt{2}$ **(2)** $5\sqrt{2}$ **(3)** $4\sqrt{3}$ **(4)** $\sqrt{10}$

6 How many points are equidistant from 2 parallel lines and also equidistant from 2 points on one of these lines?

(1) 1 **(2)** 2 **(3)** 3 **(4)** 4

7 If the midpoints of the sides of a triangle are connected, the area of the triangle formed is what part of the area of the original triangle?

(1) $\frac{1}{4}$ **(2)** $\frac{1}{5}$ **(3)** $\frac{1}{2}$ **(4)** $\frac{3}{8}$

Use this space for computations.

8 Which equation represents a line parallel to the line whose equation is $2x + 3y = 12$?

(1) $6y + 4x = 2$ **(3)** $4x - 6y = 2$

(2) $6x + 4y = 2$ **(4)** $6x + 4y = -2$

9 $\triangle DEF$ is the image of $\triangle ABC$. The perimeter of $\triangle DEF$ is twice as large as $\triangle ABC$. What type of transformation has taken place?

(1) dilation **(3)** reflection

(2) rotation **(4)** translation

10 In the accompanying diagram lines l and m are parallel.

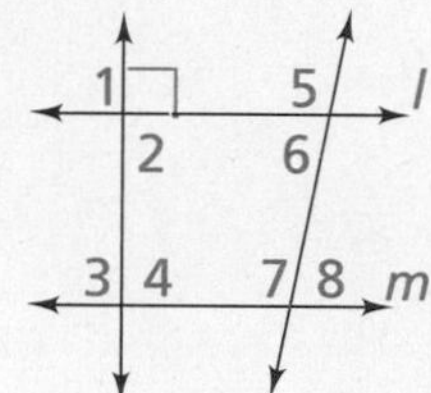

Which angle is congruent to angle 8?

(1) 3 **(2)** 4 **(3)** 5 **(4)** 6

11 In the figure of the accompanying regular octagon $\overline{AB} \cong \overline{AC}$, find $m\angle ACB$.

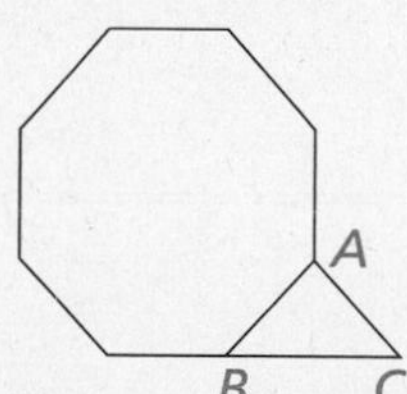

(1) 135° **(3)** 30°

(2) 45° **(4)** 90°

12 In an *A*-frame house, the 2 congruent sides extend from the ground to form a 34° angle at the peak. What angle does each side form with the ground?

(1) 156° **(2)** 146° **(3)** 73° **(4)** 78°

Use this space for computations.

13 Find the value of x.

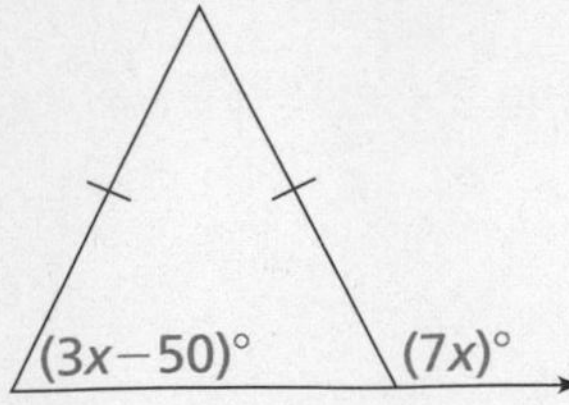

(1) $x = 23$ **(3)** $x = 13$

(2) $x = 40$ **(4)** $x = 5$

14 Which diagram shows plane PQR and plane QRS intersecting only in $\overleftrightarrow{QR}$?

(1)

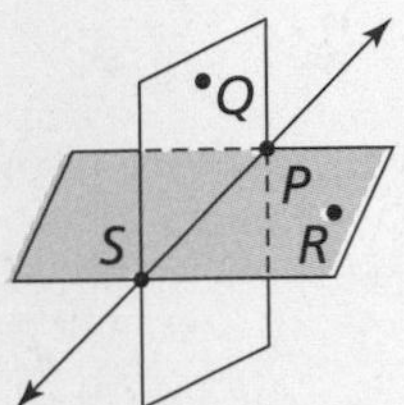

(3)

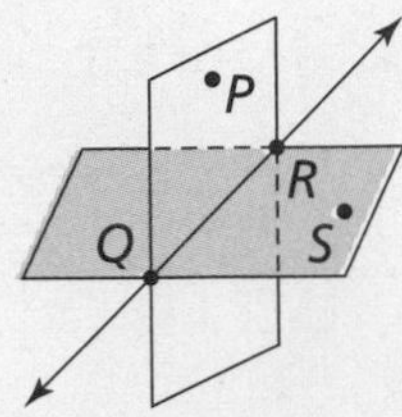

(2)

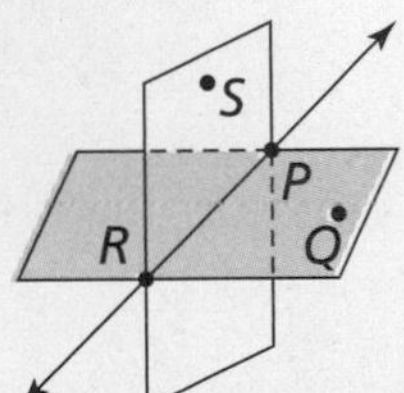

(4)

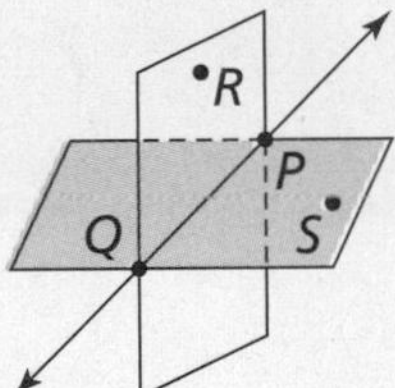

15 Which statement provides a counterexample of the following faulty definition? *A square is a figure with 4 congruent sides.*

(1) A 6-sided figure can have 4 congruent sides.

(2) Some triangles have all sides congruent.

(3) A square has 4 congruent angles.

(4) A rectangle has 4 sides.

16 What other information do you need in order to prove the triangles congruent using the SAS congruence postulate?

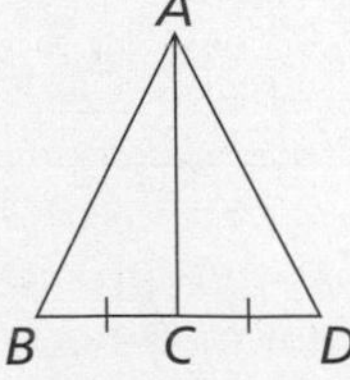

(1) $\angle BAC \cong \angle DAC$

(2) $\angle CBA \cong \angle CDA$

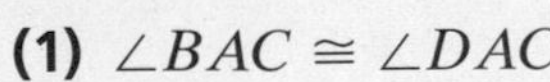

(3) $\overline{AC} \perp \overline{BD}$

(4) $\overline{AC} \cong \overline{BD}$

17 Each unit on the map represents 1 mile. What is the actual distance from Oceanfront to Seaside?

Use this space for computations.

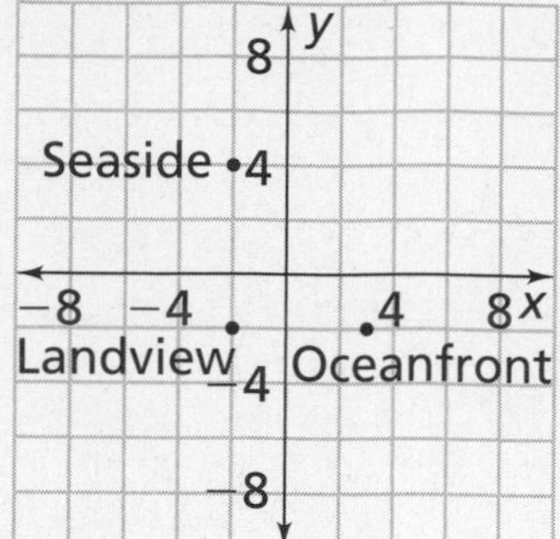

(1) 10 miles

(2) 50 miles

(3) about 8 miles

(4) about 40 miles

18 In the figure shown, $m\angle AED = 120°$. Which of the following statements is false?

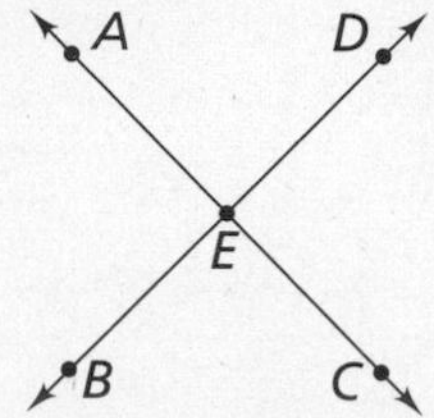

(1) $m\angle AEB = 60°$

(2) $\angle BEC$ and $\angle CED$ are adjacent angles.

(3) $m\angle BEC = 120°$

(4) $\angle AED$ and $\angle BEC$ are adjacent angles.

19 State whether $\triangle ABC$ and $\triangle AED$ are congruent. Justify your answer.

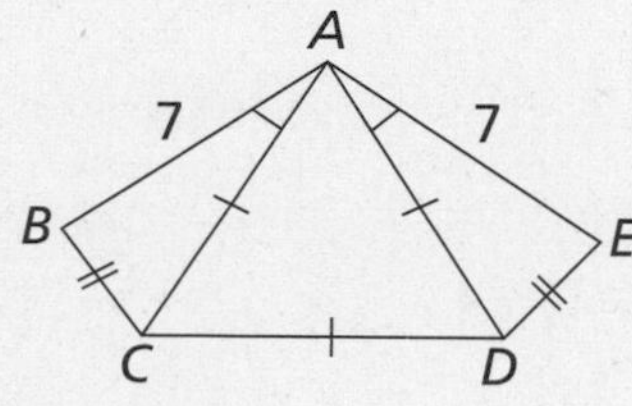

(1) Yes, by either SSS or SAS.

(2) Yes, by SSS only.

(3) Yes, by SAS only.

(4) No, there is not enough information.

20 Which construction is a line perpendicular to the given line through the given point?

Use this space for computations.

(1)

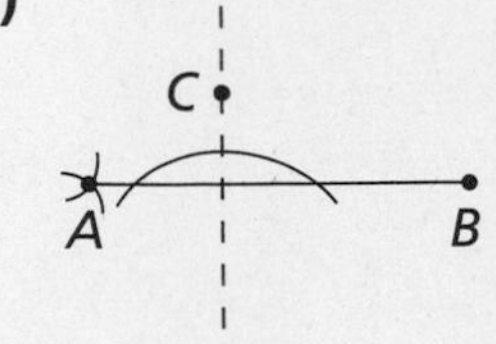

(3)

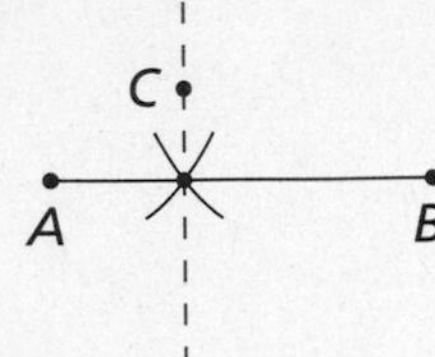

(2)

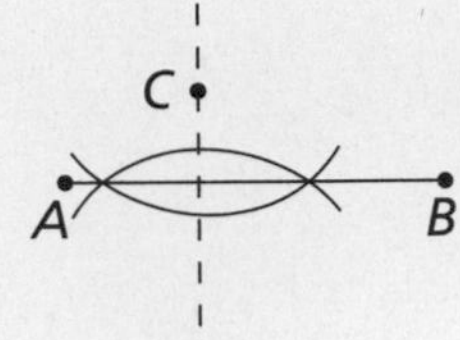

(4)

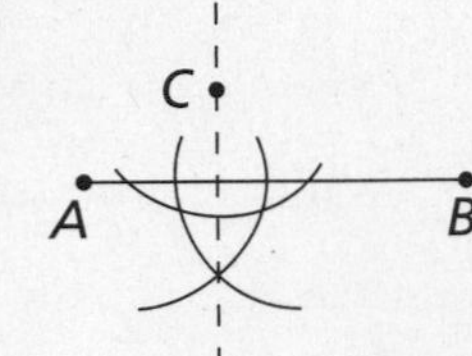

21 The Polygon Angle-Sum Theorem states: The sum of the measures of the interior angles of an n-gon is

(1) $\frac{n-2}{180}$.

(2) $(n-1)180$.

(3) $\frac{180}{n-1}$.

(4) $(n-2)180$.

22 The two rectangles are similar. Which is a correct proportion for corresponding sides?

4 m, 12 m; 8 m, x

(1) $\frac{12}{8} = \frac{x}{4}$ **(3)** $\frac{12}{4} = \frac{x}{20}$

(2) $\frac{12}{4} = \frac{x}{8}$ **(4)** $\frac{4}{12} = \frac{x}{8}$

23 Which Venn diagram is **NOT** correct?

Use this space for computations.

(1)

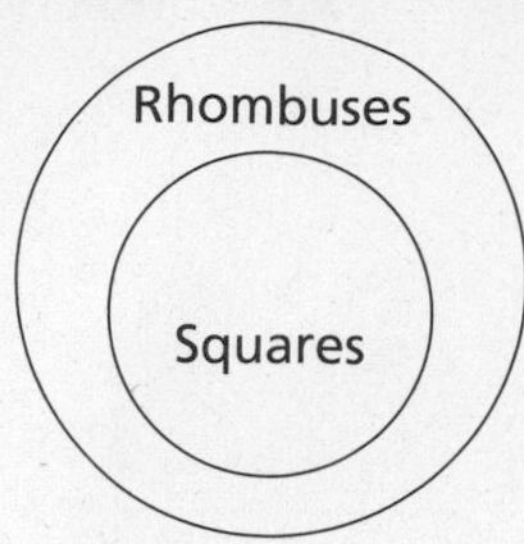

(3)

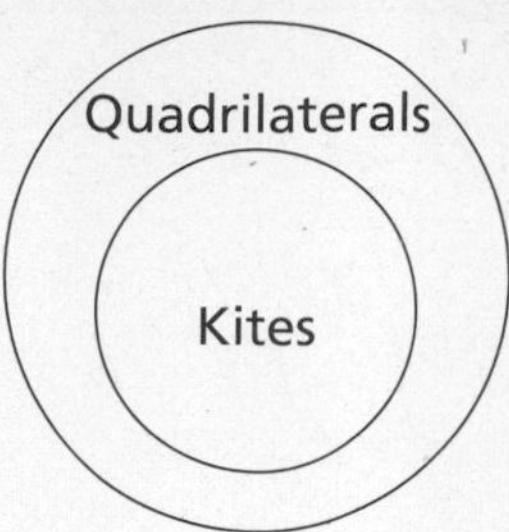

(2)

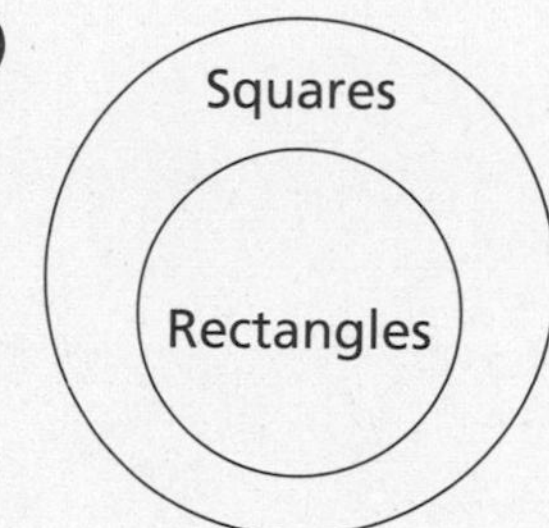

(4)

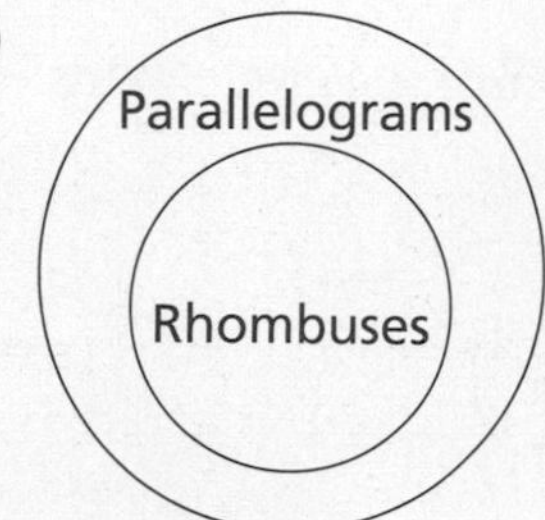

24 Which group contains triangles that are all similar?

(1)

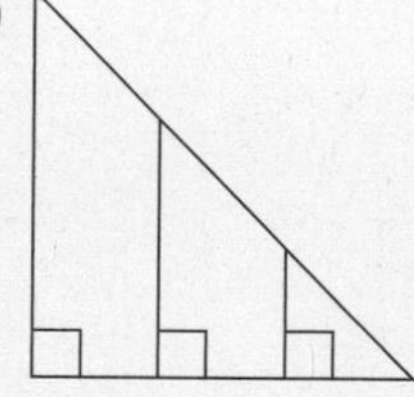

(3)

(2)

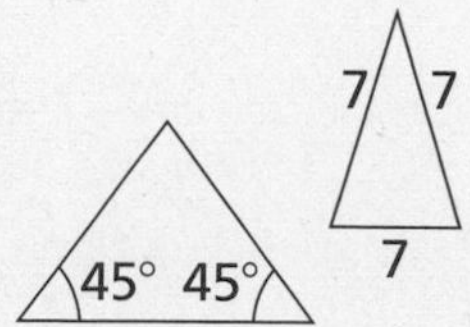

(4)

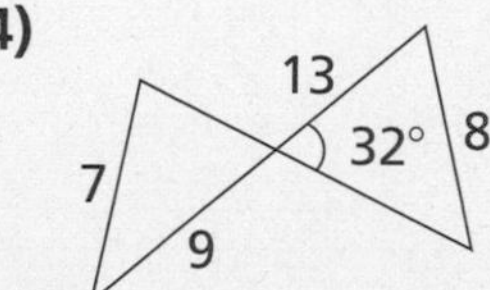

Use this space for computations.

25 In the figure below, $\overline{AB}$ is tangent to the circle. Find the value of x. If necessary, round your answer to the nearest tenth.

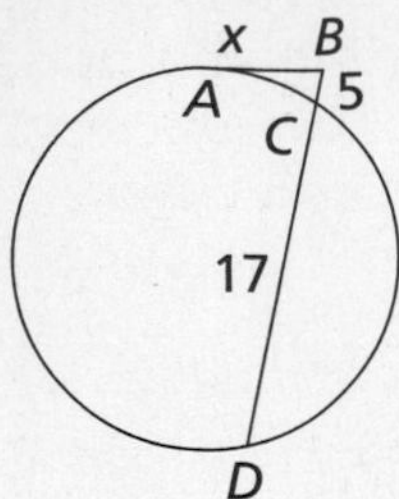

(1) 19.34 **(2)** 10.49 **(3)** 110 **(4)** 9.22

26 In the figure below, O is the center of the circle. Which statement is **NOT** true?

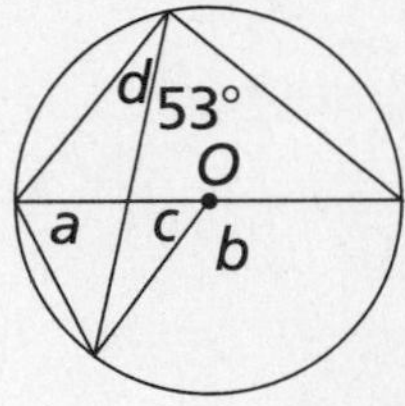

(1) $a = 53°$ **(2)** $b = 106°$ **(3)** $c = 73°$ **(4)** $d = 37°$

27 Describe the locus that the figure represents.

•A

l

•B

(1) all points 1 cm from line l

(2) all points equidistant from line l

(3) all points equidistant from point A and point B

(4) none of these

28 What is true about the following statement and its converse?
If 2 sides of a triangle are congruent, then the angles opposite these sides are congruent.

(1) The statement is true but its converse is false.

(2) The statement is false but its converse is true.

(3) The statement and its converse are both true.

(4) The statement and its converse are both false.

Part II

Use this space for computations.

Answer all questions in this part. Each correct answer will receive 2 credits. Clearly indicate the necessary steps, including appropriate formula substitutions, diagrams, graphs, charts, etc. For all questions in this part, a correct numerical answer with no work shown will receive only 1 credit.

29 A low-wattage radio station can be heard only within a certain distance from the station. On the graph below, the circular region represents that part of the city where the station can be heard, and the center of the circle represents the location of the station. Write an equation that represents the boundary for the region where the station can be heard?

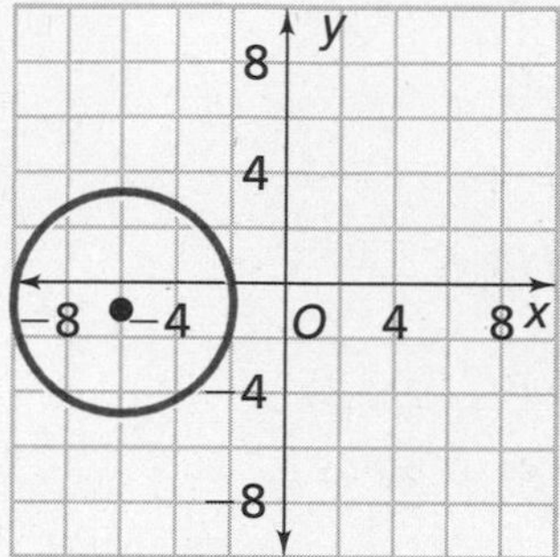

30 You live in New York City, which has approximate latitude and longitude coordinates of 50N, 75W. Your friend lives in Salt Lake City, with coordinates of 40N, 111W. You plan to meet halfway between the two cities. Find the coordinates of the halfway point.

31 Find the surface area of the following triangular prism.

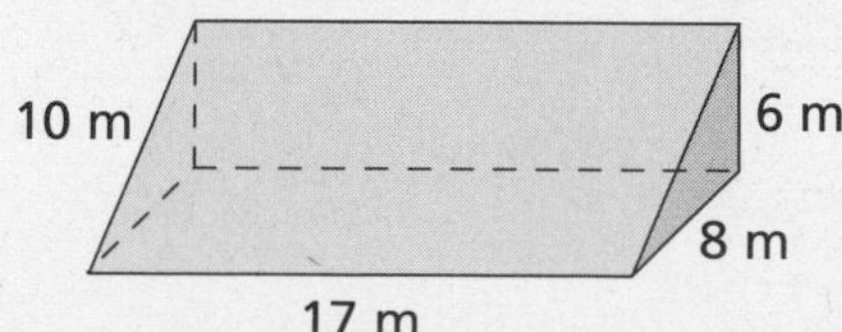

Use this space for computations.

32 Find the lengths of the diagonals of this trapezoid in terms of a, b, and c.

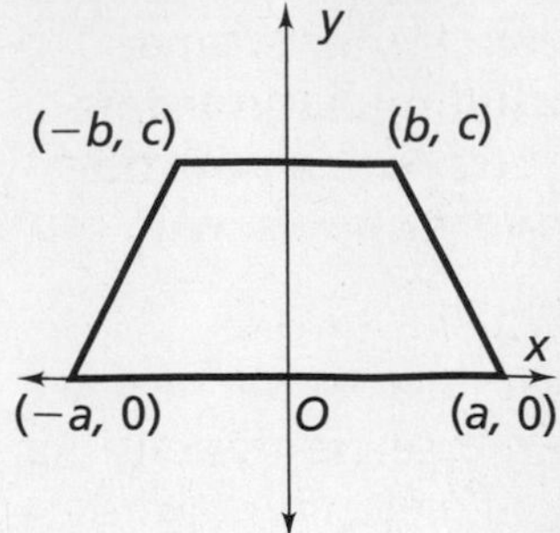

33 Complete this statement: For parallelogram $ABCD$, $\overline{BO} \cong$ __?__.
Then state a definition or theorem that justifies your answer.

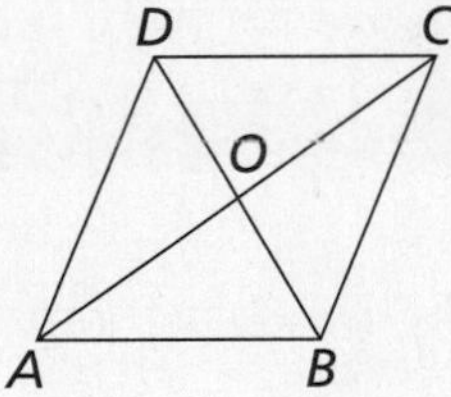

34 Draw the image of $\triangle ABC$ reflected in the x-axis.

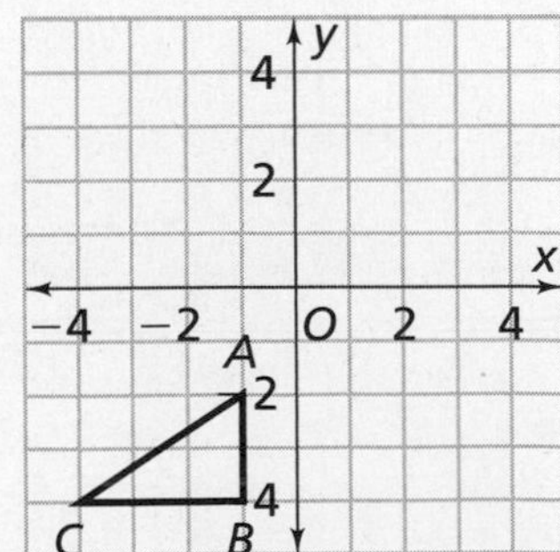

Part III

Use this space for computations.

Answer all questions in this part. Each correct answer will receive 4 credits. Clearly indicate the necessary steps, including diagrams, graphs, charts, etc. For all questions in this part, a correct numerical answer with no work shown will receive only 1 credit.

35 Find the measure of each numbered interior and exterior angle. State the theorem or postulate that supports each step.

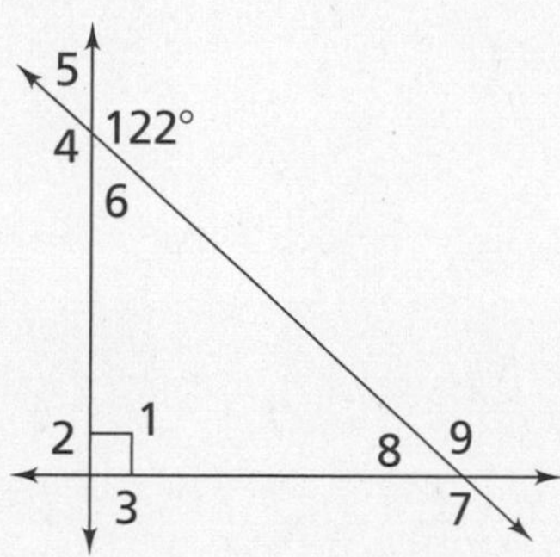

36 Write the equation $10x + 5y = 5$ in slope-intercept form. Then graph the line.

37 A log cabin is shaped like a rectangular prism. A model of the cabin has a scale of 1 centimeter to 0.5 meters.

1. If the model is 14 cm by 20 cm by 7 cm, what are the dimensions of the actual log cabin? Explain how you find the dimensions.
2. What is the volume of the actual log cabin? Explain how you find the volume.

Part IV

Use this space for computations.

Answer the following 6-credit question in this part. Clearly indicate the necessary steps, including diagrams, graphs, charts, etc. A correct answer with no work shown will receive only 1 credit.

38 Write a paragraph proof.
Given: *ABCD is an isosceles trapezoid*

Prove: $\angle D \cong \angle C$

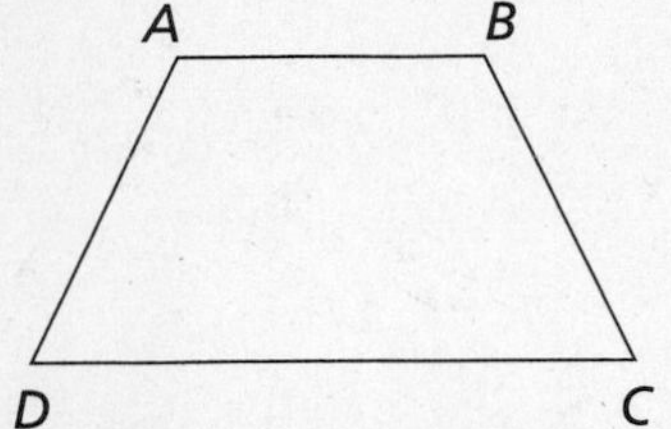

Sample

Geometry Examination

This sample exam has four parts with a total of 38 questions. Part I of this test contains 28 multiple-choice questions worth 2 points each. Parts II, III, and IV of the exam are open-response questions. There will be six 2-credit, three 4-credit, and one 6-credit open-response questions for these parts of the exam. You will need to solve the problems completely on a separate sheet of paper. You will have the use of a graphing calculator, ruler, and compass while taking the sample examination.

Sample Geometry Examination

Part I

Use this space for computations.

Answer all questions in this part. Each correct answer will receive 2 credits. No partial credit will be allowed. For each question, write on the separate answer sheet the numeral preceding the word or expression that best completes the statement or answers the question.

1 If $m\angle DEF = 118$, then what are $m\angle FEG$ and $m\angle HEG$?

(1) $m\angle FEG = 118, m\angle HEG = 62$

(2) $m\angle FEG = 62, m\angle HEG = 128$

(3) $m\angle FEG = 62, m\angle HEG = 118$

(4) $m\angle FEG = 72, m\angle HEG = 118$

2 Sarah has 78 feet of fencing to make a rectangular vegetable garden. Which dimensions will give Sarah the garden with the greatest area?

(1) 20 ft, 19 ft

(3) 21 ft, 18 ft

(2) 22 ft, 17 ft

(4) 23 ft, 16 ft

3 Plans for a bridge are drawn on a coordinate grid. One girder of the bridge lies on the line $y = 4x + 4$. A perpendicular brace passes through the point $(1, -7)$. Write an equation of the line that contains the brace.

(1) $y + 1 = \frac{1}{4}(x - 7)$

(3) $y + 7 = 4(x - 1)$

(2) $y + 7 = -\frac{1}{4}(x - 1)$

(4) $x + 7 = 4(y - 1)$

4 If $\triangle STU \cong \triangle KLM$, then all of the following must be true, **except**

(1) $\overline{ST} \cong \overline{KM}$.

(3) $\overline{TU} \cong \overline{LM}$.

(2) $\angle S \cong \angle K$.

(4) $\angle T \cong \angle L$.

5 Based on the given information, what can you conclude, and why?

Given: $\angle A \cong \angle E$, $\overline{AC} \cong \overline{CE}$

Use this space for computations.

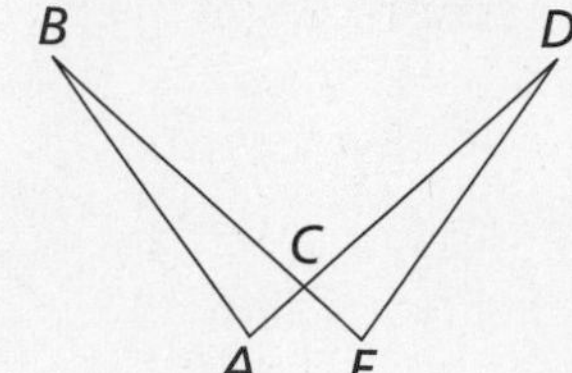

(1) $\triangle ABC \cong \triangle CED$ by SAS

(2) $\triangle ABC \cong \triangle EDC$ by ASA

(3) $\triangle ABC \cong \triangle EDC$ by SAS

(4) $\triangle ABC \cong \triangle CED$ by AAS

6 Which statement is true?

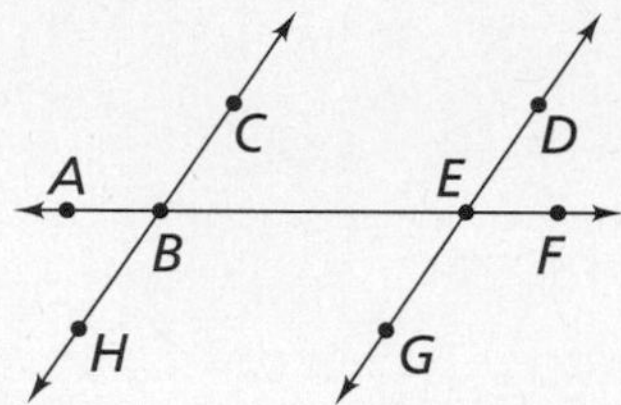

(1) $\angle FEG$ and $\angle DEB$ are same-side interior angles.

(2) $\angle FEG$ and $\angle CBE$ are alternate angles.

(3) $\angle CBE$ and $\angle DEB$ are alternate angles.

(4) $\angle CBE$ and $\angle DEB$ are same-side interior angles.

7 Write an equation in point-slope form, $y - y_1 = m(x - x_1)$, of the line through points (8, 1) and (7, 6). Use (8, 1) as the point (x_1, y_1).

(1) $(y + 1) = 5(x + 8)$

(2) $(y - 1) = -5(x - 8)$

(3) $(y + 1) = -5(x + 8)$

(4) $(y - 1) = 5(x - 8)$

8 Allison is planning to cover the lateral surface of a large cylindrical garbage can with decorative fabric for a theme party. The can has a diameter of 3 feet and a height of 3.5 feet. How much fabric does she need? Round to the nearest square foot.

(1) 123 ft^2 **(2)** 61 ft^2 **(3)** 33 ft^2 **(4)** 66 ft^2

Use this space for computations.

9 $WXYZ$ is a parallelogram. Name an angle congruent to $\angle XWZ$.

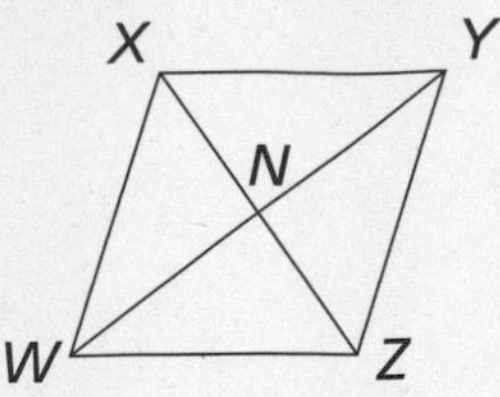

(1) $\angle XYW$ (2) $\angle WXY$ (3) $\angle WYZ$ (4) $\angle XYZ$

10 If $\angle A \cong \angle D$ and $\angle C \cong \angle F$, which additional statement does **NOT** allow you to conclude that $\triangle ABC \cong \triangle DEF$?

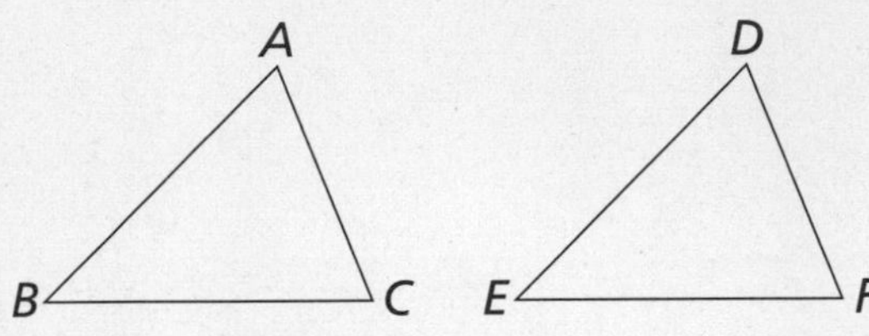

(1) $\overline{BC} \cong \overline{EF}$ (3) $\overline{AC} \cong \overline{DF}$

(2) $\angle B \cong \angle E$ (4) $\overline{AB} \cong \overline{EF}$

11 Which diagram shows the most useful positioning of a square in the first quadrant of a coordinate plane?

(1)
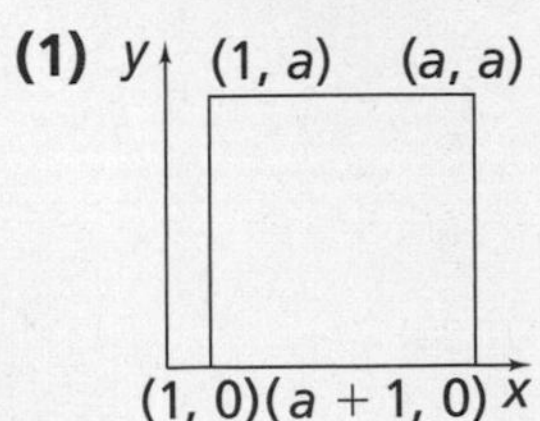

(3)
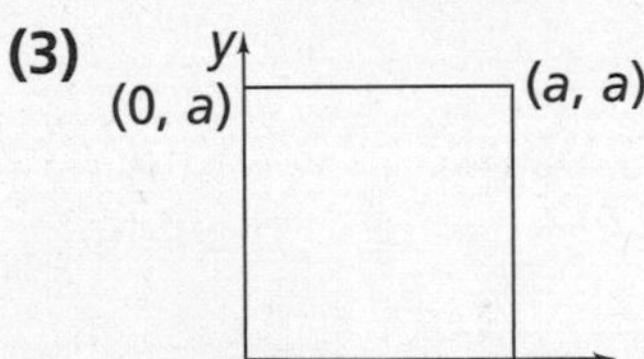

(2)
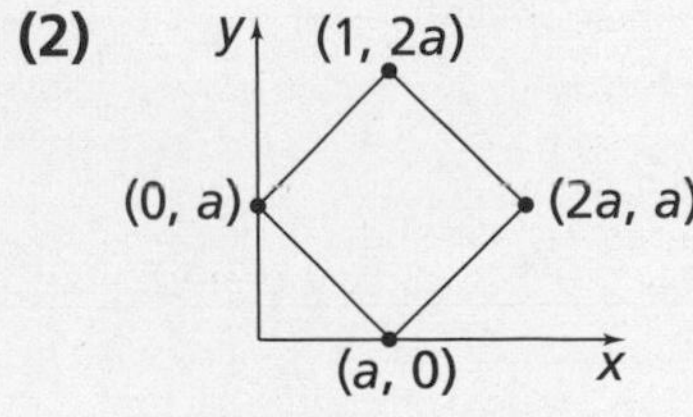

(4)
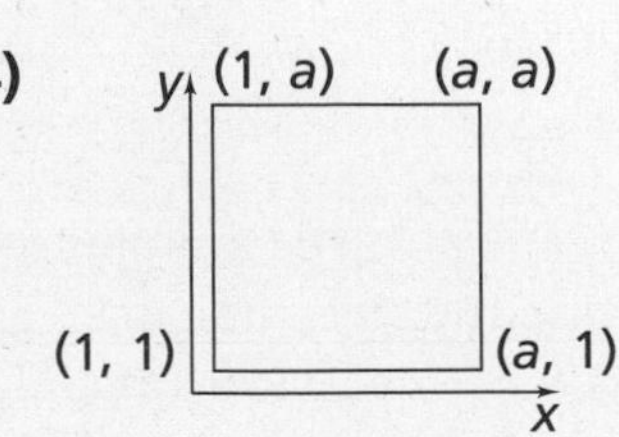

12 Which diagram suggests a correct construction of a line parallel to a given line q?

Use this space for computations.

(1)

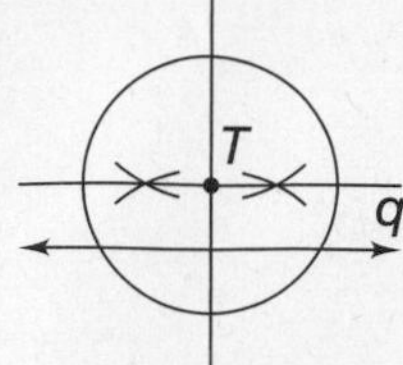

(3)

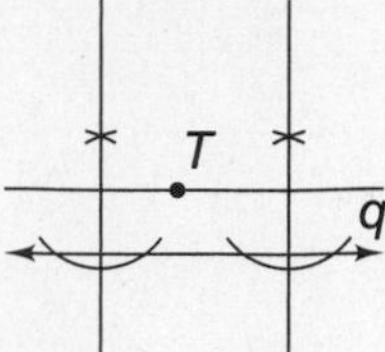

(2)

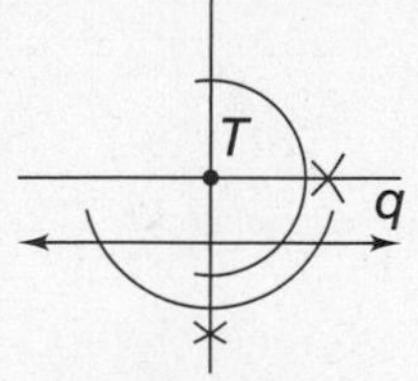

(4)

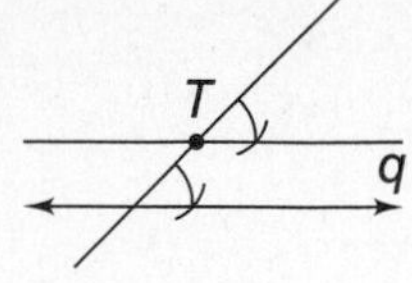

13 Judging by appearance, classify the figure in as many ways as possible.

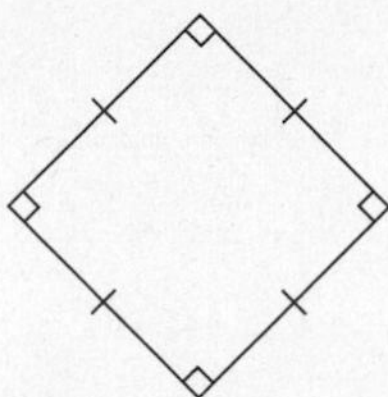

(1) rectangle, square, quadrilateral, parallelogram, rhombus

(2) rectangle, square, parallelogram

(3) rhombus, trapezoid, quadrilateral, square

(4) square, rectangle, quadrilateral

14 Find the slant height of the cone to the nearest whole number.

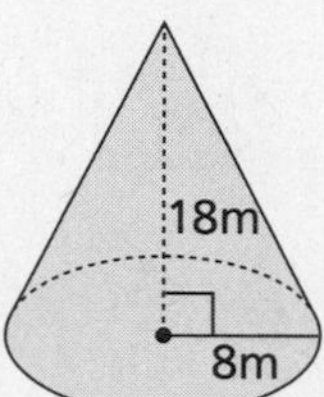

(1) 20 m **(2)** 19 m **(3)** 17 m **(4)** 22 m

Use this space for computations.

15 Find the volume of the cylinder in terms of π.

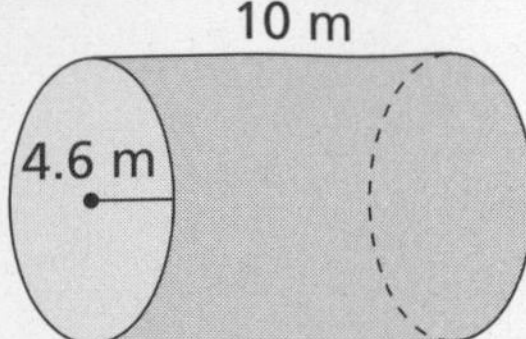

(1) $105.8\pi\ m^3$ **(2)** $92\ m^3$ **(3)** $211.6\pi\ m^3$ **(4)** $973.36\pi\ m^3$

16 $ABCDE \sim GHJDF$ Complete the statements.

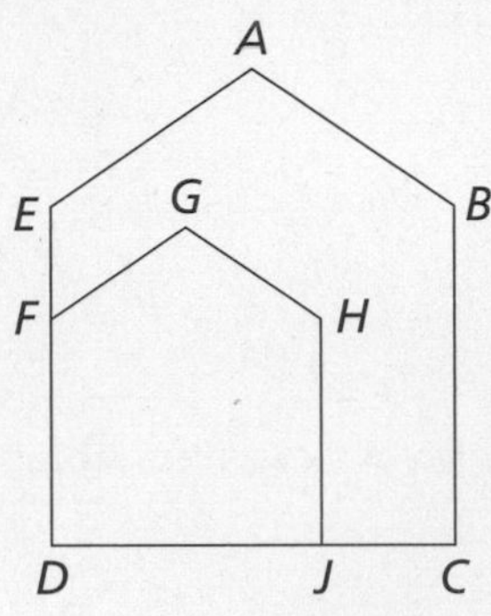

I $\angle H \cong \angle ?$

II $\frac{GH}{DJ} = \frac{AB}{?}$

(1) $\angle B$; DC **(2)** $\angle E$; AE **(3)** $\angle E$; DC **(4)** $\angle B$; AE

For questions 17–18 assume that lines that appear to be tangent are tangent. *O* is the center of the circle. Find the value of *x*.

17 $m\angle O = 122$

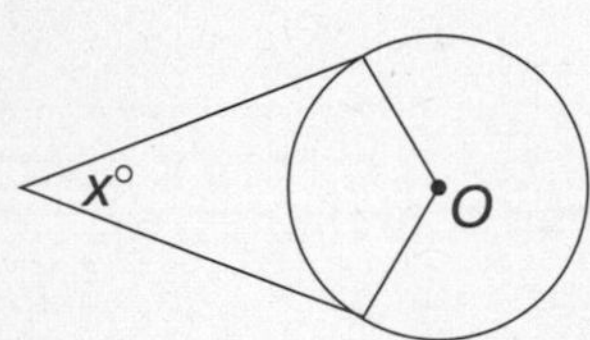

(1) 244 **(2)** 302 **(3)** 61 **(4)** 58

18 $m\angle P = 17$

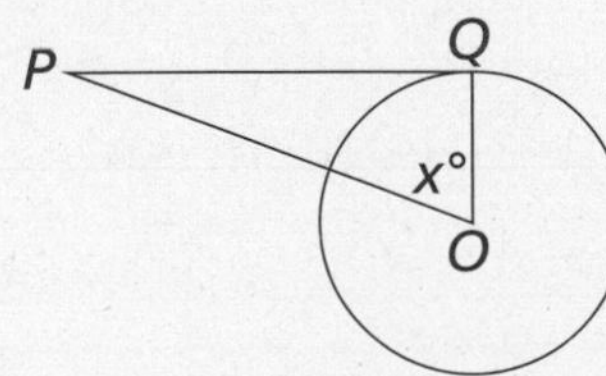

(1) 107 **(2)** 36.5 **(3)** 73 **(4)** 34

19 In the diagram below, A is the center of the circle, and $\overline{NA} \cong \overline{PA}$, $\overline{MO} \perp \overline{NA}$, $\overline{RO} \perp \overline{PA}$, $\overline{MN} = 9$ feet, find x.

Use this space for computations.

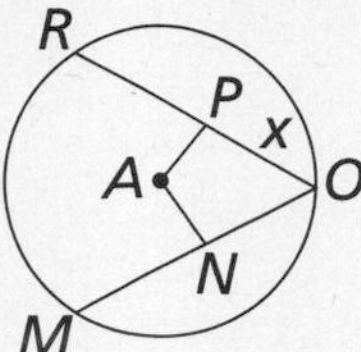

(1) 4.5 ft **(2)** 9 ft **(3)** 81 ft **(4)** 18 ft

20 Find the length of the midsegment.

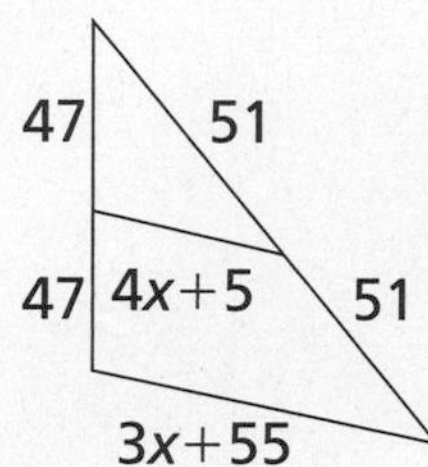

(1) 82 **(2)** 49 **(3)** 50 **(4)** 41

21 Find the midpoint of the hypotenuse in the figure below.

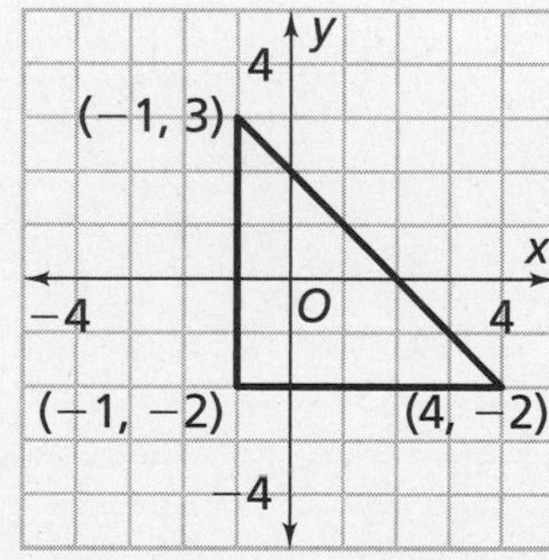

(1) $\left(\frac{3}{2}, -2\right)$ **(2)** $\left(\frac{3}{2}, \frac{1}{2}\right)$ **(3)** $\left(-1, \frac{1}{2}\right)$ **(4)** $\left(\frac{1}{2}, \frac{3}{2}\right)$

22 Where is the center of the largest circle that you could draw inside a given triangle?

(1) the point of concurrency of the altitudes of the triangle

(2) the point of concurrency of the perpendicular bisectors of the sides of the triangle

(3) the point of concurrency of the bisectors of the angles of the triangle

(4) the point of concurrency of the medians of the triangle

Use this space for computations.

23 What is the contrapositive of the statement *If you have sea water, you can make salt*?

(1) If you can make salt, you do not have sea water.

(2) If you can't make salt, you do not have sea water.

(3) If you do not have sea water, you can make salt.

(4) If you have sea water, you can't make salt.

24 In $\triangle ACE$, G is the centroid and $BE = 15$. Find BG and GE.

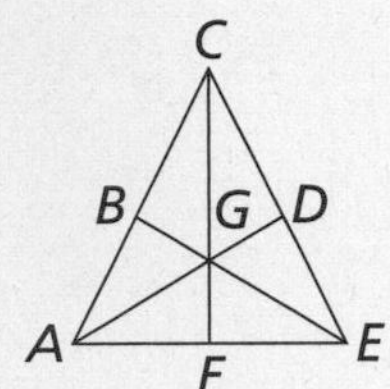

(1) $BG = 3\frac{3}{4}, GE = 11\frac{1}{4}$

(2) $BG = 5, GE = 10$

(3) $BG = 10, GE = 5$

(4) $BG = 7\frac{1}{2}, GE = 7\frac{1}{2}$

25 Name a median for $\triangle ABC$.

(1) $\overline{AD}$

(2) $\overline{CE}$

(3) $\overline{AF}$

(4) $\overline{BD}$

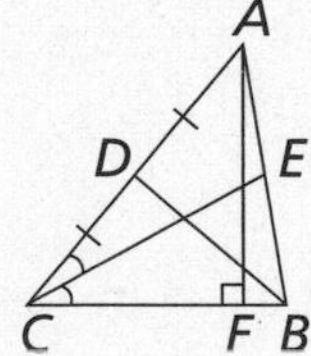

Use this space for computations.

26 What is the negation of the statement *Miguel's team won the game*?

(1) It was not Miguel's team that won the game.

(2) Miguel's team lost the game.

(3) Miguel's team did not win the game.

(4) Miguel's team did not play the game.

27 Pierre built the model shown in the diagram below for a social studies project. He wants to be able to show the inside of his model, so he sliced the figure as shown. Describe the cross section he created.

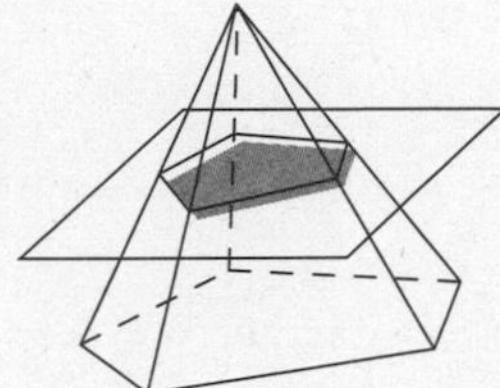

(1) hexagon

(2) pentagon

(3) pyramid

(4) rectangle

28 Find the volume of the sphere. Round your answer to the nearest integer.

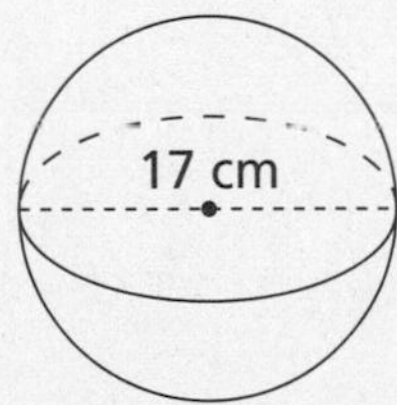

(1) 20,580 cm^3

(2) 2,573 cm^3

(3) 303 cm^3

(4) 643 cm^3

Sample Geometry Examination

Part II

Use this space for computations.

Answer all questions in this part. Each correct answer will receive 2 credits. Clearly indicate the necessary steps, including appropriate formula substitutions, diagrams, graphs, charts, etc. For all questions in this part, a correct numerical answer with no work shown will receive only 1 credit.

29 Find the surface area of the pyramid shown to the nearest whole number.

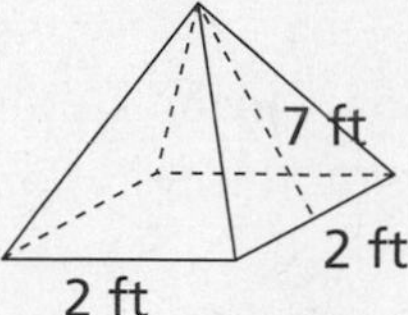

30 Explain why the triangles are similar. Then find the value of x.

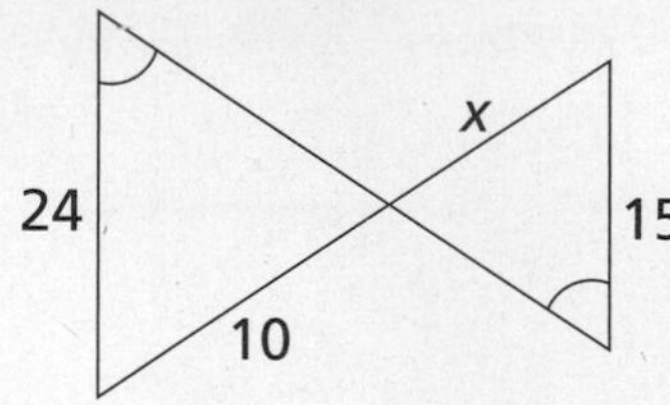

31 In the diagram below, $\overleftrightarrow{CD}$ and $\overleftrightarrow{EF}$ intersect at B, $\overline{AB} \perp \overleftrightarrow{CD}$.

1. Is $\angle EBA \cong \angle ABF$?

2. Explain your reasoning.

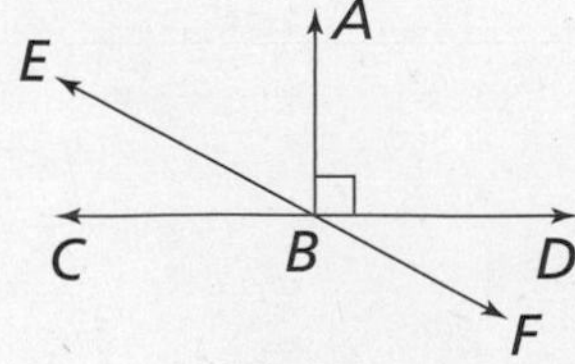

32 Find midpoint M of $\overline{AB}$.

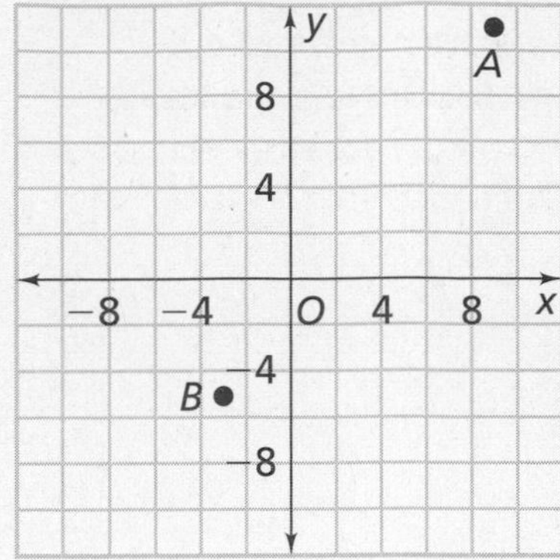

Use this space for computations.

33 Sketch the graph of the system of equations given below and name the intersecting points, if any.

$$x^2 + y^2 = 64$$
$$y = 8$$

34 Find an equation or equations for the set of all points in the coordinate plane 3 units from the graph of $x = 5$. Sketch the graph.

Sample Geometry Examination

Part III

Use this space for computations.

Answer all questions in this part. Each correct answer will receive 4 credits. Clearly indicate the necessary steps, including diagrams, graphs, charts, etc. For all questions in this part, a correct numerical answer with no work shown will receive only 1 credit.

35 Write a proof.
Given: $AB \cdot BE = CB \cdot BD$
Prove: $\triangle ABC \sim \triangle DBE$

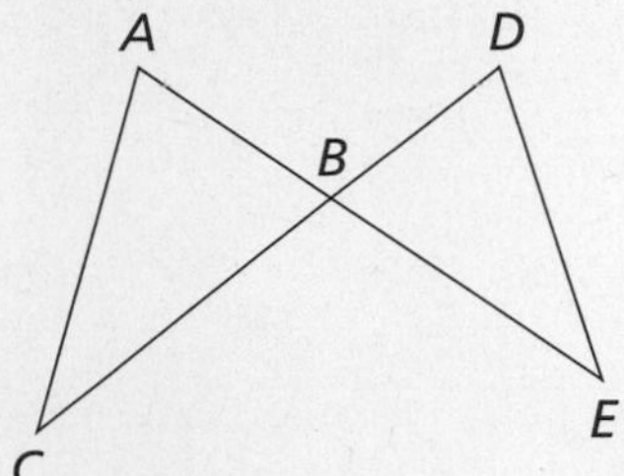

36 Write a paragraph proof to justify the following statement algebraically: *In a triangle, if the sum of the measures of two angles is equal to the measure of the third angle, then the triangle is a right triangle.*

37 In the figure, $\overline{A'B'}$ is the image of $\overline{AB}$ after a reflection in line k.

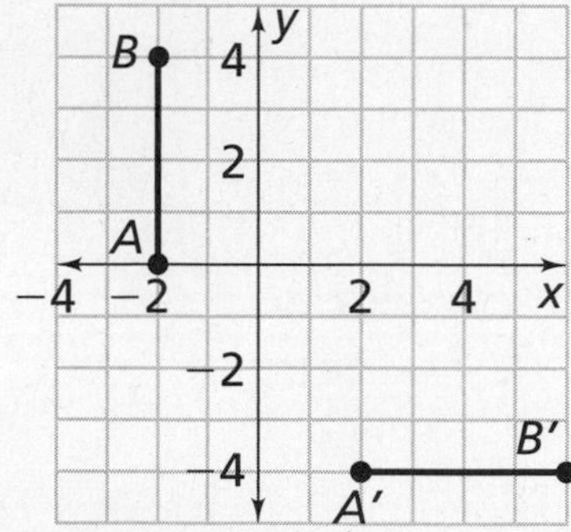

1 Find and name two points that line k passes through.

2 Explain how you know that line k passes through those two points.

3 Graph line k and the point C (3, −2) and show its image as a reflection in line k.

Part IV

Use this space for computations.

Answer the following 6-credit question in this part. Clearly indicate the necessary steps, including diagrams, graphs, charts, etc. A correct answer with no work shown will receive only 1 credit.

38 The chord-tangent theorem states that the measure of the angle formed by a chord and a tangent segment that intersect at the tangent's point of contact is equal to one half the measure of the intercepted arc. Below are three possible cases of this theorem.

Given that Case I is true, prove **Case II** of the chord-tangent theorem.

Case I **Case II** **Case III**

B B B
Y Y
O X O X O X
A C A C A C

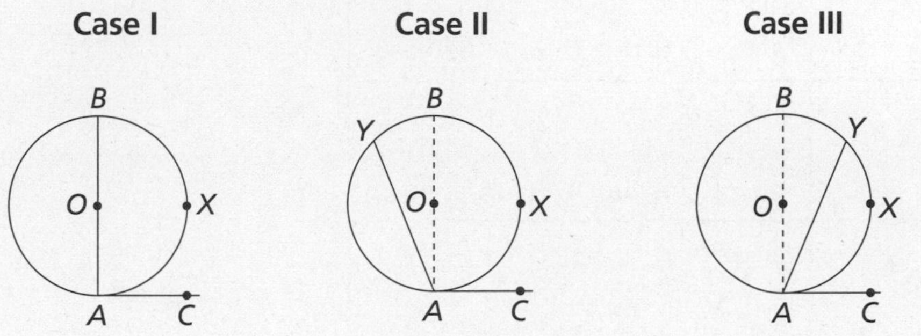

MATHEMATICS REFERENCE SHEET

The following reference sheet was taken from the New York State Education Department Web site.

Volume	
Cylinder	$V = Bh$ where B is the area of the base
Pyramid	$V = \frac{1}{3}Bh$ where B is the area of the base
Right Circular Cone	$V = \frac{1}{3}Bh$ where B is the area of the base
Sphere	$V = \frac{4}{3}\pi r^3$

Lateral Area (L)	
Right Circular Cylinder	$L = 2\pi rh$
Right Circular Cone	$L = \pi rl$ where l is the slant height

Surface Area	
Sphere	$SA = 4\pi r^2$

SELECTED ANSWERS

SELECTED ANSWERS

Diagnostic Test

Chapter 1

1 (2) **3** (4) **5** (3) **7** (4)

Chapter 2

1 (2) **3** (2) **5** (4) **7** (4) **9** (2)

Chapter 3

1 (4) **3** (4) **5** (3) **7** (2) **9** (4)

Chapter 4

1 (3) **3** (2) **5** (4) **7** (3)

Chapter 5

1 (4) **3** (1) **5** (2) **7** (3) **9** (1)

Chapter 6

1 (2) **3** (2) **5** (4) **7** (2) **9** (1)

Chapter 7

1 (1) **3** (2) **5** (3) **7** (1) **9** (2)

Chapter 8

1 (3) **3** (1) **5** (3) **7** (1) **9** (3)

Chapter 9

1 (2) **3** (1) **5** (1) **7** (3) **9** (3)

Chapter 1

Lesson 1.1

1 (1) **3** (2) **5** *No* **7** *No* **9** *Yes* **11** *No* **13** Answers may include: plane *DFE*, plane *DFB*, plane *BFE* **15** point *J* and *H* **17** point *H* **19** line *p*, or $\overleftrightarrow{JH}$ **21** 5 **23** 2 **25** *R* **27** *X* **29** $c = 4.5$ **31** Carlton is between Bradley and Ames.

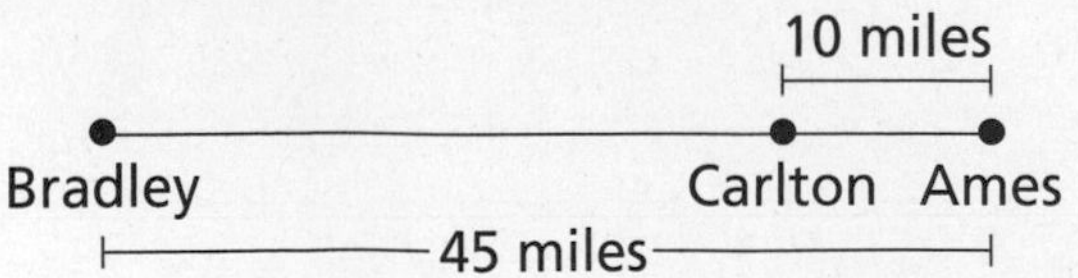

Lesson 1.2

1 (4) **3** (3) **5** (3) **7** (3) **9** (3) **11** 34° **13** $(90 - x)°$ **15** 138.5° **17** 68° **19** 29° **21** false **23** false **25** The measure of each angle is 45° **27** 120°

Lesson 1.3

1 (1) **3** (4) **5** 147° **7** 105° **9** 75° **11** 75° **13** 49° **15** 90° **17** 131° **19** 96° **21** 96° **23** 128° **25** Converse of the Same-Side Interior Angles Theorem

Lesson 1.4

1 (2) **3** (4)

5

7

9

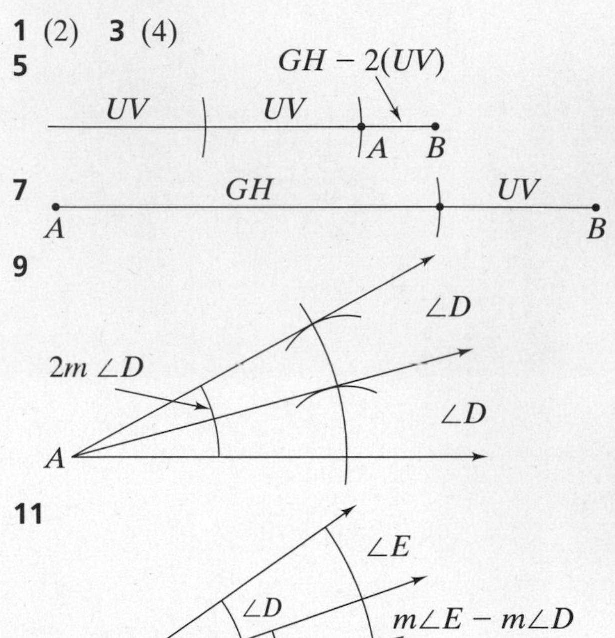

11

13

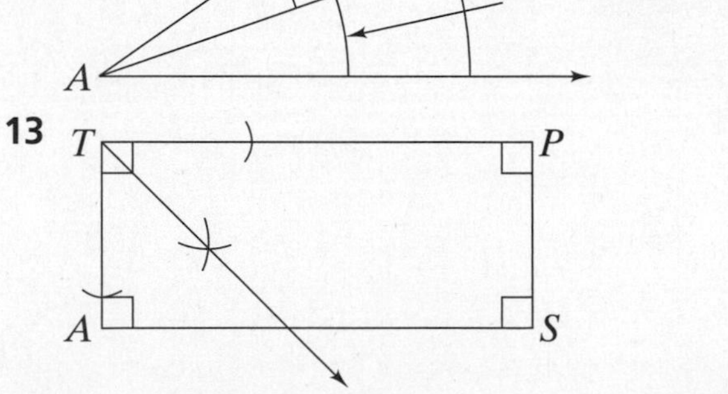

15 Check students' sketches.

17

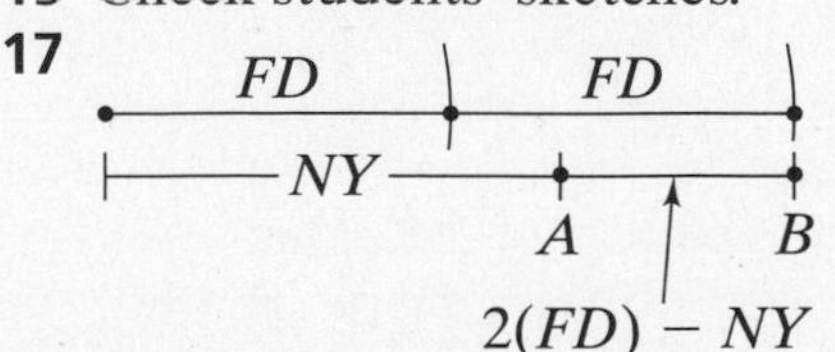

Lesson 1.5

1 (4) **3** (4)

5

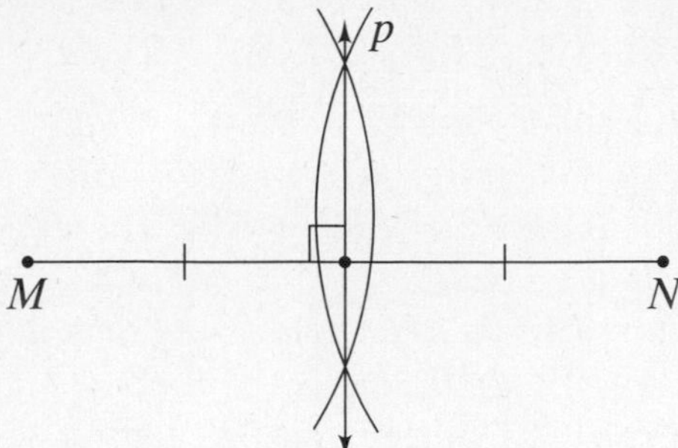

7

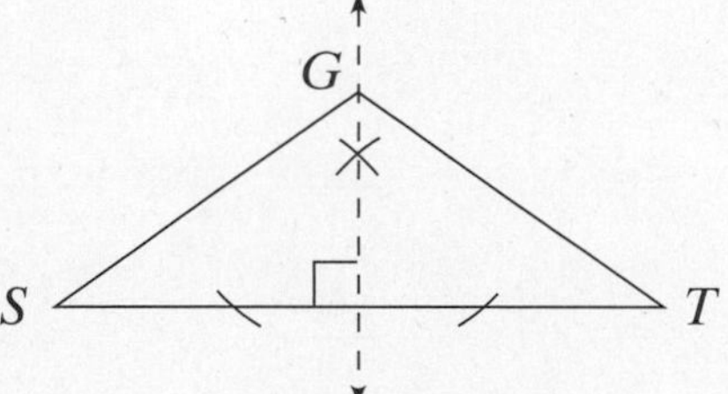

9

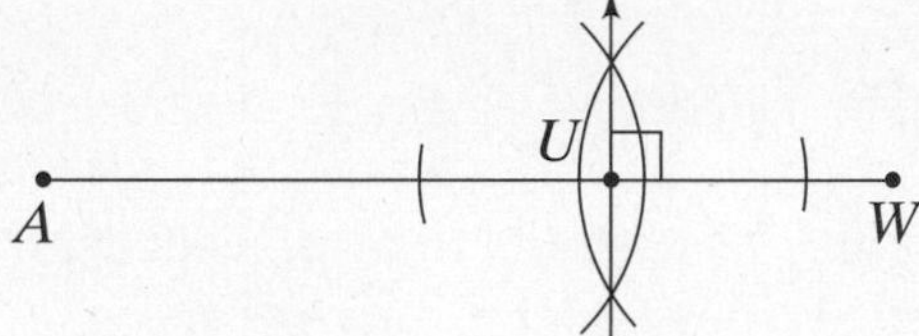

11

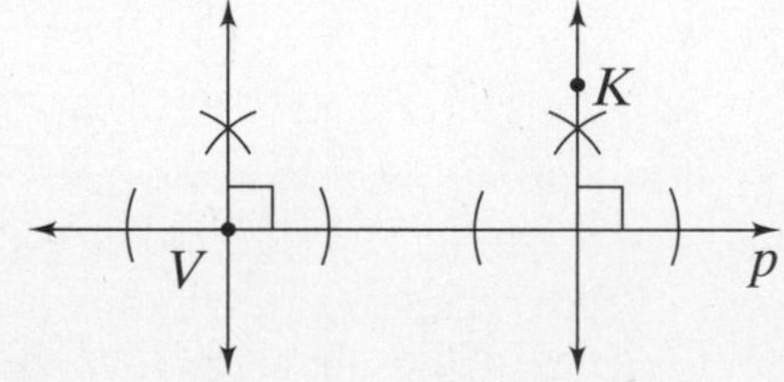

13

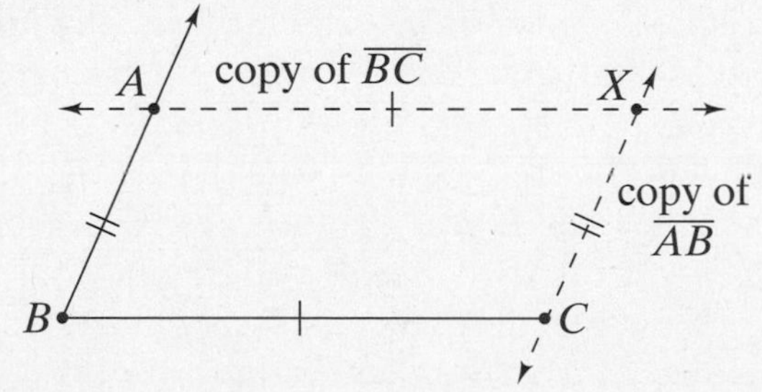

Lesson 1.6

1 (1) **3** (2) **5** (2)

7 none

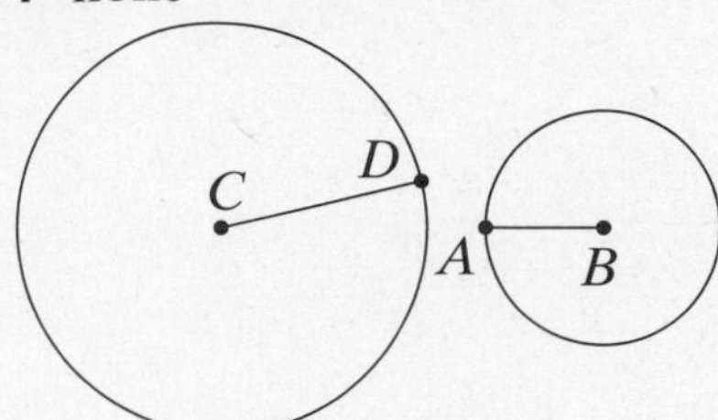

9 points *W, X, Y,* and *Z*

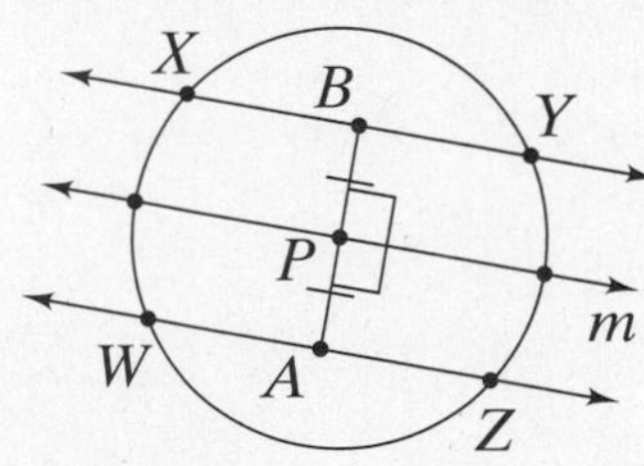

11 line *p*

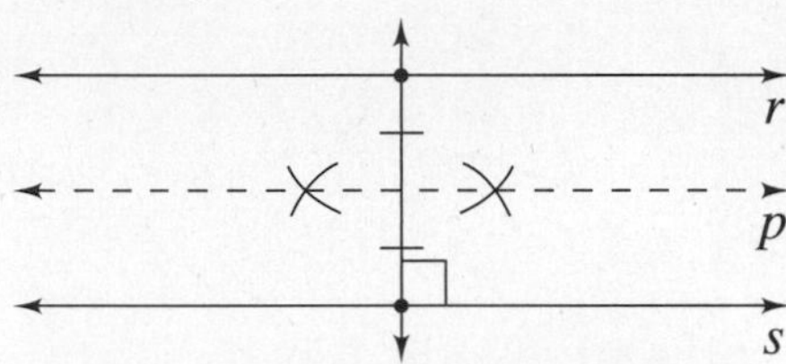

13 $x = -1$ and $x = 7$ **15** $y = 4.5$ **17** $y = \frac{2}{3}x$ **19** $y = -\frac{4}{3}x + 6.5$ **21** all points inside the circle with radius 3 and center at the origin **23** all points in the half plane to the left of or on the graph of $x = -1$ or to the right of or on the graph of $x = 5$.

Lesson 1.7

1 (4) **3** (1) **5** (3) **7** Let *d* represent the distance between *m* and *n;* two points *P* and *Q*

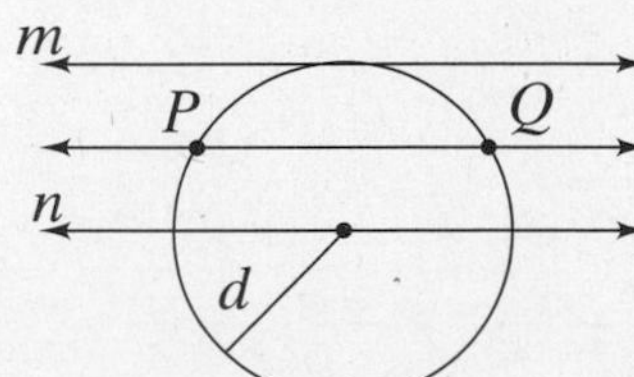

9 four

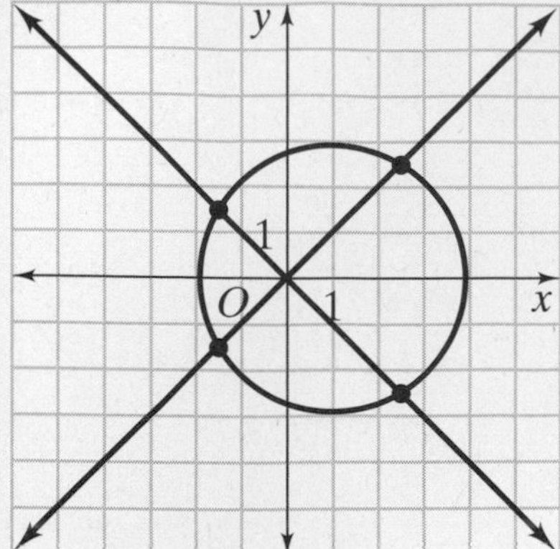

11 two points X and Y

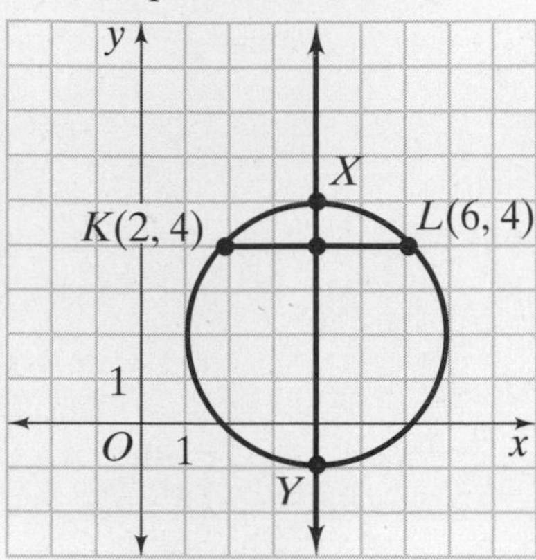

13 $P(2, 6)$ **15** $P(1, 4)$ **17** $P(3.5, 3)$ **19** 0
21 The locus is two circles centered at the origin, one with radius 6 and one with radius 4.

Chapter 1 Preparing for the Geometry Exam

1 (1) **3** (3) **5** (3) **7** (1) **9** (2) **11** (2)
13 (1) **15** (2)
17

R
S
A

19 A segment of the line $x = 1$ with endpoints at $(-1, 3)$ and $(1, 3)$.

Chapter 2

Lesson 2.1

1 (3) **3** (2) **5** (1) **7** (3) **9** (2)
11 T; *Perpendicular lines do not form right angles.*; F **13** T; *The supplement of an acute angle is not an obtuse angle.*; F **15** T; *There exists more than one bisector of an angle.*; F
17 T; *The complement of an acute angle is not an acute angle.*; F **19** F; *Twenty-seven is not a prime number.*; T **21** F; *A straight angle is 180°.*; T
23 Three collinear points **25** $\frac{1}{2} + \frac{1}{2} = 1$
27 $1 + 3 = 4$ **29** $6 + (-4) = 2$ **31** 50° and 40° **33** $x = \frac{1}{2}$; $x^2 = \frac{1}{4}$ **35** A circle with radius 1: $A = \pi$, $C = 2\pi$ **37** $a = 1$, $b = 2$, and $c = 3$; $1^2 + 2^2 \neq 3^2$

Lesson 2.2

1 (1) **3** (4) **5** (4) **7** (4) **9** T and T is T
11 F or T is T **13** T or F is T **15** T and T is T
17 All right angles are not equal, and squares do not have all sides equal. F and F is F.

Lesson 2.3

1 (2) **3** (2) **5** If you have a good job, then you will earn a good salary. *You have a good job* is the hypothesis, *you will earn a good salary* is the conclusion. **7** Two angles of a triangle are equal if it is an isosceles triangle; True. Inverse: If a triangle is not isosceles, then two angles are not equal. Converse: If two angles of a triangle are equal, then it is isosceles. Contrapositive: If two angles of a triangle are not equal, then it is not isosceles. **9** If you want lower taxes, elect Harris; Unknown. Inverse: If you do not want lower taxes, then don't elect Harris. Converse: If you elect Harris, then you want lower taxes. Contrapositive: If you do not elect Harris, then you do not want lower taxes. **11** If two angles are supplementary, then the sum of their measures is 180°; if the sum of the measures of two angles is 180°; then the angles are supplementary. **13** If two lines in the same plane are not parallel, then the two lines intersect. True. **15** If two circles have the same radius, then they have the same area. If two circles have the same area, then they have the same radius. Two circles have the same radius if and only if they have the same area.

Lesson 2.4

1 Inductive **3** Deductive **5** Deductive
7 $\angle 1$ and $\angle 2$ are supplementary, and $\angle 2$ and $\angle 3$ are supplementary by the definition of supplementary angles. Therefore, $m\angle 1 + m\angle 2 = m\angle 2 + m\angle 3$. By subtracting $m\angle 2$ from both sides, you get $m\angle 1 = m\angle 3$.

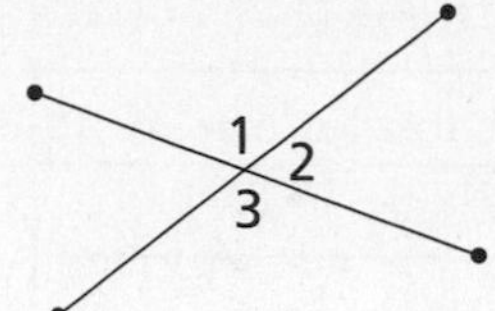

Chapter 2 Preparing for the Geometry Exam

1 (2) **3** (3) **5** (4) **7** (1) **9** (2) **11** (1)
13 (3) **15** (1) **17** (1)
19

Statements	Reasons
1. RT = 42	1. Given
2. RS + ST = RT	2. Segment Addition Axiom
3. $x + 7 + 3x - 5 = 42$	3. Substitution
4. $4x + 2 = 42$	4. Algebra (combining like terms)
5. $4x = 40$	5. Subtraction Property of Equality
6. $x = 10$	6. Division Property of Equality

21 The angles shown will change but will always remain equal to each other. By construction of parallel lines, the corresponding angles will always be equal.

Chapter 3

Lesson 3.1

1 (3) **3** (4) **5** (3) **7** 75° **9** 155 **11** $\angle 1$ and $\angle 2$ **13** $\angle 3$ **15** $\angle 2$ **17** $x = 90°, y = 34°, z = 51°$; acute, scalene
19

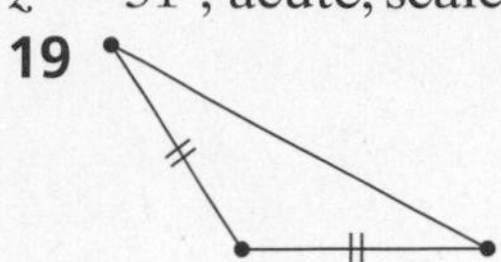

21 $s = 20°$ **23** $a = 115°, b = 30°$
25 $x = 14$

Lesson 3.2

1 (4) **3** (2) **5** The distance from Denver to St. Paul is greater than 333 miles and less than 1713 miles. **7** $\angle T$
9

Statements	Reasons
1. Draw TW such that TP = WP	1. By construction
2. $m\angle 1 = m\angle 2$	2. Base angles of an isosceles triangle are congruent
3. $m\angle OTP = m\angle 4 + m\angle 2$	3. Angle Addition Axiom
4. $m\angle OTP > m\angle 2$	4. Comparison Property of Inequality
5. $m\angle OTP > m\angle 1$	5. Substitution
6. $m\angle 1 > m\angle 3$	6. An exterior angle of a triangle is greater than either remote interior angle.
7. $m\angle OTP > m\angle 3$	7. Transitive Property of Inequality

SELECTED ANSWERS

11 $\overline{AB}, \overline{BC}, \overline{AC}$ **13** $\overline{BC}, \overline{AB}, \overline{AC}$
15 Answers may vary. Sample answer: 4, 5, and 9

Lesson 3.3

1 (2) **3** (4) **5** $\triangle ABC \sim \triangle MBN$, AA Similarity Postulate **7** 10 **9** $21\frac{1}{3}$ **11** 8
13 $4\frac{7}{9}$ **15** $\triangle JEF \sim \triangle QRF$; SSS Similarity
17 $\angle 1 \cong \angle 2$ is given. $\angle ACB \cong \angle DCE$ because intersecting lines form congruent vertical angles. Therefore, $\triangle ACB \sim \triangle DCE$ by AA Similarity.
19

Statements	Reasons
1. $\frac{XR}{RQ} = \frac{YS}{SQ}$	1. Given
2. $\frac{XR + RQ}{RQ} = \frac{YS + SQ}{SQ}$	2. Property of Proportions
3. $\frac{XQ}{RQ} = \frac{YQ}{SQ}$	3. Segment Addition Postulate
4. $\angle Q \cong \angle Q$	4. Reflexive Property
5. $\triangle XQY \sim \triangle RQS$	5. SAS Similarity
6. $\angle QXY \cong \angle QRS$	6. Corresponding angles of similar triangles are congruent.
7. $\overline{RS} \parallel \overline{XY}$	7. If two lines are cut by a transversal such that corresponding angles are congruent, then the lines are parallel.

21 251.875 m

Lesson 3.4

1 (1) **3** (4) **5** $\triangle FDE \cong \triangle IHG$; AAS
7 $\triangle XYZ \cong \triangle BCA$; ASA **9** Check students' work. **11** $\overline{AB} \cong \overline{CD}, \angle BAC \cong \angle ACD$
$\overline{BC} \cong \overline{DA}, \angle ABC \cong \angle ADC$
$\overline{CA} \cong \overline{AC}, \angle BCA \cong \angle DAC$
13 $\overline{AB} \cong \overline{AD}, \angle BAC \cong \angle DAC$
$\overline{CB} \cong \overline{CD}, \angle ABC \cong \angle ADC$
$\overline{AC} \cong \overline{AC}, \angle ACB \cong \angle ACD$

15

Statements	Reasons
1. $\angle ABC \cong \angle DCB$, $\angle DBC \cong \angle ACB$	1. Given
2. $\overline{BC} \cong \overline{BC}$	2. Reflexive Property
3. $\triangle ABC \cong \triangle DCB$	3. ASA

17

Statements	Reasons
1. $\overline{AB} \cong \overline{DC}$	1. Given
2. $\overline{BC} \cong \overline{BC}$	2. Reflexive Property
3. $AB + BC = DC + BC$	3. Addition Property of Equality
4. $AB + BC = AC$, $BC + CD = BD$	4. Segment Addition Postulate
5. $\overline{AC} \cong \overline{BD}$	5. Substitution
6. $\angle G \cong \angle E$, $\angle 2 \cong \angle 3$	6. Given
7. $\triangle GAC \cong \triangle EDB$	7. AAS

19 Yes. $\overline{AE} \cong \overline{EC}$ and $\overline{BE} \cong \overline{DE}$.
By Vertical Angle Theorem $\angle AEB \cong \angle DEC$.
The triangles are congruent by SAS.

Lesson 3.5

1 (3) **3** (3) **5** Given **7** $m\angle BAC = m\angle 1 + m\angle 2$ **9** Definition of a right angle
11

Statements	Reasons
1. $\overline{AD} \cong \overline{CE}$, $\angle DAC \cong \angle ECA$	1. Given
2. $\overline{AC} \cong \overline{AC}$	2. Reflexive Property
3. $\triangle ACD \cong \triangle CAE$	3. SAS
4. $\overline{AE} \cong \overline{CD}$	4. CPCTC
5. $\overline{ED} \cong \overline{ED}$	5. Reflexive Property
6. $\triangle CED \cong \triangle ADE$	6. SSS

13 1. By construction
2. Definition of angle bisector
3. Given
4. Reflexive Property
5. AAS
6. CPCTC

15

Statements	Reasons
1. $\overline{AD} \cong \overline{BE}$, $\angle DAB \cong \angle EBA$	1. Given
2. $\overline{AB} \cong \overline{AB}$	2. Reflexive Property
3. $\triangle DAB \cong \triangle EBA$	3. SAS
4. $\overline{BD} \cong \overline{AE}$	4. CPCTC

17

Statements	Reasons
1. $\angle 4 \cong \angle 5$	1. Given
2. $\overline{BD} \cong \overline{BD}$	2. Reflexive Property
3. $\angle 2 \cong \angle 3$	3. Given
4. $\angle 3 \cong \angle 1$	4. Intersecting lines form congruent vertical angles.
5. $\angle 1 \cong \angle 2$	5. Substitution
6. $\triangle DAB \cong \triangle DCB$	6. ASA
7. $BA = BC$	7. CPCTC

19 Given: $\overrightarrow{CD}$ is the $\perp$ bisector of $\overline{AB}$
Prove: $\overline{CA} \cong \overline{CB}$

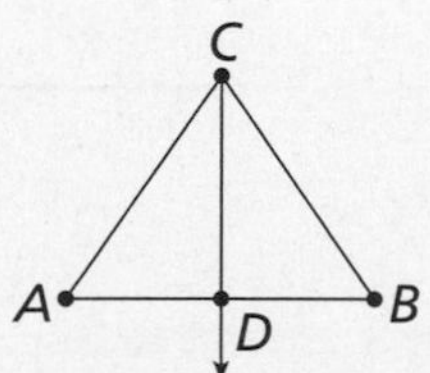

Statements	Reasons
1. Draw $\overline{AC}$ and $\overline{BC}$	1. Two points determine a line segment
2. $\overline{AD} \cong \overline{BD}$	2. Definition of perpendicular bisector
3. $\angle ADC \cong \angle BDC$	3. Perpendicular lines form right angles and all right angles are congruent.
4. $\overline{CD} \cong \overline{CD}$	4. Reflexive Property
5. $\triangle ADC \cong \triangle BDC$	5. SAS
6. $\overline{AC} \cong \overline{BC}$	6. CPCTC

Chapter 3 Preparing for the Geometry Exam

1 (3) **3** (4) **5** (4) **7** (3) **9** (3) **11** (3)
13 (2) **15** (1) **17** (2) **19** (4)

21

Statements	Reasons
1. $\overline{AE} \cong \overline{CD}$, $\angle AED \cong \angle CDE$	1. Given
2. $\overline{ED} \cong \overline{ED}$	2. Reflexive Property
3. $\triangle EAD \cong \triangle DCE$	3. SAS
4. $\angle A \cong \angle C$	4. CPCTC
5. $\overline{AB} \cong \overline{CB}$	5. Given
6. $\triangle ABE \cong \triangle CBD$	6. SAS

Chapter 4

Lesson 4.1

1 (3) **3** (1) **5** (3) **7** (4) **9** $\overline{EF} \| \overline{AC}$, $\overline{DE} \| \overline{CB}$, $\overline{DF} \| \overline{AB}$ **11** $2\frac{3}{8}$
13

Statements	Reasons
1. $\triangle DEF$ is medial triangle of $\triangle ABC$	1. Given
2. $\overline{DE} = \frac{1}{2}\,\overline{BC}$, $\overline{EF} = \frac{1}{2}\overline{AB}$, $\overline{DF} = \frac{1}{2}\,\overline{AC}$	2. Triangle Midsegment Theorem
3. $\overline{AD} = \frac{1}{2}\,\overline{AB}$, $\overline{AE} = \frac{1}{2}\,\overline{AC}$	3. Definition of midpoint
4. $\overline{DE} = \overline{DE}$	4. Reflexive
5. $\triangle ADE \cong \triangle DEF$	5. SSS Postulate

15 27 in. **17** 13.5 **19** 29
21 $PR = 100$, $TU = 50$

Lesson 4.2

1 (4) **3** (4) **5** (1)
7

Statements	Reasons
1. $\triangle RST$ with M midpoint of $\overline{SR}$ and N midpoint of $\overline{ST}$	1. Given
2. $\overline{MN} \| \overline{RT}$	2. Midsegment is parallel to the third side of the triangle.
3. $\angle MNR \cong \angle NRT$, $\angle NMT \cong \angle MTR$	3. Alternate interior angles of two parallel lines cut by a transversal are equal.
4. $\triangle MNW \sim \triangle TRW$	4. AA

9 10 **11** Centroid (Center of Gravity)
13 These segments are concurrent. (See accompanying figure)

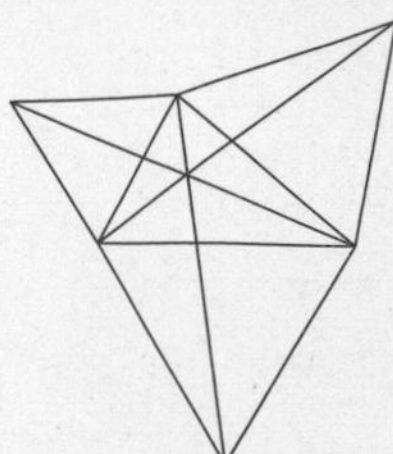

Lesson 4.3

1 (2) **3** (3) **5** (4) **7** (1) **9** (2) **11** 8 ft
13 29.4 ft **15** $\frac{2\sqrt{3}}{3}$ **17** $4\sqrt{3}$ **19** $16\sqrt{2}$
21 $\sqrt{2} : 1 = \frac{\sqrt{2}}{1}$ **23** $6\sqrt{3}$ **25** 2

Lesson 4.4

1 (2) **3** (3) **5** (1) **7** (2) **9** (3) **11** (2)
13 y **15** a **17** c **19** $x = 6$, $y = 6\sqrt{3}$
21 $x = 4.8$, $y = 3.6$ **23** $x = 4\sqrt{30}$, $y = 4\sqrt{70}$
25 $\frac{600\sqrt{13}}{13} \approx 166.41$

Chapter 4 Preparing for the Geometry Exam

1 (2) **3** (3) **5** (4) **7** (2) **9** (3) **11** (2)
13 (2) **15** (1) **17** (2) **19** (2)
21 The area of the square built upon the hypotenuse is equal to the sum of the areas built upon the two legs. This relationship holds for any similar figures built upon the sides of the right triangle. For example, the area of the semicircle built upon the hypotenuse is equal to the sum of the areas of the semicircles built upon the legs. **23** $64\sqrt{3} \approx 110.85$

Chapter 5

Lesson 5.1

1 (2) **3** (4) **5** (1) **7** $n = 51.4°$
9 $x = 120°$, $y = 60°$ **11** 3 **13** 17 **15** 5
17 6 sides, hexagon **19** 8 sides, octagon
21 decagon, $a = 144°$

Lesson 5.2

1 (3) **3** (1) **5** (1)
7 $m\angle K = 138°, m\angle L = 42°, m\angle M = 138°$
9 50° **11** *sometimes true* **13** *sometimes true*
15 *always true* **17** *ABCD* cannot be a trapezoid or a kite, since it is a parallelogram. *ABCD* can be a square only if the sides are congruent and the interior angles are 90°. *ABCD* is a rhombus if and only if its sides are all congruent.

Lesson 5.3

1 (3) **3** (4) **5** (1)
7

Statements	Reasons
1. Kite $DEFG$; $\overline{EF} \cong \overline{FG}$	1. Given
2. $\overline{DF} \perp \overline{EG}$	2. Diagonals of a kite are perpendicular
3. $\angle EHF$ and $\angle GHF$ are right $\angle s$	3. $\perp s$ form right angles
4. $\triangle EHF$ and $\triangle GHF$ are right triangles	4. Definition of right triangles
5. $\overline{FH} \cong \overline{FH}$	5. Reflexive Property
6. $\triangle EHF \cong \triangle GHF$	6. HL
7. $EH \cong GH$	7. CPCTC

9 In rectangle $KLMN$, $\overline{KL} \cong \overline{NM}$ because opposite sides of a rectangle are congruent. $\overline{LM} \cong \overline{LM}$ by the reflexive property. $\angle KLM$ and $\angle LMN$ are right angles since rectangles have four right angles. $\triangle KLM$ and $\triangle LMN$ are congruent by SAS. Therefore $\overline{KM} \cong \overline{LN}$ by CPCTC, proving the diagonals of a rectangle are congruent.

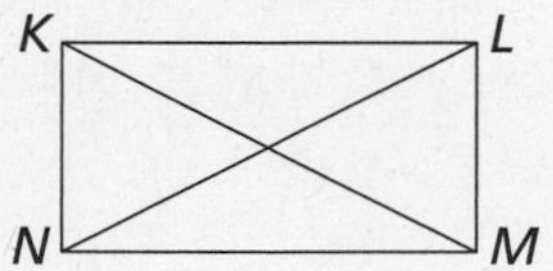

Chapter 5 Preparing for the Geometry Exam

1 (2) **3** (1) **5** (2) **7** (4) **9** (1)
11 (4) **13** (1) **15** (2)
17 $90° + 105° + 135° + 115° + x = 540°$; $445° + x = 540°$; $x = 95°$
19 Assume that the quadrilateral *PUNT* is a rectangle. By the definition of rectangle, $\overline{PT} \cong \overline{UN}$ and $\overline{PU} \cong \overline{TN}$. Since $\overline{UT}$ is congruent to itself by the Reflexive Property, $\triangle PUT \cong \triangle NTU$. But this contradicts what was given, that $\triangle PUT \not\cong \triangle NTU$. Therefore, the assumption that the quadrilateral *PUNT* is a rectangle was false. This proves that *PUNT* is not a rectangle.

CHAPTER 6

Lesson 6.1

1 (2) **3** (1) **5** (3) **7** (2) **9** $y = -2x - 1$
11 $y = -\frac{3}{5}x + \frac{2}{5}$ **13** $y = 7$ **15** $x = -11$
17 $y = 0$, or the x-axis **19** $3x + 5y = 15$
21 Yes; An equation for the line containing P and Q is $y = \frac{7}{8}(x + 3) - 1$; $\frac{7}{8}(93 + 3) - 1 = 7(12) - 1 = 83$. So, (93, 83) is on the line.

Lesson 6.2

1 (4) **3** (3) **5** (1) **7** $y = x$ **9** $y = -3x + 4$
11 $y = 2x - 8$ **13** $y = \frac{3}{2}x + \frac{5}{2}$
15 slope of $\overline{JK} = -1$, slope of $\overline{LM} = -1$, parallel
17 slope of $\overline{JK} = 3$, slope of $\overline{LM} = 0$, neither
19 slope of $\overline{JK} = -\frac{1}{6}$, slope of $\overline{LM} = -\frac{1}{5}$, neither
21 slope of $\overline{JK} = 2$, slope of $\overline{LM} = -\frac{1}{2}$ perpendicular **23** slope of $\overline{JK} = -\frac{1}{4}$, slope of $\overline{LM} = -\frac{1}{4}$, parallel

Lesson 6.3

1 (3) **3** (4) **5** (3) **7** $(-1, 1)$ and $(3, 9)$
9 no solution **11** $(-1, -6)$ and $(6, 8)$
13 $(-4, 3)$ and $(3, -4)$

15 One parabola has vertex (0, 1) and opens up. The other parabola has vertex (0, −2) and opens down. These parabolas cannot intersect.

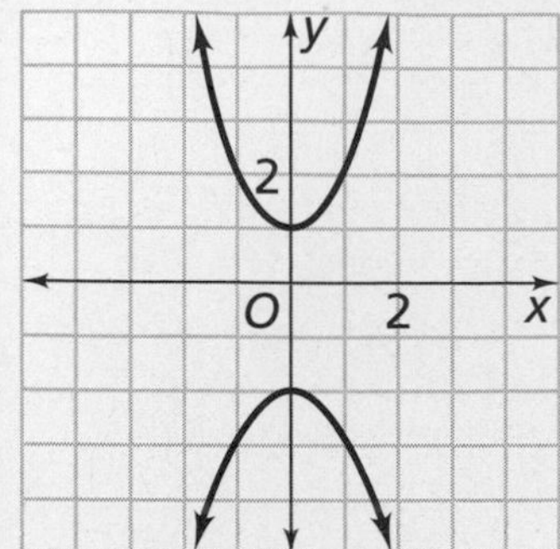

17 one point of intersection

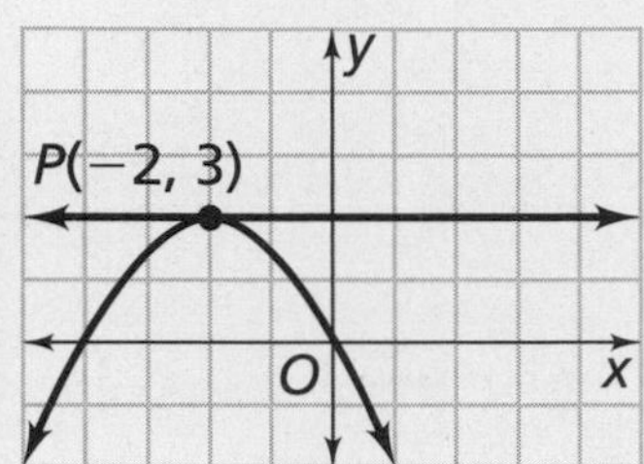

19 no points of intersection

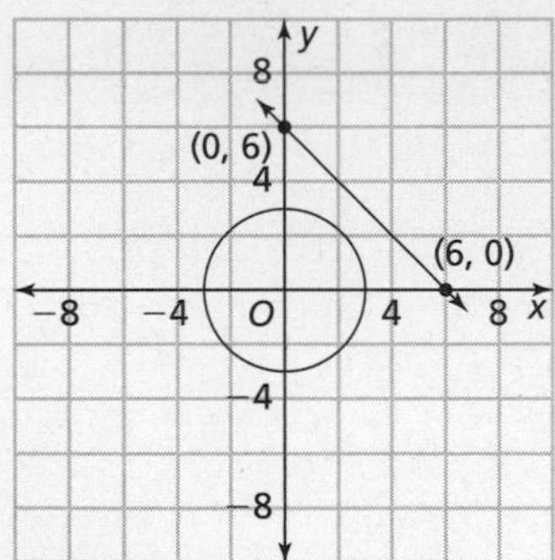

21 The system has no solution when $k < 4$, the system has 1 solution when $k = 4$, and the system has 2 solutions when $k > 4$.

Lesson 6.4

1 (2) **3** (4) **5** (1) **7** midpoint: (1.5, 6.5); length: $\sqrt{514}$ **9** midpoint: (5.5, 1); length: $5\sqrt{5}$
11 $\sqrt{113} \approx 10.63$ **13** 7 **15** $\sqrt{34} \approx 5.83$
17 midpoint. (0, 2); $y = -x + 2$ **19** midpoint (3, −2); $y = \frac{2}{3}x - 4$ **21** $\frac{5\sqrt{2}}{4}$

Lesson 6.5

1 (3) **3** (4) **5** $AB = AD = BD = CD = \sqrt{5}$. The quadrilateral is a rhombus because it has four congruent sides. **7** (2, −2) **9** The line joining the midpoints has slope $m = 0$. The base has slope 0. Therefore, the line joining the midpoint and the base are parallel. **11** Length of the segment connecting (3, 9) and (−6, 3): $\sqrt{9^2 + 6^2} = \sqrt{81 + 36} = \sqrt{117}$.
Length of the segment connecting (−4, 9) and (5, 3) is also $\sqrt{9^2 + 6^2} = \sqrt{81 + 36} = \sqrt{117}$.
Therefore the diagonals are congruent.
13 The length of each side is $\sqrt{2a^2 + 2a + 1}$. Therefore the quadrilateral is a rhombus, since a quadrilateral with 4 congruent sides is a rhombus.

Lesson 6.6

1 (4) **3** (3) **5** (2) **7** Center (0, 0); $r = 3$; (0, 3)

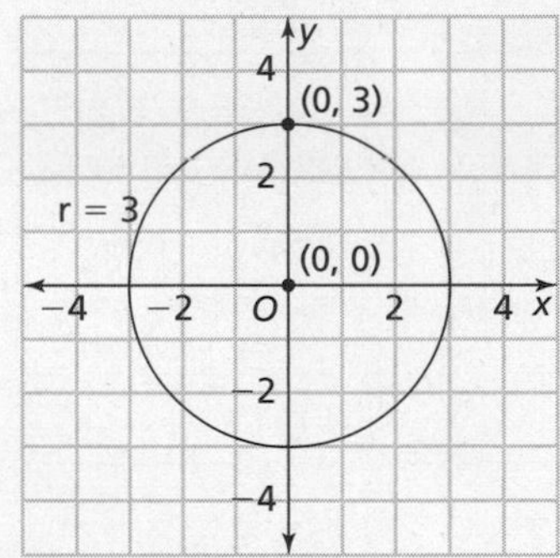

9 Center (−2, 2), $r = 2$; (−4, 2)

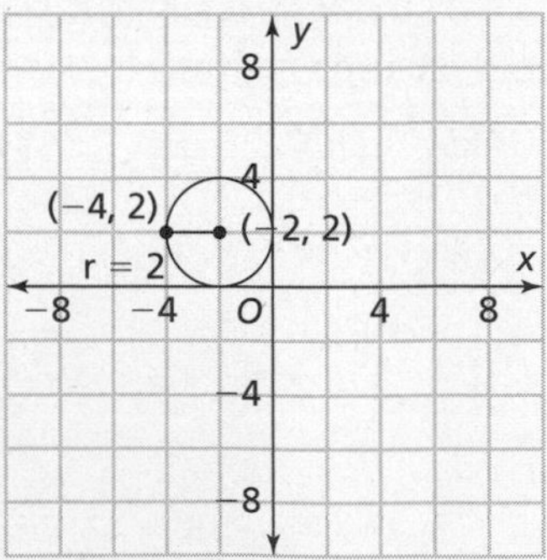

11 Center (2, 1); $r = 5$; (7, 1)

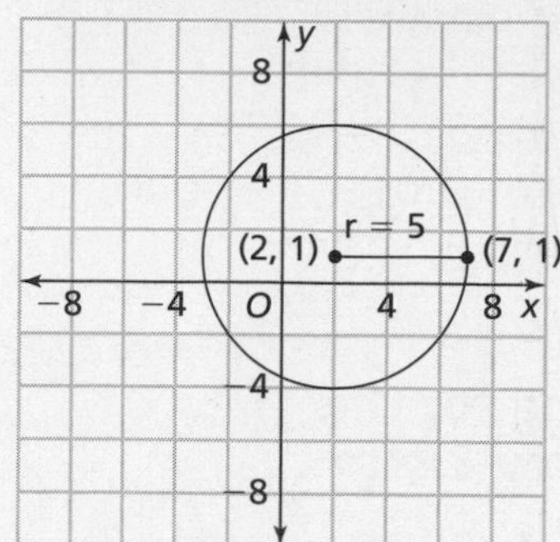

13 $(x + 5)^2 + (y - 2)^2 = 5^2$
15 $(x - 1)^2 + (y + 3)^2 = 3^2$

Chapter 6 Preparing for the New York Geometry Exam

1 (3) **3** (4) **5** (2) **7** (2) **9** (1) **11** (4)
13 (4) **15** $(x - 1)^2 + (y - 1)^2 = 25$
17 The slopes of both bases are 0, therefore they are parallel. The lengths of the nonparallel sides are:

$\sqrt{(a - 0)^2 + (c - 0)^2} = \sqrt{a^2 + c^2}$ and
$\sqrt{(a - (a + b)^2 + (c - 0)^2} = \sqrt{a^2 + c^2}$.

Since the nonparallel sides are equal length, and the bases are parallel, the figure is an isosceles trapezoid.

CHAPTER 7

Lesson 7.1

1 (2) **3** (2) **5** (2)
7

9 $R'(1, -1)$, $S''(5, -1)$, and $T'(5, -3)$
11 $E'(1, 5)$, $U'(-1, 5)$, $D'(3, 9)$, $P'(5, 9)$
13 $B(-3, 2)$, $C(3, -2)$, $D(3, 2)$

15

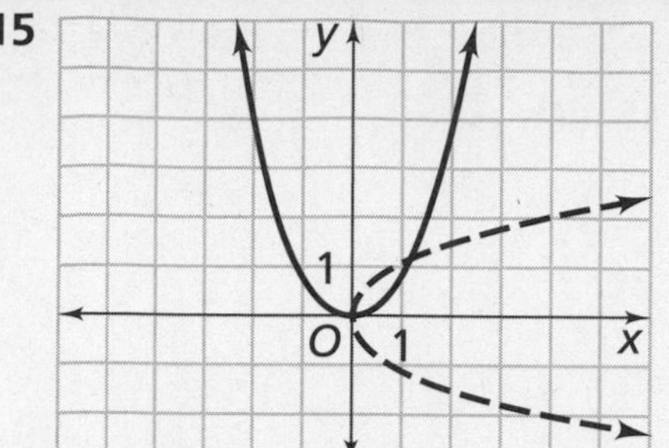

Lesson 7.2

1 (2) **3** (1) **5** (2) **7** $A'(-4, -1)$
9 $C'(-7, 8)$ **11** $E'(3, -4)$
13

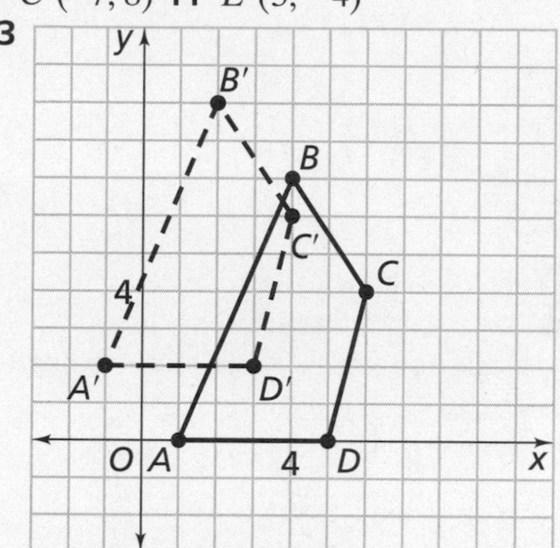

15

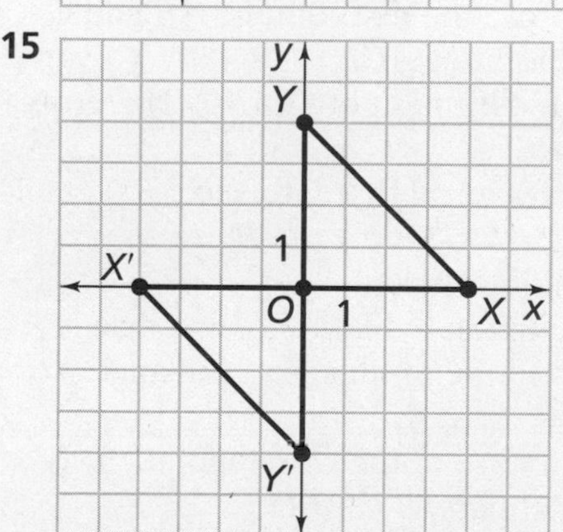

17

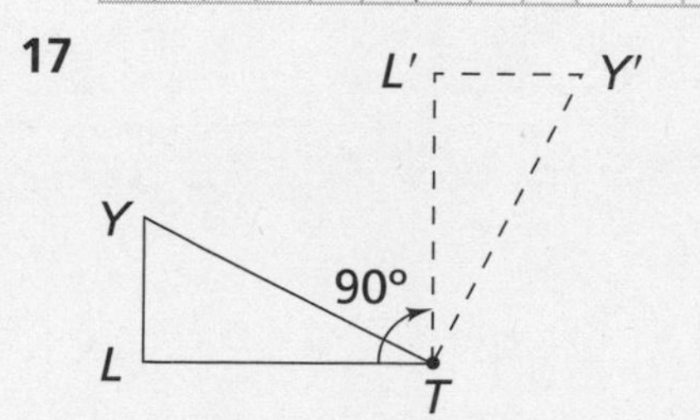

Lesson 7.3

1 (1) **3** (3) **5** (1) **7** (3)

9 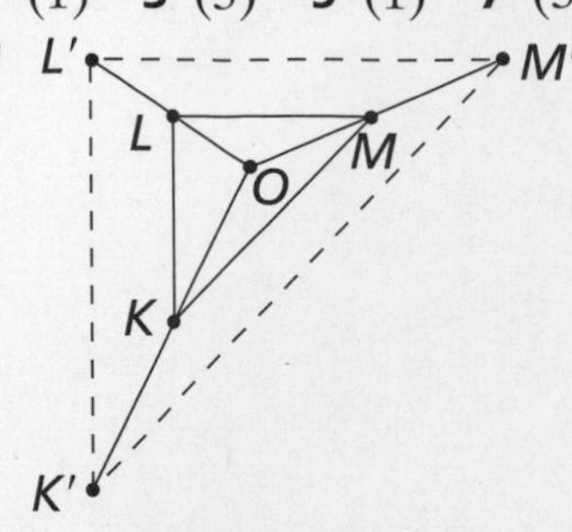

11 $A'(-3, 1.5)$, $B'(4.5, 1.5)$, and $C'(-3, 7.5)$,

13 $X''(3, -3)$ and $Y''(21, 6)$

Lesson 7.4

1 (4) **3** (3) **5** (3) **7** $B''(6, -6)$

Lesson 7.5

1
1. Construct $\triangle ABC$ with vertices $A(0, 0)$, $B(x_1, y_1)$, $C(x_2, y_2)$.
2. Apply a dilation with a scale factor of 0.5 to points B and C.
   $D_{0.5}(B) = B'\left(\frac{x_1}{2}, \frac{y_1}{2}\right)$
   $D_{0.5}(C) = C'\left(\frac{x_2}{2}, \frac{y_2}{2}\right)$
3. B' is therefore the midpoint of $\overline{AB}$ and C' is the midpoint of $\overline{AC}$.
4. $\overline{B'C'}$ is a midsegment of $\triangle ABC$. Therefore, $\overline{B'C'} = \frac{1}{2}\overline{BC}$.
5. $\overline{AC}$ is a transversal that intersects $\overline{B'C'}$ and $\overline{BC}$, and $\angle AB'C'$ and $\angle ACB$ are corresponding angles.
6. The image under a dilation of an angle is congruent to the preimage of the angle, so $\angle AB'C' \cong \angle ACB$.
7. By the converse of the Corresponding Angles Postulate, $B'C' \parallel BC$.

3 Let Q be the origin and let the coordinates of S be $(x_1, 0)$ and the coordinates of T be $(0, y_1)$. Then $R_{Q, 90°}(x_1, 0) = R(0, x_1)$ and $R_{Q, 90°}(0, y_1) = P(y_1, 0)$. $QS = RQ = x_1$ and $QT = QP = y_1$. Therefore, $R_{Q, 90°}(\triangle PQR) = \triangle TQS$. Since a reflection is an isometry, $\triangle PQR \cong \triangle TQS$.

Chapter 7 Preparing for the New York Geometry Exam

1 (1) **3** (3) **5** (2) **7** (3) **9** (2) **11** (3)
13 (2) **15** (4) **17** (3)

19 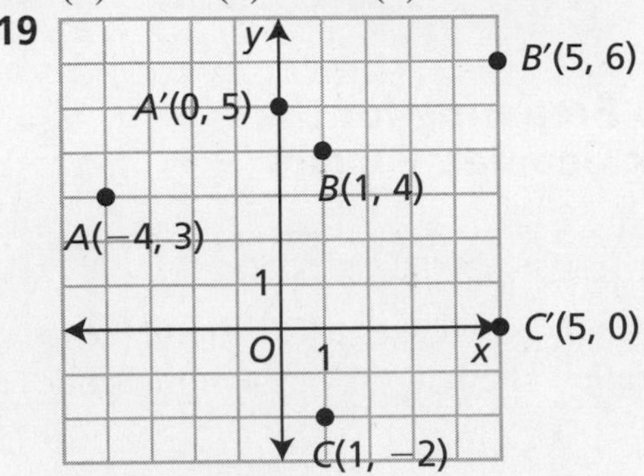

The transformation is a slide. The transformation has no effect on the distance of A' from the library. The transformation increases the distance of B' and C' from the library.

21 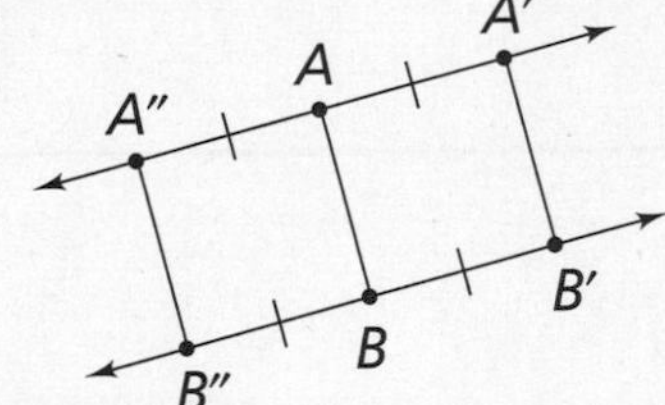

Chapter 8

Lesson 8.1

1 (1) **3** (3)

5

Statements	Reasons
1. $\overline{BG} \cong \overline{BF}; \overline{DB} \cong \overline{BE}$	1. Given
2. $\angle BGF \cong \angle BFG$	2. If two sides of a triangle are ≅, the angles opposite those sides are ≅.
3. $m\angle BGF = \frac{1}{2}m(\overset{\frown}{BE} + \overset{\frown}{DA})$ $m\angle BFG = \frac{1}{2}m(\overset{\frown}{DB} + \overset{\frown}{EC})$	3. A measure of an angle formed by intersecting chords is half the sum of the intercepted arcs.
4. $\frac{1}{2}m(\overset{\frown}{BE} + \overset{\frown}{DA}) = \frac{1}{2}m(\overset{\frown}{DB} + \overset{\frown}{EC})$	4. Substitution
5. $m\overset{\frown}{DA} \cong m\overset{\frown}{CE}$	5. Multiplication and Subtraction Property of Equality

7

Statements	Reasons
1. $\overset{\frown}{AC} \cong \overset{\frown}{BD}$	1. Given
2. $m\angle B = \frac{1}{2}m\overset{\frown}{AC}$ $m\angle C = \frac{1}{2}m\overset{\frown}{BD}$	2. The measure of an inscribed angle is half its intercepted arc.
3. $m\angle B = m\angle C$	3. Substitution
4. $\overline{AB} \parallel \overline{CD}$	4. If two lines are cut by a transversal such that alternate interior angles are congruent, then the lines are parallel.

Lesson 8.2

1 (2) **3** (3) **5** (1) **7** 80° **9** 120° **11** 220°

Lesson 8.3

1 (1) **3** $x = 4$

5

Statements	Reasons
1. $\overline{EC} \cong \overline{EB}; \overline{AE} \cong \overline{DE}$	1. A tangent segment drawn to a circle from an exterior pt. are congruent
2. $EC = EB; AE = DE$	2. Definition of congruence
3. $AE + EB = DE + EC$	3. Addition Property of Equality
4. $AB = AE + EB$; $DC = DE + EC$	4. Segment Addition Axiom
5. $AB = DC$	5. Substitution
6. $\overline{AB} \cong \overline{DC}$	6. Segments of equal length are congruent.

7 $x = 5$

Chapter 8 Preparing for the New York Geometry Exam

1 (4) **3** (2) **5** (3) **7** (2) **9** (2) **11** (2) **13** (2) **15** (3) **17** (1)

19

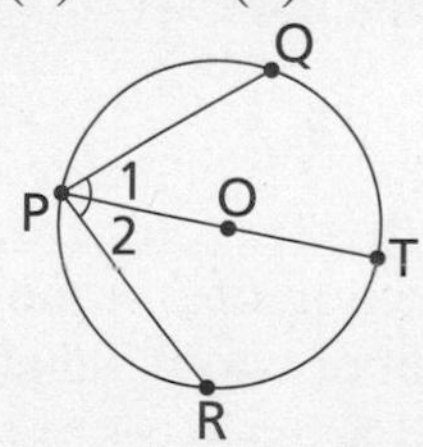

Statements	Reasons
1. $\overline{PQ}$ & $\overline{PR}$ are chords of circle O, $\overline{PT}$ bisects $\angle P$	1. Given
2. $m\angle 1 = m\angle 2$	2. Definition of angle bisector
3. $\widehat{QT} \cong \widehat{TR}$	3. ≅ inscribed angles have ≅ arcs.
4. $m\widehat{PQ} = 180° - m\widehat{QT}$ $m\widehat{PR} = 180° - m\widehat{RT}$	4. Measure of a semicircle is 180°. Properties of algebra
5. $m\widehat{PR} = 180° - m\widehat{QT}$	5. Substitution
6. $\widehat{PQ} \cong \widehat{PR}$	6. Substitution
7. $\overline{PQ} \cong \overline{PR}$	7. ≅ arcs have ≅ chords.

CHAPTER 9

Lesson 9.1

1 (4) **3** (1) **5** Answers may vary. Sample answer: A, D, and E **7** Answers may vary. Sample answer: plane EFC **9** Answers may vary. Sample answer: plane AEC and plane CDE
11 Answers may vary. Sample answer: $\overleftrightarrow{CE}$
13 Answers may vary. Sample answer: $\overleftrightarrow{CD}$
15 4 **17** T **19** F **21** T

Lesson 9.2

1 (1) **3** (3) **5** The intersection of 2 or more planes is a line. **7** Definition of two parallel planes **9** By definition, 2 adjacent faces of a cube are perpendicular. **11** The shortest distance between 2 planes is the perpendicular distance between them.

Lesson 9.3

1 (1) **3** 136 in.^2 **5** 80 m^2 **7** L.A. = 60 m^2; S.A. = 96 m^2

Lesson 9.4

1 (3) **3** (3) **5** 113.5 m^2 **7** 490.7 sq. units **9** 49.28π cm^2 **11** 1.25 gallons **13** Answers will vary. Sample answer: A cylinder with height = 2 and radius 6

Lesson 9.5

1 (1) **3** (1) **5** one family-sized can **7** 6739.2 lb

Lesson 9.6

1 (2) **3** (4) **5** (1) **7** S.A = 100π in.^2; V = $\frac{500}{3}\pi$ in.^3 **9** $V = 2{,}304\pi$ cm^3 **11** $2{,}303.1\pi$ cm^3 **13** 12π cm **15** 16 cm **17** 9π cm^2 **19** 121.5π in.^3

Chapter 9 Preparing for the New York Geometry Exam

1 (4) **3** (2) **5** (1) **7** (4) **9** (2) **11** (4) **13** (2) **15** (1) **17** (3) **19** 667.73 cm^3 **21** 138.2 ft^2; $2,625.70; 207.3 ft^3

Sample Geometry Examination I

Part I

1 (1) **3** (2) **5** (2) **7** (1) **9** (1) **11** (2) **13** (1) **15** (1) **17** (3) **19** (1) **21** (4) **23** (2) **25** (2) **27** (3)

Part II

29 Circle with center (−6, −1) and radius of 4. Equation of circle $(x + 6)^2 + (y + 1)^2 = 16$ **31** 456 m^2 **33** $\overline{BO} \cong \overline{OD}$; the diagonals of a parallelogram bisect each other.

Part III

35

Statements	Reasons
1. $m\angle 1 = m\angle 2 = m\angle 3 = 90°$	1. Perpendicular lines meet to form right angles.
2. $m\angle 4 = 122°$	2. Vertical angles are equal in measure.
3. $m\angle 5 = m\angle 6 = 58°$	3. Vertical angles are equal in measure.
4. $m\angle 8 = 90 - 58 = 32°$	4. The acute angles of a right triangle are complementary.
5. $m\angle 7 = 180° - m\angle 8$	5. The sum of supplementary angles = 180°.
6. $m\angle 7 = m\angle 9 = 148°$	6. Vertical angles are equal in measure.

37 1. Use the scale of 1 cm to 0.5 meters. The dimensions of the actual cabin are 7 m by 10 m by 3.5 m.
2. The volume of the cabin is 245 cubic meters.

Sample Geometry Examination 2

Part I

1 (3) **3** (2) **5** (2) **7** (2) **9** (4) **11** (3) **13** (1) **15** (3) **17** (4) **19** (1) **21** (2) **23** (2) **25** (4) **27** (2)

Part II

29 $4(\frac{1}{2})\,bh + s^2 = 4(7) + 4 = 32\text{ ft}^2$ **31** No. $m\angle CBA = 90°$ because perpendicular lines form right angles. $m\angle EBA < 90°$ and $m\angle ABF > 90°$, so the angles cannot be congruent. **33** The graphs intersect at (0, 8).

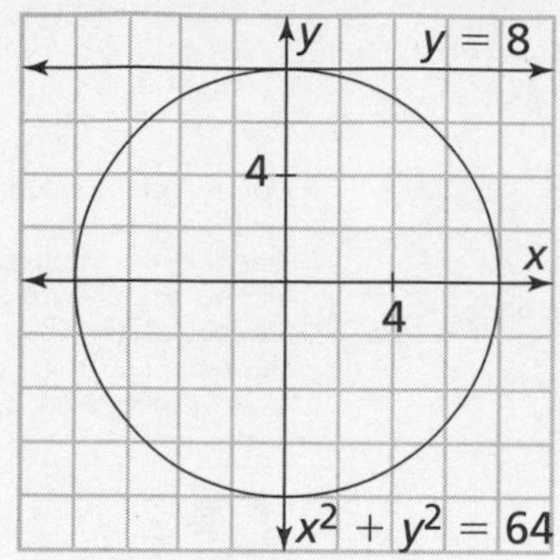

Part III

35

Statements	Reasons
1. $AB \cdot BE = CB \cdot BD$	1. Given
2. $\frac{CB}{BE} = \frac{AB}{BD}$	2. Property of Proportions
3. $\angle ABC \cong \angle DBE$	3. Vertical $\angle s$ are $\cong$.
4. $\triangle ABC \sim \triangle DBE$	4. SAS ~ Theorem

37 1. (0, −2) and (2, 0)
2. The line that contains the two points is the perpendicular bisector of $\overline{AA'}$ and $\overline{BB'}$.
3.

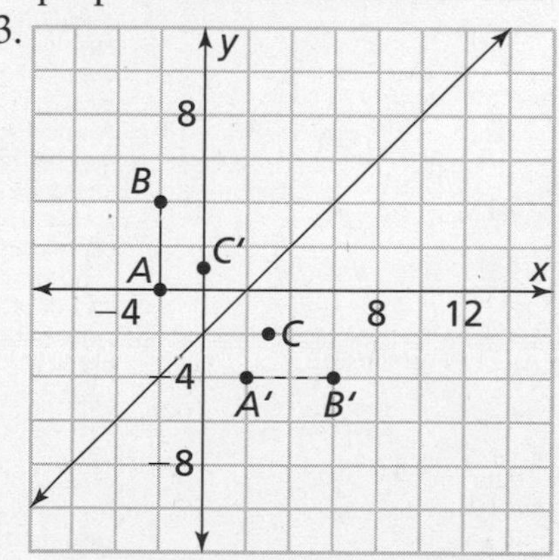

INDEX

INDEX

Q

R

S

INDEX

ACKNOWLEDGMENTS

Staff Credits:

The people who make up the ***High School Brief Review***—representing design, editorial, educational technology, marketing, production services, and publication processes—are listed below. Bold type denotes the core team members.

Jane Breen, Stacey Clark, Bob Craton, **Daren Hastings, Ted Kechris,** Courtney Marsh, **Andrea Niles,** Jennifer Scuppi

Additional Credits:

Quarasan, Inc.: Chicago, IL;
Kathy Osmus, Bob Burnham, and Diane Folliard

GGS Book Services-PMG: York, PA

Cover Image:

Punchstock

Geometry June, 2011

Part I

Answer all 28 questions in this part. Each correct answer will receive 2 credits. No partial credit will be allowed. For each question, write on the separate answer sheet the numeral preceding the word or expression that best completes the statement or answers the question. [56]

Use this space for computations.

1 Line segment AB is shown in the diagram below.

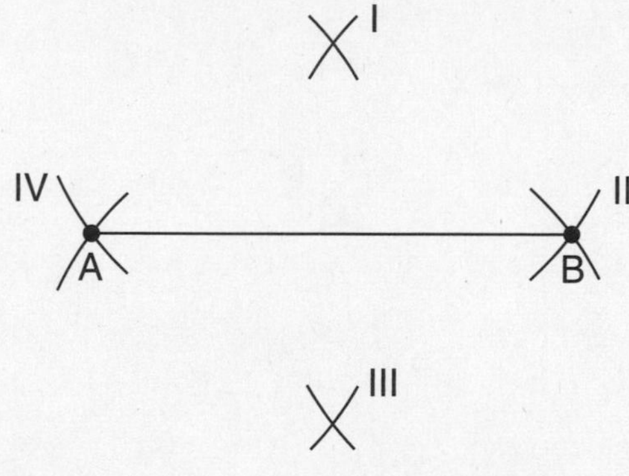

Which two sets of construction marks, labeled I, II, III, and IV, are part of the construction of the perpendicular bisector of line segment AB?

(1) I and II
(2) I and III
(3) II and III
(4) II and IV

2 If $\triangle JKL \cong \triangle MNO$, which statement is always true?

(1) $\angle KLJ \cong \angle NMO$
(2) $\angle KJL \cong \angle MON$
(3) $\overline{JL} \cong \overline{MO}$
(4) $\overline{JK} \cong \overline{ON}$

Use this space for computations.

3 In the diagram below, $\triangle A'B'C'$ is a transformation of $\triangle ABC$, and $\triangle A''B''C''$ is a transformation of $\triangle A'B'C'$.

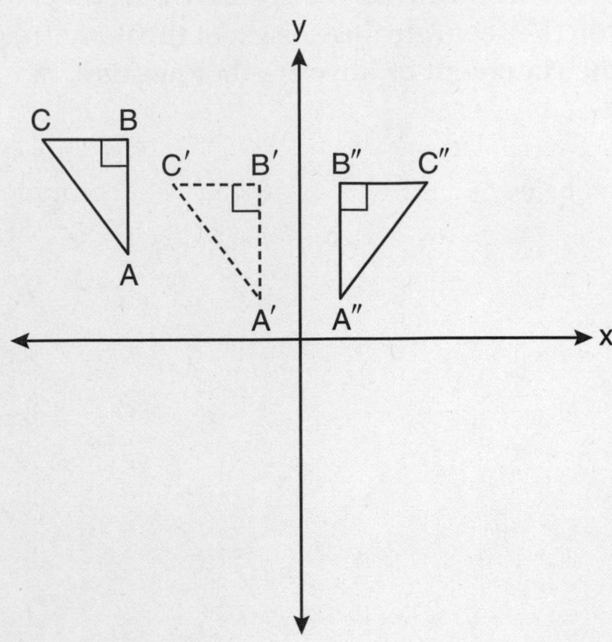

The composite transformation of $\triangle ABC$ to $\triangle A''B''C''$ is an example of a

(1) reflection followed by a rotation

(2) reflection followed by a translation

(3) translation followed by a rotation

(4) translation followed by a reflection

Use this space for computations.

4 In the diagram below of $\triangle ACE$, medians $\overline{AD}$, $\overline{EB}$, and $\overline{CF}$ intersect at G. The length of $\overline{FG}$ is 12 cm.

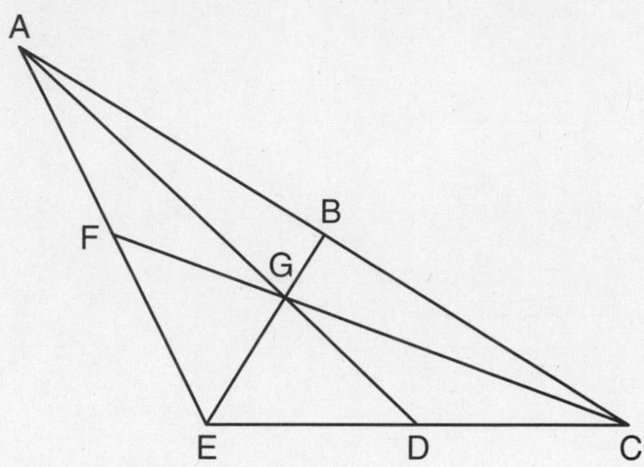

What is the length, in centimeters, of $\overline{GC}$?

(1) 24
(2) 12
(3) 6
(4) 4

5 In the diagram below of circle O, chord $\overline{AB}$ is parallel to chord $\overline{CD}$.

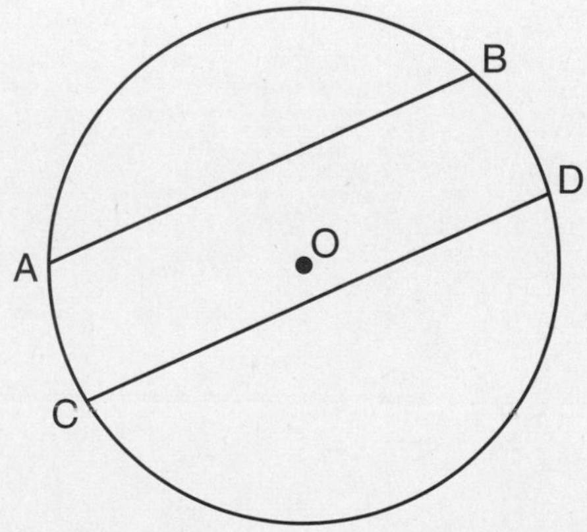

Which statement must be true?

(1) $\overset{\frown}{AC} \cong \overset{\frown}{BD}$
(2) $\overset{\frown}{AB} \cong \overset{\frown}{CD}$
(3) $\overline{AB} \cong \overline{CD}$
(4) $\overset{\frown}{ABD} \cong \overset{\frown}{CDB}$

Use this space for computations.

6 In the diagram below, line p intersects line m and line n.

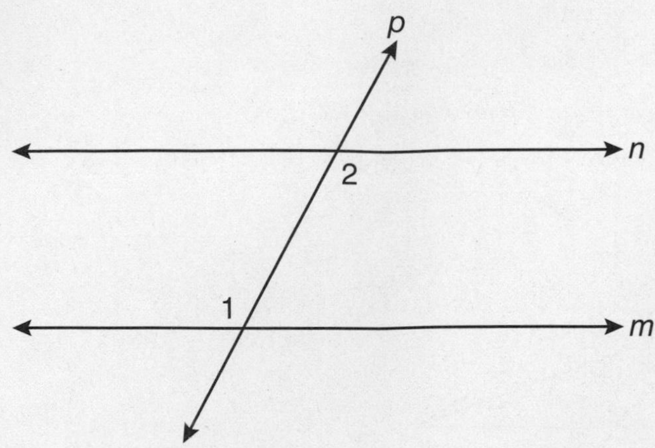

If m$\angle 1 = 7x$ and m$\angle 2 = 5x + 30$, lines m and n are parallel when x equals

(1) 12.5

(2) 15

(3) 87.5

(4) 105

7 In the diagram of $\triangle KLM$ below, m$\angle L = 70$, m$\angle M = 50$, and $\overline{MK}$ is extended through N.

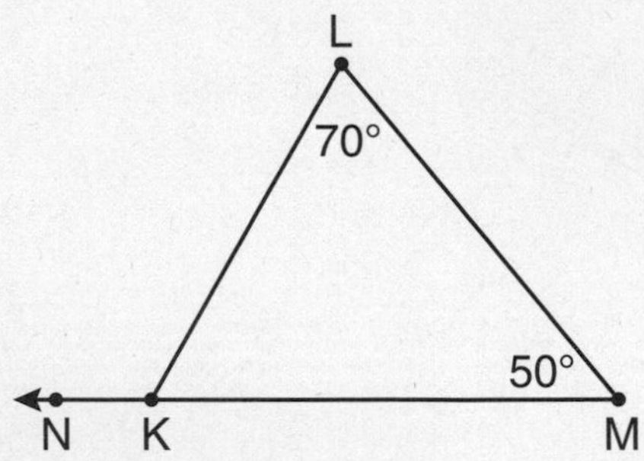

What is the measure of $\angle LKN$?

(1) 60°

(2) 120°

(3) 180°

(4) 300°

Use this space for computations.

8 If two distinct planes, $\mathcal{A}$ and $\mathcal{B}$, are perpendicular to line c, then which statement is true?

(1) Planes $\mathcal{A}$ and $\mathcal{B}$ are parallel to each other.

(2) Planes $\mathcal{A}$ and $\mathcal{B}$ are perpendicular to each other.

(3) The intersection of planes $\mathcal{A}$ and $\mathcal{B}$ is a line parallel to line c.

(4) The intersection of planes $\mathcal{A}$ and $\mathcal{B}$ is a line perpendicular to line c.

9 What is the length of the line segment whose endpoints are $A(-1,9)$ and $B(7,4)$?

(1) $\sqrt{61}$

(2) $\sqrt{89}$

(3) $\sqrt{205}$

(4) $\sqrt{233}$

10 What is an equation of circle O shown in the graph below?

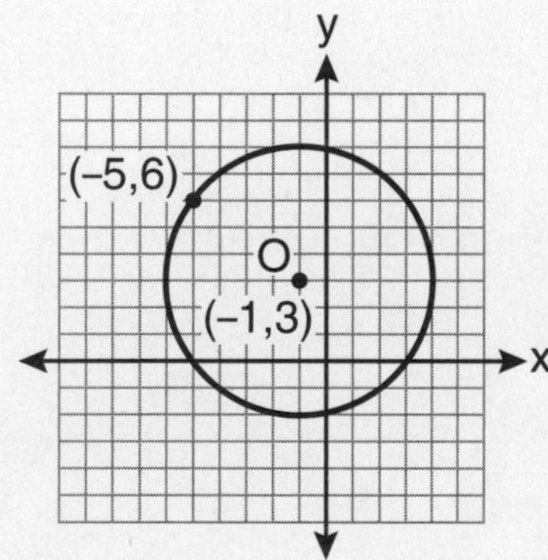

(1) $(x + 1)^2 + (y - 3)^2 = 25$

(2) $(x - 1)^2 + (y + 3)^2 = 25$

(3) $(x - 5)^2 + (y + 6)^2 = 25$

(4) $(x + 5)^2 + (y - 6)^2 = 25$

Use this space for computations.

11 In the diagram below, parallelogram $ABCD$ has diagonals $\overline{AC}$ and $\overline{BD}$ that intersect at point E.

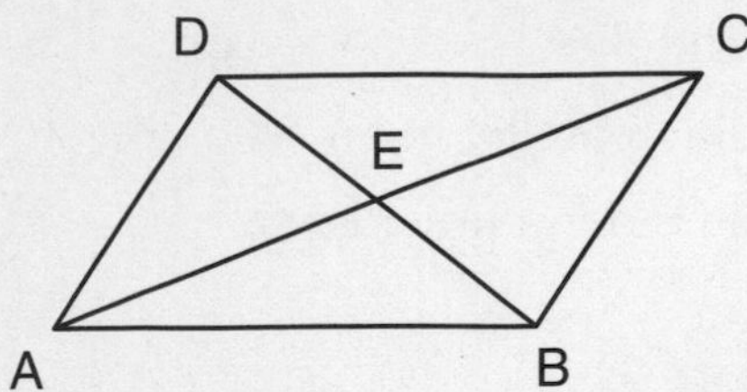

Which expression is *not* always true?

(1) $\angle DAE \cong \angle BCE$
(2) $\angle DEC \cong \angle BEA$
(3) $\overline{AC} \cong \overline{DB}$
(4) $\overline{DE} \cong \overline{EB}$

12 The volume, in cubic centimeters, of a sphere whose diameter is 6 centimeters is

(1) 12π
(2) 36π
(3) 48π
(4) 288π

13 The equation of line k is $y = \frac{1}{3}x - 2$. The equation of line m is $-2x + 6y = 18$. Lines k and m are

(1) parallel
(2) perpendicular
(3) the same line
(4) neither parallel nor perpendicular

Use this space for computations.

14 What are the center and the radius of the circle whose equation is $(x - 5)^2 + (y + 3)^2 = 16$?

(1) $(-5,3)$ and 16
(2) $(5,-3)$ and 16
(3) $(-5,3)$ and 4
(4) $(5,-3)$ and 4

15 Triangle ABC has vertices $A(0,0)$, $B(3,2)$, and $C(0,4)$. This triangle may be classified as

(1) equilateral
(2) isosceles
(3) right
(4) scalene

16 In rhombus $ABCD$, the diagonals $\overline{AC}$ and $\overline{BD}$ intersect at E. If $AE = 5$ and $BE = 12$, what is the length of $\overline{AB}$?

(1) 7
(2) 10
(3) 13
(4) 17

Use this space for computations.

17 In the diagram below of circle O, $\overline{PA}$ is tangent to circle O at A, and $\overline{PBC}$ is a secant with points B and C on the circle.

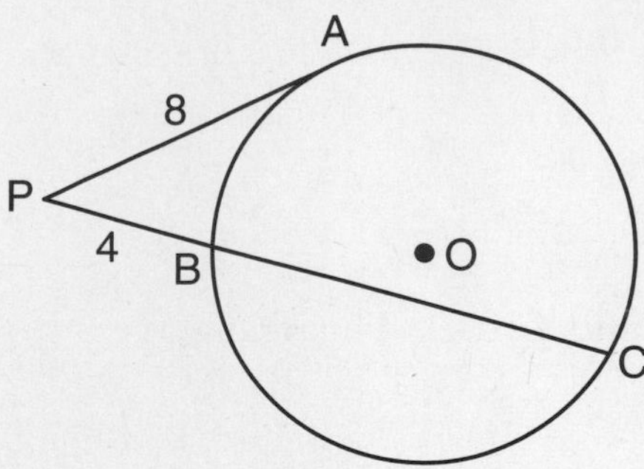

If $PA = 8$ and $PB = 4$, what is the length of $\overline{BC}$?

(1) 20 (3) 15

(2) 16 (4) 12

18 Lines m and n intersect at point A. Line k is perpendicular to both lines m and n at point A. Which statement *must* be true?

(1) Lines m, n, and k are in the same plane.

(2) Lines m and n are in two different planes.

(3) Lines m and n are perpendicular to each other.

(4) Line k is perpendicular to the plane containing lines m and n.

19 In $\triangle DEF$, $m\angle D = 3x + 5$, $m\angle E = 4x - 15$, and $m\angle F = 2x + 10$. Which statement is true?

(1) $DF = FE$ (3) $m\angle E = m\angle F$

(2) $DE = FE$ (4) $m\angle D = m\angle F$

Use this space for computations.

20 As shown in the diagram below, $\triangle ABC \sim \triangle DEF$, $AB = 7x$, $BC = 4$, $DE = 7$, and $EF = x$.

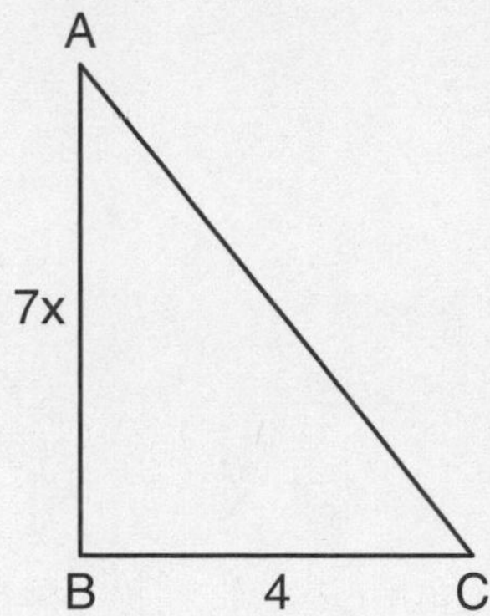

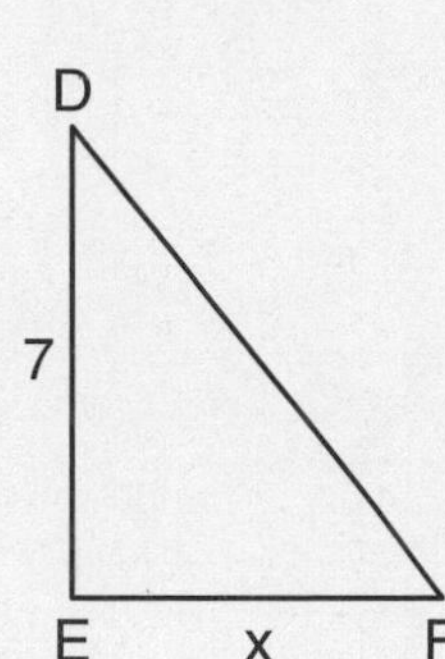

What is the length of $\overline{AB}$?

(1) 28 (3) 14

(2) 2 (4) 4

21 A man wants to place a new bird bath in his yard so that it is 30 feet from a fence, *f*, and also 10 feet from a light pole, *P*. As shown in the diagram below, the light pole is 35 feet away from the fence.

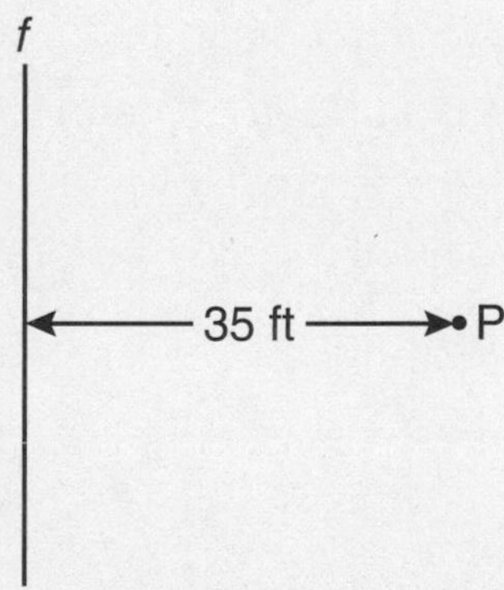

How many locations are possible for the bird bath?

(1) 1 (3) 3

(2) 2 (4) 0

Use this space for computations.

22 As shown on the graph below, $\triangle R'S'T'$ is the image of $\triangle RST$ under a single transformation.

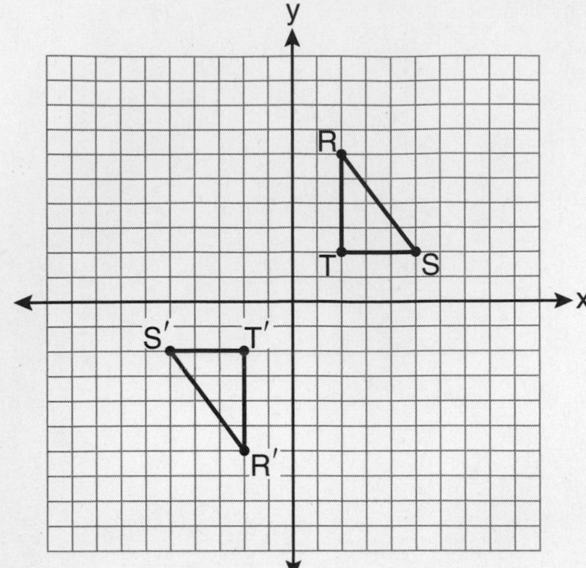

Which transformation does this graph represent?

(1) glide reflection
(2) line reflection
(3) rotation
(4) translation

23 Which line is parallel to the line whose equation is $4x + 3y = 7$ and also passes through the point $(-5,2)$?

(1) $4x + 3y = -26$
(2) $4x + 3y = -14$
(3) $3x + 4y = -7$
(4) $3x + 4y = 14$

Use this space for computations.

24 If the vertex angles of two isosceles triangles are congruent, then the triangles must be

(1) acute
(2) congruent
(3) right
(4) similar

25 Which quadrilateral has diagonals that always bisect its angles and also bisect each other?

(1) rhombus
(2) rectangle
(3) parallelogram
(4) isosceles trapezoid

26 When $\triangle ABC$ is dilated by a scale factor of 2, its image is $\triangle A'B'C'$. Which statement is true?

(1) $\overline{AC} \cong \overline{A'C'}$
(2) $\angle A \cong \angle A'$
(3) perimeter of $\triangle ABC$ = perimeter of $\triangle A'B'C'$
(4) 2(area of $\triangle ABC$) = area of $\triangle A'B'C'$

Use this space for computations.

27 What is the slope of a line that is perpendicular to the line whose equation is $3x + 5y = 4$?

(1) $-\frac{3}{5}$ (3) $-\frac{5}{3}$

(2) $\frac{3}{5}$ (4) $\frac{5}{3}$

28 In the diagram below of right triangle ABC, altitude $\overline{BD}$ is drawn to hypotenuse $\overline{AC}$, $AC = 16$, and $CD = 7$.

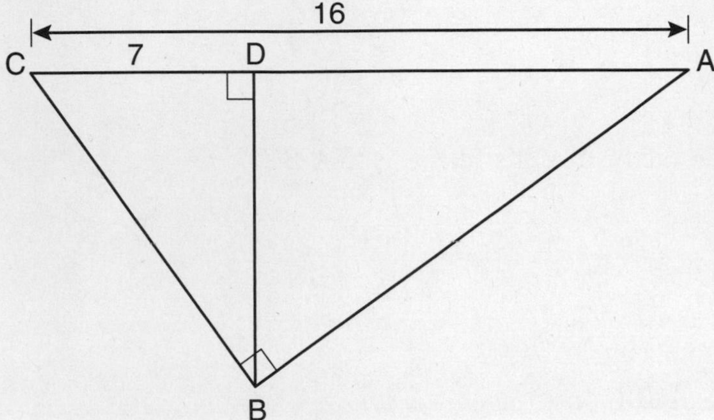

What is the length of $\overline{BD}$?

(1) $3\sqrt{7}$ (3) $7\sqrt{3}$

(2) $4\sqrt{7}$ (4) 12

Part II

Answer all 6 questions in this part. Each correct answer will receive 2 credits. Clearly indicate the necessary steps, including appropriate formula substitutions, diagrams, graphs, charts, etc. For all questions in this part, a correct numerical answer with no work shown will receive only 1 credit. All answers should be written in pen, except for graphs and drawings, which should be done in pencil. [12]

29 Given the true statement, "The medians of a triangle are concurrent," write the negation of the statement and give the truth value for the negation.

30 Using a compass and straightedge, on the diagram below of $\overleftrightarrow{RS}$, construct an equilateral triangle with $\overline{RS}$ as one side. [Leave all construction marks.]

R

S

31 The Parkside Packing Company needs a rectangular shipping box. The box must have a length of 11 inches and a width of 8 inches. Find, to the *nearest tenth of an inch*, the minimum height of the box such that the volume is *at least* 800 cubic inches.

32 A pentagon is drawn on the set of axes below. If the pentagon is reflected over the y-axis, determine if this transformation is an isometry.
Justify your answer. [The use of the set of axes below is optional.]

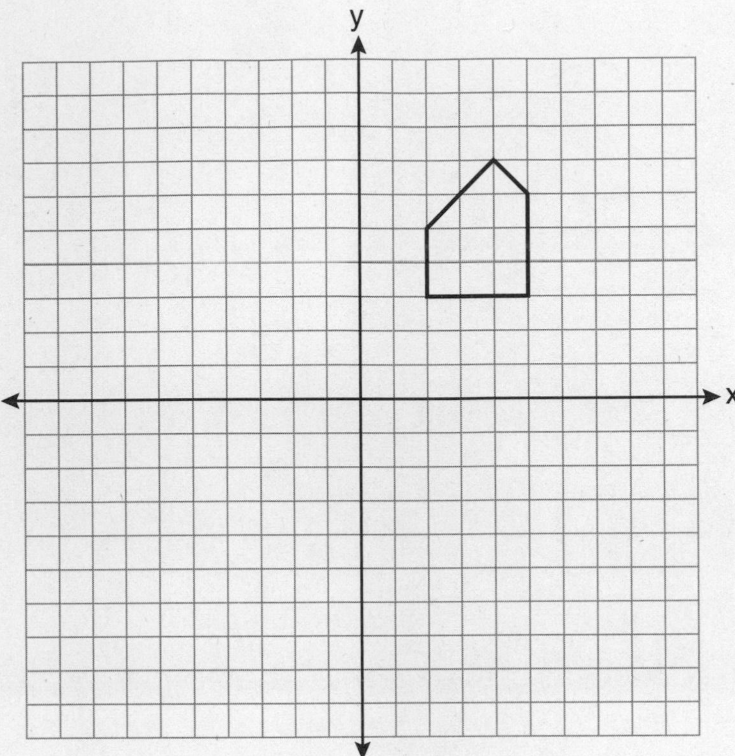

33 In the diagram below of $\triangle ABC$, D is a point on $\overline{AB}$, E is a point on $\overline{BC}$, $\overline{AC} \parallel \overline{DE}$, $CE = 25$ inches, $AD = 18$ inches, and $DB = 12$ inches. Find, to the *nearest tenth of an inch*, the length of $\overline{EB}$.

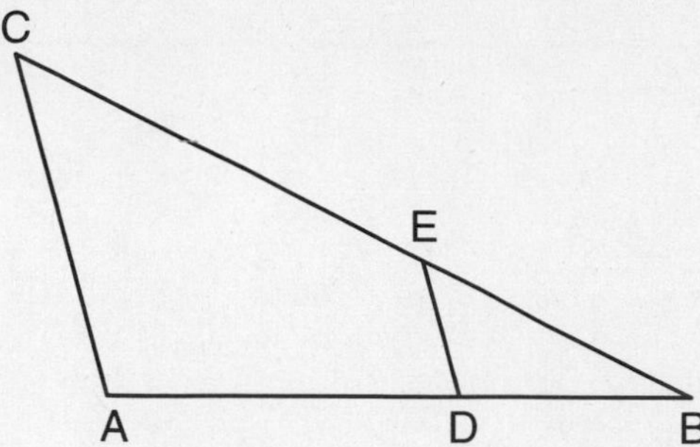

34 In circle O, diameter $\overline{RS}$ has endpoints $R(3a,2b - 1)$ and $S(a - 6,4b + 5)$. Find the coordinates of point O, in terms of a and b. Express your answer in simplest form.

Part III

Answer all 3 questions in this part. Each correct answer will receive 4 credits. Clearly indicate the necessary steps, including appropriate formula substitutions, diagrams, graphs, charts, etc. For all questions in this part, a correct numerical answer with no work shown will receive only 1 credit. All answers should be written in pen, except for graphs and drawings, which should be done in pencil. [12]

35 On the set of coordinate axes below, graph the locus of points that are equidistant from the lines $y = 6$ and $y = 2$ and also graph the locus of points that are 3 units from the y-axis. State the coordinates of *all* points that satisfy *both* conditions.

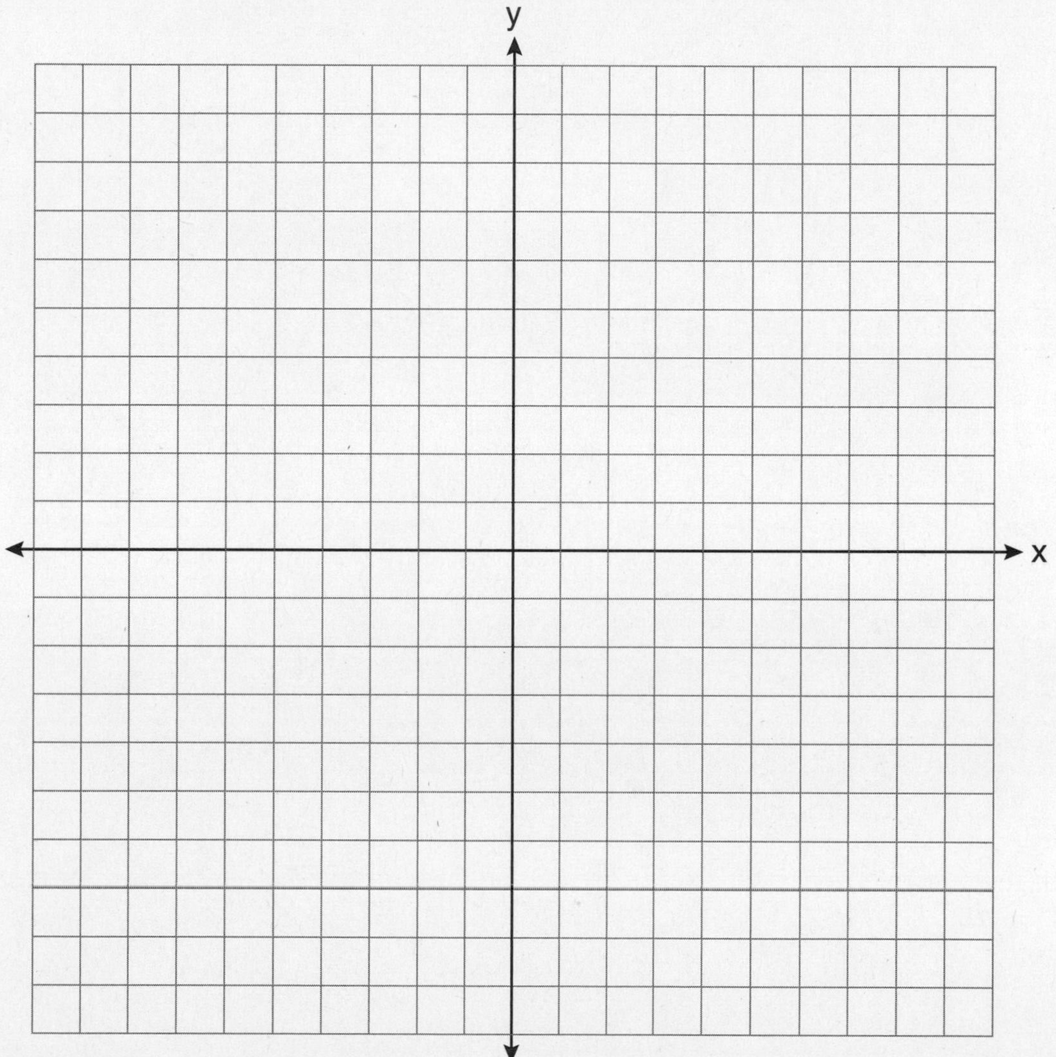

36 In the diagram below, tangent $\overline{ML}$ and secant $\overline{MNK}$ are drawn to circle O. The ratio $m\widehat{LN}:m\widehat{NK}:m\widehat{KL}$ is 3:4:5. Find $m\angle LMK$.

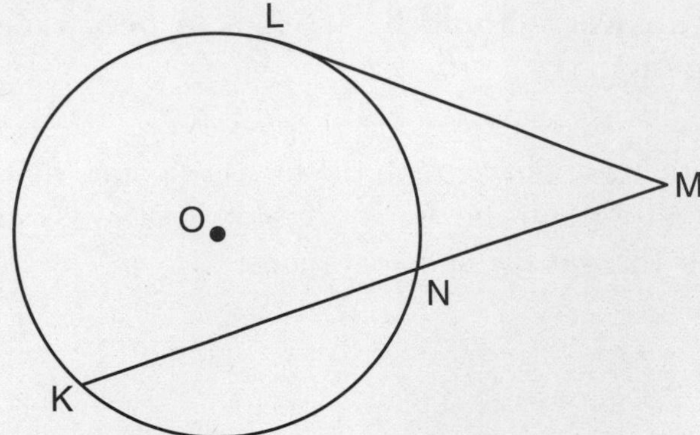

37 Solve the following system of equations graphically.

$$2x^2 - 4x = y + 1$$
$$x + y = 1$$

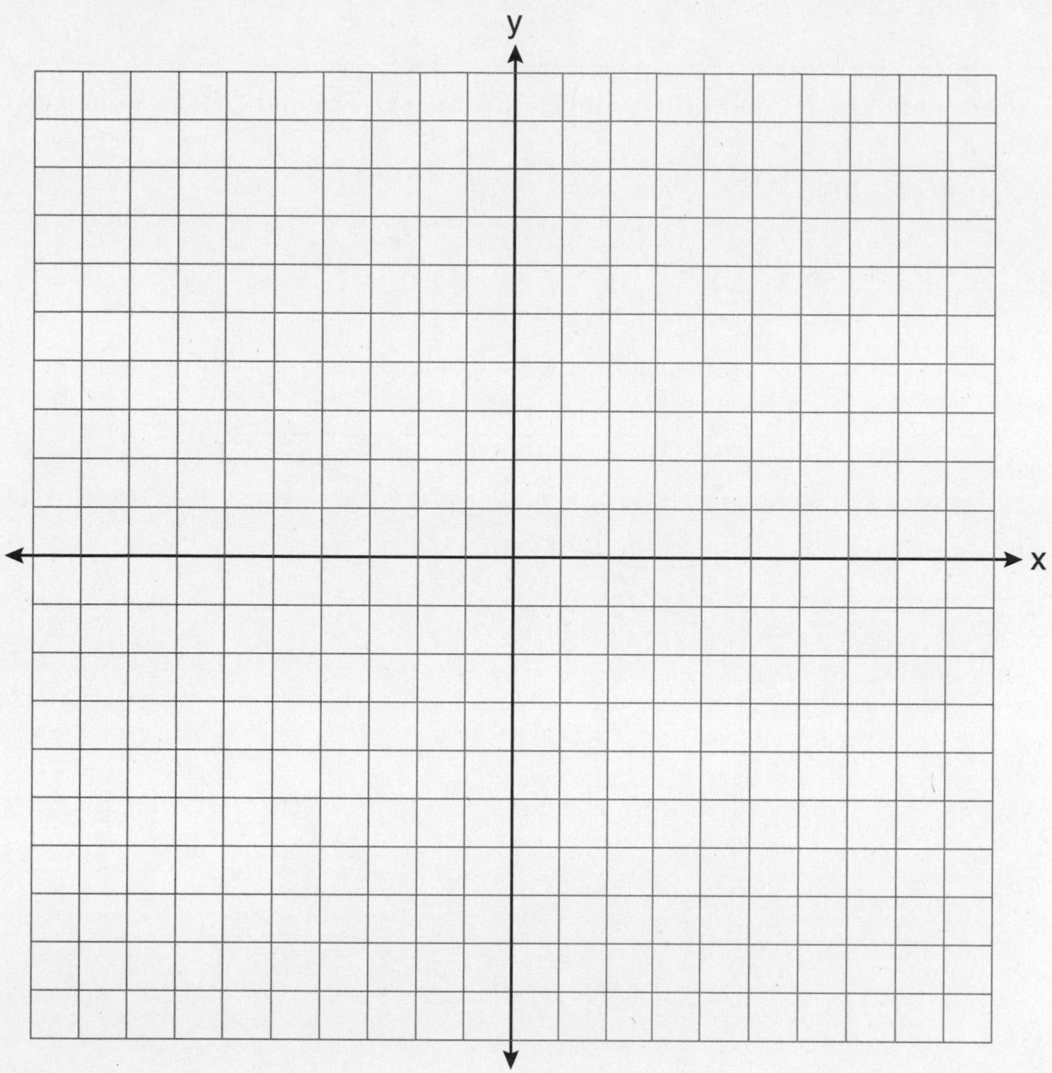

Part IV

Answer the question in this part. A correct answer will receive 6 credits. Clearly indicate the necessary steps, including appropriate formula substitutions, diagrams, graphs, charts, etc. A correct numerical answer with no work shown will receive only 1 credit. The answer should be written in pen. [6]

38 In the diagram below, $\overline{PA}$ and $\overline{PB}$ are tangent to circle O, $\overline{OA}$ and $\overline{OB}$ are radii, and $\overline{OP}$ intersects the circle at C.

Prove: $\angle AOP \cong \angle BOP$

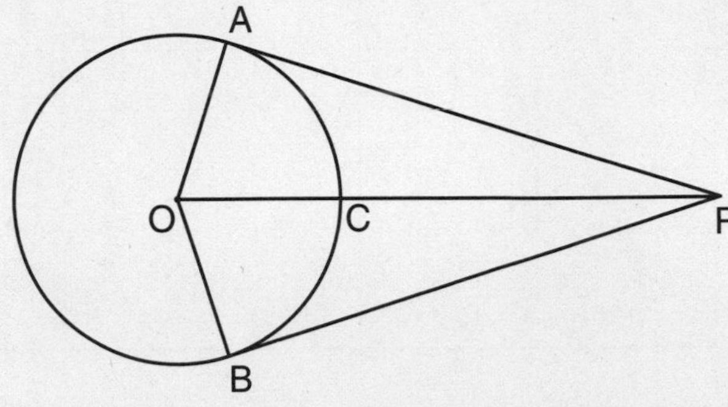

Tear Here

The University of the State of New York

REGENTS HIGH SCHOOL EXAMINATION

GEOMETRY

Thursday, June 23, 2011—9:15 a.m. to 12:15 p.m., only

ANSWER SHEET

Student .... **Sex:** ☐ **Male** ☐ **Female** **Grade** ......

Teacher .... **School** ....

Your answers to Part I should be recorded on this answer sheet.

Part I

Answer all 28 questions in this part.

1	8	15	22 ....
2	9	16	23 ....
3	10	17	24 ....
4	11	18	25 ....
5	12	19	26 ....
6	13	20	27 ....
7	14	21	28 ....

Your answers for Parts II, III, and IV should be written in the test booklet.

The declaration below must be signed when you have completed the examination.

I do hereby affirm, at the close of this examination, that I had no unlawful knowledge of the questions or answers prior to the examination and that I have neither given nor received assistance in answering any of the questions during the examination.

Tear Here

____

Signature

Geometry January, 2011

Part I

Answer all 28 questions in this part. Each correct answer will receive 2 credits. No partial credit will be allowed. For each question, write on the separate answer sheet the numeral preceding the word or expression that best completes the statement or answers the question. [56]

Use this space for computations.

1 In the diagram below, $\overline{AB}$, $\overline{BC}$, and $\overline{AC}$ are tangents to circle O at points F, E, and D, respectively, $AF = 6$, $CD = 5$, and $BE = 4$.

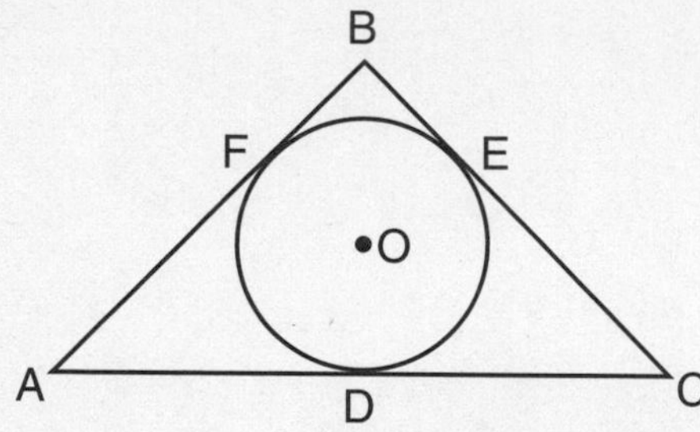

What is the perimeter of $\triangle ABC$?

(1) 15

(2) 25

(3) 30

(4) 60

2 Quadrilateral $MNOP$ is a trapezoid with $\overline{MN} \parallel \overline{OP}$. If $M'N'O'P'$ is the image of $MNOP$ after a reflection over the x-axis, which two sides of quadrilateral $M'N'O'P'$ are parallel?

(1) $\overline{M'N'}$ and $\overline{O'P'}$

(2) $\overline{M'N'}$ and $\overline{N'O'}$

(3) $\overline{P'M'}$ and $\overline{O'P'}$

(4) $\overline{P'M'}$ and $\overline{N'O'}$

Use this space for computations.

3 In the diagram below of $\triangle ABC$, D is the midpoint of $\overline{AB}$, and E is the midpoint of $\overline{BC}$.

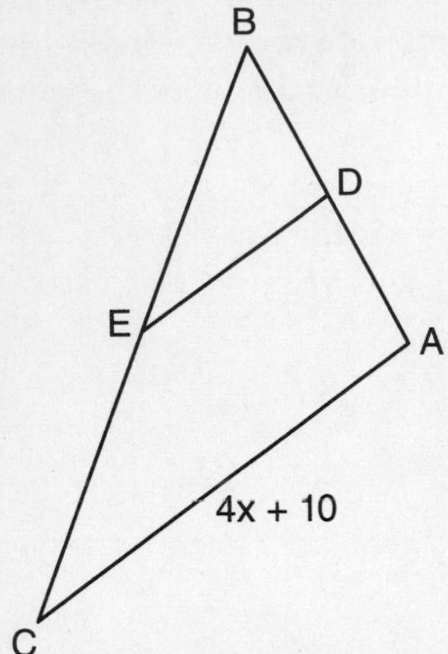

If $AC = 4x + 10$, which expression represents DE?

(1) $x + 2.5$

(2) $2x + 5$

(3) $2x + 10$

(4) $8x + 20$

4 Which statement is true about every parallelogram?

(1) All four sides are congruent.

(2) The interior angles are all congruent.

(3) Two pairs of opposite sides are congruent.

(4) The diagonals are perpendicular to each other.

Use this space for computations.

5 The diagram below shows a rectangular prism.

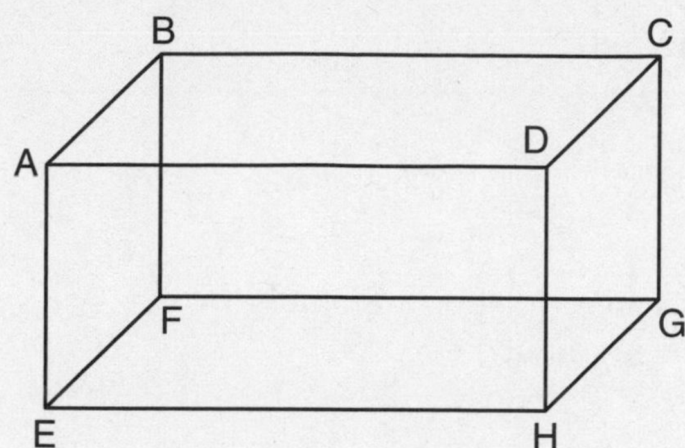

Which pair of edges are segments of lines that are coplanar?

(1) $\overline{AB}$ and $\overline{DH}$

(2) $\overline{AE}$ and $\overline{DC}$

(3) $\overline{BC}$ and $\overline{EH}$

(4) $\overline{CG}$ and $\overline{EF}$

6 A line segment has endpoints $A(7,-1)$ and $B(-3,3)$. What are the coordinates of the midpoint of $\overline{AB}$?

(1) (1,2)

(2) (2,1)

(3) (−5,2)

(4) (5,−2)

Use this space for computations.

7 What is the image of the point $(-5,2)$ under the translation $T_{3,-4}$?

(1) $(-9,5)$
(2) $(-8,6)$
(3) $(-2,-2)$
(4) $(-15,-8)$

8 When writing a geometric proof, which angle relationship could be used alone to justify that two angles are congruent?

(1) supplementary angles
(2) linear pair of angles
(3) adjacent angles
(4) vertical angles

9 Plane $\mathcal{R}$ is perpendicular to line k and plane $\mathcal{D}$ is perpendicular to line k. Which statement is correct?

(1) Plane $\mathcal{R}$ is perpendicular to plane $\mathcal{D}$.
(2) Plane $\mathcal{R}$ is parallel to plane $\mathcal{D}$.
(3) Plane $\mathcal{R}$ intersects plane $\mathcal{D}$.
(4) Plane $\mathcal{R}$ bisects plane $\mathcal{D}$.

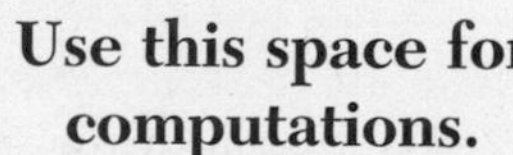

10 The vertices of the triangle in the diagram below are $A(7,9)$, $B(3,3)$, and $C(11,3)$.

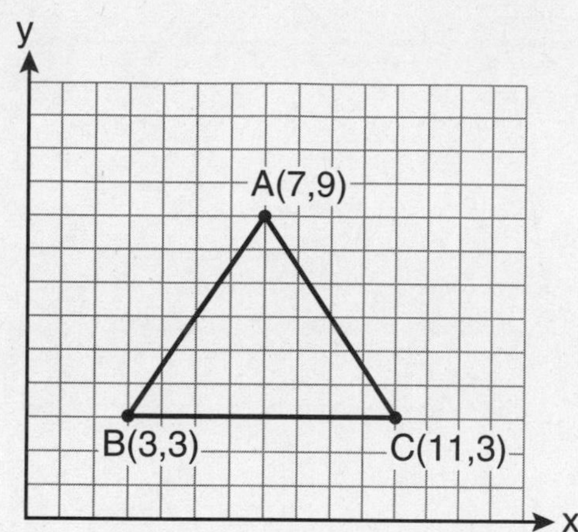

What are the coordinates of the centroid of $\triangle ABC$?

(1) (5,6) (3) (7,5)

(2) (7,3) (4) (9,6)

11 Which set of numbers does *not* represent the sides of a right triangle?

(1) {6, 8, 10} (3) {8, 24, 25}

(2) {8, 15, 17} (4) {15, 36, 39}

Use this space for computations.

12 In the diagram below of rhombus $ABCD$, $m\angle C = 100$.

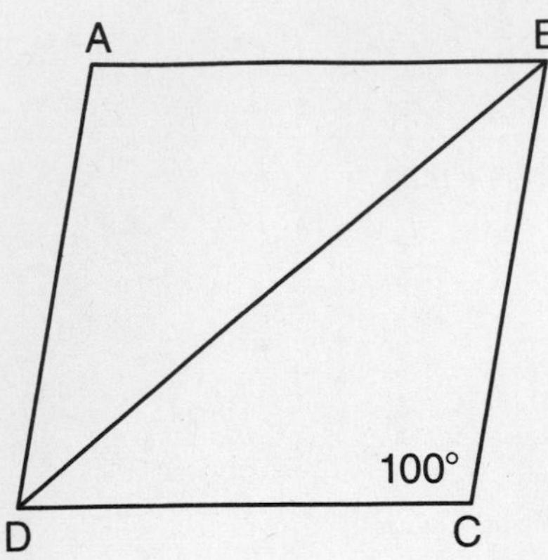

What is $m\angle DBC$?

(1) 40 (3) 50

(2) 45 (4) 80

13 In the diagram below of circle O, radius $\overline{OC}$ is 5 cm. Chord $\overline{AB}$ is 8 cm and is perpendicular to $\overline{OC}$ at point P.

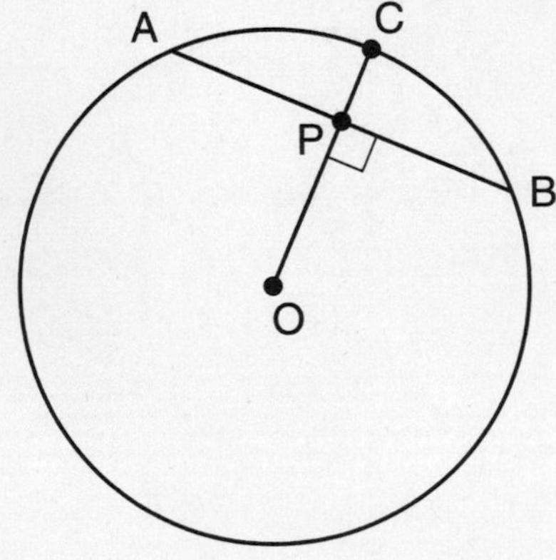

What is the length of $\overline{OP}$, in centimeters?

(1) 8 (3) 3

(2) 2 (4) 4

Use this space for computations.

14 What is an equation of the line that passes through the point $(-2,3)$ and is parallel to the line whose equation is $y = \frac{3}{2}x - 4$?

(1) $y = \frac{-2}{3}x$

(2) $y = \frac{-2}{3}x + \frac{5}{3}$

(3) $y = \frac{3}{2}x$

(4) $y = \frac{3}{2}x + 6$

15 In scalene triangle ABC, $m\angle B = 45$ and $m\angle C = 55$. What is the order of the sides in length, from longest to shortest?

(1) $\overline{AB}, \overline{BC}, \overline{AC}$

(2) $\overline{BC}, \overline{AC}, \overline{AB}$

(3) $\overline{AC}, \overline{BC}, \overline{AB}$

(4) $\overline{BC}, \overline{AB}, \overline{AC}$

16 What is an equation of a circle with center $(7,-3)$ and radius 4?

(1) $(x - 7)^2 + (y + 3)^2 = 4$

(2) $(x + 7)^2 + (y - 3)^2 = 4$

(3) $(x - 7)^2 + (y + 3)^2 = 16$

(4) $(x + 7)^2 + (y - 3)^2 = 16$

Use this space for computations.

17 What is the volume, in cubic centimeters, of a cylinder that has a height of 15 cm and a diameter of 12 cm?

(1) 180π (3) 675π

(2) 540π (4) $2{,}160\pi$

18 Which compound statement is true?

(1) A triangle has three sides and a quadrilateral has five sides.

(2) A triangle has three sides if and only if a quadrilateral has five sides.

(3) If a triangle has three sides, then a quadrilateral has five sides.

(4) A triangle has three sides or a quadrilateral has five sides.

19 The two lines represented by the equations below are graphed on a coordinate plane.

$$x + 6y = 12$$

$$3(x - 2) = -y - 4$$

Which statement best describes the two lines?

(1) The lines are parallel.

(2) The lines are the same line.

(3) The lines are perpendicular.

(4) The lines intersect at an angle other than 90°.

Use this space for computations.

20 Which diagram shows the construction of the perpendicular bisector of $\overline{AB}$?

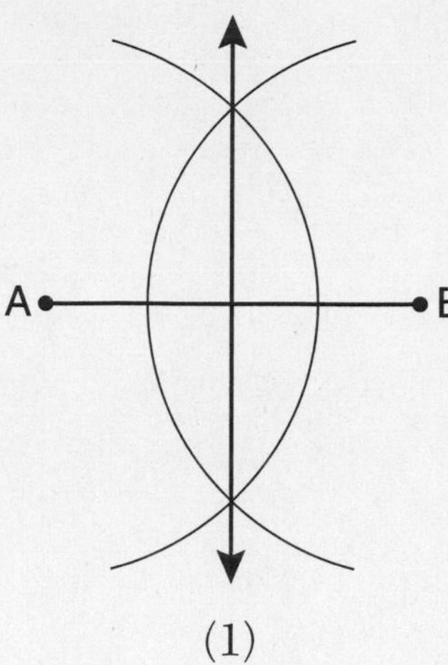

(1)

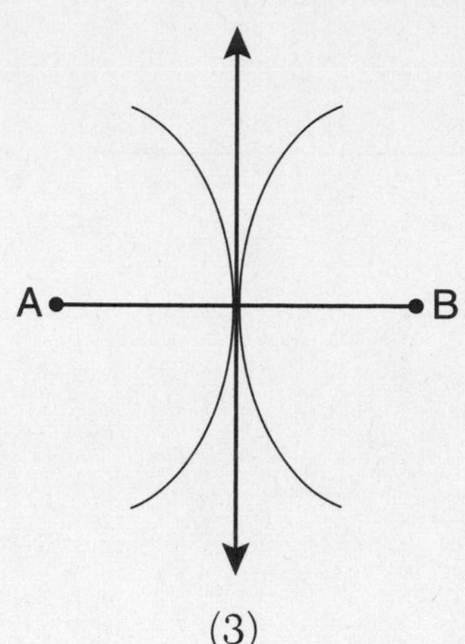

(3)

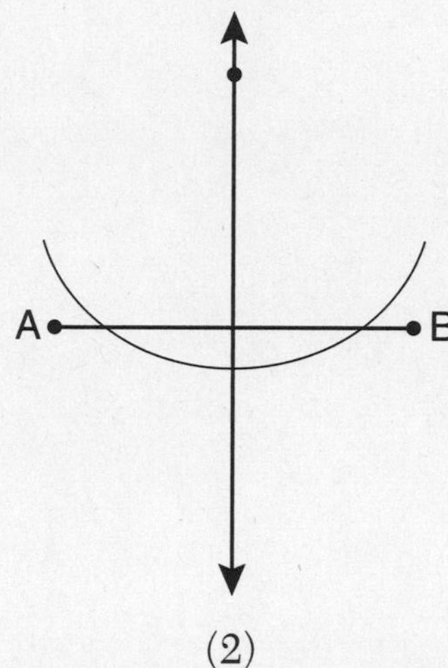

(2)

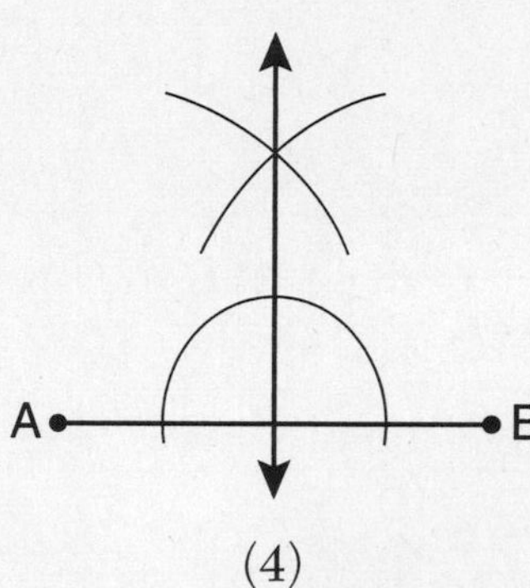

(4)

21 In circle O, a diameter has endpoints $(-5,4)$ and $(3,-6)$. What is the length of the diameter?

(1) $\sqrt{2}$
(2) $2\sqrt{2}$
(3) $\sqrt{10}$
(4) $2\sqrt{41}$

Use this space for computations.

22 In the diagram below of quadrilateral $ABCD$, $\overline{AB} \parallel \overline{CD}$, $\angle ABC \cong \angle CDA$, and diagonal $\overline{AC}$ is drawn.

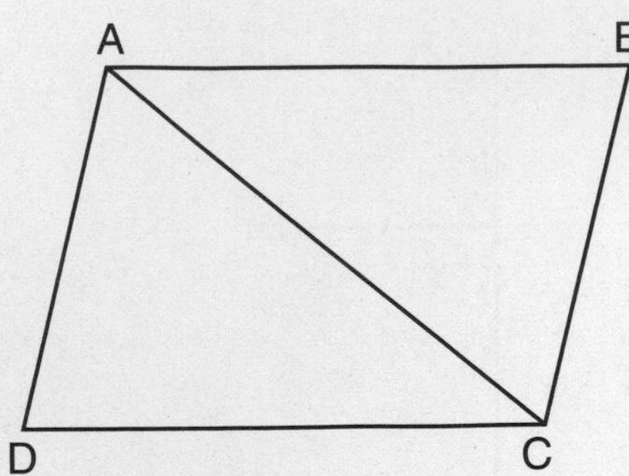

Which method can be used to prove that $\triangle ABC$ is congruent to $\triangle CDA$?

(1) AAS
(2) SSA
(3) SAS
(4) SSS

23 In the diagram below of right triangle ABC, $\overline{CD}$ is the altitude to hypotenuse $\overline{AB}$, $CB = 6$, and $AD = 5$.

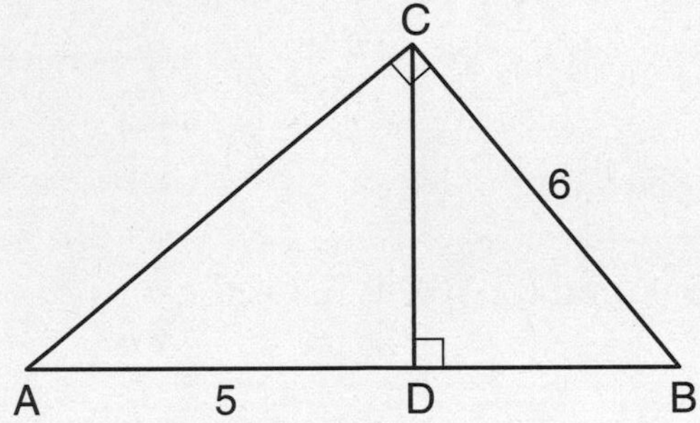

What is the length of $\overline{BD}$?

(1) 5
(2) 9
(3) 3
(4) 4

Use this space for computations.

24 In the diagram below, quadrilateral *JUMP* is inscribed in a circle.

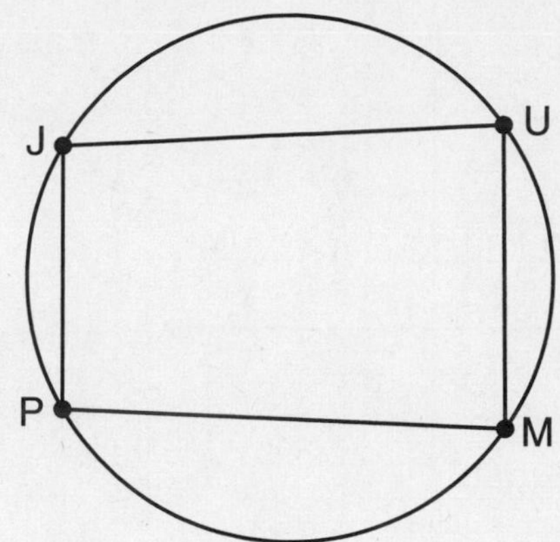

Opposite angles *J* and *M* must be

(1) right
(2) complementary
(3) congruent
(4) supplementary

Use this space for computations.

25 Which graph represents a circle with the equation $(x - 3)^2 + (y + 1)^2 = 4$?

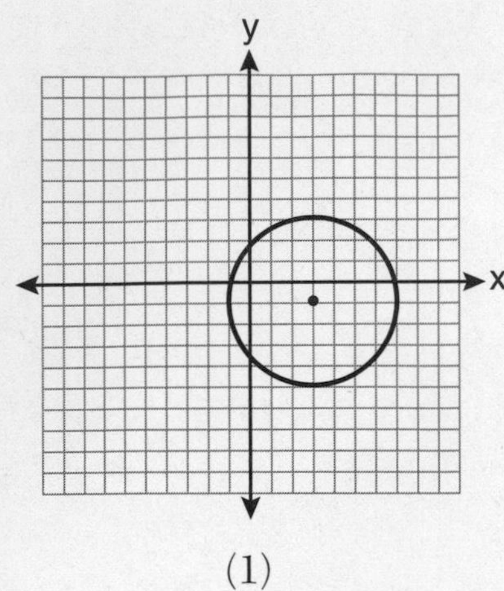

(1)

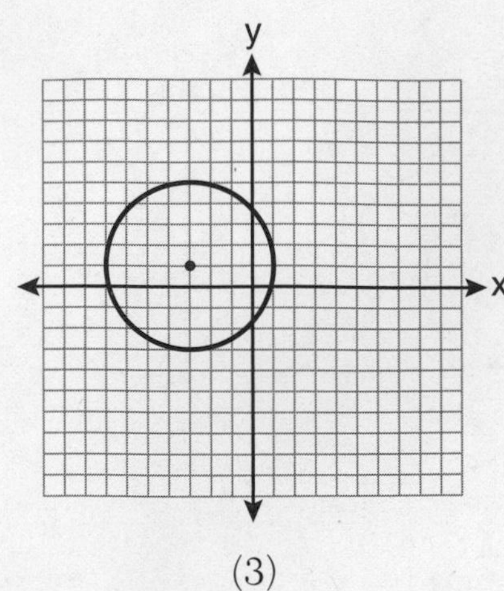

(3)

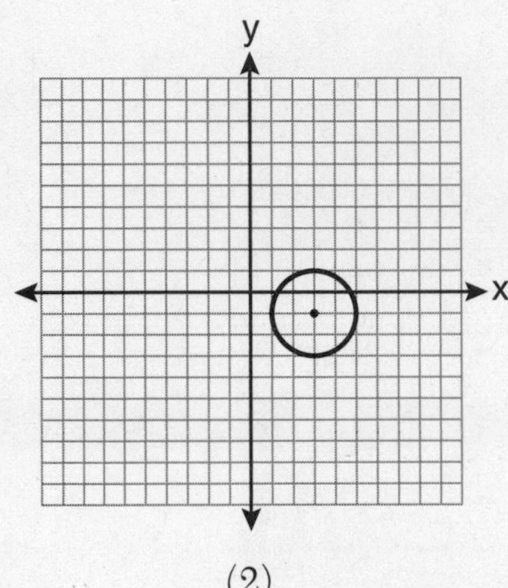

(2)

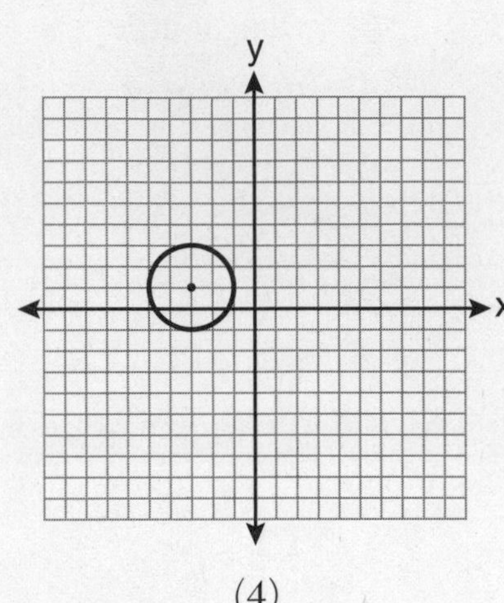

(4)

26 The point $(3,-2)$ is rotated 90° about the origin and then dilated by a scale factor of 4. What are the coordinates of the resulting image?

(1) $(-12,8)$ (3) $(8,12)$

(2) $(12,-8)$ (4) $(-8,-12)$

Use this space for computations.

27 In the diagram below of $\triangle ABC$, side $\overline{BC}$ is extended to point D, $m\angle A = x$, $m\angle B = 2x + 15$, and $m\angle ACD = 5x + 5$.

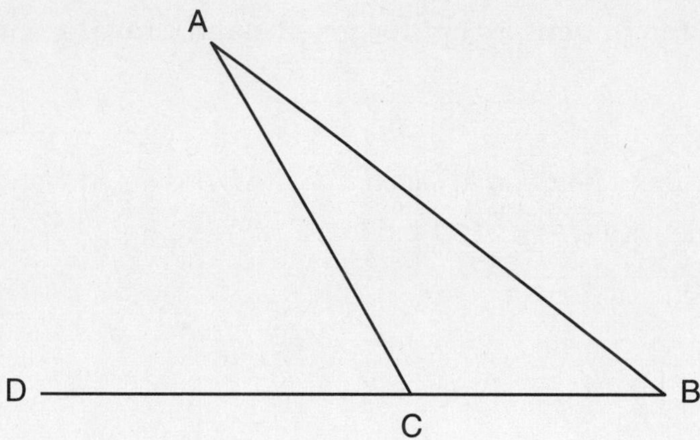

What is $m\angle B$?

(1) 5 (3) 25

(2) 20 (4) 55

28 Point P lies on line m. Point P is also included in distinct planes $\mathcal{Q}$, $\mathcal{R}$, $\mathcal{S}$, and $\mathcal{T}$. At most, how many of these planes could be perpendicular to line m?

(1) 1 (3) 3

(2) 2 (4) 4

Part II

Answer all 6 questions in this part. Each correct answer will receive 2 credits. Clearly indicate the necessary steps, including appropriate formula substitutions, diagrams, graphs, charts, etc. For all questions in this part, a correct numerical answer with no work shown will receive only 1 credit. All answers should be written in pen, except for graphs and drawings, which should be done in pencil. [12]

29 In the diagram below of $\triangle ACD$, B is a point on $\overline{AC}$ such that $\triangle ADB$ is an equilateral triangle, and $\triangle DBC$ is an isosceles triangle with $\overline{DB} \cong \overline{BC}$. Find $m\angle C$.

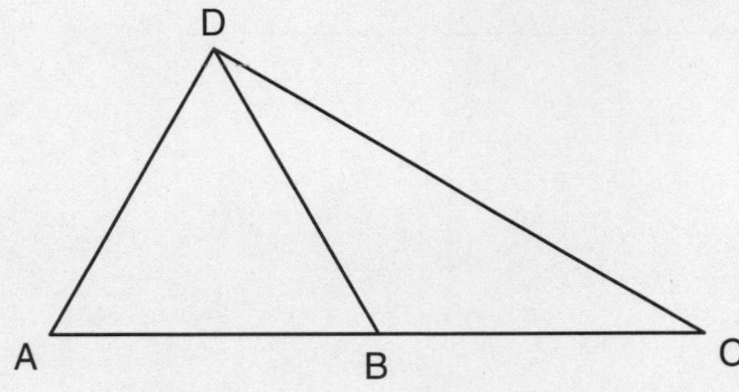

30 Triangle ABC has vertices $A(-2,2)$, $B(-1,-3)$, and $C(4,0)$. Find the coordinates of the vertices of $\triangle A'B'C'$, the image of $\triangle ABC$ after the transformation $r_{x\text{-axis}}$.
[The use of the grid below is optional.]

31 Find, in degrees, the measures of both an interior angle and an exterior angle of a regular pentagon.

32 In the diagram below of circle O, chord $\overline{AB}$ bisects chord $\overline{CD}$ at E. If $AE = 8$ and $BE = 9$, find the length of $\overline{CE}$ in simplest radical form.

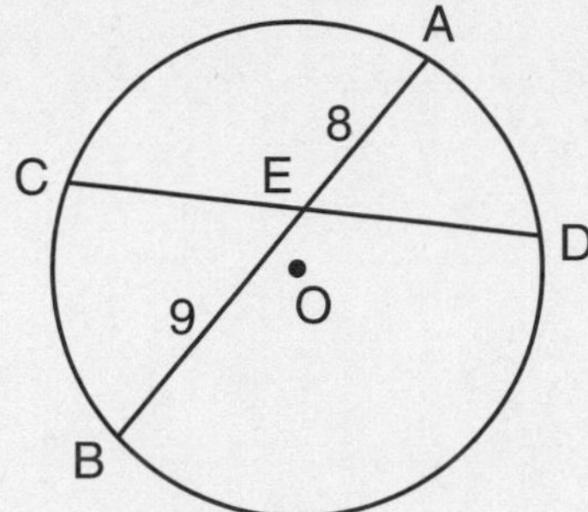

33 On the diagram below, use a compass and straightedge to construct the bisector of $\angle ABC$. [Leave all construction marks.]

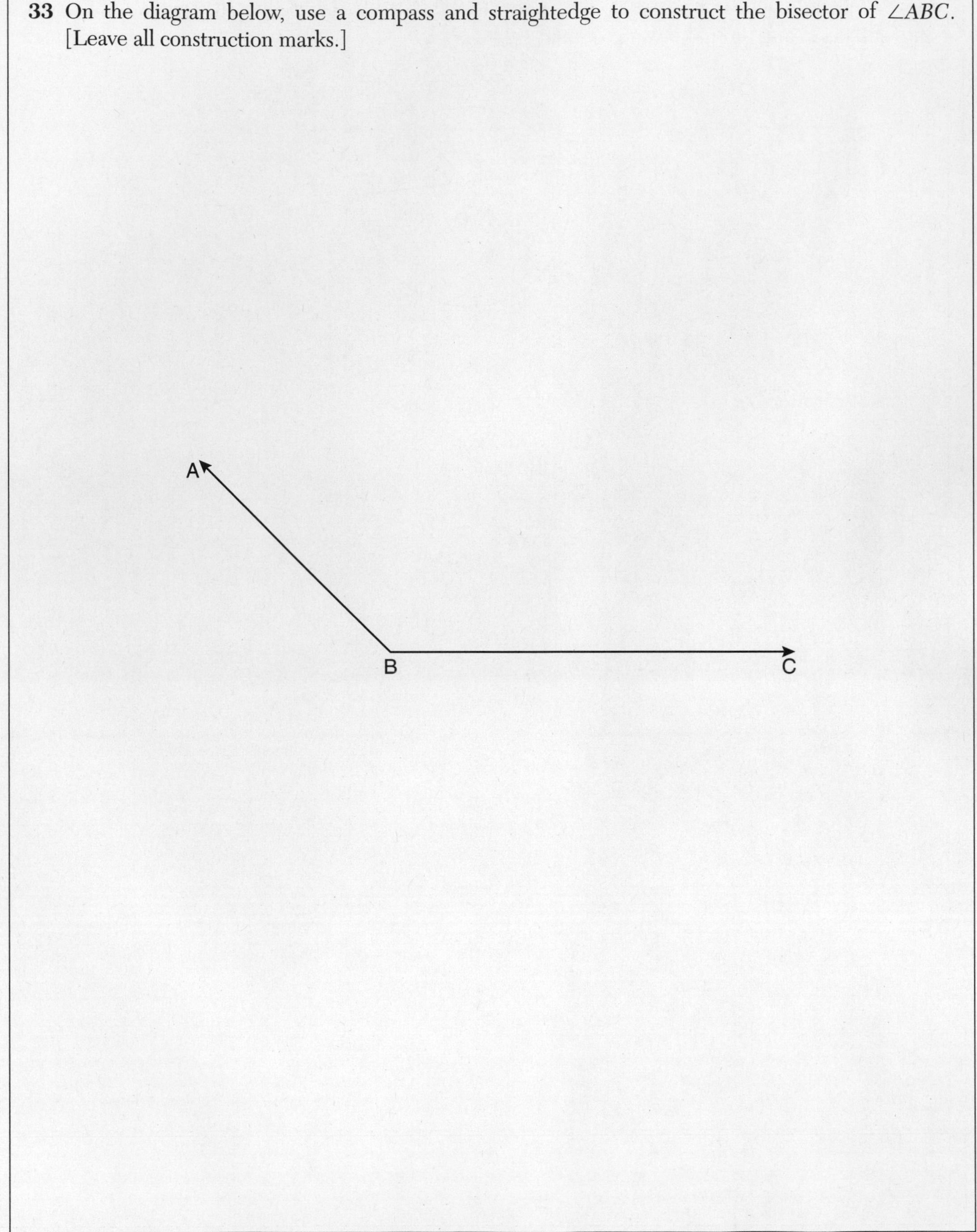

34 Find the slope of a line perpendicular to the line whose equation is $2y - 6x = 4$.

Part III

Answer all 3 questions in this part. Each correct answer will receive 4 credits. Clearly indicate the necessary steps, including appropriate formula substitutions, diagrams, graphs, charts, etc. For all questions in this part, a correct numerical answer with no work shown will receive only 1 credit. All answers should be written in pen, except for graphs and drawings, which should be done in pencil. [12]

35 On the set of axes below, graph the locus of points that are four units from the point (2,1). On the same set of axes, graph the locus of points that are two units from the line $x = 4$. State the coordinates of all points that satisfy both conditions.

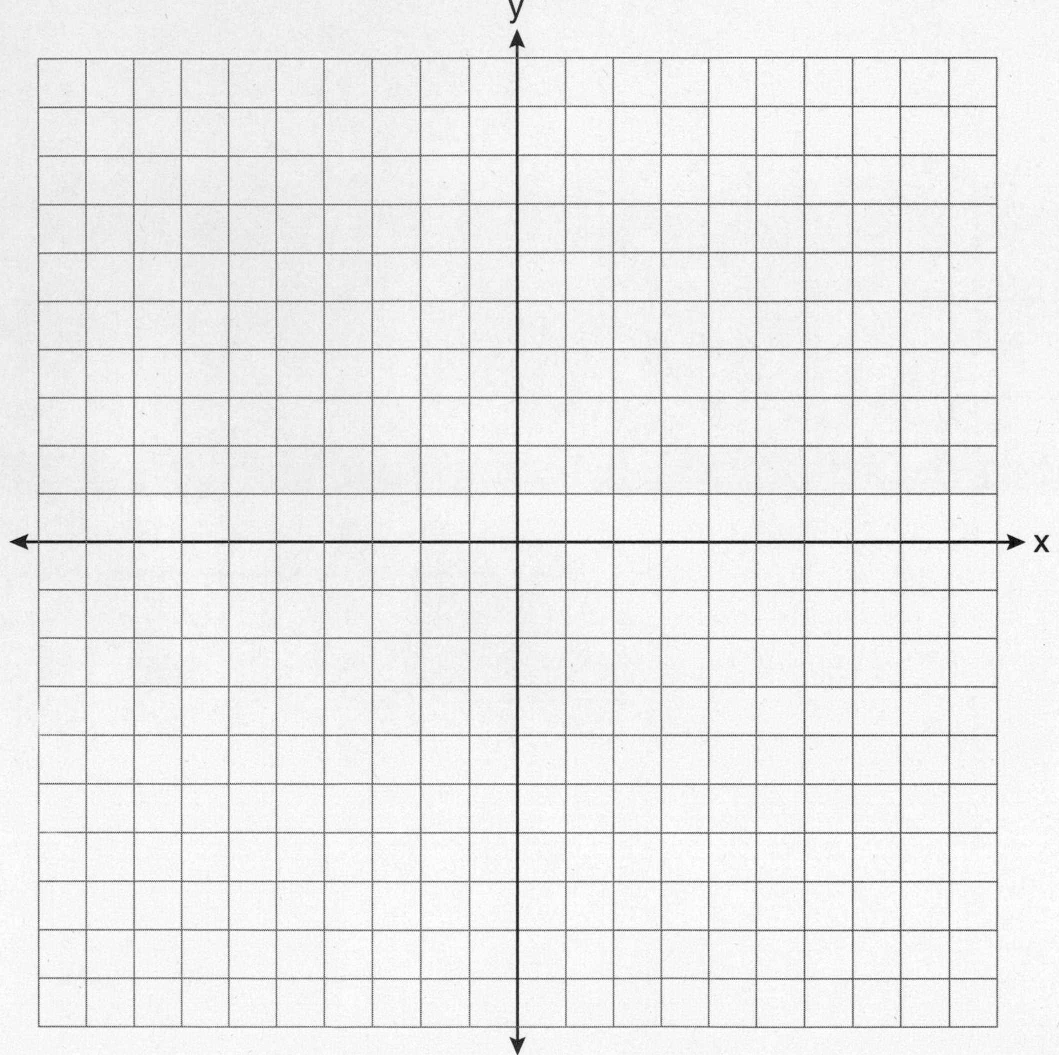

36 In the diagram below, $\overline{BFCE}$, $\overline{AB} \perp \overline{BE}$, $\overline{DE} \perp \overline{BE}$, and $\angle BFD \cong \angle ECA$. Prove that $\triangle ABC \sim \triangle DEF$.

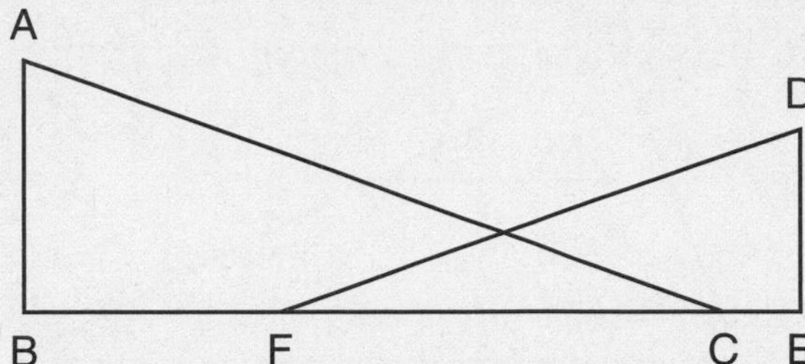

37 In the diagram below of $\triangle ADE$, B is a point on $\overline{AE}$ and C is a point on $\overline{AD}$ such that $\overline{BC} \parallel \overline{ED}$, $AC = x - 3$, $BE = 20$, $AB = 16$, and $AD = 2x + 2$. Find the length of $\overline{AC}$.

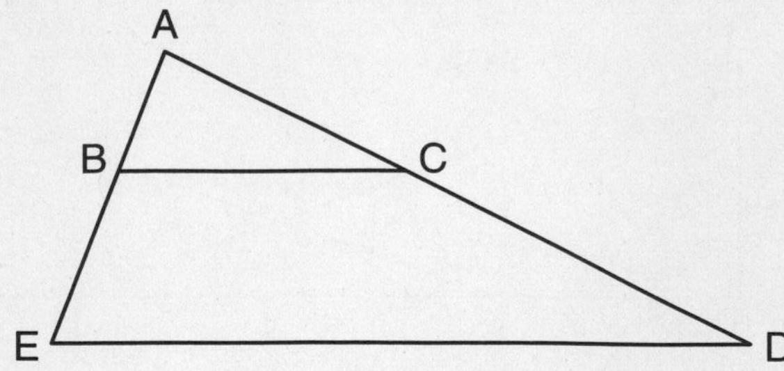

Part IV

Answer the question in this part. A correct answer will receive 6 credits. Clearly indicate the necessary steps, including appropriate formula substitutions, diagrams, graphs, charts, etc. A correct numerical answer with no work shown will receive only 1 credit. The answer should be written in pen. [6]

38 Quadrilateral $MATH$ has coordinates $M(1,1)$, $A(-2,5)$, $T(3,5)$, and $H(6,1)$. Prove that quadrilateral $MATH$ is a rhombus and prove that it is *not* a square.
[The use of the grid on the next page is optional.]

Question 38 continued

Tear Here

The University of the State of New York

REGENTS HIGH SCHOOL EXAMINATION

GEOMETRY

Thursday, January 27, 2011 — 9:15 a.m. to 12:15 p.m., only

ANSWER SHEET

Student .... **Sex:** ☐ **Male** ☐ **Female** **Grade** .....

Teacher .... **School** ....

Your answers to Part I should be recorded on this answer sheet.

Part I

Answer all 28 questions in this part.

1	8	15	22 ....
2	9	16	23 ....
3	10	17	24 ....
4	11	18	25 ....
5	12	19	26 ....
6	13	20	27 ....
7	14	21	28 ....

Your answers for Parts II, III, and IV should be written in the test booklet.

The declaration below must be signed when you have completed the examination.

I do hereby affirm, at the close of this examination, that I had no unlawful knowledge of the questions or answers prior to the examination and that I have neither given nor received assistance in answering any of the questions during the examination.

Tear Here

____

Signature

Geometry August, 2010

Part I

Answer all 28 questions in this part. Each correct answer will receive 2 credits. No partial credit will be allowed. For each question, write on the separate answer sheet the numeral preceding the word or expression that best completes the statement or answers the question. [56]

Use this space for computations.

1 In the diagram below, $\triangle ABC \cong \triangle XYZ$.

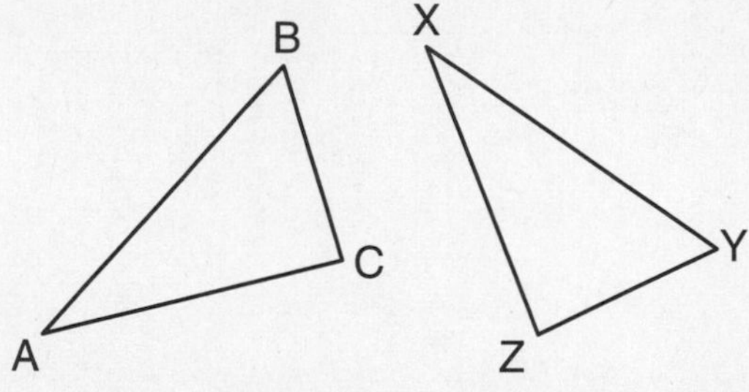

Which two statements identify corresponding congruent parts for these triangles?

(1) $\overline{AB} \cong \overline{XY}$ and $\angle C \cong \angle Y$

(2) $\overline{AB} \cong \overline{YZ}$ and $\angle C \cong \angle X$

(3) $\overline{BC} \cong \overline{XY}$ and $\angle A \cong \angle Y$

(4) $\overline{BC} \cong \overline{YZ}$ and $\angle A \cong \angle X$

2 A support beam between the floor and ceiling of a house forms a 90° angle with the floor. The builder wants to make sure that the floor and ceiling are parallel. Which angle should the support beam form with the ceiling?

(1) 45°

(2) 60°

(3) 90°

(4) 180°

Use this space for computations.

3 In the diagram below, the vertices of $\triangle DEF$ are the midpoints of the sides of equilateral triangle ABC, and the perimeter of $\triangle ABC$ is 36 cm.

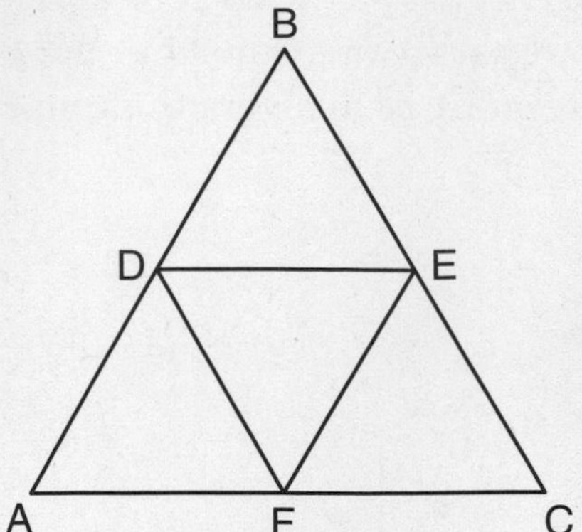

What is the length, in centimeters, of $\overline{EF}$?

(1) 6 (3) 18
(2) 12 (4) 4

4 What is the solution of the following system of equations?

$$y = (x + 3)^2 - 4$$
$$y = 2x + 5$$

(1) $(0,-4)$ (3) $(-4,-3)$ and $(0,5)$
(2) $(-4,0)$ (4) $(-3,-4)$ and $(5,0)$

Use this space for computations.

5 One step in a construction uses the endpoints of $\overline{AB}$ to create arcs with the same radii. The arcs intersect above and below the segment. What is the relationship of $\overline{AB}$ and the line connecting the points of intersection of these arcs?

(1) collinear

(2) congruent

(3) parallel

(4) perpendicular

6 If $\triangle ABC \sim \triangle ZXY$, $m\angle A = 50$, and $m\angle C = 30$, what is $m\angle X$?

(1) 30

(2) 50

(3) 80

(4) 100

Use this space for computations.

7 In the diagram below of $\triangle AGE$ and $\triangle OLD$, $\angle GAE \cong \angle LOD$, and $\overline{AE} \cong \overline{OD}$.

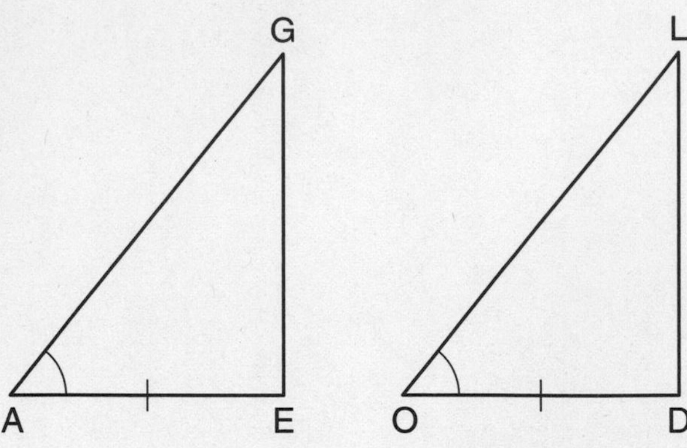

To prove that $\triangle AGE$ and $\triangle OLD$ are congruent by SAS, what other information is needed?

(1) $\overline{GE} \cong \overline{LD}$

(2) $\overline{AG} \cong \overline{OL}$

(3) $\angle AGE \cong \angle OLD$

(4) $\angle AEG \cong \angle ODL$

8 Point A is not contained in plane $\mathcal{B}$. How many lines can be drawn through point A that will be perpendicular to plane $\mathcal{B}$?

(1) one

(2) two

(3) zero

(4) infinite

9 The equation of a circle is $x^2 + (y - 7)^2 = 16$. What are the center and radius of the circle?

(1) center = (0,7); radius = 4

(2) center = (0,7); radius = 16

(3) center = (0,−7); radius = 4

(4) center = (0,−7); radius = 16

Use this space for computations.

10 What is an equation of the line that passes through the point (7,3) and is parallel to the line $4x + 2y = 10$?

(1) $y = \frac{1}{2}x - \frac{1}{2}$

(2) $y = -\frac{1}{2}x + \frac{13}{2}$

(3) $y = 2x - 11$

(4) $y = -2x + 17$

11 In $\triangle ABC$, $AB = 7$, $BC = 8$, and $AC = 9$. Which list has the angles of $\triangle ABC$ in order from smallest to largest?

(1) $\angle A, \angle B, \angle C$

(2) $\angle B, \angle A, \angle C$

(3) $\angle C, \angle B, \angle A$

(4) $\angle C, \angle A, \angle B$

12 Tangents $\overline{PA}$ and $\overline{PB}$ are drawn to circle O from an external point, P, and radii $\overline{OA}$ and $\overline{OB}$ are drawn. If $m\angle APB = 40$, what is the measure of $\angle AOB$?

(1) 140°

(2) 100°

(3) 70°

(4) 50°

13 What is the length of the line segment with endpoints $A(-6,4)$ and $B(2,-5)$?

(1) $\sqrt{13}$

(2) $\sqrt{17}$

(3) $\sqrt{72}$

(4) $\sqrt{145}$

Use this space for computations.

14 The lines represented by the equations $y + \frac{1}{2}x = 4$ and $3x + 6y = 12$ are

(1) the same line
(2) parallel
(3) perpendicular
(4) neither parallel nor perpendicular

15 A transformation of a polygon that always preserves both length and orientation is

(1) dilation
(2) translation
(3) line reflection
(4) glide reflection

16 In which polygon does the sum of the measures of the interior angles equal the sum of the measures of the exterior angles?

(1) triangle
(2) hexagon
(3) octagon
(4) quadrilateral

Use this space for computations.

17 In the diagram below of circle O, chords $\overline{AB}$ and $\overline{CD}$ intersect at E.

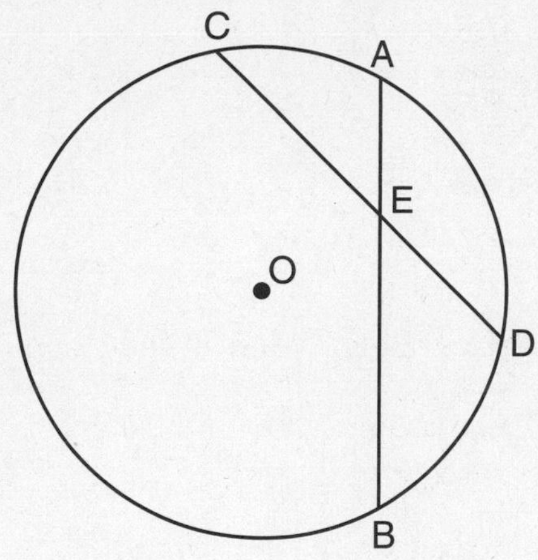

If $CE = 10$, $ED = 6$, and $AE = 4$, what is the length of $\overline{EB}$?

(1) 15
(2) 12
(3) 6.7
(4) 2.4

18 In the diagram below of $\triangle ABC$, medians $\overline{AD}$, $\overline{BE}$, and $\overline{CF}$ intersect at G.

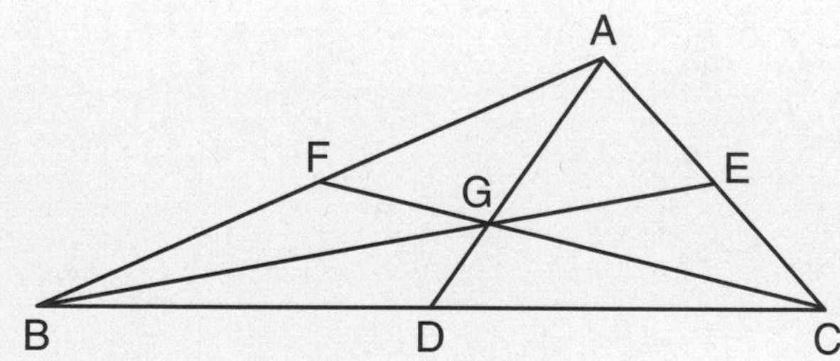

If $CF = 24$, what is the length of $\overline{FG}$?

(1) 8
(2) 10
(3) 12
(4) 16

Use this space for computations.

19 If a line segment has endpoints $A(3x + 5, 3y)$ and $B(x - 1, -y)$, what are the coordinates of the midpoint of $\overline{AB}$?

(1) $(x + 3, 2y)$
(2) $(2x + 2, y)$
(3) $(2x + 3, y)$
(4) $(4x + 4, 2y)$

20 If the surface area of a sphere is represented by 144π, what is the volume in terms of π?

(1) 36π
(2) 48π
(3) 216π
(4) 288π

21 Which transformation of the line $x = 3$ results in an image that is perpendicular to the given line?

(1) $r_{x\text{-axis}}$
(2) $r_{y\text{-axis}}$
(3) $r_{y = x}$
(4) $r_{x = 1}$

Use this space for computations.

22 In the diagram below of regular pentagon $ABCDE$, $\overline{EB}$ is drawn.

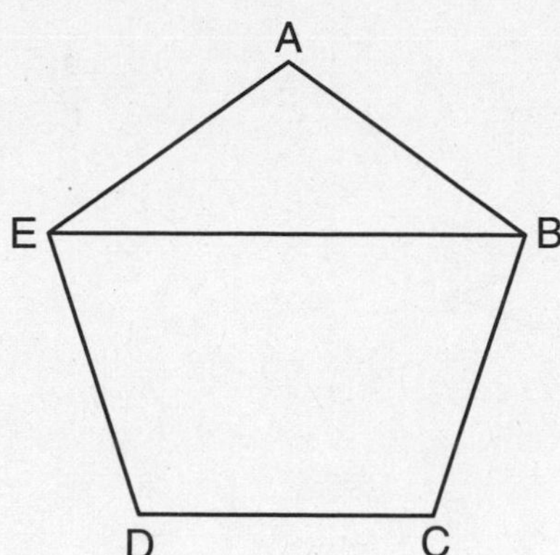

What is the measure of $\angle AEB$?

(1) 36°
(2) 54°
(3) 72°
(4) 108°

23 $\triangle ABC$ is similar to $\triangle DEF$. The ratio of the length of $\overline{AB}$ to the length of $\overline{DE}$ is 3:1. Which ratio is also equal to 3:1?

(1) $\frac{m\angle A}{m\angle D}$
(2) $\frac{m\angle B}{m\angle F}$
(3) $\frac{\text{area of } \triangle ABC}{\text{area of } \triangle DEF}$
(4) $\frac{\text{perimeter of } \triangle ABC}{\text{perimeter of } \triangle DEF}$

24 What is the slope of a line perpendicular to the line whose equation is $2y = -6x + 8$?

(1) -3
(2) $\frac{1}{6}$
(3) $\frac{1}{3}$
(4) -6

Use this space for computations.

25 In the diagram below of circle C, $m\overset{\frown}{QT} = 140$ and $m\angle P = 40$.

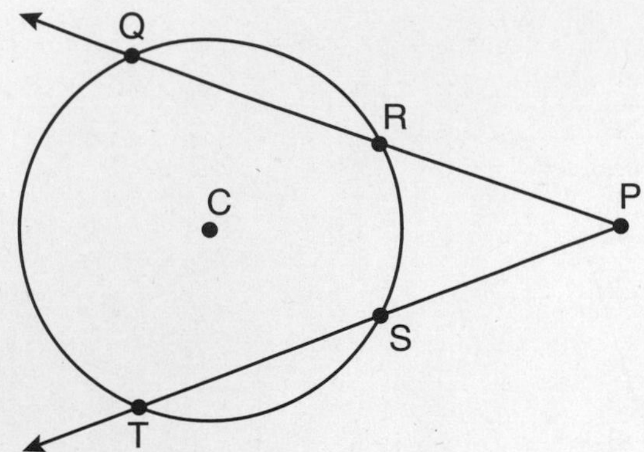

What is $m\overset{\frown}{RS}$?

(1) 50 (3) 90

(2) 60 (4) 100

26 Which statement is logically equivalent to "If it is warm, then I go swimming"?

(1) If I go swimming, then it is warm.

(2) If it is warm, then I do not go swimming.

(3) If I do not go swimming, then it is not warm.

(4) If it is not warm, then I do not go swimming.

Use this space for computations.

27 In the diagram below of $\triangle ACT$, $\overleftrightarrow{BE} \parallel \overline{AT}$.

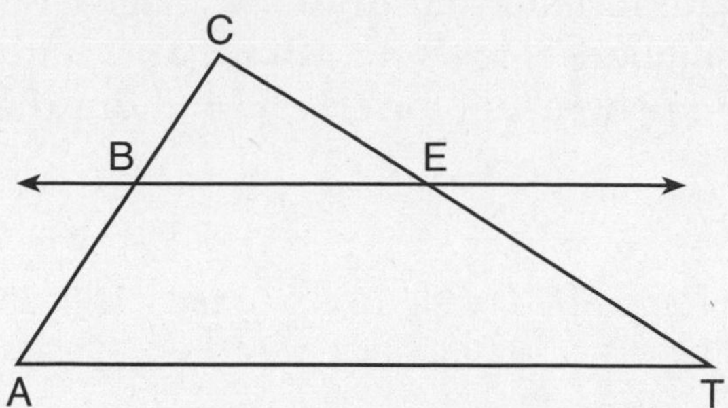

If $CB = 3$, $CA = 10$, and $CE = 6$, what is the length of $\overline{ET}$?

(1) 5 (3) 20

(2) 14 (4) 26

28 Which geometric principle is used in the construction shown below?

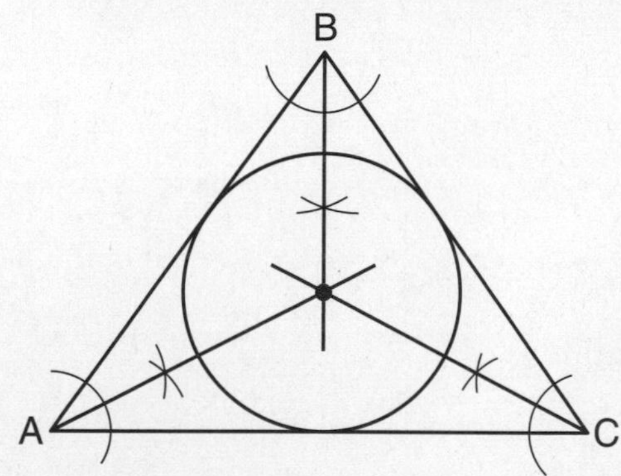

(1) The intersection of the angle bisectors of a triangle is the center of the inscribed circle.

(2) The intersection of the angle bisectors of a triangle is the center of the circumscribed circle.

(3) The intersection of the perpendicular bisectors of the sides of a triangle is the center of the inscribed circle.

(4) The intersection of the perpendicular bisectors of the sides of a triangle is the center of the circumscribed circle.

Part II

Answer all 6 questions in this part. Each correct answer will receive 2 credits. Clearly indicate the necessary steps, including appropriate formula substitutions, diagrams, graphs, charts, etc. For all questions in this part, a correct numerical answer with no work shown will receive only 1 credit. All answers should be written in pen, except for graphs and drawings, which should be done in pencil. [12]

29 The diagram below shows isosceles trapezoid $ABCD$ with $\overline{AB} \parallel \overline{DC}$ and $\overline{AD} \cong \overline{BC}$. If $m\angle BAD = 2x$ and $m\angle BCD = 3x + 5$, find $m\angle BAD$.

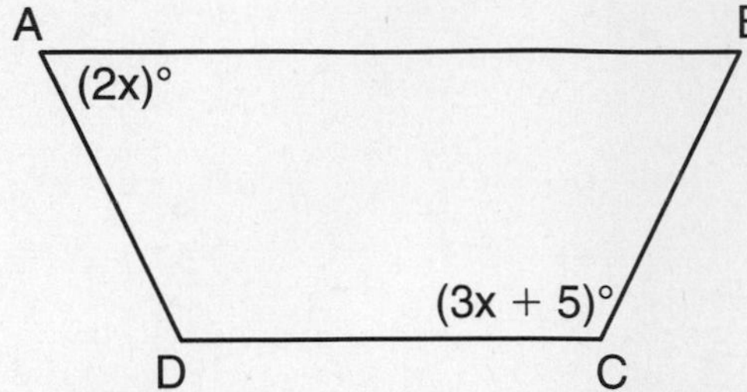

30 A right circular cone has a base with a radius of 15 cm, a vertical height of 20 cm, and a slant height of 25 cm. Find, in terms of π, the number of square centimeters in the lateral area of the cone.

31 In the diagram below of $\triangle HQP$, side $\overline{HP}$ is extended through P to T, $m\angle QPT = 6x + 20$, $m\angle HQP = x + 40$, and $m\angle PHQ = 4x - 5$. Find $m\angle QPT$.

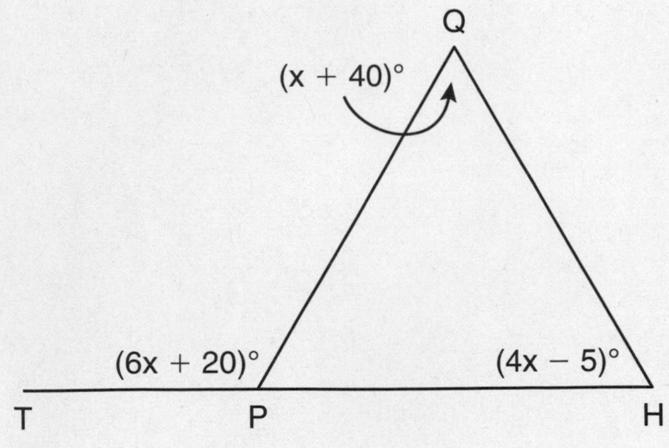

32 On the line segment below, use a compass and straightedge to construct equilateral triangle *ABC*. [Leave all construction marks.]

A ———————————— B

33 In the diagram below, car A is parked 7 miles from car B. Sketch the points that are 4 miles from car A and sketch the points that are 4 miles from car B. Label with an **X** all points that satisfy both conditions.

Car A • Car B •

34 Write an equation for circle O shown on the graph below.

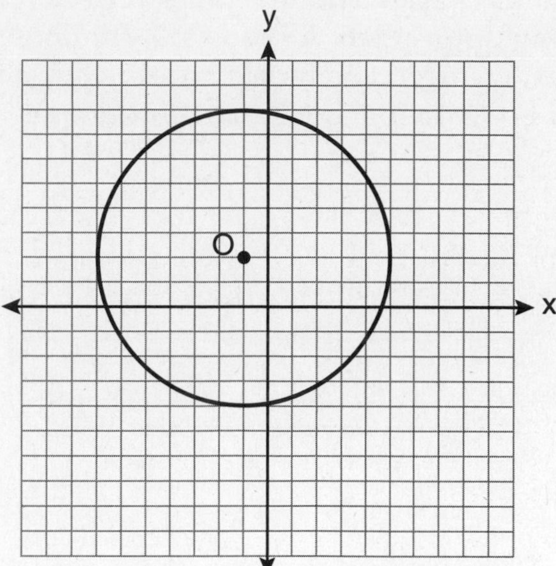

Part III

Answer all 3 questions in this part. Each correct answer will receive 4 credits. Clearly indicate the necessary steps, including appropriate formula substitutions, diagrams, graphs, charts, etc. For all questions in this part, a correct numerical answer with no work shown will receive only 1 credit. All answers should be written in pen, except for graphs and drawings, which should be done in pencil. [12]

35 In the diagram below of quadrilateral $ABCD$ with diagonal $\overline{BD}$, $m\angle A = 93$, $m\angle ADB = 43$, $m\angle C = 3x + 5$, $m\angle BDC = x + 19$, and $m\angle DBC = 2x + 6$. Determine if $\overline{AB}$ is parallel to $\overline{DC}$. Explain your reasoning.

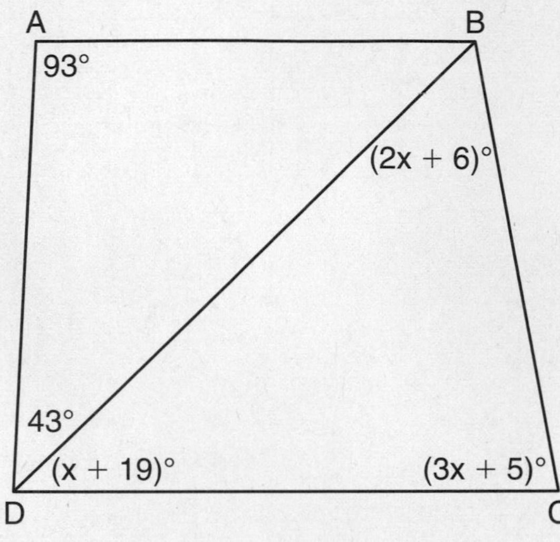

36 The coordinates of the vertices of $\triangle ABC$ are $A(1,3)$, $B(-2,2)$, and $C(0,-2)$. On the grid below, graph and label $\triangle A''B''C''$, the result of the composite transformation $D_2 \circ T_{3,-2}$. State the coordinates of A'', B'', and C''.

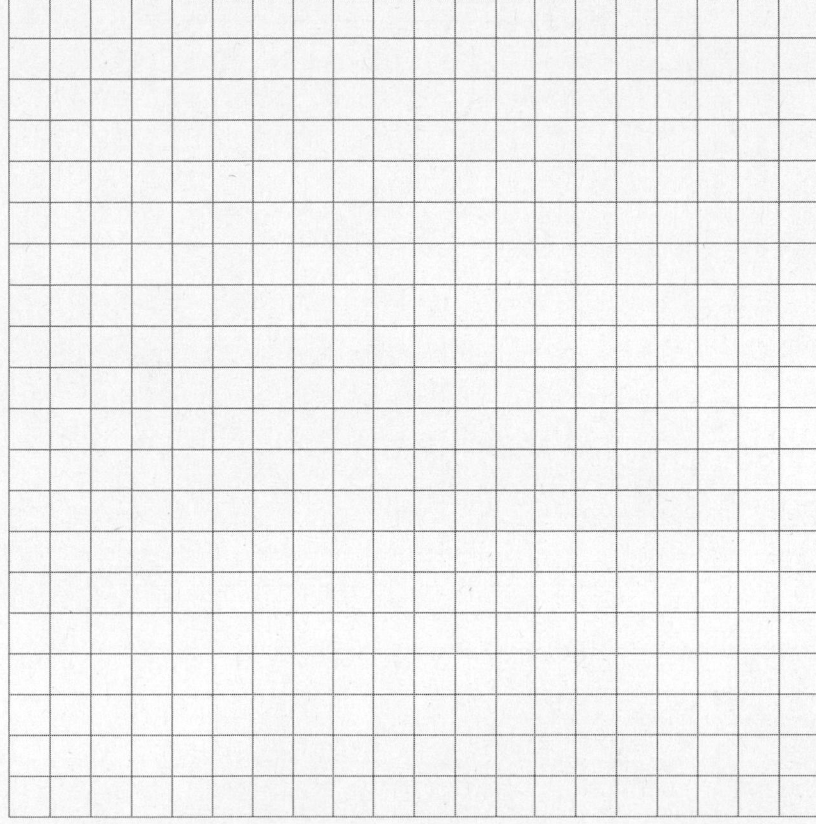

37 In the diagram below, $\triangle RST$ is a 3-4-5 right triangle. The altitude, h, to the hypotenuse has been drawn. Determine the length of h.

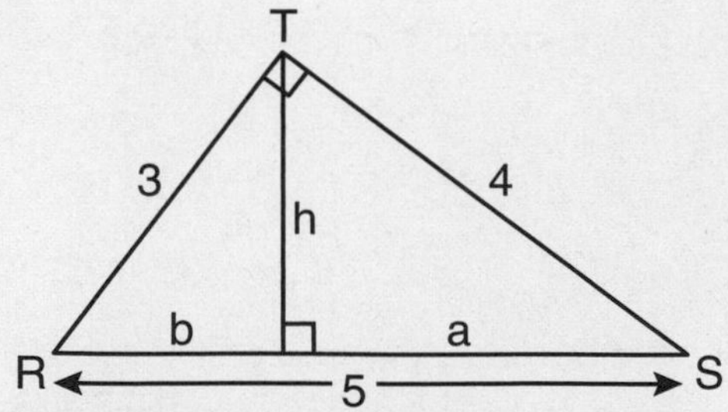

Part IV

Answer the question in this part. A correct answer will receive 6 credits. Clearly indicate the necessary steps, including appropriate formula substitutions, diagrams, graphs, charts, etc. A correct numerical answer with no work shown will receive only 1 credit. The answer should be written in pen. [6]

38 Given: Quadrilateral $ABCD$ has vertices $A(-5,6)$, $B(6,6)$, $C(8,-3)$, and $D(-3,-3)$.

Prove: Quadrilateral $ABCD$ is a parallelogram but is neither a rhombus nor a rectangle.

[The use of the grid below is optional.]

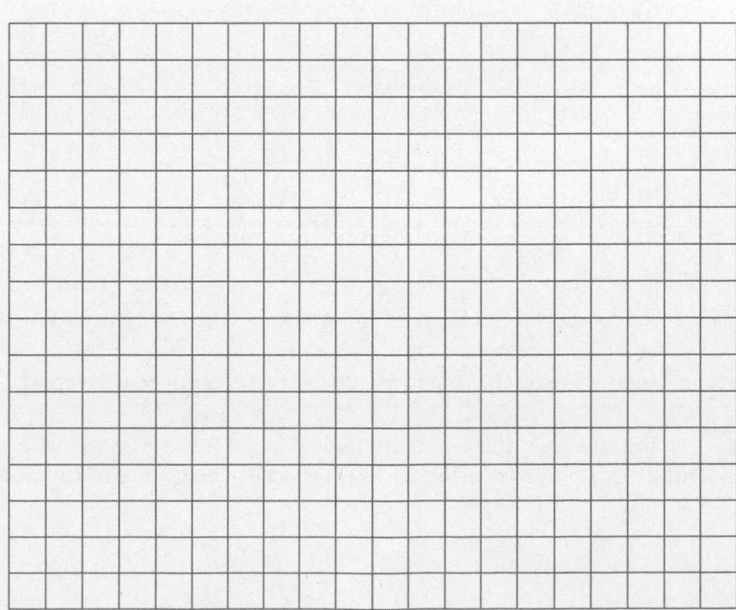

Tear Here

The University of the State of New York

REGENTS HIGH SCHOOL EXAMINATION

GEOMETRY

Wednesday, August 18, 2010 — 8:30 to 11:30 a.m., only

ANSWER SHEET

Student .... Sex: ☐ Male ☐ Female Grade ....

Teacher .... School ....

Your answers to Part I should be recorded on this answer sheet.

Part I

Answer all 28 questions in this part.

1	8	15	22 ....
2	9	16	23 ....
3	10	17	24 ....
4	11	18	25 ....
5	12	19	26 ....
6	13	20	27 ....
7	14	21	28 ....

Your answers for Parts II, III, and IV should be written in the test booklet.

The declaration below must be signed when you have completed the examination.

I do hereby affirm, at the close of this examination, that I had no unlawful knowledge of the questions or answers prior to the examination and that I have neither given nor received assistance in answering any of the questions during the examination.

Tear Here

____

Signature

Geometry June, 2010

Part I

Answer all 28 questions in this part. Each correct answer will receive 2 credits. No partial credit will be allowed. For each question, write on the separate answer sheet the numeral preceding the word or expression that best completes the statement or answers the question. [56]

Use this space for computations.

1 In the diagram below of circle O, chord $\overline{AB} \parallel$ chord $\overline{CD}$, and chord $\overline{CD} \parallel$ chord $\overline{EF}$.

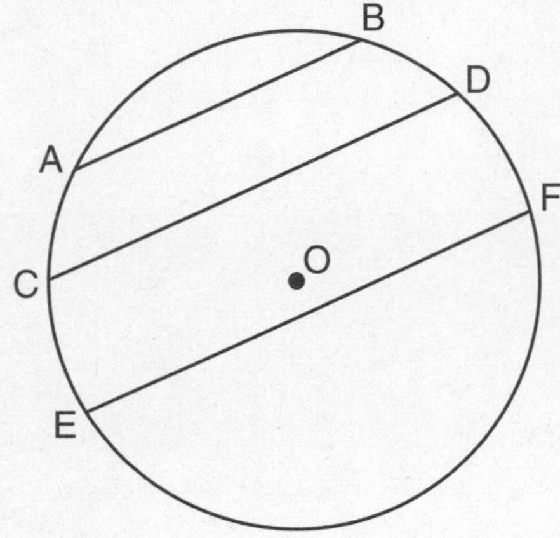

Which statement must be true?

(1) $\overset{\frown}{CE} \cong \overset{\frown}{DF}$ (3) $\overset{\frown}{AC} \cong \overset{\frown}{CE}$

(2) $\overset{\frown}{AC} \cong \overset{\frown}{DF}$ (4) $\overset{\frown}{EF} \cong \overset{\frown}{CD}$

2 What is the negation of the statement "I am not going to eat ice cream"?

(1) I like ice cream.

(2) I am going to eat ice cream.

(3) If I eat ice cream, then I like ice cream.

(4) If I don't like ice cream, then I don't eat ice cream.

Use this space for computations.

3 The diagram below shows a right pentagonal prism.

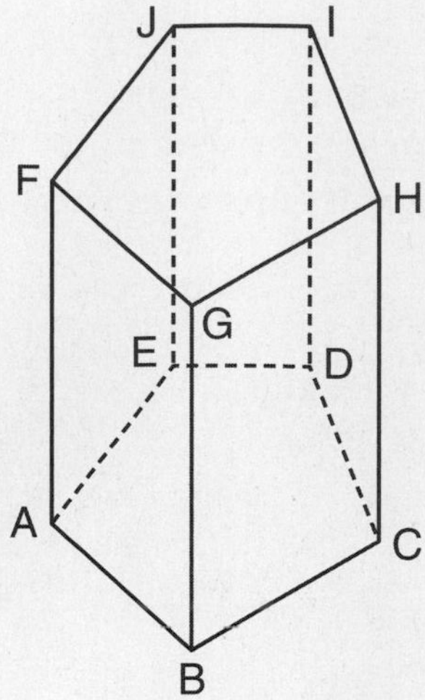

Which statement is always true?

(1) $\overline{BC} \parallel \overline{ED}$

(2) $\overline{FG} \parallel \overline{CD}$

(3) $\overline{FJ} \parallel \overline{IH}$

(4) $\overline{GB} \parallel \overline{HC}$

4 In isosceles triangle ABC, $AB = BC$. Which statement will always be true?

(1) $m\angle B = m\angle A$

(2) $m\angle A > m\angle B$

(3) $m\angle A = m\angle C$

(4) $m\angle C < m\angle B$

5 The rectangle *ABCD* shown in the diagram below will be reflected across the *x*-axis.

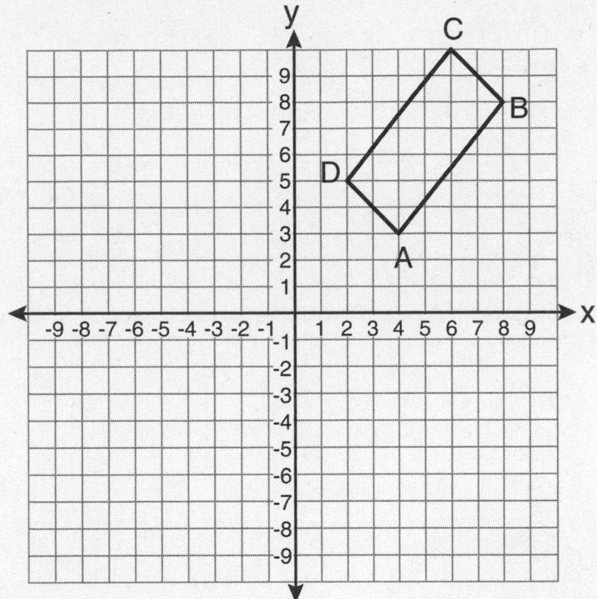

What will *not* be preserved?

(1) slope of $\overline{AB}$

(2) parallelism of $\overline{AB}$ and $\overline{CD}$

(3) length of $\overline{AB}$

(4) measure of $\angle A$

6 A right circular cylinder has an altitude of 11 feet and a radius of 5 feet. What is the lateral area, in square feet, of the cylinder, to the *nearest tenth*?

(1) 172.7

(2) 172.8

(3) 345.4

(4) 345.6

Use this space for computations.

7 A transversal intersects two lines. Which condition would always make the two lines parallel?

(1) Vertical angles are congruent.

(2) Alternate interior angles are congruent.

(3) Corresponding angles are supplementary.

(4) Same-side interior angles are complementary.

8 If the diagonals of a quadrilateral do *not* bisect each other, then the quadrilateral could be a

(1) rectangle

(2) rhombus

(3) square

(4) trapezoid

9 What is the converse of the statement "If Bob does his homework, then George gets candy"?

(1) If George gets candy, then Bob does his homework.

(2) Bob does his homework if and only if George gets candy.

(3) If George does not get candy, then Bob does not do his homework.

(4) If Bob does not do his homework, then George does not get candy.

Use this space for computations.

10 In $\triangle PQR$, $PQ = 8$, $QR = 12$, and $RP = 13$. Which statement about the angles of $\triangle PQR$ must be true?

(1) $m\angle Q > m\angle P > m\angle R$

(2) $m\angle Q > m\angle R > m\angle P$

(3) $m\angle R > m\angle P > m\angle Q$

(4) $m\angle P > m\angle R > m\angle Q$

11 Given:

$$y = \frac{1}{4}x - 3$$

$$y = x^2 + 8x + 12$$

In which quadrant will the graphs of the given equations intersect?

(1) I

(2) II

(3) III

(4) IV

Use this space for computations.

12 Which diagram shows the construction of an equilateral triangle?

(1)

(3)

(2)

(4)

13 Line segment AB is tangent to circle O at A. Which type of triangle is always formed when points A, B, and O are connected?

(1) right

(2) obtuse

(3) scalene

(4) isosceles

Use this space for computations.

14 What is an equation for the circle shown in the graph below?

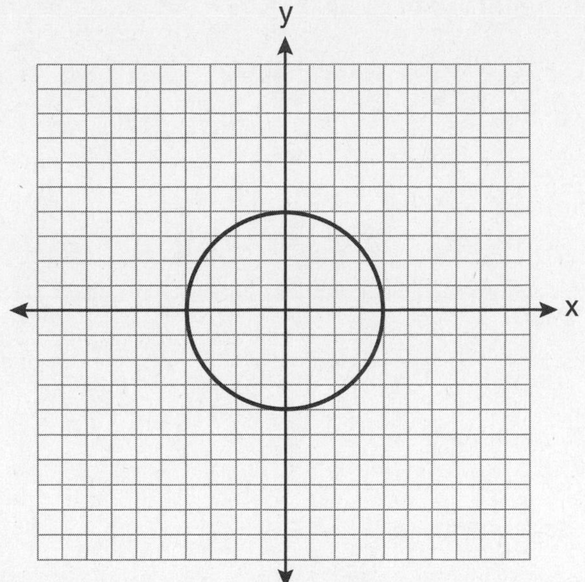

(1) $x^2 + y^2 = 2$
(2) $x^2 + y^2 = 4$
(3) $x^2 + y^2 = 8$
(4) $x^2 + y^2 = 16$

15 Which transformation can map the letter **S** onto itself?

(1) glide reflection
(2) translation
(3) line reflection
(4) rotation

16 In isosceles trapezoid $ABCD$, $\overline{AB} \cong \overline{CD}$. If $BC = 20$, $AD = 36$, and $AB = 17$, what is the length of the altitude of the trapezoid?

(1) 10
(2) 12
(3) 15
(4) 16

Use this space for computations.

17 In plane $\mathcal{P}$, lines m and n intersect at point A. If line k is perpendicular to line m and line n at point A, then line k is

(1) contained in plane $\mathcal{P}$

(2) parallel to plane $\mathcal{P}$

(3) perpendicular to plane $\mathcal{P}$

(4) skew to plane $\mathcal{P}$

18 The diagram below shows $\overline{AB}$ and $\overline{DE}$.

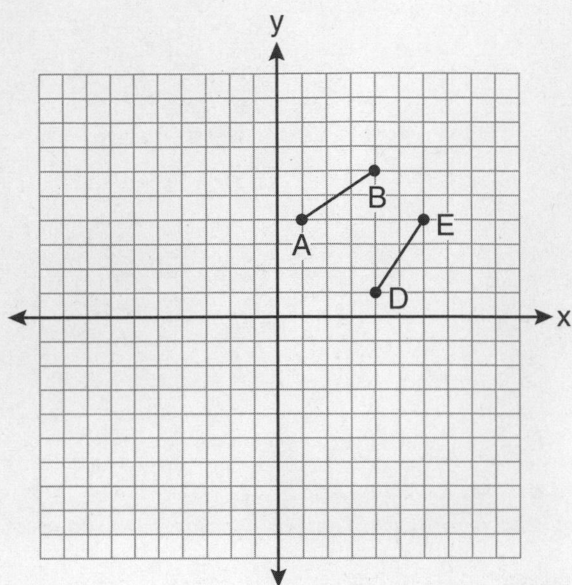

Which transformation will move $\overline{AB}$ onto $\overline{DE}$ such that point D is the image of point A and point E is the image of point B?

(1) $T_{3,-3}$

(2) $D_{\frac{1}{2}}$

(3) R_{90°

(4) $r_{y=x}$

Use this space for computations.

19 In the diagram below of circle O, chords $\overline{AE}$ and $\overline{DC}$ intersect at point B, such that $m\widehat{AC} = 36$ and $m\widehat{DE} = 20$.

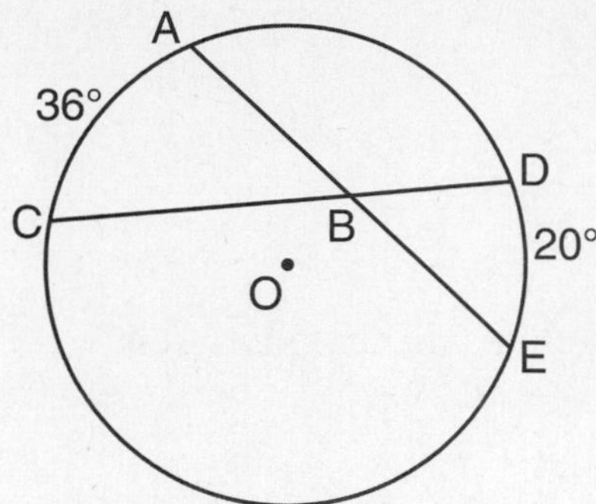

What is $m\angle ABC$?

(1) 56 (3) 28

(2) 36 (4) 8

20 The diagram below shows the construction of a line through point P perpendicular to line m.

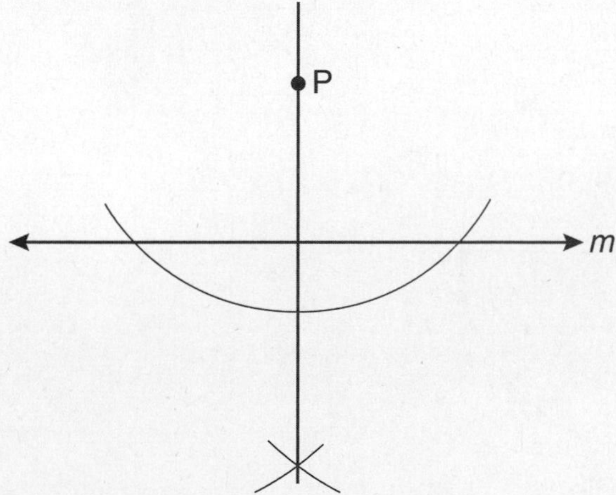

Which statement is demonstrated by this construction?

(1) If a line is parallel to a line that is perpendicular to a third line, then the line is also perpendicular to the third line.

(2) The set of points equidistant from the endpoints of a line segment is the perpendicular bisector of the segment.

(3) Two lines are perpendicular if they are equidistant from a given point.

(4) Two lines are perpendicular if they intersect to form a vertical line.

Use this space for computations.

21 What is the length, to the *nearest tenth*, of the line segment joining the points $(-4,2)$ and $(146,52)$?

(1) 141.4
(2) 150.5
(3) 151.9
(4) 158.1

22 What is the slope of a line perpendicular to the line whose equation is $y = 3x + 4$?

(1) $\frac{1}{3}$
(2) $-\frac{1}{3}$
(3) 3
(4) -3

23 In the diagram below of circle O, secant $\overline{AB}$ intersects circle O at D, secant $\overline{AOC}$ intersects circle O at E, $AE = 4$, $AB = 12$, and $DB = 6$.

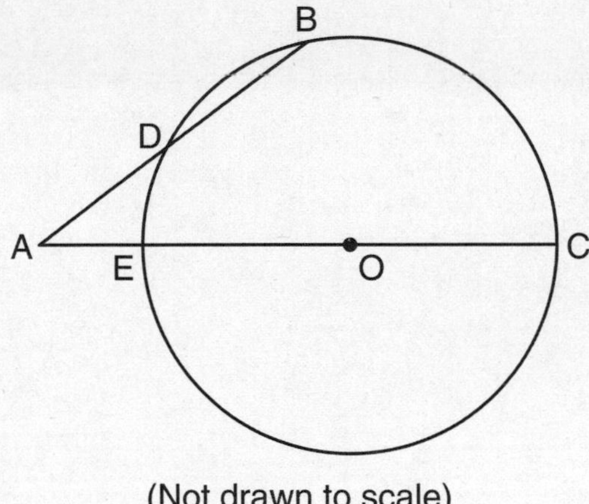

(Not drawn to scale)

What is the length of $\overline{OC}$?

(1) 4.5
(2) 7
(3) 9
(4) 14

Use this space for computations.

24 The diagram below shows a pennant in the shape of an isosceles triangle. The equal sides each measure 13, the altitude is $x + 7$, and the base is $2x$.

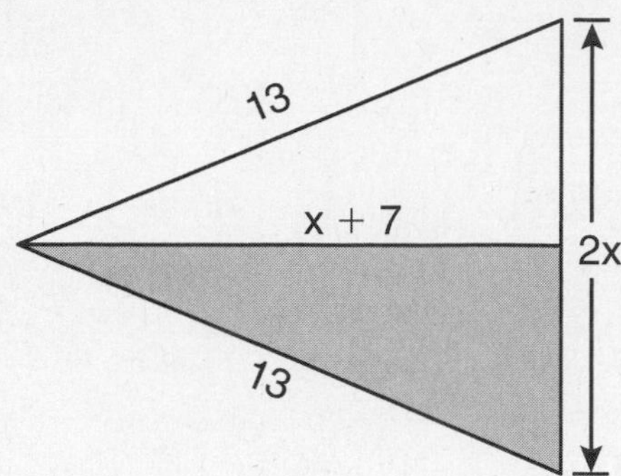

What is the length of the base?

(1) 5
(2) 10
(3) 12
(4) 24

25 In the diagram below of $\triangle ABC$, $\overline{CD}$ is the bisector of $\angle BCA$, $\overline{AE}$ is the bisector of $\angle CAB$, and $\overline{BG}$ is drawn.

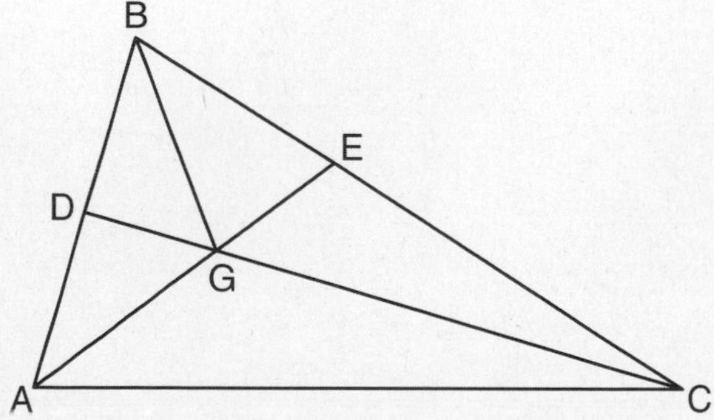

Which statement must be true?

(1) $DG = EG$
(2) $AG = BG$
(3) $\angle AEB \cong \angle AEC$
(4) $\angle DBG \cong \angle EBG$

Use this space for computations.

26 In the diagram below of circle O, chords $\overline{AD}$ and $\overline{BC}$ intersect at E.

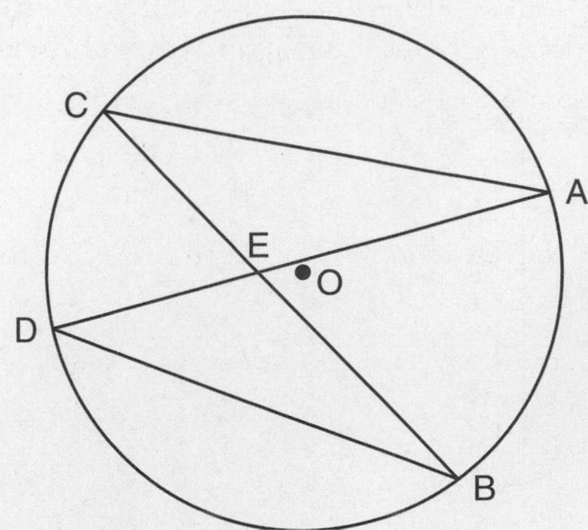

Which relationship must be true?

(1) $\triangle CAE \cong \triangle DBE$
(2) $\triangle AEC \sim \triangle BED$
(3) $\angle ACB \cong \angle CBD$
(4) $\overset{\frown}{CA} \cong \overset{\frown}{DB}$

27 Two lines are represented by the equations $-\frac{1}{2}y = 6x + 10$ and $y = mx$. For which value of m will the lines be parallel?

(1) -12
(2) -3
(3) 3
(4) 12

28 The coordinates of the vertices of parallelogram $ABCD$ are $A(-3,2)$, $B(-2,-1)$, $C(4,1)$, and $D(3,4)$. The slopes of which line segments could be calculated to show that $ABCD$ is a rectangle?

(1) $\overline{AB}$ and $\overline{DC}$
(2) $\overline{AB}$ and $\overline{BC}$
(3) $\overline{AD}$ and $\overline{BC}$
(4) $\overline{AC}$ and $\overline{BD}$

Part II

Answer all 6 questions in this part. Each correct answer will receive 2 credits. Clearly indicate the necessary steps, including appropriate formula substitutions, diagrams, graphs, charts, etc. For all questions in this part, a correct numerical answer with no work shown will receive only 1 credit. All answers should be written in pen, except for graphs and drawings, which should be done in pencil. [12]

29 Tim is going to paint a wooden sphere that has a diameter of 12 inches. Find the surface area of the sphere, to the *nearest square inch*.

30 In the diagram below of $\triangle ABC$, $\overline{DE}$ is a midsegment of $\triangle ABC$, $DE = 7$, $AB = 10$, and $BC = 13$. Find the perimeter of $\triangle ABC$.

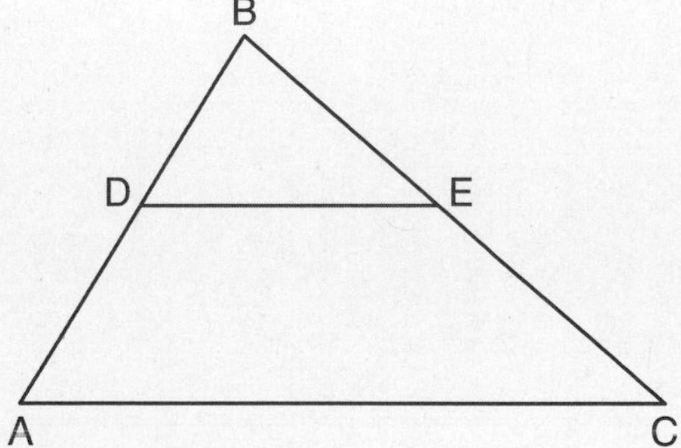

31 In right $\triangle DEF$, $m\angle D = 90$ and $m\angle F$ is 12 degrees less than twice $m\angle E$. Find $m\angle E$.

32 Triangle XYZ, shown in the diagram below, is reflected over the line $x = 2$. State the coordinates of $\triangle X'Y'Z'$, the image of $\triangle XYZ$.

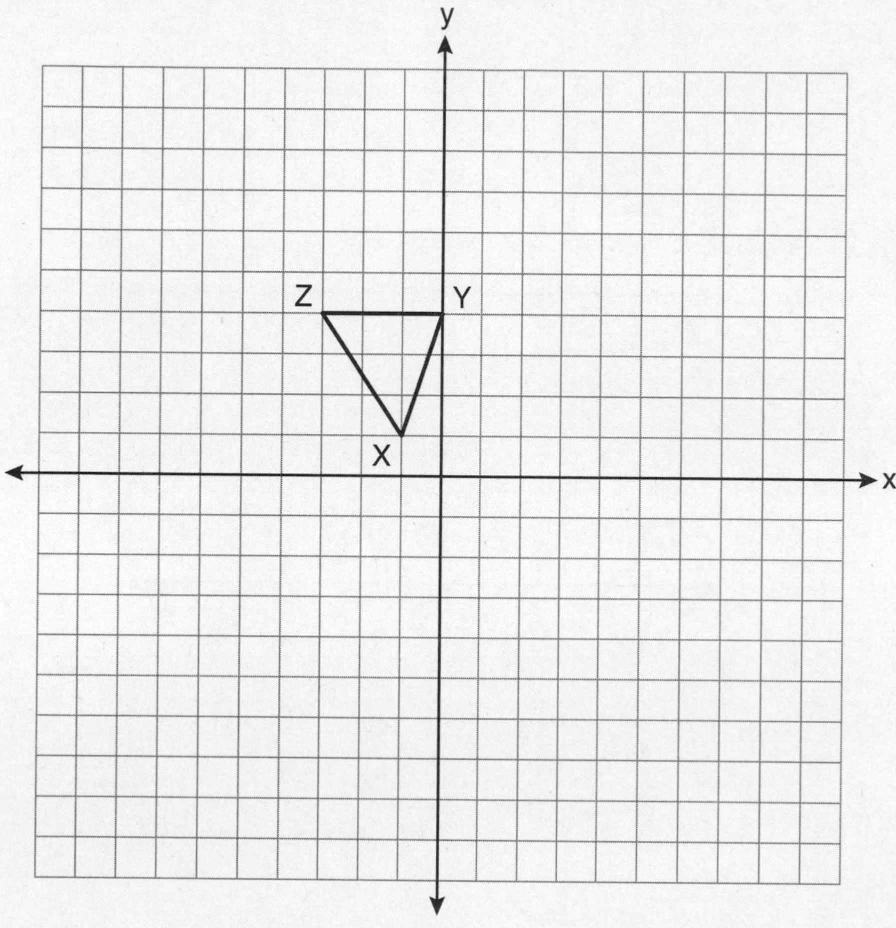

33 Two lines, $\overleftrightarrow{AB}$ and $\overleftrightarrow{CRD}$, are parallel and 10 inches apart. Sketch the locus of all points that are equidistant from $\overleftrightarrow{AB}$ and $\overleftrightarrow{CRD}$ and 7 inches from point R. Label with an **X** each point that satisfies both conditions.

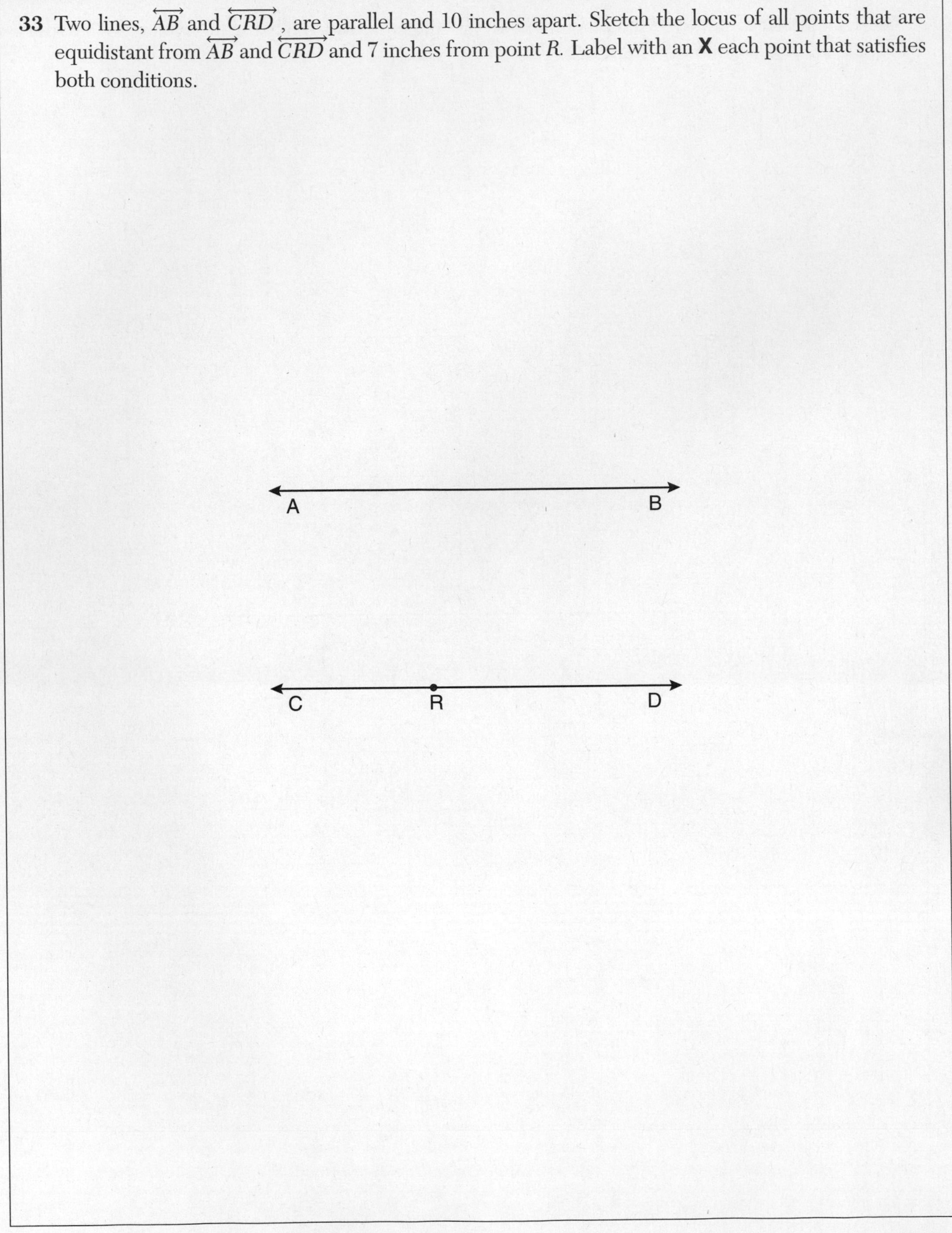

34 The base of a pyramid is a rectangle with a width of 6 cm and a length of 8 cm. Find, in centimeters, the height of the pyramid if the volume is 288 cm^3.

Part III

Answer all 3 questions in this part. Each correct answer will receive 4 credits. Clearly indicate the necessary steps, including appropriate formula substitutions, diagrams, graphs, charts, etc. For all questions in this part, a correct numerical answer with no work shown will receive only 1 credit. All answers should be written in pen, except for graphs and drawings, which should be done in pencil. [12]

35 Given: Quadrilateral $ABCD$ with $\overline{AB} \cong \overline{CD}$, $\overline{AD} \cong \overline{BC}$, and diagonal $\overline{BD}$ is drawn

Prove: $\angle BDC \cong \angle ABD$

36 Find an equation of the line passing through the point (6,5) and perpendicular to the line whose equation is $2y + 3x = 6$.

37 Write an equation of the circle whose diameter $\overline{AB}$ has endpoints $A(-4,2)$ and $B(4,-4)$. [The use of the grid below is optional.]

Part IV

Answer the question in this part. A correct answer will receive 6 credits. Clearly indicate the necessary steps, including appropriate formula substitutions, diagrams, graphs, charts, etc. A correct numerical answer with no work shown will receive only 1 credit. The answer should be written in pen. [6]

38 In the diagram below, quadrilateral $STAR$ is a rhombus with diagonals $\overline{SA}$ and $\overline{TR}$ intersecting at E. $ST = 3x + 30$, $SR = 8x - 5$, $SE = 3z$, $TE = 5z + 5$, $AE = 4z - 8$, $m\angle RTA = 5y - 2$, and $m\angle TAS = 9y + 8$. Find SR, RT, and $m\angle TAS$.

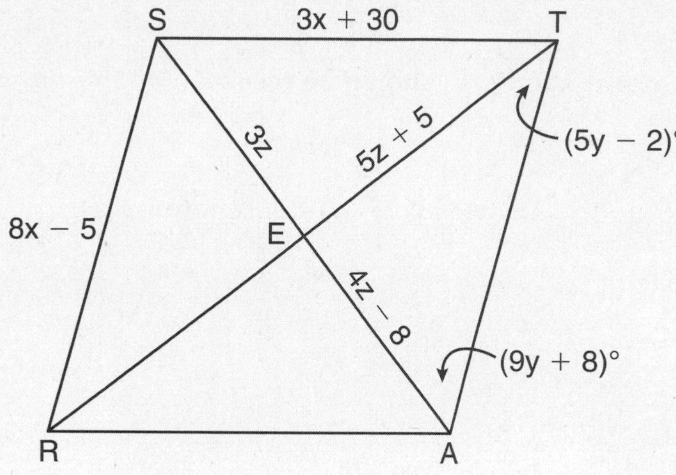

Tear Here

The University of the State of New York

REGENTS HIGH SCHOOL EXAMINATION

GEOMETRY

Thursday, June 17, 2010—1:15 to 4:15 p.m., only

ANSWER SHEET

Student .... Sex: ☐ Male ☐ Female Grade ....

Teacher .... School ....

Your answers to Part I should be recorded on this answer sheet.

Part I

Answer all 28 questions in this part.

1	8	15	22 ....
2	9	16	23 ....
3	10	17	24 ....
4	11	18	25 ....
5	12	19	26 ....
6	13	20	27 ....
7	14	21	28 ....

Your answers for Parts II, III, and IV should be written in the test booklet.

The declaration below must be signed when you have completed the examination.

I do hereby affirm, at the close of this examination, that I had no unlawful knowledge of the questions or answers prior to the examination and that I have neither given nor received assistance in answering any of the questions during the examination.

Tear Here

____

Signature

Geometry January, 2010

Part I

Answer all 28 questions in this part. Each correct answer will receive 2 credits. No partial credit will be allowed. For each question, write on the separate answer sheet the numeral preceding the word or expression that best completes the statement or answers the question. [56]

Use this space for computations.

1 In the diagram below of trapezoid $RSUT$, $\overline{RS} \parallel \overline{TU}$, X is the midpoint of $\overline{RT}$, and V is the midpoint of $\overline{SU}$.

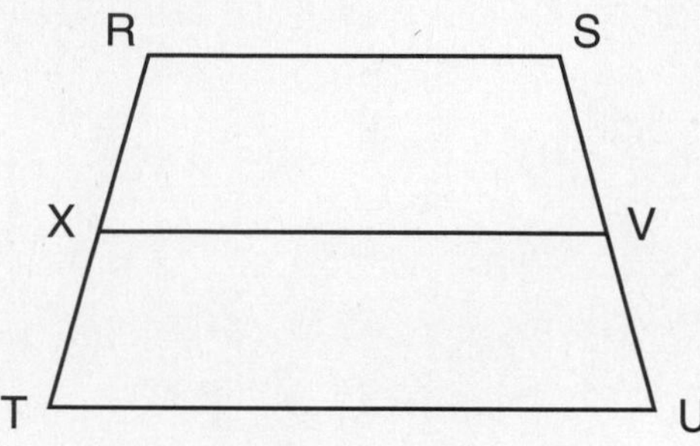

If $RS = 30$ and $XV = 44$, what is the length of $\overline{TU}$?

(1) 37 (3) 74

(2) 58 (4) 118

2 In $\triangle ABC$, $m\angle A = x$, $m\angle B = 2x + 2$, and $m\angle C = 3x + 4$. What is the value of x?

(1) 29 (3) 59

(2) 31 (4) 61

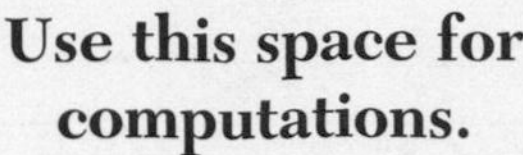

3 Which expression best describes the transformation shown in the diagram below?

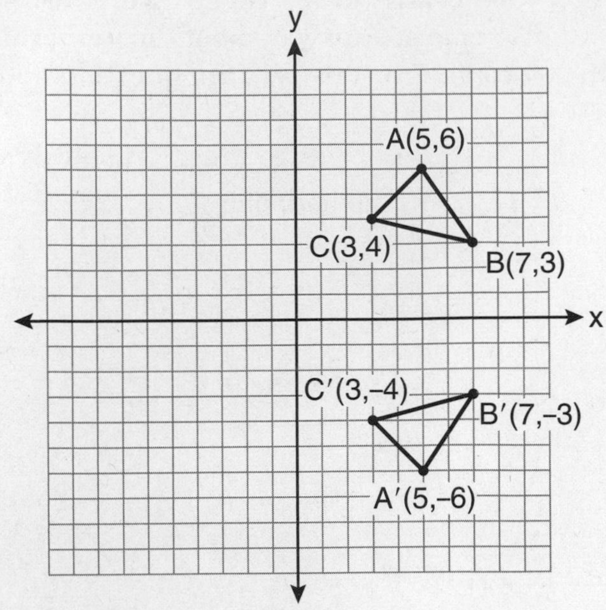

(1) same orientation; reflection

(2) opposite orientation; reflection

(3) same orientation; translation

(4) opposite orientation; translation

4 Based on the construction below, which statement must be true?

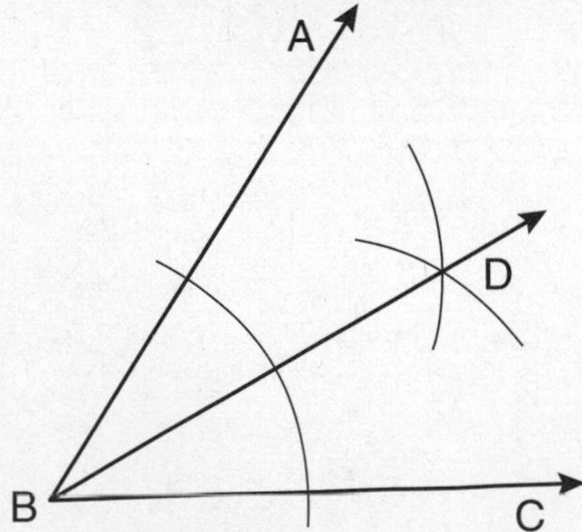

(1) $m\angle ABD = \frac{1}{2}m\angle CBD$ (3) $m\angle ABD = m\angle ABC$

(2) $m\angle ABD = m\angle CBD$ (4) $m\angle CBD = \frac{1}{2}m\angle ABD$

Use this space for computations.

5 In the diagram below, $\triangle ABC$ is inscribed in circle P. The distances from the center of circle P to each side of the triangle are shown.

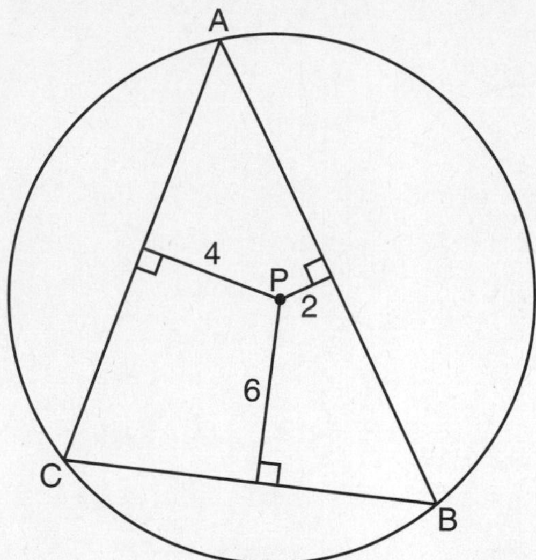

Which statement about the sides of the triangle is true?

(1) $AB > AC > BC$
(2) $AB < AC$ and $AC > BC$
(3) $AC > AB > BC$
(4) $AC = AB$ and $AB > BC$

6 Which transformation is *not* always an isometry?

(1) rotation
(2) dilation
(3) reflection
(4) translation

7 In $\triangle ABC$, $\overline{AB} \cong \overline{BC}$. An altitude is drawn from B to $\overline{AC}$ and intersects $\overline{AC}$ at D. Which statement is *not* always true?

(1) $\angle ABD \cong \angle CBD$
(2) $\angle BDA \cong \angle BDC$
(3) $\overline{AD} \cong \overline{BD}$
(4) $\overline{AD} \cong \overline{DC}$

Use this space for computations.

8 In the diagram below, tangent $\overline{PA}$ and secant $\overline{PBC}$ are drawn to circle O from external point P.

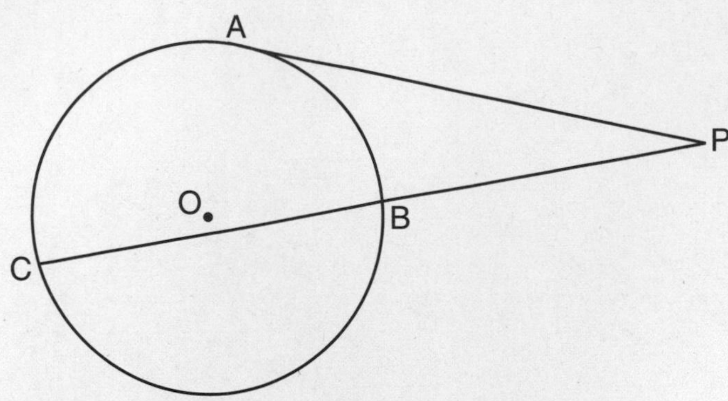

If $PB = 4$ and $BC = 5$, what is the length of $\overline{PA}$?

(1) 20
(2) 9
(3) 8
(4) 6

9 Which geometric principle is used to justify the construction below?

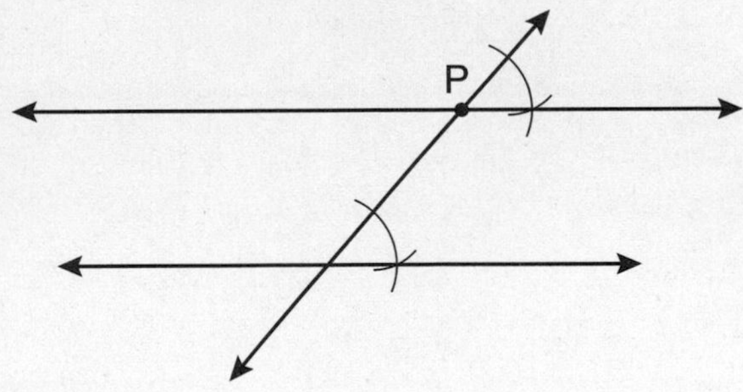

(1) A line perpendicular to one of two parallel lines is perpendicular to the other.
(2) Two lines are perpendicular if they intersect to form congruent adjacent angles.
(3) When two lines are intersected by a transversal and alternate interior angles are congruent, the lines are parallel.
(4) When two lines are intersected by a transversal and the corresponding angles are congruent, the lines are parallel.

Use this space for computations.

10 Which equation represents the circle whose center is $(-2,3)$ and whose radius is 5?

(1) $(x - 2)^2 + (y + 3)^2 = 5$

(2) $(x + 2)^2 + (y - 3)^2 = 5$

(3) $(x + 2)^2 + (y - 3)^2 = 25$

(4) $(x - 2)^2 + (y + 3)^2 = 25$

11 Towns A and B are 16 miles apart. How many points are 10 miles from town A and 12 miles from town B?

(1) 1

(2) 2

(3) 3

(4) 0

12 Lines j and k intersect at point P. Line m is drawn so that it is perpendicular to lines j and k at point P. Which statement is correct?

(1) Lines j and k are in perpendicular planes.

(2) Line m is in the same plane as lines j and k.

(3) Line m is parallel to the plane containing lines j and k.

(4) Line m is perpendicular to the plane containing lines j and k.

Use this space for computations.

13 In the diagram below of parallelogram $STUV$, $SV = x + 3$, $VU = 2x - 1$, and $TU = 4x - 3$.

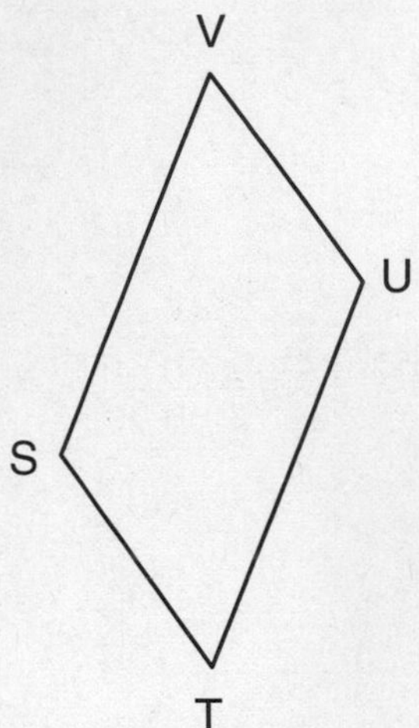

What is the length of $\overline{SV}$?

(1) 5
(2) 2
(3) 7
(4) 4

14 Which equation represents a line parallel to the line whose equation is $2y - 5x = 10$?

(1) $5y - 2x = 25$
(2) $5y + 2x = 10$
(3) $4y - 10x = 12$
(4) $2y + 10x = 8$

Use this space for computations.

15 In the diagram below of circle O, chords $\overline{AD}$ and $\overline{BC}$ intersect at E, $m\widehat{AC} = 87$, and $m\widehat{BD} = 35$.

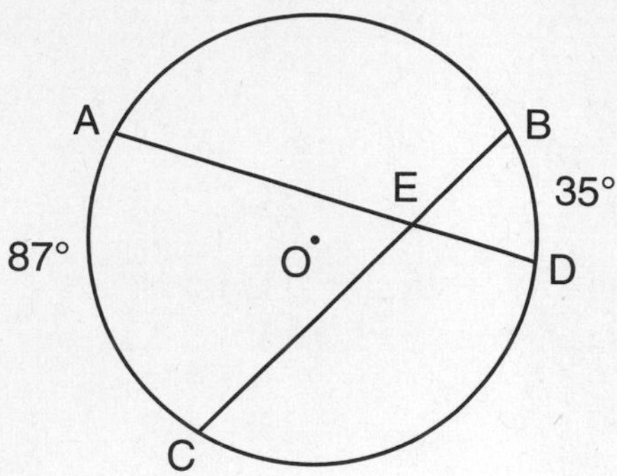

What is the degree measure of $\angle CEA$?

(1) 87
(3) 43.5
(2) 61
(4) 26

16 In the diagram below of $\triangle ADB$, $m\angle BDA = 90$, $AD = 5\sqrt{2}$, and $AB = 2\sqrt{15}$.

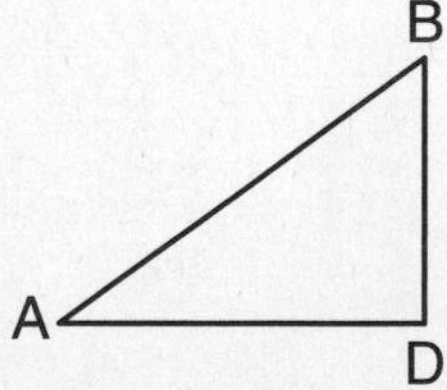

What is the length of $\overline{BD}$?

(1) $\sqrt{10}$
(3) $\sqrt{50}$
(2) $\sqrt{20}$
(4) $\sqrt{110}$

Use this space for computations.

17 What is the distance between the points $(-3,2)$ and $(1,0)$?

(1) $2\sqrt{2}$
(2) $2\sqrt{3}$
(3) $5\sqrt{2}$
(4) $2\sqrt{5}$

18 What is an equation of the line that contains the point $(3,-1)$ and is perpendicular to the line whose equation is $y = -3x + 2$?

(1) $y = -3x + 8$
(2) $y = -3x$
(3) $y = \frac{1}{3}x$
(4) $y = \frac{1}{3}x - 2$

19 In the diagram below, $\overline{SQ}$ and $\overline{PR}$ intersect at T, $\overline{PQ}$ is drawn, and $\overline{PS} \parallel \overline{QR}$.

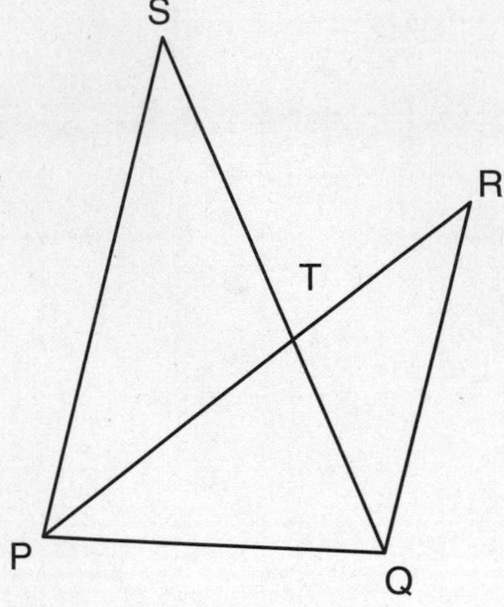

Which technique can be used to prove $\triangle PST \sim \triangle RQT$?

(1) SAS
(2) SSS
(3) ASA
(4) AA

Use this space for computations.

20 The equation of a circle is $(x - 2)^2 + (y + 4)^2 = 4$. Which diagram is the graph of the circle?

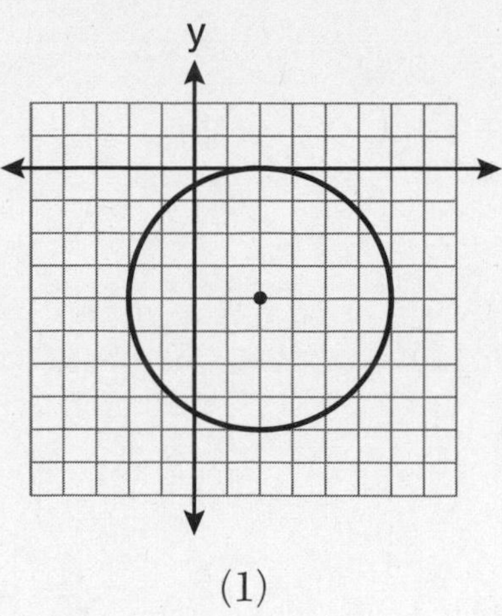

(1)

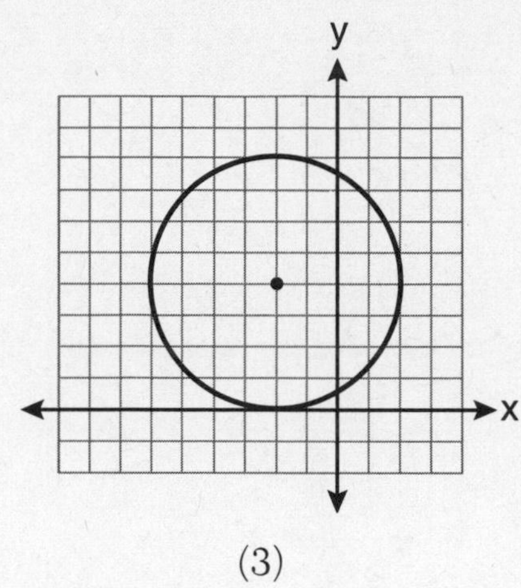

(3)

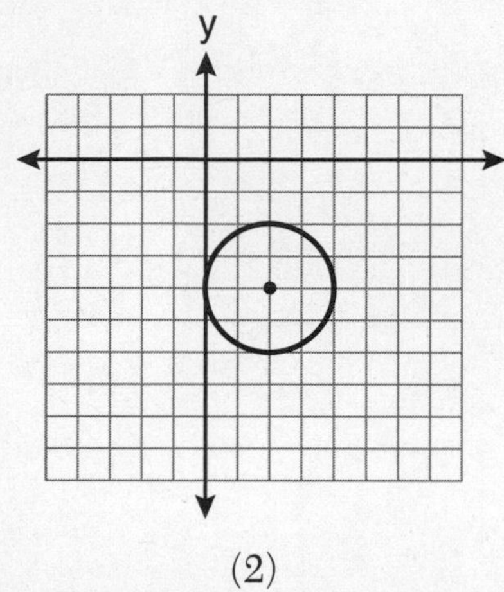

(2)

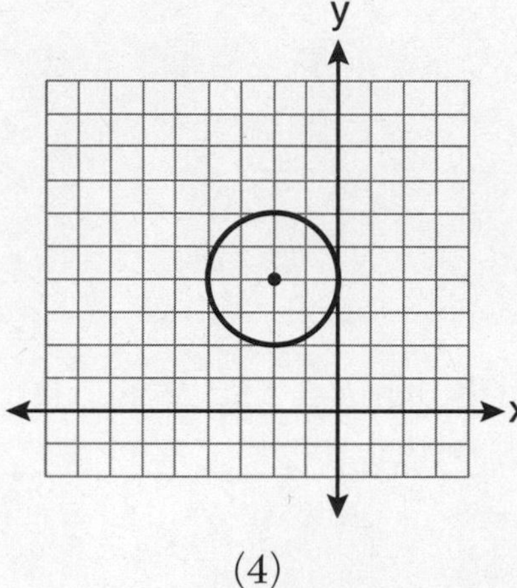

(4)

Use this space for computations.

21 In the diagram below, $\triangle ABC$ is shown with $\overline{AC}$ extended through point D.

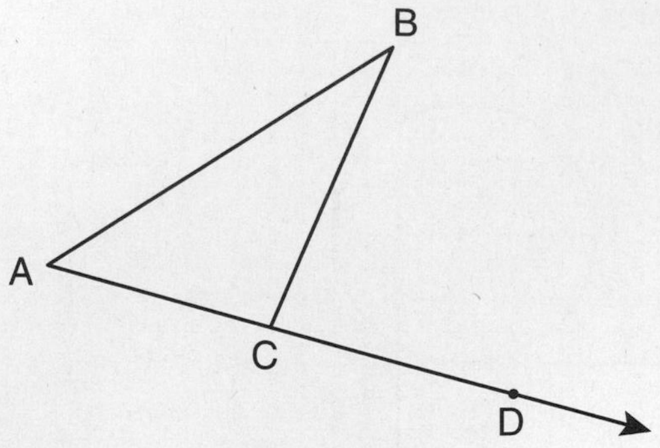

If $m\angle BCD = 6x + 2$, $m\angle BAC = 3x + 15$, and $m\angle ABC = 2x - 1$, what is the value of x?

(1) 12
(2) $14\frac{10}{11}$
(3) 16
(4) $18\frac{1}{9}$

22 Given $\triangle ABC \sim \triangle DEF$ such that $\frac{AB}{DE} = \frac{3}{2}$. Which statement is *not* true?

(1) $\frac{BC}{EF} = \frac{3}{2}$
(2) $\frac{m\angle A}{m\angle D} = \frac{3}{2}$
(3) $\frac{\text{area of } \triangle ABC}{\text{area of } \triangle DEF} = \frac{9}{4}$
(4) $\frac{\text{perimeter of } \triangle ABC}{\text{perimeter of } \triangle DEF} = \frac{3}{2}$

Use this space for computations.

23 The pentagon in the diagram below is formed by five rays.

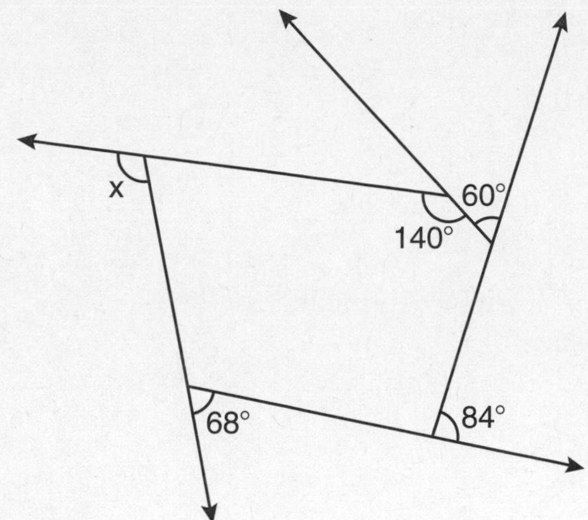

What is the degree measure of angle x?

(1) 72
(2) 96
(3) 108
(4) 112

24 Through a given point, P, on a plane, how many lines can be drawn that are perpendicular to that plane?

(1) 1
(2) 2
(3) more than 2
(4) none

25 What is the slope of a line that is perpendicular to the line whose equation is $3x + 4y = 12$?

(1) $\frac{3}{4}$
(2) $-\frac{3}{4}$
(3) $\frac{4}{3}$
(4) $-\frac{4}{3}$

Use this space for computations.

26 What is the image of point $A(4,2)$ after the composition of transformations defined by $R_{90^\circ} \circ r_{y=x}$?

(1) $(-4,2)$
(2) $(4,-2)$
(3) $(-4,-2)$
(4) $(2,-4)$

27 Which expression represents the volume, in cubic centimeters, of the cylinder represented in the diagram below?

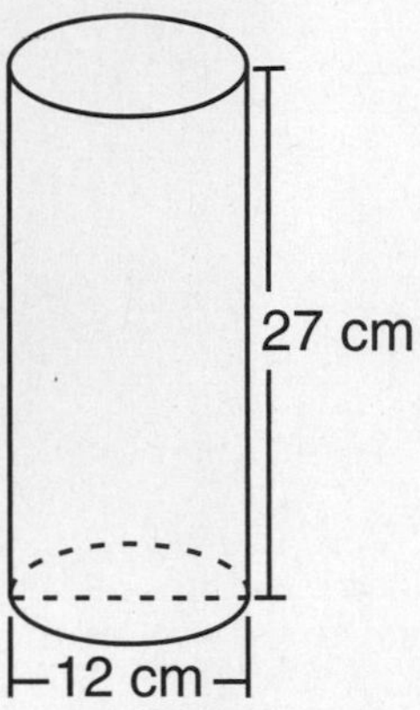

(1) 162π
(2) 324π
(3) 972π
(4) $3,888\pi$

28 What is the inverse of the statement "If two triangles are not similar, their corresponding angles are not congruent"?

(1) If two triangles are similar, their corresponding angles are not congruent.
(2) If corresponding angles of two triangles are not congruent, the triangles are not similar.
(3) If two triangles are similar, their corresponding angles are congruent.
(4) If corresponding angles of two triangles are congruent, the triangles are similar.

Part II

Answer all 6 questions in this part. Each correct answer will receive 2 credits. Clearly indicate the necessary steps, including appropriate formula substitutions, diagrams, graphs, charts, etc. For all questions in this part, a correct numerical answer with no work shown will receive only 1 credit. All answers should be written in pen, except for graphs and drawings, which should be done in pencil. [12]

29 In $\triangle RST$, $m\angle RST = 46$ and $\overline{RS} \cong \overline{ST}$. Find $m\angle STR$.

30 Tim has a rectangular prism with a length of 10 centimeters, a width of 2 centimeters, and an unknown height. He needs to build another rectangular prism with a length of 5 centimeters and the same height as the original prism. The volume of the two prisms will be the same. Find the width, in centimeters, of the new prism.

31 In the diagram below of circle C, $\overline{QR}$ is a diameter, and $Q(1,8)$ and $C(3.5, 2)$ are points on a coordinate plane.

Find and state the coordinates of point R.

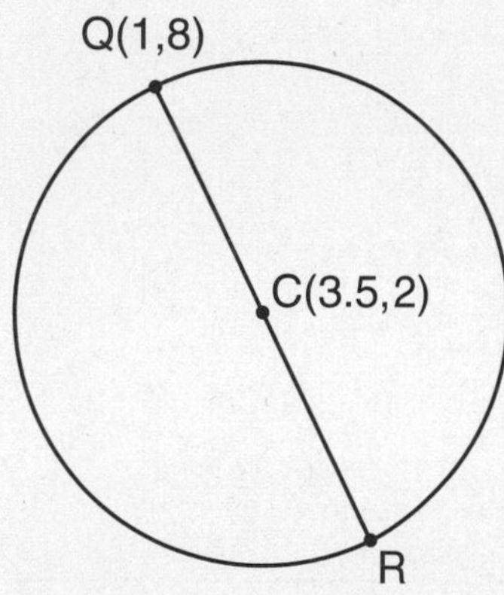

32 Using a compass and straightedge, and $\overline{AB}$ below, construct an equilateral triangle with all sides congruent to $\overline{AB}$. [Leave all construction marks.]

A B

33 In the diagram below of $\triangle ACD$, E is a point on $\overline{AD}$ and B is a point on $\overline{AC}$, such that $\overline{EB} \parallel \overline{DC}$. If $AE = 3$, $ED = 6$, and $DC = 15$, find the length of $\overline{EB}$.

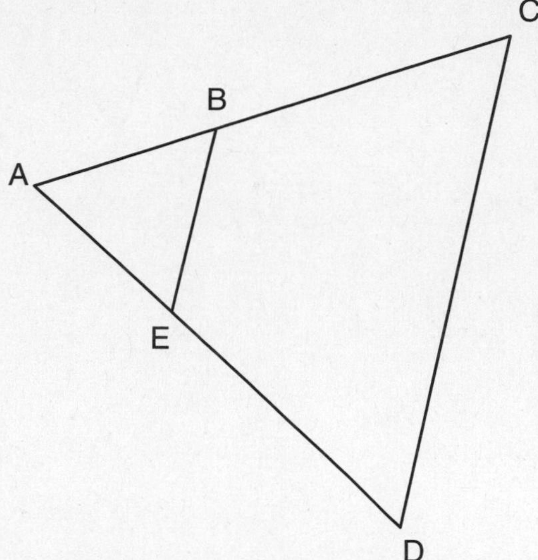

34 In the diagram below of $\triangle TEM$, medians $\overline{TB}$, $\overline{EC}$, and $\overline{MA}$ intersect at D, and $TB = 9$. Find the length of $\overline{TD}$.

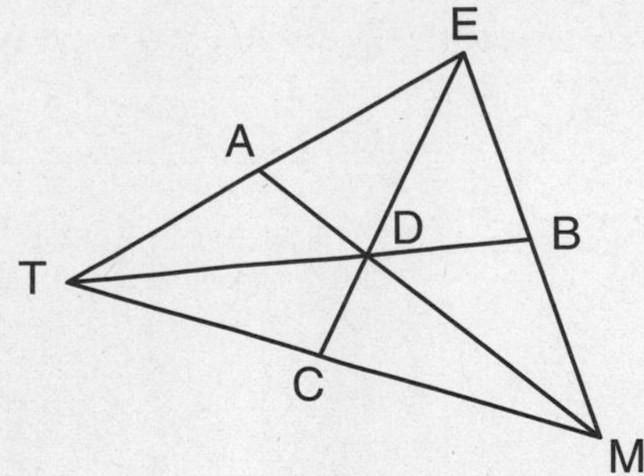

Part III

Answer all 3 questions in this part. Each correct answer will receive 4 credits. Clearly indicate the necessary steps, including appropriate formula substitutions, diagrams, graphs, charts, etc. For all questions in this part, a correct numerical answer with no work shown will receive only 1 credit. All answers should be written in pen, except for graphs and drawings, which should be done in pencil. [12]

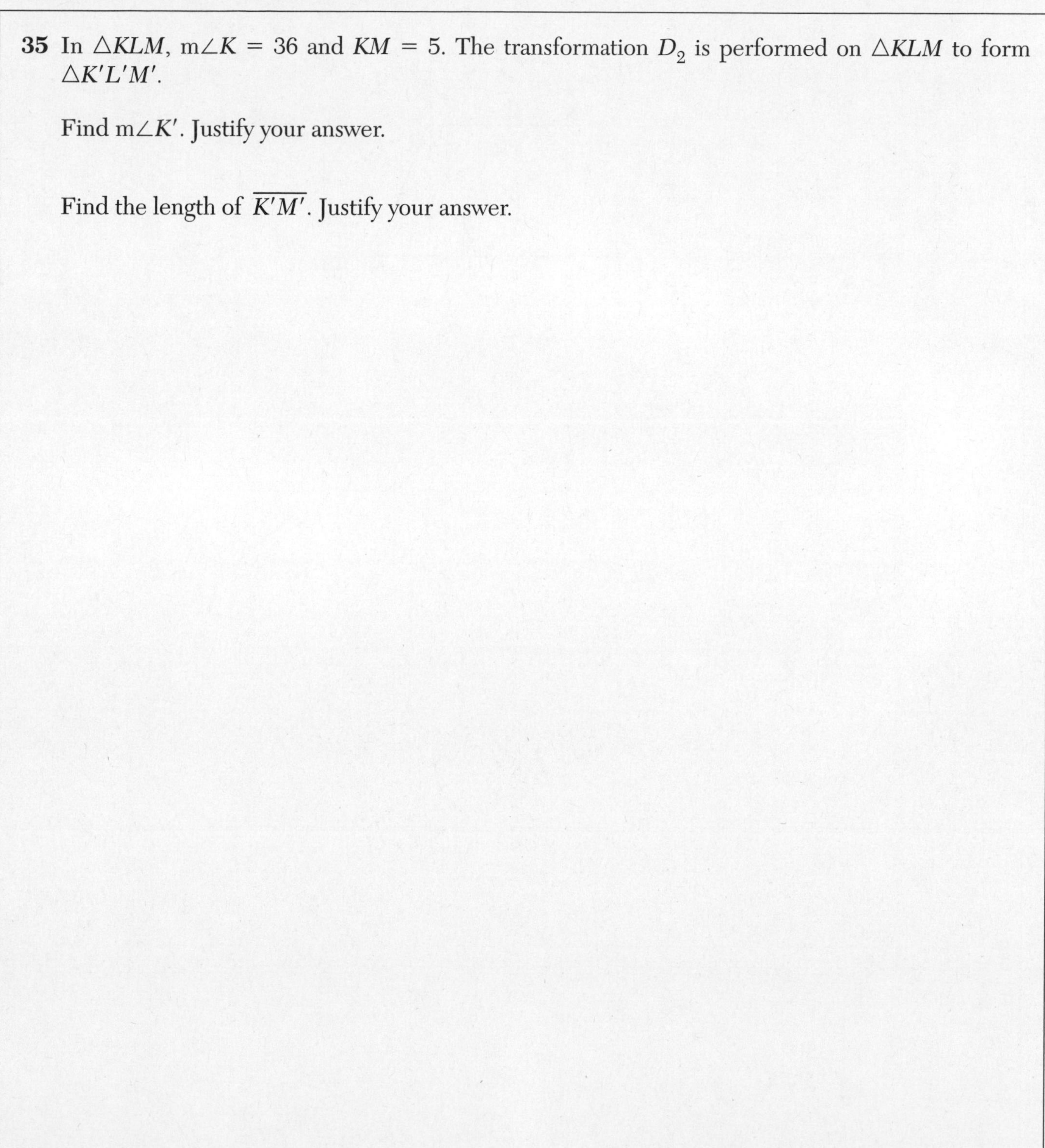

35 In $\triangle KLM$, $m\angle K = 36$ and $KM = 5$. The transformation D_2 is performed on $\triangle KLM$ to form $\triangle K'L'M'$.

Find $m\angle K'$. Justify your answer.

Find the length of $\overline{K'M'}$. Justify your answer.

36 Given: *JKLM* is a parallelogram.

$\overline{JM} \cong \overline{LN}$

$\angle LMN \cong \angle LNM$

Prove: *JKLM* is a rhombus.

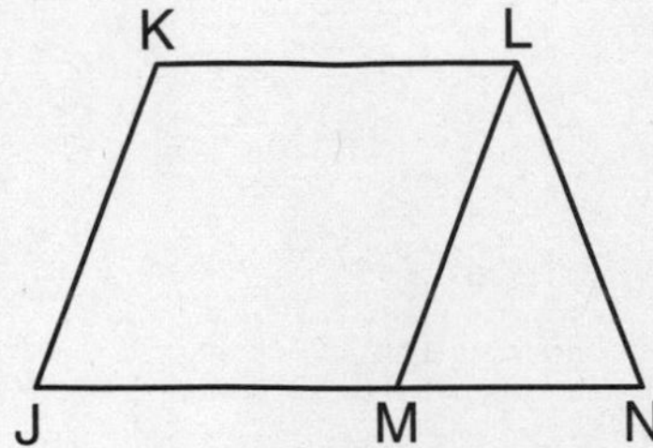

37 On the grid below, graph the points that are equidistant from both the x and y axes and the points that are 5 units from the origin. Label with an **X** all points that satisfy both conditions.

Part IV

Answer the question in this part. A correct answer will receive 6 credits. Clearly indicate the necessary steps, including appropriate formula substitutions, diagrams, graphs, charts, etc. A correct numerical answer with no work shown will receive only 1 credit. The answer should be written in pen. [6]

38 On the set of axes below, solve the following system of equations graphically for all values of x and y.

$$y = (x - 2)^2 + 4$$
$$4x + 2y = 14$$

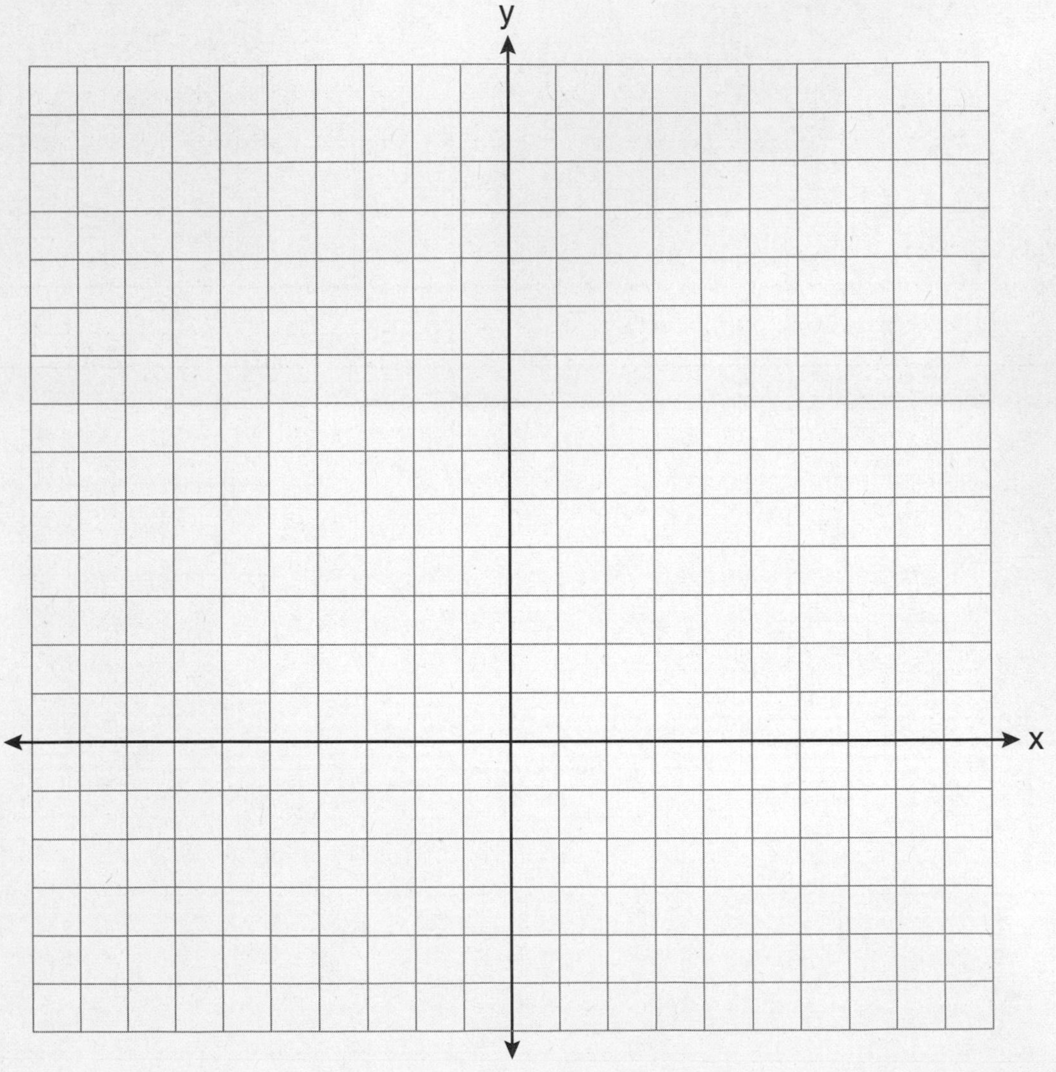

Tear Here

Reference Sheet

Volume	Cylinder	$V = Bh$ where B is the area of the base
	Pyramid	$V = \frac{1}{3}Bh$ where B is the area of the base
	Right Circular Cone	$V = \frac{1}{3}Bh$ where B is the area of the base
	Sphere	$V = \frac{4}{3}\pi r^3$

Lateral Area (L)	Right Circular Cylinder	$L = 2\pi rh$
	Right Circular Cone	$L = \pi rl$ where l is the slant height

Surface Area	Sphere	$SA = 4\pi r^2$

Tear Here

Geometry August, 2009

Part I

Answer all 28 questions in this part. Each correct answer will receive 2 credits. No partial credit will be allowed. For each question, write on the separate answer sheet the numeral preceding the word or expression that best completes the statement or answers the question. [56]

Use this space for computations.

1 Based on the diagram below, which statement is true?

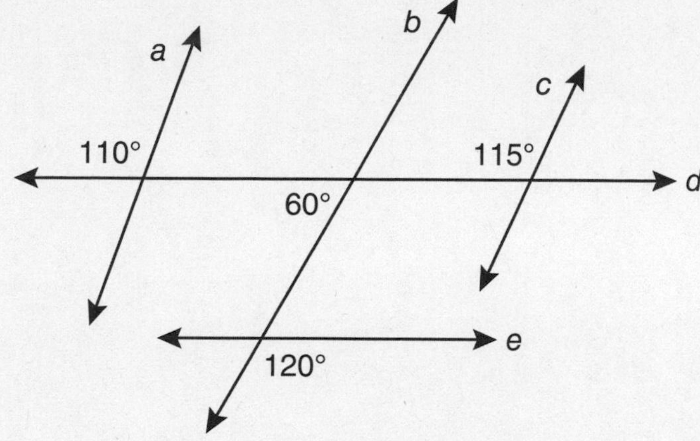

(1) $a \parallel b$

(2) $a \parallel c$

(3) $b \parallel c$

(4) $d \parallel e$

2 The diagram below shows the construction of the bisector of $\angle ABC$.

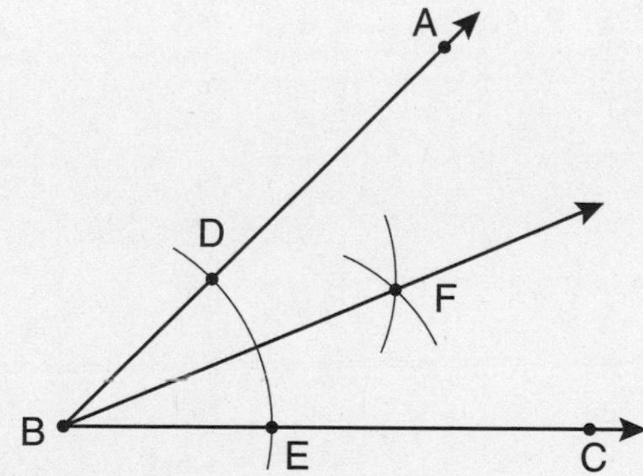

Which statement is *not* true?

(1) $m\angle EBF = \frac{1}{2} m\angle ABC$

(2) $m\angle DBF = \frac{1}{2} m\angle ABC$

(3) $m\angle EBF = m\angle ABC$

(4) $m\angle DBF = m\angle EBF$

Use this space for computations.

3 In the diagram of $\triangle ABC$ below, $\overline{AB} \cong \overline{AC}$. The measure of $\angle B$ is 40°.

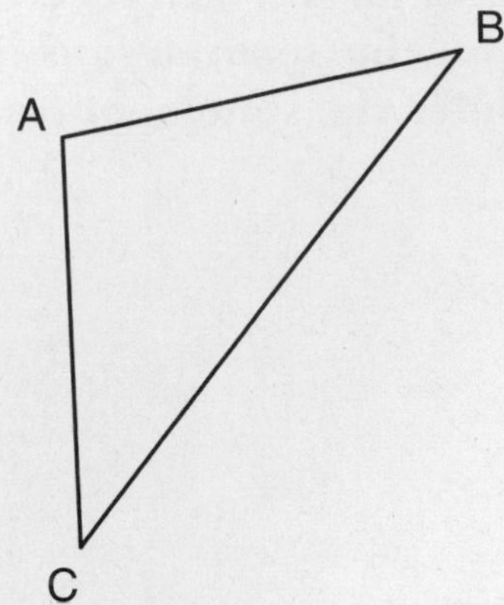

What is the measure of $\angle A$?

(1) 40° (3) 70°

(2) 50° (4) 100°

4 In the diagram of circle O below, chord $\overline{CD}$ is parallel to diameter $\overline{AOB}$ and $m\overset{\frown}{AC} = 30$.

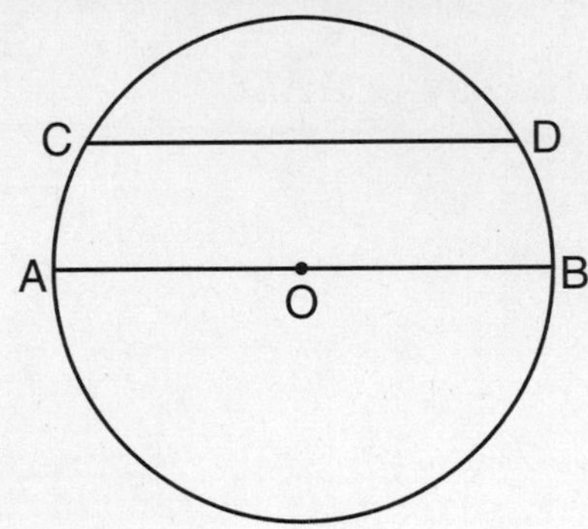

What is $m\overset{\frown}{CD}$?

(1) 150 (3) 100

(2) 120 (4) 60

Use this space for computations.

5 In the diagram of trapezoid $ABCD$ below, diagonals $\overline{AC}$ and $\overline{BD}$ intersect at E and $\triangle ABC \cong \triangle DCB$.

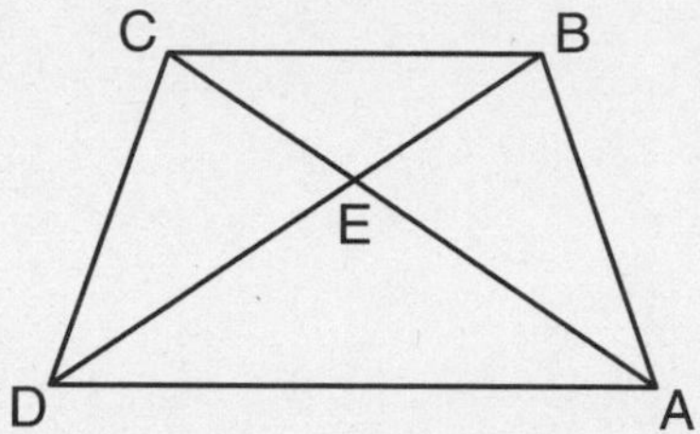

Which statement is true based on the given information?

(1) $\overline{AC} \cong \overline{BC}$

(2) $\overline{CD} \cong \overline{AD}$

(3) $\angle CDE \cong \angle BAD$

(4) $\angle CDB \cong \angle BAC$

6 Which transformation produces a figure similar but *not* congruent to the original figure?

(1) $T_{1,3}$

(2) $D_{\frac{1}{2}}$

(3) $R_{90°}$

(4) $r_{y=x}$

7 In the diagram below of parallelogram $ABCD$ with diagonals $\overline{AC}$ and $\overline{BD}$, m$\angle 1 = 45$ and m$\angle DCB = 120$.

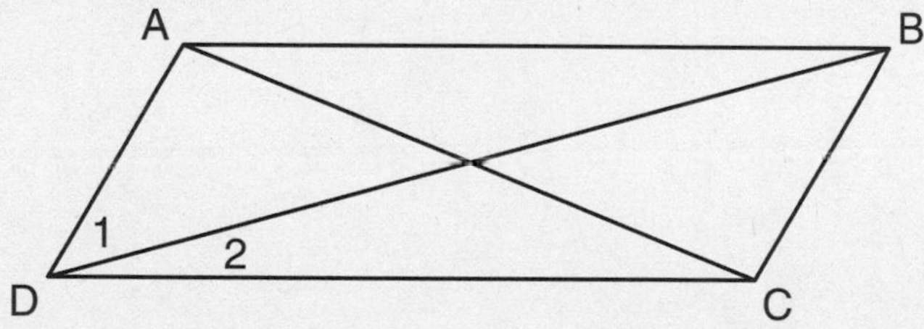

What is the measure of $\angle 2$?

(1) 15°

(2) 30°

(3) 45°

(4) 60°

Use this space for computations.

8 On the set of axes below, Geoff drew rectangle $ABCD$. He will transform the rectangle by using the translation $(x,y) \rightarrow (x + 2,y + 1)$ and then will reflect the translated rectangle over the x-axis.

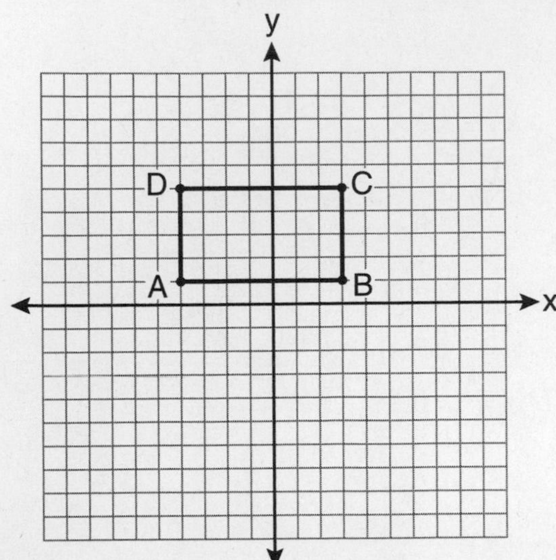

What will be the area of the rectangle after these transformations?

(1) exactly 28 square units

(2) less than 28 square units

(3) greater than 28 square units

(4) It cannot be determined from the information given.

9 What is the equation of a line that is parallel to the line whose equation is $y = x + 2$?

(1) $x + y = 5$

(2) $2x + y = -2$

(3) $y - x = -1$

(4) $y - 2x = 3$

10 The endpoints of $\overline{CD}$ are $C(-2,-4)$ and $D(6,2)$. What are the coordinates of the midpoint of $\overline{CD}$?

(1) (2,3)

(2) (2,−1)

(3) (4,−2)

(4) (4,3)

Use this space for computations.

11 What are the center and the radius of the circle whose equation is $(x - 3)^2 + (y + 3)^2 = 36$?

(1) center = $(3,-3)$; radius = 6

(2) center = $(-3,3)$; radius = 6

(3) center = $(3,-3)$; radius = 36

(4) center = $(-3,3)$; radius = 36

12 Given the equations:

$$y = x^2 - 6x + 10$$
$$y + x = 4$$

What is the solution to the given system of equations?

(1) (2,3)

(2) (3,2)

(3) (2,2) and (1,3)

(4) (2,2) and (3,1)

13 The diagonal $\overline{AC}$ is drawn in parallelogram $ABCD$. Which method can *not* be used to prove that $\triangle ABC \cong \triangle CDA$?

(1) SSS

(2) SAS

(3) SSA

(4) ASA

Use this space for computations.

14 In the diagram below, line k is perpendicular to plane $\mathcal{P}$ at point T.

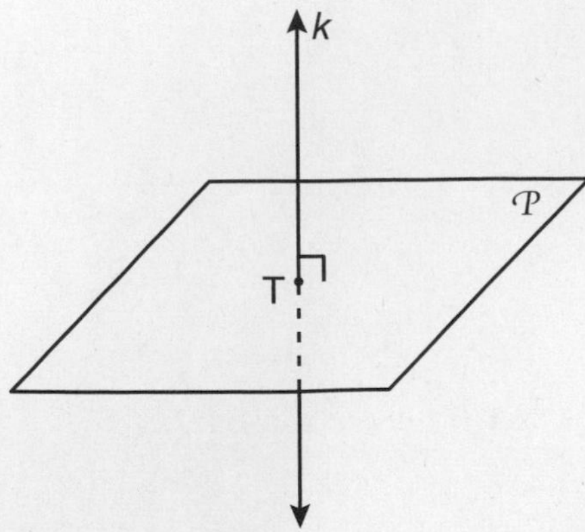

Which statement is true?

(1) Any point in plane $\mathcal{P}$ also will be on line k.

(2) Only one line in plane $\mathcal{P}$ will intersect line k.

(3) All planes that intersect plane $\mathcal{P}$ will pass through T.

(4) Any plane containing line k is perpendicular to plane $\mathcal{P}$.

15 In the diagram below, which transformation was used to map $\triangle ABC$ to $\triangle A'B'C'$?

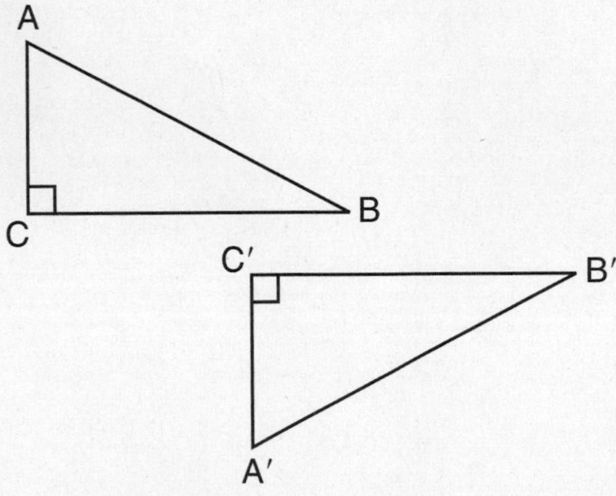

(1) dilation

(2) rotation

(3) reflection

(4) glide reflection

Use this space for computations.

16 Which set of numbers represents the lengths of the sides of a triangle?

(1) {5, 18, 13}
(2) {6, 17, 22}
(3) {16, 24, 7}
(4) {26, 8, 15}

17 What is the slope of a line perpendicular to the line whose equation is $y = -\frac{2}{3}x - 5$?

(1) $-\frac{3}{2}$
(2) $-\frac{2}{3}$
(3) $\frac{2}{3}$
(4) $\frac{3}{2}$

18 A quadrilateral whose diagonals bisect each other and are perpendicular is a

(1) rhombus
(2) rectangle
(3) trapezoid
(4) parallelogram

19 If the endpoints of $\overline{AB}$ are $A(-4,5)$ and $B(2,-5)$, what is the length of $\overline{AB}$?

(1) $2\sqrt{34}$
(2) 2
(3) $\sqrt{61}$
(4) 8

Use this space for computations.

20 In the diagram below of $\triangle ACT$, D is the midpoint of $\overline{AC}$, O is the midpoint of $\overline{AT}$, and G is the midpoint of $\overline{CT}$.

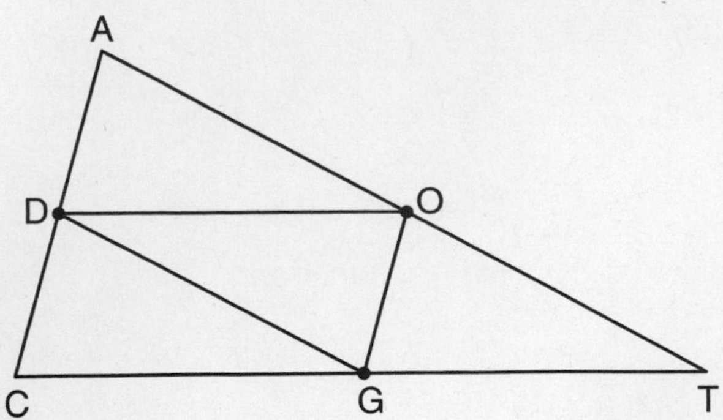

If $AC = 10$, $AT = 18$, and $CT = 22$, what is the perimeter of parallelogram $CDOG$?

(1) 21
(2) 25
(3) 32
(4) 40

21 Which equation represents circle K shown in the graph below?

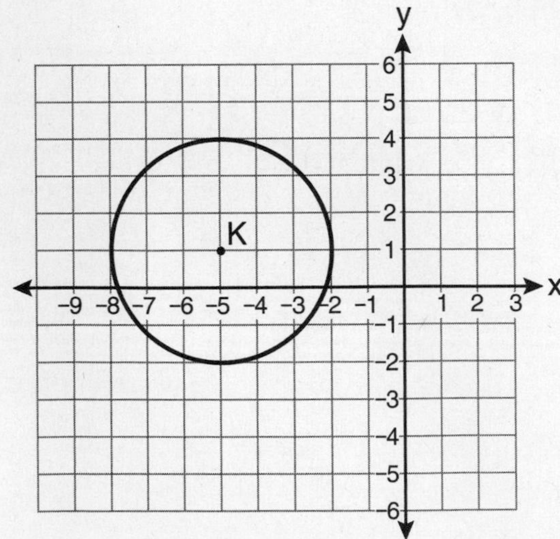

(1) $(x + 5)^2 + (y - 1)^2 = 3$
(2) $(x + 5)^2 + (y - 1)^2 = 9$
(3) $(x - 5)^2 + (y + 1)^2 = 3$
(4) $(x - 5)^2 + (y + 1)^2 = 9$

Use this space for computations.

22 In the diagram below of right triangle ACB, altitude $\overline{CD}$ is drawn to hypotenuse $\overline{AB}$.

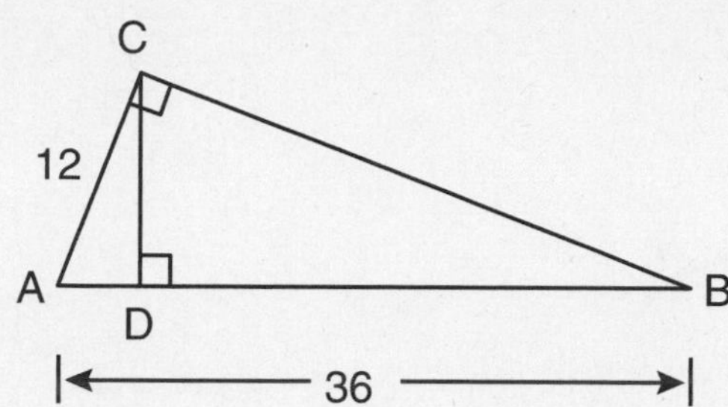

If $AB = 36$ and $AC = 12$, what is the length of $\overline{AD}$?

(1) 32 (3) 3

(2) 6 (4) 4

23 In the diagram of circle O below, chord $\overline{AB}$ intersects chord $\overline{CD}$ at E, $DE = 2x + 8$, $EC = 3$, $AE = 4x - 3$, and $EB = 4$.

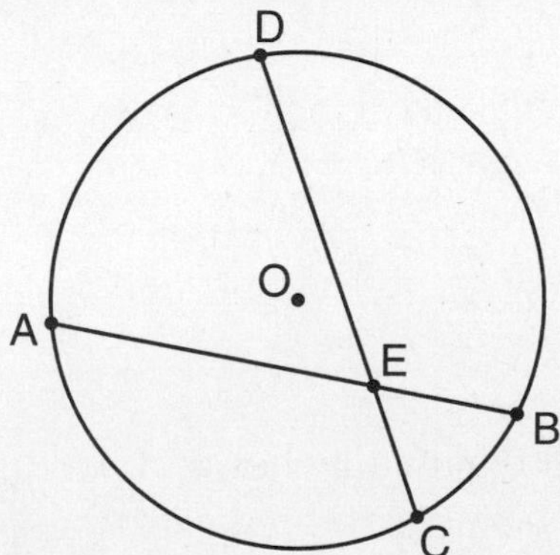

What is the value of x?

(1) 1 (3) 5

(2) 3.6 (4) 10.25

24 What is the negation of the statement "Squares are parallelograms"?

(1) Parallelograms are squares.

(2) Parallelograms are not squares.

(3) It is not the case that squares are parallelograms.

(4) It is not the case that parallelograms are squares.

Use this space for computations.

25 The diagram below shows the construction of the center of the circle circumscribed about $\triangle ABC$.

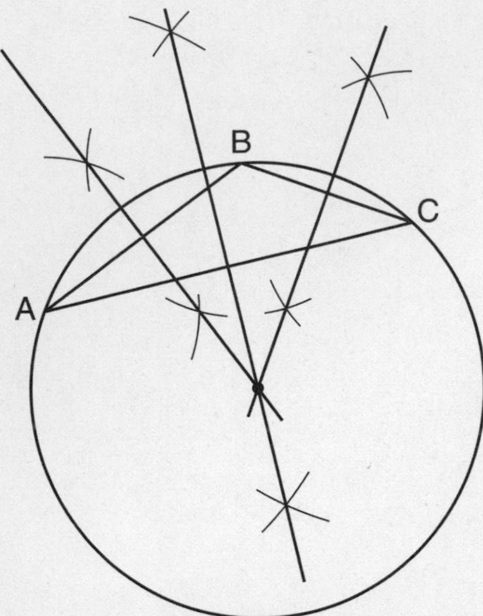

This construction represents how to find the intersection of

(1) the angle bisectors of $\triangle ABC$

(2) the medians to the sides of $\triangle ABC$

(3) the altitudes to the sides of $\triangle ABC$

(4) the perpendicular bisectors of the sides of $\triangle ABC$

26 A right circular cylinder has a volume of 1,000 cubic inches and a height of 8 inches. What is the radius of the cylinder to the *nearest tenth of an inch*?

(1) 6.3 (3) 19.8

(2) 11.2 (4) 39.8

27 If two different lines are perpendicular to the same plane, they are

(1) collinear (3) congruent

(2) coplanar (4) consecutive

Use this space for computations.

28 How many common tangent lines can be drawn to the two externally tangent circles shown below?

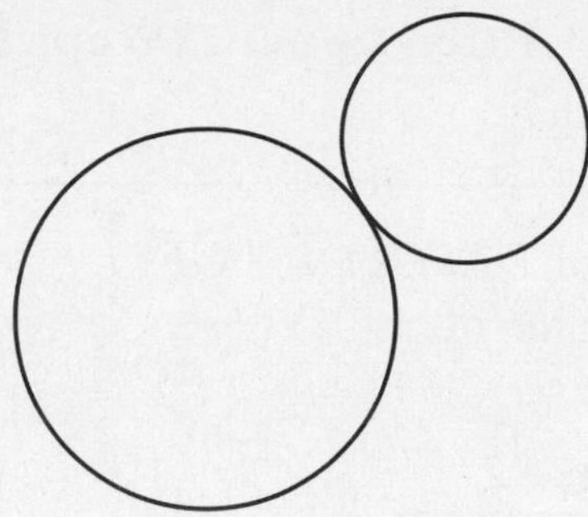

(1) 1

(2) 2

(3) 3

(4) 4

Part II

Answer all 6 questions in this part. Each correct answer will receive 2 credits. Clearly indicate the necessary steps, including appropriate formula substitutions, diagrams, graphs, charts, etc. For all questions in this part, a correct numerical answer with no work shown will receive only 1 credit. All answers should be written in pen, except for graphs and drawings, which should be done in pencil. [12]

29 In the diagram below of isosceles trapezoid *DEFG*, $\overline{DE} \parallel \overline{GF}$, $DE = 4x - 2$, $EF = 3x + 2$, $FG = 5x - 3$, and $GD = 2x + 5$. Find the value of x.

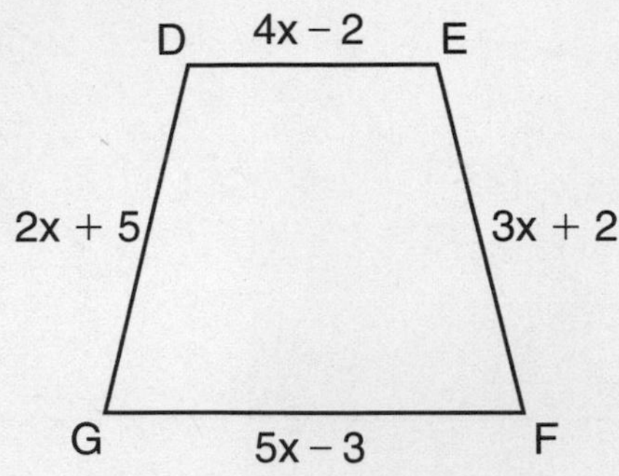

30 A regular pyramid with a square base is shown in the diagram below.

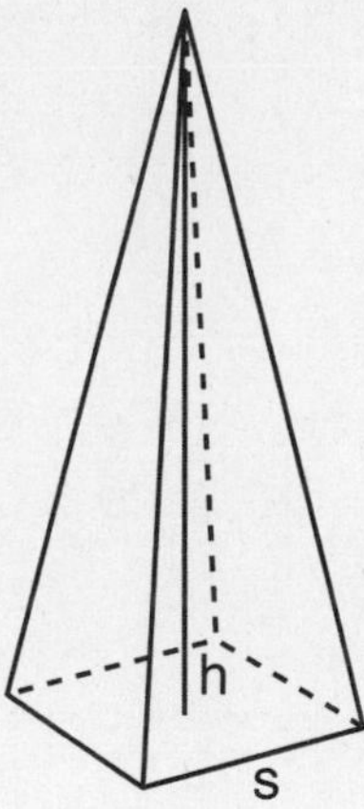

A side, s, of the base of the pyramid is 12 meters, and the height, h, is 42 meters. What is the volume of the pyramid in cubic meters?

31 Write an equation of the line that passes through the point $(6,-5)$ and is parallel to the line whose equation is $2x - 3y = 11$.

32 Using a compass and straightedge, construct the angle bisector of $\angle ABC$ shown below. [Leave all construction marks.]

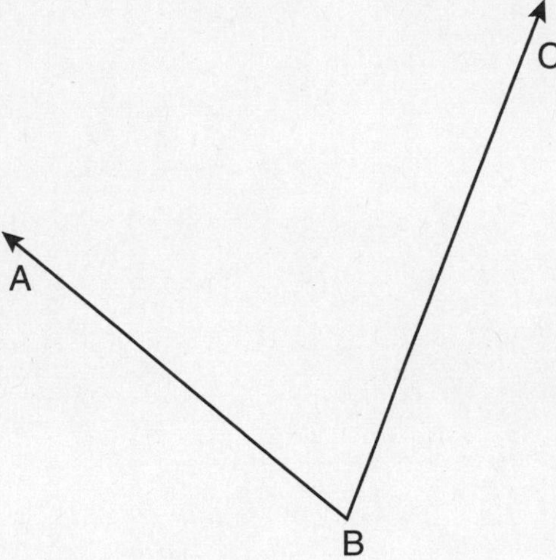

33 The degree measures of the angles of $\triangle ABC$ are represented by x, $3x$, and $5x - 54$. Find the value of x.

34 In the diagram below of $\triangle ABC$ with side $\overline{AC}$ extended through D, $m\angle A = 37$ and $m\angle BCD = 117$. Which side of $\triangle ABC$ is the longest side? Justify your answer.

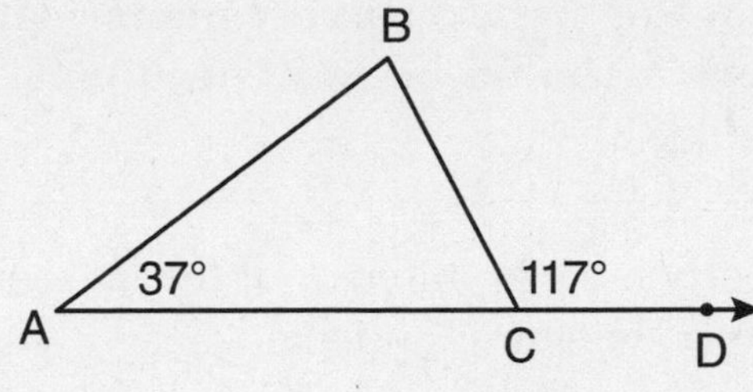

(Not drawn to scale)

Part III

Answer all 3 questions in this part. Each correct answer will receive 4 credits. Clearly indicate the necessary steps, including appropriate formula substitutions, diagrams, graphs, charts, etc. For all questions in this part, a correct numerical answer with no work shown will receive only 1 credit. All answers should be written in pen, except for graphs and drawings, which should be done in pencil. [12]

35 Write an equation of the perpendicular bisector of the line segment whose endpoints are $(-1,1)$ and $(7,-5)$. [The use of the grid below is optional.]

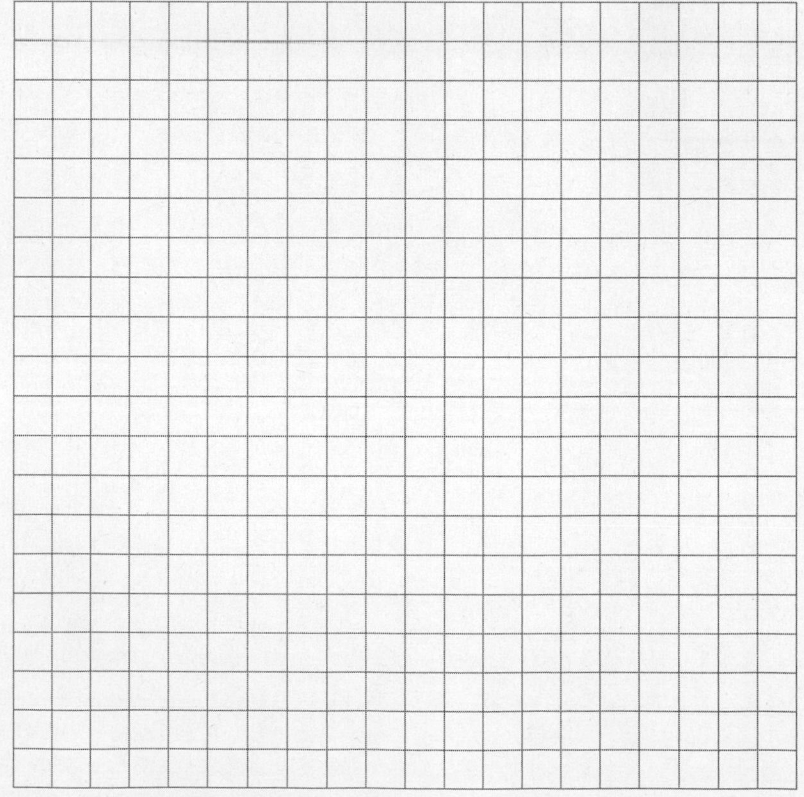

36 On the set of axes below, sketch the points that are 5 units from the origin and sketch the points that are 2 units from the line $y = 3$. Label with an **X** all points that satisfy *both* conditions.

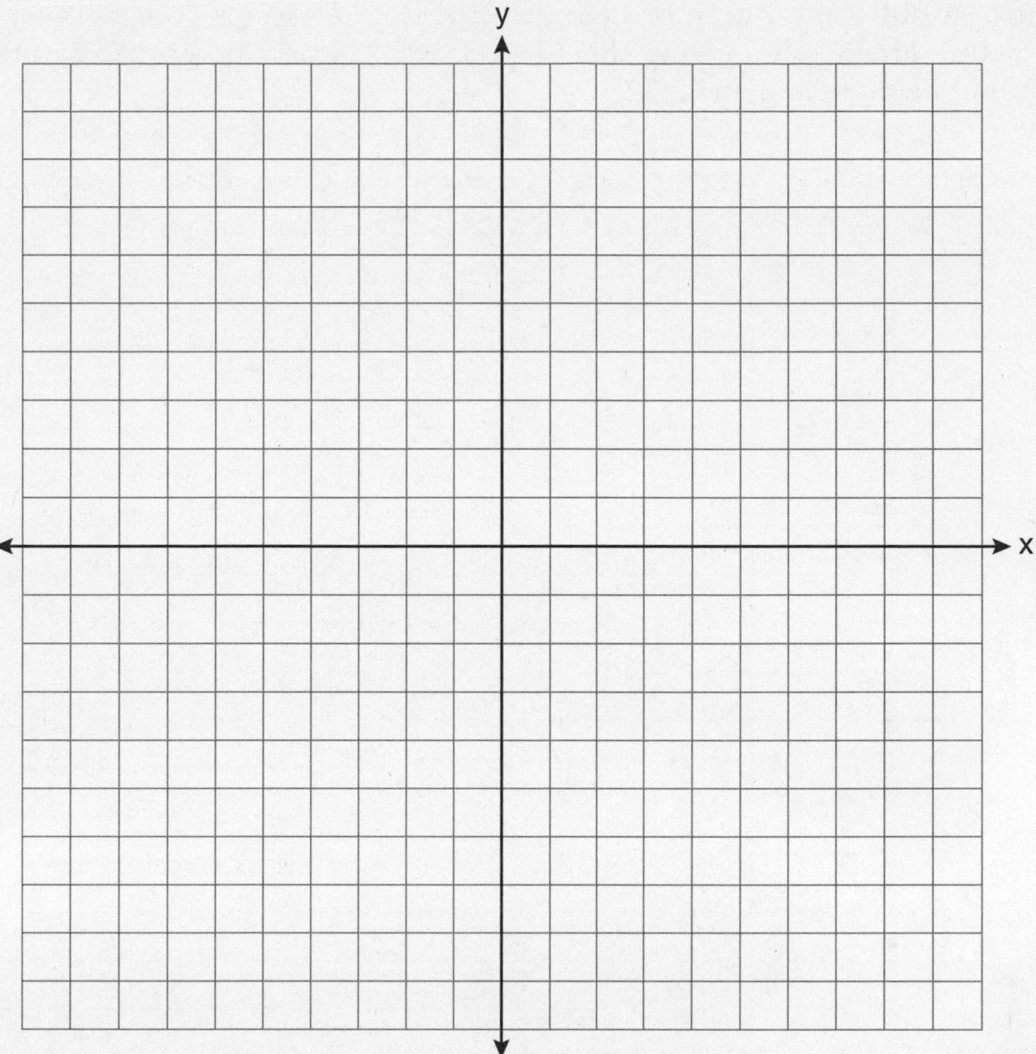

37 Triangle *DEG* has the coordinates $D(1,1)$, $E(5,1)$, and $G(5,4)$. Triangle *DEG* is rotated 90° about the origin to form $\triangle D'E'G'$. On the grid below, graph and label $\triangle DEG$ and $\triangle D'E'G'$. State the coordinates of the vertices D', E', and G'. Justify that this transformation preserves distance.

Part IV

Answer the question in this part. A correct answer will receive 6 credits. Clearly indicate the necessary steps, including appropriate formula substitutions, diagrams, graphs, charts, etc. A correct numerical answer with no work shown will receive only 1 credit. The answer should be written in pen. [6]

38 Given: Quadrilateral *ABCD*, diagonal $\overline{AFEC}$, $\overline{AE} \cong \overline{FC}$, $\overline{BF} \perp \overline{AC}$, $\overline{DE} \perp \overline{AC}$, $\angle 1 \cong \angle 2$

Prove: *ABCD* is a parallelogram.

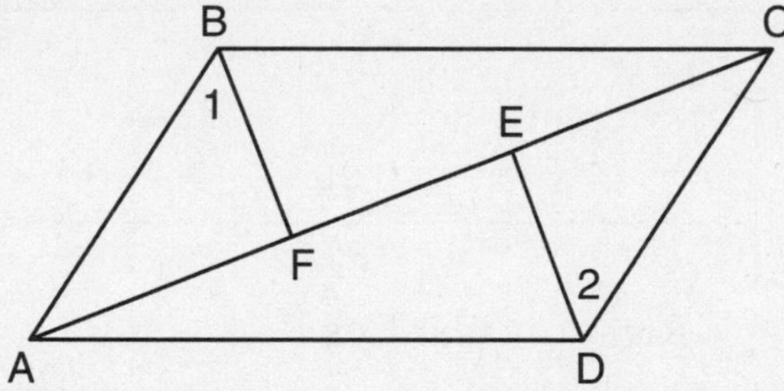

Tear Here

Reference Sheet

Volume	Cylinder	$V = Bh$ where B is the area of the base
	Pyramid	$V = \frac{1}{3}Bh$ where B is the area of the base
	Right Circular Cone	$V = \frac{1}{3}Bh$ where B is the area of the base
	Sphere	$V = \frac{4}{3}\pi r^3$

Lateral Area (L)	Right Circular Cylinder	$L = 2\pi rh$
	Right Circular Cone	$L = \pi rl$ where l is the slant height

Surface Area	Sphere	$SA = 4\pi r^2$

Tear Here